State of the Environment:

A View toward the Nineties

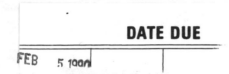

The Conservation Foundation is a nonprofit research and communications organization dedicated to encouraging human conduct to sustain and enrich life on earth. Since its founding in 1948, it has attempted to provide intellectual leadership in the cause of wise management of the earth's resources. The Conservation Foundation is affiliated with World Wildlife Fund.

State of
the Environment:

A View toward the Nineties

A Report from The Conservation Foundation
Sponsored by the Charles Stewart Mott Foundation

Washington, D.C.

State of the Environment: A View toward the Nineties

Cover design by Sally A. Janin
Typography by Rings-Leighton, Ltd., Washington, D.C.
Printed by Exspeedite Printing Service, Inc., Silver Spring, Maryland

The Conservation Foundation
1250 Twenty-Fourth Street, N.W.
Washington, D.C. 20037

Library of Congress Cataloging-in-Publication Data
State of the environment: a view toward the nineties.
    Includes bibliographies and index.
    1. Environmental protection—United States. 2. Environmental policy—United States. I. Conservation Foundation.
TD171.S73 1987   363.7'00973   87-15193
ISBN 0-89164-098-3

Contents

PART 1: STATUS AND TRENDS

x

BOXES

6. AGRICULTURE AND THE ENVIRONMENT IN A CHANGING WORLD ECONOMY

7. AMERICA'S WASTE: MANAGING FOR RISK REDUCTION

8. TOXICS IN THE AIR: REASSESSING THE REGULATORY FRAMEWORK

9. PROTECTION OF BIOLOGICAL DIVERSITY: THE CHALLENGES OF A BROADENING PERSPECTIVE

FIGURES

1. UNDERLYING TRENDS

2. CONVENTIONAL POLLUTANTS

3. TOXIC AND HAZARDOUS POLLUTANTS

4. NATURAL RESOURCES: LAND, WATER, AND ENERGY

5. PROTECTED LANDS, CRITICAL AREAS, AND WILDLIFE

6. AGRICULTURE AND THE ENVIRONMENT IN A CHANGING WORLD ECONOMY

7. AMERICA'S WASTE: MANAGING FOR RISK REDUCTION

8. TOXICS IN THE AIR: REASSESSING THE REGULATORY FRAMEWORK

9. PROTECTION OF BIOLOGICAL DIVERSITY: THE CHALLENGES OF A BROADENING PERSPECTIVE

Acknowledgments

In preparing this report, The Conservation Foundation sought the advice of a variety of outside experts and drew heavily on its own interdisciplinary staff of scientists, economists, lawyers, political scientists, and policy analysts. Panels composed of industry, environmental, government, and academic representatives helped chart the direction of the four issue chapters and provided useful comments on chapter drafts. Many other outside experts also reviewed and commented on chapter drafts. A wide variety of government officials in Washington and throughout the country gave unstintingly of their time and shared information with project staff.

Edwin H. Clark II, vice-president of The Conservation Foundation, directed the project; Michael Mantell, who directs the Foundation's Land, Heritage, and Wildlife Program, managed the effort. J. Clarence Davies, executive vice-president of The Conservation Foundation, provided continual review. John H. Noble, Foundation vice-president for planning and evaluation, assisted in several portions of the report. In addition to Messrs. Clark and Mantell, the principal authors of the chapters were: Sharon Green (Underlying Trends); Kathy Cox, Julia Doerman, Abby Goldsmith, Daniel Grossman, and German Reyes (Traditional Environmental Contaminants; Toxic and Hazardous Pollutants); Cecilia Danks, Abby Goldsmith, Sharon Green, Cameryl Hill, and Katherine L. Muller (Natural Resources: Land, Water, and Energy; Protected Lands, Critical Areas, and Wildlife); Robert G. Healy, Thomas E. Waddell, and Kenneth A. Cook (Agriculture and the Environment in a Changing World Economy); Frances H. Irwin (America's Waste: Managing for Risk Reduction); Richard A. Liroff (Toxics in the Air: Reassessing the Regulatory Framework; and Robert L. Peters (Protection of Biological Diversity: The Challenges of a Broadening Perspective). Additional Foundation staff who contributed to the report include Gordon L. Binder, Philip C. Metzger, Phyllis Myers, Rice Odell, and William E. Shands. Foundation librarian Barbara K. Rodes provided valuable research assistance.

The experts who served on the panels for each issue chapter include Malcolm Bale, Pierre Crosson, Paul Kindinger, John Miranowski, David Pimentel, Ned Raun, Stephen Rawlins, and R. Neil Sampson (Agriculture and the Environment in a Changing World Economy); Bart Carhart, E. William Colglazier, W. David Conn, Sister Margreen Hoffman, Jim O'Leary, Suellen Pirages, and Steffan Plehn (America's Waste: Managing for Risk Reduction); William Becker, David Doniger, Charles Elkins, Neil Orloff, Elizabeth Raisbeck, Phil Reed, Donald Smith, and Gordon Strickland (Toxics in the Air: Reassessing the Regulatory Framework); Michael Bean, F. William Burley, William J. Chandler, Robert Davison, Kathryn S. Fuller, Edward T. LaRoe, Thomas E. Lovejoy, Richard Miller, Russell A. Mittermeier, Elliot Norse, Whitney Till, and David Wilcove (Protection of Biological Diversity: The Challenges of a Broadening Perspective).

Additional review or assistance was provided by Curtis H. Freese, Leonard Gianessi, Barbara J. Lausche, Howard Levinson, Gerald A. Lieberman, Jeffrey G. Miller, Mark J. Plotkin, Richard Smith, Konrad von Moltke, and R. Michael Wright.

Neither the members of the panels nor the other outside reviewers bear any direct responsibility for the contents of the report. The diversity of their backgrounds was intended to, and did, produce a diversity of views that stimulated exploration of topics. We are very grateful to them for the time and effort they contributed to the report.

The manuscript was typed with great patience under tight deadlines by Charmaine Chong, Sharon Jonas, Joy Patterson, Carol L. Plotnick and Marsha G. White.

The report was edited by staff member Bradley B. Rymph and free-lance editor Lindsay Edmunds. Crucial editorial and production assistance was provided by Barton G. Brown, David Elwell, Fannie Mae Keller, and Stacy C. Roberts. Rings-Leighton, Ltd., of Washington, D.C., typesetters, and Exspeedite Printing Service, Inc., of Silver Spring, Maryland, printers, met frequently shifting deadlines to enable production of this book on a tight schedule.

Finally, we are deeply grateful for the support of the Charles Stewart Mott Foundation, which made this report possible.

Executive Summary

Twice before in this decade—with *State of The Environment 1982* and *State of the Environment: An Assessment at Mid-Decade* (1984)—The Conservation Foundation has reviewed the United States' progress in improving the condition of its environment and the management of its natural resources. In those reports, the Foundation has carefully examined some of the vital issues still to be faced. This report continues that focus with two important changes: It intentionally takes a long-term view of the nation's environmental picture in an effort to ask the questions and provide the information that policy makers and other concerned individuals will need as the nation approaches the 1990s. In addition, it takes a more global approach, recognizing that the United States increasingly must formulate its environmental policies with a careful appreciation of their interrelationships with the rest of the world.

The report is divided into two parts. The first five chapters describe and analyze a wide range of environmental conditions and trends.

- Chapter 1 deals with such underlying trends as population, economic growth, public opinion, and environmental expenditures.
- Chapter 2 covers trends in conventional environmental pollutants in the air and water and on the land.
- Chapter 3 assesses the situation with toxic substances and hazardous and nuclear wastes.
- Chapter 4 summarizes what is happening to the use and condition of the nation's land, water, and energy resources.
- Chapter 5 deals with wildlife and such protected lands and critical areas as parks, wilderness, and wetlands.

The second part of the report examines four environmental issues that are not being fully addressed by existing environmental protection and management programs.

- Chapter 6 assesses the problems facing the nation's agricultural sector and the interactions between agricultural production and environmental quality, both at home and abroad.
- Chapter 7 provides a broad overview of waste production and management in the United States. It suggests that there may be more rational approachs to dealing with these problems than are provided by existing programs.
- Chapter 8 evaluates the risks associated with three types of air pollution not being dealt with rigorously under current air pollution control laws: air toxics, indoor air, and accidental releases.
- Chapter 9 assesses the importance and implications of switching from past wildlife policies aimed predominantly at protecting individual species to expanded approaches addressing biological diversity.

PART I. STATUS AND TRENDS

Chapter 1. Underlying Trends

Three separate but interacting conditions determine the quality of a nation's environment: (*a*) the natural environmental endowment, (*b*) the stress induced by population growth and economic development, and (*c*) the amount of protection afforded by the nation. All three conditions can be difficult to measure. Nevertheless, an understanding of basic, underlying stresses and protective efforts is necessary if one is to adequately comprehend the widely varied environmental issues that will face the United States and the rest of the world in the coming years.

Population

The world's population, growing at a rate of 1.67 percent per year, has topped 5 billion people, with another 80 to 85 million—a population almost one-third the size of the United States—being added annually. Most of this growth is occurring in less-developed countries, which are commonly experiencing growth rates of over 2 percent while most of the more developed countries have natural growth rates of less than 1 percent. The world's population is also becoming more concentrated in urban areas, with cities such as Mexico City and São Paulo projected to contain over 24 million people each by the year 2000.

The U.S. population growth rate continues to decline gradually, reaching a level of 0.99 percent in 1986. The national average, however, hides regional differences. The South and West continue to grow rapidly, while areas in the North and East continue to lose population. Suburban areas continue to grow most rapidly.

Economy

The U.S. economy has recovered from the recession of the early 1980s, but not as vigorously as anticipated. The recovery has brought a continued structural shift in the economy from "dirty" manufacturing industries to "clean" services, a shift that may have environmental benefits. But some high technology industries are also producing environmental problems, such as widespread groundwater contamination by toxic substances in California'a Silicon Valley. The regional distribution of the nation's economic growth has been uneven. For example, oil-producing areas such as Texas have suffered from the decresed price of oil, while oil-importing areas have benefited.

The most significant economic issues facing the United States are the substantial deficits in the federal budget and in the nation's foreign trade. Fiscal problems are constraining environmental improvement efforts at all levels of government, as the federal government transfers increasing responsibilities to state and local governments at the same time that it has been decreasing financial support to those governments. Globally, high international debts rung up by many developing countries are causing those countries to exploit their natural resources for short-term economic benefit with little concern for possible long-term environmental problems.

Public Opinion

The U.S. public continues to strongly support environmental programs, and the majority of Americans indicate a willingness to pay for these programs. This support is reflected both in opinion polls and in voting patterns for candidates and ballot referenda. Other countries, including the less-developed countries, are also showing increasing concern about environmental quality and reflecting this concern in increased environmental protection efforts.

Environmental Expenditures

In constant 1982 dollars, the United States (including governments, industry, and personal consumption expenditures) spent over $600 billion for air and water pollution control (relatively evenly divided between the two) between 1972 and 1984. Expenditures grew at an average annual rate of 4.7 percent between 1972 and 1980 and then slowed to a rate of 0.8 percent from 1980 to 1984. Among federal expenditures, outlays for water pollution control and other media fell in the 1980s, while expenditures for the Superfund program increased significantly. While some industries have caught up with the backlog of investments made to comply with industrial-effluent limitations, many investments remain to be made.

Enforcement

The intensity of federal enforcement efforts has fluctuated during this decade. In the early 1980s, U.S. Environmental Protection Agency (EPA) civil enforcement activities fell sharply. Since 1983, activities generally have increased. Superfund enforcement expenditures have grown significantly, from $3 million in 1981 to $45 million in 1985. Two types of enforcement that have increased steadily during the 1980s are criminal enforcement activities and citizen enforcement intitiatives. However, the compliance of federal and other government facilities with environmental statutes continues to present a major problem.

Chapter 2. Traditional Environmental Contaminants

Most pollution control efforts in the United States over the past 15 years have focused on controlling the discharge of conventional pollutants into the air and water and on cleaning up some of the most obvious problems associated with the disposal of solid wastes on the land. These programs have achieved some substantial successes, but they still have not attained some of the goals established over a decade ago.

Air Quality

The nation has seen some significant improvements in air quality since 1975. The ambient concentrations of all five "conventional" pollutants have declined, with the most substantial progress being made in the levels of sulfur dioxide and carbon monoxide, which have dropped 30 to 40 percent. Nitrogen dioxide has shown the least improvement, with national ambient levels falling only 10 percent from 1975 to 1984. Some of the improvements result from changes in economic activity, but the national regulatory programs can take substantial credit as well.

Nevertheless, significant problems remain. Many areas of the country still suffer from unhealthy air. EPA estimates that some 368 air quality control areas, containing an estimated 80 million people, had not achieved compliance with the health-based ozone standards by 1984. Average annual particulate levels also exceeded national standards in a number of regions. Further, the nation has yet to begin to deal with such problems as acid deposition and the threat of climate changes resulting from increasing levels of carbon dioxide, and it has made relatively little progress in addressing such other problems as diminished visibility near national parks and protecting the earth's ozone layer.

Water Quality

The available information on the nation's water quality continues to indicate that while many waters are becoming cleaner, others are degrading. The greatest improvements have occurred in levels of fecal coliform and dissolved oxygen. However, for some contaminants such as chlorides, nitrates and certain toxic metals (arsenic, cadmium, and mercury), more river segments are degrading than are improving.

Two causes of the nation's remaining surface water quality problems are the failure of many municipal wastewater treatment plants to meet the standards set forth in 1972, and the lack of controls on nonpoint sources of pollution such as storm water runoff from farmland and urban streets. Other problems include discharges of toxic contaminants, water pollution resulting from the fallout of air pollutants, and the quality of a number of lakes and extuaries.

Current laws have done little to protect the nation's groundwater. The few surveys that have been conducted indicate that contamination is probably more widespread than most people have realized. The causes are diverse. Septic tanks, animal feedlots, and leaking sewers can cause high levels of pathogens; hazardous waste disposal, industrial spills, and pesticide application add toxic chemicals; and many other sources add some of the over 200 other substances that have been found in groundwater.

Solid Waste

Two of the solid waste problems of greatest concern a decade ago—open dumps and ocean dumping—have been largely brought under control. However, solid waste management remains a serious problem. Waste generation rates continue to be high; in some cases, such as with sludges resulting from wastewater treatment and some forms of air pollution control, those rates have increased significantly. Many communities are running out of space to dispose of their wastes and finding it increasingly difficult to site new landfills or other disposal facilities. As a result, an increasing number of states and communities are implementing recycling programs.

Chapter 3. Toxic and Hazardous Pollutants

As the United States has progressed in cleaning up many conventional pollution problems, it has become increasingly aware of the dangers of toxic pollutants and hazardous wastes in the environment. These problems often prove more difficult to deal with than the more conventional pollutants.

Toxic Substances

Because of a lack of adequate testing and the difficulties of assessing toxicity, relatively little is known about the dangers associated with the approximately 70,000 chemicals in commercial use in the United States. Over 1,500 new chemicals are now introduced each year.

Pesticides are one of the most widely used group of toxic chemicals, and their residues are found widely in the air and water as well as on the land and in food. Even after the use of some persistent pesticides such as DDT has been banned, they have continued to show up for many years in people, wildlife, and the environment. However, monitoring demonstrates that pesticide regulatory efforts have been successful in reducing the concentrations, if not the prevalances, of these substances.

Over the past decade, the total volume of pesticides used in the United States has declined, a trend that is likely due in part to the increasing use of highly concentrated substances. Although increasing attention is beginning to be paid to the problems caused by pesticides used in the agricultural sector, limited attention has been paid to their uses elsewhere, which now account for a quarter of total pesticide consumption.

Another significant area of accomplishment in managing toxic substances is the dramatically lower lead levels found in the air and water. This improvement is predominantly due to the reduced lead levels in gasoline. The environmental levels of other toxic metals, however, show no strong trends.

Use of asbestos, one of the few substances with essentially irrefutable evidence demonstrating that it causes cancer in humans, is declining rapidly. Some of the highest concentrations of asbestos have been found in schoolrooms. In reaction, in 1986 Congress passed legislation requiring all schools to inspect for asbestos-containing materials and to develop and implement plans to control the threat of asbestos.

Hazardous Waste

The federal government continues to have problems collecting good information about the amount of hazardous waste generated in the United States, how it is currently managed, and how much risk it potentially poses. The most recent estimates tend to converge on an industrial generation rate equivalent to approximately 2,400 pounds per American per year, with most wastes disposed of at the industrial sites where they are generated. However, in some states, the generation rate may be twice as high. The federal government also is attempting to grapple with the problem of cleaning up sites where hazardous wastes have been improperly disposed of in the past. This job has proved to be more difficult and expensive than originally thought, with the result that, in the program's first eight years, only a handful of the almost 1,000 sites listed on EPA's priority list were sufficiently cleaned up that they could be taken off the list.

Nuclear Waste

The United States continues to produce significant amounts of nuclear wastes despite its failure to find acceptable methods of disposing of them. Increasing amounts of spent reactor fuel from nuclear power plants and high level wastes from military facilities are being stored temporarily until agreement is reached on permanent treatment methods or disposal sites. States are now obligated by federal law to dispose of their low-level nuclear wastes within their own borders or in a state with which they have a compact. The total amount of waste generated annually is not increasing rapidly (in part because of the slow down in the construction of nuclear power plants), but the problem of disposal continues to be one of the most politically and scientifically controversial environmental problems the nation faces.

(The issues associated with hazardous and nuclear wastes are discussed in greater detail in chapter 7.)

Chapter 4. Natural Resources: Land, Water, and Energy

The United States is well endowed with land, water, and energy resources. Yet these resources continue to be placed under stress by the nation's increasing population and economic growth. Americans have begun to recognize that, as abundant as U.S. natural resources are, they are not limitless.

As population and economic growth continue in the coming years, the nation will require new, long-term management strategies as it strives to keep pace with this growth and to deal with the resulting, increasing stresses.

Land

The United States is rich in land, with nearly 9.4 acres per capita—about 1.4 times the global average and several times more than in most developed countries. Nearly a third of this land (over 700 million acres) is owned by the federal government, 7 percent is owned by state and local governments, and the rest is privately held.

The largest land uses are: forest, 29 percent; pastureland and rangeland, 26 percent; and cropland, 21 percent. The predominant changes in land use from 1974 to 1982 were the reclassification of forestland to wildlife and recreation areas, and a decline in pastureland and rangeland, with a corresponding increase in cropland.

In 1984, 76 percent of the U.S. population lived on the 16 percent of the land in metropolitan areas. Urban areas have grown rapidly since World War II. In 1950, 5.9 percent of U.S. land was designated as "metropolitan"; by 1980, the figure was 16 percent. Most of this growth has occurred in suburbs, which increasingly are the site of commercial and industrial, as well as residential, development.

The nation's cropland base totals about 469 million acres. About 383 million acres were actually used for crops in 1982, but federal programs have resulted in much land being idled since then—for example, 49 million acres in 1986. Soil erosion continues to be a serious problem, with soil conservation practices in use on only about half of the nation's farmland. In many cases, the most erodible land is not receiving the most attention.

The amount of rangeland and pastureland in the nation has declined slowly since 1950, to a total of 597 million acres and 1982. Almost three-fifths of this land was in nonfederal ownership, and about 60 percent of this nonfederal land was judged to be in only fair or poor condition.

A total of 655 million acres of the nation's land is covered by forests, with two-thirds of this forestland classified as commercial timberland. The production of forest products from this commercial timberland has increased rapidly since the mid-1980s following many years of only moderate growth. The outlook for the future is uncertain, both because of conflicting demands being placed on the nation's forests and because of changes in the quality of the timber resources.

Water Quantity

The United States is a water-rich country. It receives about 18,000 gallons of rainfall per person every day, only 2.5 percent of which is actually consumed.

Water withdrawals per capita increased from an average of 1,200 gallons per day in 1950 to about 2,000 gallons per day in 1980. Steam electrical generation and irrigation are the primary uses of this water. In certain areas, increasing withdrawals are reducing in-stream flows to detrimental levels and are lowering groundwater levels.

Energy

Increased fuel prices, the worldwide economic recession, and greater energy efficiency together caused U.S. energy consumption to fall over 10 percent between 1979 and 1983, most noticeably in the industrial sector. With the recovery of the U.S. economy, energy consumption picked up as well, rising 5.1 percent from 1983 to 1984 before declining slightly in 1985.

The nation also became more self-sufficient in its energy production over this period, with net imports falling to 14 percent of total consumption in 1985. However, imports have been rising rapidly since then.

The aggregate numbers on energy consumption hide some important shifts among different forms of energy. In general, the composition of the U.S. fuel supply is gradually shifting from oil and gas toward nuclear power and coal used in the production of electricity. Still, in 1985, oil and natural gas accounted for nearly two-thirds of all energy consumed in the United States, whereas coal provided 23.7 percent and nuclear energy only 5.6 percent.

Chapter 5. Protected Lands, Critical Areas, and Wildlife

Appreciation for natural resources is not limited to those that are commercially valuable. In the United States, land has long been preserved for purposes other than growing or harvesting crops, livestock, and timber.

The demands for conserving critical resources have, in recent times, expanded and diversified. Increasing numbers of Americans participate in outdoor activities and are concerned about protecting a broadening array of natural, cultural, and scenic resources. The far-reaching importance of these resources for human enjoyment, for maintenance of a healthy environment, and for fostering sustainable economic growth is the driving force behind increased preservation efforts by private organization and all levels of government.

Parks and Recreation

The total amount of federal lands designated for resource protection and recreational use has increased significantly since 1960, reaching 716 million acres by 1985. The largest increase resulted from the designation of protected areas in Alaska in 1980, and since then the increases have been modest (a total of 12.9 million acres representing a 1.8 percent increase). Americans use these lands extensively, with a total of 6.3 billion visitor hours logged in 1985.

Although they receive less attention than federally owned lands, state parks and other state lands actually play a bigger role in satisfying the public's recreational demands. On less than one-seventh the acreage of national parks, state parks and related areas reported more than twice the visitation in 1985. City and community parks have the smallest acreage and the highest visitation of all public recreation areas. Both state and local recreation areas suffer from diminishing funds and increased usage.

In response to the growing interest in outdoor recreation, and the increasing demands on outdoor lands to provide it, the president established a Commission on Americans Outdoors to conduct a comprehensive evaluation of the nation's recreational resources and to make recommendations for future recreational needs and means for financing them. Among the most noteworthy of the commission's recommendations were that governments should spend at least $1 billion annually to acquire, develop, and protect open spaces and that governments should create a nationwide system of greenways—scenic highway, river, and trail corridors linking communities.

In fiscal year 1984, federal, state, and local governments together spent $10 billion for all park and recreation activities and programs. Between fiscal years 1978 and 1984, direct spending by federal and state governments for parks and recreation declined, while local government spending increased.

Wetlands

The United States has lost more than half of its original wetlands in the 48 contiguous states, leaving only 95 to 99 million acres. An additional

223 million acres (primarily tundra) are found in Alaska.

The Fish and Wildlife Service estimates that between the 1950s and the mid-1970s, an average of almost one half million acres of wetlands were converted to other uses annually. Since then the loss rate may have slowed to 300,000 acres per year.

Since the early 1970s, increasing efforts have been made by all levels of government and by private groups to stem these wetland losses. The most common of these have involved regulation, economic incentives for wetlands protection, and acquisition of priority wetlands by both governmental and nongovernmental organizations.

Wildlife

An encouraging note with respect to natural resources in the United States is the admittedly fragmented and uncertain evidence that many wildlife species may be slowly increasing. For instance, selected species on Forest Service lands have shown stabilizing, and in a few cases, increasing trends since 1960.

Surveys of nongame bird populations show that most bird populations generally seem to be holding steady. According to the annual Breeding Bird Survey, 16 percent of the species analyzed in the United States and Canada showed increasing trends, 11.2 percent showed decreasing trends, and the remaining 73 percent showed no change. Many of the declining species are coastal or wetland species or migrate to Central and South America to overwinter. Thus, habitat loss and degradation in these areas are suspected causes for the declines.

Trends in commercial fish catches since 1973 show increases, partly because of increased landings of menhaden, used for industrial purposes. Shellfish landings, however, increased in the late 1970s, then declined rapidly in the early 1980s. Thirty percent of all marine finfish used for food is caught recreationally.

Nongame species (that is, species not harvested for sport or commercial purposes), which make up the huge majority of wildlife, are facing threats as great, if not greater, than game species. Eighty-five percent of all the vertebrate species listed as endangered in 1976 were nongame. As of November 1986, 928 species had been listed under the Endangered Species Act, at least in some locations, and 425 of those were U.S. species. Some 3,900 potentially endangered species still await action. As of August 1986, 197 recovery plans had been completed, covering 56 percent of listed species.

PART II. ISSUES

Chapter 6. Agriculture and the Environment in a Changing World Economy

In stark contrast to the 1970s, when U.S. agriculture prospered, the 1980s brought an assortment of severe economic problems that have been financially painful for farmers and costly to taxpayers. Throughout the transition from agricultural boom to bust, however, resource and environmental problems associated with agriculture have remained serious in the United States and in other nations.

The internationalization of U.S. agriculture—by far the most significant economic development in the sector since 1970—was the major cause of the growth of the 1970s and the decline of the 1980s. U.S. crop farmers became heavily dependent on rapidly increasing exports during the 1970s. But the onset of the world recession, along with a rapid appreciation in the value of the dollar and high price levels established by the government, constricted U.S. agricultural exports beginning in 1982, triggering severe economic problems. The U.S. share of international grain markets declined; farm incomes and land values fell; surplus crops strained storage capacity; and the cost of the government's agricultural support programs reached record levels. Agriculture's financial problems were further exacerbated by high interest payments on debts incurred during the expansion of the 1970s.

The United States has not been alone in experiencing significant change in its agricultural sector over the past decade. For example, the European Economic Community and China have rapidly increased their wheat production, Brazil its soybean and citrus production, and Central America its cattle production. All these changes have vastly reduced former markets for U.S. goods and in some instances created lower cost competitors.

The developments in U.S. and world agriculture have raised two broad issues for conservationists and environmentalists. First, many people are concerned about the sustainability of agricultural resource use in the United States and in other countries, particularly because of agriculture's growing dependence on chemicals and energy, the depletion of groundwater in some areas by irrigation, the continuing displacement of topsoil through erosion, and damage to soil quality from compaction, salinization, and the continued use of pesticides and fertilizers.

Concerns have also been raised about the environmental side effects of agriculture: contamination of groundwater by pesticides and fertilizers, pollution of surface waters with sediment and agricultural chemicals, hazards that pesticides and other agricultural chemicals may pose to the health of farmers and consumers, and destruction of wildlife habitat as new lands are brought into production. For the most part, the costs of these problems to society have not been rigrously quantified. Clearly they vary among countries, though in many cases they appear large.

The Food Security Act of 1985 contained several measures designed to help U.S. agriculture adapt to changing conditions in world agricultural trade. Perhaps of even greater significance, Congress established potentially important linkages between conventional agricultural support programs and resource conservation goals, notably soil conservation and wetlands protection. Such linkages may be applicable to other environmental problems associated with agriculture in the United States and may be adaptable to policies in other nations that export agricultural commodities—particularly other industrial countries.

Clearly, agricultural production levels and farming practices affect the environment in virtually every country in the world. The challenge for policy makers in the United States and in other countries is to make the mitigation of these effects a central part of the policies they devise to help farmers adjust to a dynamic world economy.

Chapter 7. America's Waste: Managing for Risk Reduction

About 50,000 pounds of air, water, and solid waste are generated for each person in the United States every year. Only about 3 percent of this waste is generated directly by households through garbage, wastewater, automobiles, and wood stoves. The rest results from manufacture and distribution of goods for human use.

The crucial question is determining how to prevent the damage or reduce the risk that can be caused by the huge amounts of waste produced in modern societies. Instead of solving the waste problem, many waste management facilities today only move waste from one place or one time to another. The failure of these approaches to keep wastes that can cause harm from entering the air, water, and soil in ways that people may be exposed to them has been increasingly evident in recent years. For instance, sewage treatment plants may release volatile organic wastes to the air, while landfills may leak wastes into water used for drinking.

At least 11 national laws control wastes. But they and the regulations that emerge often are only indirectly related to the longer term risk or damage wastes may cause. This is partly because relatively little is known about how many wastes behave in the environment or the damages they can cause. The science of assessing these risks is still relatively undeveloped. In addition, some wastes are difficult to control—for example, runoff from city streets—and, as a result, remain significant sources of pollution.

Choosing waste management techniques that prevent damage or reduce risk can be very difficult. No method of management is without risk. Persistent chemicals and metals can accumulate in the environment when dispersed, but dispersal probably remains the most common method of handling waste. Efforts to contain wastes on land almost always result in some leakage. Wastes can be treated so that they are largely degraded into less harmful substances before entering the environment. But releases during the treatment process and the inevitable residues—often in very concentrated form—must be carefully managed. Recycling wastes and reducing the amount of waste produced both offer promising opportunities to reduce risk over the long term since much less waste remains to cause damage. Recycling can have the same short-term risks that treatment has, however, and thus must be well managed. Reduction is the method most likely to reduce risk as long as substitute processes and products are carefully evaluated for their own risk. The extent it can be used varies greatly by industry, and it is not yet known what percentage of wastes can be removed from waste streams in this way.

The United States' present institutional structure and the resulting incentives can get in the way of selecting the means to reduce or manage a waste so as to prevent the most damage. That structure also may make it difficult to compare different options. An environmental agency or department concerned solely with water or air measures its success by how well it keeps waste out of the particular environmental medium under its care, regardless of the longer term consequences for the rest of the environment. Economic incentives may not encourage the least risky choice. Land disposal has been popular because it was long the least expensive and least regulated means of managing waste. That is now changing, but it is not clear whether incentives are yet adequate to encourage a significant shift to treatment and reduction. Also, barriers such as inadequate information about both wastes and the means of managing them must be surmounted.

Damage from waste is most likely to be prevented and risk avoided when managing it receives as much care as is given to manufacturing or buying a product, rather than being handled as an afterthought.

Chapter 8. Toxics in the Air: Reassessing the Regulatory Framework

Since the early 1970s, the United States' national air pollution control programs have focused largely on reducing routine outdoor emissions of the most common pollutants from major industries and motor vehicles. But these are not the only—or perhaps even the most serious—problems. Americans live in a chemical fog, and the time has come to reassess the regulatory framework for air pollution.

Human exposures to air pollution transcend the artificial boundaries between indoor air and outdoor air, between occupational and nonoccupational environments, and between routine emissions and accidental releases. Information that has emerged in recent years makes it clear that:

- contamination of indoor environments may be a much more serious problem than was realized a decade ago and must be moved much higher on public and private research agendas;
- much more attention must be paid to assessing hot spots of routine toxic emissions; and
- greater emphasis must be placed on understanding the causes of, and on preventing, industrial accidents.

At present, federal authority to deal with toxic air pollutants is widely dispersed throughout the government. Much responsibility lies with EPA, but important duties are also vested in other federal agencies. Federal action against toxic airborne pollutants has been fragmented and slow, and much better integration of federal efforts is needed. The slow pace of federal efforts to address risks from airborne toxic substances has prompted some state and local governments to move ahead of the federal government in developing innovative policies. These initiatives are a reminder of the vitality and responsiveness of these governments. The state and local innovations also provide important tests for new approaches that ultimately might be applicable nationwide.

In sorting out this confusion and establishing priorities, it seems entirely appropriate to establish as management principles the ideas that (a) big risks should be managed before small ones, (b) dollars should be spent where they will buy the biggest reductions in risk, and (c) the likely speed and effectiveness of risk reduction activities should be weighed when designing risk management programs. These principles suggest an orderly approach to cleaning up the air. They recognize the impossibility of either achieving zero risk from air pollution or acting against all significant risks simultaneously and quickly.

Yet while these principles may be appealing, their practical application creates some thorny problems. Information and analytical methods available may be inadequate. The needed institutions may not be in place. Political support may be lacking. A given approach may be regarded as unfair by those who believe government should protect them from all risks that they incur involuntarily. Decision makers also may have difficulty reconciling the desirability of targeting the biggest, most controllable risks with the delays that inevitably accompany the analysis needed to choose such targets in the first place.

When the environmental decade of the 1970s began, the United States launched itself in a headlong rush to clean up the nation's air and water. It is now evident that airborne toxic substances present a complex problem that requires a more systematic analysis of threats to human health and the environment. In managing these risks, much greater attention will have to be paid to distinguishing significant from insignificant risks. And, if this new generation of risks is to be adequately addressed, new forms of creative partnerships will be needed among agencies, among different levels of government, and between the public and private sectors.

Chapter 9. Protection of Biological Diversity: The Challenges of a Broadening Perspective

Preservation of the biological diversity of the earth is gaining recognition as a goal of resource management. Efforts to preserve biological diversity embrace three types of conservation:
- protection of individual species;
- protection of communities of species and the ecosystems of which they are a part, such as tropical forests, wetlands, and virgin prairies; and
- preservation of diverse gene pools within species.

There is no consensus on how many species exist in the world or the rate at which they are disappearing. According to one authority, 15 to 20 percent of the species that inhabited the earth in 1980 are likely to be lost by the turn of the century; this could mean a loss of 4.5 to 6 million species. Although this estimate is vigorously disputed by some, great losses will surely be suffered as tropical forests are cleared.

The losses could be very costly. Biological diversity provides immense benefits to agriculture in the form of new and hardier crops; to human health in the form of more effective drugs; to the stability of ecosystem processes such as the recycling of nutrients and the degradation of environmental pollutants; and to the human spirit by providing opportunities for outdoor recreation and aesthetic enjoyment.

The threats to biological diversity are immense. Hunting and harvesting are typically assumed to be the main culprits. Probably more important, however, are habitat destruction—for example, as tropical forests are cleared and wetlands are drained for agriculture—and the degradation of habitat as a result of chemical contamination.

The two principal ways to counter these threats are species management and habitat management. Species management includes such approaches as protection programs for species in the wild (for example, hunting, trading, and predator control regulations, supplemental feeding and breeding initiatives); preserving a few members of the species in captivity; and attempting to propagate species in captivity for release to the wild.

Habitat management includes such approaches as establishing and managing reserves, ensuring that development and agricultural practices in nonreserved areas provide better habitat, and attempting to restore degraded habitats,

How to use these approaches most effectively raises a number of policy issues. What should energies be focused on trying to save? What strategies should be preferred to maximize effective protection? How should broader constituencies be built for conservation? No single approach is likely to be sufficient by itself, and all techniques have costs that are often difficult to measure.

Information—about where species are concentrated, how and where they are most threatened, how to design and manage reserves—will permit more efficient allocation of limited available resources. Scientific knowledge must continue to be sought and technical solutions developed. Yet the constituency for protecting biological diversity as such remains thin, so a strategy is needed to bridge science and policy. A vision of the richness of life on earth should be part of that strategy. So should an awareness of the economic benefits of diversity. Only by carefully establishing priorities can those committed to biological diversity lead the enlarged coalition that is necessary for effective action.

Overview

As the United States approaches the 1990s, two factors above all characterize the state of affairs in environmental policy:

- First, the country faces an array of environmental problems even more daunting than pollution crises of the past generation.
- Second, current policies and institutions, having addressed the easiest matters, seem increasingly unable to deal with these emerging problems.

In short, the programs our country has created to tackle environmental problems are not up to the job ahead. We must critically examine and then change our policies and institutions, or prepare to face serious threats to public health, the environment, and the national economy.

To be sure, the United States does not now face an environmental crisis. Progress continues in abating some kinds of pollution problems in some places, and in the short haul no impending disasters can be predicted from a failure to address any of the lengthy list of environmental issues. Looming ahead, however, is a set of complex, diffuse, long-term environmental problems portending immense consequences for the economic well-being and security of nations throughout the world, including our own. These problems challenge our country's leadership to establish a new course for U.S. environmental policy at home and abroad.

PROGRESS CONTINUES

This report, like The Conservation Foundation's two previous *State of the Environment* reports, documents continuing progress over nearly two decades in improving some aspects of environmental quality. Levels of particulates, sulfur dioxide, nitrogen dioxide, and other air pollutants, for example, are trending downward in comparison with levels that were prevalent a decade or more ago. While ozone levels also seem to be dropping, this pollutant remains especially difficult to control; it is anticipated that many communities will not achieve compliance with federal health-based standards for exposure to ozone by the end of 1987, as the law requires. Millions of Americans are affected.

In water quality, too, there are some signs of improvement. Monitoring indicates that levels of fecal coliform and dissolved oxygen are decreasing in some bodies of water. People are swimming and fishing in rivers that once presented hazards to health. Some signs of improved quality are appearing in the Great Lakes—especially Lake Erie, once virtually written off as a dying body of water.

Toxic wastes released into the air or water or disposed of on land still present health and environmental risks, but at least some consideration is now being given to the effects of *new* chemicals *before* they enter commerce. In the natural resource area, substantial amounts of land have been protected in parks, wilderness areas, and wildlife refuges. For some endangered wildlife—the whooping crane and the peregrine falcon, for example—the threat of extinction has diminished.

In other words, determined actions to improve environmental quality during the 17 years since Earth Day have yielded positive results.

As significant as these developments are, perhaps the most important step forward has been the broad recognition by the U.S. public that the relationship between people and their natural surroundings, between human well-being and a healthy environment, must be a matter of ongoing concern. More than any other factor, the evolution of public attitudes, manifested in deep-seated political support for environmental programs, underlies the environmental progress this country has made.

Also encouraging is the fact that many of the worst effects of the minimalist federal environmental policies prevalent in the early 1980s have been reversed. Integrity and good management have been restored at the U.S. Environmental Protection Agency (EPA). The rhetoric of confrontation, so prevalent during the early Reagan years, has softened somewhat. The State Department's Agency for International Development has taken an active role in U.S. efforts to protect the environment of developing countries. Under U.S. government pressure and new leadership, the World Bank, too, has taken major steps to improve its environmental performance in the developing world.

To be sure, bastions in federal and state governments and elsewhere continue to preach the discredited line that the market, in and of itself, will safeguard the environment. More sensible is the widespread and growing recognition of the need for monitoring, analysis, and intervention, as well as for effective partnerships among different levels of government, to improve and protect the environment and to assure continuing supplies of the resources we need to survive and prosper.

A CONFOUNDING SET OF PROBLEMS, OLD AND NEW

Notwithstanding evident progress, the need for environmental action is at least as great as it has ever been. Problems long recognized remain unsolved, and new ones continually appear. Public understanding of environmental threats lags well behind reality, and political consensus on how to meet new needs is not apparent. Past successes belie a growing incongruity between where the problems are greatest, and where priorities and money for cleanup are directed.

If citizens or policy makers or corporate leaders in the early 1970s once believed that the primary job in environmental protection would end when the air and water were cleaned of a handful of known contaminants, this belief has been dispelled. With greater knowledge and with heightened public awareness, the catalog of environmental problems confronting the country has grown, making obsolete the notion that a simple checklist of environmental problems can be dealt with once and for all.

The following examples suggest the range of problems and the difficulties in fashioning and implementing responses.

• *Although current air quality programs have helped clean the air in the vicinity of emission sources, many pollutants escape and are carried much longer distances in the upper atmosphere than previously thought, before they fall to earth.* Acid rain is the most publicized example. Another instance is the large amount of toxic chemicals, like PCBs in the Great Lakes, that come from pollution settling out of the air. The disparity between the geographic scope of environmental problems and the jurisdictions of the governments that must deal with the problems is becoming an acute weakness in efforts to improve environmental quality. The jurisdictions creating the problems have no incentive to do anything about them, while those jurisdictions on the receiving end have no power over far-off sources.

 • *Indoor air pollution is another serious problem current programs do not address.* Most people spend most of their time indoors, and pollutants inside are found in much higher concentrations than levels outside. One source, smoking, is notoriously difficult to curb. Other sources of indoor pollutants, such as materials or building systems widely used in new construction throughout the country, may not have ready substitutes. The national debate has not really begun about how to respond to the discovery that indoor air pollution often far exceeds minimum health standards for air outdoors.

 • *Growing conflicts surround the allocation of fresh water supplies.* Especially in the West, state water allocation systems established in the last century have allocated all the available water, and then some, to uses such as irrigation, ranching, and mining. Today, as values are changing, Indian tribes, urban populations, and others are asserting new claims on fresh water for recreation, industrial expansion, and preservation of aquatic environments. Mechanisms that can adjust water allocations to the emerging situation are woefully inadequate. The shift from an era of water development to an era of water management will have substantial and widespread impact throughout the West.

 • *Groundwater is becoming increasingly contaminated.* About half the population depends on unseen groundwater resources for drinking water. Hundreds of thousands of Americans at one time or another have had to switch to bottled water. Experience has demonstrated that it is usually far less costly and far less complicated to protect groundwater from contamination than to clean up polluted supplies later. Effective protection will require modifying and controlling widespread, often diffuse activities, such as use of septic tanks and pesticide, herbicide, and fertilizer applications.

 • *The review and reregistration of approximately 600 basic pesticide ingredients in use in this country are far behind where they should be.* Although this process was mandated in legislation in 1972, EPA estimates that it may take well into the next century to complete the job. In the meantime, environmental experts cite potential threats from pesticides as among the most important risks to public health and the environment. EPA itself has courageously identified these risks as far more serious than those posed by many problems on which EPA spends far more effort and money.

 • *After eight years and $1.5 billion, the Superfund program to clean up toxic waste dumps has yielded disappointing results.* Distressingly little is known about how many toxic waste sites there are and how serious a risk each poses. No one has yet satisfactorily determined the standards to which sites should be cleaned, and the prospects of having agreement on these standards in any reasonable time are dim. Too few scientifically and legally defensible standards exist for troublesome chemicals. No one can yet say with authority that waste sites once sealed will remain so permanently.

With these fundamental questions unresolved, the task confronting EPA has been daunting, helping to explain why only 13 official cleanups had been achieved by mid-1987. Some cleanup efforts have begun at half the sites included on the National Priority List, and the agency has undertaken 1,000 emergency actions where the sites posed imminent threats. But the Superfund program may well result in many billions of dollars being spent with little net reduction in risk to public health and the environment. Hazardous waste cleanup, to which the nation has assigned a high priority backed by a $9 billion program, is hobbled by excessively onerous processes for fixing liability and mixing federal and private funding.

Superfund affords the best example of the lasting legacy of congressional mistrust of EPA, dating to the early years of the Reagan administration. The most promising, cheapest, and quickest solution to the cleanup of hazardous waste dumps is to obtain voluntary settlements. EPA has the legal authority and funds to foster such settlements, but Congress, which is highly suspicious of a repetition of sweetheart deals between regulators and industries, has created a climate hostile to settlements. As a result, there is little prospect the law's goals or timetables will be met or that its funding will stretch as far as had been hoped.

• *Degradation of wildlife refuges and national parklands continues.* More and more, the country's wildlife refuges and national parklands are threatened by energy, commercial, and other developments outside their borders. These developments not only diminish the visual and recreational amenities that parks and refuges provide to many millions of visitors each year, but also threaten the very survival of wildlife and undermine other natural and cultural resources these parks and refuges were established, at least in part, to protect. It often comes as a shock even to frequent visitors to the national parks to learn that some of the wildlife they are accustomed to seeing may soon no longer be there, as development in adjacent areas closes off vital habitat. Some major species, including the gray wolf and the mountain sheep, are likely to disappear from such parks as Yellowstone and Zion. Over the next century or two, Yosemite may lose between 8 and 15 of the 20 mammalian species that exist there now; Bryce Canyon may lose all its current large mammalian species. Climate change could wreak further havoc on parkland wildlife as changes in vegetation, temperature, and water availability alter habitat, even as surrounding development closes off potential escape routes.

• *Soil erosion continues at rates that are unacceptably high in the long term if the nation's farmlands are to continue supporting high levels of agricultural production.* An estimated 106 million acres (or 25 percent of U.S. cropland) exceed the average tolerable erosion levels each year. One especially costly dimension of this problem is the variety of problems caused by eroding soils when they leave the farm: for example, waterways polluted by pesticides and fertilizers carried off by erosion; reservoirs and harbors that silt up faster than predicted; recreational opportunities and wildlife habitat that are lost. The Conservation Foundation has estimated these losses off the farm (that is, not counting on-farm damages) at $6 billion per year.

• *Long after their values for flood control and fish and wildlife enhancement have been established, wetlands continue to be lost at a rapid rate.* With 50 percent of the nation's original endowment of wetlands now gone, draining, flooding, filling, cultivation, and development continue to destroy an estimated 300,000 to 500,000 acres per year. Some 80 percent of these losses have been attributable to agriculture. At the same time, many of the approaches used to manage wetlands are burdensome, costly, and inefficient. New programs are urgently needed to protect and manage the nation's wetlands more effectively.

• *After decades of environmental action by federal, state, and local governments and by citizen groups across the country, degradation of the American landscape is proceeding unchecked.* A steady, perceptible degradation of the countryside from urban sprawl and haphazard development continues to erode the distinctive qualities that differentiate one place from another. No national plan, no federal agency, can orchestrate protection of what Americans value about their communities; redefining the process and standards by which we build our landscape is ultimately a matter for local action. More than any other issue the poor quality of urban development—even in areas such as Florida, Colorado, and California— stands in stark contrast to the nation's lofty environmental aspirations. More than 20 years after the White House Conference on Natural Beauty, it is difficult to point to an example of urbanization in which the environment has not been degraded.

These examples hardly exhaust the list of problems. Carbon dioxide buildup in the atmosphere and the projected, accompanying climate change; depletion of the protective ozone shield; the loss of biological diversity; waste of energy; disposal of nuclear wastes; pollution at public facilities; loss of historic structures; threats to continuing productivity of national forests and rangeland; controversy surrounding the use of Alaska's abundant natural resources and the designation of wilderness areas there and in the continental United States; industrial and chemical accidents—these are but a few of the dozens of issues that require urgent attention.

THE DIFFICULTY OF FASHIONING RESPONSES

For many of the long-standing environmental issues, there is at least a track record of programmatic successes and failures on which to build. Yet, in virtually every instance, the easy steps have been taken, the obvious solutions applied. The difficulty of making further progress on these issues, as well as on problems more recently recognized, is compounded by a number of factors:

• *The nation's budget situation provides a major source of conflict.* Competition among federal activities, including environmental programs, for a share of the U.S. budget is fierce. States and localities are little better off, for they have been asked to pick up many programs that the federal government has pared in efforts to reduce budget deficits.

• *The process by which policies are set and decisions made leaves much to be desired.* Better information is a requisite for better decisions. Yet the degree of uncertainty surrounding the data on which environmental decisions are based is often frightening. For example, many of the air quality models used to support regulatory decisions have enormous margins of error. Equally lacking is information about how well programs work; compliance statistics are notoriously incomplete, and monitoring of program implementation is problematic at best. Little evaluation has been done, for example, on the municipal sewage-treatment program to determine how much actual improvement in water quality has been brought by the billions of dollars the nation has invested. In addition, decisions are still too often made in the confrontational manner that has polarized environmental decision making in the past.

• *Many issues cut across the boundaries of traditional programs, thus requiring herculean efforts at integration and cooperation among multiple offices, agencies, and levels of government whose activities, as often as not, are competitive or adversarial.* Each of dozens of regulatory programs—for underground storage tanks, old hazardous waste sites, new hazardous waste sites, indoor air pollution, outdoor air pollution, workplace air pollution, and on and on—concentrates only on its narrowly defined mission, generally ignoring often critical ecological interrelationships. Several different permitting systems exist at federal and state levels to regulate activities in wetlands, for example; as part of these programs, agencies use at least one-half dozen different definitions of wetlands, making compliance difficult and helping create interagency confusion and battles.

• *Some of today's problems are less visible, less tangible, and thus more difficult to mobilize for than those with which the country has been grappling over the past two decades.* Public outrage in this country over foul, dirty water or over brown-colored smog—problems people could readily see—helped marshal a constituency for environmental cleanup. The 1972 clean water legislation set a goal of "swimmable and fishable waters," a powerful image capable of capturing public attention and motivating action. People could see results. But no one can see acid rain or carbon dioxide or the ozone layer or indoor air pollutants or groundwater. Though the effects of these recently identified problems may be felt all the same, experts with access to sophisticated equipment and computer programs are increasingly needed to identify environmental problems and convince officials and the public of their scope and consequences.

• *The sources of many environmental problems are becoming far more diffuse.* Basic U.S. pollution control laws have relied on the states for their implementation and are premised on the assumption that damage caused by pollution occurs primarily in the state in which the pollution arises. Two decades ago, consensus for action in a community could develop over nailing a specific culprit—take action, and the problem would go away. Technology could reduce a power plant's emissions. A manufacturing plant could be required to treat its effluents. If pollution sources were numerous, they nonetheless were discernible, and strategies or controls for correcting the problems were available even if results fell short of expectations.

But it is much harder to target those who are responsible for the environmental problems now being recognized. Few strategies can be easily devised, few controls readily applied. No single culprit is causing the buildup of carbon dioxide and other gases in the atmosphere; countless individuals and economic activities, highly decentralized, are responsible. Similarly, depletion of ozone in the upper atmosphere can be laid at no one's doorstep in particular. Responsibility is shared widely. Tropical forests are falling, endangering wildlife, not only because of ill-conceived development projects but even more because of the activities of countless subsistence farmers eking out their living from the forests. Radon, a health hazard only recently recognized as such in this country, occurs naturally. Human activities are not to blame for the basic problem, though decisions by innumerable local officials over the years unknowingly have allowed homes to be sited in places of high exposure; the drive to create more energy efficient buildings has exacerbated the situation.

• *Some of the problems now confronting the country are likely to cause environmental and economic damage on a global scale.* Among these are climate warming; the threat of depletion of the earth's ozone layer, with its potential for increasing the incidence of skin cancer; the rampant loss of tropical forests and other highly productive ecosystems; and inadequate coordination and control of agricultural, chemical, and other goods traded in international commerce. No one country can solve these problems on its own. Different cultures and languages can turn the simplest transactions into complex undertakings. Above all, the weakness of international institutions, arising from jealously guarded national sovereignty, means that implementation would remain extremely difficult at best, even if nations could agree on cooperative measures.

SETTING A NEW COURSE

When a new presidential administration takes office in January 1989, it will hold the potential for a fresh start and new leadership. It would be well advised to avoid the mistakes of ideology, single-mindedness, and confrontation that in the past have interfered with constructive development and implementation of sound environmental policy. This will be true for the broad range of environmental issues facing this country— pollution control, land management, wildlife protection, and so forth. The new administration should set a high priority on constructing an active, effective partnership among diverse interests. Numerous successful efforts at collaborative problem solving among business representatives, leaders of public interest groups, and officials at all levels of government show that such an approach is promising.

Unquestionably, the new administration would do well to begin the difficult process of overhauling the nation's current approach to pollution control. The administration will find no readily mobilized constituency for such a massive restructuring; too many interested parties—in Congress, conservation groups, industry, the legal profession, and elsewhere—have a stake in the current, heavily fragmented system. Federal legislative responsibility for the environment is split up among Congress's many committees, with little coordination of efforts.

Many of today's environmental problems defy traditional categorization. Acid rain, global climate change, groundwater pollution, toxic substances, hazardous waste—none of these problems fits into the way pollution control programs have been conceived in the past.

One important step forward in overcoming this fragmented approach is already being taken by EPA. The agency is devoting increased attention to risk assessment, the setting of priorities based on analysis of how many

people are affected how seriously by multiple sources of exposure to contaminants. Setting priorities, however, requires consideration not only of
environmental effects but also of factors such as feasibility and costs of curbing problems, and this could generate substantial conflict as various interests
in Congress, EPA, and the public argue over what should be the priorities.

Regardless of the controversy, however, public consideration of a new
approach to environmental protection is essential. Merely patching up current policies and institutions, helpful as it might be in the short term, simply
will not be adequate for the country in the long term. Fundamental changes
in concepts, in laws, and in the organizational structure of legislative and
executive branch activities are essential if further progress is to be made
on long-standing environmental issues and newly recognized ones alike.

The Conservation Foundation in the 1980s, even while it has pointed to
the nation's unmet environmental needs, has repeatedly emphasized the
indisputable achievements of the nation's environmental reforms of the
1970s. Those achievements deserve recognition, for they vindicate significant efforts and large financial sacrifices. Yet with time the victories over
conventional air and water pollutants loom less large in the unfolding picture of both accumulated toxic wastes and emerging new problems that
threaten groundwater, tropical and temperate forests, the upper atmosphere,
climate, and life on earth.

In the face of budget deficits, trade barriers, arms control, and other
prominent national issues, even ensuring that the environment is on the
agenda may not be simple. But the task is no less important for its difficulty. Achieving a prosperous and sustainable economy built on healthy
and productive natural systems is critical as the nation prepares to move
into the 1990s.

William K. Reilly
President
The Conservation Foundation
September 1987

PART I
Status and Trends

Chapter 1

Underlying Trends

Three separate but interacting conditions determine the quality of a nation's environment: (*a*) the natural environmental endowment, (*b*) the stress induced by population growth and economic development and (*c*) the amount of protection afforded by the nation.

Of these conditions, only the first is fixed or "given." Some areas are plentifully endowed with high-quality natural resources that can be exploited without significant depletion. Different natural environments have different abilities to resist or assimilate insults; for example, fast-flowing streams are better able to assimilate some pollutants than sluggish lakes. Some areas, on the other hand, are both fragile and impoverished in terms of their natural attributes. Ironically, no objective way to measure natural environmental endowments has yet been proposed.

Not surprisingly, the final two conditions also can be difficult to measure. Nevertheless, an understanding of basic, underlying stresses and protective efforts is necessary if one is to adequately comprehend the widely varied environmental issues that will face the United States and the rest of the world in the coming years.

STRESSES

Environmental stress results not only from the amount of population growth and economic development, which can be measured reasonably accurately, but also from how this growth and development occur, which can be much harder to quantify. The number of people and the size and structure of the economy in any society determine how natural resources are used and,

1

in that usage, the volume and type of contaminants that are generated—in short, the overall demands placed by a society on its environment. Changing trends in population size and demographics and in economic health may result in either positive or negative changes in environmental stresses, depending on the nature of the shift. Thus, only by looking at changes in this context can society begin to address the most pressing current issues and plan for future needs.

Population

In the mid-1980s, trends in U.S. population growth and distribution did not deviate significantly from previously observed directions. Overall, population growth rates gradually declined, people from the North and East continued to move to the South and West, and growth was concentrated in suburban areas.

Growth

As of mid-1986, the population of the United States reached an estimated 241 million people, up some 14 million from mid-1980 estimates—an average growth rate of under 1 percent per year.[1] Since the mid-1950s, the rate of population growth (which includes both natural growth, or births minus deaths, and net immigration) has steadily fallen and is projected to decline still further[2] (figure 1.1).

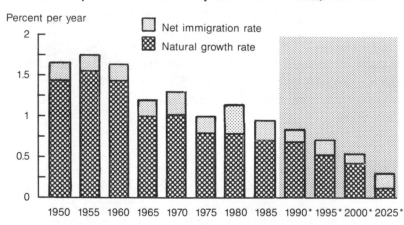

Figure 1.1
U.S. Population Past and Projected Growth Rates, 1950–2025

* Projected growth rate.

Source: U.S. Bureau of the Census.

The decline in the net growth rate between the 1950s and the 1980s is primarily due to the reduced number of children being born per woman. However, following a 15-year decline, the total number of children born in the United States actually increased between 1975 and 1985. This echo of the "baby boom" of the 1950s "reflects larger numbers of women in the childbearing ages rather than an increase in fertility rates."[3]

Since 1972, the average number of children born to an American woman during her child-bearing years (the "total fertility rate") has been smaller than the number (2.1) required to eventually sustain zero population growth or population replacement.[4] In 1985, the U.S. total fertility rate was approximately 1.8, as it has been since 1977.[5] However, even at this low rate, it would take another 40 years for the natural growth rate to fall to zero, assuming no net immigration. At a net immigration rate of 450,000 people per year, it would take 60 years to reach zero population growth.[6]

Immigration has increased consistently since 1970, with an exceptionally large influx of immigrants in 1980. Because of the decline in natural growth rates, immigration has become relatively more significant. The approximately 577,000 immigrants in 1985 accounted for approximately 26 percent of total population growth that year.[7]*

The U.S. trend does not reflect population changes occurring throughout the world, however. According to one estimate, the world's population reached five billion in 1986, up from four billion in 1975.[9] The United Nations estimates that the world's population grew an average of 1.67 percent per year from 1980 to 1985.[10] This is equivalent to adding about five New York Citys per year to the world's population.[11]

However, the average growth rate, like any average, masks significant differences between different regions of the world. All of the more-developed countries show relatively low population growth rates. In Western Europe, for instance, the population growth rate was 0.26 percent per year between 1980 and 1985, while the United States and Canada grew at a combined rate of 0.8 percent per year. Similarly, the population in Eastern Europe and the USSR increased at an annual rate of 0.84 percent during the same period.[12]

In contrast, the less-developed countries experienced very high fertility and population growth rates, although in many cases these too have somewhat diminished during the past decade. Africa grew the fastest between 1980 and 1985, with a rate of 3.01 percent, followed by Latin America (which includes South and Central America and the Caribbean) at 2.30 percent per year. Asia and Oceania had a growth rate of 1.73 percent annually during the same time period, although China grew at the relatively

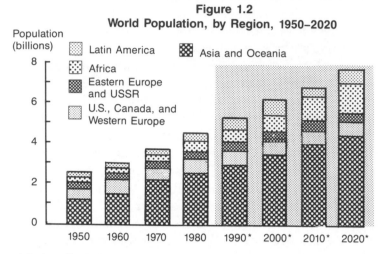

Figure 1.2
World Population, by Region, 1950–2020

* Projected.
Source: United Nations.

low rate of 1.17 percent per year[13] due to its strict population growth policies since the early 1970s.

As a result of this disparity in growth, less-developed nations will continue to comprise an increasing proportion of world population in coming years (figure 1.2). They represented approximately 72 percent of the world's population in 1970 but will account for 92 percent of the increase between 1970 and 2020.[14] The less-developed nations here are considered to include Latin America, Africa, Asia (except for Japan), and Oceania (except for Australia and New Zealand).

In 1984, in a significant reversal of earlier policies, the United States announced its new population and family planning policy for less-developed countries at the International Conference on Population held in Mexico City. Although it supports voluntary family planning programs, the United States declared it will not support coercive population control programs nor provide assistance to multilateral or nongovernmental organizations that perform or promote abortion. The consensus eventually reached by the 146 participating governments affirmed that "governments have a

*These figures, based on the Census Bureau's revised methodology, include 200,000 undocumented entrants per year into the United States since 1980 as well as 160,000 legal emigrants, resulting in a net increase in immigration of 76,000 per year.[8] This estimate, however, is very uncertain.

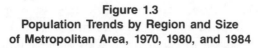

Figure 1.3
Population Trends by Region and Size
of Metropolitan Area, 1970, 1980, and 1984

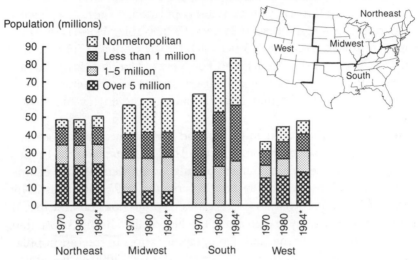

* Estimated population.

Source: U.S. Bureau of the Census.

responsibility to make universally available the information and means for couples and individuals to make decisions about the number and spacing of their children."[15] The conference accommodated the U.S. policy by deploring the use of coercion and agreeing that abortion should not be promoted as a method of family planning. The outcome of this policy has been that the United States has cut off contributions to a number of international family planning and aid organizations.[16]

Distribution

Within the United States, two major population distribution trends have occurred since 1970. The first relates to regional shifts in population—people moving primarily from the Northeast and Midwest to the South and West (figure 1.3). For example, comparing 1950 and 1984, the Northeast dropped from 26.1 percent of the population to 21.0 percent, and the Midwest dropped from 29.4 to 25 percent. The South, on the other hand, grew from 31.2 to 34.1 percent and the West from 13.3 to 19.8 percent.[17] During the 1970s, Wyoming, Arizona, Nevada, Texas, and Florida grew most rapidly, whereas New York, the District of Columbia, and Rhode Island all experienced net decreases in population.[18]

Between 1980 and 1985, Alaska joined the five fastest growing states, while Wyoming dropped out of this group and became the 13th fastest growing state. Five states (Michigan, Iowa, West Virginia, Ohio, and Pennsylvania) and the District of Columbia lost population.[19] The fastest growing metropolitan areas in the 1980-1985 period were Naples, Florida (36.0 percent); Anchorage, Alaska (35.3 percent); Ocala, Florida (32.3 percent); Midland, Texas (32.1 percent); and Fort Peirce, Florida (31.4 percent). However, in some cities (such as Houston and Midland, Texas) growth slowed somewhat in the mid-1980s because of the energy production slowdown.[20]

Projections of what future migration and growth patterns will look like depend at least in part on whom is asked. The U.S. Bureau of the Census (BOC), for example, tends to make population projections that assume future trends will be the same as those experienced in the recent past. The Bureau of Economic Analysis (BEA) bases its projections on anticipated future economic activity in each state. The National Planning Association (NPA) combines economic and demographic factors to forecast population growth.[21] Estimates by these experts differ significantly. For example, projections of population in the year 2000 put New York at 14,990,200 (BOC), 18,696,200 (NPA), or 18,971,000 (BEA). Texas's population at the turn of the century is projected to be 20,739,400 (BOC), 18,801,800 (NPA), or 19,339,000 (BEA).[22] Such wide variability can confound long-term planning for environmental needs such as water supply, sewage treatment, and transportation.

The second trend is the fairly consistent high growth—albeit lower than in the 1970s—of suburban areas in comparison to central cities (figure 1.4).[23]* In some parts of the country, this growth is based on movement away from central cities to suburbs and rural areas. In other areas, this trend reflects migration from nonmetropolitan areas, with growth not necessarily confined to suburban areas. With few exceptions, the major metropolitan areas in the South and West experienced growth in both the central cities and suburbs during the 1980-1984 period (figure 1.4). While suburban

---

*Large metropolitan areas are defined here as those with a population of over one million, according to the 1980 U.S. Census. Metropolitan area growth rates are defined by calculating a population-weighted average of central city and suburban growth rates. The largest city in the metropolitan statistical area (MSA) is designated a central city, as are other cities in the area if they meet minimum population size and specified place-of-work requirements.[24] The remaining area of an MSA constitutes the suburbs.

Figure 1.4
Population Change in Central Cities, Suburbs, and Large Metropolitan Areas of the United States, 1980–1984*

☐ Entire metropolitan area

▨ Central cities

■ Suburbs

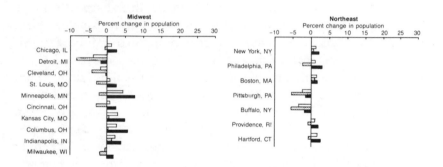

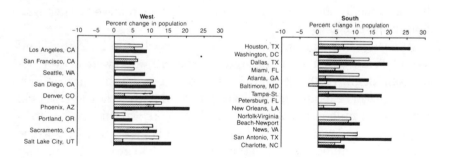

* 1984 data are provisional estimates.

Source: U.S. Bureau of the Census.

areas generally grew faster than downtown areas, they grew from a smaller population base. Thus, the overall metropolitan area growth rates are lower than those for the suburbs alone. For example, Houston suburbs grew 25.9 percent, while the metropolitan area as a whole increased by 15.0 percent. Other notable increases were in Dallas, with 19.4 percent growth in the suburbs and 14.2 percent overall, and Tampa-St. Petersburg, with 17.7 percent growth in the suburbs and 12.2 percent overall.[25]

In contrast, metropolitan areas in the Northeast and Midwest grew much more slowly, if at all. Some, such as New York City, Philadelphia, and St. Louis, managed to turn their decreases of the 1970s to small rates of increase in the 1980s.[26] Generally, growth in the suburbs contributed significantly to growth rates in these regions (and, in some cases, offset declines in the central cities). For instance, while only two large (over one million people) central cities in the Northeast and three large cities in the Midwest grew between 1980 and 1984, five of seven metropolitan areas in the Northeast and seven of ten metropolitan areas in the Midwest experienced an overall net increase in population during the same period.[27] The decline of northeastern and midwestern central cities thus resulted both from movement to the suburbs and an exodus to the South and West.

In other parts of the world, the trend seems to be very much toward the growth of large cities. In the less-developed countries, some 34 percent of the population lives in urban areas, as compared with 72 percent of the population of more-developed countries.[28] But the urban proportion of less-developed countries is expected to increase dramatically in the future, primarily due to high natural growth rates and rural-to-urban migration in these regions.[29]

As a result, most of the world's largest cities will soon be in the Third World. While only 4 of the 10 largest cities in the world were in developing countries in 1970, the United Nations projects that by the year 2000 8 of them will be located in the developing world. The 6 largest cities will have over 15 million people each; only New York was this large in 1970 (figure 1.5). In 1950 the average size of the 35 largest urban areas in the world was 4.1 million; by 1980 the average size had grown to 8 million; and by the year 2000 the average size is projected to be 12.1 millon people.[30]

Implications

For the United States and similar countries, the environmental implications of population trends are both positive and negative. On the positive side, reduced population growth rates may reduce resource consumption rates, the development of natural lands, and, in conjunction with

Figure 1.5
Population in the World's Largest Urban Areas, 1970, 1985, and 2000

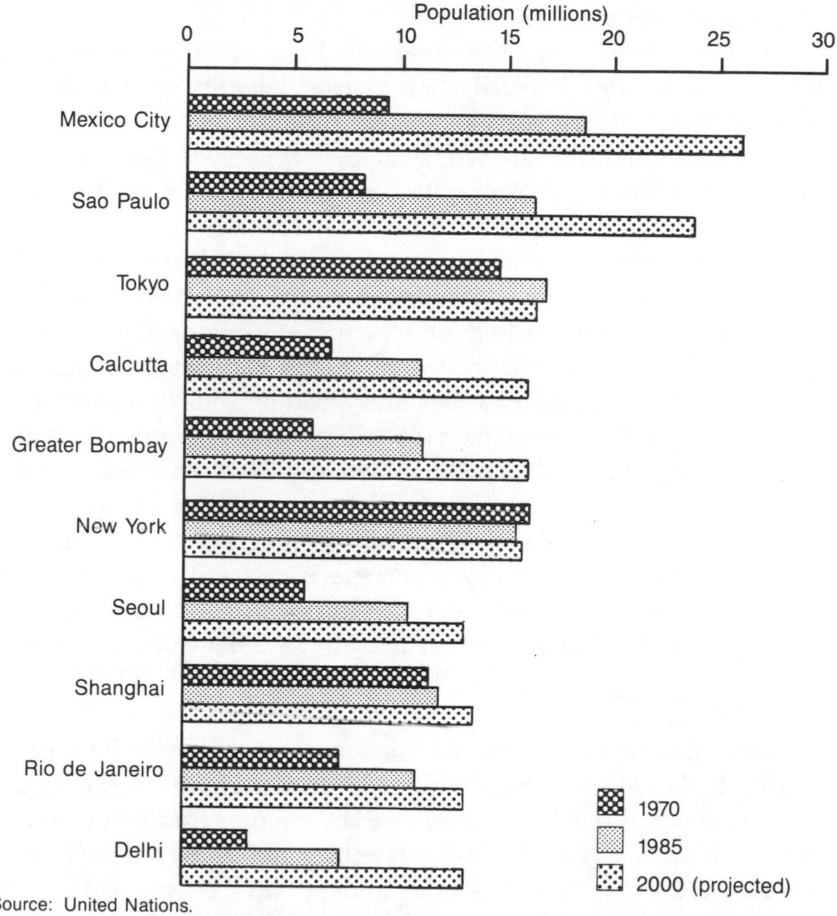

Population (millions)

	1970
	1985
	2000 (projected)

Source: United Nations.

improvements in control technology, pollution. In the United States, the slowdown in central city population growth in the Northeast and Midwest means that the number of people living in the areas where the highest pollution levels have been experienced is not growing significantly. The new booming Sunbelt regions tend to house less industrial manufacturing than do Frostbelt regions; even where such plants are constructed, they tend to be newer and, therefore, less polluting. However, it is not only the large industrial polluters that create serious pollution problems but automobiles, "high-technology" firms, and small businesses as well. The southern and western regions are as likely to experience these problems as the older cities in the Northeast and Midwest; they may be even more vulnerable, due to current demographic and economic trends, as well as environmental factors.

The shift is also placing stresses on limited water supplies. Many of the fastest-growing states are already short of water. For instance, Arizona and the rest of the southern Colorado River basin already consume more water than is naturally available. In many areas, the development associated with population dispersion is also eating up prime farmland and valuable wildlife habitat and creating conflicts with other rural land uses.

In less-developed countries, the environmental implications of current population trends are almost uniformly negative. Many Third World cities are plagued by overcrowding and substandard living conditions, as well as industrial pollutants, inadequate water supplies and sewage treatment, air pollution from automobiles, and other environmental contaminants.[31] The high population growth rates can only put more pressure on natural resources and increase urban pollution levels in these countries. And the high growth rates these cities are experiencing means that increasing portions of the world's total population will be subjected to these environmental problems. The rural areas are deteriorating as well because of rapid deforestation and significant erosion.[32] The growth and distribution of population in developing countries remains a fundamental problem.

Economy

Economic pressures are the second fundamental stress on environmental quality. In the United States, the early 1980s saw the most severe recession since the end of World War II,[33] followed by vigorous growth in 1984 and slower but positive rates of growth since that time. However, the United States, because of its unique position in the world economy, faces major obstacles to attaining and maintaining a strong economy in the near future.

Growth

Although the constant-dollar growth rate for the U.S. gross national product (GNP) grew at an average annual rate of 2.67 percent between 1970 and 1985, annual growth rates ranged from − 2.6 percent in 1982 to + 6.4 percent in 1984[34] (figure 1.6). Unemployment rates have fluctuated as well, from a low of 4.9 percent in 1970 and 1973 to a peak of 9.7 percent in 1982 during the recession, with a mean of 6.9 percent for the 1970-1985 period.[35] However, inflation has dropped considerably since the late 1970s

Figure 1.6
Percentage Growth in U.S. Gross National Product,
in Constant Dollars, 1970–1985

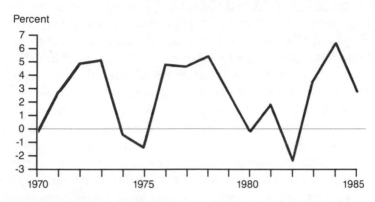

Source: U.S. Bureau of Economic Analysis.

and early 1980s. The rate of change in consumer prices fell from a high of 13.5 percent in 1980 to 3.8 percent in 1985.[36]

While the economy made a strong comeback in 1984 from the recession, the recovery has not continued quite as expected. Growth in GNP slowed considerably in 1985 (to 2.7 percent), and the Congressional Budget Office projects that real GNP growth will be only slightly higher during the remainder of the decade.[37] Although growth in employment was higher than average for a recovery period, productivity (especially in the non-manufacturing sector) appears to have been significantly lower than is normal during such periods.[38]

What do these trends imply about environmental conditions? At the aggregate level, an answer is difficult. On one hand, the economic slowdown of the early 1980s, for all its costs, may have temporarily benefited the environment. Lower industrial production probably resulted in less industrial pollution and less energy consumption. On the other hand, government budget reductions significantly hampered some environmental agencies and programs (see "Environmental Expenditures" section).

How any future economic growth affects environmental quality depends on the pattern of growth. Business investments in the near future will probably have mostly positive or neutral environmental implications because of the stricter controls usually placed on new sources. However, the net effect depends on the extent to which any reduction in per-unit pollution is offset by increased pollution due to increases in overall industrial output.[39]

Over the past several decades, the economy has undergone a structural shift from an economy with a roughly even split between manufacturing and services to a service-based economy. For instance, in 1950, goods-producing industries accounted for 49 percent of employment, and services comprised 51 percent. By 1980, these figures had shifted to 33 and 66 percent, respectively.[40] Figure 1.7 shows that, while the manufacturing sectors have maintained positive average growth rates, the highest growth rates have been in sectors such as communications; personal, business, and other services; electric, gas, and sanitary services; and finance, insurance, and real estate.[41] It is reasonable to expect that these relatively clean industries will continue to grow faster than the goods-producing industries.

Within the manufacturing sector, the growth over the past 15 years has been and should continue to be primarily in the technology-based industries, such as computers and communications equipment, rather than in smoke-stack industries.[42] While these high-technology industries have often been considered less environmentally damaging than traditional heavy industries, they can also cause serious environmental problems. Though they may emit less conventional air and water pollution, they may still release toxic substances. For example, in California's Silicon Valley, which is the proto-type of new industrial development, 7 locations were on the list of approved priority areas for Superfund cleanup as of 1986; another 13 were proposed.[43] The primary problem was toxic contamination of the groundwater with solvents.[44]

Regional Distribution

Economic growth, like population growth, does not occur evenly throughout the country. The past decade has seen a distinct shift in the locus of economic growth from the Northeast and Midwest to the South and West.[45] This trend was interrupted in the mid-1980s, at least temporarily, because of the fall in energy prices (which has particularly hurt boom states such as Texas), the glut of office and condominium space in Sunbelt cities, and the shutdown of many southern textile mills.[46] While the Frostbelt has begun to make a comeback, the long-term outlook suggests that economic influence will continue to shift toward the South and West.[47]

To the extent that high economic growth rates continue in the western states, stresses will be placed on water supplies and other environmental elements in that region. The siting of industrial facilities outside established industrial areas may consume prime agricultural land or wildlife habitat.

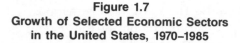

Figure 1.7
Growth of Selected Economic Sectors
in the United States, 1970–1985

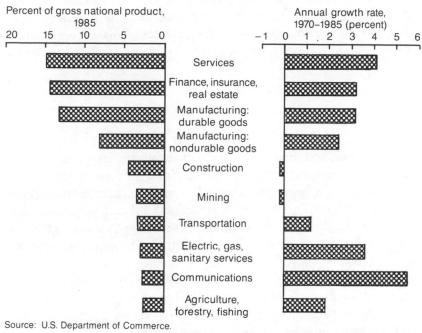

Percent of gross national product, 1985

Annual growth rate, 1970–1985 (percent)

Source: U.S. Department of Commerce.

New industrial plants, particularly in areas with no major prior development, may also have indirect environmental impacts associated with an influx of new people to an area, such as increased vehicular air pollution and inadequate water and sewage systems.[48]

Foreign Trade

Another factor confounding the current U.S. economic situation is the rapidly expanding trade deficit that developed in the mid-1980s. The trade balance for goods and services shifted from a peak surplus in 1981 of $28 billion to a record deficit in 1984 of more than $64 billion. Three major factors contributed to the growth of the deficit: the high value of the dollar in the early 1980s compared with other major currencies (making U.S. goods relatively more expensive), the slow economic recovery of many industrialized countries after the 1980-1982 recession (reducing their demand for imports), and the Third World's international debt crisis.[49]

The environmental implications of the trade deficit have not been thoroughly analyzed. At the most basic level, however, the deficit means that the United States is shifting some of its environmental stress abroad by consuming goods and natural resources produced in other countries rather than at home. This reduction of domestic environmental stresses may bring a concomitant increase in regions that often have much less capacity to resist them.[50]

International Conditions

Economic conditions in other countries are as unsettled as they are in the United States, and their effect on the environment is even more uncertain. The world economy suffered severely from the most recent recession; since then, the five largest industrialized countries' economies showed strong growth in 1984 but grew more slowly in 1985.[51] Many developing countries showed a similar trend; oil-exporting countries and countries that hold large foreign debts have been especially hard hit by economic conditions in the 1980s.[52]

The prices that developing countries receive for commodities are, in real terms, at the lowest level in 50 years.[53] These low prices combined with high interest payments and the high cost of oil and other imports have contributed to extremely serious foreign exchange problems for many lower-income nations. To recover from these problems, as well as to provide for rapidly expanding populations, some countries have been pushed to exploit aggressively their natural resources, accelerating the destruction of tropical and other forest lands, grasslands, fisheries, and other natural resources.[54] For example, an estimated 29,000 to 36,000 square miles of tropical rain forest are being cleared annually, and perhaps another 39,000 square miles are being grossly disrupted.[55] These local trends threaten to deplete the ecological systems on which economic development is based, thus transforming renewable resources into nonrenewable resources.[56]

Manufacturing by U.S. companies and affiliates is also increasing in many countries, often to supply the U.S. market.[57] While the growth of manufacturing abroad may result in fewer pollution or siting problems in the United States, international redistribution of industry may result in greater environmental impacts in other countries, especially in those countries that have less stringent environmental regulations than the United States.[58]

One of the most significant shocks to the world's economic system in the 1980s has been the substantial fall in oil prices. The rapid price increases experienced during the 1970s were a major cause of the rapid inflation and other economic problems experienced during that decade. But the rapid drop in prices during the 1980s has created some significant economic problems as well—particularly for the energy industry and oil-exporting states and countries.[59]

The fall in oil prices produced far-reaching effects, one being a transfer of benefits from producers to consumers of energy. On one hand, energy users benefit significantly from cheaper energy, especially energy-intensive industries such as trucking, airlines, and electric utilities.[60] States and countries heavily dependent on imports also gain from the lower prices.

On the other hand, lower oil prices dramatically affect the economies of oil-producing areas both in the United States and abroad. While the rest of the country enjoys an unexpected windfall, states such as Texas, Alaska, Oklahoma, Louisiana, and California suffer from a variety of economic woes: unemployment in Louisiana, for instance, reached 13.2 percent in March 1986 compared with a rate of 7.2 percent nationally.[61] The American Petroleum Institute reported that, based on a survey conducted in March 1986, the number of active oil rigs was less than half the December 1985 level, spending plans for 1986 for exploration and production were curtailed by at least 25 percent from 1985, and employment in exploration and production had declined by nearly 100,000 jobs since 1985.[62]

The declining oil prices are also wreaking havoc among oil exporting nations' economies. The Organization of Petroleum Exporting Countries (OPEC), which was so successful with its pricing policies in the 1970s, has lost much of its power due to development of new non-OPEC sources of oil, decreased worldwide consumption, increased energy conservation and efficiency, and an inability of its members to come to agreement on production quotas and prices, along with lower oil prices.[63] Non-OPEC countries such as Mexico and Egypt are also facing major financial problems.[64]

The collapse in oil prices, however, should translate into greater economic growth, lower inflation, and lower interest rates over the long term in oil-importing areas. It may also stimulate increased energy consumption, which could create significant environmental impacts and increase again the dependence of U.S. consumers on foreign supplies, with all the security risks that would entail.[65] However, the structural energy conservation measures implemented over the past decade—such as home insulation and greater fuel efficiency in appliances and automobiles—should preclude a return to former energy consumption growth rates.[66]

Some experts expect that depressed world oil prices will be sustained for the rest of the decade, followed by moderate annual increases between 1990 and 1995.[67] However, events of the 1970s clearly showed that, if nothing else, the future is unpredictable. During that decade, a surprising number of reputable energy forecasters, including industry analysts, government experts, and academic researchers, were far off the mark.[68] Energy prices showed a surprisingly strong vulnerability to political events in the 1970s, a factor that energy planners still may not be fully taking into account.[69]

Fiscal Policy

The federal government made two extremely significant shifts in its economic policies in the 1980s. The first was its approaches to dealing with the government's rapidly increasing budget deficit. The second was a major change in the structure of federal taxation, put in place by the Tax Reform Act of 1986.

The budget deficit, the largest in U.S. history and sizable enough to double the nation's debt in five years,[70] threatens to disrupt substantially the funding of governmental programs. Because of large increases in interest payments to service the outstanding debt (these increased at an average annual rate of 18.4 percent per year from 1980 through 1985)[71] and the Reagan administration's commitment to increased defense expenditures, domestic programs such as those to protect the environment are being squeezed particularly hard.

To counter the large deficits, Congress in 1985 enacted the Balanced Budget and Emergency Deficit Control Act (commonly known as the Gramm-Rudman-Hollings Act), mandating significant annual reductions in the federal deficit to balance the budget by 1991.[72] At the time of its passage, environmentalists expressed concerns that such budget reductions would only serve to increase the ultimate cost of dealing with problems such as toxic wastes, acid rain, and water pollution.[73] A few years later, however, it is still unclear whether the targets set in the law can be met, and if so, how the reductions will be allocated.

The primary impact of the second shift, substantial tax reform, will be not on total federal revenues but on private investment and expenditure decisions.[74] These decisions can have, of course, significant environmental impacts. As a group of environmentalists stated in a letter to the House and Senate tax committees, "Tax policy is environmental policy."[75]

The changes brought on by the Tax Reform Act will affect both personal expenditure and business investment decisions.[76] Higher after-tax income for many taxpayers is likely to result in an increase in personal consumption expenditures. This shift could have negative environmental impacts, though their exact nature and seriousness are impossible to predict. The impact would depend largely on what products consumers chose to buy; a shift to larger, less energy-efficient automobiles, for example, would have greater environmental repercussions than would increased purchase of personal computer equipment. In addition, charitable donations for environmental purposes may decline since taxpayers who don't itemize deductions will no longer be able to deduct donations when figuring their tax obligations, and the after-tax cost of such donations will be higher even when they are deducted.[77]*

Environmentalists have focused primarily, however, on the way the new tax law is likely to affect business expenditures. Here the elimination of some special tax breaks may have decidedly beneficial environmental effects, and the elimination of the investment tax credit along with other changes may generally reduce pressures to exploit natural resources and convert environmentally valuable lands for "economic" purposes.[79]

Some of the most significant changes will affect the agricultural sector, where the new bill eliminates the special tax breaks that promoted the clearing and drainage of lands for agricultural purposes. The elimination of special tax treatment for capital gains will further reduce the incentives for such land conversion, and the bill contains a provision that specifically excludes the conversion of highly erodible lands and wetlands from any capital gains advantages that Congress may adopt in the future. A final change limits special tax advantages for soil conservation expenditures to those that are consistent with conservation plans approved by the Soil Conservation Service or a comparable agency.[80] This provision should eliminate at least the most flagrant abuses of this tax break, which has sometimes been applied to expenditures that had little relation to actual soil conservation needs and could even be environmentally destructive.[81]

Other major changes include the reduction of rapid depreciation benefits for electric utilities and the elimination of tax-exempt financing for many commercial developments.[82] Both should reduce incentives to construct new facilities, promote more efficient use of existing facilities, and reduce the conversion of environmentally valuable lands. At the same time, some

---

*The drop in the tax rate means that the percentage of every donation that is deducted will decline. Thus, for a taxpayer who was taxed at a rate of 50 percent under the old law and is now subject to a 28 percent tax rate, the cost of a donation will be 44 percent higher.[78]

of the tax benefits for historic preservation, private timber raising, and some renewable resource (for example, wind and geothermal) energy investments were retained,[83] although the importance may be reduced because of generally lower tax rates.

Environmentalists did not get all environmentally destructive tax breaks eliminated in the new bill. For instance, the oil and gas industries retained most tax advantages promoting the rapid exploitation of these resources in the United States.[84] Nevertheless, the changes that were made probably will reduce unnecessary environmental degradation and natural resource exploitation.

States also have experienced their share of fiscal distress. State treasuries experienced large revenue growth in the late 1970s, as evidenced by the high year-end balances that occurred in this period.[85] These large ending balances contributed to a citizen-led tax revolt—exemplified by California's Proposition 13 (a statewide initiative passed in 1978 that reduced property tax rates dramatically)[86]—towards the end of the decade. With the 1982-1983 recession, however, many state budgets were severely constrained, and many states raised tax rates.[87] After the recession, most state budgets recovered fairly well. However, in the mid-1980s, significant regional differences have emerged. While New England and mid-Atlantic states are thriving, states dependent on farming and energy are experiencing economic and fiscal difficulties as a result of the decline in oil prices and the soaring foreign trade deficit.[88]

Since the early 1970s, Congress has steadily increased the management responsibilities of state governments. A 1986 estimate done for the National Conference of State Legislatures listed 145 federal laws enacted since 1972 that require state action.[89] Another study lists 29 major federal statutes that regulate state and local governments, 14 of which concern some aspect of the environment.[90] A 1984 study put the cost of implementing existing federal mandates at about $200 billion.[91] However, federal funding authorizations to state governments have not followed the same trend. In recent years state governments have been given more fiscal responsibility and less financial support from the federal government.[92] The result has been "the gradual overburdening of state resources and capabilities in environmental management."[93]

Most, if not all, cities have also faced fiscal challenges in recent years. A reduction in the amount of federal money available to municipal governments has directly affected individual cities' abilities to provide basic services such as water and sewage treatment, solid waste disposal, health and welfare benefits, job training, and parks and recreation.

Surprisingly, however, one researcher found that, by some measures, many of the large, older cities that experienced fiscal crises in the 1970s, had, by 1982, seen their financial conditions improve, despite the drop in federal aid. This apparent improvement was due primarily to fiscal restraint by city officials—a reaction to the fiscal woes of the 1970s as well as the cutbacks in federal funding and economic recession in the early 1980s.[94] To meet stringent fiscal goals, many municipalities were forced to eliminate nonessential services and reduce the scope of basic services, as well as increase revenues through taxes, user fees, and other revenue-raising means.[95]

One strategy employed by many cities has been to cancel or delay capital expenditures for infrastructural improvements to bridges, highways, mass transit, water and sewer lines, wastewater treatment plants, schools, libraries, and police and fire stations. In addition, cities have attempted to lower the cost and increase the efficiency of service delivery through a variety of means.[96]

Nevertheless, most studies show continuing severe fiscal problems in many cities. For instance, the National League of Cities found that, of 660 cities surveyed, 56 percent expected expenditures to exceed revenues in 1986, up from 24 percent in 1984.[97] This trend could be exacerbated by proposed cutbacks in general revenue sharing and other federal funds that support urban programs; fiscal problems in Farm Belt and oil states may exacerbate the fiscal situation in cities because of reductions in grants to cities.[98]

RESPONSES

The multitude of stresses placed on the environment has stimulated significant responses in countries around the world. These responses are usually led by changes in public opinion as people become more concerned about the deteriorating conditions around them. The degree of concern appears to be correlated with economic well-being. As incomes increase, people become less concerned about simple survival and more concerned about the quality of that survival.

The shift in public opinion is followed by an increase in government environmental protection efforts. But passing laws and announcing programs do not, in themselves, improve the environment. Laws and programs must be vigorously implemented, and that implementation generally is reflected in greater environmental protection expenditures and increased government enforcement of environmental laws and regulations.

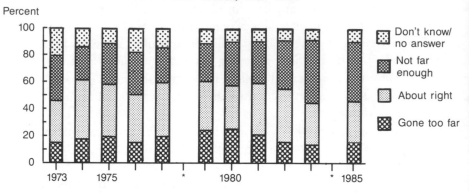

Figure 1.8
Public Support for Environmental Programs
in the United States, 1973–1985

Responses were to the question, "At the present time, do you think environmental protection laws and regulations have gone too far, or not far enough, or have struck about the right balance?"

* Data for 1978 and 1984 are not available.

Source: *Public Opinion*, The Roper Organization, and *Time*/Yankelovich.

Public Opinion

In most countries, the viability of government programs to conserve and protect the environment depends on strong public support. The durability of this public support is one of the remarkable characteristics of environmental programs in the United States. Since Earth Day in 1970, many observers and politicians have predicted that public attention would quickly fade as some new fad caught the public's fancy.[99] Much to the surprise of many, and partially stimulated by the current administration's environmental policies, the public's support for environmental programs appears to be "stronger than ever."[100]

By 1980, a gradual, but discernible, upward trend had occurred in the percentage of people who thought that environmental protection programs had "gone too far" (figure 1.8). Since then, this trend has reversed. The number of people who think environmental protection laws and regulations have gone too far is as low as it was in the early 1970s. By the mid-1980s, almost half the people thought these laws and regulations had not gone far enough; this proportion had seldom exceeded one-third previously. And positions seem to have hardened. The percentage who "don't know" has stabilized since 1980 and is smaller than at any time during the 1970s.

The events of the 1980s appear to have strongly crystallized people's opinions about the need for greater efforts to protect the environment.

Other recent public opinion polls reinforce these conclusions. A September 1985 *Time*/Yankelovich poll found that 73 percent of the respondents favored "strictly enforcing pollution regulations against an industrial plant in your area, even if workers might be laid off as a result."[101] The same survey found that 50 percent of those surveyed felt that business compliance with environmental laws and regulations had been poor, and 63 percent of those questioned thought that government enforcement efforts were not strict enough.[102] The strength of this concern was demonstrated by a 1983 public opinion poll in which 60,000 people ranked environmental crime in seventh place, after murder but ahead of heroin smuggling and skyjacking.[103] (see "Enforcement" section)

Similarly, the public feels strongly that industry should pay for environmental cleanup. A May 1986 Harris poll reported that, when asked who should pay for an injury to a person living near a landfill when it cannot be determined that the injury was caused by wastes from a specific company, 58 percent of the public thought that the companies using the landfill should pay and another 31 percent felt that the industry producing the waste should pay; only 5 percent thought that the government should compensate the victim.[104] More generally, a large majority of Americans favor "imposing high taxes on companies which pollute the environment, even if these companies' products would be higher priced because of the tax."[105] And a 1986 *New York Times*/CBS poll found that 66 percent of the people agreed with the statement that "protecting the environment is so important that requirements and standards cannot be too high, and continuing environmental improvements must be made regardless of cost."[106] This represented a steady increase over the 58 percent who agreed with the statement in 1983 and the 45 percent who agreed in 1981.[107]

On the other hand, people do not necessarily identify pollution and other environmental issues as the most serious issues facing the country.[108] Concerns about the economy and peace usually head this list. Are these results inconsistent with the results summarized above? One expert explains the apparent discrepancy by distinguishing between the salience of the environmental issue and its strength. Salience, according to this analysis, "has to do with how much immediate, personal interest people have in the issue," whereas strength "refers to the degree to which people regard the issue as a matter of national concern and are committed to improving the situation or solving the problem."[109] According to this analysis, although many people feel very strongly about environmental issues, they are immediate concerns for only a few. This distinction is emphasized by the results of the 1983 ABC News/*Washington Post* poll, in which three of four respondents showed strong support for environmental programs, yet most of those polled "don't think that air pollution, unsafe drinking water, or toxic wastes are serious problems in the area where they live."[110]

Another measure of public opinion toward environmental issues is voting behavior. Pollsters have begun to find that voters are basing their decisions on environmental issues.[111] For instance, a 1986 Harris survey found that as much as 10 percent of the electorate would not vote for a candidate who favored antienvironmental positions, even though they agreed with the candidate on other issues.[112] This margin could be crucial in a close election. Success of state initiatives and referenda on environmental issues is yet another indicator of public opinion.[113] Such referenda have been responsible for California's Coastal Conservation Initiative; bills requiring returnable containers ("bottle bills") in Michigan and Maine; measures restricting nuclear power and/or nuclear waste disposal in Montana, Massachusetts, Maine, Oregon, South Dakota, and Washington; and a host of other environmental initiatives.[114]* In the 1986 elections, California, Massachusetts, New York, and New Jersey all passed measures relating to the cleanup and prevention of toxic contamination.[116]

Other countries also show a high level of support for environmental programs. A 1982 poll of European Community countries found that, in 9 of 10 countries surveyed, over 50 percent of the respondents felt that priority should be given to protecting the environment even if this meant restricting economic growth. In Japan, a similar study showed that only 11 percent of the population thought that economic growth should be given priority over environmental concerns.[117] The growth in West Germany, France, New Zealand, Australia and other, developed countries of political parties based on environmental platforms[118]—the so-called "Green" parties—reflects this concern.

While many Third World countries showed little awareness of or concern about the quality of the environment in the early 1970s, citizens,

---

*In addition, seven states—Oregon, Vermont, Iowa, Connecticut, Delaware, Massachusetts, and New York—have enacted legislation requiring returnable containers. Most of these laws were enacted by the state legislatures rather than through statewide votes, although Massachusetts passed its bill through both the legislature and a statewide vote. In 1979, a measure to repeal the bottle bill in Maine was overwhelmingly defeated.[115]

governments, and international development organizations alike are gradually addressing environmental issues. For instance, nongovernmental organizations organized for wildlife and natural area protection are active in Costa Rica, India, Kenya, Malaysia, and several South American countries.[119] Nearly all developing countries have established governmental agencies with environmental control responsibilities.[120] Taiwan, for example, established its Bureau of Environmental Protection in 1982. In the December 1986 Taiwanese legislative elections, environmental protection was a major issue, a sign that the public clearly supports cleaning up the environment.[121]

Environmental Expenditures

The strong U.S. public support for environmental improvement resulted in the adoption, during the 1970s, of a host of strong environmental protection laws. These, in turn, have stimulated significant increases in environmental expenditures by both government and the private sector. In real terms, total pollution control expenditures rose to 2 percent of GNP in the United States by 1976 and maintained that level for several years, falling off somewhat after 1979.[122] While total pollution control and abatement spending increased at an average annual rate of 4.7 percent between 1972 and 1980, it slowed to a rate of 0.8 percent between 1980 and 1984.[123]*

During the 12 years from 1972 through 1984, the United States spent a total of $557 billion for pollution control, equivalent to $739 billion in constant 1982 dollars. The bulk of the expenditures were for water and air (42 percent each), with the remainder going primarily to solid waste. These expenditures were slightly offset due to cost recovery by businesses.[125]

The distribution of constant dollar expenditures between sectors gradually changed during this period (figure 1.9). In 1972, business was responsible for 65 percent ($28 billion in 1982 dollars) of the expenditures, government for 27 percent ($11.7 billion), and personal consumption for the remaining 8 percent ($3.3 billion). By 1975, these proportions had shifted to 61 percent ($32.6 billion), 28 percent ($15 billion), and 11 percent ($5.9 billion), respectively. In the decade that followed, business's contribution gradually stabilized at about 63 percent of the annual pollution control expenditures.[126] Between 1980 and 1984, the government's share dropped

---

*Pollution abatement and control expenditures also form the basis for a significant manufacturing industry. According to one estimate, in 1985, business investments in pollution control technologies resulted in $19 billion in sales and almost $2.6 billion in corporate profits and created close to 167,000 jobs.[124]

Figure 1.9
Pollution Abatement and Control Expenditures in Constant Dollars,
by Sector, 1972–1984

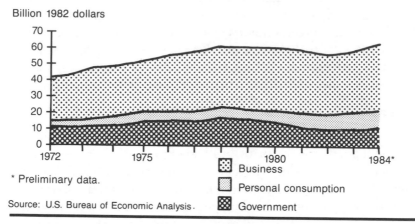

* Preliminary data.

Source: U.S. Bureau of Economic Analysis.

from 25 percent to about 20 percent, primarily due to changes in spending for sewer system construction, which in constant dollars was lower in 1984 than in 1972. The contribution by private individuals grew to 16 percent in the 1980s and can be explained in large part by higher spending to purchase motor vehicle emission control devices.[127]

New plant and equipment expenditures for pollution control and abatement by business also reached their peak in the mid-1970s (when adjusted for inflation), declining slowly until 1980 and then more rapidly from 1980 to 1983. They rebounded slightly in 1984[128] (figure 1.10). The percentage of total new plant and equipment spending allocated to pollution abatement declined at a steady rate throughout the same period, falling to 2.1 percent in 1984 from the 1975 peak of 4.2 percent[129] (figure 1.11).

The fall in total pollution control spending between 1979 and 1982 was felt primarily in water pollution control, although expenditures for all media dipped in the early 1980s (figure 1.12). In real terms, expenditures for water pollution control peaked in 1978, while those for controlling solid waste and air pollution continued their slight upward trend after falling in 1982. Expenditures for water pollution control facilities were 31 percent lower in 1984 than they were in the peak year of 1978, though operating expenses rose 23 percent over the same period. Both business and public facilities showed decreased investment for water pollution control devices during this period.[130]

Figure 1.10
Percent of Business Investment in New Plants
and Equipment for Pollution Abatement, 1973–1984

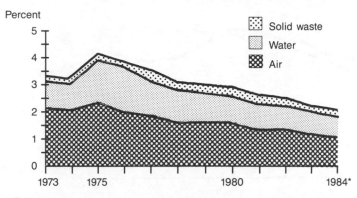

* Estimate.

Source: U.S. Department of Commerce.

Figure 1.11
New Plant and Equipment Expenditures for Pollution Abatement
in Constant Dollars, 1973–1984

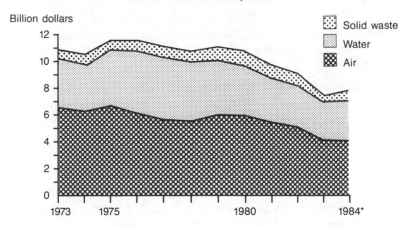

* Estimate.

Source: U.S. Department of Commerce.

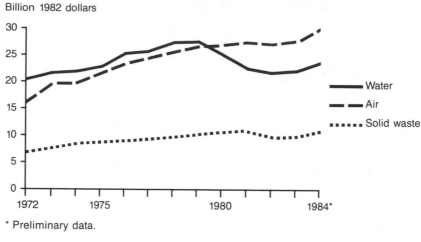

Figure 1.12
Pollution Abatement and Control Expenditures
in the United States, by Media, 1972–1984

Billion 1982 dollars

Water
Air
Solid waste

1972   1975   1980   1984*

* Preliminary data.

Source: U.S. Bureau of Economic Analysis.

Several factors explain the falloff in expenditures. One is that many industries have caught up with the backlog of investments made to comply with industrial-effluent limitations. A second is the slowdown in economic growth and total business investment during the late 1970s and early 1980s. A third factor is the diminished availability of federal funds to support the construction of municipal wastewater treatment plants. Between 1970 and 1977, federal government outlays (in 1983 constant dollars) rose from about $0.5 billion to $6.0 billion annually, and after 1972 the federal government paid 75 percent of the construction cost for these facilities.[131] In 1984, only $3 billion in federal funds was available, and, beginning in fiscal year 1985, the federal share of expenditures had dropped to 55 percent of the cost.[132]

However, ample evidence indicates that many investments still need to be made. Many facilities are not yet in compliance with their water pollution control permits. A 1986 survey by the U.S. Environmental Protection Agency (EPA) estimated that $76.2 billion (in 1986 dollars) in capital investments would be necessary to provide adequate municipal wastewater treatment capabilities in 2005.[133]

The federal government has reduced its funding not only for municipal wastewater treatment plants but for pollution control in general. Aside

Figure 1.13
U.S. Environmental Protection Agency
Budget Trends, 1971–1987

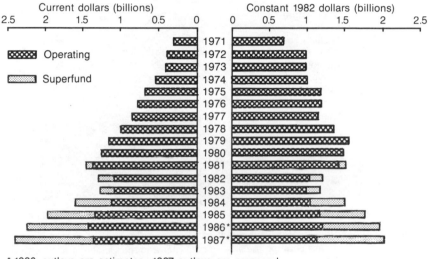

* 1986 outlays are estimates; 1987 outlays are proposed.

Source: U.S. Environmental Protection Agency.

from the Superfund program, under which EPA is responsible for cleaning up inactive hazardous waste sites and spills threatening public health and the environment,[134] EPA's inflation-adjusted operating budget peaked in 1979, at over twice the 1971 level (figure 1.13). Constant dollar funding levels for operating programs fell considerably in the early 1980s and have only partially recovered since that time. Superfund expenditures, however, have increased steadily since the program began in 1981; outlays accounted for 38 percent of EPA's estimated 1986 budget and for 43 percent of the proposed 1987 budget.[135]

EPA's budget cuts have been echoed throughout many of the federal environmental programs (figure 1.14). Expenditures for natural resource and environmental programs fell 9 percent from their 1980 peak of nearly $14 billion to $12.6 billion in 1984, even without taking inflation into account. The reductions have primarily taken place in pollution abatement and control programs and, to a lesser extent, in water resource and recreation resource programs. Outlays rose by 6 percent in 1985, to $13.4 billion, but the Reagan administration projects they will fall steadily for the rest

Figure 1.14
Federal Outlays for Environment and
Natural Resource Programs, 1965–1990

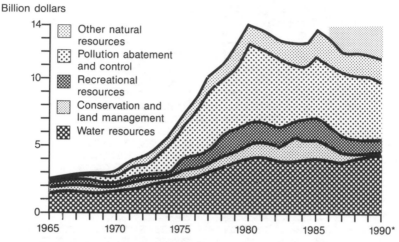

Billion dollars

Other natural resources
Pollution abatement and control
Recreational resources
Conservation and land management
Water resources

* 1986–1990 data represent estimated outlays.
The transitional quarter between the July 1 fiscal year and the October 1 fiscal year in 1976 is not included.

Source: Office of Management and Budget.

of the decade. Only outlays for water resource programs are expected to increase.[136] In current dollars, expenditures for all federal natural resource and environmental programs rose from 1.6 percent of the federal budget in 1970 to 2.45 percent in 1977, but fell gradually to 2.35 percent in 1980 and then dropped quickly to 1.48 percent in 1984.[137]

State and local governments also play an important role in administering environmental programs. For instance, in 1983-1984, states spent $5.7 billion on natural resources, including agriculture (8.7 percent of total governmental spending on natural resources), $1.4 billion on parks and recreation (14.9 percent of the total), and $246 million on sewerage (2.1 percent of the total). In the same year, local governments spent $1.8 billion on natural resources (2.7 percent of total governmental expenditures), $7.0 billion on parks and recreation (70 percent of the total), $11.3 billion on sewerage (97.9 percent of the total), and $4.7 billion on other sanitation services (100 percent of the governmental outlays for this purpose). In 1983-1984, state and local governments spent over five times more than the federal government for parks and recreation ($35.33 per capita versus

$6.52 per capita) and made all of the expenditures for sewerage ($48.76 per capita) and for sanitation ($19.94 per capita). In contrast, the federal government far outspent state and local governments for natural resource programs ($245.07 per capita compared with $31.42).[138]

As indicated above, the federal government is increasingly allocating more responsibilities to the states while reducing the financial assistance it provides to carry out these responsibilities. A prime example is the issue of funding for municipal wastewater treatment plants, which could affect water quality in many urban areas of the United States for years to come. Although state and local governments paid the majority of the costs of constructing wastewater treatment facilities prior to and during the 1960s, the 1970s saw great increases in the federal contribution to this program, as authorized by the Clean Water Act of 1972.[139] In the 1980s, the federal government has tried to phase out its role as a primary funding source, beginning with the reduction of the federal share of funding for construction from 75 percent to 55 percent. As of 1986, 2,930 projects had yet to be financed,[140] and federal funding under the Clean Water Act will be phased out by 1994.[141] Given these conditions, it is likely that many municipalities will not be able to meet the July 1, 1988, deadline for compliance with the act established by EPA.[142]

Given current fiscal realities, it does not appear likely that environmental programs will soon regain the resources they had available in the late 1970s, although some program areas, such as toxic waste cleanup, are likely to fare better than others. The trend toward shifting funding responsibility from the federal government to the state and local levels is likely to continue, as the federal government confronts record budget deficits. In the absence of new and innovative funding mechanisms, these budget constraints could well have a profound impact on the quality of the U.S. environment in the remaining years of this century.

Expenditures for pollution control in many other countries have followed trends in the United States. In 1985, the Organization for Economic Cooperation and Development (OECD) found that in countries such as Austria, Denmark, and Japan outlays were relatively high in the 1970s when pollution control programs were newly instituted but have since diminished as facilities have come into compliance with pollution control requirements. In some countries, expenditures have fluctuated or continued to increase over the past decade, possibly reflecting the gradual adoption of new requirements. In southern European countries, where pollution abatement and control investments began more recently, much remains to be accomplished. In most countries, operation and maintenance expenditures should continue to increase even after capital investments are largely completed. [143]

In many countries, environmental programs have been criticized on the basis of their alleged economic impacts. However, in a 1984 study, OECD found that the macroeconomic effects of pollution control requirements were relatively small, ranging from slightly positive to slightly negative, depending on the country and the parameter examined. [144] In a later report, OECD estimated that in five major OECD countries, total industrial pollution control expenditures comprised less than 1 percent of gross domestic product in 1980 in each of the countries studied. [145]

Enforcement

In the United States, the majority of dischargers have come into compliance with the law with no enforcement action taken against them. [146] But a vigorous enforcement program has been necessary both to stimulate such "voluntary" compliance and to deal with the more recalcitrant firms. Unfortunately, no clear measures exist that convey how vigorous or effective enforcement programs have been, or that even describe the rate of noncompliance. [147]

One reason is that enforcement actions involve a wide range of approaches. Traditional enforcement responses include informal notifications, formal notice of violation, administrative orders (with or without penalties), civil actions, and criminal prosecution. [148] But environmental laws also provide for citizen lawsuits against polluters, blacklisting companies in violation so that they cannot receive government contracts, and other measures. [149] Enforcement actions may result in the imposition of compliance schedules, penalties, and, in some cases, jail sentences. Due to this wide variety of actions, uniform data are difficult to collect and interpret.

A second reason is that much of the enforcement responsibility lies at the state or local level. In recent years, states have been increasingly responsible for implementing federally enacted environmental laws and regulations; by 1984 approximately 70 percent of EPA's day-to-day responsibilities for environmental enforcement had been delegated to the states. [150] However, while efforts to compile data into a national data base were under way in the late 1970s, this effort lagged in the early 1980s so that consistent and comprehensive data describing state enforcement efforts are not now available. [151]

A third reason is that compliance may not always be clearly defined, thus aggravating efforts to measure the effectiveness of enforcement efforts. [152] Disputes about what constitutes compliance focus on interpretation of ambiguous terms (such as "feasible and prudent"), the proper application and interpretation of statistical methods, and the tension between assuring initial installation of equipment and continued compliance with environmental standards.[153] More importantly, though, the data document the intensity of enforcement efforts but say little, if anything, about how stringent the enforcement is or whether efforts are being made to attack major problems.

In spite of these problems, the effort devoted by the federal government to enforcement can be determined generally by certain indicators. These include enforcement budgets and the number of enforcement actions undertaken. In addition, information is available on citizen suits.

EPA's Enforcement Budget

According to a 1984 Congressional Budget Office report, EPA's enforcement budget, measured in constant dollars, has varied widely (figure 1.15).

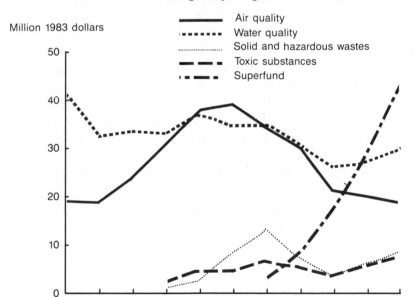

Figure 1.15
U.S. Environmental Protection Agency
Enforcement Budget, by Program, 1975–1985

Million 1983 dollars

Air quality
Water quality
Solid and hazardous wastes
Toxic substances
Superfund

Data through 1983 reflect actual obligations; 1984 and 1985 data reflect budget authority.

Source: Congressional Budget Office.

The air quality enforcement budget peaked in 1980 and has declined steadily since then, while the water quality budget peaked in 1975. Enforcement budgets for solid and hazardous wastes programs, which began in 1978, have been no higher than between one-half and one-third of the funding levels for air and water and fell sharply between 1981 and 1983, before returning in 1985 to about the same level of spending as in 1980.

Since 1981, an increasing proportion of enforcement-related expenditures have been devoted to the Superfund program, which grew from $3 million in 1981 to $45 million in 1985.[154]

Between 1975 and 1985, the total budget for enforcement activities (excluding Superfund) grew from a low of $51 million (in constant 1983 dollars) in 1976 to $88 million in 1981. Between 1981 and 1983, enforcement expenditures dropped nearly 40 percent (to $53 million), before rising by 20.8 percent to $64 million in 1985.[155] As a percent of the total EPA operating budget, enforcement has ranged from a low of 8.0 percent in 1979 to a high of 10.5 percent in 1985.[156]

EPA Enforcement Actions

Figures 1.16, 1.17, and 1.18 trace the progress of civil enforcement by EPA and the U.S. Department of Justice (DOJ) in various program areas. As shown in figure 1.16, administrative orders have been used primarily in the water, hazardous waste, and toxic substance and pesticide programs. Generally, the use of administrative orders—quantitatively, the most frequently used formal enforcement tool—has increased since the early 1980s in all programs. Some have attributed the relative lack of overall enforcement activity between 1981 and 1983 to confusion among staff about expectations of agency management, low morale, and a loss of public confidence.[157]

Administrative orders issued in the water program peaked in 1984 due to an unusually active year in EPA's Region 4 (headquartered in Atlanta). They then dropped 37 percent from 1984 to 1985 and a further 4 percent in 1986.[158] The number of orders issued by the air program has been fairly consistent, but there has been a steady increase in the number of orders generated in the hazardous waste (except for 1986) and toxic substance and pesticide areas.[159]

Civil suits also have been an important tool in promoting compliance with environmental activities. The number of cases referred by EPA to DOJ and the number of cases filed in court by DOJ are two measures of civil enforcement activities. In general, cases referred and cases filed fell significantly between 1980 and 1982 (figure 1.17).

Figure 1.16
Administrative Orders Issued by the U.S. Environmental Protection Agency, by Program, 1980–1986

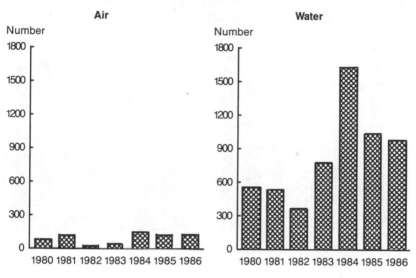

Air

Water

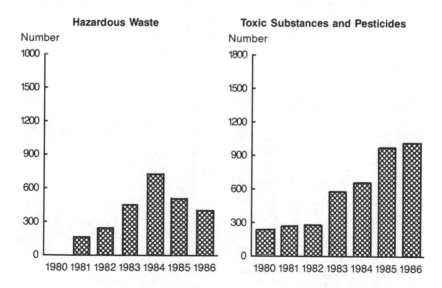

Hazardous Waste

Toxic Substances and Pesticides

Source: U.S. Environmental Protection Agency.

Figure 1.17
U.S. Environmental Protection Agency Enforcement
Cases, by Program, 1980–1986

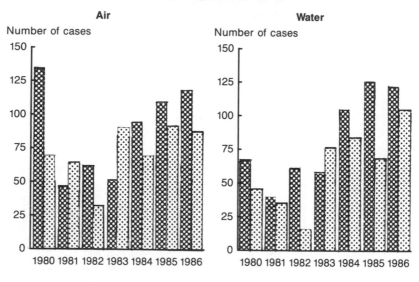

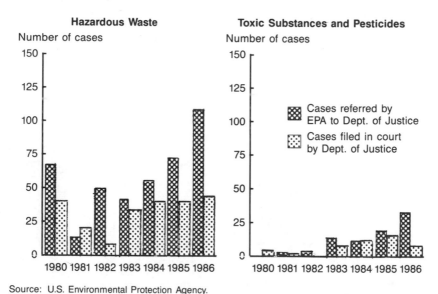

Source: U.S. Environmental Protection Agency.

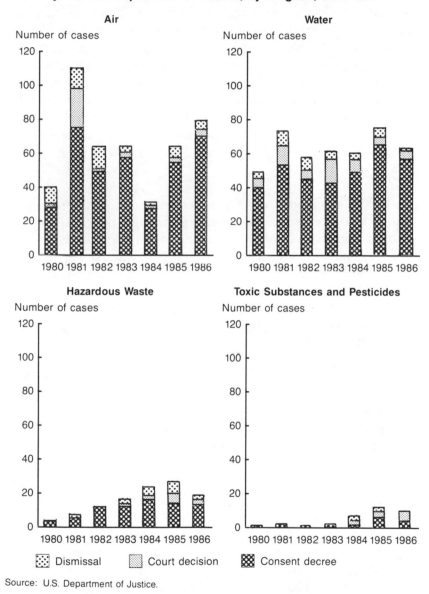

Figure 1.18
Disposition of Environmental Enforcement Cases Brought by the U.S. Department of Justice, by Program, 1980–1986

Source: U.S. Department of Justice.

The pattern in the cases disposed of (figure 1.18) lags behind the pattern in the number of cases referred because of the time required to reach settlement or complete a trial. In the air program, the number of cases completed between 1980 and 1986 fluctuated, ranging from a high of 109 cases in 1981 to a low of 37 cases in 1984. The number of water cases disposed of during that period did not vary much, although small peaks occurred in 1981 and 1985. Hazardous waste, toxic substance, and pesticide cases increased gradually from 1980 to 1985, then dropped off in 1986.

A consent decree is clearly the predominant outcome in all program areas. Such a decree avoids the court rendering a decision on the merits of the case. Many cases are dismissed after the court or the agency determines that the case does not have enough substance to make pursuit of it worthwhile. Only a relatively few cases are actually decided by the courts.

Criminal Suits

In 1982, EPA significantly strengthened environmental enforcement programs by establishing a federal program providing for criminal prosecution of environmental crimes.[160] The threat of criminal prosecution, particularly against company executives, is thought to have a strong deterrent effect.[161] Criminal measures tend to be used only ''in areas of agency priority where civil and administrative enforcement have not significantly benefited compliance.''[162] Although criminal cases may be brought under a number of environmental statutes, the majority involve hazardous wastes, brought under the Resource Conservation and Recovery Act (RCRA) and, to a lesser extent, the Toxic Substances Control Act.[163]

This trend is reflected in the increased number of criminal cases referred to DOJ by EPA since 1980. Since fiscal year 1982, when referrals reached a low of 20 cases, criminal referrals have steadily increased: 45 cases were referred in fiscal year 1986.[164] Between October 1, 1982, and September 30, 1986, a total of 217 indictments were handed down, 41 against corporations and 176 against individuals; these have resulted in 176 pleas and convictions.[165] Criminal prosecution from fiscal years 1983 through 1986 resulted in a total of over $3.2 million in fines and almost 41 years of jail time collectively served.[166] The increase in incarceration of corporate officials over the past few years has been attributed to increased public awareness and concern for environmental protection, experience gained in seeking incarceration as a deterrent, and increased willingness by judges to impose jail terms as a form of punishment.[167] The rise in activity was accompanied by increased hiring of prosecutors and investigators (especially those with criminal justice experience) and greater emphasis within EPA and DOJ on prosecuting environmental criminal cases.[168]

Private Party Enforcement Actions

Citizen suits also have become more common.[169] Eleven federal environmental laws authorize private suits against polluters for noncompliance with statutory requirements, as well as suits against the government for failure to perform a nondiscretionary duty.[170]

A 1984 study conducted for EPA found that, between 1978 and mid-1984, nearly 350 citizen enforcement actions, including both notices of intent to sue and lawsuits themselves, were initiated under the six major statutes administered by EPA (figure 1.19).* Some 189 of these actions

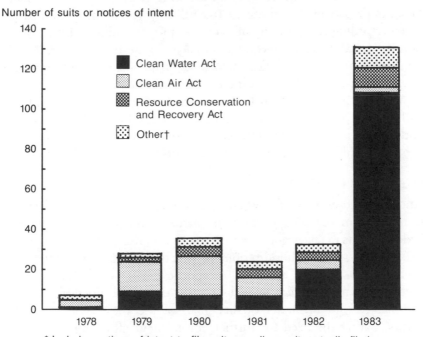

Figure 1.19
Citizen Suits Filed under Five
Environmental Statutes, 1978–1983*

Number of suits or notices of intent

■ Clean Water Act
▨ Clean Air Act
▧ Resource Conservation and Recovery Act
⠿ Other†

* Includes notices of intent to file suit as well as suits actually filed.
† Includes Toxic Substances Control Act, Safe Drinking Water Act, and suits citing more than one of these five statutes.

Source: Environmental Law Institute.

*As of April 30, 1984, 93 notices or suits had been filed for the first seven months of the fiscal year, as compared with 131 for all of fiscal year 1983.[172]

resulted in litigation.[171] Citizen suits filed under the Clean Water Act increased dramatically during this period, especially from 1982 to 1983 and accounted for the bulk of suits filed. Suits under RCRA and other environmental statutes increased gradually, while those under the Clean Air Act declined after 1980.[173] The study concluded that the sharp rise in citizen suit activity beginning in 1982 was directly related to a perceived lack of EPA enforcement activity, and that the emphasis on violations of the Clean Water Act reflected the greater availability of discharge information.[174] Citizen suit activity under RCRA has increased in recent years as implementation of the program has begun.

The National Environmental Policy Act (NEPA) was the first of recent environmental laws to support substantial numbers of citizen suits— primarily regarding the adequacy of environmental impact statements (EISs) and assessments and the need for an EIS in cases in which agencies had failed to prepare one.[175] In the 1970s, NEPA litigation focused on basic issues regarding the authority of agencies, proper timing of EISs, scope of review, and direct and secondary impacts. In the 1980s, NEPA litigation has become more sophisticated, focusing on questions such as the proper role of worst-case analysis and the effects of cumulative impacts.[176]

Almost 1,500 lawsuits were filed between 1974 and 1984 under NEPA, with quite a bit of activity in the law's early years, followed by a decline and then an increase again in the early 1980s (figure 1.20). As a percentage of EISs filed, the number of lawsuits peaked in 1983.[177]

Government Facilities Compliance

Another major issue is effective enforcement against government-owned facilities, from local sewage treatment plants to federal defense facilities. Federal efforts to take vigorous enforcement actions against local governments involve clear political problems. But these actions are sometimes necessary. For example, a 1986 EPA report estimated that 37 percent of the nation's major publicly owned sewage treatment facilities were not in compliance with the water quality goals of the Clean Water Act,[178] demonstrating the need for further enforcement efforts against those facilities.

EPA has identified some 5,000 federal facilities that have the potential to affect the environment; this number will likely increase as the regulated universe is broadened to include facilities such as small quantity generators. Data on the number of actual violations have not been available to date,

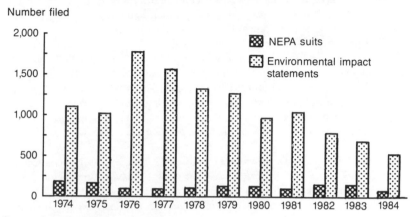

Figure 1.20
Impact Statements and Lawsuits Filed under the
National Environmental Policy Act, 1974-1984

Number filed

NEPA suits

Environmental impact statements

Source: Council on Environmental Quality,
       U.S. Environmental Protection Agency.

but EPA plans to remedy this situation with a new data system to track compliance rates in fiscal year 1988.[179]

Enforcement efforts against federal facilities can run into a variety of problems. Although federal facilities are subject to pollution control requirements to the same extent as private parties,[180] EPA relies on administrative remedies rather than judicial actions, and penalties are not usually imposed.[181] National security concerns frequently arise in situations involving Department of Defense installations. On a practical level, the Department of Justice runs into conflicts when having to represent an offending agency as well as EPA.

As with enforcement against private parties, states with delegated or approved federal programs play a big role in enforcing environmental statutes at federal facilities. States generally have a much broader range of tools at their disposal than EPA to pursue violations at federal facilities.[182]

Given that government-owned facilities can be significant sources of some serious environmental contamination problems, bringing them into compliance remains a major challenge under most of the pollution control programs.

REFERENCES

Text

1. U.S. Department of Commerce, Bureau of the Census, *Estimates of the Population of the United States to May 1, 1986*, Current Population Reports, series P-25, no. 989 (Washington, D.C.: U.S. Government Printing Office, 1986), p. 2.

2. U.S. Department of Commerce, Bureau of the Census, *Estimates of the Population of the United States and Components of Change: 1970 to 1985*, series P-25, no. 990 (Washington, D.C.: U.S. Government Printing Office, 1986), p. 9; U.S. Department of Commerce, Bureau of the Census, *Statistical Abstract of the United States 1986* (Washington, D.C.: U.S. Government Printing Office, 1986), p. 7; and information provided by Gregory Spencer, U.S. Department of Commerce, Bureau of the Census, August 1986.

3. U.S. Bureau of the Census, *Estimates of the Population and Components of Change*, p. 1.

4. Ibid., pp. 2-3; and U.S. Department of Health and Human Services, National Center for Health Statistics, *Vital Statistics of the United States*, vol. 1, *Natality* (Washington, D.C.: U.S. Government Printing Office, 1978), pp. 1-9, table 1-6.

5. U.S. Bureau of the Census, *Estimates of the Population and Components of Change*, p. 3.

6. Ibid., p. 2; and Gregory Spencer, *Projections of the Population of the United States by Age, Sex, and Race: 1983-2080*, prepared for the U.S. Department of Commerce, Bureau of the Census, Current Population Reports, series p. 25, no. 952 (Washington, D.C.: U.S. Government Printing Office 1984), p. 12.

7. U.S. Bureau of the Census, *Estimates of the Population and Components of Change*, pp. 4-5.

8. Ibid., pp. 4-5, 9.

9. Personal communication with James Brackett, U.S. Agency for International Development, January 1987.

10. United Nations, Department of International Economic and Social Affairs, *World Population Prospects: Estimates and Projections as Assessed in 1982*, Population Studies no. 86 (New York: United Nations, 1985), p. 44.

11. Ibid., p. 42; and United Nations, Department of International Economic and Social Affairs, *Estimates and Projections of Urban, Rural, and City Populations, 1950-2025: The 1982 Assessment* (New York: United Nations, 1985), p. 146. Estimates are based on 1985 population of New York/Northeastern New Jersey.

12. United Nations, *World Population Prospects*, p. 44.

13. Ibid. These numbers differ from estimates by other experts. For instance, the Population Reference Bureau estimates that average annual natural growth rates as of mid-1986 were as follows: Africa, 2.8 percent; Asia, 1.8 percent (China, 1.0 percent, Asia without China, 2.2 percent); Oceania, 1.2 percent; Latin America, 2.3 percent. See Population Reference Bureau, ''1986 World Population Data Sheet: Demographic Data and Estimates For the Countries and Regions of the World'' (Washington, D.C.: Population Reference Bureau, April 1986).

14. United Nations, *World Population Prospects*, p. 42.

15. World Resources Institute and International Institute for Environment and Development, *World Resources 1986* (New York: Basic Books, 1986), pp. 23-24.

16. Ibid.

17. U.S. Bureau of the Census, *Statistical Abstract 1986*, p. 9, table 10.

18. Philip M. Hauser, "The Census of 1980," *Scientific American* 245, no. 5 (1980):56.

19. U.S. Department of Commerce, Bureau of the Census, *State and Metropolitan Data Book, 1986: Metropolitan Areas, Central Cities, States* (Washington, D.C.: U.S. Government Printing Office, 1986), p. xxvi.

20. U.S. Department of Commerce, "California's Bay Area Population Edges Out Philadelphia for No. 4 Spot, Census Bureau Estimates Show," news release, July 30, 1986, p. 2.

21. "Trends: The States in 1990," *American Demographics* 5, no. 12 (1983):23; and Eugene Carlson, "Why the Experts Don't Agree on Future Population Figures," *Wall Street Journal*, June 3, 1986.

22. Carlson, "Why the Experts Don't Agree".

23. U.S. Department of Commerce, Bureau of the Census, *Patterns of Metropolitan Area and County Population Growth: 1980 to 1984*, Current Population Reports, series P-25, no. 976 (Washington, D.C.: U.S. Government Printing Office, 1985), p.8. 24. Ibid, p. 12.

25. Ibid, pp. 22, 26, 37.

26. U.S. Bureau of the Census, *Statistical Abstract 1986*, pp. 21-23, table 24.

27. U.S. Bureau of the Census, *Patterns of Metropolitan Area and County Population Growth*, pp. 17-39.

28. Population Reference Bureau, "1986 World Population Data Sheet," April 1986.

29. Rafael M. Salas, *The State of World Population 1986* (New York: United Nations, 1986), pp. 2-3.

30. United Nations, Department of International Economic and Social Affairs, *Estimates and Projections of Urban, Rural and City Populations, 1950-2025: The 1982 Assessment* (New York: United Nations, 1985), p. 61.

31. For more information, see World Resources Institute, "Third World Cities—the Environment of Poverty," *Journal '85*, pp. 45-57.

32. Lester R. Brown et al., *State of the World* (New York: W.W. Norton, 1984), pp. 8-11.

33. U.S. Congress, Congressional Budget Office, *The Economic Outlook: A Report to the Senate and House Committees on the Budget-Part I* (Washington, D.C.: U.S. Government Printing Office, 1984), p. 79.

34. U.S. Department of Commerce, Bureau of Economic Analysis, unpublished data from "GNP (Revised Estimates), Current and Constant (1982) Dollars 1986," table 1.2.

35. U.S. Department of Labor, Bureau of Labor Statistics, "Employment Status of the Civilian Nonindustrial Population 16 Years and Over, 1952 to Date," *Employment and Earnings* 33, no. 7 (1986):10, table A-3.

36. U.S. Department of Commerce, Bureau of the Census, *Statistical Abstract 1986*, p. 477; and U.S. Department of Labor, Bureau of Labor Statistics, *CPI Detailed Report: December 1985* (Washington, D.C.: U.S. Government Printing Office, 1986), p. 1.

37. U.S. Congress, Congressional Budget Office, *The Economic and Budget Outlook: An Update* (Washington, D.C.: U. S. Government Printing Office, 1986), p. 6, table I-2.

38. U.S. Congress, Congressional Budget Office, *The Economic and Budget Outlook: Fiscal Years 1987-1991* (Washington, D.C.: U.S. Government Printing Office, 1986), pp. 31, 35, figures 1-8, 1-10.

39. Robert G. Healy, *America's Industrial Future: An Environmental Perspective* (Washington, D.C.: The Conservation Foundation, 1982), pp. 30-31.

40. David Clark, *Post-Industrial America: A Geographical Perspective* (New York: Methuen, 1985), pp. 22-23.

41. U.S. Department of Commerce, Bureau of Economic Analysis, unpublished data from "Gross National Product by Industry in Constant Dollars," 1986, table 6.2.

42. While there are a number of ways to define high-technology and smokestack industries, there is no general agreement on standard definitions for these terms. The U.S. Department of Commerce published the following definitions in the *1986 Industrial Outlook*: "Hi-tech" products include "guided missiles and spacecraft, communications equipment, electronic components; aircraft and parts, computing and accounting machines; drugs and medicines, industrial inorganic chemicals; professional and scientific instruments, engines, turbines and parts, plastic materials, and synthetic resins, rubber and fibers." Smokestack industries include sectors that produce "motor vehicles and equipment, iron and steel products; primary copper, aluminum, primary lead, primary zinc, industrial and farm machinery and machine tools." See U.S. Department of Commerce, International Trade Administration, *1986 U.S. Industrial Outlook: Prospects for Over 350 Manufacturing and Service Industries* (Washington, D.C.: U.S. Government Printing Office, 1986), pp. 27, 30.

43. See William Pat Patterson, "The 'New Silicon Valleys," *Industry Week*, January 20, 1986, pp. 48-54. All sites listed are in Santa Clara County, except one that is in neighboring San Mateo County. Information provided by U.S. Environmental Protection Agency, Region 9, November 1986; U.S. Environmental Protection Agency, Office of Emergency and Remedial Response, "CERCLIS V 1.2, L.1-Site Location Listing," November 1986 (unpublished); and U.S. Environmental Protection Agency, Office of Emergency and Remedial Response, *National Priorities List Fact Book, June 1986* (Washington, D.C.: U.S. Government Printing Office, 1986), pp. 51-54.

44. Personal communication, John Dover, U.S. Environmental Protection Agency, Region 9, November 1986.

45. Philip L. Rones, "An Analysis of Regional Employment Growth, 1973-85," *Monthly Labor Review* 109, no. 7 (1986):3; and Bernard L. Weinstein and Harold T. Gross, "An Economic Role Reversal," *State Legislatures* 12, no. 4 (1986):22-24.

46. John D. Kasarda, Michael D. Irwin, and Holly L. Hughes, "The South Is Still Rising," *American Demographics* 8, no. 6 (1986):33; Neal R. Peirce and Gregory Peterson, "A Tale of Two Souths," *National Journal*, December 13, 1986, pp. 3015-16; and Weinstein and Gross, "An Economic Role Reversal," pp. 22-24.

47. Kasarda, Irwin and Hughes, "The South Is Still Rising," p. 33.

48. Healy, *America's Industrial Future*, pp. 33-34.

49. Virgil Ketterling, "Industry Trends in International Trade," in U.S. International Trade Administration, *1986 U.S. Industrial Outlook*, p. 14; see also Alan O. Maurer and Gorti V. L. Narasimham, "Global Trends in U.S. Trade: 1980-1985," in U.S. International Trade Administration, *1986 U.S. Industrial Outlook*, pp. 25-32; and Roger A. Sedjo, "Third World Debts Create U.S. Trade Deficits," *Resources*, no. 80 (1985):14.

50. Healy, *America's Industrial Future*, pp. 36-37.

51. World Bank, *World Development Report 1986* (New York: Oxford University Press, 1986), pp. 1-3.

52. Ibid., pp. 1-3, 24-26.

53. Hobart Rowen, "Globally, Slow Pace Continues," *Washington Post*, January 11, 1987.

54. Lester R. Brown et al., *State of the World 1986* (New York: W.W. Norton, 1986), pp. 5-11; and World Commission on Environment and Development, *Mandate, Key Issues,*

Strategy and Workplan (Geneva: World Commission on Environment and Development, 1984), pp. 26-27.

55. Norman Mayers, "Tropical Deforestation and Mega-Extinction Spasm," in Michael Soule, *Conservation Biology: The Science of Scarcity and Diversity* (Sunderland, Mass.: Sinauer Associates, 1986), p. 399.

56. Brown et al., *State of the World 1986*, pp. 8-11.

57. Donald B. Thompson, "Exodus: Where is U.S. Industry Going? It's Heading Where Many American Manufacturers Have Already Gone—Offshore," *Industry Week*, January 6, 1986, pp. 28-31.

58. Healy, *America's Industrial Future*, pp. 36-37.

59. Edward R. Fried, "World Oil Markets: New Benefits, Old Concerns," *Brookings Review* 4, no. 3 (1986):36.

60. "The Impact of $15 a Barrel Oil," *Petroleum Economist* (April 1986):116.

61. Stephen Koepp, "Cheap Oil," *Time*, April 14, 1986, p. 62; see also Nicholas D. Kristof, "Bakersfield Runs on a Leaner Mix," *New York Times*, July 6, 1986; and David Maraniss, "The Newly Jobless Wait for Houston to Boom Again," *Washington Post*, July 21, 1986.

62. American Petroleum Institute, "Results of the API Crude Oil Price Effects Survey" (Washington, D.C.: American Petroleum Institute, May 7, 1986, photocopy), p. 1.

63. World Resources Institute and International Institute for Environment and Development, *World Resources 1986*, p. 117.

64. "The Impact of $15 a Barrel Oil," p. 116.

65. Fried, "World Oil Markets: New Benefits, Old Concerns," pp 37-38; see also Douglas R. Bohi and Michael A. Toman, "International Planning for Future Oil Crises," *Resources*, no. 84 (1986), p. 13.

66. Stephen Koepp, "Cheap Oil," p. 68.

67. U.S. Department of Energy, Energy Information Administration, Office of Energy Markets and End Use, *Annual Energy Outlook 1985*, DOE/EIA-0383(85) (Washington, D.C.: U.S. Government Printing Office, 1986), p. 13.

68. Edward Kutler, "Energy Forecasting: The Troubled Past of Looking to the Future," *Public Opinion* 8, no. 6 (1985/1986):47-52.

69. Michael J. Coda, "Energy: Ten Years After," *Resources*, no. 75 (1984):1-4.

70. Based on 1980-1985 data in Council of Economic Advisors, "Annual Report of the Council of Economic Advisors," in *Economic Report of the President* (Washington, D.C.: U.S. Government Printing Office, 1986), p. 339. While the budget deficit is the largest in history in absolute terms, as a percentage of GNP it is less than half of the size of the debt incurred by the federal government in the 1940s. Sylvia Nasar, "The $2-Trillion Debt Headache," *Fortune*, November 10, 1986, p. 42.

71. "Annual Report of the Council of Economic Advisors," p. 344.

72. 2 USC §901 et seq., supp. 1985.

73. Environmental Safety et al., *The Environmental Solution to the Deficit Dilemma*, (n.p., n.d.), p. 7.

74. 26 USCA §1 et seq.

75. Brent Blackwelder, "Environmental Impacts of Tax Reform," *Environmental Law Reporter* 16 (1986):10322.

76. Brent Blackwelder and David Campbell, "Tax Reform and the Environment," p. 1 (photocopy).

77. "Taxing Times for America's Charities," *U.S. News and World Report*, December 22, 1986, pp. 56-57.

78. Randy Abeles, Alex Darragh, and David Brint, "Tax Reform in a Nutshell," *Business Facilities* 19, no. 10 (1986):39.

79. Blackwelder and Campbell, "Tax Reform and the Environment," pp. 4-7.

80. F. Kaid Benfield, Justin R. Ward, and Anne E. Kinsinger, "Assessing the Tax Reform Act: Gains, Questions and Unfinished Business" (Washington, D.C.: Natural Resources Defense Council, 1986), pp. 10-13; and Blackwelder, "Environmental Impacts of Tax Reform," p. 10323.

81. "Conferees Approve Tax Reform Bill," *Land Letter*, September 1, 1986, p. 5.

82. Ibid., p. 4; and Blackwelder, "Environmental Impacts of Tax Reform," pp. 10323-24.

83. Blackwelder, "Environmental Impacts of Tax Reform," pp. 10322-23; and "Preservationists Not Unhappy with Partial Tax Credit Plan," *Land Use Planning Report*, November 3, 1986, p. 338.

84. Blackwelder and Campbell, "Tax Reform and the Environment," p. 4.

85. As measured by the U.S. average year-end balance as a percent of general fund expenditures, a commonly used measure of fiscal health. See National Governors' Association and National Association of State Budget Officers, *Fiscal Survey of the States* (Washington, D.C.: National Governors' Association and National Association of State Budget Officers, 1986), pp. 41-42, appendix table A-4.

86. Personal communication with David Schmidt, Initiative Resource Center, March 1987.

87. Personal communication with Karen Banker, National Association of State Budget Officers, December 1986.

88. National Governors' Association and National Associaton of State Budget Officers, *Fiscal Survey of the States*, p. 21.

89. These are not just environmental laws. W. John Moore, "Mandates without Money," *National Journal*, October 4, 1986, pp. 2367-68.

90. Thad L. Beyle, ed., *State Government: CQ's Guide to Current Issues and Activities 1986-87* (Washington, D.C.: Congressional Quarterly, Inc., 1986), pp. 192-93.

91. John Moore, "Mandates without Money," p. 2367.

92. Ibid., p. 2366.

93. Jon Grand, "Environmental Management: Emerging Issues," in Council of State Governments, *The Book of the States 1984-1985*, vol. 25 (Lexington, Ky.: Council of State Governments, 1984), p. 450.

94. George E. Peterson, "Urban Policy and the Cyclical Behavior of Cities," in George E. Peterson and Carol W. Lewis, eds., *Reagan and the Cities* (Washington, D.C.: Urban Institute Press, 1986), pp. 26-29; and Robert W. Burchell et al., *The New Reality of Municipal Finance: The Rise and Fall of the Intergovernmental City* (New Brunswick, N.J.: Center for Urban Policy Research, 1984), p. 299.

95. Burchell et al., *The New Reality of Municipal Finance*, pp. 299-300; U.S. Congress, 97th Cong., 1st sess., *Emergency Interim Survey: Fiscal Condition of 48 Large Cities*, study prepared for the Joint Economic Committee (Washington, D.C.: U.S. Government Printing Office, 1982), p. 3.

96. Burchell et al., *The New Reality of Municipal Finance*, pp. 310, 312-13.

97. Douglas D. Peterson, "City Fiscal Conditions in 1986" (Washington, D.C.: National League of Cities, 1986), p. 18.

98. Ibid., p. 10; see also Linda Dove, "Oil Prices Affect Fiscal Fortunes of West and

Southwest," in Beyle, *State Government*, pp. 172-73.

99. Robert Cameron Mitchell, "Public Opinion and Environmental Politics in the 1970's and 1980's," in Norman J. Vig and Michael E. Kraft, eds., *Environmental Policy in the 1980's: Reagan's New Agenda* (Washington, D.C.: Congressional Quarterly Press, 1984), p. 52.

100. "Watt's Departure Is Helping Reagan," *Business Week*, December 19, 1983, p. 14.

101. Memo from Hal Quinley, The Policy Planning Group of Yankelovich, Kelly and White, Inc., to Dick Duncan and Walter Issacson, *Time*, "Time/Yankelovich Poll-September, 1985," table 25.

102. Ibid., tables 23 and 24.

103. Patricia Papa, "Combating Environmental Crime at EPA's National Enforcement Investigations Center," *The Environmental Forum* 3, no. 11 (1985):36.

104. Louis Harris, "Environmental Issues Could Become a Factor in Congressional Races," *The Harris Survey*, May 19, 1986, p. 3.

105. Memo from Hal Quinley to Dick Duncan and Walter Issacson, table 25.

106. Martin Plissner, "The State of the Union," CBS News/*The New York Times* Poll, January 27, 1986.

107. "A New York Times/CBS Survey Found 58% Back Environmental Laws at Any Cost," *Inside EPA Weekly Report*, April 29, 1983, p. 9; and "Poll Finds Strong Support for Environmental Code," *New York Times*, October 4, 1981.

108. Mitchell, "Public Opinion and Environmental Politics in the 1970's and 1980's," pp. 54-57.

109. Ibid., p. 55.

110. Ibid., p. 56.

111. Carl Pope, "After the Polls Close," *Sierra* 71, no. 6 (1986):56.

112. Harris, "Environmental Issues Could Become a Factor in Congressional Races," p. 1.

113. Initiative Resource Center, "Initiative Loses in R.I.," *Initiative and Referendum: The Power of the People*, Winter 1986-87, p. 3. Only 23 states and the District of Columbia have provisions for putting initiatives on the ballot. Many local jurisdictions (in all 50 states) also have such provisions. Personal communication with David Schmidt, December 1986.

114. David Schmidt, "Taking It to the Voters," *Environmental Action* 18, no. 2 (1986):21; for more discussion on California's Coastal Conservation Initiative, see Robert G. Healy, ed., *Protecting the Golden Shore: Lessons from the California Coastal Commission* (Washington, D.C.: The Conservation Foundation, 1978), pp. xx-xxi.

115. Personal communication with Jonathan Puth, December 1986.

116. Cass Peterson, "Setbacks for Feminists and Abortion Foes; Victories for Environmentalists," *Washington Post*, November 6, 1986.

117. Organization for Economic Cooperation and Development, *OECD Environmental Data Compendium 1985* (Paris: Organization for Economic Cooperation and Development, 1985), p. 265.

118. Lynton K. Caldwell, *International Environmental Policy: Emergence and Dimensions* (Durham, N.C.: Duke University Press, 1984), p. 279.

119. David Morell and Joanna Poznanski, "Rhetoric and Reality: Environmental Politics and Environmental Administration in Developing Countries," in H. Jeffrey Leonard, ed., *Divesting Nature's Capital* (New York: Holmes and Meier, 1985), pp. 139-41.

120. Ibid., p. 144.

121. Nicholas D. Kristof, "Taiwan Starts to Clean Up Its Air and Water," *New York Times*, December 29, 1986.

122. U.S. Department of Commerce, Bureau of Economic Analysis, unpublished data from "GNP (Revised Estimates), Current and Constant (1982) Dollars, 1986," table 1.1; and Kit D. Farber and Gary L. Rutledge, "Pollution Abatement and Control Expenditures," *Survey of Current Business* 66, no. 7 (1986):100-3, table 9.

123. Farber and Rutledge, "Pollution Abatement and Control Expenditures," p. 97, table 6.

124. Management Information Services, "Economic and Employment Benefits of Investments in Environmental Protection" (Washington, D.C.: Management Information Services, 1986), p. 4.

125. Farber and Rutledge, "Pollution Abatement and Control Expenditures," pp. 98, 100-103, tables 7, 9. These figures do not account for "other and unallocated" ("other" includes expenditures for abatement and control of noise, radiation and pesticide pollution; "unallocated" includes business expenditures not assigned to media).

126. Ibid., p. 97, table 6.

127. Ibid., p. 98.

128. U.S. Department of Commerce, Bureau of Economic Analysis, Environmental Economics Division, "Plant and Equipment Expenditures by Business for Pollution Abatement," *Survey of Current Business* 66, no. 2 (1986):39, table 2.

129. Ibid., pp. 40-41, table 1.

130. Farber and Rutledge, "Pollution Abatement and Control Expenditures," pp. 97-99.

131. U.S. Congress, Congressional Budget Office, *Efficient Investments in Wastewater Treatment Plants* (Washington, D.C.: U.S. Government Printing Office, 1985), pp. 3-4.

132. Ibid., p. 3; and U.S. Congress, Congressional Budget Office, *The Federal Budget for Public Works Infrastructure* (Washington, D.C.: U.S. Government Printing Office, 1985), p. 57.

133. Roy F. Weston, Inc., "1986 Needs Survey Report to Congress: Assessment of Needed Publicly Owned Wastewater Treatment Facilities in the United States," report prepared for the U.S. Environmental Protection Agency (Washington, D.C.: U.S. Government Printing Office, 1987), p. 9.

134. U.S. Congress, Congressional Budget Office, *The Budget of the Environmental Protection Agency: An Overview of Selected Proposals for 1985*, special study (Washington, D.C.: U.S. Government Printing Office, 1984), p. 57.

135. U. S. Environmental Protection Agency, Office of the Comptroller, *Summary of the 1987 Budget* (Washington, D.C.: U.S. Government Printing Office, 1986), p. 8; and information provided by Kevin Neyland, U.S. Office of Management and Budget, September 1986.

136. U.S. Office of Management and Budget, *Budget of the U.S. Government, Historical Tables, Fiscal Year 1987* (Washington, D.C.: U.S. Government Printing Office, 1986), pp. 3.3(7)-(10).

137. Ibid., pp. 3.3(7)-(9), 3.3(27)-(29).

138. These figures include money provided to state and local governments by the federal government. Expenditures are counted at the level of final expenditure. For instance, in 1983-1984, $315 million of the amount expended by state and local governments for parks and recreation was provided under the federally funded Land and Water Conservation Fund; predominantly under the Clean Water Act, the federal government transferred $2.825 billion

to state and local governments for water and sewerage facilities. U.S. Department of Commerce, Bureau of the Census, *Governmental Finances in 1983-1984*, series GF 84, no.5 (Washington, D.C.: U.S. Government Printing Office, 1985), p. 19, table 11, and p. 20, table 12.

139. U.S. Congressional Budget Office, *Efficient Investments in Wastewater Treatment Plants*, pp. 4-5; and U.S. Congressional Budget Office, *The Federal Budget for Public Works Infrastructure*, p. 56.

140. W. John Moore, "Mandates without Money," p. 2370.

141. Steven V. Roberts, "President Vetoes Clean Water Bill; Cites Budget Gap," *New York Times*, January 31, 1987.

142. Moore, "Mandates without Money," pp. 2367-70; see also U.S. Environmental Protection Agency, *1988 Budget in Brief* (Washington, D.C.: U.S. Government Printing Office, 1987), p. 22.

143. Organization for Economic Cooperation and Development, *The State of the Environment 1985* (Paris: Organization for Economic Cooperation and Development, 1985), pp. 252-53.

144. Organization for Economic Cooperation and Development, *Environment and Economics*, vol. I, Background Papers for an International Conference on Environment and Economics, Sessions 1-3, July 18-21, 1984 (Paris: Organization for Economic Cooperation and Development, 1984), pp. 123-25.

145. The countries examined were France, Germany, Japan, the Netherlands, and the United States. See Organization for Economic Cooperation and Development, *OECD Environmental Data Compendium 1985*, p. 271.

146. Clifford S. Russell, Winston Harrington, and William J. Vaughan, *Enforcing Pollution Control Laws* (Washington, D.C.: Resources for the Future, 1986), p. 7.

147. Ibid., pp. 8-9; Cheryl Wasserman, "Improving the Efficiency and Effectiveness of Compliance Monitoring and Enforcement of Environmental Policies in the United States: A National View," a report prepared for the Organization for Economic Cooperation and Development Environment Directorate, July 1986, pp. VI3-VI4; Joseph F. DiMento, *Environmental Law and American Business: Dilemmas of Compliance* (New York: Plenum Press, 1986), pp. 25-28; and Bud Ward, "Voluntary Compliance—What Is Its Status?" *The Environmental Forum* 3, no. 8 (1984):37-38.

148. Wasserman, "Improving the Efficiency and Effectiveness of Compliance Monitoring," pp. VI11-VI15.

149. Use of innovative methods, such as mediation and environmental audits, may increase in the near future. For a more complete discussion, see Richard H. Mays, "The Need for Innovative Environmental Enforcement," *The Environmental Forum* 4, no. 11 (1986):7-14.

150. U.S. Environmental Protection Agency, Office of Federal Activities, "Federal Facilities Compliance Strategy," draft, July 1986, pp. 9, 29-32.

151. U.S. Environmental Protection Agency, Office of Enforcement and Compliance Monitoring, "Summary of Enforcement Accomplishments & Fiscal Year 1985," April 1986, pp. 1-2; personal communication with Jeffrey Miller, February 1986; and "Integrated Federal-State Data Systems Proposed by EPA for All Pollution Programs in Effort to Upgrade Management," *Environment Reporter* 17, no. 13 (1986):476-77.

152. DiMento, *Environmental Law and American Business*, pp. 25-28.

153. Ibid.; Russell, Harrington and Vaughan, *Enforcing Pollution Control Laws*, pp. 8-9; and L. Kropp and David M. Flannery, "Guilty or Not Guilty—Only Your Statistician

Knows for Sure," *The Environmental Forum* 2, no. 12 (1984):23-27.

154. U.S. Congressional Budget Office, *The Budget of the Environmental Protection Agency*, pp. 84-85.

155. As with enforcement subprogram budgets, overall enforcement activity figures for 1984 and 1985 reflect budget authority rather than actual obligations but are considered fairly comparable to actual expenditures (based on the close correlation exhibited from 1977 to 1983). See U.S. Congressional Budget Office, *The Budget of the Environmental Protection Agency*, pp. 9, 84-85.

156. The figures used for the overall EPA operating budget include the air, water, solid and hazardous wastes, and toxic substances programs. They do not include Superfund, Construction Grant, or Leaking Underground Storage Tank expenditures. Activities within each program include research and development, abatement and control, and enforcement. These figures come from a source other than that used in the Environmental Expenditures Section and therefore may not be consistent. Ibid., pp. 84-85.

157. Mays, "The Need for Innovative Environmental Enforcement," p. 7; and Environmental Law Institute, *Citizen Suits: An Analysis of Citizen Enforcement Actions Under EPA-Administered Statutes*, prepared for the U.S. Environmental Protection Agency (Washington, D.C.: Environmental Law Institute, 1984), p. vii.

158. These figures are for National Pollutant Discharge Elimination System administrative orders. In Region 4, increased activitiy was due to 623 administrative orders issued to smaller industrial facilities. Personal communication with Larry Reid, U.S. Environmental Protection Agency, March 1987.

159. The decrease in hazardous waste administrative orders in 1986 was due to definitional changes, transfer of responsibilities to states, and delays in Superfund reauthorization. See U.S. Environmental Protection Agency, Office of Public Affairs, *Environmental News*, December 16, 1986, p. 5.

160. Judson W. Starr, "Countering Environmental Crimes," *Environmental Affairs* 13 (1986):380-81.

161. Ibid., p. 383; David Riesel, "Criminal Prosecution and Defense of Environmental Wrongs," *Environmental Law Reporter* 15, (March 1985):10065; and "Environmental Crimes Prosecuted," *Environ Report*, Fall 1986, p. 1.

162. U.S. Environmental Protection Agency, "Summary of Enforcement Accomplishments," p. 3.

163. "Environmental Crimes Prosecuted," pp. 1, 6.

164. U.S. Environmental Protection Agency, "Summary of Enforcement Accomplishments," p. 15; and U.S. Environmental Protection Agency, *Environmental News*, December 16, 1986, p. 2.

165. Personal communication with Joyce Blakley, U.S. Department of Justice, Environmental Crimes Unit, March 1987.

166. "Environmental Crimes Prosecuted," p. 5.

167. Ibid.; and Starr, "Countering Environmental Crimes," p. 383.

168. Starr, "Countering Environmental Crimes," pp. 381-82; and Papa, "Combating Environmental Crime at EPA's National Enforcement Investigations Center," p. 37.

169. See generally Barry Boyer and Errol Meidinger, "Privatizing Regulatory Enforcement: A Preliminary Assessment of Citizen Suits under Federal Environmental Laws," in Administrative Conference of the United States, *Recommendations and Reports 1985* (Washington, D.C.: U.S. Government Printing Office, 1985), pp. 365-504; and Jeffrey

G. Miller and Environmental Law Institute, *Citizen Suits: Private Enforcement of Federal Pollution Control Laws* (New York: Wiley Law Publications, 1987).

170. Environmental Law Institute, *Citizen Suits*, p. I-3.

171. The 350 notices or suits were filed under the Clean Air Act, §304, 42 USC §7604; Federal Water Pollution Control Act, §505, 33 USC §1365; Toxic Substances Control Act, §20, 15 USC §2619; Resource Conservation and Recovery Act, §7002, 42 USC §6972; and Safe Drinking Water Act, §1449, 42 USC §300j-8. The Noise Control Act, §12, 42 USC §4911 (also studied, but under which no actions were initiated); Marine Protection Research and Sanctuaries Act, §105(g), 33 USC §1415(g); Endangered Species Act, §11(g), 16 USC §1540(g); Deepwater Port Act, §16, 33 USC §1515; Outer Continental Shelf Lands Act, 43 USC §1349(a); and the Surface Mining Control and Reclamation Act, §520, 30 USC §1270 also contain citizen suit provisions. See Environmental Law Institute, *Citizen Suits*, pp. I-2-I-3, III-9, III-21; and "Citizen Suits—1980's Version of 70's EIS's?" *The Environmental Forum* 3, no. 8 (1984):33.

172. See Environmental Law Institute, *Citizen Suits* (1984), p. III-10.

173. Ibid.

174. Ibid., p. III-2; and Jeffrey G. Miller, "Private Enforcement of Federal Pollution Control Laws, Part III," *Environmental Law Reporter* 14, (November 1984):10425.

175. Nicolas C. Yost, "The Law that Works," *The Environmental Forum* 3, no. 9 (1985):41; and Council on Environmental Quality, *Environmental Quality 1984: 15th Annual Report of the Council on Environmental Quality* (Washington, D.C. U.S. Government Printing Office, 1986), p. 522.

176. Council on Environmental Quality, *Environmental Quality 1984*, pp. 514-15; and personal communication, Dinah Bear, Council on Environmental Quality, March 1987.

177. Council on Environmental Quality, *Environmental Quality*, annual editions, 1970-1984; information provided by Dinah Bear, September 1986; and information provided by U.S. Environmental Protection Agency, Office of Federal Activities, October 1986.

178. This figure includes municipal facilities that are on Compliance Schedule/Interim Effluents Limits (1,219) and facilities operating in "significant noncompliance" with their final permit limits (158). Management Advisory Group to the U.S. Environmental Protection Agency, Construction Grants Program, "Municipal Compliance with the National Pollutant Discharge Elimination System," a report to the U.S. Environmental Protection Agency, June 1986, pp. 11-12.

179. Telephone conversation with Jim Edward, U.S. Environmental Protection Agency, Office of External Affairs/Federal Activities, March 1987.

180. U.S. Environmental Protection Agency, "Federal Facilities Compliance Strategy," p. II-1.

181. Although penalties legally may be applied when specifically provided by statute, EPA policy precludes imposition of penalties. See ibid., p. VI-1.

182. Ibid., p. VI-19.

Figures

1.1. Projections for 1990-2025 make the following assumptions: 1.9 births per woman (fertility or ultimate lifetime births per woman), 79.6 years life expectancy, and 450,000 annual net immigration. U.S. Department of Commerce, Bureau of the Census, *Estimates of the Population of the United States and Components of Change: 1970 to 1985*, series

P-25, no. 990 (Washington, D.C.: U.S. Government Printing Office, 1986), p. 9; U.S. Department of Commerce, Bureau of the Census, *Statistical Abstract of the United States 1986* (Washington, D.C.: U.S. Government Printing Office, 1986), p. 7; and information provided by Gregory Spencer, U.S. Department of Commerce, Bureau of the Census, August 1986.

1.2. These estimates assume the following: catastrophes will not occur during the projection period; for countries with populations less than 300,000 in 1980, projections were made on the basis of assumed rates of growth for the total population; estimates were made on a country-by-country basis, with specific conditions and circumstances of each country considered; the projections were arrived at by crossing assumed levels of fertility, mortality and migration. For this figure, the medium variant estimates and projections were used. United Nations, Department of International Economic and Social Affairs, *World Population Prospects: Estimates and Projections as Assessed in 1982*, Population Studies no. 86 (New York: United Nations, 1985), p. 42.

1.3. U.S. Department of Commerce, Bureau of the Census, *Patterns of Metropolitan Area and Country Population Growth: 1980 to 1984*, Current Population Reports, series P-25, no. 976 (Washington, D.C.: U.S. Government Printing Office, 1985), pp. 57-59.

1.4. Ibid., pp. 17-39.

1.5. United Nations, Department of International Economic and Social Affairs, *Estimates and Projections of Urban, Rural and City Populations, 1950-2025: The 1982 Assessment* (New York: United Nations, 1985), pp. 144-47.

1.6. U.S. Department of Commerce, Bureau of Economic Analysis, unpublished data from "GNP (Revised Estimates), Current and Constant (1982) Dollars 1986," table 1.2.

1.7. U.S. Department of Commerce, Bureau of Economic Analysis, unpublished data from "Gross National Product by Industry in Constant Dollars," 1986, table 6.2.

1.8. Memo from Hal Quinley, The Policy Planning Group of Yankelovich, Kelly and White, Inc. to Dick Duncan and Walter Isaacson, *Time*, "Time/Yankelovich Poll-September, 1985," table 25; "Opinion Roundup-Environmental Update," *Public Opinion*, February/March 1982, p. 32; and unpublished results of survey conducted by The Roper Organization.

1.9. Kit D. Farber and Gary L. Rutledge, "Pollution Abatement and Control Expenditures," *Survey of Current Business* 66, no. 7 (1986):97, table 6.

1.10. U.S. Department of Commerce, Bureau of Economic Analysis, Environmental Economics Division, "Plant and Equipment Expenditures by Business for Pollution Abatement," *Survey of Current Business* 66, no. 2 (1986):39, table 2.

1.11. Ibid., pp. 40-41, table 1.

1.12. Farber and Rutledge, "Pollution Abatement and Control Expenditures," pp. 100-3, table 9.

1.13. U.S. Environmental Protection Agency, Office of the Comptroller, *Summary of the 1987 Budget* (Washington, D.C.: U.S. Government Printing Office, 1986), p. 8; and information provided by the Office of Management and Budget, September 1986.

1.14. U.S. Office of Management and Budget, *Budget of the U.S. Government, Historical Tables, Fiscal Year 1987* (Washington, D.C.: U.S. Government Printing Office, 1986), pp. 3.3(7)-(9).

1.15. U.S. Congress, Congressional Budget Office, *The Budget of the Environmental Protection Agency: An Overview of Selected Proposals for 1985*, special study (Washington, D.C.: U.S. Government Printing Office, 1984), pp. 84-85, tables C-3, C-4.

1.16. 1980-1984: Information provided by U.S. Environmental Protection Agency, Office of Enforcement and Compliance Monitoring, Compliance Evaluation Branch, Office of Compliance Analysis and Program Operations, October 1986. 1985-1986: U.S. Environmental Protection Agency, "FY1986 EPA Enforcement Activity Fact Sheet," in *Environmental News*, December 16, 1986, p. 2.

1.17. Cases referred: 1980-1984: Information provided by Rick Duffy, U.S. Environmental Protection Agency, Office of Enforcement and Compliance Monitoring, March 1987; 1985-1986: U.S. Environmental Protection Agency, "FY1986 EPA Enforcement Activity Fact Sheet," in *Environmental News*, December 16, 1986, p. 1. Cases filed: 1980-1986: U.S. Environmental Protection Agency, "FY1986 Enforcement Activity Fact Sheet," in *Environmental News*, December 16, 1986, p. 3.

1.18. Information provided by David Knight, U.S. Department of Justice, Land and Natural Resources Division, Environmental Enforcement Section, Environmental Enforcement Case Management System, March 1987.

1.19. Environmental Law Institute, *Citizen Suits: An Analysis of Citizen Enforcement Actions under EPA-Administered Statutes*, prepared for the U.S. Environmental Protection Agency (Washington, D.C.: Environmental Law Institute, 1984), p. III-10, figure D.

1.20. U.S. Council on Environmental Quality, *Environmental Quality*, annual editions, 1970-1984; information provided by Dinah Bear, Council on Environmental Quality, September 1986; and information provided by U.S. Environmental Protection Agency, Office of Federal Activities, October 1986.

Chapter 2

Traditional Environmental Contaminants

The major response to the increasing environmental concern in the late 1960s and early 1970s was the enactment of a series of laws at the federal, state, and local levels to deal with at least the most obvious of the nation's pollution problems. Congress enacted the Resource Recovery Act in 1970 to begin to address the problem of unsightly and nocuous dumps, the Clean Air Act in 1970 to eliminate the health and aesthetic effects of ambient air pollution, and amendments to the Federal Water Pollution Control Act in 1972 to reduce discharges of pollution from municipal wastewater treatment plants and industries.

These statutes focused initially on cleaning up what has come to be known as the conventional problems—reducing the release of particulates, sulfur dioxide, automobile-related, and other conventional pollutants to the air; decreasing the amount of suspended solids, bacteria, and oxygen-consuming materials discharged to surface waters; and promoting the use of sanitary landfills. The statutes established ambitious goals, set tight deadlines, and forced the nation to take unprecedented steps, involving the expenditure of hundreds of billions of dollars, to improve the environment.

These efforts have succeeded in substantially reducing the problems that they set out to address. Most of the air and water is cleaner than it was in 1970, and most of the dumps are gone. There are still problems, and in some places the problems have even gotten worse. And one can certainly ask whether the job could not have been accomplished cheaper and faster. All in all, however, the United States is less polluted, at least with the conventional pollutants, than it was in 1970. Considering that, as indicated in the previous chapter, the nation's gross national product has grown by approximately 50 percent during the same period, this is not a trivial accomplishment.

AIR QUALITY

Since the 1970 amendments to the Clean Air Act, the United States has invested billions of dollars to clean up the air in its dirtiest regions and to prevent deterioration of air quality in its cleanest ones. Despite population growth, economic development, and large increases in the use of motor vehicles, much progress appears to have been made in cleansing the nation's air. Energy conservation and declines in smokestack industries surely have helped protect air quality, but the nation's substantial investment in regulatory programs also has produced significant benefits.

Progress has been uneven. Levels of some pollutants appear to have dropped much more than levels of others. Many areas, including many major cities, still experience levels of pollution that have been deemed a threat to human health. Moreover, some of the easiest pollution control measures already may have been employed on the largest sources of pollution, so further progress may depend substantially on controlling more numerous smaller sources.

Policy makers' perception of air pollution problems has evolved considerably since the Clean Air Act was amended in 1970. At that time, the major programs were designed to counter the impacts on local communities of local sources of the most common pollutants. (Concern has grown over less commonly found toxic pollutants. See chapter 8.) Since then, the focus has shifted to the longer-range effects of pollution. For example, emissions that may not cause local problems can travel long distances and cause trouble elsewhere. Furthermore, the global aspects of air pollution—such as depletion of protective ozone levels in upper layers of the earth's atmosphere and warming of the earth's atmosphere because of rising levels of carbon dioxide and chlorofluorocarbons—may be solvable only through agreements reached on a worldwide scale.

Ambient Air Quality

Since 1970, efforts to control air pollution have focused on limiting emissions of five common pollutants: total suspended particulates (TSPs), sulfur dioxide, nitrogen dioxide, carbon monoxide, and the organic compounds that contribute to the formation of ozone in the lowest layers of the atmosphere.* For these pollutants, the U.S. Environmental Protection Agency (EPA) has established national ambient air quality standards† (figure 2.1). The ambient standards specify maximum allowable concentrations of these pollutants in the air. Levels above the *primary ambient standards* are considered threats to public health, and levels above the *secondary ambient standards* are deemed threats to public welfare.

Indicators of Pollution

The federal government uses several measures to assess progress in abating air pollution. These are reviewed in this section, but they should be considered with a recognition of their significant limitations.

Statements about air quality (often summarized in an index such as the Pollutant Standard Index),[1] whether they pertain to individual communities or national averages, rely on stationary monitors in a few locations. Unfortunately, monitors collect data only on a limited number of places, and often the locations of the monitors are not indicative of actual human exposure. Furthermore, data from monitors usually are not weighted to take population concentrations into account. So regulators and the public have only a limited idea of how many people are exposed to what levels of pollution. (Chapter 8 discusses the importance of monitoring personal exposures and taking indoor as well as outdoor pollution into account.) Moreover, tracking progress through the years is complicated by incomplete records, a variety of measurement techniques, and insufficient checking of data quality.[2]

Progress also can be measured by changes in emissions from industries, automobiles, and other sources. But little information is available on actual emissions, and emission estimates are precisely that—estimates. As such, they are only as accurate as the assumptions underlying them, and these assumptions change periodically.‡

---

*Ozone in the upper layers of the atmosphere protects humans from harmful ultraviolet radiation. Ozone in the lowest layers can impair breathing and produce other harmful health effects.

†In 1978 an ambient standard was established for lead. For discussion of progress in removing lead from the air, see chapter 3.

‡For example, in 1982, when EPA changed its method for estimating carbon monoxide emissions from motor vehicles, the estimated change in carbon monoxide emissions between 1970 and 1978 shifted from a slight to a substantial decline.[3]

Figure 2.1
National Ambient Air Quality Standards

Pollutant	Primary (health-related)		Secondary (welfare-related)	
	Averaging time	Concentration	Averaging time	Concentration
Particulates	Annual geometric mean	75 μg/m³	Annual geometric mean	60 μg/m³
	24-hour	260 μg/m³	24-hour	150 μg/m³
Sulfur dioxide	Annual arithmetic mean	(0.03 ppm) 80 μg/m³	3-hour	1,300 μg/m³ (0.50 ppm)
	24-hour	(0.14 ppm) 365 μg/m³		
Carbon monoxide	8-hour	(9 ppm) 10 μg/m³	None	
	1-hour	(35 ppm) 40 μg/m³	Same as primary	
Nitrogen dioxide	Annual arithmetic mean	(0.053 ppm) 100 μg/m³	Same as primary	
Ozone	Maximum daily 1-hour average	0.12 ppm (235 μg/m³)	Same as primary	
Lead	Maximum quarterly average	1.5 μg/m³	Same as primary	

Source: U.S. Environmental Protection Agency.

Explaining why changes occur in monitored ambient concentrations or estimated emissions is even more problematic. Year-to-year improvement or deterioration in air quality occurs for a number of reasons aside from the presence or absence of pollution control efforts. Some major sources of pollution may have closed or moved elsewhere, decreasing pollution levels at their old site and increasing levels at their new one. Temporary economic slowdowns may have caused an equally temporary reduction in industrial emissions. Or climatic conditions may have changed for the better or worse. For example, wet years may lower ambient concentrations of particulates, while certain meteorological conditions may promote formation of ozone. For all these reasons, care must be exercised in interpreting year-to-year changes in measurements. Somewhat greater confidence can be placed in measured longer term trends, although even with those it is difficult in most cases to identify precisely the relative influence of regulatory and nonregulatory factors on ambient levels of pollution.

Yet another measure of progress is the number of "nonattainment areas" for a pollutant. A nonattainment area is one that fails to attain an EPA established ambient standard. A major purpose of federal and state air pollution control programs is to bring areas into compliance with the ambient standards.

On a national and state-by-state basis, EPA compiles lists of counties and portions of counties that are judged "attainment," "nonattainment," or unclassifiable. In 1978, EPA published the initial designations for the over 3,000 counties in the United States.[4] A drop in the number of nonattainment counties since then suggests progress in attaining national air quality goals. However, this indicator has two limitations. First, EPA's process for redesignating an area from nonattainment to attainment is quite time-consuming.[5] Air quality in an area may be better than an ambient standard for several years before the area's designation is changed. Second, no distinctions are drawn administratively among different degrees of nonattainment. Those areas violating a national standard often and by a substantial amount are not distinguished from those areas violating one infrequently and only by a small margin. In theory, the air in both types of nonattainment area threatens human health; in reality, the air in one nonattainment area may be a far greater threat than that in the other.

The Pollutant Standard Index

The Pollutant Standard Index (PSI), developed in 1976, can be used to analyze trends in urban air quality and to make comparisons among urban areas.[6] This index compares air quality monitoring data to the primary ambient air quality standards (excluding those for lead). In theory, the higher the index reading, the more severe the pollution and the greater the threat to human health. The index is an imperfect measure of air quality, not only because it relies on fixed monitoring stations but because it focuses only on the most common pollutants.[7] Nevertheless, a decline in the highest PSI readings indicates that the most serious episodes of elevated pollution, with their attendant health risks, have been reduced. A decline in average readings also denotes progress.

PSI data are published each year by the Council on Environmental Quality (CEQ). The latest available data, for 33 cities from 1976 to 1983, and for 12 of these cities from 1976 to 1984, showed a "dramatic" downward trend in PSI for most of the urban areas analyzed.[8] The PSI is influenced heavily in many cities by measurements of ozone and carbon monoxide. CEQ attributes the drop in PSI readings to the "rapid decline" in emissions from motor vehicles of carbon monoxide and the pollutants that contribute to ozone.[9] This decline stems from strict federal limits on emissions of these pollutants from new automobiles.

Trends for Individual Pollutants

Although the national trend is very encouraging, many cities continue to exceed ambient air quality standards for at least one pollutant, and in a few the air quality in 1984 was worse than it was in 1982 (figures 2.2-2.6).* The pollutants creating the most problems are particulates, carbon monoxide, and ozone.

Particulates. Particulates are solid particles or liquid droplets small enough to remain suspended in air. They can be emitted directly or formed from gaseous precursors such as sulfur dioxide. They can irritate the human respiratory system and contribute to acute respiratory illness. Prolonged inhalation of some types of airborne particulates may increase both the incidence and the severity of chronic respiratory disease.[10]

EPA reports that average total suspended particulate (TSP) levels, measured at 1,344 sites, decreased 20 percent between 1975 and 1984, while emissions during the same period declined an average of 33 percent[11] (figures 2.7 and 2.8). Changes in ambient levels tend to differ from changes in emission estimates because ambient levels are influenced by natural dust,

---

*In general, one year's measurement does not adequately represent a city's air quality, and the change from one year to another is not necessarily representative of the overall trend in air quality. However, the data presented in figures 2.2-2.6 do, in most cases, represent the longer term levels and trends in air quality in the cities listed.

Figure 2.2
Total Suspended Particulate Levels in
Selected U.S. Metropolitan Areas, 1982 and 1984

(Highest Annual Geometric Mean)

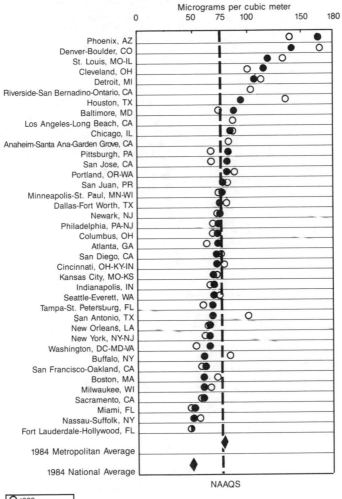

Micrograms per cubic meter

NAAQS

O 1982
● 1984
◑ The same
1982 and 1984
concentrations

Source: U.S. Environmental Protection Agency.

Figure 2.3

Sulfur Dioxide Levels in
Selected U.S. Metropolitan Areas, 1982 and 1984

(Highest Annual Arithmetic Mean)

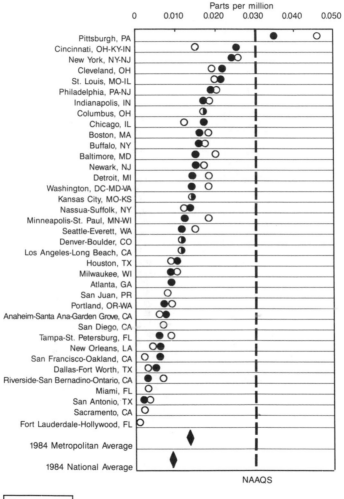

Source: U.S. Environmental Protection Agency.

Figure 2.4

Ozone Levels in
Selected U.S. Metropolitan Areas, 1982 and 1984

(One-Hour Second Highest Daily Maximum)

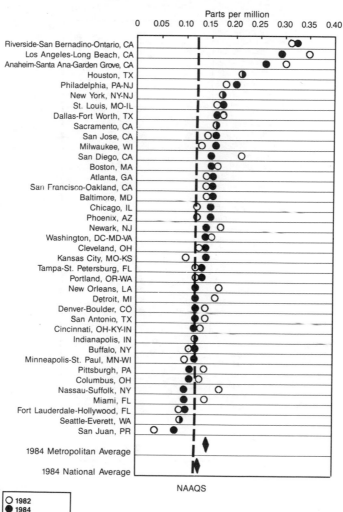

Source: U.S. Environmental Protection Agency.

Figure 2.5

**Nitrogen Dioxide Levels in
Selected U.S. Metropolitan Areas, 1982 and 1984**

(Highest Annual Arithmetic Mean)

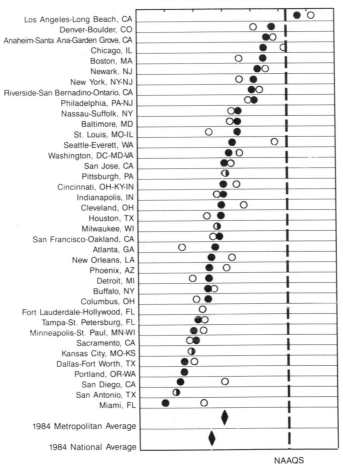

NAAQS

○ 1982
● 1984
◑ The same 1982
and 1984
concentrations

Source: U.S. Environmental Protection Agency.

Figure 2.6

Carbon Monoxide Levels in
Selected U.S. Metropolitan Areas, 1982 and 1984

(Highest Second Maximum Eight-Hour Nonoverlapping Average)

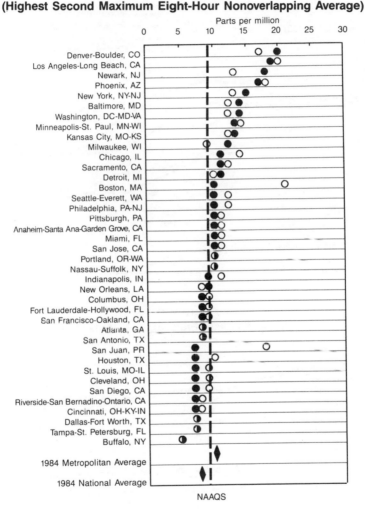

Source: U.S. Environmental Protection Agency.

Figure 2.7
U.S. Trends in Ambient Air Quality for
Five Pollutants, 1975–1984

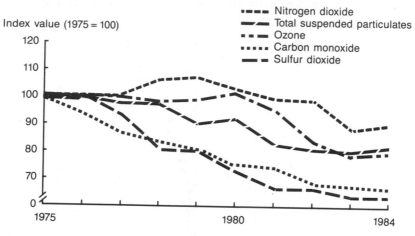

Index value (1975 = 100)

- ■■■■ Nitrogen dioxide
- ━ ◢ Total suspended particulates
- ■ ▪ ■ Ozone
- •••••• Carbon monoxide
- ━ ━ Sulfur dioxide

Source: U.S. Environmental Protection Agency.

Figure 2.8
U. S. Air Pollutant Emissions, 1970–1984

Million metric tons

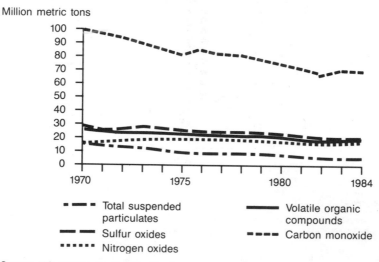

- ▪ ▪ ▪ Total suspended particulates
- ━ ━ Sulfur oxides
- •••••• Nitrogen oxides
- ━━━ Volatile organic compounds
- ▪▪▪ Carbon monoxide

Source: U.S. Environmental Protection Agency.

construction activity, and other factors not included in EPA's emission estimates.[12] The highest concentrations of particulates in 1984 generally were found in the industrial Midwest and in arid areas of the West.

A substantial decrease in particulate matter emissions since 1978 is attributed by EPA to both reduced industrial activity and installation of control equipment. Reductions are also attributed by EPA to reduced coal burning by industry (other than utilities) and installation of control equipment by coal-burning utilities.[13] Electric utilities and other industrial sources were responsible for approximately 47 percent of the particulates estimated to have been emitted in 1984[14] (figure 2.9).

In 1978, EPA listed 421 counties or portions of counties that failed to attain the primary or secondary ambient standards for particulates;[15] this number had dropped to 290 by 1985.[16] Of those, 145 failed to attain the health-based primary standard[17] (figure 2.10).

Ambient levels of TSP are assessed by monitors that measure the concentration of suspended particles ranging up to approximately 45 microns in diameter.[18] The existing TSP standard does not distinguish between larger and smaller particles, although scientists have recognized that "fine" particles, those smaller than 2.5 microns in diameter, present a more serious health risk than large particles. The fine particles are deposited in the parts of the lung that are most vulnerable to injury and can carry with them

Figure 2.9
Air Emissions, by Source and Type of Pollutant, 1970, 1977, 1984

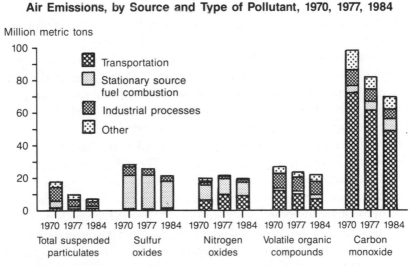

Source: U.S. Environmental Protection Agency.

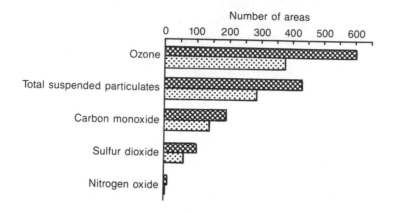

Figure 2.10
Number of Areas in the United States Not Attaining
Air Pollution Standards, by Pollutant, 1978 and 1985*

* Areas correspond to counties or portions of counties.   ⊠ March 1978

Source: U.S. Environmental Protection Agency.   ⊡ September 1985

other pollutants, such as toxic metals.[19] In 1984, EPA proposed revising the particulate air quality standard so that it would apply only to those particles equal to or smaller than 10 microns in diameter.[20] This proposal has not yet been issued as a final, legally binding revision.

The primary particulate standard was to have been achieved by December 31, 1982.[21] In the past, EPA insisted that states revise their attainment strategies for pollutants when deadlines were missed. But, in the absence of a revised TSP standard, revising state plans to reduce particulate emissions appears to have a relatively low regulatory priority.[22]

Data on particulate concentrations in other countries have been compiled by several international organizations.[23] These data have been culled from a small number of monitors, so they must be interpreted with considerable caution. They suggest that particulate concentrations have dropped in many Western European cities since 1975.[24] However, progress in reducing emissions from industrial sources reportedly has been offset somewhat by particulates generated from increased motor vehicle traffic and use of diesel-powered automobiles.[25]

The Global Environmental Monitoring System (GEMS) has reported trend data for 62 sites around the globe, in both advanced industrial nations and developing countries. The limited data indicate downward trends for particulates at 43 percent of the sites and upward trends at 10 percent.[26] In 1980, about 40 percent of the sites registered particulate concentrations higher than those recommended in guidelines established by the World Health Organization.[27] Very high concentrations measured in some cities— such as Teheran, Iran, and Calcutta, India—may be due partly to naturally high dust levels in these cities, rather than to industrial pollution.[28] The GEMS data also indicate that cities in developing countries (for example, Jakarta, Indonesia; Kuala Lampur, Malaysia; and New Delhi, India) have relatively higher concentrations of particulates than most cities in Western Europe; these are attributed to use of wood and charcoal in urban homes and small industries.[29] Relatively high levels of particulates are also found in Eastern European cities.[30]

Sulfur Dioxide. Sulfur dioxide (SO_2) is a colorless gas that, when present in high concentrations, aggravates respiratory diseases, corrodes metals and stone, reduces plant growth, and injures aquatic life.[31]

Two-thirds of all SO_2 emissions nationwide are generated by electric utilities, with most coming from a relatively small number of coal-fired power plants.[32] Fifty-three plants in 14 states account for one-half of all power plant emissions, and the 200 highest emitters produce 85 percent of all power plant emissions of SO_2. These 200 plants account for 57 percent of all SO_2 emissions nationwide.[33]

Primary ambient standards for SO_2 have been set for both annual and 24-hour concentrations of the pollutant. EPA reports that between 1975 and 1984, based on readings at 229 sites, annual mean SO_2 concentrations declined 36 percent[34] (figure 2.7). Similarly, among 224 stations measuring the "second highest 24-hour value," the average reading declined 41 percent.[35] Most of the monitors did not show the 24-hour standard being exceeded.[36]

Nationwide, EPA estimates that emissions of all sulfur oxides declined 16 percent between 1975 and 1984.[37] Decreases have come from installation of pollution control devices and reduction in the average sulfur content of fuels used. Smelters are the major source of SO_2 emissions in the Intermountain West (between the crest of the Sierras and the Continental Divide running through the Rockies). Dramatic declines in smelter emissions during the past several years, and attendant declines in violations of ambient standards, have resulted from plant closings, limited plant operations, and installation of pollution control devices.[38]

Nationwide, the 36 percent decrease in monitored ambient levels, as compared with the lower 16 percent decline in overall estimated emissions, is attributed by EPA to the fact that most monitors for SO_2 are in urban areas; thus, major emitters of SO_2 in rural areas are overlooked. In these urban areas, estimated reductions in emissions for residential and commercial sources are comparable to measured reductions in ambient levels of SO_2. EPA attributes these emission reductions to energy conservation measures and the use of cleaner fuels.[39]*

Industry and utility use of taller stacks to dissipate pollution also has contributed to the disparity between measures of ambient concentrations and estimates of emissions. Tall stacks release emissions higher in the atmosphere, reducing concentrations at nearby ground-level monitors at a faster rate than actual emissions may decline.[40]

The number of nonattainment areas for sulfur dioxide has dropped from 101 counties or portions of counties in 1978 to 60 in 1985[41] (figure 2.10). Fifty-four of these are wholly, or have portions, in violation of the primary standard.[42]

Trends in ambient levels of SO_2 in other nations are reported through the GEMS network of monitors. The number of monitors in many cities is quite limited, so great care must be taken in interpreting monitored data and making comparisons among locations. Between 1973 and 1980, for 63 sites for which five or more years of data were available, downward trends were reported at 54 percent of the sites and upward trends at 16 percent of the sites.[43] About one-quarter of the sites in the GEMS network reported annual average concentrations of SO_2 above the World Health Organization (WHO) guidelines for average concentrations, and about one-third exceeded the WHO guidelines for 24-hour concentrations.[44] Data from 1980 indicate that cities in Eastern Europe and developing nations have higher levels of SO_2 and particulate matter than most (but not all) cities with GEMS monitors in Organization for Economic Cooperation and Development countries (most of which are in Western Europe).[45] Figure 2.11, compiled from several sources, shows illustrative trends in New York and five European cities.

Nitrogen Dioxide. Emissions of nitrogen oxides contribute to several major air pollution problems. Nitric oxide, one of these compounds, forms nitrogen dioxide (NO_2). A variety of nitrogen oxides interact with volatile organic compounds to form ozone and other photochemical oxidants.[46]

---

*SO_2 levels in a number of major cities had already dropped dramatically during the 1960s, in response to local pollution control requirements.

Nitrogen oxides also contribute to formation of acidic compounds that can harm plants and animals.

EPA reports that, at 119 monitored sites, average NO_2 levels increased from 1975 to 1979, decreased through 1983, and then increased slightly in 1984, with the 1984 level 10 percent below that of 1975 (figure 2.7).[47] Trends in estimated national emissions of nitrogen oxides are similar to the ambient trends for NO_2 (figure 2.8).[48] In 1984, just over half of the nitrogen oxides emitted in the United States came from fuel burning at stationary sources (principally utilities), while nearly all the rest came from motor vehicles[49] (figure 2.9).

The Los Angeles region is the only part of the country that has failed to attain the national ambient air quality standards for NO_2. However,

Figure 2.11
Annual Average Concentrations of Sulfur Dioxide
in Selected European and U.S. Cities, 1973–1983

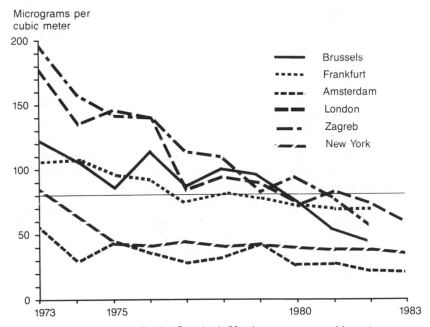

U.S. National Ambient Air Quality Standard: 80 micrograms per cubic meter.
Source: United Nations Environment Program; World Health Organization; Organization for Economic Cooperation and Development; New York Department of Environmental Conservation.

further reductions in emissions of nitrogen oxides across the country may reduce acid deposition.

Carbon Monoxide. Carbon monoxide (CO), a colorless, odorless gas, forms when fossil fuels, principally gasoline and diesel fuel, burn incompletely. CO has immediate health effects (drowsiness, slowed reflexes) at high exposure levels because it reduces the blood's capacity to carry and circulate oxygen. Very high concentrations cause death.[50]

Primary ambient standards for carbon monoxide specify both an eight-hour average (9 parts per million ppm) and a one-hour level (35 ppm) not to be exceeded more than once per year[51] (figure 2.1). Because the eight-hour standard generally is more restrictive, EPA's analysis of national ambient trends emphasizes eight-hour averages. Based on readings from 157 sites, EPA reported that the national composite average of "second highest non-overlapping 8 hour values" for CO decreased by 34 percent between 1975 and 1984.[52] The number of times the ambient standard has been exceeded at those sites has also dropped; there has been an 88 percent decrease between 1975 and 1984.[53] In its annual report for 1984, CEQ reported that, between 1976 and 1983, the number of days CO standards were violated dropped dramatically in nearly all of the 19 urban areas where the gas's emissions have the greatest impact.[54]

In 1975, 54.2 million metric tons (or 67 percent) of CO emissions came from highway vehicles. By 1984, emissions from highway vehicles had dropped to 41.4 million metric tons (or 59.2 percent of all CO emissions), even though the vehicle miles traveled increased 30 percent during this period.[55] EPA estimates that total emissions of CO dropped 14 percent between 1975 and 1984[56] (figure 2.9). The greater decrease in ambient levels (34 percent) than in emission levels (14 percent) is attributable to the fact that most CO monitors are placed in traffic-saturated areas. With newer, cleaner cars replacing older, dirtier cars, and with saturation preventing a significant increase in vehicle miles traveled, these areas experienced a substantial drop in ambient levels of carbon monoxide.[57]

The number of counties or portions of counties not attaining the carbon monoxide standard dropped from 190 in 1978 to 142 in 1985 (figure 2.10).[58]

As noted earlier, stationary monitors record data for places, not people. One must monitor individuals to fully appreciate the health risk from ambient levels of carbon monoxide. Figure 2.12, derived from EPA-sponsored research in Washington, D.C., demonstrates that commuters are exposed to significantly more CO than are noncommuters. Thirty-seven percent of those commuters who spent the most time on the road were

Figure 2.12
Commuter Exposure to Carbon Monoxide in Washington, D.C.
Winter 1982–83

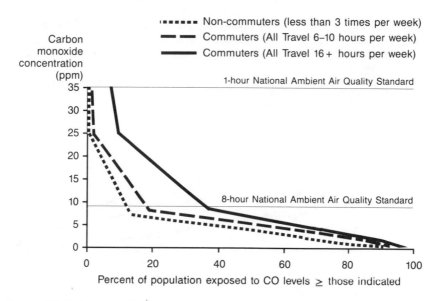

Source: U.S. Environmental Protection Agency.

exposed to CO levels greater than the eight-hour primary ambient standard, and seven percent were exposed to levels above the one-hour standard. A much lower proportion of noncommuters were exposed to these high levels.[59]

Figure 2.13 illustrates the influence of occupation on exposures to CO in the Washington, D.C., area. Fifty-seven percent of "high occupational exposure groups"—professional drivers (truck, bus, and taxi), automobile mechanics, garage workers, and policemen—were exposed to CO concentrations above the eight-hour ambient standard, and 24 percent were exposed to concentrations above the one-hour standard. Workers in other occupations and those not working outside their homes showed far lower levels of exposure.[60]

Ozone. Ozone, a principal component of smog, is produced by chemical reactions between nitrogen oxides and volatile organic compounds (VOCs) in the presence of oxygen and sunlight. Photochemical oxidants such as ozone impair breathing; irritate the eyes, nose, and throat; reduce visibility; and damage crops and other vegetation.[61]

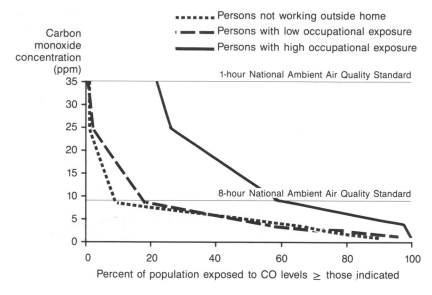

Figure 2.13
Worker Exposure to Carbon Monoxide in Washington, D.C.,
Winter 1982–83

Source: U.S. Environmental Protection Agency.

The proportions of VOCs emitted by various sources have changed dramatically since 1970. In 1970, transportation sources emitted an estimated 12.3 million metric tons of VOCs, 45 percent of all VOC emissions; by 1984, transportation emissions had dropped to an estimated 7.2 million metric tons, just 33 percent of all VOC emissions. In contrast, in 1970, industrial emissions totaled 8.7 million metric tons of VOCs, 32 percent of all estimated VOC emissions. By 1984, industrial emissions had barely changed, dropping down to 8.4 million metric tons, comprising 39 percent of all VOC emissions nationwide[62] (figure 2.9). The changing composition of the VOC emissions, like the decline in estimated CO emissions, is a tribute to the success of federal efforts to impose strict limits on emissions from new automobiles and trucks.

Between 1979 and 1984, ambient ozone levels decreased 7 percent and the estimated number of days the ozone standard was exceeded dropped 36 percent.[63]* During the 1980s, ambient levels of ozone have both

---

*Meaningful comparisons of pre- and post-1979 ambient data are not possible because EPA changed techniques for measuring ozone during 1978 and 1979.[64]

increased and decreased. Readings in 1980 and 1983 were higher than those in 1981, 1982, and 1984. EPA observes that the elevated levels in 1983 probably were attributable to meteorological conditions conducive to ozone formation.[65] Levels in 1984 were similar to those in 1981 and 1982, despite increases in both economic activity and vehicle miles traveled.

More nonattainment counties and portions of counties exist for ozone than for any other pollutant (figure 2.10). Nevertheless, the 368 such areas in 1985 represent a marked improvement from the 607 in 1978. Most major metropolitan areas in the United States are designated nonattainment for ozone, including much of the northern United States, major portions of the Gulf Coast, and coastal California. Figure 2.14 shows areas designated nonattainment for ozone as of September 1, 1985.[66]

Areas were obliged to meet the primary standard for ozone by December 31, 1982, but under certain conditions could obtain an extension of this deadline to December 31, 1987.[67] Although many of these areas developed plans that projected attainment by the extended deadline, EPA estimates that from 10 to 32 major urban areas—including Los Angeles, Chicago, Dallas, and Phoenix—will fail to do so.[68]

EPA has estimated that in 1984 approximately 80 million people lived in counties not attaining the ozone standard.[69] Unfortunately, this figure does not distinguish between those individuals who were exposed to levels of ozone greatly exceeding the standard and those who were exposed to levels barely exceeding it. Neither does it indicate whether people live in areas where the standard was exceeded on many days or just a few. So this number by itself is not a precise indicator of the risk ozone poses to the nation's population.

Recent scientific findings suggest the current ozone standard may not be sufficiently protective. The primary ambient air quality standard is supposed to be set with a "margin of safety" for especially sensitive portions of the nation's population. But EPA's Clean Air Scientific Advisory Committee has concluded that the existing one-hour standard has little or no margin of safety, and that lasting health effects might result from long-term exposure.[70] Some scientists have urged establishing an eight-hour standard, contending that such a longer-term standard is needed to protect public health.[71] Moreover, evidence indicates that ozone can significantly decrease the yield of several important agricultural crops and may cause other environmental damage.[72]

Long-Range Atmospheric Problems

Acid deposition, visibility, the destruction of the ozone layer, and rising levels of atmospheric CO_2 are long-range problems (both in terms of

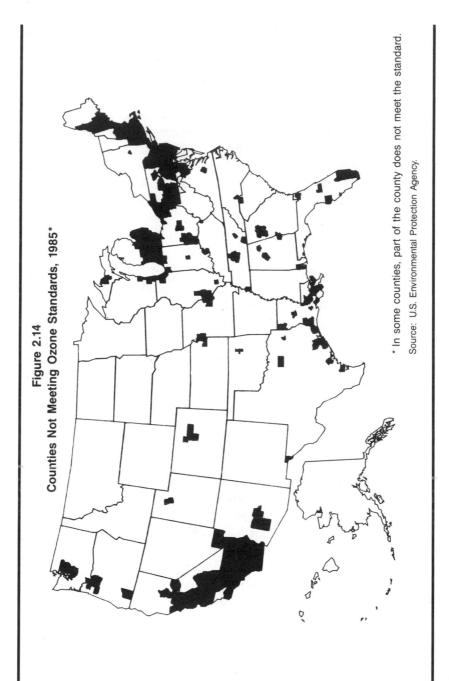

Figure 2.14
Counties Not Meeting Ozone Standards, 1985*

* In some counties, part of the county does not meet the standard.

Source: U.S. Environmental Protection Agency.

geography and years) that national programs do not address effectively. Their effects range from the aesthetic (for example, pollution-impaired visibility in national parks) to global alterations in climate and ecosystem composition.

Acid Deposition

One of the most controversial air quality issues in recent years has been what to do about acid rain, or more properly, acid deposition. Acid deposition begins with emissions of sulfur and nitrogen oxides. In the eastern United States, most sulfur oxides are emitted from burning coal at electric utility power plants.[73] In the western United States, utilities and smelters are each responsible for roughly one-quarter of the sulfur oxide emissions; smelter emissions have lessened in recent years.[74] Nationwide, most nitrogen oxides are emitted from utilities (33 percent) and highway vehicles (34 percent).[75] Nitrogen compounds are proportionately greater components of acid rain in the West than in the East.[76]

Sulfur and nitrogen oxides are transformed in the atmosphere into sulfates and nitrates.[77] The sulfates and nitrates are then removed from the atmosphere through both wet and dry deposition.[78] In wet deposition, they return to earth in the form of acid rain or snow. In dry deposition, about which data are scanty,[79] sulfur dioxide and nitrogen oxides are deposited as gases, fog and cloud droplets, or particles.[80] Acidic compounds may fall to earth a short distance from where their precursor gases were emitted or may be transported hundreds of miles before falling. For example, one model of long-distance transport suggests that about 38 percent of the sulfur deposition in the northeastern United States comes from the Midwest.[81]

Acid deposition can adversely affect aquatic systems. The adversity of the impacts depends, in part, on a system's buffering capacity. If the soil in a watershed contains limestone or other substances that neutralize acidity, the system's lakes acidify less rapidly than lakes in less-buffered watersheds.[82] Acids release metals from soils, sometimes in levels toxic to fish, and can harm other organisms.[83]

In 1986, the National Research Council (NRC) published the fifth in a series of reports on deposition of chemical pollutants.[84] The report focused on relationships among data on emissions, deposition, and environmental effects in eastern North America.* It reached the following conclusions:[86]

---

*While most attention in recent years has been given to acid deposition in the East, acid deposition is also a concern in the western United States.[85]

- In eastern North America a causal relationship exists between emissions of sulfur dioxide and (*a*) sulfate concentrations in ambient air, (*b*) reduced visibility, (*c*) wet deposition of sulfate, and (*d*) sulfate in watersheds that do not have large internal sources of sulfur. SO_2 emissions and deposition of sulfur oxides are highest in a region spanning the midwestern and northeastern United States.*
- SO_2 and other acid precursors have been emitted into the atmosphere of eastern North America in substantial amounts since the early 1900s. Prior to 1970, trends in SO_2 emissions among the several eastern regions the committee studied were the same. Since 1970, of these regions, the southeastern United States has experienced the greatest rate of increase in SO_2 emissions and related phenomena. A slightly lower rate of increase has occurred in the Midwest, while the northeastern United States has experienced modest decreases in emissions.
- Emissions of nitrogen oxides are estimated to have increased steadily since the early 1900s, with the rate of increase accelerating in the southeast since about 1950. However, reliable data do not exist on nitrate concentration trends in the atmosphere, surface waters, or wet and dry deposition.
- Data uncertainties make it difficult to reach unambiguous conclusions about trends in alkalinity and acidity in Adirondack lakes during the past 50 years.[88] The weight of chemical and biological evidence indicates that atmospheric deposition of sulfate has caused some Adirondack lakes to decrease in alkalinity.† Based on a review of sediments in low-alkalinity lakes, six of the ten Adirondack Mountain lakes for which such data exist became increasingly acidic between 1930 and 1970. Acid deposition is the most probable cause.
- Available data indicate that fish populations decline concurrently with acidification, with the strongest evidence coming from the Adirondack region.
- At higher elevations in the eastern United States, geographically widespread reductions in the width of tree rings (an indicator of growth) and increased mortality of red spruce trees began in the early 1960s. Current data do not permit adequate evaluation of the roles of acid deposition and other factors in this phenomenon.

---

*The NRC committee did not attempt to evaluate the extent to which emissions from one group of states influence acid deposition in another.[87]

†A subsequently published EPA survey of a sample of Adirondack lakes larger than 4 hectares (approximately 10 acres) estimated that about 11 percent (138) of such lakes are acidic.[89]

Committee member Dr. Arthur Johnson, elaborating on the group's work, concludes that "there is no longer reasonable doubt" that sulfur emissions affect aquatic ecosystems, although the extent of the adverse effects is not clear. Adirondack lakes have been affected, he writes, but acid deposition does not appear to have had a marked effect in New England.[90]

The NRC committee's conclusions are couched in cautious terms, as befits a scientific review of uncertain data. Yet public policy to reduce pollution often is made before unassailable scientific conclusions are available. Concern about the impacts of acid deposition on aquatic ecosystems, forests, structures that are both culturally significant and mundane, and potentially on human health has prompted Congress to consider a number of alternative strategies for reducing emissions of sulfur and nitrogen oxides. Proposed bills have addressed such questions as:

- Which pollutants should be controlled further?
- Should the whole country or only specific regions be subject to controls?
- What reductions in emissions should be required from utilities, motor vehicles, and other sources?
- By what date should reductions occur?
- Who should bear the cost of reducing emissions?
- Should measures be adopted to ease the economic and unemployment burdens a control program might place on certain regions?[91]

When it reconsiders reauthorization of the entire Clean Air Act during 1987 and 1988, the 100th Congress will surely grapple with bills offering widely different answers. For example, based on legislation introduced in past Congresses, legislators will consider whether they wish to impose controls only in 31 states east of the Mississippi River or in all 50 states; whether the total estimated reduction in emissions of sulfur and nitrogen oxides (from 1980 levels) should be 10 or 12 million tons;* and whether costs of cleanup should be borne exclusively by polluters and their customers or should be subsidized by a nationwide fee levied on electricity generation.[93]

Controls will cost billions of dollars.[94] The Congressional Budget Office estimates that the cost of abating 1 ton of SO_2 emissions will rise as emission reduction targets increase from 8 million to 12 million tons, with costs rising most steeply above 10 million tons.[95] Costs also will rise if Congress restricts use of low-sulfur coals or subsidizes the use of scrubbers to protect high-sulfur coal markets.[96]

---

*EPA estimates that in 1980 nationwide emissions of sulfur oxides totaled 23.2 million tons, and nitrogen oxide emissions totaled 20.4 million tons.[92]

Other nations have responded somewhat faster than the United States to acid deposition, motivated in part by evidence of massive forest damage on the European continent.* In July 1985, a protocol was adopted that called in principle for SO_2 emissions to be reduced from 1980 levels by at least 30 percent by 1993.[98] A total of 22 nations are now signatories to the agreement, but, for it to take effect, it must be formally ratified by 16 nations. As of early 1987, 13 nations had ratified it, and 6 more had signaled their intention to do so.† Both Great Britain and the United States have refused to sign the protocol, citing scientific uncertainty.[100]

Massive damage—such as decreased and abnormal growth, water-related stress, and death—is occurring in Europe's forests. For example, 52 to 55 percent of West Germany's forests are declining or dying.[101] (Figure 2.15 shows the damage manifested in various German tree species.) Acid rain is believed to be only one of several contributing causes. Scientists theorize that other major culprits include chronic and acute exposure to ozone, exposure to heavy metals and organic substances, and drought.[102]

Visibility

In the Clean Air Act, Congress singled out visibility as an environmental value especially deserving of protection.[103] EPA has divided visibility impairment into three categories: plume blight (clearly identifiable plumes from one or more sources); regional haze (uniform reduction in visual range in all directions); and layered discoloration by bands of gases and particulates above the earth's surface.[104]

Visibility may be impaired by gases and fine particles in the atmosphere that either scatter light or absorb it.[105] The National Park Service has found that sulfates comprise 40 to 60 percent of the fine particulates measured in eastern parks and 30 to 40 percent of the particulates measured in western parks.[106] Except in the northwestern United States, where fine carbon plays an important role, sulfates are the single most important contributor to visibility impairment in the nation's park system.[107] It appears then that controlling emissions of sulfur dioxide to reduce acid deposition would also serve to improve visibility. The NRC cautions, however, that short-

---

*Emission densities (tons per year per square mile) of sulfur dioxide often are much higher in Europe than in the United States.[97]

†The 13 ratifying countries are Bulgaria, Byelorussian SSR, Canada, Denmark, Finland, France, Hungary, Liechtenstein, the Netherlands, Norway, Sweden, Ukrainian SSR, and the Soviet Union. The 6 nations that have indicated their intention to ratify are West Germany, Belgium, Austria, Norway, Switzerland, and Czechoslovakia.[99]

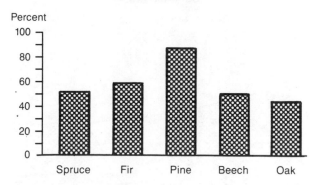

Figure 2.15
**Estimated Degree of Damage to Foliage in West Germany,
by Species, 1984**

Source: The MITRE Corporation.

and long-term variations in temperature, relative humidity, and instances of air stagnation may affect visibility. These variations can complicate the relationship between trends in visibility and trends in SO_2 emissions.[108]

National Weather Service data indicate that summertime visibility over much of the eastern United States has decreased by more than 50 percent since 1948.[109] The best visibility in the United States tends to be found in the mountain/desert West, with visibility declining sharply both farther west and farther east of this region.[110] Figure 2.16 shows the dramatic differences in visibility among western states, particularly California and its neighbors. The highest sulfate concentrations and lowest visibility occur east of the Mississippi and south of the Great Lakes, with the Ohio Valley generally having the lowest visibility.[111] Figure 2.17 shows the great visual ranges at some of the western United States's most well-known park units and the much shorter ranges in several eastern parks. In all the parks assessed, visibility tends to be better in winter than in summer.

EPA's regulatory program for protecting visibility has developed at a snail's pace. A lawsuit filed by the Environmental Defense Fund pushed the program forward somewhat in 1985.[112] EPA regulations published in 1980 had invited the Department of Interior to identify "integral vistas," views from inside national parks looking out, deserving special regulatory protection.[113] A preliminary list of such vistas was published in January 1981. After much delay, however, Interior Secretary Donald Hodel announced in late 1985 that no final list would be published.[114]

Figure 2.16
Visibility in National Parks and the Western States,
Summer 1985

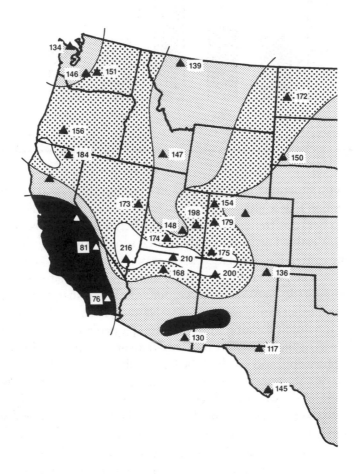

▲ = National Park System unit
Numbers = Visual range at park unit.

Source: National Park Service.

■■■	<100 Kilometers
▨▨▨	100–150 Kilometers
▨▨▨	150–200 Kilometers
☐	>200 Kilometers

Figure 2.17
Visual Ranges at Selected National Park System
Units, 1983-1986

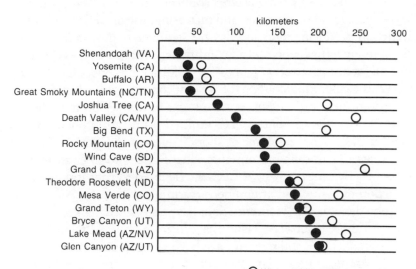

O Winter (1983–1986 Average)*
● Summer (1983–1985 Average)*

* Average of years for which data is available.

Source: National Park Service.

The Greenhouse Effect and Destruction of the Ozone Layer

In 1974, scientists initially theorized that human-made chlorofluorocarbons (CFCs) are destroying the earth's protective layer of stratospheric ozone.[115] Although ozone, the major component of smog, is undesirable near the earth's surface (as is noted earlier), its presence in the stratosphere serves to reduce the amount of ultraviolet radiation reaching the earth's surface. It thereby protects humans from skin cancer and other harmful effects, such as reduced agricultural and marine productivity.[116]

Later in the 1970s, scientists paid increasing attention to "the greenhouse effect," the idea that rising levels of carbon dioxide in the atmosphere, attributable to burning of fossil fuels, might raise atmospheric temperatures well beyond their natural levels. These increases could, among other things, melt polar ice sheets, raise sea levels, and cause shifts in agricultural productivity among different regions.[117] More recently, concerns over ozone destruction and the greenhouse effect have converged, because four gases—

CFCs, carbon dioxide, nitrous oxide, and methane—have been theorized as playing major roles in both phenomena.[118]

CFCs served as the propellant in most aerosol products until that use was banned by EPA and the U.S. Food and Drug Administration. CFCs are still used in aerosols in many other countries, however. Many countries also continue to make extensive, and increasing, use of CFCs as industrial solvents, in producing rigid and flexible synthetic foams, as the cooling fluid in many refrigerators and air conditioners, for some types of insulation, and for numerous other purposes.[119] Global emissions of CFC-11 and CFC-12, the chlorofluorocarbons of greatest concern, peaked in 1974 and declined until the early 1980s, but emissions have since been on the rise (figure 2.18).[120] Nearly all the CFCs emitted to the atmosphere are still there, for CFC-11 has a lifetime of about 75 years and CFC-12 a lifetime of 110 years.[121] Atmospheric concentrations of these two CFCs are increasing about 5 percent per year.[122] CFCs are believed to contribute to both destruction of ozone and atmospheric warming.

Carbon dioxide (CO_2) concentrations have also grown markedly. Levels monitored above Mauna Loa, Hawaii have increased from 315 ppm in 1958 to 345 ppm in 1986, and recently have been rising about 0.5 percent per year.[123] Data from measurements at the South Pole and other locations show similar results.[124] Figure 2.19 shows the substantial rise in estimated carbon dioxide emissions from the mid-1800s to the 1980s; an especially dramatic increase has occurred since the 1940s.[125] The slight dip in emissions in the early 1980s may well reflect the combined effect of rising energy prices and economic recession. The distribution of CO_2 emissions among different regions of the world has shifted markedly since 1970 (figure 2.20).[126] Growth of emissions in North America and Western Europe has slowed or declined, while emissions in developing nations have jumped considerably. The growth in the developing nations in part reflects increasing use of fossil fuels. Rising levels of carbon dioxide can warm the earth's surface but cool the upper atmosphere; cooler temperatures in the stratosphere can slow ozone depletion.[127]

Nitrous oxide is a third gas of concern. With oxygen, it forms nitric oxide, which acts as a catalyst in ozone destruction.[128] It also may contribute to atmospheric warming.[129] Most nitrous oxide is produced by activities of naturally occurring bacteria, but some may also be contributed by fertilizers and burning of fossil fuels.[130] Nitrous oxide is difficult to measure precisely, but concentrations appear to be have increased about 0.25 percent annually for the past 10 years.[131] It has a lifetime in the atmosphere of approximately 150 years.[132]

Figure 2.18
Global Emissions of Chlorofluorocarbons,
1965–1984

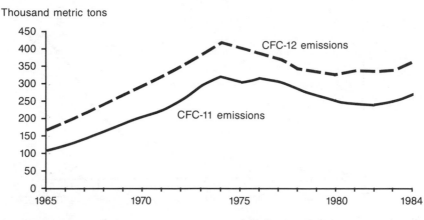

Thousand metric tons

Source: World Resources Institute.

Methane may increase rather than decrease atmospheric ozone,[133] but it may also contribute to atmospheric warming.[134] Methane is produced by fermentation in wet locations where oxygen is scarce; such areas include swamps, rice paddies, and the intestines of cattle and termites.[135] Increased cultivation of rice and growing populations of cattle may be contributing to increases in methane.[136] Increases in methane also may be caused indirectly by increased carbon monoxide from combustion processes.[137] Atmospheric concentrations of methane have been climbing for about 300 years, with a dramatic increase beginning in the late 1800s.[138]

It is quite difficult to assess the impact of these and other gases on the atmosphere.[139] The atmospheric models used to evaluate the ozone problem contain about 160 chemical reactions and more than 40 species of chemicals.[140] The oceans' role in absorbing carbon and moderating temperature changes is not known precisely.[141] Also understood poorly is the role of cloud cover and tropical forests.[142]

Growing scientific knowledge has led to shifting estimates of atmospheric changes. For example, a report from the NRC in 1979 estimated that ozone levels would fall by 18.6 percent, but this figure was revised in a 1984 report to 4 percent.[143] The scientific uncertainty is perhaps best illustrated by recent experience in Antarctica, where monitored ozone levels plummeted so low (as much as 50 percent) each September and October that the computer

Figure 2.19
Global Carbon Dioxide Emissions from Fossil Fuels, 1860–1984

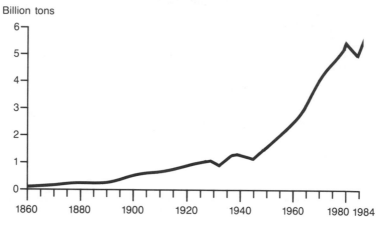

Billion tons

Source: Oak Ridge Associated Universities.

Figure 2.20
Global Emissions of Carbon Dioxide,
1950-1983

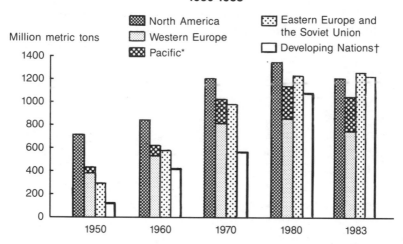

Million metric tons

North America — Western Europe — Pacific*

Eastern Europe and the Soviet Union — Developing Nations†

* Pacific includes Japan, Australia, and New Zealand.
† Developing Nations includes Africa, Latin America, Asia (except Japan), and the Middle East.

Source: Oak Ridge Associated Universities.

program used to record these levels dismissed the readings as anomalies.[144] The reason ozone levels drop precipitously in the Antarctic is still not known and was not predicted by existing models.[145] Preliminary scientific analyses of the phenomenon in late 1986 ruled out two theories of natural causes but did not provide firm proof that CFCs were the culprits.[146]

Monitored ozone levels worldwide dropped 3 percent between late 1978 and 1984, as measured by instruments aboard a National Aeronautics and Space Administration (NASA) satellite.[147] But the meaning of the decline is not clear, because 1979 was a year of considerable solar activity that might have elevated ozone levels, and a major volcanic eruption in 1982 may have confounded ozone measurements.[148] Moreover, a ground-based system of instruments has not shown such a decline.[149]

The earth's temperature has risen about 0.6 °C (1 °F) during the past 100 years, although there has been considerable regional variation in this warming trend.[150] Although this rise in temperature is consistent in magnitude with the rise one might expect from increasing concentrations of greenhouse gases,[151] it also is within the natural variability of the earth's climate.[152] However, climate modelers expect the temperature of the atmosphere to rise above its natural level of variability in the 1990s.[153] By the early 21st century, temperatures may rise well above levels not witnessed for over 100,000 years[154] (figure 2.21).

Avoiding or slowing ozone depletion will require major cooperative efforts among the nations of the world. In December 1986, representatives from 45 countries met in Geneva, Switzerland, to begin negotiating an international protocol to protect stratospheric ozone.[155] Negotiators need to find a way to reduce CFC emissions by limiting CFC production and use and encouraging development of substitute chemicals.

Because of CFCs' long lifetime in the atmosphere, just keeping their atmospheric concentrations from rising above existing levels would require an immediate and drastic reduction in emissions.[156] (For example, an estimated 85 percent reduction in emissions of CFC-12 would be needed.[157]) The Natural Resources Defense Council has suggested an 85 percent reduction in production of CFCs (and other selected chemicals) over 5 years, with total phaseout over 10 years.[158] The Environmental Defense Fund has suggested cutting back production and allowing buying and selling by countries and producers of limited rights to produce CFCs.[159] The World Resources Institute has suggested a $5 per pound tax on CFC production to encourage development and use of substitute materials.[160] E.I. du Pont de Nemours & Company, the world's largest producer of CFCs, has urged

Figure 2.21
Mean Global Temperatures, 150,000 B.C. to Present

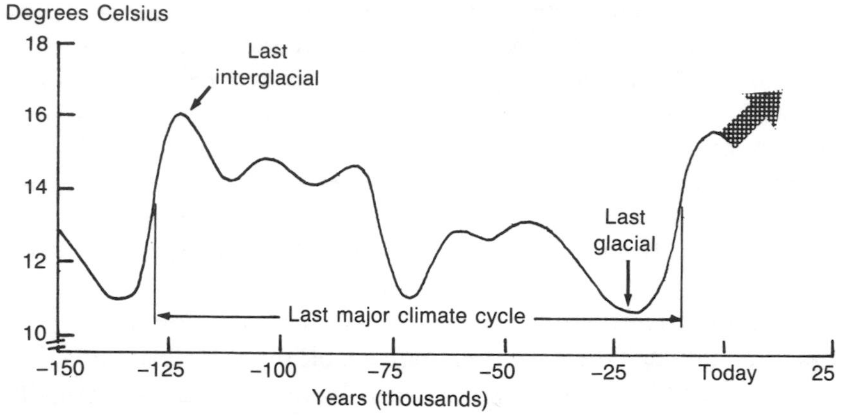

Degrees Celsius

Years (thousands)

Adapted from U.S. Department of Energy.

a worldwide limit on CFC emissions; negotiations among industry, environmentalists, and government to develop a domestic CFC policy; and incentives to industry to develop alternatives.[161]

The United States has presented the strongest governmental proposal at the Geneva negotiations: freezing CFC use at or near current levels and gradually eliminating use if additional research confirms the role of CFCs in ozone destruction.[162] EPA is under a court order to decide, in 1987, on whether to regulate CFCs domestically, regardless of international action.[163]

Some approaches to the greenhouse effect, like energy conservation, emphasize reducing gas emissions. These are preventive strategies. Other potential approaches—such as genetically engineering crops adapted to changing temperatures or building dikes around low-lying land masses that are likely to be flooded by rising waters—are adaptive.[164] No single preventive strategy, like aggressive energy conservation in countries whose energy consumption is greatest, is likely to succeed in stopping global warming. However, such a preventive strategy might at least slow the process.[165] Getting domestic and international agreement on strategies to prevent further global warming promises to be very hard, unless some headline-making event as dramatic as the seasonal ozone depletion in Antarctica occurs. Even with such an event, action would be difficult because carbon dioxide emissions are closely tied to use of fossil fuels throughout the world, other greenhouse effect gases are tied to food production, and still other gases have natural origins.

WATER QUALITY

Most of the water in the United States—both on the surface and underground—appears to be relatively clean. However, in neither case does adequate data exist to support a definitive assessment of how extensive water quality problems are or the rate at which they are improving or degrading.

Since the passage of the 1972 amendments to the Federal Water Pollution Control Act (now called the Clean Water Act),[166] U.S. businesses, government, and individuals have spent over $300 billion (constant 1984 dollars) for water pollution control (see chapter 1).[167] It appears that high levels of spending will continue, at least for a few years, as a result of the Water Quality Act of 1987. As a result, the water quality in many streams and lakes has improved, sometimes dramatically. But in most cases little more has been done than to prevent further degradation—although this is not a trivial accomplishment in view of the increases in industrial production, agricultural output, and population that have occurred over the intervening decade and a half. In some cases, however, even this fight has been lost, and water quality has gotten worse.

During the past 15 years, pollution abatement efforts have focused primarily on reducing discharges of "conventional" pollutants such as organic matter, sediment, nutrients, salts, and bacteria from point sources—industries and municipal wastewater treatment plants that discharge their wastes through sewer pipes.[168] Substantial progress has been made in reducing these discharges. At the same time, however, it is becoming clear that these conventional pollutants are not the only point-source pollutants of concern. Furthermore, point-source polluters are not the only cause of degradation of U.S. waters. Toxic pollutants can continue to cause serious water quality problems after most of the conventional discharges are cleaned up. These toxic substances come predominantly from industries and municipal wastewater treatment plants releases but can also come from nonpoint sources such as urban runoff, agricultural practices, abandoned mining operations, and atmospheric fallout.[169] Such nonpoint sources are increasingly recognized as contributing substantial amounts of both conventional and toxic pollutants to surface waters; this is recognized by the 1987 Water

Quality Act which requires the regulation of nonpoint sources.

It has become increasingly clear that existing pollution control programs have done little to protect groundwater quality. Contamination is widespread, threatening drinking water supplies for millions of Americans.[170] The sources of contamination are diverse, ranging from septic tanks to hazardous waste dumps, and from fertilizers applied on farms and lawns to leaking storage tanks.[171]

This evolution of the awareness of water quality problems is reflected in the availability of water quality data. Surface waters have been monitored for decades for a number of conventional water quality parameters, but only recently for toxic contaminants. And virtually no information on changes in groundwater quality is available.

Even the data that are collected are unsatisfactory for many purposes. They suffer from many of the same problems as those indicated for air quality data. Many are not collected with adequate quality control procedures, making them of questionable validity. These data often come from widely separated, fixed stations and do not adequately represent water quality in the intervening reaches. The stations are often located without regard to human or ecological exposure so that the data provide little information on how serious the water quality problems really are in terms of people affected or ecosystems damaged. Only a few conventional pollutants are commonly monitored, leaving substantial gaps in our knowledge of other contaminants that may present a greater risk. And the data are not processed or analyzed in a timely manner.

In a September 1986 report, the U.S. General Accounting Office (GAO) decried the poor state of knowledge about trends in the quality of the nation's waters, causes of changes in water quality, and the impact on water quality of the national program to improve treatment of municipal sewage. Reviewing some major analyses of water quality, including some of those discussed further below, GAO observed that "little conclusive information is available to the Congress to use in policy debates on the nation's water quality."[172]

Surface Water Quality

Surface water quality conditions are assessed either by the professional judgment of water quality officials or by measuring the concentration of specific contaminants. Evaluations of water quality are based on whether a body of water supports the uses for which it has been designated.

Conclusions regarding water quality are often based on subjective assessments by pollution control agency personnel and water quality experts.

In a 1982 assessment by the Association of State and Interstate Water Pollution Control Administrators (ASIWPCA), for instance, actual water quality monitoring results were used for assessing only 22 percent of the stream miles and 29 percent of the lake area.[173]

Most of the U.S surface waters have "fishable-swimmable" as their designated use. Some, including 120,000 stream miles, are designated more stringently for drinking or food processing. Another 32,000 stream miles have less stringent designations, such as use for for navigation or agriculture.[174] In the judgment of state water quality officials, the majority of U.S. surface waters satisfy their designated uses.[175]

The 1984 EPA National Water Quality Inventory estimates that, for the states submitting the biennial reports required by Section 305(b) of the Clean Water Act, the designated uses were supported in 73 percent (with 40 states reporting) of river miles; 78 percent of lake acres (with 30 states reporting, excluding the Great Lakes); and 82 percent of estuarine and coastal waters (with 12 states reporting).[176] Preliminary data for the 1986 report show that, of the areas assessed, the proportion supporting designated uses may be even lower for rivers, lakes, and estuarine and coastal waters than in 1984.[177] The National Fisheries Survey, focusing on the biological quality of the nation's waters, was carried out jointly by EPA and the U.S. Fish and Wildlife Service in 1982. This assessment found that sport fish, such as rainbow trout and largemouth bass, occur in about 73 percent of U.S. inland waters and that 67 percent of U.S. streams are suitable as sport fish habitat.[178]

The ASIWPCA survey also attempted to assess the improvement of water quality between 1972 and 1982. However, the officials could make no such assessment in almost half of the surface waters because (a) the current quality was not known, (b) the quality 10 years ago was not known, or (c) the state agencies would not supply the information.[179] For those waters that were assessed, the vast majority—67 percent of stream miles, 62 percent of lake area, and 74 percent of estuarine area—showed no change. Of the stream miles, 11 percent improved and 2 percent were degraded. Estuaries were judged to improve more than streams, but the net change in lakes and reservoirs was for the worse: only 2 percent improved while 10 percent deteriorated.[180]

Information collected by the National Shellfish Register of Classified Estuarine Waters suggests that the state assessments of improvements in estuarine waters may be overly optimistic. This register keeps track of the amount of estuary acreage closed to shellfish harvesting because of excess pollution. Between 1980 and 1985, 14 of 22 coastal states experienced a net decrease in the amount of area approved for harvest. 6 six states showed a net increase.[181]

The U.S. Geological Survey (USGS) provides comprehensive, nation-wide water quality trend information on specific contaminants through their National Ambient Stream Quality Accounting Network (NASQAN) (figure 2.22). Ambient monitoring stations located in river basins and sub-basins throughout the country have collected information on the same pollutants since 1974, with the number of stations totaling 501 in 1985. The most recent report includes data from 1974-1981.[182] Data are adjusted to reflect annual variations in stream flow and then statistically analyzed to see trends in the pollutants' concentrations.

Although NASQAN is the most comprehensive continuous quality monitoring system available, the data still do not necessarily measure water quality where it is most likely to affect people. NASQAN was originally established to measure the quantity of surface water flow. Therefore, its monitoring stations generally are located at the downstream end of a water-shed. Thus, they are often upstream of, or too far downstream from, major pollution sources to record locally severe problems. NASQAN stations are limited further because they do not measure all pollutants (including most of the potentially toxic organic chemicals) and because, in many cases, monitoring equipment may not be sophisticated enough to measure pollutants at low concentrations that are nonetheless high enough to be of concern.[183]

Dissolved Oxygen

Dissolved oxygen, usually present in clean waters at levels of 5 ppm or more, is necessary for fish and other aquatic life to survive. The decomposition of organic pollutants, such as those in municipal sewage, or chemicals, such as those in industrial wastes, depletes the natural oxygen level. Temperature can also change the amount of dissolved oxygen by affecting the solubility of oxygen.[184]

Of 369 NASQAN stations, 17 percent showed improving trends in dissolved oxygen, while 11 percent showed deteriorating trends from 1974 to 1981.[185] The improvement likely reflects the efforts to reduce oxygen-demanding wastes from industries and municipal facilities. Between 1972 and 1982, these waste loads decreased 46 percent from municipal sources and 71 percent from industries.[186]

Figure 2.22
Water Quality Trends in the United States for Selected Pollutants,
1974–1981

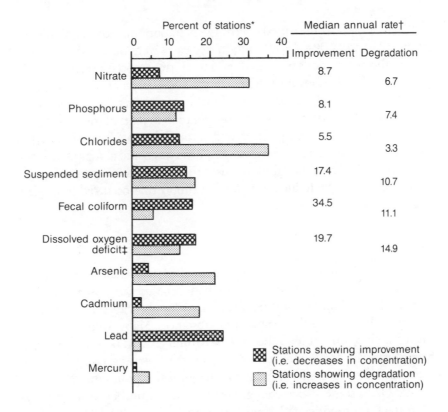

* Only includes stations showing statistically significant trends in flow-adjusted
concentrations.
† This is the median annual rate of improvement (first column) or degradation
(second column), in percent change per year, for those stations showing
statistically significant trends.
‡ The dissolved oxygen deficit is the difference between the amount of oxygen that
is dissolved in the water and the total amount that could be dissolved.

Source: U.S. Geological Survey.

Bacteria

Many bacteria are harmless, but the concentration in water of fecal coliform and fecal streptococcus bacteria from human and animal wastes indicate the potential for infection and disease. High bacteria counts force officials to close public swimming beaches and restrict shellfishing in contaminated waters.[187]

Levels of bacteria measured at NASQAN stations improved notably between 1974 and 1981. Fecal coliform decreases were observed at 15 percent of the 305 stations measured, and fecal streptococcus decreases at 23 percent of 295 stations measured. Only 5 and 3 percent of the stations, respectively, showed higher fecal coliform and fecal streptococcus levels.[188] Fecal streptococcus decreases were most common in parts of the Gulf Coast, along the central Mississippi River, and in the Columbia River. Both types of bacteria decreased in the Arkansas-Red River basin and along the Atlantic coast. The USGS attributes these trends to the improved treatment of municipal wastes and the reduction in feedlot runoff that occurred in the late 1970s.[189]

Suspended Solids

Brown, turbid water caused by suspended solids such as soil sediment and other particles can significantly reduce beneficial uses of water by people and can harm aquatic wildlife. These particles also can carry nutrients, pesticides, bacteria, and other harmful substances. Many rivers have always carried high sediment loads because of natural erosion occurring in their watersheds. But erosion from cropland, construction sites, rangeland, and forestland has elevated sediment to a major water pollutant.[190]

NASQAN stations detected almost the same number of increases as decreases for suspended sediment between 1975 and 1981.[191] Some of the decreasing trends are felt to be caused by the presence of upstream reservoirs that serve as sediment traps, such as those in the Missouri River basin. Stations detecting increasing levels of sediment appear to be in regions with expanding or intensifying land use for agriculture and silviculture. Such areas include the Columbia River basin in Oregon and Washington, the Arkansas and Red River basins in Oklahoma, and the tributaries to the Mississippi River near the confluence of the Missouri and Ohio rivers. In the Pacific Northwest, ash and mud from the eruption of Mount St. Helens in the early 1980s also increased sediment loads.[192]

Total Dissolved Solids

Dissolved solids are inorganic salts and other substances from natural and human sources after they have dissolved in water. Most commonly these dissolved substances are measured together as total dissolved solids (TDS). EPA recommends a limit of 500 mg of dissolved solids per liter for most uses.[193] High TDS levels can make water unfit to drink, adversely affect fish and other freshwater aquatic life, accelerate corrosion in water systems and equipment that uses water, and depress crop yields.[194] Levels causing these problems are more likely in regions with low annual rainfall, such as the Southwest and the High Plains.[195]

NASQAN stations showed increases in TDS at 59 percent of the stations that showed significant trends. The pattern of the trend indicates that irrigation return flow is a major culprit, especially in the semiarid basins of the West and Southwest. The water quality of the Arkansas, Red, and Colorado rivers is believed to be significantly influenced by irrigated agriculture. In the northeastern and north-central states a major source of TDS is road salt used for snow and ice control.[196]

Nutrients

Nutrients, such as phosphorus and nitrogen, can stimulate algae blooms and growth of nuisance water plants, can accelerate eutrophication (the aging of lakes and reservoirs), and can cause problems with oxygen depletion as the plants die and decompose.[197] Nutrients can over enrich water bodies, allowing algal blooms. Such blooms block light from reaching submerged aquatic vegetation, thereby killing off valuable nursery habitat for finfish and shellfish.[198] The primary sources of nutrients are fertilizer runoff from croplands and urban lawns, runoff from feedlots, and discharges from municipal wastewater treatment plants.[199]

Nationwide, nearly as many NASQAN stations reported decreases as increases in phosphorus concentrations. However, definite regional patterns exist, frequently corresponding with trends in suspended sediment concentrations. For example, phosphorus concentrations are increasing at many stations in the South, most likely due to increased agricultural activity and fertilizer use. However, in the Great Lakes and Upper Mississippi regions, concentrations are declining. One explanation may be controls on the phosphorus content controls initiated in the late 1970s.[200]

Nitrogen concentrations have increased in about three times as many stations as they have decreased. Areas dominated by cropland were most likely to show increases, reflecting the rapid increase in agricultural use of nitrogen fertilizers. The decreases were limited to scattered locations in the western half of the country—most notably, the Colorado River basin.[201]

Another significant source of the increased levels of nitrogen is atmospheric deposition of nitrate. In some cases it is the largest nitrogen source in a river basin. The increasing trends at NASQAN stations correspond well, particularly in eastern states, with overall emission rates of nitrogen that have increased since 1975.[202]

Metals and Toxic Substances

Probably the most dramatic improvement in surface water quality is the decreased levels of lead. Twenty-three percent of the 292 stations measuring lead concentrations showed statistically significant improvements between 1974 and 1981, while only 2 percent showed increasing lead levels.[203] The improvements occurred most frequently along both the East and West coasts and on tributaries to the Mississippi and Missouri rivers. Increases were found only in the Lower Mississippi basin and along the Gulf Coast. The explanation for the improvement probably lies more with the reduced use of lead in gasoline imposed by air pollution control requirements than any actions taken under the Clean Water Act. USGS has estimated that streams, on the average, carry amounts of lead equal to approximately 5 percent of the amount of lead in the gasoline consumed by the population in the stream's basin. The steepest rate of decline in both leaded gasoline consumption and lead levels in streams occurred in 1980.[204]

Trends for other metals are less encouraging. Arsenic concentrations generally increased from 1974 to 1981, most frequently in the Great Lakes and Ohio basins and in the Pacific Northwest. The relatively few decreases were scattered throughout the western states. USGS found that little correlation exists between arsenic trends and the natural occurrence of arsenic in soils and other natural materials. Thus, the explanation probably lies in the arsenic released by such human activities as fossil fuel (particularly coal) burning and the use of detergents, herbicides, and fertilizers. As with lead, atmospheric deposition is probably the main source, with arsenic being emitted in large amounts to the atmosphere by coal-burning electric power plants and nonferrous smelters.[205]

Cadmium measurements also showed predominantly deteriorating trends. Seventeen percent of the 285 NASQAN stations measuring cadmium showed statistically significant concentrations, while 2 percent showed improvements.[206] The improvements were found predominantly in the Great Plains states, while the increased concentrations were found in the Great Lakes, Upper Mississippi, and Texas Gulf regions. Again, no significant relationships were found between these trends and naturally occurring cadmium, suggesting the importance of human sources. USGS analyses again found that atmospheric deposition was probably a significant source, with fossil fuel combustion being a major contributor.[207]

USGS found few significant trends—either up or down—for the other metals (chromium, iron, manganese, selenium, mercury, and zinc) it measured, and those that it did find showed no particular geographical pattern.[208]

USGS also established a network of 160 to 180 pesticide monitoring network stations to analyze water and sediment samples for 11 chlorinated hydrocarbon insecticides, 7 organophosphate insecticides, and 4 herbicides.[209] Fewer than 1 percent of their water samples showed detectable amounts of most of these chemicals. The exceptions are the herbicide atrazine, which was detected in almost 5 percent of the samples, and the insecticides Lindane and Diazinon, which were detected in 1 to 2 percent of the samples. The organochlorine insecticides, which are not water soluble, were much more likely to be found adsorbed onto sediments. Dieldrin, DDD, and DDE (the latter two being degradation products of DDT [dichloro-diphenyl-trichloro-ethane]), were found in 10 to 20 percent of the sediment samples. DDT itself and chlordane were found in 8 to 10 percent of the samples.[210] EPA banned all three of these in the early to mid 1970s, and USGS found that the frequency of detection gradually decreased from 1975 to 1980.[211] They found no trends for other pesticides or herbicides over this period.

Some evidence on the prevalence of toxic contamination is provided by state assessments of water quality conditions. State officials listed toxic substances as the fourth most frequent cause of continuing pollution in "waters of concern";[212] 30 of 35 states cite violations of water quality standards or use impairments resulting from these substances. In another study, 41 states perceived toxic materials as a major problem, with at least 14,000 miles of streams and rivers in 39 states, 638,000 acres of lakes in 16 states, and 920 square miles of estuaries in 8 states affected.[213] (These figures are likely to be underestimated, because the reporting officials tend to focus on hot spots or known acute situations.) The National Fisheries Survey reported toxic contamination of fish populations in 10 percent of all waters.[214]

Groundwater Quality

Relatively little is known about the quality of the nation's groundwater, despite the importance of the resource. That groundwater is sometimes seriously contaminated from human activities is a fairly recent realization. Every state has experienced contamination episodes from a variety of sources, and, though most of the nation's groundwater probably remains relatively unaffected by human activities, contamination often occurs in groundwater that is or could be tapped for human use.[215]

Incidents of groundwater contamination and well closures have been increasingly documented over the past several years. Water in 8,000 private, public, and industry wells was reported in 1984 to be unusable or degraded due to some form of contamination.[216] The Council on Environmental Quality reported the closing of hundreds of wells affecting millions of people between 1978 and 1981 due to contamination by toxic organic chemicals.[217] And a 1984 EPA survey of rural water quality found that approximately two-thirds of the supplies tested exceeded EPA's drinking water standards for at least one contaminant.[218]

In 1984, the Office of Technology Assessment (OTA) listed some 175 organic chemicals, more than 50 inorganic chemicals (metals, nonmetals, and inorganic acids), a number of biological organisms, and various radionuclides that had been identified in groundwater. Most of the substances had been found as a result of research projects, by routine monitoring, or in response to complaints.[219]

All groundwater contains some impurities, even if it is completely unaffected by human activities. The types and concentrations of natural impurities depend on the nature of the geological material through which the groundwater moves and the quality of the recharge water. But many human activities contaminate groundwater as well. Figure 2.23 shows some of the more important sources of groundwater contamination, many of which also are a direct or indirect source of water pollution.

Biogical Contaminants

Biological contaminants include bacteria, viruses, parasites, and other biological agents that can cause illness. OTA found reports of several different types of bacteria and viruses in groundwater, including those that cause typhoid, tuberculosis, cholera, and hepatitis.[220]

In 1984, approximately 4,900 year-round groundwater supplies (10 percent of the total) were reported by the states to exceed EPA's drinking water

Figure 2.23
Major Sources of Groundwater Contamination

Waste Disposal
Hazardous waste sites
   Impoundments
   Sanitary landfills
   Septic tanks
   Underground injection wells
Application of Wastes
Radioactive wastes
Municipal sewers

Materials Handling and Storage
Underground storage tanks
Above-ground storage tanks
Materials stockpiles
Materials transport and transfer incl. pipelines

Mining
Coal mining (surface and underground)
Noncoal mining (surface and underground)
Oil, gas, and geothermal wells

Agriculture
Pesticides
Fertilizers
Irrigation
Livestock

Other
New and abandoned wells
Salt water intrusion
Urban stormwater runoff
Deicing salts
Household operations
Atmospheric deposition

Source: The Conservation Foundation.

standard for microbiological contaminants.[221] EPA's Rural Water Survey* reported that 30 percent of the nation's rural groundwater systems exceeded microbiological drinking water standards; of those, about 40 percent were small individual or intermediate systems. Larger rural community systems exceeded EPA standards only 15.5 percent of the time.[223]

Inorganic Substances

Inorganic substances include metals, salts, and other compounds that do not contain carbon. OTA listed 37 inorganic substances that had been found in groundwater, including some 27 metals.[224] EPA has established primary drinking water standards for 10 inorganic compounds, and these were exceeded in an estimated 1,500 to 3,000 groundwater supplies between

*This survey tested for 40 groundwater contaminants (microbial, physical, chemical, and radioactive) in 2,654 households selected to be representative of rural populations in the United States. The results of this study are reported as national statistics.[222]

1975 and 1985. The most commonly exceeded standards were for fluoride (in 1,000 to 2,000 supplies) and for nitrate (in 500 to 600 supplies).[225] EPA's Rural Water Survey also found contamination by a variety of inorganic substances in wells serving rural households. Although natural causes are responsible for much of this inorganic contamination, human sources can create significant amounts as well.

Metals. Selenium and arsenic were the toxic elements most often reported to exceed EPA drinking water standards in groundwaters.[226] EPA's Rural Water Survey found mercury, lead, cadmium, silver, and selenium in 5 to 25 percent of the wells serving rural households,[227] although there were notable regional variations. The survey reported mercury concentrations above drinking water standards in almost one-quarter of rural wells nationwide and up to nearly one-third of rural wells in the north central region. Lead levels exceeded EPA's standards in about one-tenth of the nation's rural wells.* Cadmium levels exceeded EPA standards in about one-sixth of all rural wells, with the highest prevalence—about 27 percent—in rural wells in the West. Selenium levels were excessive in about one-seventh of rural wells, with the highest prevalence in the north central (26 percent) and western (41 percent) regions. Silver levels were higher than the standards in about 5 percent of the rural wells tested.[228]

Iron and manganese, which are not known to have any toxic effects, were also relatively common, particularly in the north central region. The other elements tested for—chromium, barium, magnesium, and arsenic— were found to exceed standards in less than 1 percent of rural wells. These national statistics, however, may understate conditions in certain local settings.[229] Near Knott, Texas, for example, 26 percent of the tested wells had elevated levels of arsenic. This arsenic was thought to result from pesticides applied to cotton crops.[230]

Nitrates. Nitrates may be the most common groundwater contaminant in the United States.[231] Though low levels of nitrates are natural, resulting from the decomposition of vegetation and geological deposits, higher levels may indicate that contamination is occurring from other sources such as septic tanks, animal wastes, fertilizers, and municipal landfills.

USGS recently analyzed the occurrence of nitrate-nitrogen† in samples

---

*The actual measurement for lead was higher (16 percent nationwide), but the researchers found their sampling methods may have distorted that number upwards.

†Nitrate measured as elemental nitrogen.

collected over 25 years from nearly 124,000 wells across the country. The results do not represent a random survey of wells, and for several reasons noted below may overstate the problem of nitrate contamination. Nevertheless, the analysis does indicate that nitrate contamination is a common problem. The agency found that approximately 20 percent of the wells it reviewed had nitrate-nitrogen concentrations greater than 3 milligrams per liter (mg/l), a level that may indicate contributions by human activities (though natural levels in some locations, especially the semiarid West, are known to exceed this figure). About 6 percent of the total wells had concentrations exceeding 10 mg/l, EPA's drinking water standard. Groundwaters in wells shallower than 100 feet were most likely to have elevated nitrate concentrations, probably because most sources of nitrates are at or near the land surface.[232]

Six states—Arizona, Delaware, Kansas, New York, Oklahoma, and Rhode Island—and Puerto Rico had nitrate levels exceeding 3 mg/l in at least one-third of their test wells. Arizona, California, Kansas, New York, Oklahoma, and Rhode Island exceeded the 10 mg/l EPA drinking water standard in about 10 percent of the wells. The highest of these was Rhode Island, with more than 10 mg/l in 36 percent of its test wells.[233]

Special surveys that EPA has conducted, however, have not found such high nitrate concentrations. The Rural Water Survey, for instance, found that only 2.7 percent of wells supplying rural homes nationwide had water supplies containing nitrates in excess of EPA standards, although 5.8 percent in the north central region had excessive nitrates.[234]

One explanation for the differences in these two studies is that the USGS data base was not a random sample of wells. Some portion of the wells were sampled because of suspected contamination, and there was little sampling consistency from state to state.

Total Dissolved Solids. At least two-thirds of the United States is underlain by aquifers known to produce waters containing at least 1,000 mg/l of TDS. The bulk of these dissolved solids come from natural salts in the soils, and, in general, natural salinity levels tend to increase with groundwater depth.[235] TDS content in groundwater is also a function of the age of the water and the relative solubility of minerals in the geological material.[236] The highest natural salt concentrations in groundwater are typically found in the West, particularly where ancient seas left salt deposits as they evaporated.[237] High salt levels are also found in coastal regions experiencing seawater intrusion, in the vicinity of geothermal springs, and beneath heavily irrigated saline soils.[238]

Organic Substances

Although many organic substances occur in nature (the most notable being petroleum), tens of thousands of synthetic organic compounds have been developed in laboratories over the past several decades. These are used in such common products as dyes, food additives, detergents, plastics, solvents, and pesticides.[239] For years, little groundwater monitoring was done for contamination from organic chemicals. However, in recent years, the discovery of synthetic organic chemicals in groundwater supplies has caused major concern.

OTA found that 175 different organic chemicals have been measured in groundwater supplies. Particularly disturbing is the discovery that the concentrations of synthetic organic chemicals in groundwater are often orders of magnitude higher than those found in water drawn from the most contaminated surface drinking water supplies.[240] For example, concentrations of trichloroethylene (TCE) in groundwater is 27,300 parts per billion (ppb), whereas the highest concentration reported for a surface water supply is 160 ppb.[241]

EPA conducted a number of studies between 1966 and 1981 testing for up to 14 volatile organic compounds.[242] Some of these compounds, such as TCE and vinyl chloride, were found more frequently in raw groundwater than in treated water.[243] All of the surveys found carbon tetrachloride and 1,2-dichloroethane in some of the drinking water supplies tested. An analysis of about 500 randomly selected samples from the Groundwater Supply Survey showed that approximately 20 percent of the nation's supplies may have at least one volatile organic compound present at detectable levels, and that 5.6 percent have three or more present.[244]

The Council on Environmental Quality reviewed detailed information on drinking water contamination from organic chemicals in 34 states and found problems in at least 1 state in each of the 10 EPA regions. They identified major problems in almost all states east of the Mississippi, as well as in sparsely populated western states such as Idaho, Arizona, and New Mexico.[245] They concluded that the contamination of drinking water supplies by toxic organic chemicals is a greater problem for groundwater supplies than for surface water.[246] Solvents such as TCE, tetrachloroethylene, chloroform, and carbon tetrachloride occur most frequently—both singly and together—at high concentrations.

Radionuclides

Almost all groundwater contains some amount of naturally occurring radioactive substances. The types and levels of these substances vary geographically, depending on local geology.[247] Approximately 20 radionuclides are known to occur in groundwater, originating from both natural radiation and from radioactive substances resulting from human activity.[248]

Activities associated with nuclear power generation can release both natural and human-produced radiation into the environment.[249] Atmospheric testing of nuclear weapons and use of radionuclides in medical and other scientific research provide additional conduits for the release of radioactivity.[250] Radionuclides are also a natural by-product of other activities such as phosphate mining and production of phosphoric acid.[251]

Sources of Water Quality Problems

As described earlier in this chapter, water pollution is catagorized as coming from point sources, such as industries or municipal wastewater treatment plants that discharge directly into surface waters, or nonpoint sources, such as runoff from agricultural fields, urban streets, timbered lands, and construction sites, leakage from septic tanks, and deposition of atmospheric pollutants.[252] The same distinction is often made for sources of groundwater pollution, although a nonpoint source in one case can be classified as a point source in the other.

Point-Source Discharges

The nation's pollution abatement efforts have primarily focused on reducing discharges to surface water from industrial and municipal point sources.[253] For industries, EPA sets nationally applicable effluent limitations based on the availability of pollution abatement technologies and whether firms in the industry can afford to install the technology. Municipal wastewater treatment plants are required by statute to achieve secondary treatment or better. Each discharger must obtain a National Pollutant Discharges Elimination System permit specifying the amount of pollution that the particular facility can discharge.[254]

Municipal Wastewater Discharges. Municipal wastewater discharges continue to contribute to a significant portion of the pollutants carried in U.S. rivers and streams, in spite of Clean Water Act amendments in 1972 that called for secondary treatment at all municipal sewage treatment plants by 1977 (with some extensions up to 1983) (figure 2.24).[255] In 1982 when ASIWPCA asked state officials for the primary reasons why their streams did not support the designated uses, municipal discharges ranked first in 19 states (only nonpoint sources ranked higher) and second in another 20.[256]

Municipal treatment facilities must handle substantial volumes of different types of wastes. In 1986, 172 million people sent 27,692 million

---

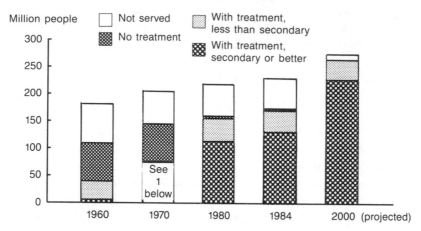

Figure 2.24
U.S. Population Served by Municipal Wastewater Systems, by Level of Treatment, 1960–2000

¹Available data for 1970 do not distinguish between type of treatment.

Source: U.S. Department of Commerce; U.S. Environmental Protection Agency.

gallons of pollutants to 15,438 municipal facilities daily.[257] In addition to normal domestic sewage, wastewater treatment plants must handle a wide variety of toxic and other nonconventional substances disposed of by households and businesses.[258]

A recent EPA study, for instance, identifies about 160,000 industrial and commercial facilities that discharged wastes containing hazardous constituents to publicly owned treatment works (POTWs). These businesses discharge an estimated 3,200 million gallons of wastewater, or approximately 12 percent of the total POTW flow, daily. This flow contains an estimated 92,000 metric tons of hazardous pollutants annually.[259]

Thirty industries were found to discharge 62,000 metric tons annually of hazardous metal constituents at raw discharge levels and 3,300 metric tons per year of the hazardous metal constituents.[260] These industries also discharge between 37,000 and 52,000 metric tons annually of priority organic constituents at raw discharge levels and approximately 20,000 metric tons per year of organic constituents.[261] Some of these substances can substantially disrupt the effective operations of a municipal plant. More typically, 8 to 18 percent of the wastes will be released to the receiving waters through the plant's effluent.[262] The rest will either be removed in the treatment sludge, biodegraded, or released to the air.

In an assessment of the impact of these discharges on ambient water quality levels, an EPA contractor concluded that even if the receiving waters were completely pure, large numbers of municipal treatment plants would be exceeding water quality standards for many of the toxic chemicals investigated—65 percent for cadmium, 47 percent for silver, 35 percent for lead, 33 percent for copper, 30 percent for cyanide, and 4 to 10 percent for mercury, zinc, chromium, and nickel.[263] If any of those substances are already dissolved in the receiving waters, the frequency of noncompliance would be even higher.

These results assume that the facilities are discharging into streams containing their average annual flow. In most cases the worst water quality problems occur during low flow periods. When low stream flows were analyzed, the prevalence of noncompliance shot up dramatically—for example, from 65 to 84 percent for cadmium, 35 to 64 percent for lead, and 10 to 28 percent for mercury.[264]

Another problem many plants must deal with is very high flows during storms, particularly a problem in cities with sewage systems built before 1900, where stormwater runoff is likely to be carried in the domestic sewer pipes. Such systems result in overwhelming volumes of waste being delivered to treatment plants during wet weather, forcing the sewers to overflow, discharging raw sewage directly into receiving waters.[265] In 1986, EPA estimated it would cost $15.2 billion to remedy the combined sewer overflow problem.[266]

Industrial Discharges. EPA's 1984 National Water Quality Inventory blames industrial discharges for impairing the designated use of 10 percent of the nation's lake area and 11 percent of its stream miles.[267] One assessment estimates that they contribute about one-third of the total point source loading of oxygen-demanding wastes (measured as biochemical oxygen demand, or BOD).[268] Nevertheless, industries have been much more successful than municipal facilities in reducing their discharges. EPA estimates that 78 percent of industries were in compliance with their discharge permits, compared with 76 percent of municipal facilities in 1982.[269]

Another study looked at how industries dispose of the hazardous wastes they generate. It found that the organic chemicals industry, the largest generator of hazardous wastes, discharges half (about 31 million metric tons a year) of its hazardous wastes to surface waters under its water discharge permits.[270] Most of these wastes, however, are not included among the toxic pollutants identifed by the Clean Water Act.[271] Over 70 percent are substances considered "hazardous" under the Resource Conservation and Recovery Act, but not listed among the Clean Water Act's "priority pollutants."[272]

EPA does not as a matter of course estimate trends in industrial loadings to surface waters or how these loadings have changed over time. The last published estimate, produced by the agency's Office of Research and Development, indicated that industrial discharges of most conventional pollutants declined by 70 percent or more from 1972 to 1977.[273] Unfortunately, trends since then cannot be evaluated since data are unavailable.

It is known, however, that industries have reduced their discharges of toxic pollutants to some degree. An EPA contractor estimates that 75 percent of toxic organics and 88 percent of toxic metals are reduced in direct discharge.[274] Even though few facilities were required, until recently, to reduce such discharges, many of the pollutants apparently are removed by the treatment systems adopted to control conventional pollutants.[275]

Nonpoint Sources

A more ubiquitous problem than point-source pollution, for both surface water and groundwater, is presented by nonpoint sources. These include seepage, stormwater runoff from agricultural lands and urban streets, septic tanks, atmospheric deposition, and a number of other sources that do not discharge wastewater through pipes or other structural conveyances. According to a recent Resources for the Future estimate, they are responsible for a majority of many conventional pollutants—nearly 100 percent of sediment, 82 percent of nitrogen, and 84 percent of phosphorous—reaching the nation's surface waters.[276]

Most states have identified nonpoint sources as the primary reasons why their streams do not support their designated uses.[277] Nonpoint sources ranked first in 26 states and second in 13 others. Forty states reported that nonpoint sources need to be controlled if water quality is to continue to improve.[278]

A more recent study assessed the extent to which nonpoint sources affected water quality in 22 percent of the nation's river miles, 39 percent of its lake acreage, and 59 percent of its estuarine areas (these percentages exclude Alaska). Of the assessed waters, state officials considered 29 percent of both lakes and rivers and 13 percent of estuaries to be moderately or severely impaired due to nonpoint-source pollution.[279] They estimated that nutrients and sediment were the major nonpoint source pollutants, accounting for

60 percent of the impacts in rivers and 81 percent in lakes.[280] Of the waters affected by nonpoint source pollutants, sediment was thought to affect more river miles than any other pollutant (47 percent), while nutrients were thought to be the major pollutant in lakes and estuaries (59 percent of lake acres).[281]

EPA and the U.S. Fish and Wildlife Service found that nonpoint sources adversely affect fish communities in 30 percent of the nation's lakes and rivers, with agricultural sources being the most frequent culprit.[282] In contrast, point sources harm fish in only 20 percent of the waters.

These sources do not only affect the quality of surface waters. State officials and others have identified numerous instances in which they were a cause of groundwater contamination as well. In one survey, 34 states identified nitrates as the most common contaminant of groundwater; 31 states reported contamination from organic chemicals (other than petroleum). Approximately half of the states reported groundwater contamination due to bacteria, petroleum, pesticides, and inorganic chemicals.[283]

Agriculture is the predominant source of the problem for both surface water and groundwater (see chapter 6), contributing most of the sediment, nitrogen, phosphorus, and BOD, as well as a large amount of the pesticides, bacteria, and dissolved solids that are degrading U.S. surface waters.[284] State officials identified agriculture as the most widespread source of water pollution in 60 percent of the states, causing problems in 64 percent of the river miles and 57 percent of the acres area assessed.[285]

Agricultural sources of water pollution have substantial economic impact. Costs include sedimentation in lakes, loss of valuable reservoir capacity, lessened navigational space in channels and harbors, increased water treatment costs, decreased recreational opportunities, and so forth. A recent Conservation Foundation study estimated that the total off-site cost of soil erosion amounts to $6.1 billion a year, $2.2 billion of which results from cropland erosion alone.[286]

Agricultural pollution can cause significant groundwater contamination as well. For instance, EPA has identified groundwater contamination from at least 17 pesticides in 23 states as a result of normal agricultural use.[287] A 1985 EPA briefing reported that at least 100,000, and possibly more than 200,000, people have consumed water from wells known to be contaminated with such pesticides as dibromochloropropane, aldicarb, and ethylenedibromide.[288] The agency suggested that the number of affected people would be higher if other pesticides were included. California, for instance, has found some 57 different pesticides in its groundwaters, although the state believes that some of these resulted from spills or leakage rather than from normal pesticide application.[289] Officials in Iowa also recently reported a systematic deterioration of shallow groundwater throughout the state from pesticide contamination.[290]

SOLID WASTE

Solid waste management in the United States apparently has improved markedly since 1970. Generation rates for several types of solid wastes have declined. Implementation of the Marine Protection, Research and Sanctuaries Act has substantially reduced the amount of wastes (with the exception of municipal sewage sludge) dumped into the ocean. Open dumps and open burning are now uncommon. And, with the implementation of the hazardous waste provisions of the Resource Conservation and Recovery Act (RCRA), the vast majority of the more hazardous substances have been diverted from the solid waste stream to be disposed of in more secure facilities.

Nevertheless, solid wastes remain a major economic, environmental, and political problem. Acceptable disposal sites are becoming increasingly scarce in many metropolitan areas. Existing and abandoned disposal sites are a potential source of groundwater, surface water, and even air pollution. To many, the only satisfactory answers are waste reduction, recycling, and resource recovery. But even these activities can be very expensive and can cause health risks and environmental problems of their own.

No precise definition of a solid waste exists, and little real information is available on the magnitude of the problem. The term is often applied to materials that are either not solid or not truly waste.* Sludges from wastewater treatment plants or air pollution scrubbers may be counted as solid waste even though they are over 90 percent water. Containers of waste liquids such as crude oil and even wastewater disposed of in an impoundment rather than a stream may be included as well.

When a material becomes a waste is often not clear. If an industrial plant reprocesses some of the waste materials produced in one operation (for instance, a metal fabrication plant returning metal cuttings to its smelter) the materials are often not counted as wastes. If, however, the plant producing the materials ships them to another facility for resmelting, they

---

*Solid waste is defined in the Resource Conservation and Recovery Act as any discarded material that is abandoned to disposal or incineration; recycled in a manner constituting disposal (such as land application); burned for energy recovery or reclaimed (such as recovering lead from batteries); or is an inherently waste-like material that is ordinarily disposed of, or incinerated, or the recycling of which may be hazardous to human health and the environment.[291]

may well be counted as wastes that are recycled. The question of what should be counted as an agricultural waste is even more uncertain. Is animal manure that is spread on fields as a soil conditioner and fertilizer a waste? How about corn stalks? They formerly were a nuisance that had to be plowed under before the next crop could be planted, but on many fields they are now left on the surface to reduce erosion.

Even if the definition could be made precise, it would be very difficult to collect data on how much solid waste was actually being produced. Even for municipal waste, most estimates are based on extrapolations from small samples or are estimated from mathematical "materials balance" models.[292] The estimates produced by such techniques may differ widely. Information on industrial, agricultural, and mining wastes is even less certain, for most of these wastes are disposed of on-site by the generator with no data produced about the amount or characteristics of the wastes generated.

The solid waste problem has traditionally been left to local governments. This is still predominately the case, although any hazardous materials are now being rigorously controlled under RCRA or the Superfund program,[293] and some other specific types of wastes are regulated under other federal programs. Federal laws have tended to focus on those wastes deemed to create the greatest "health risks" (see chapter 7), but EPA and others are evaluating the need for the federal government to expand its efforts to deal with the nation's solid waste problem.[294]

Generation

Chapter 7 estimates that the United States produces approximately 50,000 pounds of waste per person per year. Of this, some 26,000 pounds, or 51 percent, might be considered solid waste. Air or water pollutants constitute the rest. But the effort to control these last two types of pollution increases the amount of solid wastes by creating sludges or by causing dischargers to divert waste streams to solid waste handling facilities rather than releasing them to the air and the water.

Municipal and Industrial Wastes

Although municipal garbage is normally thought of as the most important solid waste problem, it does not constitute the largest amount of waste generated. Mining, agriculture, silviculture, and industry all produce greater amounts. Nevertheless, municipal wastes are often the most obvious, costly, and politically difficult wastes to deal with.

Municipal solid waste includes postconsumer solid waste and food and yard waste from residential, commercial, and institutional sources. The

United States generates an estimated 150 million tons per year of these wastes, equivalent to 1,300 pounds per person per year. Annually, the amount of waste increases approximately 2 percent. Wastes discarded after energy and materials recovery increased 66 percent between 1960 and 1980.[295] The composition of the waste is also changing over time, with plastics and paper becoming much more predominant and metals and food waste much less. Because of the increased prevalence of lightweight plastics, the volume of municipal wastes is probably increasing faster than the weight.

Industries are estimated to be producing anywhere from 55 to 400 million tons of waste per year.[296] The uncertainty results from a lack of rigorous studies of industrial solid waste, as well as the fact that much of the waste is disposed of on-site directly by the plant generating it. Therefore, it is never seen by the professional waste management industry.

Mining

Mining can generate large amounts of wastes, some of which can create significant pollution problems. Noncoal mining is responsible for the largest amount of solid waste—an estimated 1,000 to 2,000 million tons each year (about 13,000 pounds per person).[297] More than 85 percent of this waste is produced by copper, iron ore, phosphate, and uranium mining (uranium mill tailings are not included). Several different types of waste are produced during the mining process. The largest amount is "mine waste," which is the soil or rock that is removed while gaining access to the ore.[298] Tailings are generated by physical and chemical processes to remove desired ores from the surrounding rocks.

The volume of these wastes has probably diminished over the past decade because of the decrease in minerals mined in this country. Iron ore production, for instance, decreased 35 percent from 1975 to 1984.[299] Production of other major minerals also decreased, although the use of lower-grade ores may have led to an increase in the amount of waste produced per unit of final product.

In contrast to most noncoal minerals, the total production of coal has increased over the past decade.[300] The output of surface mines, potentially the largest source of mine wastes, rose 46 percent from 1975 to 1984. Since the passage of the Surface Mine Control and Reclamation Act (SMCRA) in 1977, however, miners have been required to fill in the excavated mines with the overburden stripped from the mines to return the ground surface to its approximate original contour.[301] Because the overburden materials are being replaced, they probably should no longer be considered as wastes.

Production of underground mines is also increasing—over 25 percent between 1975 and 1984.[302] An estimated 25 percent of the coal extracted from underground mines is rejected as waste, resulting in the production of about 120 million tons of waste in 1985.[303]

Agriculture and Silviculture

Agriculture and silviculture operations produce substantial amounts of waste, most of which is left where it is produced.

In many cases it is not clear whether substances should be considered wastes or not. For instance, crop residues are now intentionally left on fields to control soil erosion (see chapter 6). However, the U.S. cropland that is not managed under some such system of conservation tillage is probably producing around 500 million tons (4,100 pounds per person) of crop residue wastes annually.[304]

Another major source of agricultural waste is the manure produced by the 110 million head of cattle and 600 million other animals raised on U.S. farms and rangeland.[305] Some 1.5 to 2 billion tons of manure (about 260 million tons dry weight), or 1,500 pounds per person, is produced annually.[306] About 50 percent of all animal manure is economically recoverable and thus probably should not be considered waste.[307] Because of changing domestic eating habits, the amount of livestock raised in the United States has fallen in recent years—about 10 percent between 1974 and 1984—and thus the amount of animal wastes has probably declined as well.[308]

Silviculture operations also produce large amounts of relatively innocuous wastes, much of which is left where the trees are harvested. EPA estimated that 83 million tons (dry weight) of logging residues and 86 million tons (dry weight) of milling residues were produced in 1970. Apparently no more recent estimates are available.[309] Most of the milling wastes are reused and for this reason might be excluded from the total. Similarly, the logging wastes left on-site may help to control erosion and are likely to cause little harm (except for the potential risk of fire). Industrial timber production has increased relatively little over the past one to two decades. Fuel wood consumption, however, has grown rapidly (over 750 percent since 1970) and is now equal to almost one-third of the industrial timber product.[310]

Sludges and Other Pollution Control By-Products

Air and water pollution control facilities such as scrubbers, precipitators, and wastewater treatment plants generate substantial amounts of sludges and other solids that must be disposed of as solid wastes.

Coal-fired electric utilities produce approximately 50 million tons per year of air pollution control sludge.[311] The amount generated depends on the number of coal-fired plants with scrubbers installed and the type of coal they burn. For the most part, only new generating plants are required to install scrubbers, and the number of such facilities has grown slowly since 1980. Many of these are burning low-sulfur coal, which generates less sludge (the amount of sludge varies directly with the sulfur content of the coal). Because of the switch to low-sulfur coals, the amount of sludge generated may have actually decreased in recent years. Fly ash generation increases with the total coal consumption and therefore has risen over the past several years.[312] Industrial boilers and processes generate another 50 million tons or so of air pollution control sludge, primarily in the food, lumber and wood, paper, chemicals, petroleum, stone, clay and glass, and primary metals industries.[313]

Wastewater treatment plants produce about 26 million tons of sludge a year, 18 million from industrial plants and 7.6 million from municipal sewage facilities.[314]* Ninety percent of the industrial sludge is produced by four industries: iron and steel, inorganic chemicals, pulp and paper, and food processing.[316] Drinking water treatment plants produce another 4.4 million tons per year.

Other Wastes

Two other major sources of solid wastes are incinerator and furnace residues and demolition wastes. Coal-fired electric utilities produce more than 14 million tons of bottom ash and 3.9 million tons of boiler slag annually.[317]†️ The amount of these residues is probably increasing because of the increased dependence on coal for electrical production and the higher ash content of many low-sulfur coals that increasingly are being used.

Demolition wastes are generated during the destruction of buildings and other structures. EPA estimated that 82 million tons of these wastes were created in 1971, but no more recent estimates exist. The generation rate depends largely on construction activity. Thus, it is highly influenced by economic cycles.[319]

---

*All quantities are reported in dry weight, although wastewater sludge actually averages 93 to 99.5 percent water and air pollution control sludge averages 50 percent water when produced.[315]

†Bottom ash is the noncombustible materials that are too dense to escape from the boiler in the flue gas stream, while boiler slag forms when noncombusted inorganic materials melt and reform.[318]

Management

Although even less information is available on solid waste management techniques than on the amounts of waste generated, it is evident that these wastes are being managed more carefully now then they were in the past. Open dumps and open burning are prohibited; ocean dumping is limited by the Marine Protection, Research and Sanctuaries Act of 1972; and hazardous constituents are being diverted from the waste stream to be handled by special hazardous waste management and disposal facilities.[320]

But the solid waste management problem, as discussed in chapter 7, has not been solved. Municipal solid waste collection and disposal are often two of the more contentious issues local governments must deal with. Furthermore, increased attention is being focused on how waste disposal practices contaminate surface water and groundwater, pollute the air, destroy wildlife habitat, or create aesthetic nuisances.

Municipal and Industrial Solid Wastes

Approximately 85 percent of municipal solid wastes are currently disposed of in sanitary landfills—facilities in which the waste is covered by dirt, usually at least daily, to reduce the aesthetic nuisance and health risks it may cause[321] (figure 2.25). Recent studies for EPA estimate that approximately 10,000 municipal landfills are currently in operation, down significantly from the number thought to be in operation only a few years ago.[322] Some of the difference probably results from more accurate estimation techniques. But the availability of landfills is a national problem.

In a recent study, over 75 percent of 43 responding states admitted a problem of insufficient solid waste landfill capacity in their state.[323] Nationally, the number of new landfills sited decreased from 559 in 1981 to 416 in 1983—a 25 percent drop over three years.[324] Some states have particularly serious problems. In Connecticut no new municipal waste landfills have been permitted since 1978.[325] Officials predict that all of the nine major landfills will reach capacity at the same time, and the capacity shortage should become critical in late 1988. As another example, the total number of landfills in New Jersey fell from 310 in 1977 to 128 in 1984.[326] The problems are not limited to the Northeast. Concerns about groundwater contamination and the leasing of public lands to private companies have made it increasingly difficult to site new landfills even in the sparsely populated state of Arizona.[327]

Little is known about how industries are disposing of their solid wastes, although a recent EPA survey identified 3,500 industrial landfills.[328] The

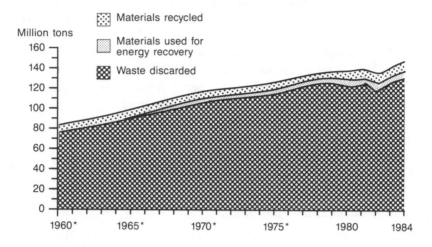

Figure 2.25
Municipal Solid Waste Generation in the United States,
Recovery and Disposal, 1960–1984

* Data for 1960–1975 are for every five years only; data are not available for individual other years.

Source: Franklin Associates, Ltd.

number could be much higher because, as noted previously, most industrial solid wastes are thought to be disposed of at the plant site where they are generated, and no information is collected on the disposal techniques.

Because of landfill capacity problems, many local governments are paying more attention to recycling and resource recovery options. Increased costs—for both waste management and industrial raw materials—along with regulatory pressures are forcing industries to explore such opportunities as well. An estimated 10 percent of solid wastes are currently recycled or reused.[329]

Nine states (Oregon, Vermont, Maine, Massachusetts, Michigan, Iowa, Connecticut, Delaware, and New York) have passed "bottle bills" (laws requiring deposits on beverage containers) to reduce the amount of glass and other beverage containers going to the municipal solid waste stream.[330] A 1984 EPA study of municipal wastes estimates that, partially as a result of the bottle bills, about 8 percent of discarded glass (one million tons) and 40 percent of discarded aluminum (643,000 tons) is being recycled.[331] About half of all aluminum beverage containers are being recycled. Some

20 percent of paper and paperboard discards are recycled, accounting for 85 percent of the materials recycled from the municipal waste stream. Only two types of plastic are currently recycled on a wide scale—polyester (PET, or polyethylene tetraphthalate), soft drink containers and polyethylene milk jugs. In 1984, approximately 63,000 tons were recycled, equal to only two-thirds of 1 percent of the gross plastic discarded.

Total industrial waste recycling is more difficult to estimate. But the National Association of Recycling Industries reports that in 1984, 44 percent of copper, 33 percent of aluminum, 48 percent of lead, 22 percent of zinc, 29 percent of iron and steel, 43 percent of stainless steel, and 4 percent of rubber were recovered by the recycling industry and sold as raw materials.[332] EPA estimates that 4 percent of industrial hazardous wastes are being recycled.[333]

Many states and municipalities are resorting to burning solid waste for energy, both to reduce the volume of waste requiring disposal and to generate steam or electricity.[334] Four to five percent of municipal wastes currently are disposed of in this manner, up from an estimated 1 percent in 1977.[335] These resource recovery or "waste-to-energy" facilities reduce the waste to approximately 30 to 40 percent of its original weight and 10 to 15 percent of its original volume.[336] Over 70 resource recovery facilities are now in existence, compared with an estimated 20 in 1977. Another 120 are in the planning or construction phase.[337]

About 25 percent of municipal wastewater sludge is currently incinerated. However, very little is burned for energy recovery because the amount of energy required to dry a sludge sufficiently to be burned is greater than the amount of energy recovered from burning sludge.[338]

Mining

Most mining wastes are simply dumped on the ground where they are generated. As previously noted, the primary exception is waste from surface coal mines, since the SMCRA mandates that this material be used to fill in or "reclaim" the excavated ground.

For noncoal minerals, EPA reports that approximately 35 percent of mine waste and mill tailings are recovered after generation. This estimate, however, is misleading. Almost half of these wastes are simply reprocessed using acid leaching to recover materials that were not previously extracted. Solutions of acids and cyanide are sprayed over the wastes to dissolve valuable materials, and the leachate is then collected for recovery of the desirable elements. Most of the waste, however, remains. Other noncoal mining wastes are used as agricultural lime replacements, road and building construction materials, and as constituents of bricks, ceramics, and wallboard.[339]

Agriculture and Silviculture

Most agricultural and silvicultural wastes are left in the field or forest where they are created. As indicated above, an increasing amount of many of the agricultural wastes are intentionally left on the land to control erosion. Eventually, if they are not carried into streams by stormwater runoff, they decompose and contribute to soil fertility. Animal wastes similarly are predominantly spread on the land as a fertilizer and soil conditioner. But some agricultural wastes are now being recycled in other ways.[340]

Much of what was formerly discarded from lumbering activities is also now being used in some beneficial way. The most recent estimate from EPA indicated that almost 70 percent of mill residues—the wood wastes created by lumber, plywood, and wood pulp production—were burned for fuel or used as raw material for another product in 1970.[341]

Pollution Control Sludge

Pollution control sludges can, depending on their constituents, be disposed of in landfills, by land spreading, through incineration, or by processing to produce commercially useful materials. Landfills are the most common disposal technique, used for 25 percent of municipal sewage sludge and probably for a larger proportion of industrial air and water pollution control sludges.[342] If they do not contain hazardous levels of contaminants, these sludges can also be disposed of by spreading them on agricultural and other lands.

EPA estimates that 19,000 land application units existed in 1984, ranging in size from fewer than 10 acres to 100 acres or more. The majority of these units (12,000) were used to dispose of one-quarter of the nation's municipal sewage sludge.[343] If carefully applied, sludge can help reclaim disturbed lands, serve as a soil conditioner, and partially reduce the need for commercial fertilizers on cropland.[344]

Approximately 5,600 units were used to dispose of industrial wastewater sludges, primarily in Wisconsin, Michigan, Indiana, North Carolina, and Maryland. These lands are not generally used for crop production because the industrial sludges often contain metals and other chemicals that may be toxic if introduced into the food chain and because the application rate typically exceeds the nutrient needs of crops. The petroleum industry also disposes of oil and gas wastes on 726 land application units, primarily in Nebraska, California, and Texas. Another 450 land application units receive animal wastes and 170 receive drinking water treatment sludges.[345]

Many sludges are incinerated. EPA estimates that this is how one-quarter of municipal sewage sludge is disposed of.[346] The proportion of industrial sludges managed in this manner is probably lower.[347] The sludges may be incinerated with other solid waste, but little opportunity exists for recovering usable energy because of the sludge's high water content.

Some air and water pollution control sludges and incinerator residues are recycled by the industries producing them, depending on the value and concentration of materials trapped in the sludges and residues. Industries that use precious metals, for example, may find it economically feasible to recover the metals trapped in the wastewater sludge or sell the sludge to other industries for recovery.[348]

Municipal sludges may also be processed by composting and drying to make them usable as soil conditioners. EPA estimates that this is the fate of approximately 20 percent of municipal wastewater sludge that ends up as fertilizer.[349]

Finally, a few coastal cities (among them, New York, Los Angeles, and Boston) continue to haul or pipe their municipal wastewater sludge off-shore for disposal in the ocean.[350] Though most coastal cities have discontinued this practice, it still is the only form of ocean dumping that has increased over the past decade—accounting for 4 percent of the total municipal sludge produced in 1984.[351] No industrial sludge is known to be disposed of in this manner.

Other Wastes

Ocean dumping used to be a common method for disposing of other types of wastes as well but, because of restrictions imposed by EPA and the Army Corps of Engineers, is no longer used for construction debris, bottom ash, or boiler slag.[352] Construction debris are frequently buried in sanitary landfills used for other wastes as well. Fly ash, bottom ash, and boiler slag from the utility industry are recycled as components of building materials. In 1983, 14 percent of fly ash, 20 percent of bottom ash, and 64 percent of boiler slag in cement were used predominantly in cement and concrete products, in structural fills and road base, and to control snow and ice.[353]

REFERENCES

Text

1. U.S. Council on Environmental Quality, *Environmental Quality 1984, 15th Annual Report of the Council on Environmental Quality* (Washington D.C.: U.S. Government Printing Office, 1986), p. 13.

2. U.S. General Accounting Office, *Problems in Air Quality Monitoring System Affect Data Reliability* (Washington, D.C.: U.S. Government Printing Office, 1982), pp. 5-16; and U.S. General Accounting Office, *Air Quality; Do We Know What It Is?* (Washington, D.C.: U.S. Government Printing Office, 1979), pp. 5-17.

3. The Conservation Foundation, *State of the Environment 1982* (Washington, D.C.: The Conservation Foundation, 1982), pp. 50-51.

4. For details on how areas are designated and on controversies over these designations, see "When is an Attainment Not An Attainment Area?," *Environmental Law Reporter* 16 (1986):10041-48; and 43 Fed. Reg. 8964 (1978).

5. The procedures for changing a designation include a state submitting two years of data on ambient air quality revealing no violations of the ambient standard (in the case of a request for redesignating a particulate nonattainment area); review and approval by both an EPA regional office and EPA headquarters; publication of a notice of proposed rule making; receipt of public comments on the proposed rule making; and publication of the final rule making in the *Federal Register*. EPA's procedures for redesignation of TSP nonattainment areas are defined in a September 30, 1985, memorandum, "Total Suspended Particulate (TSP) Redesignations," from Gerald A. Emison, director, EPA Office of Air Quality Planning and Standards, to the directors of Air Divisions in EPA regional offices.

6. U.S. Council on Environmental Quality, *Environmental Quality 1984*, p. 13.

7. For criticism of PSI, see Robert W. Crandall, *Controlling Industrial Pollution: The Economics and Politics of Clean Air* (Washington, D.C.: The Brookings Institution, 1983), pp. 21-22.

8. U.S. Council on Environmental Quality, *Environmental Quality 1984*, p. 13.

9. Ibid., p. 25.

10. The Conservation Foundation, *State of the Environment 1982*, p. 50.

11. U.S. Environmental Protection Agency, Office of Air Quality Planning and Standards, *National Air Quality and Emissions Trends Report, 1984* (Research Triangle Park, N.C.: U.S. Environmental Protection Agency, 1986), p. 1-5.

12. Ibid.

13. Ibid., p. 3-7.

14. U.S. Environmental Protection Agency, Office of Air Quality Planning and Standards, *National Air Pollutant Emission Estimates, 1940-1984* (Research Triangle Park, N.C.: U.S. Environmental Protection Agency, 1986), p. 11.

15. 43 Fed. Reg. 8964 (1978).

16. U.S. Environmental Protection Agency, Office of Air Quality Planning and Standards, *Maps Depicting Nonattainment Areas Pursuant to Section 107 of the Clean Air Act—1985* (Research Triangle Park, N.C.: U.S. Environmental Protection Agency, 1985), p. vi.

17. Conservation Foundation calculation, based on U.S. Environmental Protection Agency,

Office of Air Quality Planning and Standards, *Maps Depicting Nonattainment Areas Pursuant to Section 107 of the Clean Air Act—1985*.

18. U.S. Environmental Protection Agency, *National Air Quality and Emissions Trends Report, 1984*, p. 3-5.

19. National Commission on Air Quality, *To Breathe Clean Air* (Washington, D.C.: U.S. Government Printing Office, 1981), p. 74; and 49 Fed Reg. 10411 (1984).

20. 49 Fed. Reg. 10408 (1984).

21. 42 USC §7502(a)(1).

22. EPA issued a proposed rule revising its regulation governing state implementation plan programs for particulate matter in March 1984. This rule has not yet been made final. See 50 Fed. Reg. 13130 (1985).

23. Burton G. Bennett et al., "Urban Air Pollution Worldwide," *Environmental Science and Technology* 19 (1985):298-304; and World Resources Institute and International Institute for Environment and Development, *World Resources 1986: An Assessment of the Resource Base that Supports the Global Economy* (New York: Basic Books, 1986), pp. 161-81; and Organization for Economic Cooperation and Development, *OECD Environmental Data Compendium 1985* (Paris: Organization for Economic Cooperation and Development, 1985), pp. 13-41.

24. Organization for Economic Cooperation and Development, *OECD Environmental Data Compendium 1985*, pp. 34-36.

25. World Resources Institute and International Institute for Environment and Development, *World Resources 1986*, p. 163.

26. Bennett et al., "Urban Air Pollution Worldwide," p. 304.

27. Ibid., p. 303.

28 Ibid., p. 302.

29. World Resources Institute and International Institute for Environment and Development, *World Resources 1986*, p. 164.

30. Ibid.

31. See ibid., pp. 171-72, 213; and World Health Organization, *Sulfur Oxides and Suspended Particulate Matter: Executive Summary*, Health Criteria no. 8 (Geneva: World Health Organization, 1979), pp. 4-6.

32. U.S. Environmental Protection Agency, *National Air Quality and Emissions Trends Report, 1984*, p. 3-12.

33. Ibid.

34. Ibid., p. 3-11.

35. Ibid.

36. Ibid.

37. Ibid., p. 3-12.

38. U.S. General Accounting Office, *Air Pollution: Sulfur Dioxide Emissions from Nonferrous Smelters Have Been Reduced* (Washington D.C.: U.S. General Accounting Office, 1986), p. 4.

39. U.S. Environmental Protection Agency, *National Air Quality and Emissions Trends Report, 1984*, p. 3-12.

40. Ibid., p. 3-17.

41. U.S. Environmental Protection Agency, Office of Management Systems and Evaluation, *Environmental Progress and Challenges: An EPA Perspective* (Washington, D.C.:

U.S. Government Printing Office, 1984), p. 16; and U.S. Environmental Protection Agency, *Maps Depicting Nonattainment Areas Pursuant to Section 107 of the Clean Air Act—1985*, p. vi.

42. Conservation Foundation calculation, based on U.S. Environmental Protection Agency, *Maps Depicting Nonattainment Areas Pursuant to Section 107 of the Clean Air Act—1985*.

43. Bennett et al., "Urban Air Pollution Worldwide," p. 304.

44. Ibid., pp. 303-4.

45. World Resources Institute and International Institute for Environment and Development, *World Resources 1986*, p. 164.

46. U.S. Environmental Protection Agency, *National Air Quality and Emissions Trends Report, 1984*, p. 3-27.

47. Ibid.

48. Ibid., p. 3-29.

49. Ibid., p. 3-30.

50. The Conservation Foundation, *State of the Environment: An Assessment at Mid-Decade* (Washington, D.C.: The Conservation Foundation, 1984), p. 93.

51. U.S. Environmental Protection Agency, *National Air Quality and Emissions Trends Report, 1984*, p. 3-21.

52. Ibid.

53. Ibid.

54. U.S. Council on Environmental Quality, *Environmental Quality 1984*, pp. 42-47.

55. U.S. Environmental Protection Agency, *National Air Pollutant Emission Estimates, 1940-1984*, p. 15; and U.S. Environmental Protection Agency, *National Air Quality and Emissions Trends Report, 1984*, p. 3-24.

56. U.S. Environmental Protection Agency, *National Air Quality and Emissions Trends Report, 1984*, p. 3-24.

57. Ibid.

58. U.S. Environmental Protection Agency, *Environmental Progress and Challenges*, p. 16; and U.S. Environmental Protection Agency, *Maps Depicting Nonattainment Areas Pursuant to Section 107 of the Clean Air Act—1985*, p. vi.

59. T.D. Hartwell et al., *Study of Carbon Monoxide Exposure of Residents of Washington, D.C. and Denver, Colorado*, prepared for U.S. Environmental Protection Agency, Environmental Monitoring Systems Laboratory (Research Triangle Park, N.C.: U.S. Environmental Protection Agency, 1984), p. 182.

60. Hartwell et al., *Study of Carbon Monoxide Exposure of Residents of Washington, D.C. and Denver, Colorado*, p. 182; and Gerald Akland et al., "Measuring Human Exposure to Carbon Monoxide in Washington, D.C. and Denver, Colorado, during the Winter of 1982-1983," *Environmental Science & Technology* 19 (1985):915.

61. The Conservation Foundation, *State of the Environment: An Assessment at Mid-Decade*, p. 94.

62. U.S. Environmental Protection Agency, *National Air Pollutant Emission Estimates, 1940-1984*, p. 14.

63. U.S. Environmental Protection Agency, *National Air Quality and Emissions Trends Report, 1984*, pp. 1-15, 3-34.

64. Ibid., p. 1-15.

65. Ibid.

66. U.S. Environmental Protection Agency, *Maps Depicting Nonattainment Areas Pur-*

suant to Section 107 of the Clean Air Act—1985, p. vi.; and U.S. Environmental Protection Agency, *Enviromental Progress and Challenges*, p. 16.

67. 42 USC §7502(a)(2).

68. J. Craig Potter, "Clean Air Act—When, How, and What: Keynote Address," *Journal of the Air Pollution Control Association* 36 (1986):686; and "Many Cities Expected to Fail To Meet Ozone Limit by '87," *The New York Times*, June 24, 1986.

69. U.S. Environmental Protection Agency, *National Air Quality and Emissions Trends Report, 1984*, p. 4-1.

70. "CASAC Favors Current Primary Standards as Upper Limit for Revised Ozone Regulation," *Environment Reporter—Current Developments*, May 2, 1986, p. 6; and "CASAC Urges EPA to Lower Ozone Options Range, Consider 8-HR Standard," *Inside EPA*, April 25, 1986, pp. 1, 11.

71. Peter J.A. Rombout, Paul J. Lioy, and Bernard D. Goldstein, "Rationale for an Eight-Hour Ozone Standard," *Journal of the Air Pollution Control Association* 36 (1986):915.

72. Lee M. Thomas, "A Strategy for Controlling Ozone: A Keynote Address," *Journal of the Air Pollution Control Association* 36 (1986):998.

73. U.S. Congress, Office of Tecnology Assessment, *Acid Rain and Transported Air Pollutants: Implications for Public Policy* (Washington, D.C.: U.S. Government Printing Office, 1984), p. 92.

74. U.S. General Accounting Office, *Air Pollution: Sulfur Dioxide Emissions from Nonferrous Smelters Have Been Reduced*, a report to the Chairman, U.S. Congress, Committee on Energy and Commerce, House of Representatives, Subcommittee on Oversight and Investigation (Washington, D.C.: U.S. Government Printing Office, 1986), pp. 9, 21.

75 U.S. Environmental Protection Agency, *National Air Pollutant Emission Estimates, 1940-1984*, p. 13.

76. Philip Roth et al., *The American West's Acid Rain Test*, (Washington, D.C.: World Resources Institute, 1985), pp. 23, 32.

77. National Research Council, *Acid Rain Deposition: Long-Term Trends* (Washington, D.C.: National Academy Press, 1986), p. 12.

78. Ibid.

79. Ibid., p. 13.

80. U.S. Comptroller General, *An Analysis of Issues Concerning "Acid Rain"*, report to Congress (Washington, D.C.: U.S. Government Printing Office, 1984), p. 46.

81. U.S. Office of Technology Assessment, *Acid Rain and Transported Air Pollutants*, pp. 71-73.

82. The Conservation Foundation, *State of the Environment 1982*, p. 66.

83. Ibid., p. 67.

84. The first four were *Atmosphere-Biosphere Interactions: Toward a Better Understanding of the Consequences of Fossil Fuel Combustion* (1981); *Acid Deposition: Atmospheric Processes in Eastern North America* (1983); *Acid Deposition: Processes of Lake Acidification* (1984); and *Acid Depostion Effects on Geochemical Cycling and Biological Availability of Trace Elements* (1985).

85. Roth et al., *The American West's Acid Rain Test*.

86. National Research Council, *Acid Deposition*, p. 6-9; and Arthur H. Johnson, "Acid Deposition: Trends, Relationships, and Effects," *Environment* 28, no. 4 (1986):10.

87. National Research Council, *Acid Deposition*, p. 21.

88. The Conservation Foundation, *State of the Environment 1982*, pp. 36-37.

89. U.S. Environmental Protection Agency, Office of Research and Development, *Characteristics of Lakes in the Eastern United States*, vol. 1 (Washington, D.C.: U.S. Environmental Protection Agency, 1986), pp. xxvi, 12.

90. Johnson, "Acid Rain Deposition," p. 38.

91. These questions are adapted from U.S. Office of Technology Assessment, *Acid Rain and Transported Air Pollutants*, pp. 16-18.

92. U.S. Environmental Protection Agency, *National Air Quality and Emissions Trends Report, 1984*, pp. 3-16, 3-30.

93 See the following bills introduced in the 99th Congress: S.2813 (Senator Proxmire), S.2203 (Senator Stafford), and H.R. 4567 (Representative Waxman).

94. U.S. Congress, Congressional Budget Office, *Curbing Acid Rain: Cost, Budget, and Coal-Market Effects* (Washington, D.C.: U.S. Government Printing Office, 1986), pp. xx-xxi.

95. Ibid., p. xix.

96. Ibid.

97. National Acid Precipitation Assessment Program, *Annual Report 1984 to the President and Congress* (Washington, D.C.: National Acid Precipitation Assessment Program), p. 19.

98. Helmut Weidner, *Clean Air Policy in Europe: A Survey of 17 Countries* (Geneva: World Commission on Environment and Development, 1986), p. 24. This study is part of the forthcoming book Helmut Weidner, *Clean Air Policy in Europe: A Survey of Regulations, Problems and Abatement Measures in 21 Countries*, (Berlin: Edition Sigma, 1987).

99. Personal communication, Chris Rose, World Wildlife Fund International, to Konrad von Moltke, The Conservation Foundation.

100. World Resources Institute and International Institute for Environment and Development, *World Resources, 1986*, pp. 220-21.

101. Ibid., pp. 204, 219.

102. Ibid., pp. 204, 206, 219.

103. 42 USC §7491.

104. National Commission on Air Quality, *To Breathe Clean Air*, p. 174.

105. Ibid., p. 175.

106. U.S. Congress, House of Representatives, Committee on Interior and Insular Affairs, Subcommittee on National Parks and Recreation, *Hearings on Impacts of Air Pollution on National Park Units*, 99th Cong, 1st sess., May 20 and 21, 1985, p. 542.

107. Ibid., p. 546.

108. National Research Council, *Acid Deposition*, p. 12.

109. U.S. Congress, *Hearing on Impacts of Air Pollution on National Park Units*, p. 540.

110. John Trijonis, "Patterns and Trends in Data for Atmospheric Sulfates and Visibility," in National Research Council, *Acid Deposition*, p. 112.

111. Ibid.

112. See EPA regulations implementing settlement in lawsuit 50 Fed. Reg. 28544 (1985).

113. 45 Fed. Reg. 80084 (1980); and 46 Fed. Reg. 3646 (1981).

114. "Hodel Decides Not to List Integral Vistas; McClure Charges EPA Regulations 'Unlawful'," *Environment Reporter—Current Developments*, November 1, 1985, p. 1,133.

115. Alan S. Miller, Natural Resources Defense Council, testimony before the U.S. Congress, Senate, Committee on Environment and Public Works, Subcommittee on Toxic Substances and Environmental Oversight, *Hearing on the Impact of Chlorofluorocarbon Emissions on the Stratosphere*, 97th Cong., 1st sess., July 23, 1981, p. 2.

116. James G. Titus and Stephen Seidel, "Overview of the Effects of Changing the Atmosphere," in James G. Titus, ed., *Effects of Changes in Stratospheric Ozone and Global Climate* (Washington, D.C.: U.S. Environmental Protection Agency and United Nations Environment Programme, 1986), p. 3; and papers cited therein.

117. Titus and Seidel, "Overview of the Effects of Changing the Atmosphere," pp. 8-15; and papers cited therein.

118. Lois R. Ember et al., "Tending the Global Commons," *Chemical and Engineering News* 64, no. 47 (1986):16.

119. The Conservation Foundation, *State of the Environment 1982*, p. 75.

120. World Resources Institute and International Institute for Environment and Development, *World Resources, 1986*, p. 319.

121. Ember et al., "Tending the Global Commons," p. 22.

122. Ibid.

123. Ibid., p. 20.

124. R.B. Castow and C.D. Keeling, "Atmospheric Carbon Dioxide Concentration, the Observed Airborne Fraction, the Fossil Fuel Airborne Fraction, and the Difference in Hemispheric Airborne Fractions," in B. Bolen, ed., *SCOPE 16: Global Carbon Modelling* (London: John Wiley and Sons, 1981).

125. Ralph M. Rotty, *A Look at 1983 CO_2 Emissions from Fossil Fuels* (Oak Ridge, Tenn.: Oak Ridge Associated Universities, Institute for Energy Analysis, 1986); and William C. Clark, ed., *Carbon Dioxide Review, 1982* (New York: Oxford University Press, 1982), pp. 378, 456-60.

126. Rotty, *A Look at 1983 CO_2 Emissions From Fossil Fuels*, p. 9.

127. Titus and Seidel, "Overview of the Effects of Changing the Atmosphere," p. 4.

128. Ember et al., "Tending the Global Commons," p. 22.

129. Ibid., pp. 29-30.

130. Ibid., p. 22.

131. Ibid.

132. Ibid.

133. Ibid., p. 23

134. Ibid., pp. 29-30.

135. Ibid., p. 23.

136. Michael C. MacCracken and Frederick M. Luther, eds., *Projecting the Climatic Effects of Increasing Carbon Dioxide*, prepared for U.S. Department of Energy, Office of Energy Research, Office of Basic Energy Sciences, and Carbon Dioxide Research Division (Washington, D.C.: U.S. Department of Energy, 1985), p. xxii.

137. Ember et al., "Tending the Global Commons," p. 23.

138. Ibid.

139. See, generally, Jill Jager, "Floating New Evidence in the CO2 Debate," *Environment* 11, no. 4 (1986):6-41.

140. Ember et al., "Tending the Global Commons," p. 21.

141. Ibid., p. 32; and Michael Shepard, "The Greenhouse Effect: Earth's Climate in Transition," *EPRI Journal* 28, no. 7 (1986):8-9.

142. MacCracken and Luther, eds., *Projecting the Climatic Effects of Increasing Carbon Dioxide*, p. xx; Shepard, "The Greenhouse Effect," p. 6; and Ember et al., "Tending the Global Commons," p. 21.

143. National Research Council, *Causes and Effects of Changes in Stratospheric Ozone:*

Update 1983 (Washington, D.C.: National Academy Press, 1984).

144. Ember et al., "Tending the Global Commons," pp. 16, 25-26.

145. Titus and Seidel, "Overview of the Effects of Changing the Atmosphere," pp. 4-5.

146. Richard A. Kerr, "Taking Shots at Ozone Hole Theories," *Science* 234 (1986):817-18.

147. Ember et al., "Tending the Global Commons," pp. 18-19; and Linwood B. Callis and Murali Natarajan, "Ozone and Nitrogen Dioxide Changes in the Stratosphere during 1979-84," *Nature* 323 (1986):772-77.

148. Ember et al., "Tending the Global Commons," p. 20.

149. Ibid., p. 19.

150. James E. Hansen, testimony before the U.S. Congress, Senate, Committee on Environment and Public Works, Subcommittee on Environmental Pollution, *Hearing on Ozone Depletion, the Greenhouse Effect, and Climate Change*, 99th Cong., 2nd sess., June 10 and 11, 1986, p. 86.

151. Ibid.

152. Ibid.

153. Ibid., pp. 86, 92.

154. Ibid., p. 95.

155. Barry Meier, "Hard Choices Await Industry as Ozone-Layer Fears Rise," *Wall Street Journal*, December 2, 1986. See also Mark Crawford, "United States Floats Proposal to Help Prevent Global Ozone Depletion," *Science* 234 (1986):927-29.

156. Ember et al., "Tending the Global Commons," p. 49.

157. Ibid.

158. David D. Doniger and David A. Wirth, "Cooling the Chemical Summer," *The Amicus Journal* 8, no. 2 (1986):14.

159. Daniel J. Dudek, "Industry Needs Incentives Not to Pollute," *New York Times*, November 16, 1986.

160. "U.S. Tax on Chlorofluorocarbons Sought to Help Save Ozone Layer," *Washington Post*, November 30, 1986.

161. See Rochelle L. Stanfield, "Attitudes about Ozone Are Changing," *National Journal*, November 1, 1986, p. 2,638.

162. "U.S. Tax on Chlorofluorocarbons Sought to Help Save Ozone Layer," *Washington Post*.

163. In Section 157 of the Clean Air Act, 42 USC §7457(b), Congress specifically authorized EPA to regulate substances that "may reasonably be anticipated to affect the stratosphere, especially ozone in the stratosphere, if such effect in the stratosphere may reasonably be anticipated to engandger public health or welfare." See "Science Board Forms Panel to Review EPA Efforts to Protect Earth's Ozone Layer," *Environment Reporter—Current Developments*, February 7, 1986, pp. 1,842-1,843.

164. Ember et al., "Tending the Global Commons," pp. 37-47. See also Thomas C. Schelling, "Anticipating Climate Change," *Environment* 26, no. 8 (1984):6-9, 28-35.

165. Sandra L. Postel, "Atmospheric Warm-up," *Environmental Science and Technology* 20 (1986):1,208-9.

166. 33 USC §§1251 et seq.

167. Kit D. Farber and Gary L. Rutledge, "Pollution Abatement and Control Expenditures," *Survey of Current Business* 66, no. 7 (1986):100-3; Water Quality Act of 1987 (P.L. 100-1).

168. U.S. Department of the Interior, Geological Survey, *National Water Summary 1984:*

Hydrologic Events, Selected Water Quality Trends, and Ground-Water Resources, Water Supply Paper 2275 (Washington, D.C.: U.S. Government Printing Office, 1985), pp. 51-55.

169. U.S. Environmental Protection Agency, Office of Water Regulations and Standards, *National Water Quality Inventory: 1984 Report to Congress* (Washington, D.C.: U.S. Environmental Protection Agency, 1985), p. 47.

170. U.S. Council on Environmental Quality, *Contamination of Groundwater by Toxic Organic Chemicals* (Washington, D.C.: U.S. Government Printing Office, 1981), p. 4.

171. U.S. Congress, Office of Technology Assessment, *Protecting the Nation's Groundwater from Contamination*, vol. 1 (Washington, D.C.: U.S. Office of Technology Assessment, 1984), p. 6.

172. U.S. General Accounting Office, *The Nation's Water: Key Unanswered Questions About the Quality of Rivers and Streams* (Washington, D.C.: U.S. General Accounting Office, 1986), pp. 3-4.

173. Association of State and Interstate Water Pollution Control Administrators, *America's Clean Water*, a report prepared for the U.S. Environmental Protection Agency (Washington, D.C.: Assocation of State and Interstate Water Pollution Control Administrators, 1984).

174. Association of State and Interstate Water Pollution Control Administrators, *America's Clean Water*, p. 4.

175. Ibid, pp. 4-5.

176. U.S. Environmental Protection Agency, *National Water Quality Inventory, 1984*, p. 2.

177. "Environmental Results," preliminary data provided by the U.S. Environmental Protection Agency, July 1986.

178. Robert D. Judy, Jr., et al., *1982 National Fisheries Survey*, vol. 1, *Technical Report: Initial Findings*, prepared for U.S. Department of the Interior, Fish and Wildlife Service, and U.S. Environmental Protection Agency, Office of Water, FWS/OBS- 84/06 (Washington, D.C.: U.S. Government Printing Office, 1984), p. v.

179. The Conservation Foundation, *State of the Environment: An Assessment at Mid-Decade*, p. 107.

180. Association of State and Interstate Water Pollution Control Administrators, *America's Clean Water*.

181. U.S. Department of Commerce, National Oceanic and Atmospheric Administration, and U.S. Department of Health and Human Services, Food and Drug Administration, *1985 National Shellfish Register of Classified Estuarine Waters* (Springfield, Va.: National Technical Information Service, 1985), p. 8.

182. Richard A. Smith, Richard B. Alexander, and M. Gordon Wolman, *Analysis and Interpretation of Water-Quality Trends in Major U.S. Rivers, 1974-1981*, prepared for U.S. Department of the Interior, Geological Survey, Water Supply Paper 2307 (Reston, Va.: U.S. Geological Survey, 1986).

183. The Conservation Foundation, *State of the Environment: An Assessment at Mid-Decade*, pp. 107-9.

184. Smith, Alexander, and Wolman, *Analysis and Interpretation of Water Quality Trends in Major U.S. Rivers*, p. 23.

185. Ibid., p. 11a.

186. Ibid., pp. 23-24.

187. The Conservation Foundation, *State of the Environment: An Assessment at Mid-Decade*, p. 112.

188. Smith, Alexander, and Wolman, *Analysis and Interpretation of Water Quality Trends in Major U.S. Rivers*, p. 11a.

189. Ibid., pp. 27-28.

190. Edwin H. Clark II, Jennifer A. Haverkamp, and William Chapman, *Eroding Soils: The Off-Farm Impacts* (Washington D.C.: The Conservation Foundation, 1985), pp. 61-84.

191. U.S. Geological Survey, *National Water Summary 1984*, p. 66.

192. Ibid., pp. 68-69.

193. The Conservation Foundation, *State of the Environment 1982*, p. 103.

194. U.S. Geological Survey, *National Water Summary 1984*, p. 465.

195. The Conservation Foundation, *State of the Environment: An Assessment at Mid-Decade*, pp. 112-13.

196. U.S. Geological Survey, *National Water Summary 1984*, p. 29.

197. U.S. Department of the Interior, Geological Survey, *National Water Summary 1983: Hydrologic Events and Issues*, Water Supply Paper 2250 (Washington D.C.: U.S. Government Printing Office, 1984), p. 55.

198. U.S. Environmental Protection Agency, *Chesapeake Bay Program Technical Studies: A Synthesis* (Washington D.C.: U.S. Environmental Protection Agency, 1982).

199. Ibid., p. i; and U.S. Geological Survey, *National Water Summary 1984*, p. 63.

200. U.S. Geological Survey, *National Water Summary 1984*, p. 70.

201. Ibid., p. 71.

202. Ibid., p. 72.

203 Smith, Alexander, and Wolman, *Analysis and Interpretation of Water Quality Trends in Major U.S. Rivers*, p. 11a.

204. Ibid., pp. 29-30.

205. Ibid., pp. 30-31.

206. Ibid., p. 11a.

207. Ibid., pp. 31-32.

208. Ibid., p. 32.

209. Robert J. Gilliom, Richard B. Alexander, and Richard A. Smith, *Pesticides in the Nation's Rivers, 1975-1980, and Implications for Future Monitoring*, prepared for U.S. Department of the Interior, Geological Survey, Water Supply Paper 2271, (Washington, D.C.: U.S. Government Printing Office, 1985), pp. 1, 5.

210. Ibid., table 2, p. 6.

211. Ibid., p. 21.

212. U.S. Environmental Protection Agency, Office of Water Regulations and Standards, *National Water Qaulity Inventory: 1982 Report to Congress*, EPA 440/2-84-006 (Washington, D.C.: U.S. Environmental Protection Agency, 1984), pp. 21-22.

213. Association of State and Interstate Water Pollution Control Administrators, *America's Clean Water*, p. 10.

214. "Report Surveys Water Quality for Fish," *EPA Journal* 10, no. 3 (1984):25.

215. For an overview, see The Conservation Foundation, *Groundwater Protection* (Washington D.C.: The Conservation Foundation, 1987).

216. U.S. Environmental Protection Agency, Office of Groundwater Protection, *Groundwater Protection Strategy* (Washington, D.C.: U.S. Environmental Protection Agency, 1984), p. 16.

217. U.S. Council on Environmental Quality, *Contamination of Ground Water by Toxic Organic Chemicals* (Washington, D.C.: U.S. Government Printing Office, 1981), p. xii.

218. U.S. Environmental Protection Agency, Office of Drinking Water, *National Statistical Assessment of Rural Water Conditions*, Executive Summary (Washington, D.C.: U.S. Environmental Protection Agency, 1984), p. 19.

219. U.S. Office of Technology Assessment, *Protecting the Nation's Groundwater from Contamination*, vols. 1 and 2, OTA-0-276 (Washington, D.C.: U.S. Office of Technology Assessment, 1984), p. 23.

220. Ibid., p. 34.

221. U.S. Environmental Protection Agency, Office of Drinking Water, "FY 1984 Status Report: The National Public Water System Program" (Washington, D.C.: U.S. Environmental Protection Agency, 1984, photocopy), p. 10.

222. U.S. Environmental Protection Agency, *National Statistical Assessment of Rural Water Conditions*, Executive Summary, p. 4.

223. Ibid., p. 7.

224. U.S. Office of Technology Assessment, *Protecting the Nation's Groundwater from Contamination*, vols. 1 and 2, pp. 29-30.

225. Rip G. Rice, *Safe Drinking Water: The Impact of Chemicals on a Limited Resource* (Alexandria, Va: Drinking Water Research Foundation, 1985), p. 162.

226. Ibid.

227. U.S. Environmental Protection Agency, *National Statistical Assessment of Rural Water Conditions*, Executive Summary, p. 5.

228. Ibid., p. 8.

229. Ibid., p. 9.

230. Texas Department of Agriculture, *Pesticide Safety for Texas* (Austin, Tex.: Texas Department of Agriculture, 1984), p. 9.

231. Vladmir Novotny and Gordon Chesters, *Handbook of Nonpoint Pollution* (New York: Von Nostrand Reinhold, 1981), p. 287.

232. U.S. Geological Survey, *National Water Summary 1984*, p. 95.

233. Ibid., p. 96.

234. U.S. Environmental Protection Agency, *National Statistical Assessment of Rural Water Conditions*, Executive Summary, p. 8.

235. James J. Geraghty et al., *Water Atlas of the United States* (Syosset, N.Y.: Water Information Center, 1983), p. 39.

236. Ibid., p. 36.

237. Ibid., figure 9.

238. Ibid., p. 38.

239. National Research Council, Commission on Life Science, Board on Toxicology and Environmental Health Hazards, *Toxicity Testing: Strategies to Determine Needs and Priorities* (Washington D.C.: National Academy Press, 1984), p. 3.

240. U.S. Council on Environmental Quality, *Contamination of Groundwater by Toxic Organic Chemicals*, p. 17.

241. Ibid., p. xvi.

242. Rice, *Safe Drinking Water*, p. 164.

243. U.S. Council on Environmental Quality, *Contamination of Groundwater by Toxic Organic Chemicals*, p. 26.

244. Rice, *Safe Drinking Water*, p. 165.

245. U.S. Council on Environmental Quality, *Contamination of Groundwater by Toxic Organic Chemicals*, p. 33.

246. Ibid., p. 35.

247. U.S. Office of Technology Assessment, *Protecting the Nation's Groundwater from Contamination*, vols. 1 and 2, p. 35.

248. Ibid., pp. 31, 281.

249. James Wilson, ed., *The Fate of Toxics in Surface and Ground Waters: The Proceedings of the Second National Water Conference* (Philadelphia: Academy of Natural Sciences, 1984).

250. Ibid., pp. 146-47.

251. Gary H. Lyman, Carolyn G. Lyman, and Wallace Johnson, "Association of Leukemia with Radium Groundwater Contamination," *Journal of the American Medical Association* 254, (1985):621.

252. U.S. Geological Summary, *National Water Summary 1983*, pp. 51-55.

253. Ibid.

254. The Conservation Foundation, *State of the Environment: An Assessment at Mid-Decade*, p. 117.

255. U.S. Environmental Protection Agency, Comptroller General, "Wastewater Dischargers Are Not Complying with EPA Pollution Control Permits" (Washington, D.C.: U.S. General Accounting Office, 1983).

256. Association of State and Interstate Water Pollution Control Administrators, *America's Clean Water*, p. 10.

257. U.S. Environmental Protection Agency, Office of Municipal Pollution Control, *1986 Needs Survey Report to Congress: Assessment of Needed Publicly Owned Wastewater Treatment Facilities in the United States*, EPA 430/9-87-001 (Washington, D.C.: U.S. Environmental Protection Agency, 1987), p. 1m and appendix C-4.

258. The Conservation Foundation, *State of the Environment: An Assessment at Mid-Decade*, p. 118.

259. U.S. Environmental Protection Agency, Office of Water Regulations and Standards, *Report to Congress on the Discharge of Hazardous Wastes to Publicly Owned Treatment Works*, EPA/530-SW-86-004 (Washington, D.C.: U.S. Environmental Protection Agency, 1986), p. E-3.

260. Ibid.

261. Ibid., p. E-4.

262. Ibid., p. E-5.

263. JRB Associates, "Addendum to the Report Entitled: Assessment of the Impacts of Industrial Discharges on Publicly Owned Treatment Works," prepared for the U.S. Environmental Protection Agency, February 1983 (unpublished), p. 3-4, table 3.2.

264. Ibid., p.3-6, table 3.2

265. U.S. Environmental Protection Agency, Office of Water Program Operations, *Report to Congress on Control of Combined Sewer Overflow in the United States* (Washington, D.C.: U.S. Environmental Protection Agency, 1978), table 5-1, pp. 5-4 to 5-6.

266. U.S. Environmental Protection Agency, *1986 Needs Survey Report to Congress*, p. 17.

267. U.S. Council on Environmental Quality, *Environmental Quality 1984*, pp. 89-90.

268. Smith, Alexander, and Wolman, *Analysis and Interpretation of Water Quality Trends in Major U.S. Rivers*, p. 23.

269. U.S. Council on Environmental Quality, *Environmental Quality 1984*, p. 84.

270. U.S. Environmental Protection Agency, *Report to Congress on the Discharge of Hazardous Wastes to Publicly Owned Treatment Works*, p. 3-35.

271. Ibid., p. 3-25.

272. Ibid., p. 3-26.

273. U.S. Environmental Protection Agency, *National Water Quality Inventory 1982*, p. 14.

274. JRB Associates, "Addendum to the Report Entitled: Assessment of the Impacts of Industrial Discharges on Publicly Owned Treatment Works," p. 2-7.

275. U.S. Environmental Protection Agency, Office of Water Regulations and Standards, Effluent Guidelines Division, *Fate of Priority Pollutants in Publicly Owned Treatment Works*, Final Report, vol. 1 (Washington, D.C.: U.S. Environmental Protection Agency, 1982).

276. Leonard P. Gianessi et al., *Nonpoint Source Pollution: Are Cropland Controls the Answer?* (Washington, D.C.: Resources for the Future, 1986), table 1.

277. Association of State and Interstate Water Pollution Control Administrators, *America's Clean Water*, p. 10.

278. Ibid., p. 123.

279. Ibid., p. 5.

280. Ibid., p. 10.

281. Ibid., pp. 10-11.

282. "Report Surveys Water Quality for Fish," *EPA Journal*.

283. Association of State and Interstate Water Pollution Control Administrators, *America's Clean Water*, p. 17.

284. The Conservation Foundation, *State of the Environment: An Assessment at Mid-Decade*, pp. 124-25.

285. Association of State and Interstate Water Pollution Control Administrators, *America's Clean Water*, p. 7.

286. Clark, Haverkamp, and Chapman, *Eroding Soils*, p. 175.

287. U.S. Environmental Protection Agency, Office of Groundwater, *Pesticides in Groundwater: Background Document* (Washington, D.C.: U.S. Environmental Protection Agency, 1986), p. 9.

288. U.S. Environmental Protection Agency, Office of Drinking Water and Office of Pesticide Programs, "Joint Ground-Water Survey," briefing paper, January 22, 1985.

289. California Assembly, Office of Research, *The Leaching Fields: A Nonpoint Threat to Groundwater* (Sacramento: California Joint Publications Office, 1985), p. iii.

290. "Iowa Study Shows 'Systematic Deterioration' of Ground Water Quality Due to Pesticides," *Groundwater Monitor*, April 15, 1986.

291. 40 CFR §261.2, review effective July 5, 1985; and 42 USCA §§6901 et seq. (1983).

292. Franklin Associates, Ltd., *Characterization of Municipal Solid Waste in the United States, 1960 to 2000: Final Report*, prepared for U.S. Environmental Protection Agency, Office of Solid Waste and Emergency Response (Prairie Village, Kan.: Franklin Associates, 1986), pp. 1-1, 1-2.

293. 42 USCA §§9601 et seq. (1983); and 42 USCA §§6901 et seq. (1983).

294. Association of State and Territorial Solid Waste Management Officials, *National Solid Waste Survey* (Washington, D.C.: Association of State and Territorial Solid Waste Management Officials, 1984); and Florida State University, Institute of Science and Public Affairs, Hazardous Waste Management Program, *Proceedings of U.S. EPA Working Meeting Concerning Requirements for the Monitoring and Management of Hazardous Waste at RCRA Subtitle D Facilities*, prepared for the U.S. Environmental Protection Agency (Tallahassee, Fla.: Florida State University, 1985), p. 4.

295. Franklin Associates, *Characterization of Municipal Solid Waste in the United States*, pp. 1-6. 1-8, 1-12, table 1-1.

296. National Solid Wastes Management Association, "Basic Data: Solid Waste Amounts, Composition and Management Systems Technical Bulletin –85-6," October 1, 1985, citing National Solid Wastes Management Association, "NewsFacts," 1984.

297. U.S. Environmental Protection Agency, Office of Solid Wastes and Emergency Responses, *Report to Congress: Wastes from the Extraction and Beneficiation of Metallic Ores, Phosphate Rock, Asbestos, Overburden from Uranium Mining and Oil Shale*, EPA/530-SW-85-033 (Washington, D.C.: U.S. Government Printing Office, 1985), p. ES-6.

298. Ibid., pp. ES-4, ES-5.

299. U.S. Department of Commerce, Bureau of the Census, *Statistical Abstract of the United States 1986* (Washington, D.C.: U.S. Government Printing Office, 1985), p. 710.

300. Ibid., p. 707.

301. 30 USCA §§1201 et seq. (1983).

302. U.S. Department of Commerce, Bureau of the Census, *Statistical Abstract 1986*, p. 707.

303. William Doyle, *Deep Coal Mining Waste Disposal Technology* (Park Ridge, N.J.: Noyes Data Corp., 1976), pp. 165, 312.

304. U.S. Environmental Protection Agency, Office of Research and Development, *Environmental Outlook 1980*, EPA-600/8-80-003 (Washington, D.C.: U.S. Government Printing Office, 1980), p. 585, citing U.S. Environmental Protection Agency, Office of Water and Waste Management, *EPA Activities under the Resource Conservation and Recovery Act: Fiscal Year 1978*, SW-755 (Washington, D.C.: U.S. Government Printing Office, 1979), pp. 1-2; and U.S. Department of Agriculture, *Agricultural Statistics 1985* (Washington, D.C.: U.S. Government Printing Office, 1985), pp. 372, 470.

305. Ibid., pp. 257, 270, 280, 346, and 361.

306. Information provided by Jim Krieder, U.S. Department of Agriculture, Soil Conservation Service, October 1986.

307. Donald Van Dyne and Conrad Gilbertson, *Estimating U.S. Livestock and Poultry Manure and Nutrient Production*, prepared for U.S. Department of Agriculture, Economic Statistics and Cooperative Service, ESCS-12 (Springfield, Va.: National Technical Information Service, 1978), p. 5.

308. U.S. Department of Agriculture, *Agricultural Statistics 1985*, pp. 256, 269, 280.

309. U.S. Environmental Protection Agency, *Environmental Outlook 1980*, p. 583.

310. U.S. Bureau of the Census, *Statistical Abstracts 1986*, p. 675.

311. Utility Solid Waste Activities Group, Edison Electric Institute, and National Rural Electric Cooperative Association, *Report and Technical Studies on the Disposal and Utilization of Fossil-Fuel Combustion By-Products*, vol. 1, prepared for U.S. Environmental Protection Agency (Washington, D.C.: Utility Solid Waste Activities Group, 1982), pp. 18, 21.

312. Ibid.

313. JRB Associates, Inc., *Inventory of Air Pollution Control, Industrial Wastewater Treatment and Water Treatment Sludge*, prepared for U.S. Environmental Protection Agency (McLean, Va.: JRB Associates, Inc., 1983), p. 3-4.

314. Ibid., p. 3-18; and personal communication with Al Rubin, U.S. Environmental Protection Agency, Office of Water, May 1986.

315. *Use and Disposal* of Municipal Wastewater Sludge, 1985; and Richard Goodwin,

"Air Pollution Cleaning Wastes: Dry Versus Wet," *Journal of Energy Engineering* 109, no. 3 (1983):131.

316. JRB Associates, *Inventory of Air Pollution Control*, pp. 3-15 and 5-2.

317. American Coal Ash Association, *Ash at Work* 17, no. 3 (1984):4.

318. Utility Solid Waste Activities Group, Edison Electric Institute, and National Rural Electric Cooperative Association, *Report and Technical Studies on the Disposal and Utilization of Fossil-Fuel Combustion By-Products*, p. 17.

319. U.S. Environmental Protection Agency, *Environmental Outlook 1980*, p. 586.

320. 33 USCA §§1401 et seq. (1983).

321. Franklin Associates, *Characterization of Municipal Solid Waste in the United States*, pp. S-1, S-2.

322. Westat, Inc., *Final Report: National Survey of Hazardous Waste Generators and Treatment, Storage and Disposal Facilities Regulated under RCRA in 1981*, prepared for U.S. Environmental Protection Agency, Office of Solid Waste (Rockville, Md.: Westat, Inc., 1984), p. 49; and Florida State University, *Proceedings of U.S. EPA Working Meeting Concerning Requirements for the Monitoring and Management of Hazardous Waste at RCRA Subtitle D Facilities*, p. 4.

323. Gary Brown, Scotty Fallah, and Cassie Thompson, *Census of State and Territorial Subtitle D Non-Hazardous Waste Programs: Final Report* (Rockville, Md.: Westat, Inc., 1986), appendix A.

324. Association of State and Territorial Solid Waste Management Officials, *National Solid Waste Survey*, p. 42.

325. Brown, Fallah and Thompson, *Census of State and Territorial Subtitle D Non-Hazardous Waste Programs*, p. A-2.

326. New Jersey Department of Environmental Protection, Division of Water Management, *Proposed New Jersey Solid Waste Management Plan Update 1985-2000* (Trenton, N.J.: New Jersey Department of Environmental Protection, 1985), p. 73.

327. Brown, Fallah, and Thompson, *Census of State and Territorial Subtitle D Non-Hazardous Waste Programs*, appendix A.

328. Ibid., p. 49.

329. Peter Steinhart, "Down in the Dumps," *Audubon* 88, no. 3 (1986):107.

330. Personal communication with Jonathan Puth, November 1986.

331. Franklin Associates, *Characterization of Municipal Solid Waste in the United States*, pp. 3-7, 3-9, 3-14, 3-19.

332. National Association of Recycling Industries, Statistical Services, *Annual Review of Scrap Metal for 1984* (New York: National Association of Recycling Industries, 1986); and information provided by National Association of Recycling Industries, August 1986.

333. U.S. Environmental Protection Agency, *Report to Congress: Minimization of Hazardous Waste*, Executive Summary and Fact Sheet (Washington, D.C.: U.S. Environmental Protection Agency, 1986), p. 3.

334. Bureau of National Affairs, "State Solid Waste Management Programs Vary Widely But Face Similar Problems, Such as Capacity, Siting Limits," *BNA Environmental Reporter*, October 3, 1986, p. 845.

335. Franklin Associates, *Characterization of Municipal Solid Waste in the United States*; and U.S. Council on Environmental Quality, *Environmental Quality 1979* (Washington, D.C.: U.S. Government Printing Office, 1979), p. 276.

336. Environmental Planning Lobby, *The Financial and Environmental Impact of Garbage Incineration* (Albany, N.Y.: Environmental Planning Lobby, 1985), p. 2.

337. E. Berenyi and R. Gould, *Resource Recovery Yearbook 1986-1987* (New York: Governmental Advisory Associates, 1986), p. vi.

338. U.S. Environmental Protection Agency, Intra-Agency Sludge Task Force, *Environmental Regulations and Technology: Use and Disposal of Municipal Wastewater Sludge*, EPA-625/10-84-003 (Washington, D.C.: U.S. Environmental Protection Agency, 1984), p. 45.

339. U.S. Environmental Protection Agency, *Wastes from the Extraction and Benefication of Metallic Ores*, pp. 3-5, 3-7, 3-10, and 3-19.

340. Renewable Energy Institute, *Annual Renewable Energy Technology Review: Progress Through 1984* (Washington, D.C.: Renewable Energy Institute, 1986), p. 49.

341. U.S. Environmental Protection Agency, *Environmental Outlook 1980*, p. 583.

342. U.S. Environmental Protection Agency, *Environmental Regulations and Technology*, p. 37; and JRB Associates, *Inventory of Air Pollution Control*, pp. 4-18 and 4-21.

343. EPA Subtitle D draft, 1986, p. 75.

344. U.S. Environmental Protection Agency, *Environmental Regulations and Technology*, p. 10.

345. EPA Subtitle D draft, pp. 67, 69, 70.

346. U.S. Environmental Protection Agency, *Environmental Regulations and Technology*, p. 47.

347. JRB Associates, *Inventory of Air Pollution Control*, pp. 4-18, 4-21.

348. Ibid., p. 4-20.

349. U.S. Environmental Protection Agency, *Environmental Regulations and Technology*, p. 27.

350. Ibid., p. 56.

351. Ibid., p. 56; and U.S. Environmental Protection Agency, Office of Water Regulations and Standards, *Report to Congress January 1981-December 1983 on Administration of the Marine Protection, Research, and Sanctuaries Act of 1972, as Amended (P.L. 92-532) and Implementing the International London Dumping Convention* (Washington, D.C: U.S. Environmental Protection Agency, January 1981-December 1983), pp. 9-10.

352. U.S. Council on Environmental Quality, *Environmental Quality 1979*, p. 162; and U.S. Environmental Protection Agency, *Report to Congress on·Administration of the Marine Protection, Research, and Sanctuaries Act of 1972 and Implementing the International London Dumping Convention*, p. 9.

353. National Ash Association, *Ash at Work*, p. 4.

Figures

2.1. U.S. Environmental Protection Agency, Office of Air Quality Planning and Standards, *National Air Quality and Emissions Trends Report, 1983* (Research Triangle Park, N.C.: U.S. Environmental Protection Agency, 1985), pp. 2-1, 2-2.

2.2–2.6. The final order was determined according to the following criteria: (*a*) in cases when the 1984 data were not given, the final order was based on the 1982 reported data point; (*b*) when one or more cities had similar data points, the city assigned to be first is the one with the largest 1982 value; and (*c*) when concentration for 1982 and 1984 were the same, the city assigned to be first in the list is the one with the highest 1983 value.

U.S. Environmental Protection Agency, Office of Air Quality Planning and Standards, *National Air Quality and Emissions Trends Report, 1984* (Research Triangle Park, N.C.: U.S. Environmental Protection Agency, 1986), pp. 4-8 to 4-55.

2.7. Information provided by U.S. Environmental Protection Agency, Office of Air Quality Planning and Standards, May 1984. Data for ambient trends were taken from EPA's National Aerometric Data Bank (NADB). This information is submitted to EPA by state and local governments and various federal agencies. For a monitoring site to be included in this analysis, the site had to contain at least five out of the seven years of data in the period 1975 to 1982, and each of these years had to satisfy annual data completness criteria. For a more complete discussion of criteria and procedures used to select data for ambient trends, see U.S. Environmental Protection Agency, Office of Air Quality Planning and Standards, *National Air Pollutant Emission Estimates, 1981* (Research Triangle Park, N.C.: U.S. Environmental Protection Agency, 1981), pp. 17-19. Estimates for 1983 and 1984, which are selected on similar criteria, were provided the U.S. EPA's Monitoring and Data Analysis Division at the Research Triangle Park, North Carolina.

2.8. The trend in TSP is adversely affected by an artifact error caused by the manufacture of collection filters by different vendors. For example, the filters used in 1979, 1980, and 1981 were found to record higher values than the filters used in 1978 and 1982. The alkalinity of the 1978 and 1982 filters was found to be similar, so that TSP data for these years should be comparable. U.S. Environmetal Protection Agency, Office of Air Quality Planning and Standards, *National Air Pollutant Emission Estimates 1940-1984* (Research Triangle Park, N.C.: U.S. Environmental Protection Agency, 1986), p. 2; and U.S. Council of Environmental Quality, *Environmental Quality 1984* (Washington, D.C.: U.S. Government Printing Office, 1986), p. 583.

2.9. U.S. Environmetal Protection Agency, *National Air Pollutant Emission Estimates 1940-1984*, pp. 11-15.

2.10. A combination of a change in the ozone standard in 1978 and a recalibration of the monitoring equipment in 1979 accounts for much of the improvement in nonattainment between 1978 and 1983. U.S. Environmental Protection Agency, Office of Management Systems and Evaluation, *Environmental Progress and Challenges: An EPA Perspective* (Washington, D.C.: U.S. Government Printing Office, 1984), p. 16; and U.S. Environmental Protection Agency, Office of Air Quality Planning and Standards *Maps Depicting Nonattainment Areas Pursuant to Section 107 of the Clean Air Act—1985* (Research Triangle Park, N.C.: U.S. Environmental Protection Agency, 1985), p. vi.

2.11. Data for the 1975-1982 period was taken from the following sources: Monitoring and Assessment Research Center, *Air Pollution Concentrations in Selected Urban Areas, 1973-1980*, preliminary report prepared for the United Nations Environmental Programme and the World Health Organization (London: Monitoring and Assessment Research Center, 1983), statistical appendix. Data are annual avarage sulfur dioxide concentrations. Data (same period as above) for selected urban areas from around the world were taken from the UNEP-sponsored Global Environmenal Monitoring System (GEMS). Only data collected from monitoring sites located in central city commercial areas were chosen for the graphic: 19 for SO_2, 20 sites for suspended particulate matter (SPM). Each site had to have representative data for five or more years to be selected. Data from 1973 to 1980 were obtained from The Conservation Foundation, *State of the Environment: An Assessment at Mid-Decade* (Washington, D.C.: The Conservation Foundation, 1984), p.95; New York's estimates were provided by Peter Sattler, New York State Department of Environmental Conservation; and Organization for Economic Cooperation and Development, *OECD Environmental Data—Compendium 1985* (Paris, France: Organization for Economic Cooperation and Development 1985), pp. 26-28.

2.12. U.S. Environmental Protection Agency, Environmental Monitoring Systems Laboratory, *Study of Carbon Monoxide Exposure of Residents of Washington, D.C., and Denver, Colorado* (Research Triangle Park, N.C.: U.S. Environmental Protection Agency, 1984), p. 182.

2.13. U.S. Environmental Protection Agency, *Study of Carbon Monoxide Exposure of Residents of Washington, D.C., and Denver, Colorado*, p. 182.

2.14. U.S. Environmental Protection Agency, *Maps Depicting Nonattainment Areas Pursuant to Section 107 of the Clean Air Act—1985*, pp. 4-207.

2.15. Gordon J. McDonald, *Climate Change and Acid Rain* (McLean, Va.: The MITRE Corporation, 1985), p. 33.

2.16 Air Resources Specialists, Inc., *National Park Service Visibility Monitoring and Data Analysis Project: Winter 1983-Winter 1986*, draft report, vol. 1, prepared for National Park Service, Air Quality Division (Denver, Colorado) (Fort Collins, Colo.: Air Resources Specialists, 1986), unnumbered pages.

2.17. Air Resources Specialists, *National Park Service Visibility Monitoring and Data Analysis Project*.

2.18. World Resources Institute and International Institute for Environment and Development, *World Resources 1986: An Assessment of the Resource Base that Supports the Global Economy* (New York: Basic Books, 1986), p. 319.

2.19. Data from 1860 to 1949 were obtained from William C. Clark, ed., *Atmospheric Concentrations of Carbon Dioxide—Institute for Energy Analysis, Oak Ridge Associated Universities, Carbon Dioxide Review, 1982* (New York: Oxford University Press, 1982), pp. 456-60. Data from B.B. Castow and C.D. Keeling, "Atmospheric Carbon Dioxide Concentration, the Observed Airborne Fraction, the Fossil Fuel Airborne Fraction, and the Difference in Hemispheric Airborne Fractions," in B. Bolen, ed., *SCOPE 16: Global Carbon Modeling* (London: John Wiley and Sons, 1981), p. 434. Data for the 1950-1984 period were obtained from Ralph M. Rotti of the Oak Ridge Associate Universities, Institute for Energy Analysis, through personal communication and his paper, "A Look at 1983 CO_2 Emissions Fossil Fuels," which has been accepted for publication in *Thellus*. Estimates for 1984 are preliminary.

2.20. Rotti, "A Look at 1983 CO_2 Emissions Fossil Fuels."

2.21. Clark, *Mean Global Temperature*, pp. 448-456. To provide a much clear view of future trends, The Conservation Foundation added the arrow indicating projected temperature changes.

2.22. Richard A. Smith, Richard B. Alexander, and M. Gordon Wolman, *Analysis and Interpretation of Water Quality Trends in Major U.S. Rivers, 1974-81*, prepared for U.S. Department of Interior, Geological Survey, Water Supply Paper 2307 (Reston, Va.: U.S. Geological Survey, 1986), p. 11a, table 1.

2.23. U.S. Environmental Protection Agency, Office of Municipal Pollution Control, *1984 Needs Survey Report to Congress: Assessment of Needed Publicly Owned Wastewater Facilities in the United States*, EPA 430/9-84-001 (Washington, D.C.: U.S. Environmental Protection Agency, 1985), tables 12, 14, 15, 16, 19, 26, and 32.

2.24. The Conservation Foundation, *Groundwater Protection* (Washington D.C.: The Conservation Foundation, 1987).

2.25. Franklin Associates, Ltd., *Characterization of Municipal Solid Waste in the United states, 1960 to 2000*, prepared for the U.S. Environmental Protection Agency, Office of Solid Waste and Emergency Response (Prairie Village, Kans.: Franklin Associates, 1986), p. S-4.

Chapter 3

Toxic and Hazardous Pollutants

As the United States progressed in its efforts to control conventional pollutants during the 1970s, it began increasingly to realize that these were not the only pollution problems. Attention increasingly turned to toxic or hazardous substances*—compounds that can cause serious health and environmental damage, even in small amounts. The result was a spate of new laws and amendments to existing laws in the late 1970s—the Toxic Substances Control Act of 1976,[1] the 1976 Resource Conservation and Recovery Act[2] (which established the hazardous waste management program), the Clean Water Amendments of 1977[3] (which established the list of "priority pollutants"), and others.[4]

These initiatives raised a host of new, more difficult problems. There was no readily accepted list of which compounds were toxic. Most had not even been adequately tested for toxicity; the testing process could be long and expensive, and the results ambiguous. Many compounds are difficult and expensive to monitor, particularly at the very low concentrations required to ensure that that they pose no health threat. And traditional pollution abatement technologies are often inadequate for controlling the compounds to the extent necessary—whole new approaches, sometimes involving basic changes in production processes and raw material use, may well be needed.

---

*The terms *toxic* and *hazardous* are essentially synonymous. The same chemical will be called a toxic in one statute (for instance, the Clean Water Act or the Toxic Substances Control Act) and hazardous in another (for instance, the Clean Air Act or the Resource Conservation and Recovery Act).

These types of problems make it difficult to make any general statements about progress in controlling toxic pollutants—either in the past or in the future. Fortunately, many of the traditional pollution control devices, though designed primarily to control conventional pollutants, appear to also reduce toxic discharges. Nevertheless, this reduction is usually not to the extent needed, and much more effort to control toxic pollutants is required.

TOXIC SUBSTANCES

The number of potentially toxic substances is enormous. A registry of chemicals maintained by the Chemical Abstracts Service includes over eight million different chemical substances.[5] Most of these, however, have no current commercial application. The Toxic Substances Control Act (TSCA) Inventory lists over 63,000 chemical substances that have been used commercially since 1975,[6] and the rate at which new chemicals are introduced in the U.S. had risen to nearly 1,500 per year by 1985 (figure 3.1). Counting food additives, pesticides, drugs, cosmetics, and other substances not subject to TSCA brings the total number of commercial substances to approximately 70,000.[7]

Most of these chemicals are not thought of as toxic under normal usage.

Figure 3.1
**Trends in Pre-Manufacture Notifications (PMNs) Received
by the U.S. Environmental Protection Agency, 1979–1985**

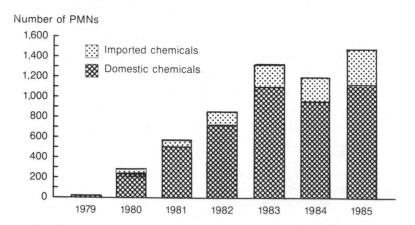

Source: U.S. Environmental Protection Agency.

Some are necessary to life or have been developed to cure illnesses. The National Institute of Occupational Safety and Health Registry of Toxic Substances lists almost 60,000 substances that are known to have toxic effects at some level of exposure.[8] Toxic effects include irritation, mutation, reproductive effects, carcinogenesis, and death. Thus it lists water because people drown in it.

Testing and Regulation

Distressingly little is known about the toxic effects of many chemicals. Manufacturers typically test for acute problems such as skin rashes, eye sensitivity, and immediate mortality of fish, algae, or the insect *Daphnia*. But chronic problems such as cancer, birth defects, and neurological damage are much more difficult to assess.[9] A National Academy of Sciences (NAS) committee evaluated a sample of commercial chemicals to determine the adequacy of the testing done to measure possible human toxicity. It found that fewer than 2 percent of the chemicals had been sufficiently tested to allow a complete health hazard assessment to be made. Sufficient information to support even a partial hazard assessment existed for another 12 percent. Adequate testing was most likely to have been conducted for drugs and pesticides. Even for those substances, however, complete or partial health assessments had been carried out on only about one-third of the chemicals. For most categories, the number of substances lacking any data is much greater than the number for which the data are considered to be minimally adequate. In short, the committee found that, for 70 percent of the substances they reviewed, no information on possible effects on human health existed. For another 16 percent, there was some information, but it was less than the amount needed for even a partial hazard assessment.[10] Chemical industry officials say that the lack of data is exaggerated because the NAS study did not include confidential test data in company files. They also point out that the committee analyzed a randomly selected subset of chemicals, and these may not be the substances in greatest use or providing the most exposure.

The NAS committee also found, however, that the frequency and quality of testing are unrelated either to the production volume or to a given substance's potential toxic effects based on its physiochemical properties (as assessed by the committee). For 20 percent of the substances reviewed, the committee had serious concerns about potential adverse human health effects; for another 32 percent, the committee had moderate concerns.[11]

Moreover, the NAS committee only looked at human health risk. In general, much less information is available on environmental hazards and effects of exposure on wildlife than is available on human health risks.

In part because of this lack of data, the number of substances regulated is quite small in comparison with the total number in use. The U.S. Environmental Protection Agency's (EPA's) regulations implementing the Resource Conservation and Recovery Act (RCRA) identify as hazardous approximately 500 process wastes and specific chemicals,[12] along with any wastes that have the characteristics of ignitability, corrosivity, reactivity, and "EP Toxicity."[13]* As amended in 1977, the Clean Water Act lists 126 chemical compounds as priority pollutants.[14] The 1986 amendments to the Safe Drinking Water Act (SDWA) require EPA to promulgate regulations for some 80 contaminants,[15] in addition to the 20 already regulated.[16] EPA has regulated only 7 substances under the toxic contaminants section of the Clean Air Act.[17]

The use of 4 existing substances (asbestos, PCBs [polychlorinated biphenyls], chlorofluorocarbons, and dioxins)[18] as well as 60 to 70 "new" chemicals has been restricted under TSCA.[19] (Manufacturers withdrew notice to produce another 80-some chemicals that were likely to be restricted.) EPA also has restricted or banned the use of 50-some pesticides under the Federal Insecticide, Fungicide and Rodenticide Act,[20] although all pesticides are also effectively restricted by the terms of their registration. The Occupational Safety and Health Administration (OSHA) adopted 400 existing standards for air contaminants in 1971.[21] Only 23 substances (at least 13 of which were among the original 400) have since been further restricted due to their highly toxic or carcinogenic nature.[22]

EPA continues to assess chemicals that are in use. For instance, scientists and regulators are currently examining tributyl tin (TBT), an organotin used since the mid-1960s, primarily in paint to protect surfaces of ships from the growth of marine organisms. Evidence exists linking TBT to the mortality and morbidity of oysters and other shellfish in waters where numerous vessels are harbored but receive little flushing by tides. TBT is similar to DDT (dichloro-diphenyl-trichloro-ethane) in that it endangers nontarget species and bioaccumulates, although it does biodegrade more completely and to less-toxic by-products.[23]

Monitoring Programs

If little is known about the toxicity of chemical substances, even less is known about the extent of human and environmental exposure. Some informa-

---

*"EP Toxicity" is a term used solely in the RCRA regulation to identify wastes that in specific extraction procedures leach hazardous concentrations of any of 14 contaminants—for example, lindane and mercury.

tion is available on production. The U.S. International Trade Commission, the U.S. Bureau of the Census, the Federal Reserve Board, and some trade associations collect data on imports, exports, and domestic production of many synthetic organic chemicals.[24] The U.S. Bureau of Mines collects information on mineral production and consumption.[25] EPA has 1977 production information for the 63,000 chemicals in the TSCA inventory and is collecting updated information for 15,000 chemicals of greatest concern.[26]

But much less information is available about the extent to which these chemicals exist in the environment. SDWA only requires that public water authorities serving communities over 25 people monitor drinking water for the contaminants regulated under that law. The U.S. Food and Drug Administration (FDA) performs a "Total Diet Study" annually to estimate the U.S. population's dietary intake of some 70 pesticides, industrial chemicals, inorganic compounds, and radionuclides.[27] The U.S. Department of Agriculture is responsible for monitoring antibiotics, pesticide residues, and other substances in meat and poultry.[28] EPA and the states monitor for a few toxic air pollutants,[29] and the U.S. Geological Survey[30] (and some states) monitor for a few toxic surface water pollutants on a widespread basis. But most information on toxic air and water pollution comes from one-time surveys.

Two other periodic surveys provide information on human exposure to toxic substances. Since 1970 EPA has conducted the National Human Adipose Tissue Survey (NHATS) to monitor selected pesticides and certain other toxic substances such as PCBs in human adipose tissue.[31] The National Center for Health Statistics sponsors the National Health and Nutrition Examination Survey (NHANES), which measures levels of lead and some pesticides in human blood and urine, among other health factors.[32] The NHANES results indicate the extent to which the test subjects have recently been exposed to toxic compounds, particularly those that are water soluble. The NHATS results are more indicative of long-term exposure to fat-soluble compounds.[33]

Attempts are being made to establish innovative programs that may take a more integrated approach to monitoring toxic substances. EPA is developing, on an experimental basis, a new strategy to determine total human exposure to environmental pollutants. The methodology is intended to measure pollutant concentrations "at human physical boundaries regardless of whether the pollutants arrive through the air, water, food or skin," by measuring levels of air pollutants in and out of doors and in drinking water.[34] Another human exposure assessment project, the

Human Exposure Assessment Location program (HEAL), has been developed under the Global Environment Monitoring Programme of the United Nations. The goal of HEAL is to improve monitoring procedures in all countries involved and to provide valid information on levels of pollutants in different media and on exposures of populations to these pollutants.[35]

Several states and federal agencies monitor the presence of certain substances in fish and other wildlife. The U.S. Fish and Wildlife Service (FWS) collects and tests representative species of birds and fish for organochlorine chemicals or their metabolites every two or three years. Fish, and occasionally birds, are also monitored for seven metals.[36] In addition, the Ocean Assessments Division of the National Oceanic and Atmospheric Administration (NOAA) has initiated the National Status and Trends Program to quantify the current status and trends of toxic contaminants in U.S. coastal and estuarine environments. Within this program the Benthic Surveillance Project will focus on toxic chemicals in sediments and bottom-dwelling fish at 52 sites. The Mussel Watch component of the program will analyze bivalves from 150 sites nationwide, corresponding where possible to sites formerly sampled by EPA.[37]

Progress in controlling toxic chemicals is impeded by a lack of basic environmental data, a deficit that monitoring programs are designed to correct. Yet the programs have several limitations. First, current monitoring efforts continue to focus on substances, such as PCBs, DDT, and lead, that have attracted interest in the past and are currently regulated. Little is being done to identify other toxic substances that may pose enough risk to the environment to warrant monitoring. Part of this lack of action stems from the costs and time required to test new and existing chemicals for their toxicity. Second, most programs are better suited to measure persistent organochlorines than to measure other potentially toxic, yet rapidly degrading, substances. Third, except for the whole animal and human adipose monitoring programs, most programs focus on only one medium of exposure. Fourth, important gaps exist in information derived through monitoring; data exist concerning emissions or ambient concentrations of toxic substances and concerning the presence of those substances in people, animals, and plants, but little is known about the exact channels through which organisms take in those substances. Finally, no system has been established to coordinate and use all the data that are being generated from all these programs within the United States, let alone the data produced by other countries. Thus, much current information is not used by all agencies involved in toxic pollutant control.

The Japanese have developed a scheme under their Chemical Substances Control Law that attempts to identify chemicals that persist in the environment. In the first phase, they select about 50 chemicals a year that they suspect are persistent and assess their presence in the environment. For those substances they find to be most persistent (10 percent or so), they conduct in-depth surveys to determine how much of each substance actually exists in the environment. In the final phase, they select one or two of the substances every two years for monitoring in wildlife and for an assessment of the effects on humans and the environment.[38] Duplicating such an approach in other countries with the selection processes coordinated would provide some of the exposure information necessary to determine how serious the threat of toxic substances really is.

Organic Chemicals

Many organic (that is, carbon-containing) substances occur naturally in the environment. However, over the last 50 years, tens of thousands of synthetic organic compounds have been introduced as plastics, pesticides, solvents, detergents, medicines, and food additives, as well as for many other commercial purposes. Nearly 225 billion pounds of synthetic organic chemicals were produced in 1985, almost 45 percent more than were produced in 1975.[39]

These organic chemicals have brought many conveniences; indeed, it is hard to imagine what life would be like without them. But many are also potentially toxic. More than 90 percent of the 165 substances listed as potential human carcinogens by the National Toxicology Program are organic compounds.[40] Of the 126 toxic compounds listed as priority pollutants by the Clean Water Act, 110 are organic.[41] Unfortunately, toxicity testing has not kept pace with the rapid development of the synthetic organics industry, and relatively little is known about the extent of exposure to and the risk posed by these chemicals.

Some evidence indicates that some organic chemicals are highly persistent and may bioaccumulate, so that the extent and duration of exposure may be much greater than was originally thought. Organic chemicals are often found in water, sediments, and wildlife far from the source of the chemical and long after the chemical is initially applied. DDT was found to accumulate to detrimental levels in raptors such as bald eagles, brown pelicans, and peregrine falcons,[42] and it is still found in the environment even though EPA banned its use in 1972.[43] Similarly, heptachlor, which was banned for most uses in 1978, still appears in some dairy and meat products,[44] and a metabolite, heptachlor-epoxide, has been detected in human breast milk and adipose tissue (figure 3.2). The Office of Technology Assessment reported in 1984 that about 175 different organic chemicals have been discovered in groundwater supplies,[45] often at levels significantly higher than those found in surface drinking water supplies.[46]

The ability of organic chemicals to spread quickly through the environment was dramatically demonstrated in 1979 when a PCB-containing transformer sprang a small leak in a meat-packing company in Billings, Montana.[47] The scraps from this facility were collected and converted into a supplement for chicken feed. The feed was shipped to poultry farms in six western states, where it was fed to both broilers and laying hens. In the latter case, the PCBs passed through to the eggs and appeared in the newly hatched chicks. By the time the problem was discovered, contaminated eggs and chickens were showing up in at least six states, and millions of eggs, 400,000 chickens, 40,000 pounds of egg products, and about

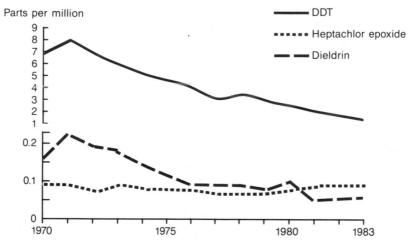

Figure 3.2
Selected Pesticides in Human Adipose Tissue
in the United States, 1970–1983

1972—Most uses of DDT cancelled.
1974—Most uses of Dieldrin cancelled.
1983—Most uses of heptachlor cancelled or registrations denied.

Source: U.S. Environmental Protection Agency.

$280,000 worth of cake mixes had to be destroyed or quarantined. Fortunately, most organic chemicals are not as long-lived as PCBs or DDT.

Pesticides

Some organic chemicals are designed to be toxic. This is the case with the chemicals used as pesticides to control unwanted insects, plants, animals, fungi, and other biological pests. Most pesticides sold commercially combine an "active ingredient," which is designed to kill certain types of pests, with one or more inert ingredients, which dilute or serve as carriers for the toxin. EPA has registered some 1,500 active ingredients, most of which are organic compounds.[48] Formulators mix these compounds with some 900 inert ingredients to create the approximately 50,000 commercial pesticides registered for use in the United States.[49]

Pesticides are, of course, designed to be biologically toxic. If humans are exposed to sufficiently high levels, they can be affected along with the insects, weeds, rodents, or other target organisms the substances are designed to control. Brief high-level exposures to some pesticides can result in acute health effects such as vomiting, dizziness, neurological disorders, or death.[50] Some compounds also are known (or suspected) to cause such problems as cancer, miscarriages, birth defects, neurological damage, sterility, and genetic mutations.[51]

While people handling or manufacturing pesticides are at the greatest risk of exposure, anyone can be exposed via water, food, or air. EPA has the responsibility to set standards ensuring that no exposure levels are high enough to cause health or environmental problems. They have suspended, canceled, or restricted 50-some pesticides, most of them organic.[52] However, as a 1986 General Accounting Office document reported, none of the older pesticide active ingredients have been fully tested and assessed for their health and environmental effects.[53] And the potential toxicity of some inert pesticide ingredients (for example, formaldehyde and carbon tetrachloride) has, until recently, largely been overlooked. EPA predicts that at its current pace, the process of reviewing older pesticides (called "reregistration") will extend past the year 2000.[54]

U.S. pesticide production increased rapidly until 1975 (figure 3.3). Through the 1950s, insecticides were the most common type of pesticide, led by DDT and other organochlorines, which were a group of synthetic, broad-spectrum pesticides providing long-lasting protection. They did not degrade rapidly and required few applications. DDT production rose from 78 million pounds in 1950 to a peak of 179 million pounds in 1963. However, insects began developing a resistance to this chemical, stimulating the development of substitutes such as dieldrin, aldrin, and heptachlor.[55] The publication of *Silent Spring* in 1962, however, brought widespread attention to how these insecticides were causing widespread damage to wildlife. As a result, emphasis has more recently been placed on developing alternatives, such as carbamates and organophosphates, which are highly toxic when first applied but break down rapidly. Because they are more toxic than earlier compounds, smaller amounts need to be used for each application. Thus, the decreasing trends in the amounts of pesticides produced after 1975 indicated in figure 3.3 do not necessarily indicate a reduction in the amount of chemical insect control. They may only indicate the shift to more toxic compounds and reduced exports of both pesticides and agricultural products.

The other major change in pesticide use has been the reliance on herbicides (figure 3.3). From 1960 to 1980, herbicide production increased almost 700 percent as chemicals replaced mechanical removal of weeds,[56] with atrazine and 2,4-D [2,4-(dichlorophenoxy)acetic acid] accounting for much of the increase. In 1982 that steady increase was reversed as production declined. Herbicide production again began to increase in 1984, but has remained below the peak levels attained in 1981.

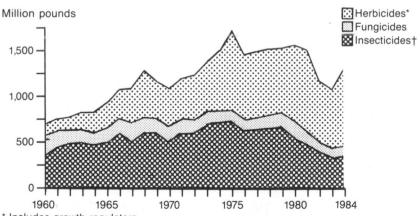

Figure 3.3
U.S. Production of Pesticides, by Type,
1960–1984

* Includes growth regulators.
† Includes rodenticides, soil conditioners, and fumigants.

Source: U.S. International Trade Commission.

Most of the pesticides (85 percent of the herbicides and 70 percent of the insecticides in 1981) used in U.S. agriculture are applied to four crops: corn, cotton, soybeans, and wheat.[57] The downward trend in pesticide production after 1980 reflects decreased production of these crops as well as the generally poor economic conditions in U.S. agriculture (see chapter 6). The sharp jump in 1984 (17 percent in total pesticide production) may indicate that these decreases are only temporary.[58]

Not all pesticides are used on agricultural lands (figure 3.4). Nonfarm uses include weed and pest control by households, government, and commercial institutions. These uses may be a significant source of human and environmental exposure, particularly to some compounds for which agricultural use has been restricted.

In 1985, almost one-quarter of all pesticides were used for such non-agricultural purposes (figure 3.5). (This figure includes wood preservatives, disinfectants, and sulfur pesticides, which total 1.5 billion pounds.)[59] As an example of the importance of nonfarm use, no chlordane and only 5.9 million pounds of toxaphene (both organochlorine pesticides) were applied to agricultural lands in 1982 because of EPA restrictions. However, 9.6 million pounds of chlordane and 10.1 million pounds of toxaphene were used for purposes other than agricultural pest control.[60] And significantly more malathion and diazinon (both organophosphates) and 2-4-D went for off-farm than for farm uses in 1982.[61]

Government agencies carry out environmental monitoring for only a few of the many pesticides currently in use. Most of these are compounds whose use has already been restricted or banned by EPA. Even so, the monitoring demonstrates how widespread and persistent some of these compounds can become. On a more positive note, the monitoring results also demonstrate that regulatory action can effectively and dramatically reduce the environmental levels of such substances.

The primary source of monitoring information is the testing for pesticide residues in food carried out by FDA and the Department of Agriculture. FDA studies of pesticide residues in typical adult diets show a decline since 1965 in the average daily intake of the organochlorines DDT and dieldrin, most uses of which were canceled in the mid-1970s. The average daily intake of toxaphene, which as the major substitute for DDT was the most heavily used insecticide in the United States from the 1960s to the mid-1970s,[62] increased over the period 1965-1982 (figure 3.6). Annual infant diet studies show similar decreases, although the levels are generally higher (in terms of micrograms of pesticide residue per kilogram of body weight) than in the adult diet.[63]

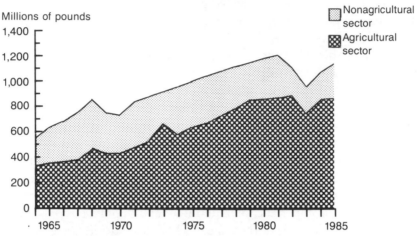

Figure 3.4
U.S. Pesticide Usage, by Sector,
1964–1985*

* Excludes wood preservatives, disinfectants and sulfur, which total
  1,500 million pounds.

Source: U.S. Environmental Protection Agency.

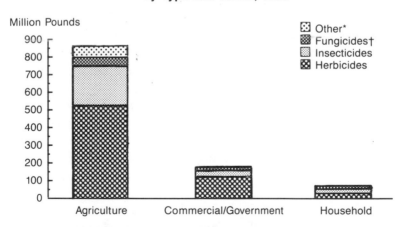

Figure 3.5
Use of Pesticides,
by Type and Sector, 1985

* Includes rodenticides, fumigants, and molluscicides.
† Does not include wood preservatives.

Source: U.S. Environmental Protection Agency.

The National Human Adipose Tissue Surveys, which can monitor for pesticides soluble in human fatty tissue, demonstrate widespread exposure to many pesticides but similarly declining body burden levels for those whose uses have been restricted (figure 3.2). Over 95 percent of the samples analyzed show residues of DDT and chlordane/heptachlor at declining levels and aldrin/dieldrin at a constant level.[64] A 1976 Canadian study on pesticide residues in human adipose tissue shows similar levels.[65]

The National Health and Nutrition Examination Survey II (NHANES II) data on levels of pesticides in urine show more recent exposure to chemicals. Pentachlorophenol, a wood preservative, was found in 79 percent of all samples. Residues of carbamate and organophosphate pesticides were found in generally fewer than 10 percent of urine samples.[66]

Figure 3.6
Adult Dietary Intake of Selected Organic Chemicals,
1965–1985*

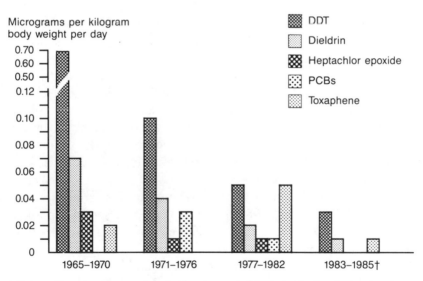

* Data points represent average intake over stated period. Missing data points indicate either unidentified analytical responses, or values less than 0.005 micrograms per kilogram body weight per day.

† Methodology for estimating average diet was different in the 1983–1985 period.

Source: U.S. Food and Drug Administration.

The limited environmental monitoring conducted generally substantiates the results of the human exposure studies—widespread though declining exposure. FWS found chlordane-related compounds in 54 percent of starlings in 1982 and at more than 90 percent of fish monitoring stations in the late 1970s and early 1980s. Toxaphene was found at 88 percent of fish monitoring stations in the early 1980s, up from 60 percent in the late 1970s.[67]

These surveys also have found pesticides such as DDT and dieldrin years after they were regulated, although at substantially reduced levels. But regional differences are marked. Birds from the eastern and western states continue to show more contamination than those from the interior.[68] Toxaphene levels increased noticeably in fish until 1976 and have remained constant since then, reflecting the heavy use of the pesticide, especially in the southern and midwestern United States.[69] In some cases, however, the changing exposure levels may reflect unexpected ways in which pesticides can travel through the environment. Toxaphene data suggest that it, like DDT, may be atmospherically transported and deposited far from where it is applied.[70] Studies of the Great Lakes also suggest large-scale atmospheric deposition.[71]

Preliminary results from the first year of NOAA's nationwide Benthic Surveillance Project (1984) indicated that chlorinated pesticides such as DDT occur in relatively low concentrations in bottom sediment and bottom-dwelling fish at the majority of sites tested. In some areas, however, such as the northeastern Atlantic Coast, relatively high levels have been found. The southern California marine ecosystem continues to have the highest concentrations of DDT (in sediments, 19 times greater than the maximum level found outside of California; in fish, 3 times greater), despite the fact that the source of contamination, a major chemical manufacturing facility, ceased discharging in 1970.[72]

The U.S. Geological Survey's (USGS's) Pesticide Monitoring Network (maintained from 1975 to 1980) shows similarly widespread exposure. Residues of dieldrin, chlordane, and DDT were found at nearly one-third of all sediment sampling stations and at fewer than 5 percent of the water-sampling stations. The herbicide atrazine was found in 24 percent of the water sampling stations. Organophosphates such as diazinon and methyl parathion, which degrade rapidly, were found at fewer than 10 percent of the water stations and at none of the sediment stations.[73]

EPA is undertaking two surveys of pesticides in the environment—one a nationwide survey of 70 pesticides in groundwater (and 90 additional detectable residues)[74] and the second a study of the highly toxic compound dioxin in fish.[75] However, the results of these surveys are not yet available. EPA's survey of pesticides in groundwater begins with a pilot project in the states of California, Minnesota, and Mississippi in March 1987. The survey is scheduled to test about 1,500 wells throughout the United States and should be completed by mid-1989.[76]

PCBs

PCBs, among the most stable compounds known, were used extensively until the 1970s as insulating fluids in electrical transformers and capacitors and in the manufacture of plastics, hydraulic fluids, lubricants, and inks. They cause such acute effects as skin rashes, vomiting, abdominal pain, and temporary blindness and are suspected of causing birth defects, miscarriages, and cancer.[77]

Because of concern over these health effects, producers agreed to limit the sale of PCBs in 1971, and Congress prohibited production completely in 1976 with TSCA.[78] However, a substantial portion of all PCBs ever produced remain in transformers, capacitors, and other electrical equipment throughout the United States.[79]

Before the toxicity and persistence of PCBs were understood, the chemical was commonly disposed of by dumping it into sewers or onto land. The bed of the upper Hudson River and Lake Michigan's Waukegan Harbor still contain large PCB concentrations, which bottom-dwelling fish pick up, making the fish unsafe to eat.[80] PCBs also slowly evaporate from landfills; air deposition is probably the largest source of PCBs entering Lake Superior and possibly the other Great Lakes.[81] However, few attempts have been made to monitor PCBs in the air or water, and hence no data on the change in levels over time are available.

A substantial decline in PCB levels from the early 1970s, with minor fluctuations up and down over the past decade, is shown by the FDA diet studies (figure 3.6). The FDA data reveal virtually no PCBs in most food products in which the chemical is expected to accumulate. Furthermore, PCB levels in the United States are substantially lower than those reported by other countries.[82]

Several wildlife-monitoring programs show that PCB concentrations have decreased since 1970, although the trends have not all been consistent.[83] In some samples, residues have increased. Exposure remains high: 83 percent of starlings sampled in both 1979 and 1982 contained detectable levels of PCBs.[84] The data from mallard ducks demonstrate some geographical differences. Ducks from the heavily populated and industrialized Atlantic Flyway show both the greatest frequency of detection (100 percent) and the highest PCB residues; the concentrations there are more than twice those in waterfowl in the Central Flyway.[85] No data are available to indicate the PCB trends in mussels either nationally or in California. California's Mussel Watch Program concentrated instead on identifying PCB "hot spots"—typically in the harbors of industrial cities.[86]

Measurements of PCBs in humans show patterns similar to those for wildlife—generally decreasing trends for the concentrations of PCBs in human fat, but an increase in the proportion of samples found to contain the substance.[87] By 1981, PCBs were being found in virtually every sample tested. The increased frequency of detection may be partially explained by improved analytical methods, but it also reflects the way in which such a persistent chemical gradually works its way through various physical, chemical, and biological cycles until it appears everywhere.

Inorganic Chemicals

Unlike the large number of synthetic organic toxic substances, many inorganic toxic compounds such as lead, asbestos, and radon occur naturally. The selenium compounds poisoning wildlife in California's Kesterson reservoir result from the weathering of the Coastal Range mountains.[88] Radon, which causes an estimated 5,000 to 20,000 cases of lung cancer a year from indoor air pollution, is released from the soils these houses are built on.[89]

But many toxic inorganic chemicals also enter the environment as a result of the mining, processing, and use of these substances. Industries may produce more toxic forms of naturally occurring inorganic elements in the manufacturing process. In the case of selenium, the above-mentioned erosion would pose little risk were it not for irrigation activities that dissolve the selenium in the soil and carry it to Kesterson reservoir.

The Clean Water Act identifies 16 inorganic substances as priority pollutants: 14 metals, cyanide, and asbestos.[90] The RCRA regulations identify 8 metals as contaminants demonstrating EP Toxicity.[91] EPA has identified 5 inorganic substances as toxic pollutants under the Clean Air Act[92] and has issued standards for 10 such compounds (including nitrate and fluoride) under SDWA.[93]

Toxic Metals

Few monitoring studies include inorganic contaminants. FDA analyzes the dietary intake of six toxic metals: lead, selenium, cadmium, zinc, arsenic, and mercury (figure 3.7). Adult intakes of these metals stabilized or declined somewhat between 1976 and 1982, while infant diets showed increasing

Figure 3.7
Dietary Intake of Metals, 1976–1982

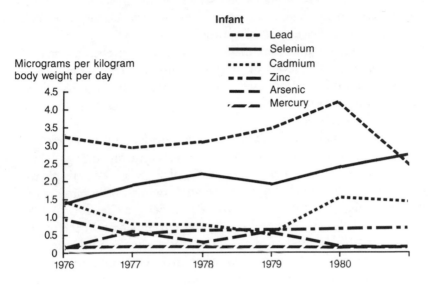

Infant

- - - - Lead
——— Selenium
· · · · · · Cadmium
- · - · Zinc
— — Arsenic
·—— Mercury

Micrograms per kilogram
body weight per day

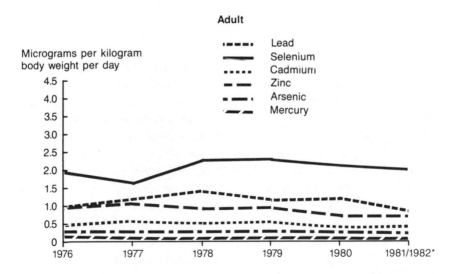

Adult

·—·—· Lead
——— Selenium
· · · · · Cadmium
— — Zinc
—·—· Arsenic
·—— Mercury

Micrograms per kilogram
body weight per day

* Only one study was performed during 1981 and 1982.

Source: U.S. Food and Drug Administration.

trends for selenium and cadmium. From 1976 to 1986, FWS analyzed fish for seven toxic metals: arsenic, cadmium, copper, lead, mercury, selenium, and zinc. Average concentrations of arsenic, cadmium, lead, selenium, and zinc decreased only slightly during this period, while mercury remained the same. Only copper decreased significantly.[94]

USGS monitors for nine trace metals in major U.S. rivers. During the period 1974-1981, the levels of arsenic, cadmium, chromium, iron, manganese, and mercury increased at more sampling stations than they decreased, whereas lead, selenium, and zinc decreased at more stations than they increased (see chapter 2).[95]

EPA and some states and localities are monitoring air for the trace metals arsenic, beryllium, cadmium, copper, chromium, manganese, molybdenum, nickel, vanadium, and zinc.[96] Only lead (as a "criteria pollutant") and mercury, beryllium, asbestos, and arsenic (as "hazardous air pollutants") are currently regulated by EPA under the Clean Air Act.[97]

Although all of these substances are of concern, much of the attention in recent years has focused on three—lead, cadmium, and asbestos.

Lead. Lead is a toxic metal that can, when ingested or inhaled in large amounts, cause convulsions, anemia, and neurological and renal (kidney) disorders; chronic exposure can cause anemia, convulsions, kidney damage, and brain damage.[98] The primary uses of lead are in automobile batteries, gasoline additives, and pigments and paints. Humans are primarily exposed to lead in food and air, although people living in older buildings may also be exposed via lead-based paint applied years before.

Use of lead in the United States gradually increased up to the early 1970s, but since then it has decreased over 40 percent[99]—primarily because of regulations limiting the lead content in gasoline and the reduced manufacture of lead-based paints. In the United States, approximately 675,000 children between six months and five years old (4 percent of that age group) have high levels of lead in their blood.[100] (Older children and adults tend to have lower blood-lead levels and less risk of physiological impairments.)

Air quality data from 92 urban monitoring sites in 11 states reveal a substantial decline (64 percent) in average ambient concentrations of lead between 1977 and 1982.[101] The decline parallels the reduced use of lead in gasoline, which plummeted 78 percent between 1970 and 1985 as a result of federal regulations.[102] This decline is expected to continue for the next few years as older cars using leaded gasoline are no longer used and as lead concentrations are reduced in leaded gasoline in response to existing EPA requirements. EPA estimates that car emissions were responsible for more than 50 percent of the average American's blood lead level in the late 1970s.[103]

Excessive lead in surface water also seems to be diminishing. Monitoring by USGS shows that lead levels decreased significantly in U.S. rivers between 1974 and 1981. The only increases were found in the Gulf Coast of Texas and the Lower Mississippi basin[104] (see chapter 2). These trends were confirmed by a study of bottom deposits in 40 lakes in the Northeast. After increasing exponentially over the past 100 years, the deposition of lead in bottom sediments began to level off or decline in the late 1970s.[105]

However, an EPA-sponsored study has indicated that lead levels in homes may be high even though the water supply contains little lead.[106] The reason is that water can dissolve lead from the solder used to join water pipes together within buildings. The problem appears to be most likely to occur in buildings less than a few years old (the available lead is eventually all leached out of the solder) and where the water is somewhat acidic. The highest lead levels occur after the water has been sitting in the pipes for a while—for instance, when the water is first turned on in the morning.

According to FDA, lead levels in the human diet have generally declined. Adult diets have shown steady declines since the late 1970s, but infant diets only began to show a marked decline in the early 1980s.[107]

Cadmium. Cadmium is a heavy metal found in various chemical forms throughout the environment. It accumulates in the body and primarily affects the kidneys, which normally contain about one-third of the accumulated metal, and the liver.[108] Commercial use of cadmium for paint pigments, additives for rubber and plastics, batteries, catalysts, antiseptics, and fungicides expanded rapidly during the 1940s and fluctuated thereafter.

The general population in the United States is exposed to cadmium mainly through food and cigarette smoke. Direct air and water exposures total less than 10 percent. Tobacco, leafy green vegetables, and some root crops and potatoes are major sources of cadmium because they rapidly take up cadium from the soil. Cadmium accumulates in soil through routes such as phosphate fertilizers, sludge application, and air deposition.[109]

Measurements of cadmium in air are few, and none indicates trends over time. About 10 percent of USGS's water quality monitoring stations detect statistically significant increasing cadmium trends; about 2 percent show decreasing trends in water; the rest report no significant trend.[110]

The adult total-diet studies, by contrast, reveal a decline over the past decade in the amount of cadmium contained in food.[111] The estimated average daily intake in the United States is about half of the acceptable level determined by the Joint Food and Agriculture Organization/World Health Organization Expert Committee on Food Additives.[112] Japan, Guatemala, and Canada report somewhat higher levels of dietary intake than the United States, while New Zealand and Hungary report lower levels. The differences are unexplained.

Only two wildlife programs report any monitoring for cadmium, and only California's Mussel Watch Program provides time-series data.[113] These data, however, demonstrate no significant trend.

United Nations blood analyses show that residents of the United States have among the lowest cadmium levels of the countries included in the survey. India is the only other country with levels as low; Mexico and Yugoslavia show the highest levels—over three times the U.S. average. Although the survey offers no explanation for these differences, the importance of smoking is clear: smokers show 1.2 to 9 times as much cadmium as nonsmokers.[114]

An analysis of cadmium levels in European countries, Japan, and the United States shows that diets in the United Kingdom, Sweden, and Finland have the lowest cadmium levels. The United States is in the middle range for cadmium intake. The highest levels were reported in West Germany, Czechoslovakia, and Romania—approximately twice that of the United States.[115] The degree and type of industrialization in these countries may contribute to the higher levels, as the cadmium concentrations in the air and the amount of cadmium deposited on land are higher in industrial than in nonindustrial areas.[116]

Asbestos

Asbestos—a generic group of naturally occurring fibrous minerals that are nonflammable, heat resistant, durable, flexible, and strong—was first used in the United States in the early 1900s as a thermal insulator for steam engines and later as fireproofing and insulating material[117] Due to its serious adverse health effects, asbestos use is declining rapidly, but it is still used for brake and clutch linings, furnace and kiln linings, some paper and plastic products, cement, plaster, paints, plumbing supplies, and roofing and flooring tiles.

Asbestos, however, is one of the few substances with essentially irrefutable evidence demonstrating that it causes cancer in humans. When inhaled by humans, asbestos fibers stick in and damage the lungs. At high exposure levels, this inhalation can cause asbestosis, a chronic lung disease.[118] After 20 to 40 years, a form of cancer called mesothelioma, which affects the lining of the chest or abdomen, may develop. This type of cancer is only known to occur in people exposed to airborne asbestos. The length of the latency period varies with the amount and duration of exposure, but asbestos-induced mesotheliomas can occur after even relatively short, low-dose exposure.

Although asbestos-caused illnesses were first related primarily to occupational exposure (people working in World War II shipyards were at particularly high risk), recent concern centers on exposures experienced by the general population and in particular by schoolchildren.[119] Deteriorating structures, especially school buildings, are a particularly dangerous exposure source because age and physical damage can disperse asbestos fibers into the air. Exposed children are at greatest risk because of the relatively long average latency between exposure to asbestos fibers and the development of asbestos-induced disease.[120]

Some of the highest asbestos concentrations have been found in schoolrooms.[121] About nine out of every one million people can expect to develop lung cancer from a lifelong exposure to typical asbestos levels in outdoor air. But the risks increase over sixfold if people spend their school days in classrooms with deteriorating asbestos surfaces.[122]

EPA and the U.S. Department of Health, Education and Welfare (now the Departments of Health and Human Services and of Education) created a program in early 1979 to help schools identify (and if necessary correct) crumbling asbestos construction materials.[123] An estimated 15 million children and 1.4 million school workers are in schools containing friable asbestos. In 1982, EPA issued a regulation requiring all public and private schools to inspect their buildings for asbestos problems by June 1983. An EPA survey indicated that 93 percent of U.S. schools had been inspected as of January 1, 1984. One-third were found to have asbestos problems, and two-thirds of those had undertaken actions to correct the problems.[124] A Government Accounting Office study found asbestos in over half of the schools it reviewed.[125] In 1986, Congress passed an amendment to TSCA, the Asbestos Hazard Emergency Response Act, requiring all schools to inspect for asbestos-containing materials and to develop and implement plans to control the threat of asbestos.[126]

Another concern is that workers may be exposed to hazardous levels of asbestos when removing or working on asbestos-containing material in old buildings. In 1986, OSHA promulgated standards for any construction activity involving exposure to asbestos. EPA issued regulations that extend protection for asbestos-abatement workers.[127]

Asbestos is another substance for which the monitoring programs provide no information on the extent or intensity of exposure. The problem in measurement in this case is not that the substance is volatile. It is not. The problems are that asbestos is difficult to detect other than in the air and that it has no demonstrated harm except when inhaled.

Regulatory Dilemmas

The dilemma of what should be done about the substantial numbers and widespread use of potentially toxic substances in the modern world has substantial economic, social, political, and public health implications. Some of these substances provide significant benefits to modern societies; prohibiting their use could lower what people perceive to be their quality of life. Restricting some could cause significant economic impacts, and the people likely to be affected are understandably concerned. In the case of asbestos, these concerns may even influence our international relations because Canada is a major source of asbestos for the United States, and the primary producers are owned by the government of Quebec.

The tradeoffs are not easy. Asbestos brake linings are apparently more effective on existing cars than any available substitute. The tradeoff then is between higher cancer risk for the workers manufacturing and repairing these linings and the safety of the motoring public, who might be involved in more accidents if the substitutes were used. Similarly, the use of PCBs reduces the risk of transformer fires, and the use of certain pesticides and food additives may decrease the risk of diseases.

The longer these chemicals continue to be manufactured and used, however, the more difficult the problem of cleaning them up is likely to become. Thus, any decisions regarding their use need to consider not only present conditions, but future costs and health risks as well.

HAZARDOUS WASTES

When disposed of on land, wastes containing potentially harmful substances are called "hazardous."* It used to be thought that land disposal of these wastes was reasonably safe, based on the implicit assumption that the substances would either degrade into harmless products or at least stay where they were put. Both assumptions were wrong. Many of the wastes do not degrade, degrade very slowly, or degrade into substances that also are hazardous. Nor do the wastes stay put. Instead, they seep into groundwater or are moved by wind or storm water and floods to other locations.

---

*As with toxic substances, a waste's "hazard" is a matter of regulatory and legislative definition.

The sad lesson has been learned: such wastes can create substantial risks for people and the environment long after their disposal. Some of the substances in the wastes can cause birth defects, cancer, genetic damage, neurological effects, or liver damage, to name a few dangers. It is hard to estimate exposure to wastes and to link this exposure to specific effects. However, under the 1986 amendments to Superfund, health assessments will be made at sites on the National Priority List.[128] These assessments should provide better information on the extent to which people are actually at risk.

In the past year, residents in several areas have succeeded in obtaining compensation from companies for health effects attributed to exposure to waste. In August 1986, a U.S. district court ordered Velsicol Chemical Company to pay more than $12.7 million to about 100 residents of Hardeman County, Tennessee. The judge held the company liable for compensatory damages for residents who could demonstrate personal health effects (for example, blurred vision and kidney and liver damage) from any of 15 chemicals (including carbon tetrachloride and benzene) that leached from a hazardous waste landfill into the groundwater that they used for drinking and washing. He also awarded punitive damages.[129] The case is being appealed. In September 1986, W. R. Grace and Company settled out of court for about $8 million in response to claims that the company's contamination of drinking water in Woburn, Massachusetts, was responsible for six leukemia deaths.[130]

Experience in attempting to manage hazardous waste under RCRA[131] and to clean it up under the Comprehensive Environmental Response, Compensation and Liability Act (CERCLA) of 1980[132] when it has not been disposed of properly has demonstrated the difficulties of preventing these wastes from causing significant risks. As a result, Congress adopted far-reaching changes to these two major waste laws in the Hazardous and Solid Waste Amendments of 1984 (HSWA)[133] and the Superfund Amendments and Reauthorization Act (SARA) of 1986.[134]

Both sets of amendments enact complex measures to shift waste management practices toward long-term prevention of damage to health and the environment by encouraging waste reduction and the use of treatment and incineration as opposed to land disposal. HSWA limits the types of wastes that can be managed on land and requires extensive protective measures such as the use of liners and groundwater monitoring at landfills and surface impoundments. It also expands the types of wastes and number of generators covered by the hazardous waste system. SARA requires that priority be given to cleanup methods that reduce the toxicity, mobility, and volume of waste rather than transfer it to another land disposal facility or try to contain it.[135] In addition, information on wastes used and released into the environment will be reported by waste generators and much of this information will be available to nearby residents.[136]

The new legislation changes the wastes that are considered hazardous and the required methods of storage, treatment, and disposal. For this and other reasons, the currently available data are not adequate to identify trends.

Generation of Hazardous Waste

Industries in the United States generate at least 2,400 pounds of hazardous waste (wet weight) per person annually,[137] including some non-RCRA-regulated wastes such as PCBs and industrial scrubber sludges. This estimate, however, does not include wastes from companies generating fewer than 1,000 kilograms a month, waste from cleaning up Superfund sites, or hazardous waste that is also nuclear, agricultural, or mining waste.[138]

Three major studies of hazardous waste generation completed between 1984 and 1986 generally agree on the total amount of waste generated, although they differ substantially in how the estimates were made. A 1985 Congressional Budget Office (CBO) estimate of 266 million metric tons (mmt) in 1983 is based on employment data.[139] A 1984 report done for EPA by Westat extrapolated a figure of 264 mmt in 1981 from a sample of hazardous waste generators.[140]* And a 1986 estimate by the Chemical Manufacturers Association (CMA) of 247 mmt in 1984 is the total amount reported in a survey of 725 plants in the chemical industry; 99.4 percent of this amount was wastewater, most of which is not regulated under RCRA.[142] As the General Accounting Office has noted, if the CMA estimate were extrapolated to other generators of hazardous waste, the result "could be significantly greater."[143]

The apparent consistency among these studies is a significant departure from earlier studies (figure 3.8). Six major studies over the past eight years have estimated the amount of hazardous waste at anywhere from 41 to 266 mmt. A major reason for the discrepancies was the difference in the types of wastes included in the estimates. This variation is likely to continue in the future as the definition of what constitutes a hazardous waste

---

*Two contractors are verifying for EPA the data submitted by the states for the 1985 biennial survey to obtain more reliable estimates than the 1981 and 1983 biennial reports provided. Future survey forms will be coordinated with the reporting releases required under SARA.[141]

Figure 3.8
Volume of Hazardous Waste Generated
in the United States: Six Estimates

Estimate in million metric tons	Explanation
56	Environmental Protection Agency (EPA) estimate (circa 1978) of volume of hazardous waste likely to be generated in 1980; 61 percent expected to come from industrial sources.
41	EPA contractor estimate in 1980 of industrial hazardous waste likely to be generated that year, with possible range set between 28 and 54 million metric tons.
250	Office of Technology Assessment (OTA) estimate in 1983 based on survey of states. If all states and territories were included, OTA suggests annual generation might range between 255 and 275 million tons.
264	EPA contractor estimate of hazardous waste in 1984 that was generated in 1981. Preliminary estimate was 150 million tons. Difference is due to difficulty of sampling because a few large plants generated and managed very large amounts of waste.
266	Congressional Budget Office (CBO) estimate of hazardous waste generated in 1983. Based on model tracking 24 types of waste produced by 70 largest waste-generating industries. Waste oils, PCBs, and industrial sludges and some other wastes besides those regulated under RCRA.
247	Chemical Manufacturers Association (CMA) estimate in 1984 based on a survey of 725 chemical plants.

continues to change. Among the continuing questions is whether or not to include wastes that are being recycled. EPA has decided not to regulate recycled oil as a hazardous waste,[144] at least in part out of fear that to do so would result in this waste being disposed of illegally.[145] The amount of waste handled illegally is not included in any of the estimates.

Estimates of the numbers of hazardous waste generators, the contributions of different industries to the total amount of hazardous waste generated, and the location of the generators also depend on the definition of hazardous waste used. The inclusion of generators of between 100 and 1,000 kilograms of waste per month under the 1984 amendments to RCRA has greatly increased the number of companies in the regulatory system. As of April 1986, an EPA report estimated the number of small-quantity generators to be about 125,000. About 63,000 generators of larger quantities of hazardous waste were already in the system.[146]

According to CBO, the chemical and allied products industries accounted for about 48 percent of the total industrial hazardous waste in 1983; metal-related industries for 28 percent; petroleum and coal products industries for 12 percent; and all other industries for 13 percent (figure 3.9).[147] Non-manufacturing industries, such as vehicle maintenance and construction, constituted 85 percent of the small-quantity generators. Manufacturing industries accounted for the remaining 15 percent (figure 3.10).[148] EPA estimates that small companies generate a total of 940,000 metric tons of hazardous waste annually, or less than 1 percent of the total.[149]

Figure 3.11 shows the distribution of the large-quantity generators. About 20 percent of those estimated to be in operation in 1985 were located in New York and New Jersey, and another 20 percent were situated in EPA's Region V. Region VIII had the smallest number.[150] How much hazardous waste a state generates is related to the degree of industrial activity.[151] In 1983, the petroleum refining and chemical industries helped to make Texas the country's largest generator, accounting for 13 percent of the national total (figure 3.12). Ohio, whose main industries are chemical and metal products, ranked second, with 7.4 percent. Pennsylvania, California, Illinois, Louisiana, New Jersey, Michigan, and Tennessee were responsible for about 5 percent each.[152]

Figure 3.9
Distribution of Industrial Hazardous Waste Generation,
by Major Industrial Group, 1983

(thousand metric tons)

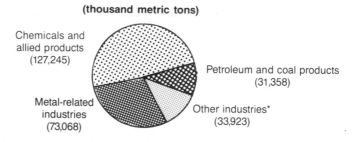

Chemicals and allied products (127,245)

Petroleum and coal products (31,358)

Metal-related industries (73,068)

Other industries* (33,923)

* Includes rubber and plastic products, miscellaneous manufacturing, motor freight transportation, wood preserving, drum reconditioning industries, nonelectrical machinery, transportation equipment, and electric and electronic machinery.

Source: Congressional Budget Office.

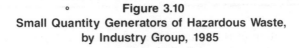

Figure 3.10
Small Quantity Generators of Hazardous Waste,
by Industry Group, 1985

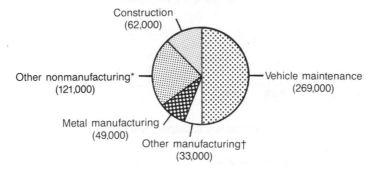

* Includes laundries, photographic processors, equipment repair shops, laboratories and schools.
† Includes printing, chemical manufacturing and formulating, furniture, and textile manufacturing.

Source: U.S. Environmental Protection Agency.

Population is also correlated with the generation of waste. Six of the most densely populated states—Texas, Pennsylvania, Illinois, Ohio, Michigan, and New Jersey—are also among the top 15 hazardous waste generating states in the United States. In terms of population density and the amount of waste generation, residents of the states of New Jersey, Rhode Island, Connecticut, and Massachusetts could be exposed to the highest levels of risk. New Jersey and Rhode Island, for example, are the states with the highest generation per square kilometer, 642 and 556 metric tons, respectively. In Louisiana, West Virginia, Tennessee, and Texas, more than 2 metric tons are generated for each state resident, about twice the average amount (figure 3.13).[153]

Some newly industralizing countries may generate more hazardous wastes per square kilometer than the United States (figure 3.14).[154] The risks there are probably very high because, not only are large amounts of hazardous waste apparently generated in small areas,* but also little care is used in disposing of the wastes properly. As a consequence, residents of countries such as South Korea, Israel, and Spain may face fairly high levels of exposure to hazardous waste.[156]

---

*Two clear examples are Brazil (which has over 90 percent of its hazardous waste generation concentrated in three states, Sao Paulo, Rio de Janeiro, and Minas Girais) and Mexico (where two-thirds of the generation is found within 40 miles of Mexico City).[155]

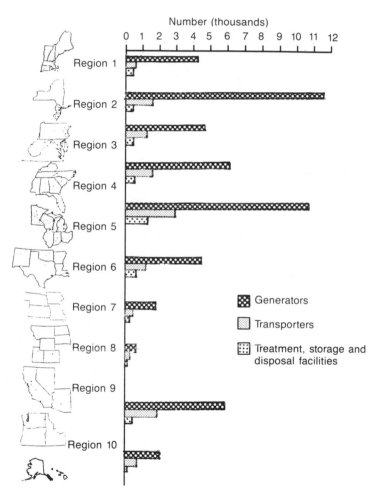

Figure 3.11
Distribution of Hazardous Waste Generators, Transporters,
and Management Facilities, by EPA Region, 1985*

* Does not include small generators (i.e., those generating less than 1000 kilograms per month).

Source: U.S. Environmental Protection Agency.

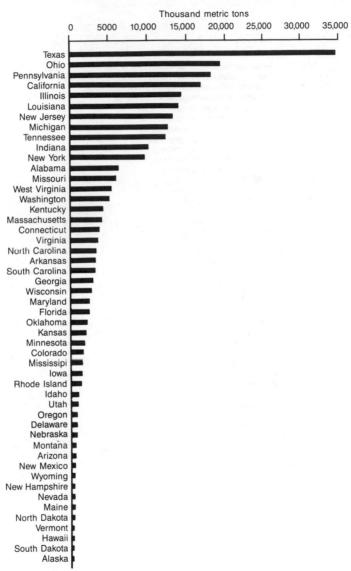

Figure 3.12
Estimated Generation of Hazardous Waste
in the United States, by State, 1983

Source: Congressional Budget Office.

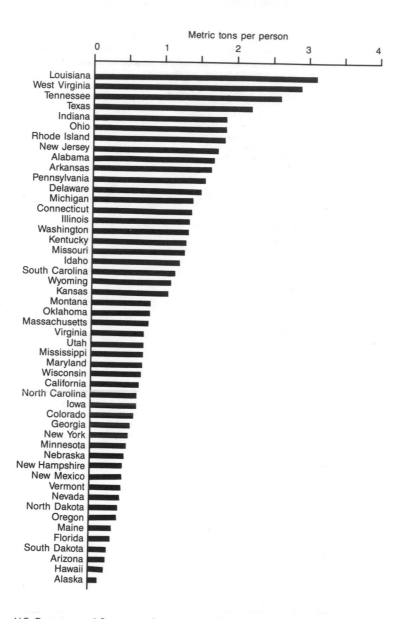

Figure 3.13
Estimated Generation of Hazardous Waste per Capita
in the United States, by State, 1983

Source: U.S. Department of Commerce; Congressional Budget Office.

Relatively little—by one estimate only 4 percent—of the waste generated in the United States in 1983 was transported away from the site where it was generated. Large generators tend to manage hazardous waste on-site since the construction and maintenance of treatment and disposal facilities is more cost effective to them than off-site transportation and management. Conversely, small generators rely more on off-site management since the waste volumes they generate do not warrant the capital expenses associated with disposing of the waste themselves. On-site facilities offer the advantage of reducing the risks associated with the transportation of hazardous waste.[157]

The regional distribution of hazardous waste transporters is closely related to that of generators and management facilities (figure 3.11). The greatest concentration of waste transporters is located in EPA's Region V. And while regions IX, II, and IV also contain relatively large numbers of hazardous waste transporters, region VIII has few.[158] EPA reports that as of April 1986, 12,885 facilities in the United States had permits to transport hazardous waste.[159]

Management of Hazardous Waste

Most RCRA-regulated hazardous waste continues to be managed on land. Many land disposal facilities have been closed, however, and the evidence indicates that some waste managers are shifting toward incineration and other forms of treatment. Large amounts of hazardous waste are apparently also being managed under the Clean Water Act.[160]

CBO estimates that two-thirds of the 266 mmt of industrial hazardous wastes generated in 1983 were managed on land: 25 percent went into deep wells, another 23 percent went into landfills (almost half of these were solid waste landfills that did not have the liners and groundwater monitoring required for hazardous waste landfills), and 19 percent went into surface impoundments. Only 1 percent of the wastes were incinerated.[161] These numbers cannot be directly compared with EPA's estimate of management practices for 1981 RCRA-regulated hazardous wastes both because different types of wastes are included and because CBO made its estimate in a different way. The EPA report found that in 1981 more than half of the wastes were disposed of by injection into deep wells and another one-third were placed in surface impoundments.[162]

The importance of wastewater treatment methods is illustrated by the CBO study. Twenty-two percent of the industrial hazardous wastes were released to sewers or surface waters.[163] The 1986 CMA survey also provides evidence of the significant contributions by non-RCRA facilities to the

Figure 3.14
Estimated Generation of Hazardous Waste in
Selected Rapidly Industrializing Nations, 1983

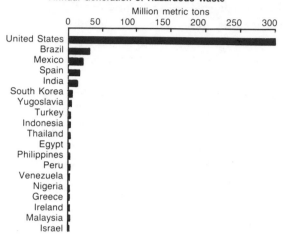

Annual Generation of Hazardous Waste

Million metric tons

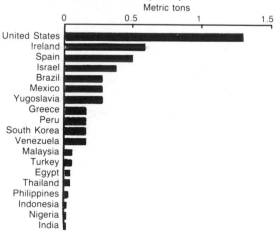

Hazardous Waste per Capita

Metric tons

Source: Original Conservation Foundation estimates.

Figure 3.14 (cont.)
Estimated Generation of Hazardous Waste in
Selected Rapidly Industrializing Nations, 1983

Hazardous Waste per Square Kilometer

Source: Original Conservation Foundation estimates.

management of hazardous waste. Of hazardous waste generated by 725 chemical plants in 1983, 99.4 percent was wastewater; only 1.7 mmt, or 0.6 percent, was solid. Most of the wastewater was discharged into non-RCRA facilities, such as wastewater treatment plants and other facilities permitted under the Clean Water Act's National Pollutant Discharge Elimination System, rather than into RCRA-regulated facilities.[164]

The 1986 National Screening Survey of Hazardous Waste Treatment, Storage, Disposal, and Recycling Facilities found that more hazardous waste was managed outside RCRA than by RCRA facilities. Including wastes regulated as hazardous under either state or federal laws (the definition of hazardous wastes varies from state to state), RCRA facilities managed 247 mmt, and other facilities managed 322 mmt. Most of the other waste was wastewater managed in tanks or solvent recovery facilities. Some of the waste was burned as fuel.[165]

Information on RCRA-permitted sites points to some movement away from the use of land for waste management as HSWA is implemented. The number of land disposal facilities fell significantly when landfills and surface impoundments were required, in November 1985, to monitor groundwater and show proof of financial responsibility,[166] although the number was declining somewhat before that date. Pennsylvania, for example, had 16 commercial treatment and disposal facilities in 1982. By 1985, 7 remained open. Only 1 was a land disposal facility and it was expected to close in two years.[167]

It is not clear just what is happening to the waste that was once handled by land disposal facilities. It may be that some is being stored. A study by the New England Congressional Institute showed that 15 percent of waste in that region was being stored at any one time.[168] Other explanations include expanded waste treatment, waste reduction, disposal in sewers or deep wells, and increased incineration. Incinerators, for instance, are operating at capacity,[169] in comparison with several years ago when the Hazardous Waste Treatment Council reported that its members were operating at 30 to 50 percent of capacity.[170]

EPA estimates that in 1984, 90 facilities were disposing of their hazardous waste through 195 deep injection wells. Of these 195 operating wells, 152 operated on a continuous basis that year, while the other 43 did not. Fifty-seven more wells were nonoperating; of these, 41 had been abandoned, 3 had been permanently sealed or were in the process of changing their type of operation, and the remaining 13 were either under construction or had their permits pending.[171] In late 1986, only 46 permitted facilities remained active.[172] Protection measures such as groundwater monitoring have not been required for deep wells,[173] but these requirements are being reconsidered.[174]

EPA has proposed to delay the land disposal ban for some wastes, because alternative types of capacity are not available.[175] A 1986 survey by ICF, a consulting firm, reports the hazardous waste management industry's views on future trends in usage and capacity of facilities. The 18 participant firms received 6.4 million wet metric tons (wmt) of hazardous waste for treatment and/or disposal in 1985, a 16 percent increase from the previous year. About 45 percent of the waste was landfilled (2.9 million wmt), and another 24 percent (1.6 million wmt) was chemically treated.[176] Comparisons with 1984 figures show increases, with the exception of underground injection, in the use of most management technologies: landfill (9 percent), chemical treatment (about 32 percent), incineration (19 percent), and resource recovery (32 percent). The amounts injected were lower in 1985 because of facility closures and the uncertainty of how RCRA regulations would apply to deep-injection wells. Closure of major competitors, growth of the cleanup business, treatment of wastes banned from land disposal, and the tightening of pretreatment standards under the Clean Water Act are some of the reasons for the larger volumes of waste now being managed.[177]

The 1986 survey shows that increased utilization of these management facilities is reducing the available capacity, especially that of incineration. ICF estimates that incinerators at the surveyed commercial firms were running at 90 percent of capacity at the end of 1985. Current landfill capacity at these commercial facilities will last for 15 years at current rates of use.[178] Use of other technologies, however, is estimated to be much lower than that of incinerators. For example, only 47 percent of the nation's existing capacity for resource recovery, 35 percent of its capacity for deep well injection, and 44 percent of its capacity for chemical treatment.[179]

ICF's most recent surveys indicate that there will be shortages of landfill capacity in some regions and that incineration capacity for solids and sludges will be limited for at least three to five years, longer if present obstacles to siting and permitting remain.[180] Incineration capacity for liquid wastes is seen as less of a problem because of alternatives such as chemical treatment, resource recovery, and waste reduction. Greater utilization of hazardous waste by newly regulated industrial boilers and furnaces and perhaps mobile incineration facilities (if the permitting problems are solved) may all help provide capacity in the future.

The speed with which EPA can grant permits to existing and new facilities will be an important factor in expanding the capacity available to manage wastes. Facilities that existed before November 1980 and notified EPA of their activities and submitted initial ("Part A") permit applications have received interim permits. These permits require monitoring, record keeping, personnel training, emergency planning, and closure procedures. Noncompliance with some provisions of interim permits apparently has been extensive.[181]

These facilities now are applying for "Part B" permits that require adherence to such design standards as liners for landfills and proper operations procedures. Until EPA makes a decision on a Part B permit application, an existing facility can continue to operate under interim permits.

As of September 1986, a total of 427 facilities had received Part B permits, a 250 percent increase since February 1984.[182] The number of permitted facilities included 389 storage and treatment sites, 27 incinerators, and 11 land disposal sites. Forty-six underground injection facilities also had permits. However, 1,130 land disposal facilities had closed or were closing (figure 3.15).[183] EPA has set November 1988 as its deadline to complete Part B permitting, but meeting this goal will be difficult.[184]

According to an extensive survey performed by EPA's Office of Solid

Waste in 1986, about 3,000 hazardous waste facilities were in operation in 1985. This estimate, the result of a census rather than projected from a sample,[185] is considerably smaller than those shown in previous EPA reports because it does not include those plants that are closing or have closed because they could not meet the groundwater monitoring and financial assurance requirements or have shifted to handling only delisted wastes. Of the 3,000 facilities, 2,585 stored waste, 1,596 treated waste, 846 recycled waste, and 433 disposed of waste on land.[186]

Cleaning Up Hazardous Waste Sites

As of June 1986, EPA had inventoried 24,269 abandoned hazardous waste sites across the United States that either cause or have the potential to cause contamination.[187] CERCLA created a fund, popularly known as Superfund, to clean up problem sites. In 1986, the Superfund Amendments provided $8.5 billion to that fund for cleaning up waste sites,[188] as well as $500 million for underground storage tanks.[189]

To qualify for cleanup under Superfund, a site must be placed on the National Priorities List (NPL) or be designated for an emergency removal action. As of June 1986, EPA had placed 951 final or proposed sites spread across 48 states on this list (figure 3.16). New Jersey had the largest number of sites on the NPL, with 97, followed by Michigan, 66; New York, 65; and Pennsylvania, 65.[190] The Great Lakes area accounted for 217 of the sites.[191] But, as of mid-1987, just 13 of these 951 sites had been cleaned up.[192] EPA had also performed 726 emergency removal actions, including 177 at NPL sites as initial cleanup measures. Other sites had been cleaned up by state and private efforts.

To determine whether a site belongs on the NPL, EPA ranks it by its potential impacts on health and environment, considering exposure through air, groundwater, and surface water. SARA requires all sites now on EPA's inventory be assessed by the end of 1987. As of June 1986, preliminary assessments had been completed on nearly 19,000 sites on the inventory. About 6,000 had been inspected, the second step in the process of evaluation for placement on the NPL.[193]

The Office of Technology Assessment estimated in a 1985 report that the NPL might eventually contain as many as 10,000 sites. This estimate was based on the assumption that, in addition to the 2,000 sites estimated by EPA to be placed on the NPL eventually, hazardous waste facilities operating in 1985 could contribute 1,000 sites, an improved site selection process could add 2,000 sites, and 5,000 or more solid waste facilities might need to be placed on the list.[194] Figure 3.17 shows potential sources of Superfund sites.

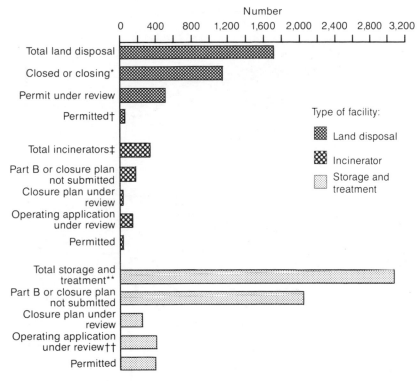

Figure 3.15
Facilities Regulated under RCRA, September 1986

* Includes 153 clean and closed facilities.
† Includes 11 land disposal and 46 underground injection permitted facilities.
‡ Includes facilities with disposal processes.
** Does not include facilities with disposal or incineration processes.
†† Does not include facilities that requested withdrawal or already have a permit.

Source: U.S. Environmental Protection Agency.

Besides facilitating important steps toward cleaning up wastes more rapidly, the new Superfund law includes several information-collecting provisions that will help EPA and others determine the extent to which people and the environment are being exposed—or are likely to be exposed—to specific wastes. SARA requires that EPA list 275 chemicals in the next five years that are the most likely to cause a hazard to human health at these sites and that the agency prepare toxicological profiles on them (at the rate of at least 25 profiles a year). Testing may be required if effects of a chemical

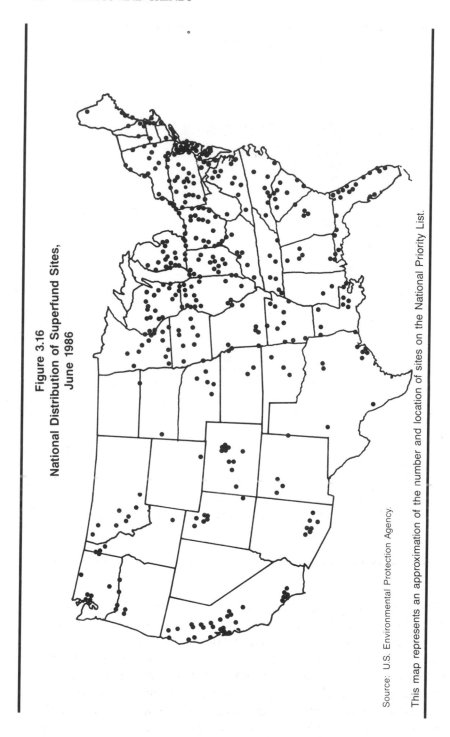

Figure 3.16
National Distribution of Superfund Sites,
June 1986

Source: U.S. Environmental Protection Agency.

This map represents an approximation of the number and location of sites on the National Priority List.

are not known.[195] SARA also requires companies to report releases into the air and water of some chemicals known to cause adverse effects, as well as the waste management methods used for them.[196] This information should help in basing selection of waste management and cleanup methods on the extent to which risk will be reduced.

NUCLEAR WASTE

Nuclear waste is classified into five categories, depending on its origin, level of radioactivity, and potential hazard. These categories are spent fuel, high-level waste, transuranic (TRU) waste, mill tailings from uranium production, and low-level waste.[197] In terms of radioactivity, spent fuel from commercial reactors constitutes over 90 percent of all nuclear waste accumulated in the United States.[198] In terms of volume, however, mill tailings account for nearly 97 percent.[199]

Spent fuel and high-level waste are long-lived and highly radioactive, requiring disposal practices that ensure indefinite isolation from the human and natural environment.[200] TRU wastes, also long-lived, vary widely in radioactivity.[201] Low-level waste has low radioactivity, some with decay periods as short as few days.[202]

The last 10 years have seen considerable effort expended to ensure that radioactive wastes are properly handled and disposed of. Laws have been enacted requiring government to find disposal sites and monitoring appropriate to each category of waste. In some instances, remedial action at abandoned sites has been required. In the case of low-level waste, measures have been taken to reduce the amount of waste generated.

Spent Fuel and High-Level Waste

Commercial power generation produces spent fuel assemblies containing fission products, unused uranium, plutonium, and TRU elements (elements with an atomic number greater than 92, the atomic number of uranium).[203] Until recently the only technology licensed by the Nuclear Regulatory Commission (NRC) for storing spent fuel rods consisted of immersing them in cooling pools at reactor sites.[204] Presently, 12,399 metric-tons-initial-heavy-metal (MTIHM)* of spent fuel, occupying a volume of approximately

---

*MTIHM refers to the mass of the uranium (and sometimes plutonium and thorium) that is contained in a fuel rod when loaded into the reactor. The total mass that must be stored, including the other atomic elements contained in the fuel and the assembly in which the fuel is held, weighs considerably more than the fuel alone. According to a U.S. Department of Energy report, a fuel assembly for a boiling water reactor weighs 319.9 kilograms, of which only 183.3 kilograms is uranium.[205]

5,300 cubic meters, are stored in such pools.[206] In 1985 nuclear plants generated 1,348 MTIHM, occupying a volume of 580 cubic meters—150 percent more than in 1975 but only 7 percent more than in 1980.[207] The relatively small increase since 1980 probably results from the decline in nuclear power plant construction.[208] Permanent disposal for this spent fuel will not be available until at least 1998, when the first nuclear waste repository is scheduled to be completed.[209] In the meantime two techniques, "reracking" of fuel (allowing more fuel to be stored in pools in the same amount of space) and transshipment of spent fuel (moving fuel from reactors where the pools are already filled to less crowded ones) are being employed to delay the date at which temporary storage capacity runs out.[210] Alternatives such as "dry storage" techiques, in which fuel is stored in containers without the use of water basins for cooling, are also being tried.[211]

High-level waste, which is a by-product of the production of nuclear weapons, is generated by fuel reprocessing—that is, the chemical separation of uranium and plutonium from the fission products and TRU elements in spent fuel.[212] Since President Carter banned commercial reprocessing of fuel in 1977, high-level waste has been generated only in the production of defense reactor fuel.[213] In the 1980s, the volume of the U.S. high-level inventory continued to increase until 1985, when it dropped from the 1984 level of 364,000 cubic meters to 357,000 cubic meters.[214] This decline was due to the use of evaporators, which removed water from the

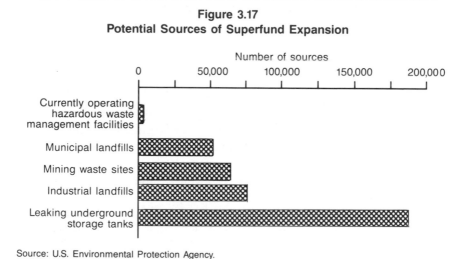

Figure 3.17
Potential Sources of Superfund Expansion

Source: U.S. Environmental Protection Agency.

waste but did nothing to reduce the radioactivity of that waste.[215] Generation was unabated, however, leading to a 9 percent growth in the inventory calculated in curies, a measure of radioactivity.[216]* High-level waste
is stored in tanks at four sites in the United States. Ninety-seven percent
of it is stored at either the Hanford Reservation in Washington state or
the Savannah River Plant in Aiken, South Carolina.[218] A recent study by
the General Accounting Office found that soil and water at these facilities
have been comtaminated by leaks from the storage tanks.[219] And, according to a private environmental organization that conducted its own study
of the Savannah River Plant, "the shallow aquifers above the Tuscaloosa
are so severely contaminated that it is reasonable to conclude that it has
been treated by the federal government as a national sacrifice area for the
U.S. nuclear weapons program."[220]

In 1982, after many years of inadequate attempts to create a national
program to dispose permanently of highly radioactive and long-lived wastes,
Congress passed the Nuclear Waste Policy Act, mandating that a disposal
facility be able to accept waste beginning in 1998.[221] The U.S. Department of Energy (DOE) was expected to plan two facilities in which spent
fuel and high-level waste would be permanently disposed of in a rock formation 1,000 to 4,000 feet underground known as a geological repository.
In May 1986 DOE nominated three sites—Yucca Mountain, Nevada; Deaf
Smith, Texas; and Hanford, Washington—for the first of two repositories.[222]
Citizens and governors of all three states strenuously opposed DOE's
plans.[223]

Congressional approval is necessary before construction can begin on
the second facility the Nuclear Waste Policy Act requires.[224] Although it
was not written into the act, the expectation of Congress was that this second site would be located in a crystalline deposit (such as granite) somewhere
east of the Mississippi River. In January 1986, DOE named 12 proposed
sites in seven north central and eastern states.[225] Citizens in these states
again protested strongly. In Maine, DOE briefing sessions drew thousands
of concerned citizens, and nine gubernatorial candidates opposed DOE's
plan.[226] In May 1986, DOE indefinitely postponed site-specific work for
the second repository and removed the proposed sites from active consideration.[227]

---

*When allowances are made for radioactive decay of the inventory, generation of new
waste in 1985 (measured in curies) exceeded 26 percent of the amount already in storage.[217]

Transuranic Waste

About 5,000 cubic meters of TRU waste* were generated in 1984,[228] primarily as a result of reprocessing of plutonium-bearing fuel and in the fabrication of nuclear weapons.[229] TRU waste is primarily stored at five sites in the United States. Two of them—Hanford Reservation and the Idaho National Engineering Laboratory in Idaho Falls, Idaho—account for 89 percent of the volume.[230] Before 1970, 194,000 cubic meters of TRU waste was buried in pits and trenches.[231] Since 1970, however, approximately 92,000 cubic meters of TRU waste has been stored in a more easily retrievable form in waste containers with a lifetime of at least 20 years so that it can be permanently disposed of at some future date.[232] Starting in 1988, DOE's Waste Isolation Pilot Plant in Carlsbad, New Mexico, is slated to begin accepting TRU waste for permanent disposal on an experimental basis. Ultimately, all stored TRU waste will be moved to the New Mexico site, although the process is not scheduled to be completed until 2013.[233]

Mill Tailings

When uranium ore is mined and uranium is extracted, large volumes of mill tailings are produced. The conventional process leaches the ore with either an acid or an alkali to produce slurries called slimes. These are decanted to remove the uranium-laden liquor and dried in mill tailings ponds. The resulting tailings piles threaten humans and the natural environment through wind dispersal and leaching into underlying soils and groundwater.[234] The radioactive components of these tailings produce decay products that include radon gas, which can be inhaled.[235] "Unconventional" methods of extracting uranium from ores, including in situ leaching of ore and recovery from mine water, may generate fewer tailings but cause other environmental impacts.[236]

Until 1978, when the Uranium Mill Tailings Radiation Control Act[237] (UMTRCA) was passed, tailings piles were typically neglected or abandoned when uranium mills closed. This act requires monitoring and management practices at operational sites and assigns to DOE the responsibility for managing "inactive" tailings piles, abandoned by milling operations conducted under contract for the Atomic Energy Commission.[238] An estimated 15.1 million cubic meters of mill tailings are at these sites, in addition to 8.2

---

*TRU waste is waste contaminated with transuranic elements that emit alpha particles (a type of positively charged radioactive emission).

million cubic meters of "subordinate waste"—soil that has been contaminated by windblown tailings, underlying ore storage areas, and tailings piles or is adjacent to abandoned piles.[239] In 1983, EPA set standards for the cleanup of these contaminated sites. The statute requires remedial action to be completed by 1990, although DOE has proposed an extension until 1993.[240]

Under UMTRCA, uranium mill tailings at active mills are now the responsibility of the company licensed by NRC to operate the site.[241] One hundred million cubic meters of mill tailings have accumulated at active sites in seven western states, with two states—New Mexico and Wyoming—jointly accounting for 79 percent of the total.[242] Like abandoned sites, these operations can threaten the environment. Of the 28 conventional uranium mills licensed in the United States, 21 have reported water contamination.[243] In 1979 a containment wall of a mill pond cracked at a uranium mine and mill site in Church Rock, New Mexico, releasing 100 tons of tailings and mud.[244]

Since its peak in 1980, production by the U.S. uranium industry has declined to such an extent that in 1985 the four conventional mills in operation represented only 11 percent of the conventional milling capacity available in the United States.[245] This decline was partially offset by more extensive use of unconventional methods—increasing from 35 percent of uranium production in 1984 to 47 percent in 1985.[246] Even so, in 1985, 1.1 million tons of mill tailings were generated—only 11 percent of the amount generated in 1980.[247] DOE attributes this decline to power plant cancellations and deferments. Although active licensed sites are probably less of a threat to the environment than inactive piles are, even licensed sites have been the cause of contamination.

Low-Level Waste

Low-level waste consists of medical fluids, power reactor liquids, and materials such as paper, clothing, plastics, and animal carcasses that have become contaminated with small amounts of radioactive substances.[248]* Over 17,000 licenses have been issued by NRC to permit facilities to handle and use radionuclides.[251]

Sixty-one percent of the 196,000 cubic meters of low-level waste disposed of in 1985 was generated by DOE's nuclear weapons fabrication and naval

---

*NRC defines low-level waste as radioactive waste that is not high-level waste, spent fuel, TRU waste, or mill tailings.[249] This approach has been criticized because one catchall category is used to encompass a broad class of materials with widely varying properties.[250]

nuclear propulsion programs, uranium enrichment operations, and research and development. Twenty-two percent was generated by commercial reactors, and the remaining 17 percent was generated by academic, medical, industrial, and non-DOE governmental generators.[252] By the end of 1985, a total of approximately 3,340,000 cubic meters of low-level waste from all sources had been buried. Since 1980, the amount of low-level waste buried annually has grown by 31 percent, with this growth due to a more than 100 percent increase in the amount of DOE waste buried annually. Over the same period the rate of commercial waste burial has declined by 19 percent.[253] The volume of medically related low-level waste diminished approximately 70 percent from 1979 to 1984. This dramatic decline has been attributed to waste treatment techniques including incineration, physical compaction, recycling, and segregation and to allowing short-lived waste to decay until it is no longer considered a hazard and can be disposed of as conventional waste.[254]*

Because most radioactive contaminants in low-level waste are shorter-lived and less concentrated than high-level and TRU waste, low-level waste needs to be isolated from the environment for only a comparatively short amount of time—between 60 and 300 years.[256]

Some low-level waste was discarded at sea until 1970, but most such waste is now buried in trenches—so-called shallow land burial (SLB).[257] Several states have prohibited SLB, however.[258] Alternatives to SLB that are under consideration include less long-lasting land disposal for waste with a short half-life; deeper, more secure containment for waste with a long half-life; and above-ground cement "vaults."[259]

Until 1979, some low-level waste generated by DOE contractors was disposed of at commercial sites, but since then it has all been disposed of at DOE facilities.[260] By 1971, six commercial facilities were in operation but operational problems, such as improper drainage, and political opposition resulted in three being closed. Presently only facilities in Beatty, Nevada; Barnwell, South Carolina; and Hanford, Washington, accept this waste.[261] In 1979, the Washington and Nevada facilities were temporarily closed because leaking waste containers trucked to the sites were seen as a health

---

*NRC plans to exempt as "below regulatory concern" radioactive wastes that contain sufficiently small quantities or low concentrations of radionuclides from low-level nuclear waste disposal requirements. While this action would reduce the quantity of waste buried at low-level waste facilities, it would also increase the amount of radioactive material entering the environment through conventional handling of solid and liquid wastes in incinerators, sewers, and landfills.[255]

threat. At the same time, South Carolina announced that the Barnwell site, which had been taking most of the waste, would cut the amount of waste it would receive in half.[262]

In 1980 Congress passed the Low-Level Radioactive Waste Policy Act (LLRWPA),[263] which attempted to solve the disposal capacity problem by encouraging states to join compacts, or coalitions, that would ''host'' regional disposal sites. As an incentive, the law permitted compacts to prohibit the disposal of waste from other states at their facilities after January 1, 1986.[264] By mid-1985, however, Congress had yet to consent to any compact, something that LLRWPA required. It was clear that no new sites would be available by January 1986,[265] and South Carolina had threatened to shut down Barnwell completely.[266] Under the Low-Level Radioactive Waste Policy Amendments Act, passed in 1985 to avert the impending waste disposal crisis, all states are required either to have their own disposal facilities or to be a member of a compact hosting one by December 31, 1992.[267] Any state or compact that fails to meet any of four milestones between the passage of the act and the date by which sites should be operational can be denied access to the three existing sites in addition to being liable for monetary penalties. As a final measure to ensure that states comply with the act, states are required, upon request of local waste generators, to take possession of and assume liability for all wastes generated within their borders after 1996 if no local or regional disposal site has yet been arranged.[268]

As of November 1986, nine compacts had been formed, seven of which had been ratified by Congress. Twelve states had not yet joined compacts; four of those did not intend to. North Dakota, Vermont, Washington, D.C., and Puerto Rico were being penalized for noncompliance.[269] By January 1988, host states for disposal facilities must be chosen and siting plans must be prepared.[270]

REFERENCES

Text

1. 15 USC §§2601 et seq. (1976).

2. 42 USC §§6901 et seq. (1976).

3. 33 USC §§1251 et seq. (as amended 1977).

4. Safe Drinking Water Act, 40 USC §§300f—300j-10 (Supp. 1977); Surface Mining Control and Reclamation Act, 30 USC §§1201 et seq. (1977); Uranium Mill Tailings Radiation

Control Act, 42 USC §§7901 et seq. (1978); and Clean Air Act, 42 USC §§7401 et seq. (Supp. 1981).

5. Information provided by the Chemical Abstracts Service, American Chemical Society, March 1987.

6. U.S. Environmental Protection Agency, Office of Toxic Substances, *Toxic Substances Control Act Chemical Substance Inventory*, 1985 ed., 5 vols. (Washington, D.C.: U.S. Government Printing Office, 1985).

7. The Conservation Foundation, *State of the Environment: An Assessment at Mid-Decade* (Washington, D.C.: The Conservation Foundation, 1984), pp. 63, 65.

8. Rodger L. Tatken and Richard J. Jewis, Sr., *Registry of Toxic Effects of Chemical Substances 1981-2* (Cincinnati: U.S. Department of Health and Human Services, National Institute for Occupational Safety and Health, 1983), p. xiii.

9. Information provided by the U.S. Environmental Protection Agency, March 1987.

10. National Research Council, *Toxicity Testing: Strategies to Determine Needs and Priorities* (Washington, D.C.: National Academy Press, 1984), p. 12.

11. Ibid., pp. 11, 13.

12. 40 CFR, §§[261.31, 261.32, and appendix 8.

13. 40 CFR, §261, subparts C and D.

14. 40 CFR, §423, appendix A.

15. U.S. Congress, "Joint Explanatory Statement of the Committee of Conference (Report 99-575)," as printed in appendix B of William J. Kelley, *The Safe Drinking Water Act Amendments of 1986* (Washington, D.C.: Bureau of National Affairs, 1986), p. 2.

16. 40 CFR, §§141.11, 141.12, 141.15.

17. "The Regulation of Toxic Air Pollutants: Critical Review Discussion Papers," *Journal of the Air Pollution Control Association* 36 (1986):990.

18. U.S. Comptroller General, *EPA's Efforts to Identify and Control Harmful Chemicals in Use*, GAO/RCED-84-100 (Washington, D.C.: U.S. General Accounting Office, 1984), p. 12.

19. U.S. Environmental Protection Agency, Office of Toxic Substances, *Chemical Control in the United States: Accomplishments under the New Chemical Program*, EPA 560/3-86-001 (Washington, D.C.: U.S. Environmental Protection Agency, 1985), p. 55, table 1.

20. 7 USC §§136 et seq.; and U.S. Environmental Protection Agency, *Suspended, Cancelled and Restricted Pesticides* (Washington, D.C.: U.S. Environmental Protection Agency, 1985), pp. 1-28.

21. 36 Fed. Reg. 10466 (1971), 29 CFR part 1910.1000, table Z-1.

22. Information provided by the U.S. Occupational Safety and Health Administration, February 1987.

23. Edward D. Goldberg, "TBT: An Environmental Dilemma," *Environment* 28, no. 8 (1986):17-20, 42-44.

24. U.S. International Trade Commission, *Synthetic Organic Chemicals: United States Production and Sales* (Washington, D.C.: U.S. Government Printing Office, ann. eds.); U.S. Department of Commerce, Bureau of the Census, *Highlights of U.S. Export and Import Trade*, FT 990, issued monthly; "Facts and Figures for the Chemical Industry," *Chemical and Engineering News*, June 9, 1983, pp. 34-44, 66-68.

25. U.S. Department of the Interior, Bureau of Mines, *Mineral Commodity Summaries* (Washington, D.C.: U.S. Department of the Interior, ann. eds.).

26. "EPA to Propose First Inventory Update," *Chemical Regulation Reporter*, March 8, 1985, p. 1427.

27. Marcia J. Gartrell et al., "Pesticides, Selected Elements, and Other Chemicals in Adult Total Diet Samples, October 1980-March 1982," *Journal of the Association of Official Analytic Chemists* 69 (1986):146-61.

28. Information provided by the U.S. Department of Agriculture, February 1987.

29. Radian Corporation, *National Air Toxics Information Clearinghouse: NATICH Data Base Report on State and Local Agency Air Toxics Activities, Final Report*, vol. 1, prepared for U.S. Environmental Protection Agency, Office of Air Quality Planning and Standards (Washington, D.C.: U.S. Environmental Protection Agency, 1986), pp. 217-50.

30. Richard A. Smith, Richard B. Alexander, and M. Gordon Wolman, *Analysis and Interpretation of Water-Quality Trends in Major U.S. Rivers, 1974-1981*, prepared for U.S. Department of the Interior, Geological Survey, Water Supply Paper 2307 (Reston, Va.: U.S. Geological Survey, 1986), pp. 8-9.

31. Information provided by the U.S. Environmental Protection Agency, Office of Toxic Substances, February 1987.

32. Arthur McDowell et al., *Plan and Operation of the Second National Health and Nutrition Survey, 1976-1980*, prepared for U.S. Department of Health and Human Services, National Center for Health Statistics, DHHS Publication no. (PHS)81-1317 (Washington, D.C.: U.S. Government Printing Office, 1981), pp. 39-40.

33. NHANES may also detect some evidence of long-term exposure to fat-soluble chemicals because low levels of residues may be released into the blood from fatty tissues and blood serum itself contains a lipid portion. Information provided by U.S. Environmental Protection Agency, Office of Toxic Substances, February 1987; and Frederick W. Kutz et al., "Toxic Substance Residues and Metabolites in Human Blood and Urine from a General Population Survey," a paper prepared by the U.S. Environmental Protection Agency, Research Triangle Institute, and National Center for Health Statistics for presentation at the 111th Annual Meeting of the American Public Health Association, November 16, 1983, Dallas, Texas.

34. Wayne R. Ott, "Total Human Exposure," *Environmental Science and Technology* 19 (1985):880-86.

35. Information provided by United Nations Environment Programme, May 1985.

36. Fish are tested every two years, and birds (starlings and mallard or black ducks) are tested every three years. The seven metals now monitored in fish are arsenic, cadmium, copper, lead, mercury, selenium, and zinc. Joel Jacknow, J. Larry Ludke, and Nancy C. Coon, *Monitoring Fish and Wildlife for Environmental Contaminants: The National Contaminant Biomonitoring Program* (Washington, D.C.: U.S. Department of the Interior, Fish and Wildlife Service, 1986), pp. 4-6.

37. National Oceanic and Atmospheric Administration, Ocean Assessments Division, "The National Status and Trends Program for Marine Environmental Quality, Program Description, FY 1986," January 1986.

38. Japan Environment Agency, Department of Environmental Health, Office of Health Studies, *Chemicals in the Environment: Report on Environmental Survey and Wildlife Monitoring in F.Y. 1982 and 1983* (Japan: Environment Agency, 1985), pp. 3-4.

39. Calculated from U.S. International Trade Commission, *Synthetic Organic Chemicals*, 1975 ed. (publ. 1977), p. 3, and 1985 ed. (publ. 1986), p. 5.

40. Information provided by the National Toxicology Program, U.S. Department of Health

and Human Services, December 1986.

41. 40 CFR §423, appendix A.

42. Jacknow, Ludke, and Coon, *Monitoring Fish and Wildlife for Environmental Contaminants*, p. 1; National Audubon Society, *Audubon Wildlife Report 1986* (New York: National Audubon Society, 1986), p. 813; and National Audubon Society, *Audubon Wildlife Report 1985* (New York: National Audubon Society, 1985), p. 513.

43. 37 Fed. Reg. 13369, July 7, 1972.

44. Ann Milner, "Banned But Not Forgotten," *Sierra*, 72, no. 4 (1986):29-32.

45. U.S. Congress, Office of Technology Assessment, *Protecting the Nation's Groundwater from Contamination*, vol. 1, OTA-0-276 (Washington, D.C.: U.S. Office of Technology Assessment, 1984), p. 23.

46. Council on Environmental Quality, *Contamination of Ground Water by Toxic Organic Chemicals* (Washington, D.C.: U.S. Government Printing Office, 1981), p. 17.

47. "Current Reports," *Chemical Regulations Reporter*, September 21, 1979, pp. 969-70.

48. EPA has registered approximately 1,500 pesticide active ingredients, but only about 1,100 have been produced in the past five years. Information provided by the U.S. Environmental Protection Agency, Office of Pesticide Programs, February 1987.

49. U.S. General Accounting Office, *Pesticides: EPA's Formidable Task to Assess and Regulate Their Risks*, GAO/RCED-86-125 (Washington, D.C.: U.S. General Accounting Office, 1986), p. 3. This report lists "over 600" active ingredients—a total that was probably arrived at by grouping similar chemicals. Information provided by the U.S. Environmental Protection Agency, Office of Pesticide Programs, February 1987.

50. George W. Ware, *Fundamentals of Pesticides* (Fresno, Calif.: Thomson Publications, 1982), p. 226.

51. See, for example, National Research Council, Committee on Prototype Explicit Analyses for Pesticides, *Regulating Pesticides* (Washington, D.C.: National Academy of Sciences, 1980), pp. 6-7, 84-89; specific chemicals listed in U.S. Department of Health and Human Services, Public Health Service, Centers for Disease Control, National Institute for Occupational Health, *Registry of Toxic Effects of Chemical Substances* (Cincinnati: National Institute for Occupational Safety and Health, 1983); and F.W. Mackison, R.S. Stricoff, and L.J. Patridge, Sr., *Occupational Health Guidelines for Chemical Hazards* (Washington, D.C.: U.S. Government Printing Office, 1981).

52. U.S. Environmental Protection Agency, *Suspended, Cancelled and Restricted Pesticides*, pp. 1-28.

53. U.S. General Accounting Office, *Pesticides: EPA's Formidable Task*, p. 3.

54. Ibid.

55. Jacknow, Ludke, and Coon, *Monitoring Fish and Wildlife for Environmental Contaminants*, p. 1.

56. Calculated from U.S. International Trade Commission, *Synthetic Organic Chemicals*, 1960 and 1980 eds.; and Ware, *Fundamentals of Pesticides*, pp. 104, 115.

57. Theodore R. Eichers, "Farm Pesticide Economic Evaluation, 1981," AERS 464 (Washington, D.C.: U.S. Government Printing Office, 1981), p. 3.

58. Calculated from U.S. International Trade Commission, *Synthetic Organic Chemicals*, 1983 ed., p. 224, and 1984 ed., p. 221.

59. U.S. Environmental Protection Agency, Office of Pesticide Programs, "Pesticide Industry Sales and Usage: 1985 Market Estimates," September 1986, table 4.

60. Robert J. Gilliom, Richard B. Alexander, and Richard A. Smith, *Pesticides in the*

Nation's Rivers, 1975-1980, and Implications for Future Monitoring, U.S. Geological Survey, Water Supply Paper 2271 (Washington, D.C.: U.S. Government Printing Office, 1985), p. 7, table 3.

61. Ibid., p. 16, table 8, and p. 20, table 11.

62. John R. Sullivan and David E. Armstrong, *Toxaphene: Status in the Great Lakes*, Priority Pollutants Status Report no. 2 (Madison, Wis.: University of Wisconsin, Sea Grant Institute, 1985), p. 34.

63. Marcia Gartrell et al., "Pesticides, Selected Elements, and Other Chemicals in Infant and Toddler Total Diet Samples, October 1978-September 1979," *Journal of the Association of Official Analytical Chemists* 68(1985):842-61; and Marcia Gartrell et al., "Pesticides, Selected Elements, and Other Chemicals in Infant and Toddler Total Diet Samples, October 1980-March 1982," *Journal of the Association of Official Analytical Chemists* 69(1986):123-45.

64. Robert S. Murphy, Frederick W. Kutz, and Sandra C. Strassman, "Selected Pesticide Residues or Metabolites in Blood and Urine Specimens from a General Population Survey," *Environmental Health Perspectives* 48(1983):81-86, table 6.

65. Jos Mes, David J. Davies, and Davida Turton, "Polychlorinated Biphenyl and Other Chlorinated Hydrocarbon Residues in Adipose Tissue of Canadians," *Bulletin of Environmental Contaminants Toxicology* 28(1982):97-104.

66. Kutz et al., "Toxic Substance Residues and Metabolites in Human Blood and Urine," table 2.

67. Jacknow, Ludke, and Coon, *Monitoring Fish and Wildlife for Environmental Contaminants*, pp. 7, 12, 13.

68. Ibid., p. 16.

69. Sullivan and Armstrong, *Toxaphene*, p. 5, figure 1.

70. Jacknow, Ludke, and Coon, *Monitoring Fish and Wildlife for Environmental Contaminants*, p. 13.

71. Sullivan and Armstrong, *Toxaphene*, p. 27.

72. U.S. Department of Commerce, National Oceanic and Atmospheric Administration, "Synopsis: NOAA Publishes Preliminary Assessment of Environmental Quality of Nation's Coastal and Estuarine Areas," photocopy, 1987.

73. Gilliom, Alexander, and Smith, *Pesticides in the Nation's Rivers, 1975-1980*, p. 5, table 1, and p. 6, table 2.

74. "Pilot Study of Water Well Contamination to Begin Sampling in Three States in March," *Chemical Regulation Reporter*, February 6, 1987, p. 1,396.

75. U.S. Environmental Protection Agency, Great Lakes National Program Office, "Dioxin in Great Lakes Fish," n.d., p. 1.

76. "Pilot Study of Water Well Contamination," p. 1,396.

77. Samuel S. Epstein et al., *Hazardous Waste in America* (San Francisco: Sierra Club Books, 1982); and The Conservation Foundation, *State of the Environment 1982* (Washington, D.C.: The Conservation Foundation, 1982), p. 121.

78. 48 Fed. Reg. (1983); and "Environmental News," U.S. Environmental Protection Agency, May 9, 1983.

79. "Current Reports," *Chemical Regulation Reporter*, June 15, 1979, pp. 420-21.

80. Steven J. Eisenreich et al., "Airborne Organic Contaminants in the Great Lakes Ecosystem," *Environmental Science and Technology* 15 (1981):30-38; and Robert V. Thomann and John P. Connolly, "Model of PCB in the Lake Michigan Lake Trout Food Chain,"

Environmental Science and Technology 18 (1984):65-71.

81. The Conservation Foundation, *State of the Environment: An Assessment at Mid-Decade*, pp. 337-38.

82. Global Environmental Monitoring System, Joint Food and Agriculture Organization/World Health Organization Food and Animal Feed Contamination Monitoring Programme, *Summary and Assessment of Data Received from the FAO/WHO Collaborating Centres for Food Contamination Monitoring* (Uppsala, Sweden: National Food Administration, 1982), p. 34.

83. The studies referred to are on pesticide residues in fish and birds. Fish: U.S. Department of the Interior, Fish and Wildlife Service, Columbia National Fisheries Research Laboratory, Columbia, Mo., unpublished data. Starlings: Donald H. White, "Nationwide Residues of Organochlorines in Starlings, 1974," *Pesticides Monitoring Journal* 10 (1976):15; and Donald H. White, "Nationwide Residues of Organochlorines in Starlings, 1976," *Pesticides Monitoring Journal* 12 (1979):197. Waterfowl: Charles R. Walker, "Occurrences of PCB in National Fish and Wildlife Monitoring Program," U.S. Fish and Wildlife Service; Donald H. White and Robert G. Heath, "Nationwide Residues of Organochlorines in Wings of Adult Mallards and Black Ducks, 1972-1973," *Pesticides Monitoring Journal* 9 (1976):184; Donald H. White, "Nationwide Residues of Organichlorines in Wings of Adult Mallards and Black Ducks, 1976-77," *Pesticides Monitoring Journal* 13 (1979):16; and Jacknow, Ludke, and Coon, *Monitoring Fish and Wildlife for Environmental Contaminants*, pp. 1-2, 9, 11.

84. Jacknow, Ludke, and Coon, *Monitoring Fish and Wildlife for Environmental Contaminants*, p. 9.

85. White, "Nationwide Residues of Organochlorine Compounds in Wings of Adult Mallard and Black Ducks 1976-77," p. 15.

86. Council on Environmental Quality, *Environmental Quality 1979* (Washington, D.C.: U.S. Government Printing Office, 1979), pp. 448-49.

87. Information provided by the U.S. Environmental Protection Agency, Exposure Evaluation Division, "National Human Adipose Tissue Survey (NHATS)."

88. J. Letey et al., *An Agricultural Dilemma: Drainage Water and Toxics Disposal in the San Joaquin Valley* (Oakland, Calif.: University of California, Division of Agricultural and Natural Resources, 1986), pp. 1, 6.

89. Isaac Turiel, *Indoor Air Quality and Human Health* (Stanford, Calif.: Stanford University Press, 1985), p. 78; and "Concern Over Radon in Homes Triggers Plan for National Survey," *Chemical and Engineering News*, April 28, 1986, pp. 19-20.

90. 40 CFR §423, appendix A.

91. 40 CFR §261.24.

92. 40 CFR §51.24.

93. 40 CFR §141.11.

94. Jacknow, Ludke, and Coon, *Monitoring Fish and Wildlife for Environmental Contaminants*, p. 13.

95. Smith, Alexander, and Wolman, *Analysis and Interpretation of Water-Quality Trends*, p. 11a, table 1.

96. Robert B. Faoro, William F. Hunt, and Karen A. Nelson, *Compilation of Benzo(a)pyrene and Trace Metal Summary Statistics, 1983-84* (Research Triangle Park, N.C.: U.S. Environmental Protection Agency, 1986).

97. John R. O'Connor, discussion paper in "The Regulation of Toxic Air Pollutants,"

Journal of the Air Pollution Control Association 36 (1986):988-93, table I.

98. The Conservation Foundation, *State of the Environment 1982*, pp. 121-22; and U.S. Department of the Interior, Bureau of Mines, "Lead," *Mineral Commodity Profiles* (Washington, D.C.: Bureau of Mines, 1983), p. 12.

99. U.S. Bureau of Mines, "Lead," p. 15, Table 11.

100. Joseph L. Annest et al., *Advance Data; Blood Lead Levels for Persons 6 Months-74 Years of Age: United States, 1976-80*, published by U.S. Department of Health and Human Services, Public Health Service, Office of Health Research, Statistics and Technology, May 12, 1982, p. 12.

101. U.S. Environmental Protection Agency, Office of Air Quality, Planning and Standards, *National Air Quality and Emissions Trends Report, 1982* (Research Triangle Park, N.C.: U.S. Environmental Protection Agency, 1984), pp. 62-63.

102. Calculated from Lew Gurman, "Deadly Lead," *Environmental Action* 17, no. 5 (1986):20.

103. Ibid.

104. Smith, Alexander, and Wolman, *Analysis and Interpretation of Water Quality Trends*, pp. 29-30.

105. Information provided by Stephen Kahl, University of Maine at Orono, Department of Geological Sciences, March 1987.

106. "EPA Study Shows 40 Million People at Risk from Lead Levels Exceeding Proposed Standard," *Environmental Reporter*, November 14, 1986, p. 1171; and "EPA Releases Draft Final Lead Report: Estimates of U.S. Citizens Affected Grows," *Environmental Reporter*, December 26, 1986, pp. 1461-1462.

107. Gartrell et al., "Pesticides, Selected Elements, and Other Chemicals in Infant and Toddler Total Diet Samples, October 1978-September 1979," p. 861; Gartrell et al., "Pesticides, Selected Elements, and Other Chemicals in Infant and Toddler Total Diet Samples, October 1980-March 1982," p. 144; Gartrell et al., "Pesticides, Selected Elements, and Other Chemicals in Adult Total Diet Samples, October 1978-September 1979," *Journal of the Association of Official Analytical Chemists* 68 (1985).875; and Gartrell et al., "Pesticides, Selected Elements, and Other Chemicals in Adult Total Diet Samples, October 1980-March 1982," p. 162.

108. Marie Vahter, "Assessment of Human Exposure to Lead and Cadmium through Biological Monitoring" (Stockholm: Karolinska Institute, 1982), p. 13.

109. R. Coleman et al., "Atmospheric Cadmium: Population Exposure Analysis," prepared for U.S. Environmental Protection Agency, Office of Air and Waste Management, Office of Air Quality Planning and Standards (Research Triangle Park, N.C.: U.S. Environmental Protection Agency, 1978), pp. 12-13, 15-16.

110. U.S. Department of the Interior, Geological Survey, *National Water Summary, 1984: Hydrological Events and Issues* (Washington, D.C.: U.S. Government Printing Office, 1984), p. 46.

111. Information provided by the U.S. Food and Drug Administration, 1984 and February 1987.

112. Global Environmental Monitoring System, *Summary and Assessment of Data Received from the FAO/WHO Collaborating Centres for Food Contamination Monitoring*, pp. 44, 77.

113. Information provided by the California State Water Resources Control Board, March 1987.

114. Vahter, "Assessment of Human Exposure to Lead and Cadmium," p. 51.

115. Konrad Von Moltke, Patricia Bauman, and Frances H. Irwin, *The Regulation of Existing Chemicals in the European Community: Possibilities for the Development of a Community Strategy for the Control of Cadmium* (Bonn, West Germany: Institut fur Europaische Umweltpolitik, 1985), p. 62, table 11.

116. Ibid., p. 32, table 3.

117. Research Triangle Institute, "Once a Blessing Now a Curse," *Hypotenuse*, July-August 1983, p. 12.

118. U.S. Environmental Protection Agency, Office of Pesticides and Toxic Substances, *Support Document Asbestos-Containing Materials in Schools: Health Effects and Magnitude of Exposure* (Washington, D.C.: U.S. Environmental Protection Agency, 1980), pp. 19, 35.

119. "Killer in the Classroom," *New York Times*, November 13, 1983.

120. Ibid; Research Triangle Institue, "Once a Blessing Now a Curse," pp. 10-19; and U.S. Environmental Protection Agency, Office of Toxic Substances, "Fifteen Toxic Chemicals Subject to Imminent Regulations," *Toxic and Hazardous Substances* (Washington, D.C.: U.S. Environmental Protection Agency, 1976), pp. 83-84.

121. National Research Council, Commission on Life Sciences, Board on Toxicology and Environmental Health Hazards, Committee on Nonoccupational Health Risks of Asbestiform Fibers, *Nonoccupational Health Risks of Asbestiform Fibers* (Washington, D.C.: National Academy Press, 1984), p. 220, table 7-6.

122. Ibid., pp. 220-223.

123. U.S. Environmental Protection Agency, Office of Management Systems and Evaluation and Office of Pesticides and Toxic Substances, "Asbestos in Schools Program Review" (Washington, D.C.: U.S. Environmental Protection Agency, 1983); and "On Asbestos Peril E.P.A. Report Cites Failure to Inspect and Report Risks," *New York Times*, February 1, 1984.

124. U.S. Environmental Protection Agency, Office of Public Affairs, *Asbestos Fact Book*, A-107/86-002, 3rd revision (Washington, D.C.: U.S. Environmental Protection Agency, 1986), p. 4.

125. U.S. General Accounting Office, *Briefing Document on GAO's Review of Asbestos in the Schools*, GAO/RCED-85-91 (Washington, D.C.: U.S. General Accounting Office, 1985), pp. 22-23.

126. Asbestos Hazard Emergency Response Act of 1986, P.L. 99-519.

127. 40 CFR §763.

128. Timothy B. Atkeson et al., "Annotated Legislative History of the Superfund Amendments and Reauthorizition Act of 1986 (SARA)", *Environmental Law Reporter: News and Analysis*, December 1986, p. 16.

129. *Sterling* v. *Velsicol Chemical Co.*, DC WTenn. no. 78-1100, August 1, 1986, from *Chemical Regulation Reporter*, August 8, 1986.

130. *Anderson* v. *W.R. Grace & Co.*, DC Mass, no. 82-1672-S, from *Chemical Regulation Reporter*, September 26, 1986.

131. 42 USCA §§6901-87 (P.L. 94-580).

132. 42 USCA §§9601-57 (P.L. 96-510).

133. 42 USCA §6901 et seq. (1983).

134. Superfund Amendments and Reauthorization Act of 1986, Pub. L. 99-499, 100 Stat. 1613 (1986).

135. "EPA Summary of Major Provisions of Superfund Reauthorization Bill Signed by

President Reagan, Covering Funding, Program, Other Provisions (Dated Oct. 17, 1986),''
Environment Reporter, October 24, 1986, p. 995.

136. Ibid., pp. 1,001-2.

137. U.S. Congress, Congressional Budget Office, *Hazardous Waste Management: Recent Changes and Policy Alternatives* (Washington, D.C.: U.S. Government Printing Office, 1985), p. 17; and U.S. Department of Commerce, Bureau of the Census, *State and Metropolitan Area Data Book 1986* (Washington, D.C.: U.S. Government Printing Office, 1986), p. 504.

138. U.S. Congressional Budget Office, *Hazardous Waste Management*, pp. 10-13; and U.S. Congress, Office of Technology Assessment, *Serious Reduction of Hazardous Waste: For Pollution Prevention and Industrial Efficiency*, OTA-ITE-317 (Washington, D.C.: U.S. Government Printing Office, 1986), p. 113.

139. U.S. Congressional Budget Office, *Hazardous Waste Management*, pp.11, 17.

140. Westat, Inc., *National Survey of Hazardous Waste Generators and Treatment, Storage and Disposal Facilities Regulated Under RCRA in 1981*, prepared for U.S. Environmental Protection Agency, Office of Solid Waste (Rockville, Md.: Westat, Inc., 1984), pp. 2, 21-38.

141. Information provided by National Governors Association, 1986.

142. Chemical Manufacturers Association, ''Results of the 1984 CMA Hazardous Waste Survey,'' January 1986, pp. 1, 9.

143. U.S. General Accounting Office, ''Statement of Eleanor Chelimsky before the Environment, Energy and Natural Resources Subcommittee, Committee on Government Operation, House of Representatives on the Condition of Information on Hazardous Waste,'' September 24, 1986, p. 6.

144. 51 Fed. Reg. 41900 (1986).

145. Ibid.

146. U.S. Environmental Protection Agency, ''Summary Report on RCRA Activities for March 1986'', draft, p. 5.

147. U.S. Congressional Budget Office, *Hazardous Waste Management*, p. 20.

148. Abt Associates, Inc., ''National Small Quantity Hazardous Waste Generator Survey,'' prepared for the U.S. Environmental Protection Agency, Office of Solid Waste, (Washington, D.C.: Chemical Manufacturers Association, 1985), pp. 32-33.

149. Ibid., pp. 28-29.

150. U.S. Environmental Protection Agency, Office of Solid Waste and Emergency Response, *The New RCRA: A Fact Book*, EPAX 86-02-0083 (Washington, D.C.: U.S. Environmental Protection Agency, 1985), p. 4.

151. U.S. Bureau of the Census, *State and Metropolitan Area Date Book*, p. 572.

152. U.S. Congressional Budget Office, *Hazardous Waste Management*, p. 22.

153. Ibid.; and U.S. Bureau of the Census, *State and Metropolitan Area Date Book*, p. 504.

154. H. Jeffrey Leonard, ''Hazardous Wastes: The Crisis Spreads—The LDCs Are Not Immune to the Problems Associated with Inadequate Disposal of Hazardous Waste'', *National Development* 27, no. 3 (1986):36.

155. Ibid., p. 38.

156. Ibid.

157. U.S. Congressional Budget Office, *Hazardous Waste Management*, p. 26.

158. U.S. Environmental Protection Agency, ''The New RCRA,'' p. 4.

159. U.S. Environmental Protection Agency, ''Summary Report on RCRA Activities for March 1986,'' p. 4.

160. U.S. Environmental Protection Agency, Office of Water Regulations and Standards, *Report to Congress on the Discharge of Hazardous Wastes to Publicly Owned Treatment Works*, EPA/530-SW-86-004 (Washington, D.C.: U.S. Environmental Protection Agency, 1986), p. 1-8.

161. U.S. Congressional Budget Office, *Hazardous Waste Management*, p. 24.

162. Westat, *National Survey of Hazardous Waste Generators*, p. 205.

163. U.S. Congressional Budget Office, *Hazardous Waste Management*, p. 24.

164. Chemical Manufacturers Association, "Results of the 1984 CMA Hazardous Waste Survey," p. 21.

165. Center for Economics Research, Research Triangle Institute, *1986 National Screening Survey of Hazardous Waste Treatment, Storage, Disposal, and Recycling Facilities: Summary of Results for TSDR Facilities Active in 1985* (Research Triangle Park, N.C.: U.S. Environmental Protection Agency, Office of Policy, Planning, and Information, Office of Solid Waste, 1986), pp. 2-3.

166. *Environment Reporter*, September 26, 1986, p. 775.

167. *Pennsylvania Hazardous Waste Facilities Plan*, (Harrisburg, Pa.: Pennsylvania Department of Environmental Resources, Bureau of Waste Management, 1986), p. 23.

168. New England Congressional Institute, "Hazardous Waste Generation and Management in New England", February 1986, p. III-2.

169. ICF, Inc., "Survey of Selected Firms in the Commercial Hazardous Waste Management Industry: 1984 Update," prepared for U.S. Environmental Protection Agency, Office of Policy Analysis, September 1985, p. 2-4.

170. Richard C. Fortuna, "Same Wastes, New Solutions," speech prepared for Bureau of National Affairs conference, September 1983, p. 16.

171. U.S. Environmental Protection Agency, *Report to Congress on Injection of Hazardous Waste*, EPA 570/9-85-003 (Washington, D.C.: U.S. Environmental Protection Agency, 1985), p. 5.

172. U.S. Environmental Protection Agency, Office of Solid Waste, "Summary Report on RCRA Permit Activities for September, 1986," October 15, 1986, photocopy, p. 3.

173. Ibid., p. 8.

174. Information provided by Gail Bingham and Timothy J. Mealey, The Conservation Foundation, 1986.

175. "Porter Calls Potential Lack of Treatment, Disposal Capacity for Waste 'Real Problem'," *Environmental Reporter—Current Developments*, September 26, 1986, p. 775.

176. ICF, "Survey of Selected Firms: 1984 Update," p. v.; and ICF, Inc., *1985 Survey of Selected Firms in the Commercial Hazardous Waste Management Industry*, prepared for the U.S. Environmental Protection Agency, Office of Policy Analysis (Washington, D.C.: U.S. Environmental Protection Agency, 1986), p. 4-3.

177. ICF, *1985 Survey of Selected Firms*, pp. 3-9 to 3-11, 4-3 to 4-4.

178. Ibid., p. 4-7.

179. Ibid., p. 4-8, and U.S. Congress, Library of Congress, Congressional Research Service, *Hazardous Waste Fact Book*, Report no. 87-56 (Washington, D.C.: Library of Congress, 1987), p. 31.

180 ICF, "Survey of Selected Firms: 1984 Update," pp. 2-4, 2-5; and ICF, *1985 Survey of Selected Firms*, pp. 2-5, 2-6, 2-7.

181. U.S. Comptroller General, *Interim Report on Inspection, Enforcement and Permitting Activities at Hazardous Waste Facilities* (Washington, D.C.: U.S. General Accounting Office, 1983), pp. 6-9.

182. Information provided by U.S. Environmental Protection Agency, Office of Solid Waste and Emergency Response, 1984; and U.S. Environmental Protection Agency, "Summary Report on RCRA Permit Activities for September, 1986," pp. 3-5.

183. U.S. Environmental Protection Agency, "Summary Report on RCRA Permit Activities for September 1986," p. 3.

184. Donald R. Cannon, Laurie A. Rich, and Mimi Bluestone, "Hazardous Waste Management: New Rules Are Changing the Game," *Chemical Week*, August 20, 1986, p. 51.

185. Center for Economics Research, Research Triangle Institute, *1986 National Screening Survey of Hazardous Waste Treatment, Storage, Disposal, and Recycling Facilities*, p. 1.

186. Ibid.

187. U.S. Environmental Protection Agency, Office of Emergency and Remedial Response, *National Priorities List Fact Book, June 1986*, HW-7.3 (Washington, D.C.: U.S. Environmental Protection Agency, 1986), p. 24.

188. *Environment Reporter*, October 24, 1986, p. 997.

189. Ibid., pp. 1,004-5.

190. U.S. Environmental Protection Agency, *National Priorities List Fact Book*, p. 19.

191. Ibid., p. 21.

192. "Sixty-four Sites Proposed in NPL Update," *Hazardous Waste Report*, February 2, 1987, p. 3.

193. Ibid., p. 24.

194. U.S. Congress, Office of Technology Assessment, *Superfund Strategy*, OTA-ITE-252 (Washington, D.C.: U.S. Government Printing Office, 1985), p. 167.

195. *Environment Reporter*, October 24, 1986, pp. 1,003-4.

196. Ibid., p. 1,002.

197. Oak Ridge National Laboratory, *Integrated Data Base for 1986: Spent Fuel and Radioactive Waste Inventories, Projections, and Characteristics*, prepared for U.S. Department of Energy, DOE/RW-0006, Rev. 2 (Washington, D.C.: U.S. Government Printing Office, 1986), p.2.

198. Ibid., p. 7.

199. Ibid., p. 158.

200. American Institute of Professional Geologists, *"Radioactive Waste: Issues and Answers* (Arvada, Calif.: American Institute of Professional Geologists, 1984), p. 12.

201. Ibid., p. 14.

202. G. John Weir, Jr., "Characteristics of Medically Related Low-Level Radioactive Waste," report prepared for U.S. Department of Energy, July 1986, photocopy, pp. 24-25.

203. U.S. Congress, Office of Technology Assessment, *Managing the Nation's Commercial High-Level Radioactive Waste*, OTA-0-171 (Washington, D.C.: U.S. Office of Technology Assessment, 1985), p. 24.

204. U.S. Department of Energy, *Spent Fuel Storage Requirements*, DOE/RL-86-5/UC-85 (Richland, Wash.: U.S. Department of Energy, 1986), p. 3.1.

205. Ibid., p. 36.

206. Oak Ridge National Laboratory, *Integrated Data Base for 1986*, pp. 15, 20.

207. Ibid., pp. 15, 32.

208. Ibid., p. 153.

209. U.S. Office of Technology Assessment, *Managing the Nation's Commercial High-Level Radioactive Waste*, p. 8.

210. U.S. Department of Energy, "Spent Fuel Storage Requirements," pp. 3.2, 3.3.

211. U.S. Office of Technology Assessment, *Managing the Nation's Commercial High-*

Level Radioactive Waste, pp. 57-58.

212. Ibid., p. 24.

213. American Institute of Professional Geologists, *"Radioactive Wastes*, p. 12.

214. Oak Ridge National Laboratory, *Integrated Data Base for 1986*, p. 64.

215. Information provided by Oak Ridge National Laboratory, Integrated Data Base Program, 1986.

216. Oak Ridge National Laboratory, *Integrated Data Base for 1986*, p. 63.

217. Ibid, pp. 73, 74, 79, 83, 86; and information provided by the Rockwell Hanford Operation of Rockwell International at Richland, Washington.

218. Oak Ridge National Laboratory, *Integrated Data Base for 1986*, p. 54.

219. U.S. General Accounting Office, *Nuclear Energy: Environmental Issues at DOE's Nuclear Defense Facilities*, GAO/RCED-86-192 (Washington, D.C.: U.S. General Accounting Office, 1986), p. 20.

220. Argon Makhijani, Robert Alvarez, and Brent Blackwelder, "Deadly Crop in the Tank Farm," cited in "Environmental Study Faults Savannah River Lab on Disposal Practices," *The Radioactive Exchange*, August 15, 1986, p. 6-7.

221. 42 USC §§10101 et seq.

222. U.S. Department of Energy, Office of Civilian Radioactive Waste Management, *OCRWM Bulletin*, June 23, 1986, p. 2.

223. Ibid., p. 3.

224. League of Women Voters, *The Nuclear Waste Primer: A Handbook for Citizens* (New York: Nick Lyons Books, 1985), p. 53.

225. Information provided by the Union of Concerned Scientists, 1987.

226. Scott Allen, "High Level Waste: If We're Not Willing to Help Dispose of High Level Nuclear Waste, Should We Be Willing to Help Produce It?," *Maine Times*, March 21, 1986, p. 1.

227. U.S. Department of Energy, *OCRWM Bulletin*, June 23, 1986, p. 3.

228. Oak Ridge National Laboratory, *Spent Fuel and Radioactive Waste Inventories, Projections, and Characteristics*, prepared for U.S. Department of Energy, DOE/RW-0006, Rev.1 (Washington, D.C.: U.S. Government Printing Office, 1985), p. 112.

229. Oak Ridge National Laboratory, *Integrated Data Base for 1986*, p. 93.

230. Ibid., p. 98.

231. Ibid., pp. 93, 98.

232. Ibid., pp. 93, 99.

233. Ibid., p. 94-95.

234. League of Women Voters, *The Nuclear Waste Primer*, pp. 37-38.

235. American Institute of American Geologists, *Radioactive Wastes*, p. 8.

236. Oak Ridge National Laboratory, *Integrated Data Base for 1986*, p. 153.

237. 42 USC §7901 et seq.

238. League of Women Voters, *The Nuclear Waste Primer*, pp. 38-39.

239. Oak Ridge National Laboratory, *Integrated Data Base for 1986*, p. 165.

240. Ibid., p. 166.

241. League of Women Voters, *The Nuclear Waste Primer*, p. 38.

242. Oak Ridge National Laboratory, *Integrated Data Base for 1986*, pp. 155, 158

243. Ibid., p. 158.

244. Oak Ridge National Laboratory, *Integrated Data Base for 1986*, p. 153; and Oak

Ridge National Laboratory, *Spent Fuel and Radioactive Waste Inventories, Projections, and Characteristics*, p. 172.

245. League of Women Voters, *The Nuclear Waste Primer*, p. 38.

246. Ibid., p. 39.

247. Ibid., p. 153.

248. U.S. Department of Energy, *Low-Level Waste Management: The National Program for Low-Level Radioactive Waste Management*, B093-0982-R-2M (Idaho Falls, Idaho: EG&G Idaho, Inc., 1983), p. 2.

249. 10 CFR §61.2.

250. The Conservation Foundation, *Toward a National Policy for Managing Low-Level Radioactive Waste: Key Issues and Recommendations* (Washington D.C.: The Conservation Foundation, 1981), p. 35.

251. Oak Ridge National Laboratory, *Integrated Data Base for 1986*, p. 119.

252. Ibid., pp. 119, 130.

253. Ibid., pp. 132-133.

254. G. John Weir, Jr., "Characteristics of Medically Related Low-Level Radioactive Waste", p. 1.

255. 51 Fed. Reg. 43368 (1986).

256. U.S. Department of Energy, *Low-Level Waste Management*, p. 2.

257. League of Women Voters, *The Nuclear Waste Primer*, p. 33.

258. "Compact Groupings, Milestone Compliance, LLRW Site Status, and Legislative Status (Congress and State)," *The Radioactive Exchange*, October 31, 1986.

259. R.D. Bennett and J.B. Warriner, *Alternative Methods for Disposal of Low-Level Radioactive Wastes*, vol. 3, prepared for U.S. Nuclear Regulatory Commission, NUREG/CR-3774 (Washington, D.C.: U.S. Government Printing Office, 1985), p. 1.

260. Oak Ridge National Laboratory, *Integrated Data Base for 1986*, p. 119.

261. League of Women Voters, *The Nuclear Waste Primer*, p. 34.

262. Ibid., p. 35.

263. 42 USC §2021b et seq.

264. League of Women Voters, *The Nuclear Waste Primer*, p. 57.

265. Colin Norman, "Low-Level Waste Deadline Looms," *Science*, August 2, 1985, pp. 448-49.

266. "S.C. State Representative Sheheen Introduces Bill to Close Barnwell," *The Radioactive Exchange*, January 31, 1985, p. 1.

267. "Congress Adopts Compact Consent Bill," *The Radioactive Exchange*, December 20, 1985, p. 8.

268. Ibid., p. 6.

269. "Compact Groupings, Milestone Compliance, LLRW Site Status, and Legislative Status (Congress and State)."

270. "Congress Adopts Compact Consent Bill," p. 8.

Figures

3.1. U.S. Environmental Protection Agency, Office of Toxic Substances, *Chemical Control in the United States: Accomplishments Under the New Chemical Program* (Washington,

D.C.: U.S. Government Printing Office, 1985), p. 61. Final data for fiscal year 1985 provided by U.S. Environmental Protection Agency, October 1986.

3.2. Information provided by U.S. Environmental Protection Agency, Office of Toxic Substances, April 1986.

3.3. U.S. International Trade Commission, *Synthetic Organic Chemicals, 1984* (Washington, D.C.: U.S. Government Printing Office, 1985), and previous annual issues.

3.4. U.S. Environmental Protection Agency, Office of Pesticide Programs, "Pesticide Industry Sales and Usage: 1985 Market Estimates," September 1986, photocopy, table 8.

3.5. Ibid., table 3.

3.6. Information provided by U.S. Food and Drug Administration, February 1986.

3.7. Marcia J. Gartrell et al., "Pesticides, Selected Elements, and Other Chemicals in Infant and Toddler Total Diet Samples, October 1978-September 1979," *Journal of the Association of Official Analytical Chemists* 68, no. 5 (1985):861; Marcia J. Gartrell et al., "Pesticides, Selected Elements, and Other Chemicals in Infant and Toddler Total Diet Samples, October 1980-March 1982," *Journal of the Association of Official Analytical Chemists* 69, no. 1 (1986):144; Marcia J. Gartrell et al., "Pesticides, Selected Elements, and Other Chemicals in Adult Total Diet Samples, October 1978-September 1979," *Journal of the Association of Official Analytical Chemists* 68, no. 5 (1985):875; and Marcia J. Gartrell et al., "Pesticides, Selected Elements, and Other Chemicals in Adult Total Diet Samples, October 1980-March 1982," *Journal of the Association of Official Analytical Chemists* 69, no. 1 (1986):162.

3.8. The basis for the 56-million-ton estimate, prepared by an EPA contractor for an environmental impact statement on the implementatiomn of the hazardous waste section of RCRA, is described in U.S. Comptroller General, *Hazardous Waste Management Programs Will Not Be effective: Greater Efforts Are Needed* (Washington, D.C.: U.S. General Accounting Office, 1979), p. 5.

The 41-million-ton estimate is made in Booz-Allen and Hamilton, Inc., and Putnam, Hayes, & Bartlett, Inc., *Hazardous Waste Generation and Commercial Hazardous Waste Management Capacity: An Assessment*, prepared for the U.S. Environmental Protection Agency, Office of Water and Waste Management, series SW-894 (Washington, D.C.: U.S. Environmental Protection Agency, 1980), pp. III-2-3.

The 250-million-ton estimate is reported in U.S. Congress, Office of Technology Assessment, *Technologies and Management Strategies for Hazardous Waste Control* (Washington, D.C.: U.S. Government Printing Office, 1983), p. 120.

The 264-million-ton estimate is made by Westat, Inc., *Final Report, National Survey and Disposal Facilites Regulated under RCRA in 1981*, prepared for U.S. Environmental Protection Agency, Office of Solid Waste (Rockville, Md.: Westat, Inc., 1984), p. 123.

The 266-million-ton estimate is reported in U.S. Congress, Congressional Budget Office, *Hazardous Waste Management: Recent Changes and Policy Alternatives* (Washington, D.C.: U.S. Government Printing Office, 1985), p. 17; and The 247-million-ton estimate (transformed into metric tons from the 272.2 short tons reported) was made in the Chemical Manufacturers Association and Engineering-Science, Inc., *Results of the 1984 CMA Hazardous Waste Survey* (Washington, D.C.: Chemical Manufacturers Association, 1986), p. 21. This estimate can also be found in U.S. Congress, Library of Congress, Congressional Research Service, *Hazardous Waste Fact Book*, Report no. 87-56 (Washington, D.C.: Library of Congress, 1987), p. 7.

3.9. Congressional Budget Office, *Hazardous Waste Management*, p. 20.

3.10. Abt Associates, Inc., *National Small Quantity Hazardous Waste Generators Survey*, prepared for the U.S. Environmental Protection Agency, Office of Solid Waste (Washington, D.C.: Chemical Manufacturers Association, 1985), pp. 32-33.

3.11. U.S. Environmental Protection Agency, Office of Solid Waste and Emergency Response, *The New RCRA: A Fact Book* (Washington, D.C.: U.S. Environmental Protection Agency, 1985), p. 4.

3.12. Congressional Budget Office, *Hazardous Waste Miangement*, p. 22.

3.13. Congressional Budget Office, *Hazardous Waste Miangement*, p. 22; and U.S. Department of Commerce, *State and Metropolitan Area Data Book 1986* (Washington, D.C.: U.S. Government Printing Office, 1986), p. 504.

3.14. Calculations are based on the asumption that the chemical and related industries in rapidly industrialized nations generate most hazardous wastes but in much lower quantities than by those based in the United States. For more details, see H. Jeffrey Leonard, "Hazardous Wastes: The Crisis Spreads—The LDCs Are Not Immune to the Problems Associated with Inadequate Disposal of Hazardous Waste," *National Development* 27, no. 3 (1986):36.

3.15. U.S. Environmental Protection Agency, Office of Solid Waste, Information Management Staff, *Summary Report on RCRA Permit Activities for September 1986* (Washington, D.C.: U.S. Environmental Protection Agency, 1986).

3.16. U.S. Environmental Protection Agency, Office of Emergency and Remedial Response, *National Priority List Fact Book* (Washington, D.C.: U.S. Environmental Protection Agency, 1986), pp. 19-20.

3.17. U.S. Comptroller General, *Cleaning Up Hazardous Wastes: An Overview of Superfund Reauthorization Issues*, a report to the U.S. Congress (Washington, D.C.: U.S. General Accounting Office, 1985), p. 10.

Chapter 4

Natural Resources: Land, Water, and Energy

The United States is well endowed with land, water, and energy resources. Yet these resources continue to be placed under stress by the increased population and economic growth (described in chapter 1).

At the same time, Americans have begun to recognize that, as abundant as U.S. natural resources are, they are not limitless. Policies that primarily emphasize the exploitation of resources are giving way to those that emphasize conservation and even preservation. A land ethic based on settlement is being replaced by policies that focus on conserving farm-, range-, and forestland and on making populated areas more livable. The era of increased exploitation of water resources has been replaced by increased emphasis on managing water use. The energy crunch of the early 1970s dramatically shifted the nation's attention to the need for using available energy supplies more wisely.

As population and economic growth continue in the coming years, the nation will require new, long-term management strategies as it strives to keep pace with this growth and to deal with the resulting, increasing stresses.

LAND

The United States is rich in land. With 2.25 billion acres, it had an average of 9.4 acres per capita in 1985.[1] In 1984, the United States had 1.4 times the per capita acreage of the world as a whole.[2]* Fifty-eight percent of the

---

*The boundaries of the United States include an additional 46 million acres of inland water surface, or about 0.2 acres per capita.[3]

nation's land is privately owned. Of this land, 67 percent is owned by individuals and married couples, 16 percent by other family groups (including family corporations), 13 percent by other corporations and partnerships, and 4 percent by miscellaneous deed holders.* Distribution of private land title is uneven; 40 percent of privately owned land is in the hands of just 0.5 percent of the landowners, whereas 78 percent of private landowners hold deeds to only 3 percent of the private land.[5]

Almost one-third of the nation's land (over 700 million acres, particularly in the West and Alaska) is federally owned (figure 4.1). This remains true even though, for much of the 19th century, considerable economic and political energy was devoted to disposing of federal lands. Between 1781 and 1985, over 1 billion acres of public land were sold or granted to homesteaders (287 million), states (328 million), railroad corporations (94 million), and other entities.[6] Other public landholders today include the state and local governments (7 percent of total land area) and Native American Indian tribes (2 percent of total land area).[7]

Land currently owned by the federal government is used for a variety of often-conflicting purposes. The Bureau of Land Management (BLM)—which manages 337 million acres of land, more than any other federal agency[8]—is required by the Federal Land Policy and Management Act of 1976 to maintain and manage its lands for multiple uses and sustained yield.[9] Energy resource development, hardrock mining, timber production, livestock grazing, recreation, and the protection of fish and wildlife habitat, cultural resources, and natural scenic and scientifically valuable areas all compete for priority on BLM lands.[10]

The U.S. Forest Service, the second largest federal land manager with 190.7 million acres, faces similar conflicts in how its land is used.[11] The other major federal land owners—the Fish and Wildlife Service (FWS, with 90.4 million acres),[12] the National Park Service (with 79.5 million acres),[13] and the Department of Defense (DOD, with 24 million acres)[14]—tend to have more specific management objectives.†

---

*These data were reported in 1978 but have probably not changed substantially since then. The patterns of private landownership vary greatly from state to state. For example, although individuals and married couples owned 67 percent of the private land nationwide in a 1980 assessment, in the Pacific region less than half of the private land was in such ownership. In the Corn Belt and Lake States regions, single and joint title holders held more than 80 percent of the private land.[4]

†FWS lists the acreage it administers, and DOD lists the acreage it controls. Although comparable to the acreage they own, the figures may not be identical.

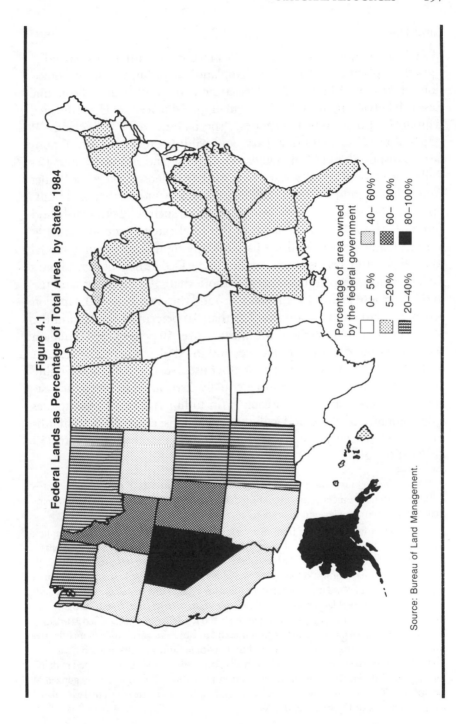

Figure 4.1

Federal Lands as Percentage of Total Area, by State, 1984

Percentage of area owned
by the federal government

0– 5%
5–20%
20–40%
40– 60%
60– 80%
80–100%

Source: Bureau of Land Management.

Land Use

Most land in the United States—76 percent—is either "forestland," "grassland pasture and range," or "cropland" according to one categorization scheme used by the U.S. Department of Agriculture's Economic Research Service (figure 4.2).* The remaining 24 percent of U.S. land area is grouped into two broad categories, "special uses" and "other land."[15] "Special uses" includes rural parks and wildlife areas (211 acres), non-farm transportation (27 million acres), defense and industrial areas (24 million acres), and farmsteads and farm roads (8 million acres).[16] The "other land" class encompasses 274 million acres and includes urban and built-up areas, and areas of miscellaneous vegetation, such as desert, marsh, and tundra.† About half of the lands in this final category are in Alaska.[18]

On a regional scale, land-use patterns vary significantly from national totals (figure 4.3). For instance, according to the Department of Agriculture's categorization, cropland accounts for more than 50 percent of land use in the Northern Plains (107 million acres) and the Corn Belt (100.4 million acres). But cropland accounts for less than 10 percent of the land in the Mountain states (43.8 million acres), where over 50 percent (304.5 million acres) is grassland pasture and range, and in Alaska, where 75.8 percent of the land (277 million acres) is for other uses, such as parks and wildlife areas.[19] Although total forest area is equally distributed between the eastern and western portions of the country (including Alaska), it encompasses larger proportions of the land in the eastern regions, especially in the northeastern (62 percent), Appalachian (57 percent), and southeastern (59 percent) regions.[20]

---

*Determinining just how much land is used for what purposes in the United States is difficult. Different sources even within the federal government, use categorization systems that differ in terminology and definitions.

†Estimates of land use come from many sources that use different statistical sampling techniques with various degrees of error. Although the rough estimates are an adequate gross representation of the uses to which land is being put, they are not precise. For example, the urban area is almost certainly overstated because city limits, being political rather than geographical boundaries, do not coincide with actual land character. On one hand, undeveloped and rural land may exist within city limits, yet be considered "urban." On the other hand, built-up areas in towns of under 2,500 residents are not classified as urban.[17] Furthermore, the character of spaces within each land-use category varies tremendously. The downtown skyscrapers of a large city, clustered single-family homes in a suburban subdivision, and the main street of a small town all occupy urban land. Land devoted to dairying is quite different from the land on a cotton plantation, yet both are categorized as agricultural. The two categories "special uses" and "other land" are combined as "other" for the purposes of figure 4.2 and 4.3.

Land use seems to change rapidly in the United States. New subdivisions and shopping centers suddenly appear on what until recently was productive farmland. New office buildings are built on formerly vacant lots. Wetlands are drained and forests cut down to provide more cropland.

Figure 4.2
Land Use in the United States

Changes in Land Use in the United States,
1974–1982

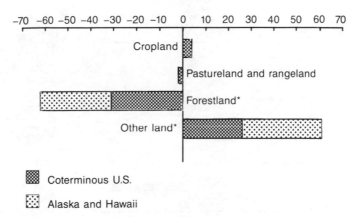

Coterminous U.S.

Alaska and Hawaii

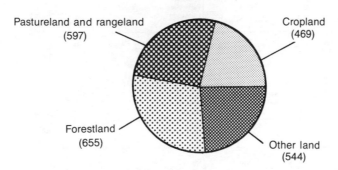

Major Uses of Land, 1982,
Total United States
(Million acres)

* Some changes, especially those in Alaska, are due to recategorization rather than changes in land use.

Source: U.S. Department of Agriculture.

Figure 4.3
Major Uses of Land in the United States, by Region, 1974–1982*

Region **Changes from 1974 to 1982**

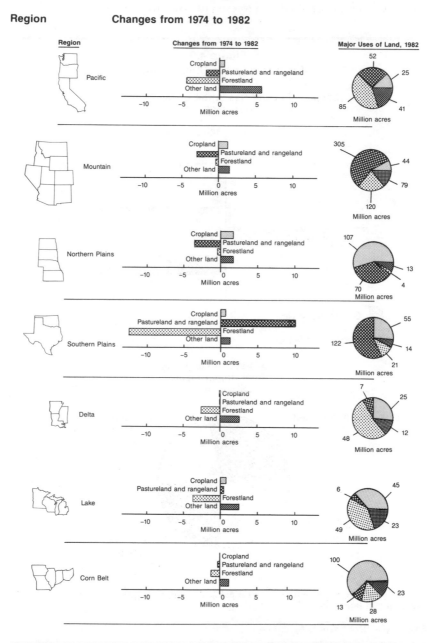

Figure 4.3 (continued)
Major Uses of Land in the United States, by Region, 1974–1982*

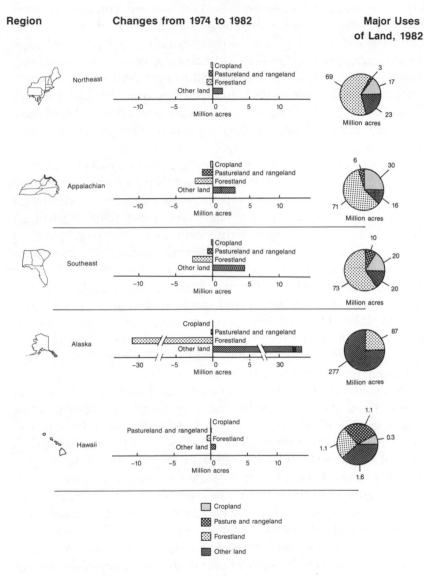

Region

Changes from 1974 to 1982

Major Uses of Land, 1982

Northeast

Appalachian

Southeast

Alaska

Hawaii

Cropland

Pasture and rangeland

Forestland

Other land

* Some changes, especially those in Alaska, are due to recategorization rather than changes in land use.

Source: U.S. Department of Agriculture.

Yet national trends in land use are difficult to identify or confirm, especially in the short term.

For the first few centuries after Europeans began to settle North America, large-scale and dramatic changes in land use occurred. Forests and prairies were converted to cropland. Even on nonagricultural land, intensive logging and livestock grazing, as well as the spread of towns, represented major departures from Native American patterns of crop production, animal husbandry, and settlement. By the beginning of the 20th century, the current pattern of land use on the North American continent had emerged. Certain trends, such as an increase in the amount of urbanized land, have continued, but the changes in this century have been gradual and, compared to the nation's total land area, relatively small.

These relatively static conditions, however, mask considerable shifting back and forth among uses. Large amounts of abandoned agricultural land are allowed to revert to forest, while large areas of forest are cleared for cropland. The shifts may be very large, even if they result in small net changes. The "other" category is the exception, tending to gain more or less irreversibly. Nearly 13 million acres were transformed into urban areas between 1970 and 1980, compared to 9 million in the 1960s.[21] New roads and highways, especially the interstate highway system, add to this total both by direct consumption of land and by making undeveloped areas more accessible. Dam building, begun on a large scale in the 1930s, has inundated millions of acres, generally agricultural, especially in the Tennessee Valley, Missouri River basin, and Columbia River basin.[22] Much of this conversion, especially to reservoirs and roads, has slowed significantly.

The predominant changes in the nation's land use from 1974 to 1982, exhibited in all regions, was a decrease in forestland and a corresponding increase in the "other" category (figure 4.2). Nearly half of these changes were in Alaska and were the result of reclassification of forestlands to recreation and wildlife areas, shifts that only reflected changes in legal designation rather than changes in actual land use or vegetative cover.[23]

Most regions also exhibited a decline in pastureland and rangeland. The exception was in the Southern Plains, where large increases represented reclassification of noncommercial forest to open rangeland.[24] Some of the decrease in pastureland and rangeland was due to actual changes in land use and was countered by increases in cropland, especially in the western regions, where cropland expanded onto semiarid rangeland to meet the demands of the export boom of the 1970s.[25]

Urban Land

In 1980, some 47 million acres (2 percent of the total area of the United States) were in urban areas, as defined by the U.S. Bureau of the Census.[26]* How urban land is used greatly influences the quality of life for most Americans and the condition of the environment in general. The urban environment affects how other lands are used, what lands are converted to other uses, and the extent of pollution in many areas.

Seventy-six percent of Americans lived in metropolitan areas by 1984. Of that proportion, roughly 41 percent lived in central cities, while 59 percent lived in suburbs.[28] Because a substantial proportion of the nation's economic activities occurs in urban areas and because those areas house much of the U.S. population, they are the sites of many of the nation's most serious pollution problems.

Urban areas have grown rapidly since World War II. In 1950, 5.9 percent of U.S. land was designated as "metropolitan"; by 1980, metropolitan areas constituted 16 percent of U.S. land.[29] While statistics on the conversion of land to urban use are uncertain because of changes in the definitions of land-use categories, the Department of Agriculture estimates that the land area used for urban development increased by about 36 percent from 1960 to 1970 (from 25.5 million acres to 34.6 million acres) and by another 37 percent between 1970 and 1980 (from 34.6 million acres to 47.3 million acres).[30] Estimates of annual conversion of rural land to urban and transportation uses are roughly 900,000 acres per year.[31]† While the total land area involved is small relative to the total land area of the United States, the impacts at local and regional levels can be significant.

As indicated in chapter 1, most of this growth has occurred in the suburbs. Suburbs, built up over the last three decades primarily as bedroom communities, increasingly have come to house offices and commercial development, resulting in a more urban atmosphere in areas traditionally thought

---

*The Department of Agriculture also includes another 11 million acres in "farmstead and ranch headquarters" and 5 million acres in "small built-up areas" in its category of urban and built-up lands.[27]

†This figure is only one-third of the 3 million acres estimated in the 1981 National Agricultural Lands Study, based on a comparison of studies done in 1967 and 1977. The 1977 study overestimated built-up areas and some land classified as built-up in 1977 was reclassified by the Soil Conservation Service as rural land in the more comprehensive 1982 National Resources Inventory.[32]

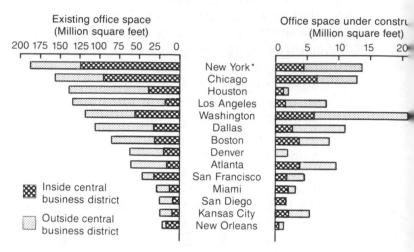

Figure 4.4
Office Space in Selected U.S. Cities, Summer 1986

Existing office space
(Million square feet)

Office space under constru
(Million square feet)

Inside central
business district

Outside central
business district

* New York central business district refers to mid-town Manhattan. Outside CBD ref
the rest of Manhattan; other boroughs are not included.

Source: The Office Network.

of as suburban.[33] Many suburban cities have "more jobs than bedroc
The hallmark of these new urban cores is the wrenching replacemer
the suburban residential way of life with the opportunities and probl
of a city."[34] Figure 4.4 illustrates the tremendous office space construc
under way as of mid-1986; most of the new space is being constructed out
of areas traditionally thought of as the city core.

Suburban growth corridors are frequently located along highway
ensure easy access, but the result in many cases has been severe traffic c
gestion due to increased intrasuburban commuting and dependenc
a few major arteries. Intrasuburban commuting was estimated to acco
for 40 to 45 percent of all work trips in large metropolitan areas in
United States in 1980, while only 30 to 33 percent of metropolitan w
trips were made entirely within a city.[35] In many cases, existing transp
tation networks are unable to handle the additional traffic.[36] Indicati
of the extent of the problem include longer commuting times, increa
response times for emergency vehicles, increased numbers of accide
and an expanded definition of the hours constituting the "rush hour

Urban Revitalization

In the face of declining financial support from the federal government, increased cooperation between private developers and public agencies has contributed significantly to urban revitalization.[38] Indianapolis, for instance, is noted for its turnaround from the 1960s, having created new jobs, new private investment in the downtown, and more tax revenue, as well as a sense of pride in the city's new image.[39] Urban waterfronts in many cities are being built into areas that are drawing economic investment and creating spaces for urban recreation.[40] Many urban areas, including Boston, Philadelphia, Baltimore, and San Francisco, have "festival marketplaces," which focus on unique cultural and historic themes, thus adding to the social and cultural environment of the city.[41]

This upsurge in historic preservation activities—the number of local historic preservation commissions increased from some 600 in the late 1970s to over 1,200 by 1986[42]—contributes substantially to the success of urban revitalization efforts. One recent study found that, in the four cities examined:

> preservation was linked to a dramatic increase in physical renovation activity, the formation of new businesses, the stimulation of investment of private funds and lending, an increase in tourism, a decrease in crime, a significant rise in property values, and an overall improvement in the quality of life.[43]

Historic preservation tax credits have played a large role in encouraging rehabilitation of historic structures, particularly since the Economic Recovery Tax Act was enacted in 1981.[44] The General Accounting Office reported that between 1982 and 1985, the National Park Service, which certifies historic structures, received nearly four times as many applications as during the 1977-1981 period.[45] Under the Economic Recovery Tax Act, taxpayers reported about $6.1 billion in rehabilitation expenditures for 1982 and 1983 together and earned an estimated $1.3 billion in tax credits.[46]

Efforts to Manage Growth

The effects of growth continue to be an important public concern and are being addressed by state and local governments in urban, suburban, and rural areas. In several places, voters have passed initiatives and referenda to control development, indicating their perceptions that locally elected officials are doing too little about the adverse effects of urban sprawl. For instance, in 1986 voters in Los Angeles passed an initiative limiting growth of high-rise development occurring in or adjacent to residential neighborhoods. This initiative grew out of concern about increased traffic, loss of affordable housing, and deterioration of neighborhood character.[47] Such ballot measures, particularly in suburbs and small towns, have become increasingly common ways of voicing public concern about planning and zoning issues.[48]

Among cities experiencing development booms, many seek to maintain urban environmental quality through growth management mechanisms requiring direct or in-kind contributions from developers to municipalities for housing, open space, employment, and infrastructural improvements. Both San Francisco and Boston, for example, have developed such programs.[49]

Citizens are also becoming concerned about the effects of high-rise development on community aesthetics. For example, city councils in Austin and Denver have enacted measures limiting building heights in some parts of the city to protect scenic vistas deemed critical to city character.[50] A number of cities around the country have instituted measures to restrict the use of signs and billboards to unclutter the local visual environment.[51]

The rapid expansion of urban areas also can create serious problems of incompatible adjoining land uses. A classic example is farmers who are pitted against the residents of newly suburbanized areas. The farmers complain of children and pets who destroy crops or harass livestock and of rising property taxes pushed up by newcomers' services. The nonfarmers get equally irate about farm machinery operating early in the morning, manure odors, and pesticide spraying. The farmers often lose such battles as the nonfarmers come to outnumber them and to dominate local government. One analyst describes the result as the "zone-out" process—suburbanites gain a numerical majority, incorporate an area, and then enact zoning regulations to ban "objectionable" agricultural land uses.[52] Farmers and other interests have counterattacked in state legislatures; since 1971, over 40 states have enacted "right-to-farm" laws, which exempt preexisting agricultural uses from nuisance suits.[53] Some experts claim that the mere existence of such laws acts as a deterrent to litigation against farmers. However, of the several cases brought to court, few thus far have been decided in favor of farmers.[54]

Another farmland protection technique is "agricultural districting," which is an effort, often initiated by farmers, to promote farming as the primary activity in a legally recognized area. Farmers within a declared district who voluntarily agree not to develop their land for a specified length of time receive a variety of benefits. These benefits include not only such guarantees as preferential taxation and protection from nuisance suits, but also the assurance that their neighbors will not sell to developers, thus preserving the "critical mass" necessary to maintain agricultural activities in an area.[55] The first agricultural district was established in New York in 1971, and by 1986 over 25 million acres in 13 states were protected.[56] Other ways used to protect farmland from development include zoning, purchase or transfer of development rights, and tax reductions for agricultural land.[57*]

State governments in many parts of the country are responding to these trends and are beginning to take a more active role in managing growth. In the early 1970s, several states enacted comprehensive laws that involved state governments directly in land-use regulation. With a decade of experience behind them, some states are refining these laws and others are developing similar initiatives suited to their own political and demographic conditions. Florida, for example, finding its growth management legislation of the 1970s inadequate, enacted several new laws in 1984 and 1985 to improve the effectiveness of state and local land-use regulation. One of these, the State and Regional Planning Act of 1984, requires each regional planning council to develop a comprehensive plan and each agency to develop a functional plan to be used in its budgetary process. All plans must be in accordance with the state plan.[60] Maryland, in response to deterioration of the Chesapeake Bay, established a critical area protection program in 1985 that seeks to control development along the shoreline. Localities in the state are developing plans consistent with statewide criteria.[61]

Assessing Trends

One trend that clearly emerges is that the fastest growth   in terms of population, economy, and land use conversion—continues to occur in suburban areas. This growth results in the expansion of metropolitan areas in general and, in many places, the gradual urbanization of suburbia.

Ascertaining the effects of that growth and how well urban land is being used, however, is more difficult. Despite the variety of indicators of urban

---

*These conflicts also are occurring in more rural areas as people continue to move into nonmetropolitan areas. Even though this movement from metropolitan to nonmetropolitan areas has slowed—the growth rates in nonmetropolitan areas fell from an average of 1.3 percent in the 1970s to 0.8 percent in the 1980s[58]—such conflicts are likely to continue to increase. People will continue to settle at the urban fringe and in even more rural areas. This can create conflicts with forest owners as well as farmers. New rural residents often object to clear-cutting of timber, burning of logging residues, and aerial application of herbicides. Particularly in the West, nonfarm rural settlement has been associated with a greater incidence of forest fires and more difficult fire management once a blaze starts.[59]

environmental quality that can be examined, solid, supportable conclusions are elusive. In most cases, the existing data do not show trends over time, are not available for many urban areas, or have only an indirect relationship to the quality of the urban environment. Moreover, overall improvement or decline in quality is a relatively subjective judgment that depends to some extent on one's personal experiences and values. A 1986 opinion poll conducted by the Gallup Organization for the Urban Land Institute found that 85 percent of the general public thinks that "a good job is being done to improve the city,"[62] a finding that would suggest that people are fairly satisfied with current policies. At the same time, the increasing demand for growth management indicates dissatisfaction with the direction development has taken in some areas. Overall, the upsurge in activity and interest in historic renovation, various aesthetic issues, and community planning portend some improved conditions for urban land use in the future.

Cropland

Although urban development is the most intensive type of land use, the widespread conversion of forestland and prairie to cropland probably has been the major ecological change in the last two centuries. Huge areas of forest, especially in the eastern and southern United States, were cleared to allow agricultural planting. As settlement moved westward, crops replaced native grasses; only isolated vestiges remain of the tall-grass prairie that once covered some 140 million acres of the plains.[63]

In 1982 the nation's cropland base totaled about 469 million acres. The three main categories of cropland, in decreasing intensity of use, were cropland used for crops (383 million acres), idle cropland (21 million acres), or cropland pasture (65 million acres).[64]* Despite mild fluctuations, partly due to federal crop programs, the acreage of total cropland in the United States, has not changed substantially since around 1920.[66] However, regional and local shifts in cropland and changes in the intensity of its use continue to have important environmental implications. From 1949 to 1969, cropland acreage (excluding cropland used for pasture) decreased from 409 to 384 million acres[67] (figure 4.5), as large areas of cropland in the South and the East were converted to pastureland, forestland, and urban and other nonagricultural uses.[68] Particularly in the South and Appalachia, a contributing factor to cropland conversion was that much of the farmland had

---

*"Cropland pasture," also called "cropland used for pasture," is long-term crop rotation of field crop and pasture. It also includes some land used for pasture that could be cropped without additional improvement.[65]

been divided into small, hilly, irregularly shaped tracts that were inappropriate for highly mechanized agriculture.[69]

Government programs encouraging farmers to take land out of production were important factors in these changes.[70] In the Southeast, about half the cropland diverted under federal farm programs was never returned to crop production.[71] These losses, however, were largely offset by new land being brought into production through drainage and irrigation in other regions. Extensive areas of the lower Mississippi Valley were converted to cropland by the clearing and draining of bottomland hardwood forests in Arkansas, Louisiana, Mississippi, and Missouri.[72] Draining wetlands, including some in the Everglades watershed basin, permitted expansion of sugar cane, vegetable, and citrus production in southern Florida[73] and contributed to cropland increases in the Corn Belt states and the prairie pothole region of Minnesota and North Dakota.[74] Irrigation allowed substantial expansion of cropland in western Texas, western Kansas, California, Washington, Idaho, and Montana.[75]

When export demand increased in the 1970s, the gradual, long-term decline in cropland acreage was reversed. Cropland, including idled land, rose from from 384 million acres in 1969 to 404 million acres in 1982.[76] Cropland used for crops reached a high of 387 million acres in 1981—a figure matched only in 1949.[77] Double-cropping, particularly with winter wheat and soybeans, also rose during this time from 3.1 million acres in 1969 to 12.4 million acres in 1982.[78] The clearing and draining of forestlands in the lower Mississippi Valley and the pocosins of North Carolina and the conversion of forestland and pastureland to cropland in the Corn Belt and Lake States continued to add to the cropland base.[79] Drainage for cropland also continued in southern Florida with the continued expansion of sugar cane, the increase in dairy operations, and the shift of citrus production southward after the freezes in the early 1980s.[80] Private irrigation (primarily from groundwater) contributed to cropland expansion in the arid West.[81] But this trend was slowed by the rise in oil prices. For instance, much of the irrigated land in northwestern Texas went out of production in the 1970s because of high pumping costs caused by the combination of increased energy prices and the rapid lowering of the water table in this part of the Ogallala Aquifer by irrigation withdrawals.[82]

With the fall in export demand, the amount of cropland has begun to decrease as well. In 1986, cropland used for crops was 31 million acres below the 1981 high, with the greatest reductions occurring in the Plains states and the Corn Belt.[83] These decreases resulted in part from federal programs encouraging farmers to idle a portion of their cropland to receive

Figure 4.5
U.S. Cropland Acreage Changes,* 1949-1982

**Increase in Cropland Acreage,
1949–69**

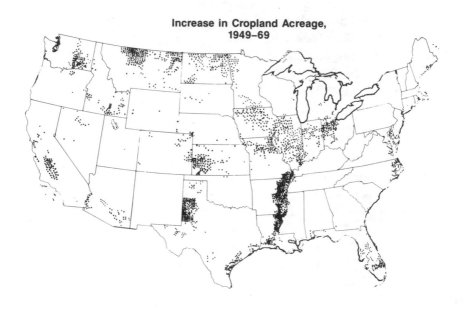

**Decrease in Cropland Acreage,
1949–69**

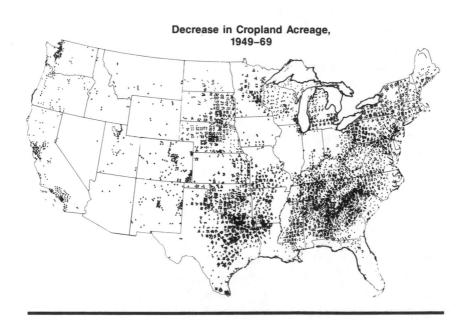

Figure 4.5 (continued)
U.S. Cropland Acreage Changes,* 1949-1982

**Increase in Cropland Acreage,
1969–82**

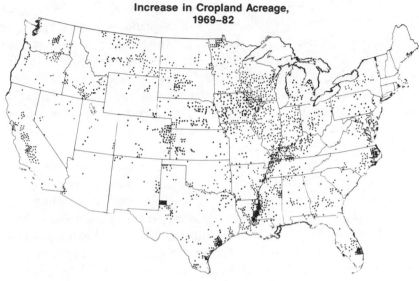

**Decrease in Cropland Acreage,
1969–82**

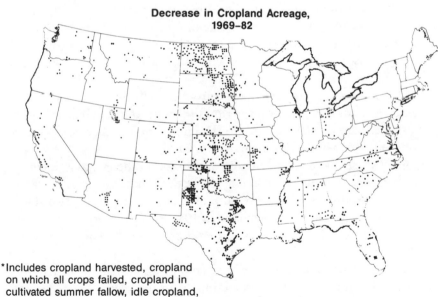

*Includes cropland harvested, cropland on which all crops failed, cropland in cultivated summer fallow, idle cropland, and cropland in cover and soil improvement crops. Excludes cropland used only for pasture.

Source: U.S. Soil Conservation Service.

•1 dot = 10,000 acre change, in counties which had a net increase or decrease in cropland acreage.

agricultural income supports. In 1983, 78 million acres of cropland were idled under the payment-in-kind (PIK) and other government programs—the largest amount of land ever diverted in a single year.[84] Most of that land went back into production the following season when the one-year PIK ended. In 1986, 49 million acres of cropland were idled as part of federal crop programs.[85] The enactment of the Food Security Act of 1985 created longer-term incentives for cropland retirement—particularly for more erodible lands.[86] By March 1987, 8.2 million acres of highly erodible cropland were scheduled to be planted to grass or trees for a 10-year period under the Conservation Reserve Program, and the Department of Agriculture had tentatively accepted another 10.6 million acres for enrollment in the program.[87]

When cropland is converted to urban uses, the loss is irreversible. Urban growth competes with agriculture for some of the nation's best land; the level, well-drained soils of prime farmland are ideal for building. The American Farmland Trust estimates that 30 percent of the dollar value of agricultural production comes from counties that are within metropolitan statistical areas or that adjoin metropolitan counties, even though those counties contain only 14 percent of the nation's cropland.[88] An estimated 38 percent of the land converted to urban uses between 1967 and 1975 was prime farmland.[89] As a percentage of total cropland, however, these losses are not large. Annually, the total amount of rural land converted to urban uses is equivalent to only about 0.2 percent of the nation's cropland.[90]

Of greater concern than cropland conversion is the high rate of cropland erosion in many areas. Of the major land-use classes, cropland has the highest annual erosion rate (figure 4.6). In the United States, sheet and rill erosion (soil carried off by flowing water) on cultivated cropland averages 4.8 tons per acre per year. Wind erosion contributes another 3.3 tons, resulting in a total loss of some 3 billion tons per year.[91] These averages, however, mask the seriousness of the erosion problems in some areas. Two-thirds of all soil erosion from U.S. cropland in 1982 took place on less than one-quarter of the land.[92] Extremely severe erosion tends to be a highly localized problem.

Soil conservation practices are used on only about half of the nation's farmland (figure 4.7). The most erodible land, however, is not receiving the most attention. Only 47 percent of highly erodible cropland receives soil conservation treatment, while 58 percent of land considered to have little or no problem with erosion receives treatment.[93] One reason farmers may use soil conservation practices where erosion rates are low is the economic advantage of some practices such as conservation tillage.

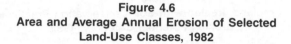

Figure 4.6
Area and Average Annual Erosion of Selected
Land-Use Classes, 1982

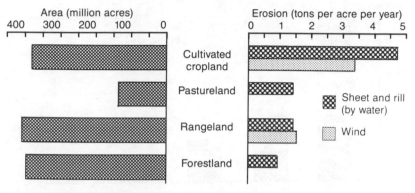

Source: U.S. Soil Conservation Service.

Conservation tillage (any of a variety of tillage or planting practices that leaves at least 30 percent of the soil surface covered by crop residue) is the single most widely used erosion control practice.[94] The Conservation Tillage Information Center estimates that conservation tillage practices were used on 100 million acres in 1985 (27 percent of the nation's planted cropland) and that the most effective technique, "no-till," was practiced on 15 percent of this land.[95] This is a substantial increase from 1970, when less than 5 percent of U.S. cropland was planted under some form of conservation tillage (figure 4.8).[96] Conservation tillage is attractive because it lowers labor and fuel costs in addition to reducing soil loss.[97]

The estimated total gross investment for conservation in U.S. agriculture has, in real terms, dropped substantially from its high in the post-World War II period (figure 4.9).* From 1936 to 1980, private and nonfederal public expenditures for land conservation were roughly equal to federal expenditures.[99] Much of the recent decline results from a decrease (in constant dollars) of federal appropriations for cost-sharing programs.[100] Increased state, county, and local expenditures for conservation have only partially offset this drop in federal funding.[101]

---

*These investments include (a) permanent improvements such as terraces, grassed waterways, and sediment basins and (b) conservative farming systems such as soil-conserving crops and rotations, conservation tillage, strip-cropping, and contour farming.[98]

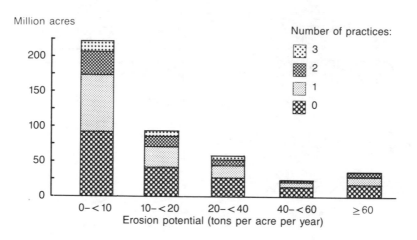

Figure 4.7
U.S. Cropland Treated with Soil Conservation Practices,*
by Erosion Potential Category, 1982

Million acres

Number of practices:

3
2
1
0

Erosion potential (tons per acre per year)

* The four major soil conservation practices sampled were conservation tillage, terracing, contour farming, and stripcropping.

Source: U.S. Soil Conservation Service.

Over the same period that land conservation investment declined, investment (primarily nongovernment) in irrigation rose dramatically. Irrigated farmland (which includes cropland, pastureland and rangeland) increased from 18.0 million acres in 1939[102] to a high of 50.3 million acres in 1978 before falling again to 44.7 million acres in 1984.[103] Although investment in drainage has not risen, drained acreage rose from 45.9 million acres in 1935 to 107.5 million acres in 1980 with the use of new, cheaper drainage systems[104]

Rangeland and Pastureland

Rangeland and pastureland ("grassland pasture and range," in the Department of Agriculture's classification scheme), account for 597 million acres, or 26 percent of the nation's land.[105]* Almost three-fifths of such land was in nonfederal ownership in 1982.[106] Land is included in this category if its natural productivity is too low to support crops or trees, generally

---

*This total does not include 65 million acres of cropland pasture.

Figure 4.8
Percent of Cropland* Treated with Conservation Tillage,†
1963–1985

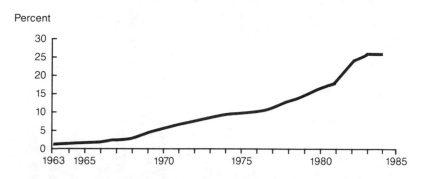

* Cropland used for crops.

† For early years, the acreage of conservation tillage (CT) may be overestimated by as much as 50 percent because the definition of CT has changed over the years. Practices that were considered CT in the 1960s or 1970s may no longer fit the current definition. The large increase between 1981 and 1982 is due in part to the difference in data sources used.

Source: U.S. Soil Conservation Service; Conservation Tillage Information Center.

because of aridity. In their natural condition, rangeland and pastureland are typically grassland, although they may include various types of shrubs and desert vegetation. The amount of pastureland and rangeland in the United States has declined slowly but constantly since 1950.[107]

Animal grazing on both pastureland and rangeland can have significant ecological effects. The interests of wildlife and of livestock ranchers can directly conflict, as when ranchers put up fences to keep wild animals off their land,[108] or when domestic and wild animals must compete for limited available food.*

Livestock grazing may also change the type of vegetation on land as the animals consume the plant species they prefer more rapidly than those plants can grow back. As a result, other species, such as shrubs, replace the native

---

*According to one highly speculative estimate, domestic cattle and sheep may even consume more range forage than did the huge herds of bison, elk, antelope, and bighorn sheep that roamed freely before the introduction of livestock. These herds have been so reduced that big-game forage requirements in the western United States are now only about 5 percent of those of domestic livestock.[109]

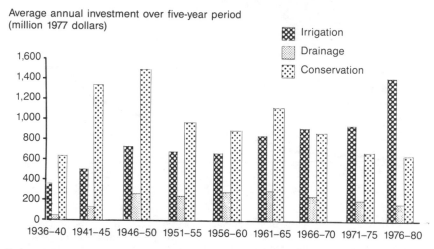

Figure 4.9
**Gross Investment for Irrigation, Drainage, and
Conservation in U.S. Agriculture, 1936–1980**

Average annual investment over five-year period
(million 1977 dollars)

Source: U.S. Department of Agriculture.

grasses. This shift may, in turn, result in a decrease in the wildlife that traditionally depend on the grasses and an increase in other species, such as deer, that can live off the shrubs.[110] The most recent estimate for grazing on public and private lands combined, made in 1976, was 213 million animal unit months per year, virtually unchanged from 1970.[111]*

The majority of the rangeland that livestock and wildlife depend on is in fair or poor condition. Rangeland condition is defined in terms of the degree of variance from the virgin or climax plant community.[114] In 1982, the Soil Conservation Service rated over 60 percent of the nonfederally owned rangeland as being in fair or poor condition (that is, having less than 50 percent of the virgin or climax plant community present) and only 4 percent as being in excellent condition (that is, having more than 75

---

*An animal unit month, the standardized measure of food consumption by livestock, is the amount of forage required to feed a 1,000-pound animal for one month. Beef production increased substantially in the early 1970s, but range grazing by cattle did not, because of the shift to grain concentrates, pasture grasses, and harvested plants.[112] In 1985, BLM and the U.S. Forest Service permitted a total of 21 million animal unit months of grazing on their land.[113]

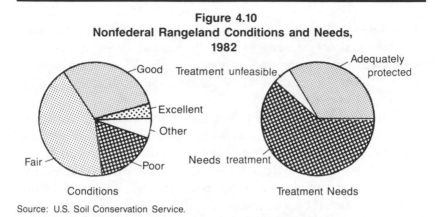

Figure 4.10
Nonfederal Rangeland Conditions and Needs,
1982

Conditions

Treatment Needs

Source: U.S. Soil Conservation Service.

percent virgin or climax plant community present) (figure 4.10). The fair-
and poor-quality land needs a wide range of treatment, including erosion
control, brush management, and reestablishment.[115] The condition of
federal rangelands is almost identical to that of nonfederal lands.[116]

Grazing on some public lands is coming under stricter control as BLM
and the Forest Service exert their authority to control grazing on public
lands, as authorized by the Taylor Grazing Act of 1934.[117] In addition,
21 states currently conduct extension programs to improve range conditions, and 4 more states are in the process of starting such programs.[118]

Forestland

The sheer magnitude of American forests overwhelmed the first European
colonists. Much of the United States' expansion well into the 19th century
involved the wholesale harvesting of these forests to clear land for growing
crops, as well as satisfying needs for firewood, building materials, masts,
and forest products.[119] Although few statistics are available, the net forest
area in the United States probably continued to decline until around the
time of World War I, when, on a national basis, natural reforestation of
formerly cleared areas in the East began to offset harvesting of new areas.[120]*
Since then, the total amount of land covered by forests has increased slightly,

---

*It should be noted, however, that forest clearing is continuing in other countries, especially
for agricultural purposes. Between 1974 and 1983 the amount of forestland and woodland
in the world declined by more than 245 million acres (2.4 percent), with a 2.5 percent increase
in cropland of over 90 million acres.[121]

so that it now accounts for 655 million acres, or 29 percent of the nation's land.[122]*

According to a 1986 Forest Service report, nearly two-thirds (481 million acres) of the nation's forested area is classified as commercial timberland. Nonindustrial, private owners own 58 percent of this land, the forest industry owns 14 percent, 18 percent is in the national forests, and other public owners own 10 percent.[124]

Until the middle 1970s, the production of forest products increased moderately, with substantial cyclical fluctuations reflecting economic conditions (figure 4.11).[125] The state of the economy, and particularly the market for new houses, has always been a major influence on the economic health of the forest products industry. But, even before the mid-1970s, the mix of products changed substantially; from 1950 to 1980, pulpwood use increased nearly threefold and plywood use more than fourfold, while lumber use showed no strong upward or downward trend.[126]

Since the mid-1970s, however, the production of forest products has increased rapidly. One of the most dramatic increases has been the use of fuelwood.[127] The Office of Technology Assessment estimates that by 1980 "about 55 percent of all wood removals in the United States were consumed for fuel purposes."[128] The forest products industry itself consumed about 60 percent of this wood energy in its manufacturing operations.[129] The Forest Service attributes the continued rapid increase in the 1980s to the increased demand for housing by the families created by the baby boom generation.[130]

Timber imports play an important role in satisfying the total demand for forest products in the United States. Canada, in particular, provided over 31 percent of the softwood lumber consumed in 1985, up from less than 20 percent in 1975.[131] But the United States is both an importer and exporter. In 1984, it exported over four times as many hardwood logs as it imported—in contrast to the early 1960s, when it was a net importer. It also exports substantial amounts of softwood logs, equivalent in value to about 15 percent of all U.S. wood products (including paper). These exports go primarily to Japan, China, and other countries in the Far East, although exports to Canada also grew 20 percent from 1983 to 1984.[132] The pattern of imports and exports is influenced by such factors as ship-

---

*This total excludes 66 million acres of forested land used for parks, recreation, and wildlife conservation.[123]

Figure 4.11
U.S. Timber Production and Consumption, 1950–1983*

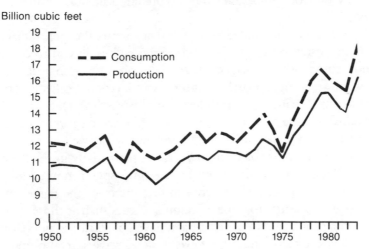

Data are in roundwood equivalents.
* 1983 data are preliminary.

Source: U.S. Forest Service.

ping costs and the supply and demand situation for different types of wood.*
According to the Forest Service, the United States is likely to remain a net
importer of forest products for some time.[134]

Yet the statistics on timber growth in the United States suggest that
wood growth in the United States is adequate to meet domestic needs.
American forests in general grow more new wood each year than is removed.
Much of that new wood, however, is from less desirable hardwood trees
in the eastern United States and the Great Lakes region.[135] Softwood supplies, particularly of valuable northwestern species such as the Douglas fir,
remain tight.[136] Even ignoring this fact, the overall situation is less encouraging than a comparison of total consumption to total growth might suggest.

One problem is that the nation expects its forests to serve a wide range
of needs, including timber production, wildlife habitat, recreational opportunities, watershed protection, employment, and wilderness preservation,

---

*Some observers have alleged that Canada strives to improve its own competitive
position—and thereby affects U.S. timber import patterns—by subsidizing its exports of
softwood lumber.[133]

among others. Sometimes these demands conflict, as when some of the remaining old-growth mature stands of northwestern forests, which could provide very valuable timber, are also the preferred habitat for the northern spotted owl.[137]

These conflicts are complicated by the fact that many of the more valuable stands are expensive to harvest. The Forest Service typically constructs the roads and assumes other management and administrative responsibilities that allow private companies to harvest these stands economically. In some cases (for example, with old-growth forests in the Northwest), the timber may be valuable enough to justify the costs.[138] However, several studies have alleged that the nation actually loses money (as well as valuable wilderness and wildlife habitat) in many cases, particularly in the Rocky Mountain region, because the Forest Service must spend more to allow the harvesting to occur than it receives in revenue from the harvests.[139] The Forest Service denies that the economics of sales such as those in the Rocky Mountains and the Northwest are as unfavorable as many critics claim and notes that the roads and other developments serve several purposes (for example, recreation and fire control) besides providing access for logging companies.[140] This ''sales-below-cost'' controversy has become a major issue among environmental groups and in Congress.[141]

The Forest Service has also been attempting to resolve use conflicts through improved planning. Under the Resource Planning Act of 1974 (as amended by the National Forest Management Act of 1976), it must prepare comprehensive development and management plans for each of 123 management units it operates.[142] Since it began this process in the late 1970s, the Forest Service has completed 65 plans and has drafts for 43 more.[143] Many of these plans are controversial, however, and, even when they are not controversial, it is not clear whether they are being implemented.

Multiple-use conflicts can involve privately owned lands as well, though usually with less intensity and in different forms. The issue on private, nonindustrial forestland frequently is not how to manage the land for commercial timber production but whether to allow that use at all. Private, nonindustrial landowners—typically farmers or investors with woodlots— owned title to 58 percent of the commercial forestland in the United States in 1983, yet this land grew only 27 percent of the softwood growing stock.[144] Although such lands have the biological capacity to produce as much timber per acre as similarly situated industrial timberland, the average productivity of private, nonindustrial forestland in most parts of the country is far less than that of its industrial counterpart.[145] This is because of generally less intense management of nonindustrial forests. In the Southeast, for example, only one of nine acres of nonindustrial, private forestland is currently being regenerated to softwoods (for example, pine stands) after harvest.[146] Many private owners in the Southeast—and elsewhere—are simply uninterested in harvesting their forests. Intensive, even-aged stand management would detract from other uses for the woods, such as hunting and recreation.[147] In addition, forest management requires more effort and outlays than many owners are willing to expend, especially since returns are often years away. The way in which nonindustrial owners of woodlands choose to manage their lands remains an important variable influencing the overall condition of American forests.

A second reason why the outlook for forest lands is not as promising as the crude statistics might indicate is that these statistics do not necessarily reflect the quality of the forests. The amount of land that grows trees is not a complete indicator of the health of forest resources. The age class, species composition, quality of timber for commercial use, and density of the canopy all affect the usefulness of a forest, whether as a sample of undisturbed nature, a home for wildlife, a place for solitude and recreation, or a supplier of timber for wood products.

In New England, the almost unmanaged growth of the forests reappearing on lands once cleared for agriculture[148] is resulting in commercially underproductive woods. Eastern forests also have experienced increasingly apparent, but unexplained, slowing of growth, particularly among conifer species. The decline in growth has been observed in both northern and southern forests, especially at high elevations. Atmospheric pollution, including acid precipitation, is a suspected cause.[149]

Forest productivity depends both on natural processes and management practices. Some potential sources of damage to forests are relatively easy to control; others are not. Major efforts to protect forests from fire have reduced the number of acres burned each year to about one-third of what it was in the early 1950s. However, the decrease in burning appears to have bottomed out; some forest fires are inevitable.*

Insect pests are a more serious problem (figure 4.12). The imported gypsy moth, for years the scourge of northern forests, continues to increase its range south and westward, defoliating 1.7 million acres in 12 states in

---

*Foresters' attitude toward fire has changed as they have recognized the ecological role of small, naturally caused fires, which reduce litter buildup, encourage reproduction of some species, and enhance the diversity of the forest. Some fires are now allowed to burn themselves out, and in some cases, fires are set and controlled to achieve management goals. Such controlled burning may, in fact, take place over many more acres than are burned by uncontrolled wildfire.[150]

Figure 4.12

U.S. Forest Acres Damaged, Planted, and Seeded, 1950–1985

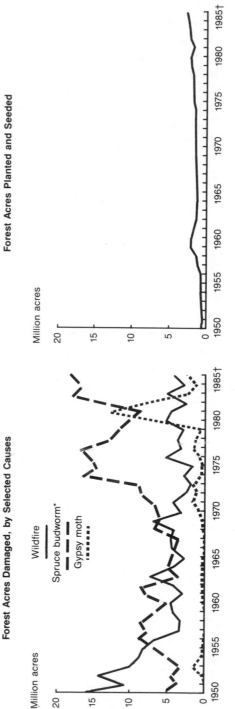

Forest Acres Damaged, by Selected Causes

Wildfire
Spruce budworm*
Gypsy moth

Forest Acres Planted and Seeded

* These data include spruce budworm and western spruce budworm.
† Preliminary data.

Source: U.S. Forest Service.

1985.[151] Defoliation by the spruce budworm has shown general decreases since 1984; however, damage due to the western spruce budworm is increasing, reaching a record 12.8 million acres defoliated in 1985.[152] The South has seen increased mortality of pines, partially due to outbreaks of bark beetles.[153] Mountain pine beetles are also a major problem in the West.[154] The amount of defoliation caused by other major pests, such as the many varieties of pine beetles, tends to show annual fluctuations corresponding to periodical serious outbreaks.[155]

Some companies are more intensively managing their forests to increase productivity. But the overall trends are not encouraging. The number of forest acres seeded or planted each year since 1950 has remained fairly constant (figure 4.12). When a forest is cut, the natural succession of vegetation from the bare site usually ends up producing another forest, but the process can take a long time, and species may change as the forest regenerates. Where softwood stands have been clear-cut, replanting ensures that the desired species continue to be available. Reforestation has been rising slowly but fairly steadily over the past 35 years. Over half the acres planted and seeded each year are owned by forest industry companies, though this proportion is declining.[156]

Clearly, what the nation wants to use its forests for and how much effort and investment it is willing to expend to increase the productivity of those forests for timber and other forest products are two fundamental issues that will determine the quality and quantity of American forests in the future. One partial answer may be to change the type of timber that the nation depends on for many of its forest products. For instance, interest has increased in using low-quality timber in the Lake States for the improvement and diversification of local and state economies. The Lake States' forests are now experiencing a resurgence of commercial harvesting of abundant aspen, valuable for particleboard and other "reconstituted" wood products.[157]

WATER QUANTITY

The nation's land resources are not the only ones that are under stress. Just as important—and just as stressed—are its freshwater resources, both on the surface and underground. The amount of water available for use by humans is only a small fraction of the total amount of water on earth. Most of the earth's water (99.99 percent) is in oceans and open seas, groundwater, soil moisture, glaciers, and ice caps.[158] Much of the world depends on precipitation and surface flow for water supply, though groundwater supplies are being increasingly tapped.[159] Many factors affect precipitation patterns. Some are short-term weather cycles. However, other cycles discovered by studying tree rings and mountain ice indicate that long-term variations in precipitation occur somewhat predictably as well.[160]

The United States is considered to be a water-rich country, receiving about 4,200 billion gallons of precipitation per day, or about 18,000 gallons of rainfall per person every day. Most (65 percent) of that rainfall returns directly to the atmosphere through evaporation or transpiration, less than one-third reaches the oceans through surface or subsurface flow, and only 2.5 percent is consumed.[161]

This general picture of water availability in the United States is not uniform, however. A closer look reveals significant regional variations. For example, land east of the Mississippi River is considerably wetter (with an average of 44 inches of rainfall annually) than is land west of the Rocky Mountains (averaging 18 inches per year).[162]

Water availability in an area can vary substantially from year to year. An area that is flooded one year can experience a drought the next. From late 1984 through much of 1986, the traditionally wetter East Coast suffered from major droughts that threatened municipal and industrial water supplies and jeopardized the short-term viability of agriculture in several states.[163] Meanwhile, the continuing, record-breaking rise of water levels in the Great Salt Lake has led Utah to approve a plan to pump water from the lake into the Utah desert.[164] And, in the arid Colorado River basin, the 1984 water-year's 20.6 million acre-foot (maf) flow volume into Lake Powell (the Upper Basin's largest storage reservoir) outstripped the previous year's 19.5 maf flow and represented the largest annual volume since 1917, a volume that is likely to be experienced no more than once every 100 years.[165]*

However, some of today's changes may represent longer-term trends, not just short-term fluctuations. On the Great Lakes, a century and a quarter of hydrologic records had led most experts to believe that the lakes' water levels would vary by less than five feet over roughly 12-year cycles. But in the summer of 1986, as water levels in four of the five Great Lakes reached or approached their historic peaks, research on water levels over the last 2,000 years suggested that the fluctuation could be five feet greater than

---

*A water-year is a 12-month period representing a full hydrologic or meteorologic cycle (in this case, October 1, 1983, through September 30, 1984.) An acre-foot is the volume of water required to cover one acre of land to a depth of one foot.[166]

was previously thought. The promise of such a further rise would jeopard-ize thousands of beaches and shoreline structures, in addition to the dozens of houses and beaches already lost to lakefront erosion, particularly in Michigan, Illinois, and New York.[167]

In most areas, of course, long-term changes in supply do not ordinarily occur quite so rapidly, but discussion of drought and surplus does raise a point that is fundamental to all water use. Water policy has traditionally assumed that the supply of water was fixed and focused on the changing human demands on the resource. But both hydrology and climate—the natural determinants of water availability—are dynamic processes. Increas-ingly, policy makers are recognizing the natural vagaries of resource availability, vagaries that are becoming more apparent and extreme as the decades of experience with American water resources lengthen into cen-turies. Neither human demand nor natural supply is in any way static; the challenge for policy makers is to seek practical and responsive ways to accommodate both.

Trends in Water Use

The two common measures of water use are withdrawal and consumption. Water is withdrawn when it is taken from a groundwater or surface water source and conveyed to the place of use. Water is consumed when it is no longer available for use because it has been removed from available supplies by evaporation or transpiration, for use in agriculture or manufac-turing, or for food preparation and drinking.[168] Withdrawals and consump-tion refer exclusively to off-stream uses of water; that is, uses that require water to be taken out of a stream channel, impoundment, or groundwater aquifer. By contrast, in-stream uses—for example, hydroelectric power generation, aquatic life, recreation, navigation, and wastewater dilution—utilize water without removing it from the source.

Water Withdrawal

The renewable water supply of the contiguous United States amounts to about 1,380 billion gallons per day (bgd).[169] Water withdrawals in the United States rose 22 percent between 1970 and 1980 (370 bgd to 420 bgd) and 37 percent in the previous decade (270 bgd to 370 bgd).[170] Thus, since 1950 water withdrawals per capita increased from an average of 1,200 gallons per day to about 2,000 gallons per day in 1980.[171]

Steam electrical generation surpassed irrigation as the largest user of water (in terms of withdrawals) in the 1960s (figure 4.13). But irrigation has increased as well, by about 7 percent in both the amount of water used and the total irrigated acreage from 1975 to 1980. An average of 2.9 acre-feet of irrigation water was applied to each of 58 million acres of farmland in 1980.[172] However, irrigated acreage dropped to about 49 million acres in 1982 (figure 4.14), most likely because of increased pumping costs, lower grain prices, and in some cases limited water supplies.[173]

In some locations, water withdrawals have decreased as a result of effi-ciency improvements.[174] Overall, experts feel that water withdrawals for irrigated agriculture may peak within the next decade even though total irrigated acreage may continue to increase into the first decade of the next century.[175]

Public water supplies, which support some industrial as well as most residential and commercial uses, have increased significantly, up 15 per-cent between 1975 and 1980.[176] In contrast, the increasing tendency of industry to recycle process water leads some experts to predict that industrial water demands in the United States actually will decline from the 1985 level of more than 396 gallons per capita per day to fewer than 264 gallons per capita per day by the year 2000.[177]

The overall increase in withdrawals from both surface water and ground-water sources has detrimental effects. The amount of water available for in-stream uses has been severely reduced in many parts of the country. For example, the 1983 National Fisheries Survey reported that low water levels are adversely affecting fish communities in 68 percent of U.S. inland water bodies.[178] Much of the Southwest has insufficient water flows to sup-port many in-stream uses in an average year. In dry years, the problem of inadequate stream flows is experienced in much of the Great Plains as well.[179]

In addition to causing pumping costs to climb, groundwater declines can reduce surface stream flow during periods of low rainfall, draw saltwater into aquifers, and speed the spread of other contaminants. Where exten-sive groundwater withdrawals occur in an aquifer composed of poorly con-solidated materials (such as sand or gravel), aquifer compaction and land subsidence may result. These conditions not only damage structures, interfere with the drainage of streams and sewers, and increase the threat of flooding, but they also reduce the capacity of the aquifer to store recharge water in some cases.[180]

Water Consumption

Water consumption, like withdrawal, has increased steadily for most water uses. About one-fourth of the water withdrawn in the United States is

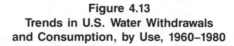

Figure 4.13
Trends in U.S. Water Withdrawals
and Consumption, by Use, 1960–1980

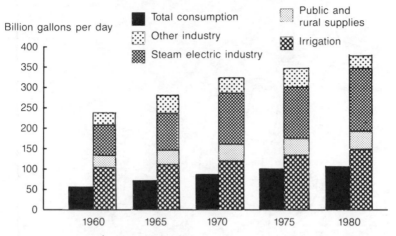

Source: U.S. Geological Survey.

irretrievably consumed, while the other three-fourths returns to surface-water or groundwater supplies.[181]

On average, the growth in water consumption appears to be slowing down. Between 1970 and 1980, consumption increased by only 14 percent, compared with a 44 percent increase for the previous decade (figure 4.13). The decline in industrial water use has caused much of the deceleration. This decline was in large part stimulated by the Clean Water Act, which made the recycling of industrial water supplies more economical than the treatment and discharge of industrial effluent.[182]

Water consumption varies with the type and efficiency of use. For example, out of 100 gallons withdrawn from a river for cooling steam electric utilities, over 98 gallons usually are returned almost immediately to the river. Fewer than 2 gallons are consumed through evaporation.[183] Overall, self-supplied industrial users (not including electric utilities) consume only 13 percent of their withdrawals (although this figure is rising because industries are reusing more of their water).[184] The efficiency of different plants varies greatly, however. One plant may use up to 20 percent more water than another in manufacturing the same product.[185] Among other water users, 59 percent of the water withdrawn for rural domestic use is consumed,[186] as is 21 percent of the water withdrawn for public supplies.[187]

Irrigation consumed an average of 55 percent of all water withdrawn

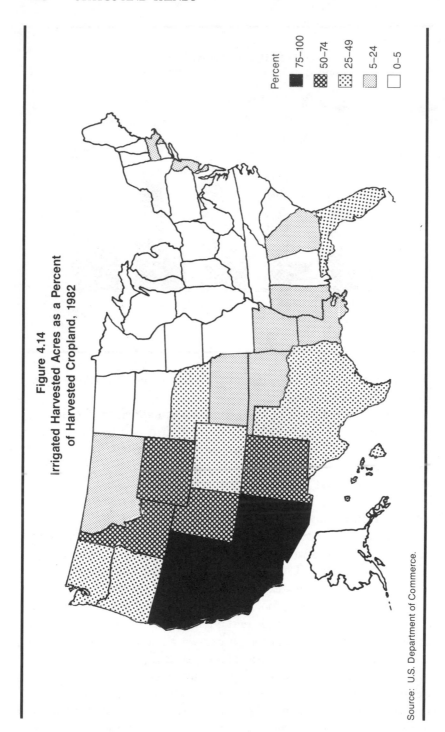

Figure 4.14
Irrigated Harvested Acres as a Percent
of Harvested Cropland, 1982

Percent
75–100
50–74
25–49
5–24
0–5

Source: U.S. Department of Commerce.

for that purpose and accounted for 83 percent of the total amount of water consumed in the United States in 1980 (figure 4.15).[188] While irrigation efficiencies tend to be low, scarcity—resulting from groundwater declines and competition with other uses—is bringing with it improvements in efficiency on an unprecedented scale. The relining of irrigation canals of the Casper Alcova Irrigation District in Wyoming will provide additional water supplies for the city of Casper.[189] It is clear that efficiency improvements of a few percentage points can result in sizable water savings. Nationwide, the Federal Interagency Task Force on Irrigation Efficiencies has determined that improving irrigation efficiencies could reduce withdrawals over the next 30 years by 13 to 18 bgd, making available 1.7 to 4.5 bgd for new uses.[190]

The full water-saving potential of improved irrigation efficiencies is suggested by an enormous proposal for agricultural water conservation, the proposed agreement between the Metropolitan Water District of Southern California (MWD) and the Imperial Irrigation District (IID). While the MWD has for more than 50 years tapped the Colorado River's flows to supply the Los Angeles and San Diego metropolitan areas, the district has only had legal claim to about half of the total amount of water it was taking.[191] The rest has belonged to Arizona. In 1985, when the Central Arizona Project began diverting Colorado River flows, Arizona began to claim its share and the MWD's day of reckoning arrived.[192]

Meanwhile, the Imperial Valley was plagued by inefficient water use. Some of the farmers in the Valley were suing the IID because the wasted water collecting in the Salton Sea was flooding their farmlands.[193] The solution to the Imperial Valley's problem may also be the solution to the MWD's, with Los Angeles paying to gain the use of the water being conserved by the Imperial Valley.

Regional consumption patterns vary as well. A minority of the runoff in the United States occurs west of the 95th meridian (the north-south line running at approximately the western boundary of Minnesota, Iowa, Missouri, Arkansas, and Louisiana).[194] However, about 80 percent of the nation's water is consumed there. In 1980, the 17 contiguous states west of the 95th meridian withdrew an average of 2,900 gallons per person per day and consumed 1,200 of these.[195] By contrast, the consumption rate in the East was only 120 gallons per capita per day—one-tenth of the amount that is consumed in the West.

As a result, many areas in the West are already consuming much of their available water (figure 4.16). In many parts of the eastern United States, average consumption levels are only 1 to 2 percent of the renewable water

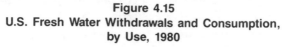

Figure 4.15
**U.S. Fresh Water Withdrawals and Consumption,
by Use, 1980**

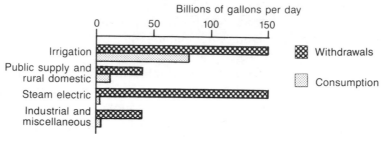

Source: U.S. Geological Survey.

supply. In the West, consumption levels equal to 30 percent or more of the renewable supply are common, and, in the lower Colorado River basin, consumption already exceeds renewable supply.[196] As a result, except during unusual floods, the Colorado River never reaches its natural mouth in the Gulf of California, ending instead 14 miles away in a saline pond.[197]

Global water use has increased steadily throughout the century, with more rapid increases since 1950. Total global use generally can be broken down into irrigation, industry, and public uses accounting for 73, 21, and 6 percent, respectively. These portions vary widely, however, with a country's level of industrialization. In developed countries, use by industry frequently rises to 40 percent or more (up to 80 percent in the case of Eastern Europe), while in the Third World, it constitutes merely 10 percent of total water use, with far more water being consumed by irrigation.[198]

Sources of Water

Most of the water withdrawn in the United States in 1980 (64 percent of total withdrawal, 77 percent of freshwater withdrawal) was from freshwater streams, lakes, and reservoirs. Groundwater was the source of 20 percent of the total supplies and 23 percent of the freshwater supplies. Almost all of the remaining withdrawals were of saline water (99 percent of which is taken from bays and estuaries). One-half billion gallons a day (about 0.1 percent) were reclaimed sewage. During the early 1970s, withdrawal of both groundwater and saline water increased much faster than did withdrawal of surface water. Between 1975 and 1980, however, these trends changed substantially, with the use of surface water increasing more rapidly than the use of either groundwater or saline water. The use of reclaimed sewage declined slightly.[199]

Groundwater

From 1950 to 1975, groundwater withdrawals increased approximately twice as quickly as did surface-water withdrawals. Much of the newly pumped groundwater was used for irrigation (for instance, in the High Plains of Texas).[200] As a result, irrigation accounts for 67 percent of current ground-water use. Public water supplies and industry each account for about 13 percent (figure 4.17). But, between 1975 and 1980, the growth of ground-water use for irrigation slowed, perhaps because of farmers' efforts to hold down the cost of pumping water from deep aquifers. Those costs have resulted from both increased energy costs and the fact that groundwater levels are declining by between 0.5 and 6.6 feet per year under 15 million acres of land irrigated by groundwater.[201]

Groundwater depletion continues to be a serious problem in many parts of the United States. Nationally, one-fourth of the amount of ground-water withdrawn was not replenished in 1975. In the Texas-Gulf region, the proportion was as high as 77.2 percent. In 1975, two-thirds of the nation's resources were experiencing greater withdrawals than there was recharge available, thus water was being taken from storage in these areas.[202] As a result, groundwater levels have declined substantially in many parts of the country: 100 feet in the past 10 years in Alabama; 400 feet in 50 years southeast of Phoenix, Arizona; 300 feet since the early 1930s in south-ern Arkansas; 200 feet since 1950 along the California coast; more than 850 feet in 116 years in northern Illinois (including 370 feet from 1953-1980 in one well); and as much as 20 feet per year throughout large areas of the Columbia Plateau in Washington state.[203]

However, groundwater levels also can recover when withdrawals are reduced. The substitution of imported surface water for groundwater in the Mendota area of California's Central Valley caused groundwater levels to rise nearly 240 feet in only 15 years (1968-1983), though some of this increase may have been attributable to widespread percolation of irriga-tion water. This rise followed a comparable drawdown over the preceding 23 years and occurred notwithstanding an intervening drop of almost 100 feet during the single drought year of 1977.[204] Similarly, after more than 40 years and almost 300 feet of groundwater decline, water level gains of

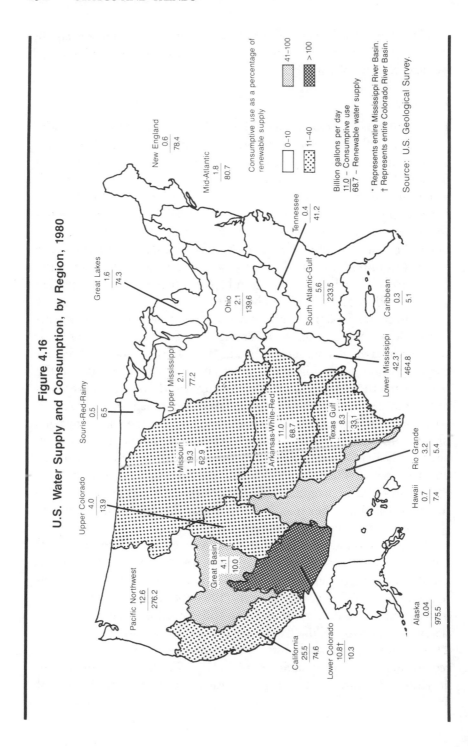

Figure 4.16
U.S. Water Supply and Consumption, by Region, 1980

Consumptive use as a percentage of
renewable supply

0-10

11-40

41-100

>100

Billion gallons per day
11.0 – Consumptive use
68.7 – Renewable water supply

* Represents entire Mississippi River Basin.
† Represents entire Colorado River Basin.

Source: U.S. Geological Survey.

New England
0.6
78.4

Mid-Atlantic
1.8
80.7

Tennessee
0.4
41.2

South Atlantic-Gulf
5.6
233.5

Caribbean
0.3
5.1

Great Lakes
1.6
74.3

Ohio
2.1
139.6

Upper Mississippi
2.1
77.2

Lower Mississippi
42.3*
464.8

Souris-Red-Rainy
0.5
6.5

Missouri
19.3
62.9

Arkansas-White-Red
11.0
68.7

Texas Gulf
8.3
33.1

Upper Colorado
4.0
13.9

Great Basin
4.1
10.0

Lower Colorado
10.8†
10.3

Rio Grande
3.2
5.4

Hawaii
0.7
7.4

Pacific Northwest
12.6
276.2

California
25.5
74.6

Alaska
0.04
975.5

up to 40 feet were observed from 1973-1983 in the Baton Rouge, Louisiana, area, due both to water conservation motivated by Clean Water Act restrictions on industrial effluent releases and to an industrial recession.[205]

Surface Water

Traditionally, when water supplies have become tight in the United States, either new reservoirs have been built or more wells have been installed to satisfy the rising demands. But for a variety of reasons—principally the diminishing economic returns from new construction and environmental objections to reservoir siting—the rate at which reservoir capacity is being added in the United States has fallen off dramatically.[206] This new reality was officially recognized by the Western Governors Association in July 1986, when they agreed that water conservation and the reallocation of existing water rights would be the principal means to meet new demands, and that new reservoirs would be built only when they represented the least-cost means to secure a new water supply.[207] One example of this new approach was provided in a June 1986 proposal by Washington state's U.S. senators. The object was to gain at least 87,000 acre-feet of water and boost instream flows in Washington's Yakima River Basin Water Enhancement Project

Figure 4.17
U.S. Fresh Groundwater Withdrawals,
by Use, 1960–1980

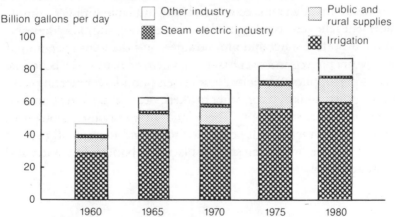

Source: U.S. Geological Survey.

by improving the efficiency of the project's existing irrigation, diversion, and storage systems.[208]

Indeed, in many areas of the country, additional reservoir capacity by itself would not substantially increase the available water supply, since increased reservoir construction is accompanied by increased evaporation. Reservoir evaporation in the United States is already equivalent to 15 percent of the total amount of offstream water consumption.[209] At some point, additional evaporation from new reservoirs built in a watershed may significantly decrease the amount of water that can be continually withdrawn.[210]

Other Sources

Other water sources—saline water and reclaimed sewage—can be used only for specific purposes. Saline water can be used in coastal facilities to generate electricity, and reclaimed sewage can provide water to irrigate golf courses, lawns, and nonfood crops. Reclaimed sewage is, however, a relatively expensive source of water compared with the surface water and groundwater the United States is accustomed to using.[211]

The emerging changes in methods of water resource management result from increasing demands on fixed but renewable water resource bases, increasing costs of water supply capacity expansion, and shifting views of appropriate government roles in water resources development and management. These new management strategies include demand management, supply management, and water reallocation.[212] Demand management employs water conservation measures, water pricing, and withdrawal permits to ensure that demands correspond with available supplies. Supply management relies on recycling and reusing existing supplies, the combined use of surface water and groundwater, and the joint operation of different water projects in a river basin as a system to increase the beneficial use of existing supplies. Water reallocation sets priorities for meeting competing water demands by using water markets, negotiating water transfers, and other voluntary transfers.[213] These innovative responses, along with efficiency improvements, will be needed more and more in all parts of the United States as increasing stress is placed on both surface water and groundwater supplies.

ENERGY

The United States can take some pride in having responded effectively to the stresses experienced during the 1970s. Today's motorist, for instance, pays much less for gasoline than was the case a few years ago and has only distant memories of long gas lines and rationing. The situation appears so rosy that the government is attempting to relax fuel-conserving speed limits and automobile fuel efficiency standards.

But the future may hold some surprises. The United States remains dependent on fuel sources that are exhaustable—and that are being gradually depleted. Due primarily to the slow pace of research and development in the 1980s, many renewable forms of energy are much more expensive to produce than conventional sources or are not yet ready for commercial exploitation. These factors, and potential increases in energy prices (see chapter 1) together may make the United States vulnerable once again to energy supply disruptions.

In addition to ensuring a secure national energy supply, the environmental consequences of energy choices also must be factored into policy making. The mix of energy sources utilized can affect levels of indoor and outdoor air pollution, contamination of streams and lakes, risk of exposure to toxic and radioactive substances, and a variety of other environmental conditions.

Energy Consumption

Increased fuel prices, the worldwide economic recession, and greater energy efficiency together caused U.S. energy consumption to fall over 10 percent between 1979 and 1983 (from 78.9 to 70.5 quads*).[216] With the recovery of the U.S. economy, energy consumption picked up as well, rising 5.1 percent from 1983 to 1984 before declining slightly in 1985.[217]†

The decline was most noticeable in the industrial sector, where energy consumption is closely related to industrial production.[218] Consumption in that sector dropped an average of 1.15 percent between 1974 and 1985. However, the other major consuming sectors—household, commercial, and transportation—also showed a leveling off, or even a slight decrease, in the early 1980s. This stabilization is a striking change from the high growth rate that had been the case a decade earlier (figure 4.18).

These recent trends demonstrate the increased efficiency with which the United States uses energy. Overall energy consumption per dollar of gross national product (in 1982 dollars) fell 13.2 percent—or 2.8 percent per year—from 1980 to 1985.[219] In general, all end-use sectors showed

---

*A quad is a quadrillion Btus. A Btu (British thermal unit) is the amount of energy required to raise the temperature of one pound of water one degree Farenheit. In one barrel of crude oil, there are approximately 5.8 billion Btus.[214] One quad is equivalent to 28 days of United States motor gasoline usage in 1985, or 30 hours of world energy consumption in 1984.[215]

†1985 energy-usage figures reported throughout this section are preliminary.

improvements. Industry consumption per unit of output (in 1977 dollars) declined an average of 3.2 percent annually from 1974 to 1984.[220] Gradual shifts in the industrial sector away from energy-intensive processing industries and toward increased emphasis on service industries is a partial explanation.[221] (See chapter 1.) Similarly, between 1974 and 1984 average consumption of energy per household dropped 2.7 percent per year[222] because of higher prices. In transportation, average automobile mileage improved 2.3 percent per year from 1974 to 1984 (figure 4.19).[223]

Energy Production and Supply

Even with its increased efficiency, the United States does not produce all the energy it consumes; net imports accounted for 14 percent of total consumption in 1985.[224] However, in the short term, the nation has become more self-sufficient. Domestic production reached a peak of 65.9 quads in 1984 (it dropped 1.7 percent in 1985), and net imports declined 40.2 percent from 20.0 quads in 1977 to 12.0 quads in 1985 (figure 4.20).[225]

The composition of U.S. energy production has shifted considerably since the early 1970s. In 1972, coal- and nuclear-generated electricity constituted 23.5 percent of total energy production; by 1985, these two sources accounted for 36.4 percent.[226] Reduced oil and natural gas output accounted for most of the shift, in addition to decreased imports and lower overall demand (figure 4.21).

Several factors argue against the trends that began in the late 1970s continuing into the future. One is the (at least temporarily) lower prices of oil and other energy sources, which should stimulate increased consumption. The second is that many of the least expensive and technologically easy conservation measures are already in place; further improvements are likely to be both more difficult and more expensive to implement.[227] The third is the shift in emphasis away from energy conservation. While further improvements in energy efficiency are certainly possible, through use of the most energy-efficient technologies for appliances, residential and commercial space, and transportation, implementation of these technologies depends on appropriate policies and economic incentives.[228]

The U.S. Department of Energy (DOE) predicts that, even in the industrial sector, recent trends of gradually declining energy use will be reversed and that energy consumption will grow by approximately 0.7 percent per year from 1985 to 1995 assuming no recession.[229] At the same time, DOE forecasts that the nation's shift away from energy-intensive industries, a return of somewhat higher energy prices, and continued replacement of old equipment with new, more energy-efficient equipment will

Figure 4.18
U.S. Energy Consumption, by End-Use Sector, 1950–1985

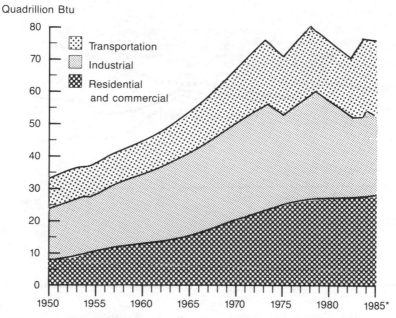

Quadrillion Btu

Transportation
Industrial
Residential
and commercial

* 1985 data are preliminary.

Source: U.S. Department of Energy.

combine to cause domestic energy use per unit of output to continue its decline through 1995.[230]

Energy Sources

The aggregate numbers on energy consumption hide some important shifts among different forms of energy, some of which may have important environmental implications. In general, the composition of the U.S. fuel supply is gradually shifting from oil and gas toward nuclear power and coal used in the production of electricity (figure 4.22). Between 1970 and 1985, for example, consumption of nuclear power increased more than 17-fold and consumption of coal for electricity doubled. In the same period, consumption of coal by industry declined 37.2 percent. Concurrently, total petroleum usage increased a meager 4.5 percent and natural gas consumption dropped by 18.5 percent.[231]

Although U.S. dependence on oil and natural gas is declining in a relative

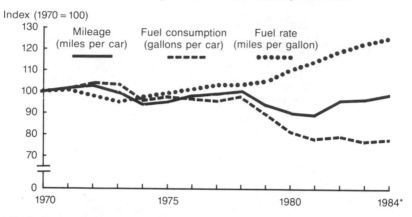

Figure 4.19
Automobile Usage in the United States, 1970–1984

Index (1970 = 100)

* Preliminary data.

Source: Federal Highway Administration.

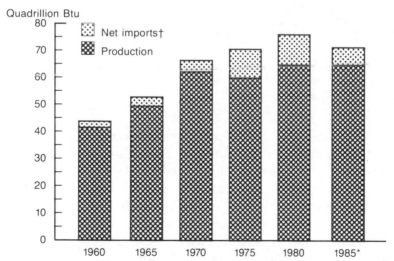

Figure 4.20
U.S. Energy Production and Net Imports, 1960–1985

Quadrillion Btu

* Preliminary data.
† Net imports = total imports less exports and adjustments.

Source: U.S. Department of Energy.

Figure 4.21
U.S. Energy Production, by Fuel Source, 1950–1985

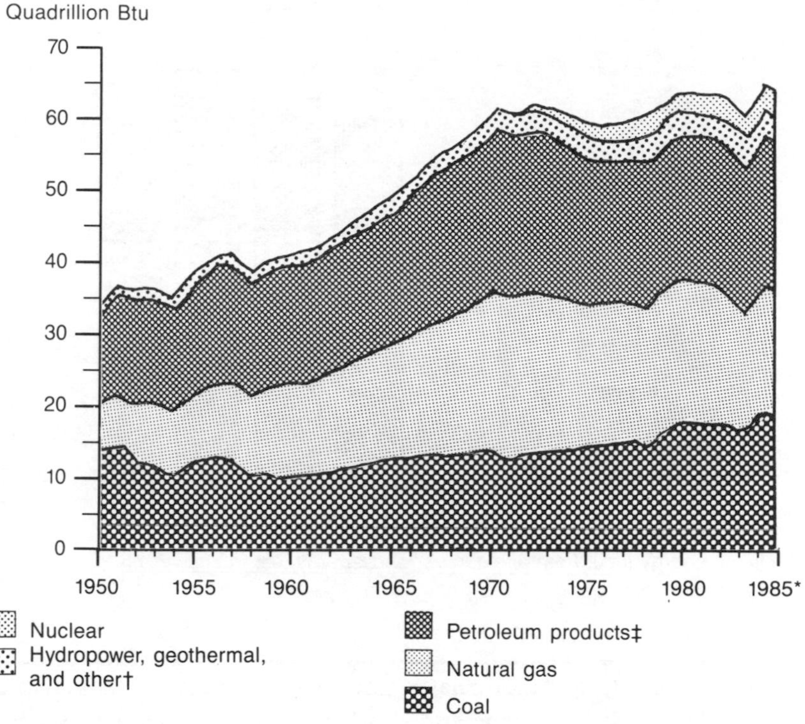

Quadrillion Btu

Nuclear

Hydropower, geothermal, and other†

Petroleum products‡

Natural gas

Coal

* Proliminary data.

† "Other" includes wood, wind, waste, and solar sources that are connected to the electric utility grid.

‡ Petroleum products include crude oil, lease condensate, and natural gas plant liquids.

Source: U.S. Department of Energy.

sense, in absolute terms the United States continues to rely heavily on these nonrenewable resources. In 1985, oil and natural gas together accounted for nearly two-thirds of all energy consumed in the United States, whereas coal provided only 23.7 percent (17.5 quads) and nuclear energy only 5.6 percent.[232]

These trends have important implications for the environment. For instance, as consumption of electricity increases and the proportion of it supplied by coal and nuclear power rises, the pollution problems associated with these sources become more pronounced. Without controls, combustion of coal can result in emissions to the atmosphere of sulfur, carbon,

Figure 4.22
U.S. Energy Consumption, by Fuel Type, 1950–1985

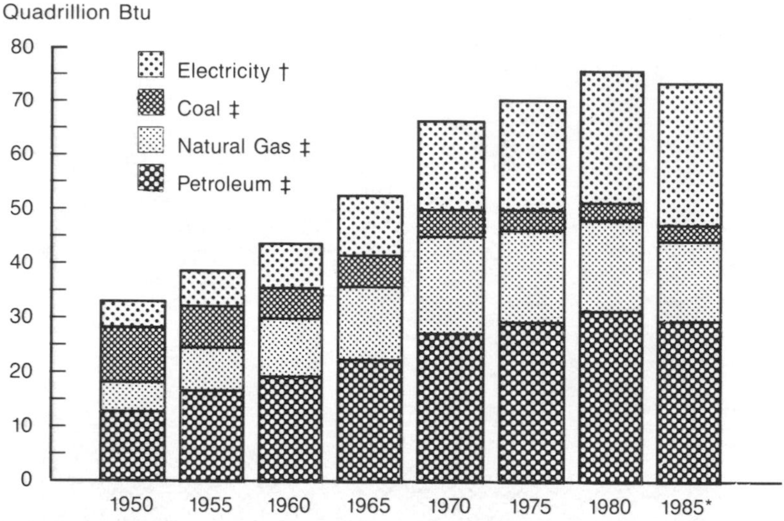

Quadrillion Btu

Legend:
- Electricity †
- Coal ‡
- Natural Gas ‡
- Petroleum ‡

* Preliminary data.
† Includes energy input from all sources, and energy lost in conversion.
‡ Includes direct use only.

Source: U.S. Department of Energy.

and nitrogen oxides and particulates, among other things.[233] (See chapter 2.) In addition, both the generation and transmission of electricity affect the environment through thermal releases and use of land for transmission lines.[234]

Oil

The United States has long relied on oil to meet a major portion of its energy needs. Because of this reliance, nearly every sector of the economy was affected by the oil price fluctuations of the 1970s and 1980s. Despite the nation's gradual shift away from oil, it will continue to be the United States' major source of energy for years to come.

As a result of the 1973-1974 oil embargo and the 1979 Organization of Petroleum Exporting Countries (OPEC) price increase, oil prices rose dramatically in the 1970s and early 1980s. These price increases resulted worldwide in greater energy conservation efforts, increased fuel efficiency, and lower energy consumption per unit of output.[235] The resulting lower consumption of oil, along with large oil inventories and a stalemate in price and production level negotiations among OPEC producers, led to depressed oil prices around the world in the mid-1980s.[236] As a result, the average price of gasoline (in constant dollars) in the United States rose from 30.3 cents in 1970 to a high of 49.7 cents in 1981 and then declined to 37.1 cents in 1985 (figure 4.23).[237] Estimates for 1986 indicate that constant dollar prices may have fallen below 30 cents per gallon, the lowest level since 1973.[238]

In response to these price shifts, oil consumption in the United States decreased after the late 1970s but now shows signs of increasing. The most dramatic effects of the higher prices were to stimulate production and decrease imports.

Production of crude oil and lease condensate (a natural gas liquid) in the United States has now apparently stabilized at about 8.5 to 9.0 million barrels per day (mbd) after falling from the 1970 level of 9.6 mbd.[239] Alaskan production (ranked second after Texas[240]) has increased steadily since it began in 1959, accounting for approximately 20 percent (1.8 mbd) of total U.S. production in 1985 (figure 4.24, left). Offshore production, how-ever, began to decline in the early 1970s and contributed only 14 percent of total production in 1985 (figure 4.24, right).[241]

Oil imports provided a total of 5.0 mbd in 1985, down from a peak of 8.8 mbd in 1977. U.S. dependence on OPEC oil has declined dramatically since the late 1970s, when as much 70 percent of imported oil was pro-vided by these countries (figure 4.25). Oil imported from Arab OPEC members was only 0.5 mbd in 1985, 19 percent of its 1980 level. Mexico, Canada, and the United Kingdom have picked up much of the slack, so that non-OPEC nations accounted for 64 percent of U.S. imports in 1985.[242] Increased energy efficiency and slowed economic activity also helped by lowering the U.S. demand for oil. Some analysts have suggested that lower oil prices in the mid-1980s could lead to renewed dependence on OPEC oil because of higher demand for oil and because of lower production in the United States and other non-OPEC countries.[243]

Oil production is an environmental issue not only in the United States but increasingly in other countries as well. It has the potential to cause both chronic and acute environmental problems, in the form of routine releases of drilling muds and the cleaning of tanks or oil spills and blowouts. Offshore drilling, in particular, poses significant risks.[244] It can result in acute releases to the marine environment, as the Santa Barbara Channel oil spill, the Amoco Cadiz accident off the coast of Brittany, and the IXTOC I blowout in the Gulf of Mexico all illustrate. Problems posed by chronic releases are less certain. Some research indicates that the species composition of marine communities can change dramatically.[245] Onshore drilling, however, also poses environmental risks, particularly the possibility that a breach in a pipeline could develop and affect terrestrial ecosystems.[246]

The implications of the recent fall in oil prices could be significant for the economy as well as the environment (see chapter 1). While many energy

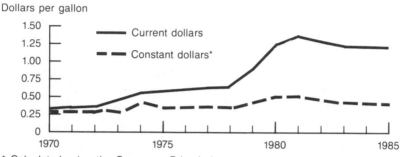

Figure 4.23
Gasoline Prices to U.S. Consumers, 1970–1985

Dollars per gallon

* Calculated using the Consumer Price Index.

Source: U.S. Department of Energy.

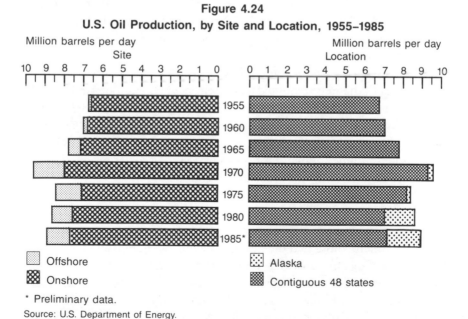

Figure 4.24
U.S. Oil Production, by Site and Location, 1955–1985

* Preliminary data.
Source: U.S. Department of Energy.

conservation measures are structural (for example, physical improvements to make cars more fuel-efficient) and therefore will probably not be reversed,[247] worldwide oil demand is likely to increase in response to lower prices.[248] Power plants and industries switch from one fuel to another (from natural gas or coal to oil) in response to price incentives.[249] One analyst estimated that, when the price of residual fuel oil (the petroleum product used predominantly by industry) plummeted from $23 per barrel in December 1985 to $13.50 per barrel in April 1986, as much as 100,000 barrels per day of additional oil demand was generated. He predicted that, if the price continues to fall, fuel switching could expand to as much as 200,000 barrels per day as plants with dual-fuel capability for coal and oil find it profitable to switch to oil. Lower prices also serve as a "lever" to create pressure on producers of other fuels, including natural gas and hydroelectric power, to lower their prices.[250]

Natural Gas

Although natural gas prices (which vary according to region, end-use, and regulatory status) have somewhat mirrored oil prices, production has not.

Figure 4.25
U.S. Oil Imports, OPEC vs. Non-OPEC, 1960–1985

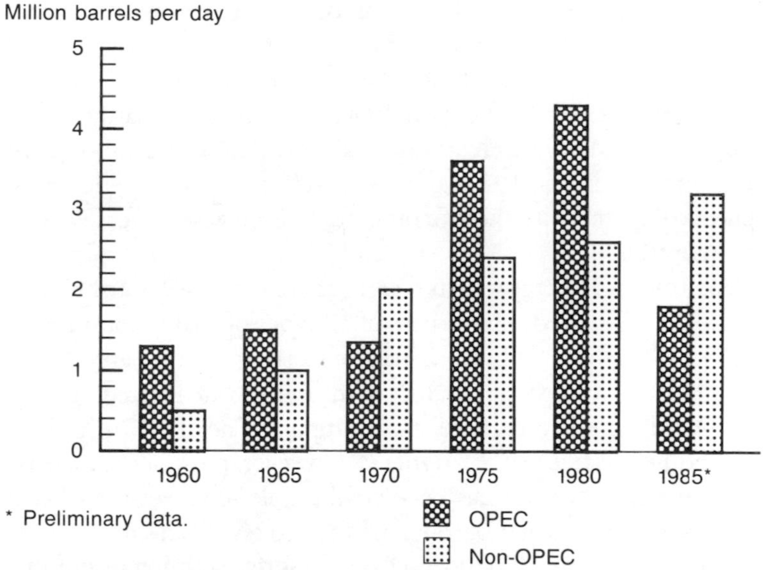

Million barrels per day

* Preliminary data.

OPEC

Non-OPEC

Source: U.S. Department of Energy.

Residential natural gas prices doubled in constant dollars between 1974 and 1983, from $0.96 per trillion cubic feet (tcf) to $2.03 per tcf, but decreased by 6.4 percent from 1983 to 1985 (figure 4.26).[251] To compete with low oil prices, natural gas suppliers continued to drop their prices in 1986.[252]

U.S. production of natural gas, however, has declined steadily since 1973, when it hit a peak of 21.7 tcf (22.3 quads). By 1985 it was down to 16.4 tcf (16.9 quads), a 24 percent drop in 12 years.[253] Net imports increased in 1985 by 10.5 percent over 1984 and constituted 5.1 percent (0.9 tcf) of U.S. consumption.[254] In 1985, 97.5 percent of imported natural gas was supplied by Canada. Proved domestic reserves of natural gas have remained relatively stable over the past decade at approximately 200 tcf, after a dramatic decline from the peak of 292.2 tcf in 1967.[255]

Coal

Coal prices also have been influenced by oil prices, rising in real terms from $16.98 per short ton to $34.90 per short ton (a 106 percent increase) between 1970 and 1982 and then falling by 11 percent between 1982 and 1985.[256] Unlike the situation with natural gas, however, the higher coal prices have stimulated substantially increased production. While 1985 coal production declined slightly from the 1984 peak level of 895.9 million short tons (equivalent to 19.9 quads), production of coal continued its general upward trend.[257] Coal production constituted about 30 percent of total U.S. energy production in 1985, up from 23.5 percent in 1970 yet down from about 41.4 percent in 1950.[258] The decline in the production of coal in the late 1950s and early 1960s was caused primarily by low petroleum prices and severe environmental impacts.[259] The subsequent production increase in the 1970s and 1980s reflects the competitiveness of coal prices compared with those of other fuels, even with increased environmental controls.

The Department of Energy reports that, as of January 1, 1984, the United States had a demonstrated reserve base of all types of coal amounting to 488.3 billion short tons. About one-half of existing reserves are considered recoverable.[260] While less than half of the reserves are located in states east of the Mississippi River, those states supported nearly two-thirds of the 1985 production (figure 4.27, right).[261] However, most of the increase in production in recent years has been attributable to expansion of coal mining in western states, where output has increased sevenfold since 1970.[262]

The majority of new coal production has used surface mining techniques (figure 4.27, left). While coal production by underground mining decreased

Figure 4.26
Natural Gas Prices to U.S. Residential Users, 1970–1985

Dollars per thousand cubic feet
7
6
5
4
3
2
1
0
Current dollars
Constant dollars*
1970
1975
1980
1985†

* Calculated using the Consumer Price Index.
† Preliminary data.

Source: U.S. Department of Energy.

Figure 4.27
U.S. Coal Production, by Mining Method and Location, 1950–1985

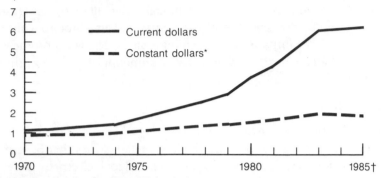

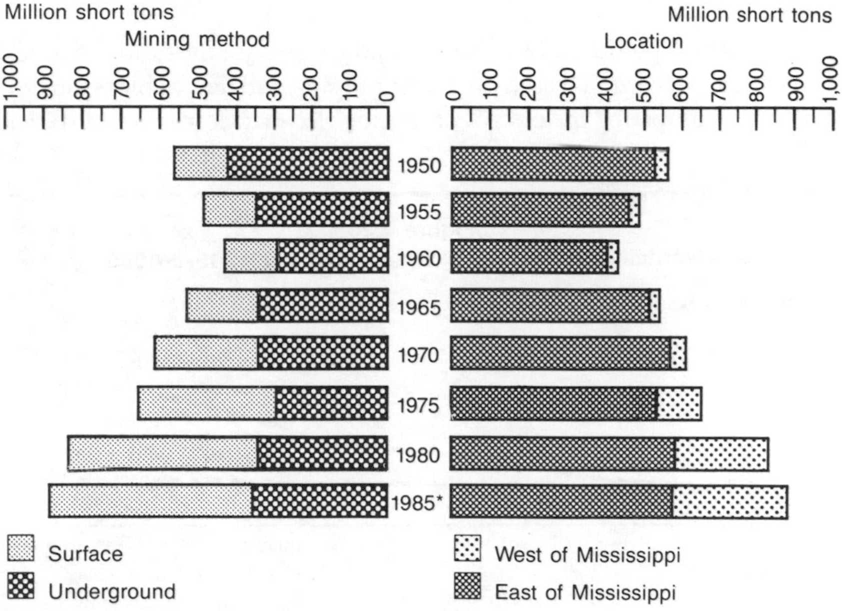

Million short tons
Mining method
Million short tons
Location
1,000
900
800
700
600
500
400
300
200
100
0
1950
1955
1960
1965
1970
1975
1980
1985*
Surface
Underground
West of Mississippi
East of Mississippi

* Preliminary data.

Source: U.S. Department of Energy.

by 16.7 percent from 1950 to 1985, coal produced by surface mines increased nearly 300 percent.[263] Most of the increase in surface mining has taken place in western states.

Coal production poses substantial environmental risks to all media: water (through acid and toxic drainage and through sedimentation), land (through erosion, subsidence, and loss of ecosystems), and air (through windblown particles).[264] The impacts of surface mining are especially worrisome in that large land areas are affected and that the amount of surface mining has been steadily increasing.

Electricity

Electricity is the most expensive energy source because of the high capital costs of generating stations and the large energy losses that occur in the conversion process. Unlike oil, natural gas, and coal, electricity prices have increased consistently—as well as substantially—since 1970. Between 1970 and 1985, residential prices rose 27 percent in real terms (more than 250 percent in current dollars), to a national average of 1.91 cents per kilowatt hour (in constant dollars) (figure 4.28).[265] Yet electricity remains competitive as an energy source, largely because of its convenience, its unique capabilities to do certain tasks, and its high end-use efficiencies relative to other energy forms.[266]

Electricity is produced by a variety of power sources, including coal, oil, natural gas, nuclear power, hydroelectric power, and renewable resources. In a study comparing the costs of producing electricity from three different

Figure 4.28
Electricity Prices to U.S. Residential Users, 1970–1985

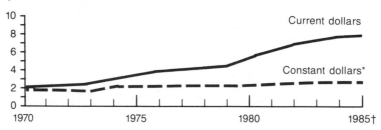

Cents per kilowatt hour

* Calculated using the Consumer Price Index.
† Preliminary data.
Source: U.S. Department of Energy.

fuels, the Atomic Industrial Forum (AIF) found that in 1975 one kilowatt hour (kwh) cost 1.2 cents when produced by nuclear power, 1.8 cents when produced by coal, and 3.3 cents when produced by oil (figure 4.29). The three fuels maintained their relative positions until 1984, when coal became the cheapest source at 3.4 cents per kwh compared with 4.1 cents per kwh for nuclear power and 7.4 cents per kwh for oil.[267] AIF attributed the relative increase in nuclear power costs to the high capitalization costs of five plants that came on-line in 1983 and 1984 and to the uneconomic performance by nuclear plants shut down in 1984 for major repairs.[268]

Nuclear Power

The escalating costs of nuclear power plant construction have also contributed to the costs of nuclear-generated electricity. The Department of Energy analyzed capital cost escalation of nuclear power plants that began construction between 1966 and 1977 and found that, in real terms, construction costs increased about 14 percent per year during that period. The study concluded that those increases were primarily due to changes in reactor design and increases in actual quantities of land, labor, and construction materials and equipment. Cost escalation was only secondarily related to length of licensing time and other delays.[269]

By May 1986, the United States had 98 operable nuclear reactors, as

Figure 4.29

Costs of Electricity Generation in the United States, by Fuel, 1975–1984

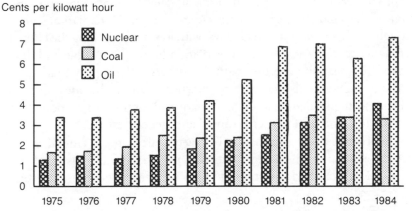

Source: Atomic Industrial Forum.

well as 32 units in some stage of planning or construction (figure 4.30).[270]* The amount of electricity generated reached a new high in 1985, up 17 percent from 1984 figures. Net generation of electricity with nuclear power grew more than 17-fold between 1970 and 1985, amounting to a record 15.5 percent of total U.S. electricity production in 1985.[271]

Uranium production dropped sharply between 1980 and 1985, falling to 11.2 million pounds in 1985.[272] Similarly, uranium exploration and development activities have fallen precipitously since the late 1970s.[273] Imports of uranium have fluctuated in recent years but have not approached the peak levels reached in 1959 and 1960. Exports remained at a fairly low level, dropping to 2.2 million pounds in 1984.[274]

While some experts support nuclear power, arguing that it does not have significant environmental effects, this view ignores the fundamental problems of operational safety and waste disposal and their potential impacts on the environment. Nuclear energy produces radioactive pollutants, which pose unique control problems. Containment is theoretically possible, but thorough experimentation cannot be conducted due to the long time periods involved.[275] Furthermore, scientists have thus far failed to adequately take human error into account. Thus, although the nuclear energy industry is heavily regulated, accidents such as the ones at Three Mile Island (in the United States) in 1979 and Chernobyl (in the Soviet Union) in 1986 have increased scrutiny of U.S. nuclear reactors.

Since it was the most serious commercial nuclear power incident to date, the catastrophic accident on April 26, 1986, at the Chernobyl nuclear reactor No. 4 near Kiev, has attracted worldwide attention. In July 1986, the Soviet government announced that the accident had been caused by human error during an experiment.[276] The incident was initially discovered when Swedish monitors detected elevated ambient radiation levels.[277] Radiation spread throughout Europe within several days, with low levels reaching the United States after several weeks.[278] By July 1986, a total of 28 people had died from acute radiation exposure, with 203 others suffering from radiation sickness.[279] Thousands more were evacuated from the area due to dangerously high radiation levels, and many will continue to be monitored for years to come for long-term cancer and genetic effects.[280]

Significantly, close examination of reactor safety in the United States since the accident in the Soviet Union has uncovered incidents involving the use of substandard materials, accidents during operations at several

---

*For 6 reactors with construction permits, the operating dates have been indefinitely deferred; for 6 other reactors, construction schedules are uncertain.

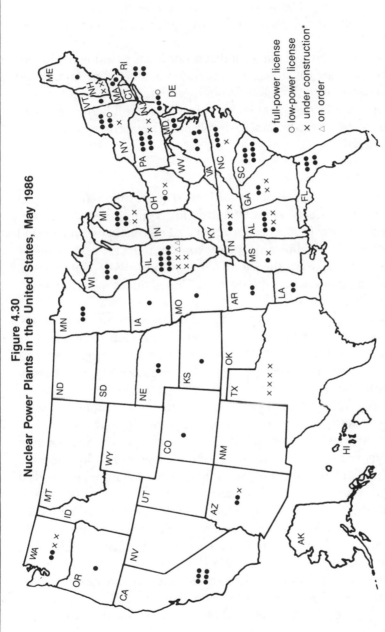

Figure 4.30
Nuclear Power Plants in the United States, May 1986

● full-power license
○ low-power license
× under construction*
△ on order

* The "under construction" category includes 6 reactors that are indefinitely delayed and may not be built. These include 1 in Mississippi, 2 in Michigan, 1 in New Hampshire, and 2 in Washington.
Placement of markers does not correspond to location of nuclear power plants.
Source: U.S. Department of Energy; Atomic Industrial Forum.

power plants, and general mismanagement at many reactors.[281] The Chernobyl accident also highlighted the inadequacy of reactor emergency safety mechanisms, evacuation plans, and treatment capabilities in the United States.[282]

Nuclear waste disposal raises another set of issues awaiting resolution. Wastes are generated at all stages of the fuel cycle, including mining and milling, reactor operation, and decommissioning.[283] While permanent disposal sites are being sought for low-, medium-, and high-level radioactive wastes, the process has become highly politicized because of the nature of the material.

Hydroelectric Power

Hydroelectric power generation in the United States followed the general trend in energy production for 1985 and declined slightly to 2.95 quads.[284] Hydroelectric power production increased 12.2 percent between 1970 and 1985, and in 1985 hydroelectric power contributed 11.4 percent of the electricity generated by the electric utility industry.[285] As of 1984, undeveloped hydroelectric capacity in the United States was estimated to be 76.4 million kilowatts.[286]

Hydroelectric power has both positive and negative environmental effects. While flood control, irrigation, increased water supply, and recreation may all be made possible with the construction of a dam,[287] negative effects can be severe. An existing ecosystem may be completely altered if mitigation measures are not implemented, resulting in environmental impacts such as disruption of fish migration patterns or flooding of prime farmland. In addition, aesthetic and cultural conditions can be affected.

One of the more controversial issues relating to hydroelectric power in recent years has been the sudden increase in "low-head" hydroelectric plants. These are small plants—ranging from a few kilowatt hours (so-called microhydro projects) up to 80 megawatts in scale—installed on streams that because of their topography or low water flow are not suitable for the large facilities installed by large power companies or the government.[288] Stimulated by high energy prices and favorable treatment by the Public Utilities Regulatory Policy Act of 1978 (PURPA),[289] permit applications to the Federal Energy Regulatory Commission (FERC) have increased from 12 to more than 1,200 per year since the enactment of PURPA.[290] At the end of 1984, FERC estimated that about 1,400 small-scale hydroelectric power stations were operating or under construction. These stations were concentrated in the West and Northeast.[291] The dramatic upsurge of interest in developing small hydroelectric projects has resulted in controversy over whether this development is the most appropriate use of the relatively few free-flowing streams remaining in many regions of the United States, as well as over what are the cumulative impacts of multiple projects on a stream.[292]

Biomass

High energy prices, combined with federal support in the late 1970s*, have also stimulated increased interest in less conventional forms of energy. Biomass—involving residues of paper, plastics, wood, animal dung, plant stalks and fibers, and food residues—is one of these.[293] The Department of Energy estimates that almost 2.88 quads of biomass energy was consumed in 1984, up 15 percent from 1981. This consumption was divided among wood (2.63 quads); waste (0.21 quads), including landfill methane, mass burning, refuse-derived fuels, and agricultural waste; and alcohol fuels (0.04 quads).[294]

The use of fuel wood has increased in both industry and households. In 1984 the industrial sector consumed 63.8 percent of the total, while the residential sector consumed 35 percent. The commercial and utility sectors combined consumed only 1.2 percent.[295] In the 1980s the South has consumed the largest proportion of wood energy (56.3 percent in 1984), largely due to the high level of industrial wood energy consumption.[296]

The waste-to-energy industry, also known as resource recovery, also has grown very quickly in the 1980s. Reports differ on the actual number of plants operating and in various stages of planning and construction, but estimates range from 209 to 269 plants—with most in the planning or construction phases.[297] Expansion of waste-to-energy systems is helped by the high cost of and public opposition to sanitary landfills and the limited number of suitable waste disposal sites available.[298] Regionally, the eastern seaboard and South have the most resource recovery facilities because of the regions' high population densities and their general shortage of appropriate alternative disposal methods, such as landfills.[299]

Although waste energy constituted only 7.2 percent of all biomass energy produced in 1984,[300] the resource recovery industry is expected to continue its high-growth pattern. One estimate predicts that the industry will process as much as 40 percent of municipal solid wastes by the end of the century (compared to 5 percent in 1986).[301] However, factors that may moderate this growth include falling energy prices, tax law revisions, and regulation of toxic emissions by resource recovery facilities.[302] (See chapters 7 and 8.)

---

*Federal financial support for these types of energy has been largely terminated in the 1980s.

Another type of waste-to-energy conversion is that which produces methane gas from landfills. As of 1984, 49 high- or medium-Btu gas recovery projects were operating or planned in the United States. Operating plants (8 high Btu and 22 medium Btu) produced 4.7 trillion Btus in heating value in 1984, almost seven times as much energy as they produced in 1980.[303] In the mid-1980s, the landfill gas recovery industry appears to be in a period of uncertainty due to falling energy prices, increased costs due to compliance with air and water emissions regulations, and tax law revisions that removed some financial incentives for alternative energy resource development.[304]

Ethanol, produced from corn, wood wastes, crop residues, or municipal solid waste, is used primarily as a fuel or fuel blend. Ethanol may replace lead as an octane enhancer as the lead content of gasoline is reduced in the mid- and late-1980s.[305] In 1984, ethanol/gasoline blends accounted for 5.6 percent of the U.S. market, although in Iowa, Nebraska, Kansas, Indiana, and Kentucky sales amounted to 20 percent or more of the gasoline market. These states all offered gasoline tax exemptions and had a large agricultural feedstock (mostly surplus corn), both of which stimulated consumption of alcohol fuels.[306]

Solar, Geothermal, and Wind Energy

While hydroelectric power and wood constitute the primary renewable energy sources used in the United States, the contributions of solar, geothermal, and wind are gradually increasing—in fact, these sources make a major contribution to some local energy supplies.[307] There is no question that solar, geothermal, wind, and other unconventional energy sources hold great potential for making the United States more energy-independent in the future. However, when and to what extent this will occur remains unclear.

Active solar energy collectors come in two types: solar thermals, which use the sun's heat for heating and cooling, and photovoltaics, which use solar cells to convert sunlight directly into electricity. In addition, passive solar building designs consist of such features as south-facing and/or double-glazed windows, skylights, movable insulation, and thermal masses (slab floors or walls filled with concrete or water).[308]

Production of solar thermal collectors increased rapidly in the late 1970s, from just over 1 million square feet in 1974 to over 20 million square feet in 1981. Production has declined somewhat since 1981 to 16.4 million square feet in 1984. Between 1974 and 1984, 137.7 million square feet of solar thermals were shipped in the United States.[309] According to the

Renewable Energy Institute, "based on an average collector output of 120,000 Btu/ft²/yr [Btu per square foot per year], approximately 17 trillion Btus (0.017 quads) of energy was produced in 1984, or the equivalent of 3.1 million barrels of oil, at a value of more than $80 million."[310]

Photovoltaic module shipments in the United States declined by 21.4 percent from 1983 to 1984, from 12,620 to 9,912 peak kilowatts of capacity. In addition, the composition of modules shipped and the end-use sector to which they were shipped shifted substantially. For instance, central-power module production declined by 3,520 kilowatts (40.0 percent), while producer shipments of all other types of modules increased slightly, resulting in a net decrease in total production of 21.5 percent. Among end-users, only the commercial sector consumed more modules from 1983 to 1984; the residential, industrial, agricultural, government, electric utility, and other sectors all decreased their consumption.[311]

In 1984, more than 200,000 homes and 15,000 nonresidential buildings in the United States were estimated to have passive solar designs.[312] However, expansion in the use of passive solar designs may be hindered by public misperceptions about their effectiveness.[313]

Geothermal energy, or heat conducted from the earth's core into concentrated hot spots or thermal reservoirs, produced 9.3 billion kwh of electricity in 1985.[314] This continued the general upward trend in geothermal electricity generation, which increased an average of 13.0 percent per year between 1980 and 1985.[315] While geothermal electricity production capability grew steadily between 1960 and 1985, geothermal and other renewable energy sources* still contributed less than 0.5 percent of the total amount of electricity generated in the United States in 1985 (although in some areas that percentage was much higher).[317] The Geysers in California, a vapor-dominated hydrothermal reservoir system, is the largest geothermal energy facility in the United States, accounting for 95 percent (1,399 megawatts) of the U.S. geothermal operating capacity in 1984.[318]

Geothermal sources also provide energy for direct uses such as space and water heating, district heating, aquaculture, commercial greenhouses, small resorts, and industrial process heating.[319] As of August 1985, about 260 geothermal sources supplying direct users in the United States were producing an estimated 1,860 billion Btus annually.[320]

Most energy produced with wind systems has been developed by electric utilities using windfarms.[321] Growth in the production of wind energy

---

*These include wood, refuse, other vegetal fuels, wind, and solar energy but exclude hydroelectric power.[316]

has been dramatic: production on California wind farms (which represents 99 percent of the U.S. capacity) went from 4,800 megawatt hours (mwh) in 1982 to 188,000 mwh in 1984 to 663,760 mwh in 1985.[322] Wind energy has become extensively developed in California because of various financial incentives and the presence of prime wind areas.[323]

While enormous potential for further commercial development of renewable resources exists, by 1984 most renewable resource energy was still provided by conventional sources such as hydroelectric power and wood energy. Renewable energy production from resource recovery, alcohol fuels, and solar, geothermal, and wind energy can be expected to increase substantially in the future. The production of energy from these and other renewable sources is projected to increase eightfold by the year 2000. In addition, although they will still constitute a small proportion of the overall U.S. energy supply, these resources are expected to account for almost 30 percent of the renewable energy supply by the year 2000 (figure 4.31).[324]

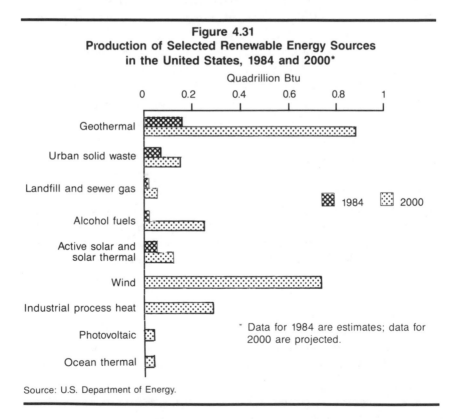

Figure 4.31
**Production of Selected Renewable Energy Sources
in the United States, 1984 and 2000***

Quadrillion Btu

Geothermal

Urban solid waste

Landfill and sewer gas

Alcohol fuels

Active solar and
solar thermal

Wind

Industrial process heat

Photovoltaic

Ocean thermal

■ 1984   ⬚ 2000

* Data for 1984 are estimates; data for
2000 are projected.

Source: U.S. Department of Energy.

Figure 4.32
Energy Consumption in Selected Countries, 1984

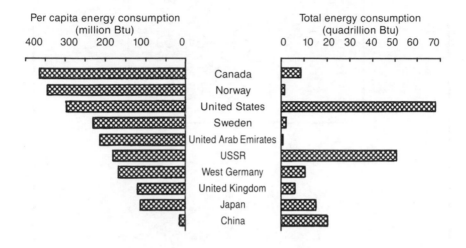

Per capita energy consumption
(million Btu)

Total energy consumption
(quadrillion Btu)

Source: World Bank.

International Trends

International trends in energy prices, consumption, and production are similar to those in the United States.* While the United States is by far the largest overall consumer of energy, many other countries have comparable per capita consumption levels (figure 4.32). World energy consumption was approximately 310.52 quads in 1984.[325] This figure does not include those fuels that are not commercially traded, such as biomass energy; thus the amounts quoted for developing countries are probably lower than may be accurate.[326] Indeed, according to the Renewable Energy Institute, biomass energy accounts for nearly half of all energy consumption in developing countries, with some countries, such as Ethiopia, relying on wood and other biomass resources for as much as 95 percent of energy consumption.[327]

---

*Figures for international energy production and consumption are from a variety of sources, which are not directly comparable with each other.

Figure 4.33

Operating Nuclear Power Plants, by Country, 1985

Numerals indicate the number of operable nuclear power plants.

Source: Atomic Industrial Forum.

The United States and the Soviet Union (in that order) were the world's two largest consumers and producers of energy in 1984. The United States produced 22.4 percent of the world's energy (a total of 292.9 quads) in 1984, and the Soviet Union contributed 20.4 percent.[328]

Crude oil and natural gas liquids are the most popular forms of energy worldwide, accounting for 45 percent of total production, followed by solid fuels (coal, lignite, peat, and oil shale), 30 percent; natural gas, 21 percent; and electricity produced from hydroelectric, geothermal, and nuclear power facilities, 4 percent.[329]

Hydroelectric power contributed approximately 21 percent of the electricity generated worldwide in 1984, or 1.953 trillion kwh.[330] In 1980, the World Energy Conference estimated that only 17 percent of the potentially exploitable hydroelectric power was being utilized.[331]

Nuclear power, however, is the fastest growing source of energy worldwide, providing an average of 15 percent of the electricity generated in 39 countries surveyed by the Atomic Industrial Forum. At the high end of the spectrum, Belgium, France, Sweden, and Taiwan all reported producing more than 40 percent of their electricity from nuclear energy. As of 1985, there were 271 operating nuclear power plants outside of the United States (figure 4.33). The Soviet Union, France, the United Kingdom, and Japan each have more than 30 operating reactors and rely heavily on nuclear power for electricity generation.[332] Nuclear power generation increased steadily through the 1970s and 1980s; by 1984, nuclear power accounted for 12.31 quads of primary energy production worldwide, a more than threefold increase over 1974 levels.[333]

REFERENCES

Text

1. U.S. Department of the Interior, Bureau of Land Management, *Public Land Statistics 1985* (Washington, D.C.: U.S. Government Printing Office, 1986), p. 1; and U.S. Department of Commerce, Bureau of the Census, *Metropolitan Area and State Data Book, 1986* (Washington, D.C.: U.S. Government Printing Office, 1986), p. 504, table C.

2. United Nations Food and Agriculture Organization, *1984 FAO Production Yearbook*, FAO Statistics Series no. 61 (Rome: U.N. Food and Agriculture Organization, 1985), pp. 47-74, tables 1 and 3.

3. U.S. Bureau of Land Management, *Public Land Statistics 1985*, p. 1; and U.S. Bureau of the Census, *Metropolitan Area and State Data Book, 1986*, p. 504, table C.

4. James A. Lewis, *Landownership in the United States, 1978*, prepared for the U.S. Department of Agriculture, Economics, Statistics, and Cooperatives Service, Agricultural

Information Bulletin no. 435 (Washington, D.C.: U.S. Government Printing Office, 1980), pp. 3-5; and U.S. Department of Agriculture, *Soil and Water Resources Conservation Act, 1980 Appraisal, part 1, Soil, Water, and Related Resources in the United States: Status, Condition, and Trends* (Washington, D.C.: U.S. Department of Agriculture, 1981), p. 21.

5. Lewis, *Landownership in the United States, 1978*, pp. 3-5.

6. U.S. Bureau of Land Management, *Public Land Statistics 1985*, pp. 4-5.

7. H. Thomas Frey and Roger W. Hexem, *Major Uses of Land in the United States: 1982*, prepared for the U.S. Department of Agriculture, Economic Research Service, Agricultural Economic Report no. 535 (Washington, D.C.: U.S. Government Printing Office, 1985), p. 14, table 14.

8. U.S. Bureau of Land Management, *Public Land Statistics 1985*, pp. 1, 6-7.

9. 43 USCA §§1701-84, as amended.

10. Katherine Barton, "Wildlife and the Bureau of Land Management," *Audubon Wildlife Report 1986* (New York: National Audubon Society, 1986), pp. 497-98.

11. U.S. Department of Agriculture, Forest Service, *Land Areas of the National Forest System as of September 30, 1985* (Washington, D.C.: U.S. Government Printing Office, 1985), p. 1.

12. U.S. Department of the Interior, Division of Realty, *Annual Report of Lands under Control of the U.S. Fish and Wildlife Service as of September 30, 1985* (Washington, D.C.: U.S. Government Printing Office, 1985), p. 3.

13. U.S. National Park Service, "National Park Service Summary of Acreages As of 12/31/86," p. 1 (photocopy).

14. Information provided by Frank Savat, U.S. Department of Defense, March 1987.

15. Frey and Hexem, *Major Uses of the Land*, pp. 18-19, appendix table 1.

16. Ibid., pp. 23-24, appendix table 4.

17. Ibid., p. '28, appendix table 7.

18. Ibid., pp. 18-19, appendix table 1.

19. As with figures 4.2 and 4.3, two categories of "special uses" and "other land" have been combined as "other" in this sentence. Ibid.

20. Ibid.

21. Ibid., p. 28, appendix table 7.

22. Phillip M. Raup, "Competition for Land and the Future of American Agriculture," in Sandra S. Batie and Robert G. Healy, eds., *The Future of American Agriculture as a Strategic Resource* (Washington, D.C.: The Conservation Foundation, 1980), pp. 49, 52-53.

23. Frey and Hexem, *Major Uses of the Land*, p. i.

24. Ibid., pp. 10, 18-19, appendix table 1.

25. Ibid., pp. 2, 6.

26. Ibid., p. 28, appendix table 7.

27. Information provided by Geography Division, U.S. Department of Commerce, Bureau of the Census; U.S. Department of Agriculture, Soil Conservation Service, *Available Federal Data on Agricultural Land Use*, prepared by the research staff of the National Agricultural Lands Study, technical paper 2 (Washington, D.C.: U.S. Department of Agriculture, 1981), p. 8, table 1; and U.S. Department of Agriculture, Soil Conservation Service, unpublished data from the 1982 National Resources Inventory, table 2a.

28. Based on July 1, 1984, estimates. See Donald Starsinic, "Patterns of Metropolitan Area and County Population Growth: 1980-1984," prepared for U.S. Department of Commerce, Bureau of the Census (Washington, D.C.: U.S. Government Printing Office, 1985), p. 2, table A and p. 7, table F.

29. U.S. Department of Commerce, Bureau of the Census, *Statistical Abstract of the United States, 1986* (Washington, D.C.: U.S. Government Printing Office, 1986), p. 19, table 20.

30. Frey and Hexem, *Major Uses of the Land*, p. 28, appendix table 7.

31. Greg C. Gustafson and Nelson L. Biles, *U.S. Cropland, Urbanization, and Landownership Patterns*, prepared for U.S. Department of Agriculture, Economic Research Service, Agricultural Economic Report no. 520 (Washington, D.C.: U.S. Government Printing Office, 1984), p. 1.

32. Ibid.; and Linda K. Lee, "Land Use and Soil Loss: A 1982 Update," *Journal of Soil and Water Conservation* 39, no. 4 (1984):226-27.

33. Ruth Eckdish Knack, "The Once and Future Suburb," *Planning* 52, no. 7 (1986):6.

34. Joel Garreau, "From Suburbs, Cities Are Springing Up in Our Backyards," *Washington Post*, March 8, 1987, p. 1.

35. Robert Cevero, *Suburban Gridlock* (New Brunswick, N.J.: Center for Urban Policy Research, 1986), p. 10; Robert T. Dunphy, "Travel Trends and the Transportation Impacts of New Projects," *Urban Land* 45, no. 7 (1986):21; see also Philip N. Fulton, "Changing Journey-to-Work Patterns: The Increasing Prevalence of Commuting within the Suburbs in Metropolitan America," paper delivered at the Annual Meeting of the Transportation Research Board, Washington, D.C., January 13, 1986.

36. Cevero, *Suburban Gridlock*, pp. 10-11.

37. Ibid.; and Lee Hockstader, "Northern Virginians Face Ordeal by Driving," *Washington Post*, September 7, 1986, pp. 1, 16-17.

38. Robert P. Duckworth, John M. Simmons, and Robert McNulty, "The Entrepreneurial American City" (Washington, D.C.: Partners for Livable Places and U.S. Department of Housing and Urban Development, 1986), p. 17; and Nina J. Gruen, "Public/Private Projects: A Better Way for Downtowns," *Urban Land* 45, no. 8 (1986):2-6.

39. Duckworth et al., "The Entrepreneurial American City," pp. 7-8.

40. See, generally, Ann Breen and Dick Rigby, eds., *Urban Waterfronts '85: Water Makes a Difference* (Washington, D.C.: The Waterfront Press, 1986).

41. George Sternlieb and James W. Hughes, "Shopping Centers Pull Up the Anchor," *American Demographics* 7, no. 8 (1985):48.

42. Information provided by Frank Gilbert, National Trust for Historic Preservation, April 1987.

43. David Listokin, *Living Cities: Report of the Twentieth Century Fund Task Force on Urban Preservation Policies* (New York: Priority Press Publications, 1985), p. 67.

44. See 26 USCA §§46(a)(2)(F), 48(g), 167(n)-(o), 191, and 280(B). For an explanation of the changes, see National Trust for Historic Preservation, *Preservation Law Reporter*, vol. 1, June 1982, pp. 11,011-16 and 11,101-6.

45. U.S. General Accounting Office, "Tax Policy and Administration: Historic Preservation Tax Incentives," fact sheet for the Chairman, U.S. House of Representatives, Committee on Interior and Insular Affairs, Subcommittee on Public Lands, GAO/GGD-86-112FS (Washington, D.C.: U.S. General Accounting Office, 1986), pp. 24-26.

46. Ibid., pp. 9, 11.

47. Rich Connell, "L.A.'s Slow-Growth Measure Wins by Wide Margin," *Los Angeles Times*, November 5, 1986, pp. 3, 26; Sam Kaplan, "Citizens Want a Hand in Zoning," *Los Angeles Times*, April 6, 1986; and Frank Clifford, "High Rise Initiative Stirs Hot Debate," *Los Angeles Times*, March 30, 1986, pp. 1, 3.

48. See, for instance, Mark A. Stein, "Growth Policy: Voters Putting the Brakes On,"

Los Angeles Times, March 10, 1986, pp. 1, 16; Gregory Longhini, "Ballot Box Zoning," *Planning* 51, no. 5 (1985):11-13; and Larry Orman, "Ballot Box Planning: The Boom in Electoral Land-Use Control," *Public Affairs Report* 25, no. 6 (1984):1-15.

49. W. Dennis Keating, "Linking Downtown Development to Broader Community Goals: An Analysis of Linkage Policy in Three Cities," *Journal of the American Planning Association* 52, no. 2 (1986):133-41; and Douglas R. Porter, "The Office/Housing Linkage Issue," *Urban Land* 44, no. 9 (1985):16-21.

50. Austin's measure was passed in 1984 by the city council. Denver's ordinance was being appealed to the Colorado Supreme Court as of fall 1985. See Christopher J. Duerksen and Mary C. Bean, "Land and the Law 1985: A Run on the Bank?' *The Urban Lawyer* 17 (1985):851-52.

51. Ibid., pp. 855-61; and Christopher J. Duerksen, "Beyond Ecology and Economics," *Urban Land* 45, no. 1 (1986):35.

52. Merle C. Prunty, "Agricultural Lands: A Southern Perspective," paper prepared for Agricultural Lands Study Workshop, Memphis, Tennessee, October 3, 1979 (Mississippi State, Miss.: Southern Rural Development Center, 1979), pp. xi, 17.

53. Hal Hiemstra and Nancy Bushwick, "How States Are Saving Farmland," *American Land Forum Magazine* 6, no. 2 (1986)61; and Edward Thompson, Jr., "Defining and Protecting the Right to Farm," *Zoning and Planning Law Report*, September and October, 1982, p. 58.

54. Ed Thompson, personal communication, December 18, 1986.

55. Jo Ann Kwong, "Farmland Preservation: The Evolution of State and Local Policies," *Urban Land* 46, no. 1 (1987):21.

56. Hiemstra and Bushwick, "How States Are Saving Farmland," p. 62.

57. Ibid., pp. 60-65; and Edward P. Thompson, Jr., "Protecting Agricultural Lands," in Russell L. Brenneman and Sarah M. Bates, *Land-Saving Action* (Covelo, Calif.: Island Press, 1984), pp. 64-73.

58. U.S. Department of Commerce, Bureau of the Census, *Patterns of Metropolitan Area and County Population Growth: 1980 to 1984*, Series P-25, no. 976 (Washington, D.C.: U.S. Government Printing Office, 1985), p. 1.

59. See, generally, Gordon Bradley ed., *Land Use and Forest Resources in a Changing Environment: The Urban/Forest Interface* (Seattle, Wash.: University of Washington Press, 1984).

60. Florida Stat. §§186.001-.911 (Supp. 1984).

61. Christopher J. Duerksen and Mary C. Bean, "Land and the Law 1986: The Perils of Prognostication," *The Urban Lawyer* 18 (1986):977-81.

62. The Gallup Organization, Inc., "Overview of the Opinion Leaders Poll on Urban America," prepared for the Urban Land Institute, May 12, 1986, p. ix.

63. Estimates of original extent of prairie: A. W. Kuchler, *Potential Natural Vegetation of the Conterminous United States*, Special Publication 36 (New York: American Geographical Society), cited in P. G. Risser et al., *The True Prairie Ecosystem* (Stroudsburg, Pa.: Hutchinson Ross, 1981), p. 13. Precise estimates of remaining prairie are unavailable. For documentation of the conversion of 92 percent of the prairie in a southern Wisconsin location to cropland/pasture rotation in the century between 1833 and 1934, as well as the virtual absence of any prairie in the area today, see A. A. Auclair, "Ecological Factors in the Development of Intensive-Management Ecosystems in the Midwestern United States," *Ecology* 57 (1976):431-44.

64. Frey and Hexem, *Major Uses of the Land*, p. 4, table 5.

65. U.S. Department of Agriculture, Economic Research Service, *Cropland Use and Supply: Outlook and Situation Report*, CUS-2 (Washington, D.C.: U.S. Government Printing Office, 1985), p. 2.

66. U.S. Department of Agriculture, *Agricultural Statistics 1980* (Washington, D.C.: U.S. Government Printing Office, 1980), p. 419, table 602; and U.S. Department of Agriculture, *Agricultural Statistics 1985* (Washington, D.C.: U.S. Government Printing Office, 1985), p. 372, table 537.

67. Information provided by the U.S. Department of Agriculture, Economic Research Service, November 1986.

68. U.S. Department of Agriculture, *Cropland Use and Supply*, pp. 14-16.

69. Information provided by the U.S. Department of Agriculture, Economic Research Service, November 1986.

70. Ibid.

71. U.S. Department of Agriculture, *Cropland Use and Supply*, p. 14.

72. Ibid.; and Ralph W. Tiner, Jr., *Wetlands of the United States: Current Status and Recent Trends*, prepared for the U.S. Department of the Interior, Fish and Wildlife Service (Washington, D.C.: U.S. Government Printing Office, 1984), p. 48.

73. Tiner, *Wetlands of the United States*, pp. 40-41; Kevin Hansen, "South Florida's Water Dilemma: A Trickle of Hope for the Everglades," *Environment* 26, no. 5 (1984):17; and information provided by Florida Agricultural Statistics Service, November 1986.

74. George A. Pavelis, *Natural Resource Capital Formation in American Agriculture: Irrigation, Drainage and Conservation, 1855-1980*, prepared for the U.S. Department of Agriculture, Economic Research Service, Natural Resources Economics Division (Washington, D.C.: U.S. Government Printing Office, 1985), p. 84; U.S. Department of Agriculture, *Cropland Use and Supply*, p. 16; and Tiner, *Wetlands of the United States*, pp. 42-43.

75. Pavelis, *Natural Resource Capital Formation in American Agriculture*, p. 83; and U.S. Department of Agriculture, *Cropland Use and Supply*, p. 16.

76. Information provided by the U.S. Department of Agriculture, Economic Research Service, November 1986.

77. Ibid.

78. U.S. Department of Agriculture, *Cropland Use and Supply*, pp. 24-25.

79. Ibid., p. 16; and Tiner, *Wetlands in the United States*, pp. 48-50.

80. Information provided by Florida Agricultural Statistics Service, November 1986.

81. The Conservation Foundation, *America's Waters: Current Trends and Emerging Issues* (Washington, D.C.: The Conservation Foundation, 1984), pp. 3-15, 75.

82. Kenneth D. Frederick and James C. Hanson, *Western Irrigation: Its Importance to the Growth and Environmental Impacts of U.S. Agriculture*, draft (Washington, D.C.: Resources for the Future, 1980), pp. 3.19, 3.25; and information provided by Texas Agricultural Statistics Service, November 1986.

83. U.S. Department of Agriculture, Economic Research Service, *Agricultural Resources: Cropland, Water and Conservation: Situation Outlook Report*, AR-4 (Washington, D.C.: U.S. Government Printing Office, 1986), pp. 9-10.

84. Ibid., p. 10; and information provided by the U.S. Department of Agriculture, Economic Research Service, November 1986.

85. U.S. Department of Agriculture, *Agricultural Resources*, p. 13; and information provided by the U.S. Department of Agriculture, Economic Research Service, November 1986.

86. 7 USC §§1281 et seq. note (1986 supp.), P.L. 99-198, commonly referred to as the "1985 Farm Bill." It provides a five-year framework for the U.S. Secretary of Agriculture to administer various agriculture and food programs.

87. Information provided by the U.S. Department of Agriculture, Soil Conservation Service, March 1987.

88. Information provided by the American Farmland Trust, November 1986, from data in "Farming on the Fringe," map.

89. Lee, "Land Use and Soil Loss," pp. 226-28; and personal communication with Linda Lee, November 1986.

90. Calculated from information in Lee, "Land Use and Soil Loss," p. 227; and information provided by the U.S. Department of Agriculture, Economic Research Service, November 1986.

91. Calculated from National Research Council, Board on Agriculture, Committee on Conservation Needs and Opportunities, *Soil Conservation: Assessing the Natural Resources Inventory*, vol. 1 (Washington, D.C.: National Academy Press, 1986), pp. 7-8.

92. U.S. Department of Agriculture, Soil Conservation Service, unpublished data from the 1982 Natural Resources Inventory, table 25a.

93. National Research Council, *Soil Conservation*, p. 77.

94. Crop rotation systems may also be considered a soil conservation practice, and, although widespread, there is no data available on the extent of its use. See U.S. Department of Agriculture, Economic Research Service, *Agricultural Resources*, pp. 2, 30.

95. Information provided by the Conservation Tillage Information Center, U.S. Department of Agriculture, Economic Research Service; and the U.S. Department of Agriculture, Soil Conservation Service, November 1986.

96. Conservation Tillage Information Center, "Conservation Tillage Information Center," pamphlet, n.d.; and information provided by the Conservation Tillage Information Center.

97. U.S. Department of Agriculture, Economic Research Service, *Agricultural Resources*, pp. 30-31.

98. George A. Pavelis, *Conservation and Erosion Control Costs in the United States*, prepared for the U.S. Department of Agriculture, Economic Research Service, Natural Resources Economics Division (Washington, D.C.: U.S. Government Printing Office, 1985), p. 13.

99. Ibid., p. 3; and Pavelis, *Natural Resource Capital Formation in American Agriculture*, pp. 80, 125.

100. Pavelis, *Conservation and Erosion Control Costs*, pp. 3-7.

101. Ibid., pp. 6-7.

102. U.S. Department of Agriculture, *Agricultural Statistics 1980*, p. 421, table 604.

103. U.S. Department of Agriculture, Economic Research Service, *Agricultural Resources*, p. 19.

104. Pavelis, *Natural Resource Capital Formation in American Agriculture*, p. 73.

105. Frey and Hexem, *Major Uses of the Land*, pp. 18-19, appendix table 1.

106. U.S. Department of Agriculture, Forest Service, *America's Renewable Resources: A Supplement to the 1979 Assessment of the Forest and Land Situation in the United States* (Washington, D.C.: U.S. Government Printing Office, 1984), p. 78, appendix table 2.

107. Frey and Hexem, *Major Uses of the Land*, p. 3, table 3.

108. Cass Peterson, "Antelopes May Roam to Home," *Washington Post*, December 12, 1983.

109. Frederic H. Wagner, "Livestock Grazing and the Livestock Industry," in Howard P. Brokaw, *Wildlife and America* (Washington, D.C.: U.S. Government Printing Office, 1978), p. 137.

110. Ibid., pp. 124-126.

111. U.S. Department of Agriculture, Forest Service, *An Assessment of the Forest and Range Land Situation in the United States*, FS-345 (Washington, D.C.: U.S. Forest Service, 1979), p. 287.

112. U.S. Forest Service, *An Assessment of the Forest and Range Land Situation in the United States*, pp. 280, 282.

113. U.S. Bureau of Land Management, *Public Land Statistics*, pp. 20-21, table 11; and U.S. Department of Agriculture, Forest Service, *Report of the Forest Service: Fiscal Year 1985* (Washington, D.C.: U.S. Forest Service, 1986), p. 27.

114. U.S. Bureau of Land Management, *Public Land Statistics*, p. 23, table 16.

115. U.S. Soil Conservation Service, National Resources Inventory, tables 36a and 12b.

116. Ibid.; and U.S. Bureau of Land Management, *Public Land Statistics*, p. 23, table 16.

117. 43 USC §§315 et seq. (1986).

118. U.S. Department of Agriculture, Extension Service, *Renewable Resources Extension Program: Second Five-Year Plan 1986-1990*, draft (Washington, D.C.: U.S. Forest Service, 1985), p. 34.

119. William Cronon, *Changes in the Land* (New York: Hill and Wang, 1983), pp. 108-26.

120. Marion Clawson, "Forests in the Long Sweep of American History," *Science* 204 (1979):1169.

121. U.N. Food and Agriculture Organization, *1984 FAO Production Yearbook*, pp. 47-58, table 1.

122. Frey and Hexem, *Major Uses of the Land*, pp. 18-19, appendix table 1.

123. Ibid.

124. U.S. Department of Agriculture, Forest Service, *Final Environmental Impact Statement: 1985-2030 Resources Planning Act Program* (Washington, D.C.: U.S. Forest Service, 1986), p. 3.2.

125. Alice H. Ulrich, *U.S. Timber Production, Trade, Consumption, and Price Statistics 1950-84*, Misc. Publ. no. 1450, prepared for the U.S. Department of Agriculture, Forest Service (Washington, D.C.: U.S. Government Printing Office, 1985), p. 12, table 3.

126. U.S. Forest Service, *America's Renewable Resources*, p. 12.

127. U.S. Forest Service, *U.S. Timber Production*, p. 12.

128. U.S. Congress, Office of Technology Assessment, *Wood Use: U.S. Competitiveness and Technology*, OTA-ITE-210 (Washington, D.C.: U.S. Office of Technology Assessment, 1983), p. 79.

129. Ibid.

130. U.S. Department of Agriculture, Forest Service, *A Recommended Renewable Resources Program: 1985-2030*, FS-400 (Washington, D.C.: U.S. Forest Service, 1986), p. 3.

131. Ibid., p. 4.

132. Ibid.

133. U.S. International Trade Commission, *Softwood Lumber from Canada* (Washington, D.C.: U.S. International Trade Commission, 1986), p. 3.

134. U.S. Forest Service, *America's Renewable Resources*, pp. 14-15; and D. R. Darr and G. L. Lindell, "Prospects for U.S. Trade in Timber Products: Implications," *Forest Products Journal* 30, no. 6 (1980):20.

135. U.S. Forest Service, *America's Renewable Resources*, p. 15; and William E. Shands

and David H. Dawson, *Policies for the Lake States Forests*, Final Report of the Lake States Policy Workshop, Rhinelander, Wisconsin, February 12-14, 1984 (Washington, D.C.: The Conservation Foundation, 1984), pp. 1-2, 5-6.

136. U.S. Forest Service, *America's Renewable Resources*, p. 15.

137. "As the Old Growth Goes, So Goes the Spotted Owl," *Wild Oregon* 10, no. 4 (1983):10-11. For more information on the controversy and proposed solutions, see U.S. Department of Agriculture, Forest Service, Pacific Northwest Region, *Draft Supplement to the Environmental Impact Statement for an Amendment to the Pacific Northwest Regional Guide*, vol. 1 (Portland, Oreg.: U.S. Forest Service, 1986), p. 5-3.

138. V. Alaric Sample, Jr., *Below Cost Timber Sales on the National Forests* (Washington, D.C.: The Wilderness Society, 1984), p. 11; and Dennis C. LeMaster, Barry R. Flamm, and John C. Hendee, eds., *Below Cost Timber Sales: A Conference on the Economics of National Forest Timber Sales*, proceedings of a conference, Spokane, Washington, February 17-19, 1986 (Washington, D.C.: The Wilderness Society, 1986), p. 2.

139. Sample, *Below Cost Timber Sales on the National Forests*, pp. 11-16; and LeMaster, Flamm, and Hendee, *Below Cost Timber Sales*, pp. 1-7.

140. Sample, *Below Cost Timber Sales on the National Forests*, p. 15; and U.S. General Accounting Office, *Congress Needs Better Information on Forest Service's Below-Cost Timber Sales*, GAO/RCED-84-96 (Washington, D.C.: U.S. General Accounting Office, 1984), pp. iii-iv.

141. See, generally, U.S. General Accounting Office, *Congress Needs Better Information on Forest Service's Below-Cost Timber Sales*, pp. 1-46; and Thomas J. Borlow et al., *Giving Away the National Forests: An Analysis of U.S. Forest Service Timber Sales Below Cost* (Washington, D.C.: Natural Resources Defense Council, 1980), pp. 21-27.

142. 16 USC §§1600-76.

143. Numbers as of February 12, 1987. Information provided by the U.S. Department of Agriculture, Forest Service, Land Management Unit, April 1987.

144. John B. Crowell, Jr., "Improved Productivity from Nonindustrial Private Forests: Dimensions of the Problem," in Jack P. Royer and Christopher D. Risbrudt, eds., *Nonindustrial Private Forests: A Review of Economic and Policy Studies* (Durham, N.C.: Duke University, 1983), p. 16.

145. Marion Clawson, *The Economics of U.S. Nonindustrial Private Forests* (Washington, D.C.: Resources for the Future, 1979), p. 88.

146. U.S. Department of Agriculture, Extension Service, *Renewable Resources Extension Program*, p. 17.

147. Clawson, *The Economics of U.S. Nonindustrial Private Forests*, p. 91.

148. Cronon, *Changes in the Land*, pp. 159-60; and Carl Reidel, *The Yankee Forest: A Prospectus* (New Haven, Conn.: Yale University, 1978), pp. 13-16. For further information, see Lloyd C. Irland, *Wildlands and Woodlots: The Story of New England's Forests* (Hanover, N.H.: University Press of New England, 1982), pp. 2-6.

149. Philip Shabecoff, "Widespread Ills Found in Forests in Eastern U.S.," *New York Times*, February 26, 1984; and Leslie Roberts, "Studies Probe Unexplained Decline in Eastern Forests," *BioScience* 34 (1984):291-92.

150. For two good discussions of the history and future of prescribed burning, see Stephen J. Pyne, "Fire Policy and Fire Research in the United States Forest Service," *Journal of Forest History* 25, no. 2 (1981):64-77; and Von J. Johnson, "Prescribed Burning: Requiem or Renaissance," *Journal of Forestry* 82, no. 2 (1984):82-90. Johnson, on p. 88, indicates

that up to 21.2 million acres of southeastern woodland was subjected to controlled burning per year in the late 1960s. This acreage is more than four times the national acreage burned by wildfires during that time period.

151. U.S. Department of Agriculture, Forest Service, Forest Pest Management, *Forest Insect and Disease Condition in the United States 1985* (Washington, D.C.: U.S. Government Printing Office, 1986), pp. 2-3.

152. Ibid., pp. 5, 7.

153. Herbert A. Knight, "The Pine Decline," *Journal of Forestry* 85, no. 1 (1987):25. See also U.S. Department of Agriculture, Forest Service, *The South's Fourth Forest: Alternatives for the Future* (review draft; final draft to be published summer 1987).

154. Mark D. McGregor, "Mountain Pine Beetle: The Conflict between People and the Beetle," in Robert C. Loomis, Susan Tucker, and Thomas Hofacker, eds., *Insect and Disease Conditions in the United States 1979-83*, prepared for U.S. Department of Agriculture, Forest Service, General Technical Report WO-46 (Washington, D.C.: U.S. Forest Service, 1985), pp. 16-23.

155. U.S. Forest Service, *Forest Insect and Disease Condition in the United States 1985*, pp. 4, 12-85.

156. U.S. Department of Agriculture, Forest Service, *1985 U.S. Forest Planting Report* (Washington, D.C.: U.S. Government Printing Office, 1986); U.S. Department of Agriculture, Forest Service, *1984 U.S. Forest Planting Report* (Washington, D.C.: U.S. Government Printing Office, 1985); U.S. Department of Agriculture, Forest Service, *1983 U.S. Forest Planting Report* (Washington, D.C.: U.S. Government Printing Office, 1984).

157. Shands and Dawson, *Policies for the Lake States Forests*, pp. 1-2.

158. World Resources Institute and the International Institute for Environment and Development, *World Resources 1986* (New York: Basic Books, 1986), p. 121.

159. Ibid., pp. 125, 127.

160. "Tree Rings, Mountain Ice Give Clues to Weather Patterns", *U.S. Water News* 2, no. 6 (1985):2

161. U.S. Water Resources Council, *The Nation's Water Resources, 1975-2000* (Washington D.C.: U.S. Government Printing Office, 1978), vol. 1, summary, p. 12; and U.S. Department of Commerce, Bureau of the Census, *Statistical Abstract of the United States: 1984* (Washington D.C.: U.S. Government Printing Office, 1984), p. 6, table 2.

162. U.S. Water Resources Council, *The Nation's Water Resources* (Washington, D.C.: U.S. Government Printing Office, 1968), p. 3-2-1.

163. U.S. Department of the Interior, Geological Survey, *National Water Summary 1985: Hydrologic Events and Surface-Water Resources*, Water Supply Paper 2300 (Washington D.C.: U.S. Government Printing Office, 1986), p. 2; and "Drought Threatens the South's Ecology," *New York Times*, August 3, 1986.

164. U.S. Geological Survey, *National Water Summary 1985*, p. 17; and "Pumping Has Its Faults," *U.S. Water News* 3, no. 1 (1986):4.

165. U.S. Department of the Interior, Geological Survey, *National Water Summary 1984: Hydrologic Events Selected Water Quality Trends and Ground-Water Resources*, Water Supply Paper 2275 (Washington D.C.: U.S. Government Printing Office, 1985), p.42.

166. Ibid., pp. 460, 464.

167. "The Great Lakes Shore-Up: Water Levels Pose Perils," *Washington Post*, July 12, 1986.

168. Wayne B. Solley, Edith B. Chase, and William B. Mann IV, *Estimated Use of Water*

in the U.S. in 1980, Geological Survey Circular 1001 (Reston, Va: U.S. Geological Survey, 1983), pp. v-vi.

169. U.S. Geological Survey, *National Water Summary 1985*, p. 64.

170. Solley, Chase, and Mann, *Estimated Use of Water in the U.S. in 1980*, p. 47.

171. Ibid., pp. 36, 47.

172. Ibid., p. 16, 46.

173. "The Growth and Decline of America's Irrigated Land", *U.S. Water News* 2, no. 6 (1985):13.

174. See, for example, "Texas Irrigators Save Millions in Water," *U.S. Water News* 1, no. 8 (1985):3; and "Irrigation Canal to be Relined," *U.S. Water News* 1, no. 8 (1985):12.

175. U.S. Geological Survey, *National Water Summary 1985*, p. 65.

176. Solley, Chase, and Mann, *Estimated Use of Water in the U.S. in 1980*, p. 8.

177. World Resources Institute and the International Institute for Environment and Development, *World Resources 1986*, p. 131.

178. "Report Surveys Water Quality for Fish," *EPA Journal* 10, no. 3 (1984):25.

179. U.S. Council on Environmental Quality, *Environmental Trends* (Washington D.C.: U.S. Government Printing Office, 1981), p. 217.

180. The Conservation Foundation, *State of the Environment: An Assessment at Mid-Decade* (Washington D.C.: The Conservation Foundation, 1984), p. 140; and James Gilluly, Aaron C. Waters, and A. O. Woodford, *Principles of Geology* (San Francisco: W. H. Freeman and Company, 1968), pp. 294-95.

181. Solley, Chase, and Mann, *Estimated Use of Water in the U.S. in 1980*, p. 36.

182. U.S. Water Resources Council, *The Nation's Water Resources, 1975-2000*, p. 34.

183. Solley, Chase, and Mann, *Estimated Use of Water in the U.S. in 1980*, p. 25.

184. Ibid., pp. 20-23.

185. World Resources Institute and the International Institute for Environment and Development, *World Resources 1986*, p. 131.

186. Solley, Chase, and Mann, *Estimated Use of Water in the U.S. in 1980*, p. 15.

187. Ibid., p. 11.

188. Ibid., p. 19.

189. "Irrigation Canal to be Relined," *U.S. Water News*, p. 12.

190. U.S. Geological Survey, *National Water Summary 1985*, p. 65.

191. Discussion, "Imperial Irrigation District Negotiations and Discussion with the Metropolitan Water District and Others," *Proceedings, Buying and Selling Water in California: How Does it Fit into the State's Water Policy Portfolio*, proceedings and summary of a conference, Santa Monica, Calif., February 27-28, 1986, pp. 55-69.

192. "When Water Kingdoms Clash," *High Country News*, September 29, 1986, pp. 19-20; and "Water from the Colorado Drawn Into Arizona as Big Project Opens," *New York Times*, November 17, 1985.

193. "Imperial Irrigation District Negotiations and Discussion with the Metropolitan Water District and Others," *Proceedings, Buying and Selling Water in California*, pp. 55-69; and "When Water Kingdoms Clash," *High Country News*, September 29, 1986, pp. 19-20.

194. U.S. Water Resources Council, *The Nation's Water Resources, 1975-2000*, p. 16.

195. Solley, Chase, and Mann, *Estimated Use of Water in the U.S. in 1980*, p. 33.

196. U.S. Department of the Interior, Geological Survey, *National Water Summary 1983: Hydrologic Events and Issues*, Water Supply Paper 2250 (Washington, D.C.: U.S. Government Printing Office, 1984), p. 27.

197. Philip Fradkin, *A River No More: The Colorado River and the West* (New York: Alfred A. Knopf, 1981).

198. World Resources Institute and the International Institute for Environment and Development, *World Resources 1986*, pp. 127-28.

199. Solley, Chase, and Mann, *Estimated Use of Water in the U.S. in 1980*, p. 47.

200. Ibid.

201. Gordon Sloggett, *Prospects for Groundwater Irrigation: Declining Levels and Rising Costs*, Agricultural Economic Report no. 478 (Washington D.C.: U.S. Department of Agriculture, 1981), p. 8.

202. U.S. Water Resources Council, *The Nation's Water Resources, 1975-2000*, p. 18.

203. U.S. Geological Survey, *National Water Summary 1983*, pp. 89, 92, 120, 227.

204. U.S. Geological Survey, *National Water Summary 1984*, pp. 107-108.

205. Ibid., p. 109.

206. U.S. Geological Survey, *National Water Summary 1983*, pp. 33-34.

207. "Western States Would Turn Off Federal Faucets," *Washington Post*, July 11, 1986.

208. U.S. Congress, *Congressional Record*, 99th Cong., 2nd sess., June 5, 1986, p. S6928.

209. U.S. Water Resources Council, *The Nation's Water Resources, 1975-2000*, p. 12.

210. U.S. Geological Survey, *National Water Summary 1983*, pp. 30-31.

211. The Conservation Foundation, *State of the Environment: An Assessment at Mid-Decade*, p. 140.

212. U.S. Geological Survey, *National Water Summary 1985*, p. 67.

213. Ibid.

214. U.S. Department of Energy, Energy Information Administration, *1982 Annual Energy Review* (Washington, D.C.: U.S. Government Printing Office, 1983), p. 221.

215. U.S. Department of Energy, Energy Information Administration, *Annual Energy Review 1985* (Washington, D.C.: U.S. Government Printing Office, 1986), p. 267.

216. Ibid., p. 5.

217. Ibid., pp. 9, 11.

218. Ibid., p. 11.

219. Ibid., p. 41.

220. Ibid., p. 45.

221. U.S. Department of Energy, Energy Information Administration, Office of Energy Markets and End Use, *Annual Energy Outlook 1985* (Washington, D.C.: U.S. Government Printing Office, 1986), p. 23; see also World Resources Institute and International Institute for Environment and Development, *World Resources 1986* (New York: Basic Books, 1986), p. 114.

222. U.S. Department of Energy, *Annual Energy Outlook 1985*, p. 19.

223. U.S. Department of Transportation, Federal Highway Administration, *Highway Statistics Annual*, annual tables 1970-1984 (Washington, D.C.: U.S. Department of Transportation, 1985), table VM-1.

224. U.S. Department of Energy, *Annual Energy Review 1985*, p. 1.

225. Ibid., pp. 5, 13.

226. Ibid., p. 1.

227. U.S. Department of Energy, *Annual Energy Outlook 1985*, p. 18; World Resources Institute and International Institute for Environment and Development, *World Resources 1985*, p. 114; and Organization for Economic Cooperation and Development, *The State of the Environment 1985* (Paris: Organization for Economic Cooperation and Develop-

ment, 1985), p. 211.

228. World Resources Institute and International Institute for Environment and Development, *World Resources 1985*, p. 114.

229. U.S. Department of Energy, Energy Information Administration, Office of Energy Markets and End Use, *Annual Energy Outlook 1985* (Washington, D.C.: U.S. Government Printing Office, 1986), p. 17.

230. Ibid., p. 23.

231. U.S. Department of Energy, *Annual Energy Review 1985*, pp. 9.

232. Ibid.

233. Organization for Economic Cooperation and Development, *Environmentally Favourable Energy Options and Their Implementation*, Environmental Monograph no. 2 (Paris: Organization for Economic Cooperation and Development, 1986), p. 26.

234. Ibid., p. 38.

235. U.S. Department of Energy, *Annual Energy Outlook 1985*, p. 13.

236. Edward R. Fried, "World Oil Markets: New Benefits, Old Concerns," *The Brookings Review* 4, no. 3 (1986):32-33.

237. Information provided by Dave Costello, U.S. Department of Energy, July 1986, based on data from U.S. Bureau of Labor Statistics.

238. Ibid.

239. U.S. Department of Energy, *Annual Energy Review 1985*, p. 103.

240. U.S. Department of Energy, Energy Information Administration, *Petroleum Supply Annual 1985* (Washington, D.C.: U.S. Government Printing Office, 1986), p. 31.

241. U.S. Department of Energy, *Annual Energy Review 1985*, p. 103.

242. Ibid., p. 107.

243. Fried, "World Oil Markets: New Benefits, Old Concerns," p. 37; and Helga Steeg, "Lower Oil Prices: The Impact on Energy Policy," *The OECD Observer*, no. 140 (1985):18.

244. Organization for Economic Cooperation and Development, *Environmentally Favourable Energy Options and Their Implementation*, p. 28.

245. Charles A. Menzie, "The Environmental Implications of Offshore Oil and Gas Activities," *Environmental Science and Technolology* 16, no. 8 (1982):454A-472A; Biliana Cicin-Sain, "Offshore Oil Development in California: Challenges to Governments and to the Public Interest," *Public Affairs Report* 27, nos. 1 and 2 (1986); Howard L. Sanders and Carol Jones, "Oil, Science and Public Policy," in Thomas C. Jackson and Diana Reische, eds., *Coast Alert: Scientists Speak Out* (San Francisco: Friends of the Earth, 1981), pp. 73-94; and Robert W. Howarth, "Oil and Fish: Can they Coexist?', in Jackson and Reische, *Coast Alert: Scientists Speak Out*, pp. 49-72.

246. Organization for Economic Cooperation and Development, *Environmentally Favourable Energy Options and Their Implementation*, p. 28.

247. Stephen Koepp, "Cheal Oil," *Time*, April 14, 1986, p. 68.

248. U.S. Department of Energy, Energy Information Administration, *The Impact of Lower World Oil Prices and Alternative Energy Tax Proposals on the U.S. Economy* (Washington, D.C.: U.S. Department of Energy, 1986), p. 5.

249. "The Impact of $15 a Barrel Oil," *Petroleum Economist* 50, no. 4 (1986):22-24; and William H. Miller, "The Luxury of Choice: Oil Price Fall Spurs Industry Fuel Switching," *Industry Week*, April 28, 1986, pp. 22-24.

250. Miller, "The Luxury of Choice," p. 24.

251. U.S. Department of Energy, Energy Information Administration, Office of Energy

Markets and End Use, *Monthly Energy Review*, February 1986, p. 99; and U.S. Department of Energy, *Annual Energy Review 1985*, p. 157.

252. Miller, "The Luxury of Choice," p. 24.

253. U.S. Department of Energy, *Annual Energy Review 1985*, p. 147.

254. Ibid., p. 149.

255. Ibid., p. 91

256. Ibid., p. 177. Prices are for cost, insurance, and freight for all types of coal at electric utility power plants.

257. Ibid., pp. 7, 165.

258. Ibid., p. 7.

259. Ibid., p. 165; and Organization for Economic Cooperation and Development, *Environmentally Favourable Energy Options and Their Implementation*, p. 25.

260. U.S. Department of Energy, *Annual Energy Review 1985*, p. 93.

261. Ibid., pp. 93, 165.

262. Ibid., p. 165.

263. Ibid.

264. Organization for Economic Cooperation and Development, *Environmentally Favourable Energy Options and Their Implementation*, p. 26; and National Wildlife Federation, Public Lands and Energy Division, *Failed Oversight: A Report on the Failure of the Office of Surface Mining to Enforce the Federal Surface Mining Control and Reclamation Act* (Washington, D.C.: National Wildlife Federation, 1985), p. 12.

265. U.S. Department of Energy, *Annual Energy Review 1985*, p. 201.

266. U.S. Department of Energy, *Annual Energy Outlook 1985*, p. 14.

267. Atomic Industrial Forum, "AIF Economic Survey: Nuclear and Coal Equal in 1983 Generating Costs," *INFO News Release*, September 21, 1984, p. 1.

268. Ibid., p. 2.

269. U.S. Department of Energy, Energy Information Administration, Office of Coal, Nuclear, Electric and Alternate Fuels, *An Analysis of Nuclear Power Plant Construction Costs* (Washington, D.C.: U.S. Department of Energy, 1986), p. ix.

270. U.S. Department of Energy, *Annual Energy Review 1985*, pp. 204-5; information provided by the U.S. Department of Energy, July 30, 1986; and Atomic Industrial Forum, "Nuclear Power Plants in the United States," *InfoData*, July 1, 1986.

271. U.S. Department of Energy, *Annual Energy Review 1985*, p. 207.

272. Ibid., p. 209.

273. Ibid., p. 87.

274. Ibid., p. 209.

275. Organization for Economic Cooperation and Development, *Environmentally Favourable Energy Options and Their Implementation*, p. 34.

276. Gary Lee, "Experiment Blamed for Accident at Chernobyl," *Washington Post*, July 25, 1986, p. A21.

277. Mark A. Fischetti, "The Puzzle of Chernobyl," *Spectrum* 23, no. 7 (1986):34.

278. U.S. Environmental Protection Agency, "Soviet Nuclear Accident: A Task Force Report," press releases, May 5-May 9, 1986; Frank Von Hippel and Thomas B. Cochran, "Estimating Long-Term Health Effects," *Bulletin of the Atomic Scientists* 43, no. 1 (1986):20-22.

279. Celestine Bohlen, "Soviets Cite Negligence at Chernobyl," *Washington Post*, July 20, 1986, p. A1.

280. "The Aftermath of Chernobyl," *Science* 33 (1986):1141-42; C. Hohensmser et al., "Chernobyl: An Early Report," *Environment* 28, no. 5 (1986):9; and Von Hippel and Cochran, "Estimating Long-Term Health Effects," p. 24.

281. Sruart Diamond, "Management Cited as Key to Nuclear Safety in U.S.," *New York Times*, May 23, 1986, p. A10; Bill Paul, "Soviet Accident Spurs Questions on Safety of U.S. Nuclear Plants," *Wall Street Journal*, May 1, 1986, p. 2; and Frederik Rose and John Emshwiller, "Power Problems: U.S. Nuclear Industry Also Has Safety Perils, Three Accidents Show," *Wall Street Journal*, May 5, 1986, p. 2.

282. See, for instance, Jerry E. Bishop and Michael Waldholz, "Soviets' Biggest Health Problem Could Take Weeks to Develop," *Wall Street Journal*, May 1, 1986, p. 22; Cass Peterson, "A Chernobyl Possible in U.S., Experts Agree," *Washington Post*, June 1, 1986, p. A17; Nancy Maxwell, "Chernobyl's Message: Look Again at Containments in the United States," *Nucleus* 8, no. 2 (1986):3; and Bill Paul, "Soviet Accident Spurs Questions on Safety of U.S. Nuclear Plants," *Wall Street Journal*, May 1, 1986, p. 2.

283. Organization for Economic Cooperation and Development, *Environmentally Favourable Energy Options and Their Implementation*, p. 34; and Cynthia Pollock, "Decommissioning Nuclear Power Plants," in Lester R. Brown et al., *State of the World 1986* (New York: W.W. Norton, 1986), pp. 119-38.

284. U.S. Department of Energy, *Annual Energy Review 1985*, p. 7.

285. Ibid., p. 185.

286. U.S. Department of Commerce, Bureau of the Census, *Statistical Abstracts of the United States 1986* (Washington, D.C.: U.S. Government Printing Office, 1985), p. 574.

287. Organization for Economic Cooperation and Development, *Environmentally Favourable Energy Options and Their Implementation*, pp. 36-37.

288. U.S. Department of Energy, *National Energy Policy Plan Projections to 2010* (Washington, D.C.: U.S. Department of Energy, 1985), p. B-7; and Tim Palmer, "What Price 'Free' Energy?" *Sierra* 68, no. 4 (1983):40.

289. U.S. Department of Energy, *National Energy Policy Plan Projections to 2010*, p. B-7.

290. "The Hydro-Beavers," *Audubon* 88, no. 1 (1986):4.

291. Renewable Energy Institute, *Annual Renewable Energy Technology Review: Progress through 1984* (Washington, D.C.: Renewable Energy Institute, 1986), pp. 125-26; and personal communication with Kevin Porter, Renewable Energy Institute, February 1987.

292. "The Hydro-Beavers"; Palmer, "What Price 'Free' Energy," pp. 40-47; Harvard Ayers, "Hydro: The Environmental Impacts," *Sierra* 68, no. 4 (1983):44-45; and Renewable Energy Institute, *Annual Renewable Energy Technology Review*, p. 127.

293. Robert L. Loftness, *Energy Handbook* (New York: Van Norstrand Reinhold, 1984), p. 80.

294. U.S. Department of Energy, *Annual Energy Review 1985*, p. 213.

295. Ibid.

296. Ibid; and U.S. Department of Energy, Energy Inforation Administration, *Estimates of U.S. Wood Energy Consumption, 1980-1983* (Washington, D.C.: U.S. Government Printing Office, 1984), pp. xii, 6, 11.

297. John D. Buchholz, "Waste-to-Energy: Analyzing the Market," *World Wastes* 29, no. 6 (1986):10; and "Report on Semiannual Survey: Resource Recovery Activities," *City Currents*, October 1985, p. 24.

298. Renewable Energy Institute, *Annual Renewable Energy Technology Review*, p. 50.

299. Buchholz, "Waste-to-Energy," p. 18.

300. U.S. Department of Energy, *Annual Energy Review 1985*, p. 213.

301. Buchholz, "Waste-to-Energy," p. 18.

302. Ibid., p. 16; and Natural Resources Defense Council, "Petition to the United States Environmental Protection Agency for the Regulation of Emissions from Municipal Solid Waste Incineration," August 5, 1986.

303. U.S. Conference of Mayors, "Resource Recovery Activities," *City Currents*, April 1985; and Jeffery L. Wingenroth and Margaret N. Davis, "State of Landfill Methane Recovery Projects," *Gas Energy Review* 12, no. 12 (1984):16, cited in Renewable Energy Institute, *Annual Renewable Energy Technology Review*, p. 53.

304. Michael J. Carolan, "Falling Oil Prices Hurt Gas Recovery," *World Wastes* 29, no. 6 (1986):26; and Brent Blackwelder, "Environmental Impacts of Tax Reform," *Environmental Law Reporter* 16 (1986):10,322-23.

305. Renewable Energy Institute, *Annual Renewable Energy Technology Review*, pp. 57-59.

306. Ibid., p. 57.

307. See, for instance, ibid., pp. 88, 184, 277-78.

308. Loftness, *Energy Handbook*, p. 334.

309. U.S. Department of Energy, *Annual Energy Review 1985*, p. 217.

310. Renewable Energy Institute, *Annual Renewable Energy Technology Review*, p. 227.

311. U.S. Department of Energy, *Annual Energy Review 1985*, p. 221.

312. Jeffry Erickson and Carlo La Porta, *Energy Innovation: Development and Status of the Renewable Energy Industries-1985* (Washington, D.C.: Solar Energy Industries Association, 1985), and U.S. Department of Energy, Office of Deputy Assistant Secretary for Renewable Energy, *Renewable Technologies Program Summaries*, DOE/CE-0105, November 1984; both cited in Renewable Energy Institute, *Annual Renewable Energy Technology Review*, p. 183.

313. Renewable Energy Institute, *Annual Renewable Energy Technology Review*, , pp. 184-5.

314. U.S. Department of Energy, *Annual Energy Review 1985*, p. 211.

315. Ibid., p. 223.

316. Ibid., p. 185.

317. Ibid.

318. Ibid., p. 211; and Renewable Energy Institute, *Annual Renewable Energy Technology Review*, p. 91.

319. Gene V. Beeland et al., "The Current Status of Geothermal Direct Use Development in the United States," in "1985 International Symposium on Geothermal Energy," unpublished proceedings, Kona, Hawaii, August 26-30, 1985, cited in Renewable Energy Institute, *Annual Renewable Energy Technology Review*, p. 88.

320. Ibid., p. 87.

321. Renewable Energy Institute, *Annual Renewable Energy Technology Review*, p. 277.

322. Ibid., pp. 277-78; and information provided by Kevin L. Porter, Renewable Energy Institute, July 1986.

323. Renewable Energy Institute, *Annual Renewable Energy Technology Review*, p. 277.

324. U.S. Department of Energy, *National Energy Policy Plan Projections to 2010*, p. B-4.

325. World Resources Institute and International Institute for Environment and Development, *World Resources 1986*, p. 103.

326. Ibid., p. 118.

327. Paul F. Bente, Jr., *International Bio-Energy Directory and Handbook 1984* (Arlington, Va.: Bio-Energy Council, 1984), cited in Renewable Energy Institute, *Annual Renewable Energy Technology Review*, p. 48.

328. U.S. Department of Energy, *Annual Energy Review 1985*, p. 231.

329. World Resources Institute, *World Resources 1986*, pp. 290, 299.

330. United Nations Department of International Economic and Social Affairs, *1984 Energy Statistics Yearbook* (New York: United Nations Publishing Division, 1986), p. 384.

331. World Energy Conference, *Survey of Energy Resources*, 1980, cited in Renewable Energy Institute, *Annual Renewable Energy Technology Review*, p. 105.

332. Atomic Industrial Forum, "1985 AIF International Survey," *INFO News Release*, June 3, 1986.

333. U.S. Department of Energy, *Annual Energy Review 1985*, p. 233.

Figures

4.1. U.S. Department of the Interior, Bureau of Land Management, *Public Land Statistics 1985* (Washington, D.C.: U.S. Government Printing Office, 1986), p. 5.

4.2. H. Thomas Frey and Roger W. Hexem, *Major Uses of Land in the United States: 1982*, prepared for the U.S. Department of Agriculture, Economic Research Service (Washington, D.C.: U.S. Government Printing Office, 1985), pp. 18-19, appendix table 1; and H. Thomas Frey, *Major Uses of Land in the United States: 1974*, prepared for the U.S. Department of Agriculture, Economics, Statistics, and Cooperatives Service (Washington, D.C.: U.S. Government Printing Office, 1979), pp. 26-27, appendix table 1.

4.3. H. Thomas Frey and Roger W. Hexem, *Major Uses of Land in the United States: 1982*, pp. 18-19, appendix table 1; and H. Thomas Frey, *Major Uses of Land in the United States: 1974*, pp. 26-27, appendix table 1.

4.4. These metropolitan areas do not necessarily conform to Bureau of the Census definitions. They are defined by The Office Network. Information provided by Kathy Gehbauer, The Office Network, October 1986.

4.5. U.S. Department of Agriculture, Economic Research Service, *Cropland Use and Supply: Outlook and Situation Report*, CUS-2 (Washington, D.C.: U.S. Department of Agriculture, 1985), pp. 15, 17.

4.6. U.S. Department of Agriculture, Soil Conservation Service, unpublished data from the 1982 National Resources Inventory, tables 16a-22a.

4.7. National Research Council, *Soil Conservation: Assessing the National Resources Inventory*, vol. 1 (Washington, D.C.: National Academy Press, 1986), p. 77, table 5-1.

4.8. For 1963-1981: Estimates provided by the U.S. Department of Agriculture, Soil Conservation Service, October 1986. For 1982-1985: Information provided by the Conservation Tillage Information Center, October 1986.

4.9. George Pavelis, *Natural Resource Capital Formation in American Agriculture: Irrigation, Drainage, and Conservation, 1855-1980* (Washington, D.C.: U.S. Department of Agriculture, Economic Research Service, 1985), pp. 62, 75, 80.

4.10. U.S. Department of Agriculture, Soil Conservation Service, *National Resources Inventory* (Washington, D.C.: U.S. Government Printing Office, 1984), tables 36a, 12b.

4.11. U.S. Department of Agriculture, Forest Service, *U.S. Timber Production, Trade, Consumption, and Price Statistics 1950-1984* (Washington, D.C.: U.S. Government Printing Office, 1985), p. 12, table 3.

4.12. Area burned by wildfire: U.S. Department of Commerce, Bureau of the Census, *Historical Census of the U.S. Colonial Times to 1970* (Washington, D.C.: U.S. Government Printing Office, 1975), p. 537; U.S. Department of Agriculture, Forest Service, *1983 Wildfire Statistics* (Washington, D.C.: U.S. Forest Service, 1985), and previous annual issues; personal communication with Karen Hanson, U.S. Forest Service, Air and Fire Management, October 1986. Area defoliated by spruce budworm: U.S. Council on Environmental Quality, *Environmental Quality 1982* (Washington, D.C.: U.S. Government Printing Office, 1982), p. 250, table A-8; U.S. Department of Agriculture, Forest Service, *Forest Insect and Disease Conditions in the United States, 1985* (Washington, D.C.: U.S. Government Printing Office, 1986), pp. 5, 7, 40, 47, and previous annual issues. Area defoliated by the gypsy moth: U.S. Council on Environmental Quality, *Environmental Quality 1982*, p. 250, table A-8; U.S. Department of Agriculture, Forest Service, *Forest Insect and Disease Conditions in the United States, 1985*, pp. 2, 12 and previous annual issues. Forest acres planted and seeded: U.S. Department of Agriculture, Forest Service, *The Outlook for Timber in the U.S.*, Forest Research Report 20 (1950-1970) (Washington, D.C.: U.S. Government Printing Office, 1974); U.S. Department of Agriculture, Forest Service, *Forest Planting, Seeding, and Silvical Treatments in the U.S., 1980 Report*, Forest Service Report FS-368 (Washington, D.C.: U.S. Government Printing Office, 1980) and previous years to 1971; U.S. Department of Agriculture, Forest Service, *1985 U.S. Forest Planting Report* (Washington, D.C.: U.S. Government Printing Office, 1986), and previous annual issues.

4.13. Wayne B. Solley, Edith B. Chase, and William B. Mann IV, *Estimated Use of Water in the United States in 1980*, Geological Survey Circular 1001 (Reston, Va.: U.S. Geological Survey, 1983), p. 47.

4.14. Information provided by U.S. Department of Commerce, Bureau of the Census, October 1986.

4.15. Solley, Chase, and Mann, *Estimated Use of Water in the United States in 1980*, pp. 11, 14, 18, 23, 36, 47.

4.16. Ibid., p. 41; U.S. Geological Survey, *Estimated Use of Water in the United States, 1960*, Geological Survey Circular 456 (Reston, Va.: U.S. Geological Survey, 1961), pp. 14-21; U.S. Geological Survey, *Estimated Use of Water in the United States, 1965*, Geological Survey Circular 556 (Reston, Va.: U.S. Geological Survey, 1968), pp. 20, 24, 28, 32, 33; U.S. Geological Survey, *Estimated Use of Water in the United States in 1970*, Geological Survey Circular 676 (Reston, Va.: U.S. Geological Survey, 1972), pp. 19, 21, 23, 25; and U.S. Geological Survey, *Estimating Water Use in the United States in 1975*, Geological Survey Circular 765 (Reston, Va.: U.S. Geological Survey, 1977), pp. 33-36.

4.17. U.S. Geological Survey, *National Water Summary 1983*, Water Supply Paper 2250 (Washington, D.C.: U.S. Government Printing Office, 1984), p. 31.

4.18. U.S. Department of Energy, Energy Information Administration, *Annual Energy Review 1985* (Washington, D.C.: U.S. Government Printing Office, 1986), p. 11.

4.19. U.S. Department of Transportation, Federal Highway Administration, *Highway Statistics Annual*, annual tables 1970-1984 (Washington, D.C.: U.S. Department of Transportation, 1985), table VM-1.

4.20. U.S. Department of Energy, *Annual Energy Review 1985*, p. 5.

4.21. Ibid., p. 7.

4.22. Ibid., p. 9.

4.23. Information provided by Dave Costello, U.S. Department of Energy, July 1986.

based on data from the U.S. Department of Labor, Bureau of Labor Statistics.

4.24. U.S. Department of Energy, *Annual Energy Review 1985*, p. 103.

4.25. Ibid., p. 107.

4.26. Ibid., p. 157; U.S. Department of Energy, Energy Information Administration, *Monthly Energy Review*, February 1986, p. 99; U.S. Department of Commerce, *Statistical Abstract of the United States 1986* (Washington, D.C.: U.S. Government Printing Office, 1985), p. 477; and U.S. Department of Labor, Bureau of Labor Statistics, *CPI Detailed Report, December 1985* (Washington, D.C.: U.S. Government Printing Office, 1986), p. 1.

4.27. U.S. Department of Energy, *Annual Energy Review 1985*, p. 165.

4.28. Ibid., p. 201; U.S. Department of Commerce, *Statistical Abstract of the United States 1986*, p. 477; and U.S. Department of Labor, *CPI Detailed Report*, p. 1.

4.29. Atomic Industrial Forum, "U.S. Electrical Generating Costs and Power Plant Performance," in "AIF Economic Survey," annual table, 1975-1985.

4.30. U.S. Department of Energy, *Annual Energy Review 1985*, pp. 204-5; information provided by the U.S. Department of Energy, July 30, 1986; and Atomic Industrial Forum, "Nuclear Power Plants in the U.S.," *Infodata*, July 1, 1986.

4.31. U.S. Department of Energy, Office of Policy, Planning, and Analysis, *National Energy Policy Plan Projections to 2010* (Washington, D.C.: U.S. Department of Energy, 1985), p. B-4.

4.32. The World Bank, *World Development Report 1986* (New York: Oxford University Press, 1986), pp. 194-95, 246.

4.33. Atomic Industrial Forum, "1985 AIF International Survey," *INFO News Release*, June 3, 1986.

Chapter 5

Protected Lands, Critical Areas, and Wildlife

Appreciation for natural resources is not limited to those that are commercially valuable. In the United States land has long been preserved for purposes other than growing and harvesting crops, livestock, and timber. From the earliest settlements, communities have set aside lands for common use. This nation, with the creation of Yellowstone National Park in 1872, was the first country to establish national parks to preserve valuable natural areas for the enjoyment of future generations.

The demands for conserving critical resources have, in recent times, expanded and diversified. Increasing numbers of Americans participate in outdoor activities and are concerned about protecting a broadening array of natural, cultural and scenic resources. Wetlands—in the past, often converted to other uses as diverse as cropland, residential and commercial developments, and highways—now are known to be among the most environmentally valuable and threatened of all U.S. lands. Declining populations of many species of game and nongame wildlife have led to increased attention to the protection of certain species and their habitats. The far-reaching importance of these resources for human enjoyment, for maintenance of a healthy environment, and for fostering sustainable economic growth is the driving force behind increased preservation efforts by private organizations and all levels of government.

PARKS AND RECREATION

Interest in outdoor recreation has grown immensely in recent decades. Since 1962, when the Outdoor Recreation Resources Review Commission

(ORRRC) completed its study of the status of the country's recreational resources, the nation has undergone major social and economic changes that have affected recreation supply and demand.[1] Increases in leisure time and personal mobility have led to a growing demand for more recreational diversity and opportunity.[2] A 1982 survey revealed that 89 percent of U.S. residents had participated in some form of recreation during the previous year.[3] By the early 1980s, almost half of the adult population practiced some form of exercise on a regular basis as compared to only 24 percent in 1960.[4]

In response to this growing interest in recreation, and the increasing demands on outdoor lands to provide it, the President's Commission on Americans Outdoors was established in 1985 to conduct a comprehensive evaluation of the nation's recreational resources, to examine changes since ORRRC, and to make recommendations for future recreational needs and means for financing them.[5]

A survey conducted in 1986 for the commission showed that 81 percent of the respondents strongly agreed that "government should preserve natural areas for use by future generations."[6] Another commission survey found that the protection of natural resources and open space was the most important recreational issue, with concern over conflicting uses of recreational lands and water a close second.[7] The most common motivations for outdoor recreation were fitness and health, sociability, excitement, and the enjoyment of nature.[8]

The 1986 survey recorded that the most enjoyed outdoor activities, in order of popularity, were swimming, walking, fishing, and baseball/softball.[9] A survey conducted by the National Park Service regarding recreation on all lands found that between 1960 and 1982 the activities that showed the largest increases in participation were bicycling (increasing from 9 to 28 percent of the respondents), camping (increasing from from 8 to 19 percent), and skiing (increasing from 2 to 9 percent).* Three primary constraints to participation in recreational activities were time, money, and access.[11]

A survey conducted for the President's Commission on Americans Outdoors, in one of its more striking findings, showed a decrease in the number of trips to public areas lasting two days or more, while shorter trips, especially those of less than six hours, increased.[12] However, 54 percent of survey respondents traveled more than one hour to a recreation site at least once

---

*Some activities that were popular in 1982, such as jogging, off-road vehicle use, and backpacking were not included in the comparison because participation was so low in 1960.[10]

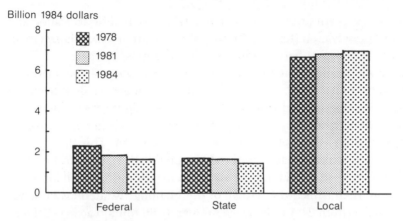

Figure 5.1

Direct Government Spending for Parks and Recreation, 1978, 1981, and 1984

Billion 1984 dollars

Source: U.S. Bureau of the Census.

a year, although the Department of the Interior found that the use of out-door areas is inversely related to the distance from home.[13]

Protected areas are owned and managed at every level of government, as well as by private organizations. In fiscal year 1984 federal, state, and local governments combined spent nearly $10 billion for parks and recreation.[14] However, between fiscal years 1978 and 1984, federal and state government funding, when converted to constant dollars, decreased (figure 5.1). Direct expenditures by local governments, however, increased during that period, and were more than four times higher than either state or federal expenditures in fiscal year 1984.

After a year of study and public forums, the President's Commission on Americans Outdoors issued over 60 recommendations. Among the most noteworthy were that federal, state, and local governments should spend at least $1 billion annually to acquire, develop, and protect open spaces; that the federal government should establish a new trust fund, earmarking a significant portion to stimulate grass-roots innovation toward this end;* that governments should create a nationwide system of greenways—scenic highway, river, and trail corridors linking communities; and that

---

*The commission recommended that this fund succeed the existing Land and Water Conservation Fund, which primarily supports the acquisiton of lands by federal, state, and local governments.[15]

federal multiple-use agencies should pay increased attention to recreational use of their lands.[16]

Federal Areas

Seven agencies administer almost all federal lands used for recreation and resource preservation (figure 5.2), with the Bureau of Land Management and the U.S. Forest Service administering the most acreage.

The total amount of federal land used for these purposes has increased significantly since 1960, although the largest changes resulted from the designation of protected areas in Alaska in 1980 (figure 5.3). Huge tracts of the federal estate in Alaska were formally classified under the Alaska National Interest Lands Conservation Act (ANILCA). This classification more than doubled the acreage of the National Park System (adding 43.6 million acres) and the Wildlife Refuge System (adding 53.8 million acres) and more than tripled the acreage of the National Wilderness Preservation System (from 23.1 million acres to nearly 80 million acres).[17]* From 1980 to 1985, acreage increases were modest—2.5 million acres for national parks, 1.7 million acres for wildlife refuges, and 8.7 million acres for wilderness.

Americans use these lands extensively, with a total of 6.3 billion visitor hours logged in 1985.[18] Eighteen percent of those surveyed by the President's Commission on Americans Outdoors reported visiting federal lands in 1986.[19] Excluding Alaska, the average time spent on federal recreational lands amounted to 15.6 hours per acre per year.† A disproportionate amount of this time (17 percent) was spent on the relatively small amount of land (5 percent) managed by the U.S. Army Corps of Engineers, Bureau of Reclamation, and Tennessee Valley Authority.[21] Although federal acreage in Alaska accounts for 44 percent (316.2 million acres) of the nation's total federal lands, visits to Alaskan federal lands are a negligible part of the total for the United States.[22]

National Park System

Recreational use of parks managed by the National Park Service has steadily increased since 1960, reaching 263.4 million recreation visits, or 1.3 billion

---

*The lands protected by ANILCA were similar in area and location to those sheltered from development by President Carter in a 1978 executive order.

†Visitation figures must be interpreted carefully. The availability and quality of data vary significantly among recreation providers and separate units.[20] Much of the data, especially on the more remote areas such as designated wilderness areas, depends on voluntary participation in visitor surveys.

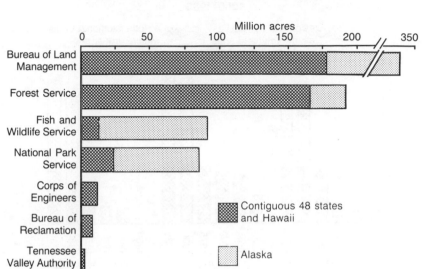

Figure 5.2
Management of Federal Lands, by Agency*, 1985

* Does not include land administered by the Department of Defense
and other agencies.

visitor hours, in 1985.²³ The integration of national parks into American
lives is evidenced by the results of a 1982 recreation survey that compared
use of parks in 1955 to use in the 1980s. In 1982-1983, 54 percent of the
respondents could recall at least one visit to a national park, compared to
37 percent in 1955.²⁴ Attendance at most well-known national parks and
monuments, however, has been fairly constant since the early 1970s. A
13.2 percent increase in overall visitor hours from 1978 to 1985 is probably
due to creation in the 1970s of new units in urban areas within easy access
of population centers.²⁵ Units in more remote areas showed a 47 percent
increase in visitation between 1978 and 1985 but still accounted for less
than 0.5 percent of total visitation.²⁶

The National Park Service manages 337 units, covering about 79.5 million
acres, that preserve many of the nation's natural, cultural, and historic
features for enjoyment by present and future generations.²⁷ The number
and diversity of units greatly expanded in the 1960s and 1970s, growing
from 176 units covering 26.2 million acres in 1960 to 333 units covering
77 million acres in 1980.²⁸ Over 85 percent of the increase in acreage (43.6

Figure 5.3

National Parks, Wildlife Areas, and Wilderness Areas, 1960–1985

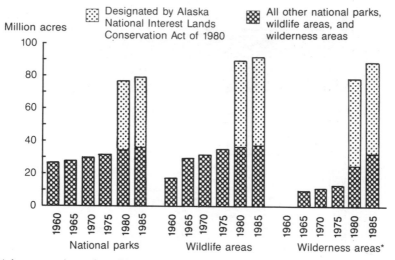

* Acreages shown for wilderness areas include some land counted in national parks and wildlife areas.

Source: National Park Service; U.S. Fish and Wildlife Service; The Wilderness Society.

million acres) was added with passage of ANILCA.[29] As a result, 70 percent of National Park System land is in Alaska (although Alaskan parks receive less than 3 percent of funds, staff, and visitation); about three-quarters of the remaining National Park System acreage is in the West.[30]

The past 25 years have been a period of tremendous change for the national parks (figure 5.4). Although the actual acreage has not increased dramatically if Alaskan land is excluded, visitation and expenditures for operation and maintenance show large increases since 1960. In the contiguous 48 states, the addition since 1960 of lakeshore and seashore units and parks in or near major metropolitan areas has broadened the range of recreational opportunities. This expansion has also produced greater geographical balance between the East and West since many of these new parks are east of the Mississippi River.[31] In 1986, Great Basin National Park in Nevada was added to the park system. With some 76,800 acres, it is the first national park established outside of Alaska in 15 years.[32]

The National Park Service predicts that the demand on its facilities will grow rapidly in the future, with recreational visits increasing by one-third between 1985 and 2000 (reaching a total of 346.7 million).[33]* The system clearly will have a major problem meeting these increased demands while striving to achieve the mandate of leaving the parks "unimpaired for future generations."[35] The challenge will be particularly significant at selected units near major metropolitan areas. Moreover, the parks also must cope with greater stresses on resources from activities on lands outside park boundaries and work more efficiently with neighboring landowners and the private sector. In a time of tight budgets, the service must face the question of how it will obtain the money required to meet its many challenges. Proposals to provide some of these funds from entrance and other user fees have generated substantial controversy in Congress. Such fees have been in effect for various park system units for some time. The questions are how high and how extensive they should be and where the revenues should be allocated. Legislation to permanently increase and expand entrance fees was introduced in 1986. However, Congress only authorized a limited one-year increase, with some of the revenue targeted for improvement of park resources.[36] An especially important issue is whether these revenues will supplement future appropriations or whether they will be used to offset future budget cutbacks.

National Forests

Americans actually use U.S. Forest Service (USFS) lands more than National Park Service lands for recreation. In 1985, USFS lands, totaling 190.7 million acres, accounted for 2.7 billion visitor hours, or 43 percent of the total visitor hours for all federal recreation lands.[37]† From 1981 to 1985, recreational use of USFS lands declined 4.4 percent.[39] The reasons for this decline are not clear and partially may be due to refinements in counting methods. However, deteriorating site conditions and site closures, caused at least in part by budget constraints, are also cited by USFS as possible contributing factors. In 1985, for example, only 29 percent of USFS facilities open for public use were managed at standard levels, compared with 74 percent in 1978.[40]‡

---

*Between 1980 and 1985, recreational visits accounted for 70 to 80 percent of the total number of visits to National Park Service units.[34]

†Ten percent of the total recreational use on USFS lands was recorded by facilities managed by the private sector to which USFS issues and manages "special use" permits.[38]

‡Standard level is the level of service at which a facility is expected to last its designed project life.[41]

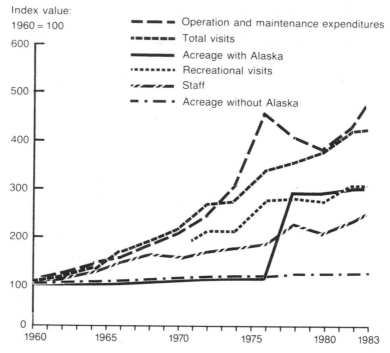

Figure 5.4

National Park Trends, 1960–1983

Index value:
1960 = 100

- – – – Operation and maintenance expenditures
- ▪▪▪▪▪▪ Total visits
- —— Acreage with Alaska
- ▪▪▪▪▪▪▪ Recreational visits
- ╱▰╱▰ Staff
- –▪–▪– Acreage without Alaska

Source: U.S. Department of the Interior.

The two most popular recreational activities on USFS lands are camping (53.1 million recreation visitor days [RVDs]* in 1985) and mechanized travel (50.4 million RVDs). Although fast growing, winter sports are a distant third at 16.2 million RVDs.[43] Visitor-day totals for dispersed areas (roads, trails, water-use areas, and general undeveloped backcountry) were consistently higher than those for developed areas for every year from 1965 through 1980.[44] Use of facilities operated by USFS, such as campgrounds and swimming, boating, and picnic sites, accounted for over one-fifth of all recreational use in 1985.[45]

Wildlife-related recreation is an important use of USFS lands. Hunting and fishing are allowed on most USFS lands (depending on the state laws).

---

*Recreation visitor days are units of measurement used by USFS. One RVD is 12 visitor hours and can include intermittent, continuous, or simultaneous use by one or more persons. There were a total of 225.4 million RVDs recorded on USFS lands in 1985.[42]

These two activities, combined with wildlife observation, accounted for 14 percent of total recreational use in 1985.[46] In comparison, off-road vehicle (ORV) use—including four-wheel-drive vehicles, motorcycles, dune buggies, three-wheel vehicles, and snowmobiles—generally constitutes an estimated 5 percent of recreational use within national forests.[47]

The President's Commission on Americans Outdoors explained why national forests are used so heavily: every resident of a major metropolitan area in the East is within a day's drive of a national forest, and in the West these areas are recreational backyards to most metropolitan centers.[48] This proximity may be one reason why USFS expects demands to increase rapidly in the future. In a 1985 assessment, USFS projected an increase of 58 to 86 percent (to between 340 and 400 million RVDs) between 1986 and 2030, with the largest increases expected in snow- and ice-related activities, water-related activities, and camping.[49] Despite the projected increase, two of nine of the proposals designed to address those trends would result in a constant or decreasing level of funding for recreation, necessitating the closing of some facilities.[50] As with the National Park Service, USFS faces the question of whether it can depend on entrance and user fees to avoid such closings. USFS has already used these fees to increase recreation receipts from $19.4 million in 1981 to $30.8 million in 1985. These receipts offset 30.2 percent of the total expenditures for the operation and maintenance of recreation facilities in 1985 (up from 21.7 percent in 1981).[51]

Bureau of Land Management

Approximately 5 percent (16.9 million acres) of Bureau of Management (BLM) lands are intensively used and managed for recreation. Included are 15 national wild and scenic rivers; 20 designated recreation, scenic, and historic trails totaling 1,600 miles; designated ORV areas; and several other recreation and conservation areas.[52] The agency also manages substantial acreage for water-based recreation, including 4 million surface acres of lakes and reservoirs, 16.3 million acres of wetlands, 15.4 million acres of riparian habitat, and 84,800 miles of permanent streams valuable for sport fishing.[53]

BLM lands are concentrated in the 11 westernmost contiguous states and Alaska. Forty-eight percent of the agency's land is in Alaska where it manages 44 percent of the state's total acreage.[54]

Camping (including trailer space) and picnic sites are the primary outdoor recreation developments at BLM recreation areas.[55] In 1985, land-, water-, and snow/ice-based activities on BLM lands accounted for 244.6 million visitor hours of use. Land-based recreation constituted 86 percent

284 STATUS AND TRENDS

of this total, with water- and snow/ice-based activities accounting for 12 and 2 percent, respectively. The most popular recreational activities on BLM lands are camping (65.4 million visitor hours), hunting (51.8 million visitor hours), and ORV travel (37.0 million visitor hours).[56]

National Wildlife Refuges

While wildlife conservation is the primary mandate of the Fish and Wildlife Service (FWS), refuge use by the general public is an important considera-tion in the agency's management.[57] From 1982 to 1986, public uses of National Wildlife Refuge System lands increased by almost 5 percent (from 30.4 million to 31.9 million visits per year) as more and more areas were opened to hunting and fishing.[58] From 1980 to 1984, 158 refuges were opened to hunting of migratory birds, upland game, or large game species, and another 42 were opened to sport fishing.[59] As of October 31, 1985, 60 percent of all refuges were open to hunting and 47 percent to fishing.[60] Critics claim that heavy recreational use in certain areas is incompatible with the agency goals of providing resting and breeding grounds for migratory birds and other wildlife.[61]

Recreational uses of national wildlife refuges include fishing, boating, wildlife observation, nature study, hunting, hiking, environmental educa-tion, photography, camping, and ORV use. Refuges recorded approximately 28.7 million visits for wildlife-oriented activities in 1986, the majority of them for so-called nonconsumptive uses; nonwildlife activities accounted for another 3.2 million. As figure 5.5 indicates, the greatest increase has been for interpretation and educational purposes and for hunting, both of which jumped about 20 percent between 1982 and 1986. Nevertheless, hunting, including trapping, remains a small component of overall use. Only nonwildlife-oriented recreation (for example, camping and ORV use) declined, with visits dropping 21 percent during this period.[62]

Wilderness Areas

Passage of the Wilderness Act in 1964 gave Congress the authority to set aside public lands under the National Wilderness Preservation System.[63] By 1986, Congress had designated 89.1 million acres to be included in this system.[64] The most recent additions include 8.3 million acres in 20 states in 1984 and almost 97,000 acres in Kentucky, Nebraska, Tennessee, and Georgia in 1985 and 1986.[65] Alaska contains the majority of the existing wilderness area (56.4 million acres) as a result of the passage of the Alaska National Interest Lands Conservation Act in 1980.[66] This act also required the review of additional federal lands in Alaska for possible inclusion as

Figure 5.5
Visitor Uses of National Wildlife Refuges, 1982–1986

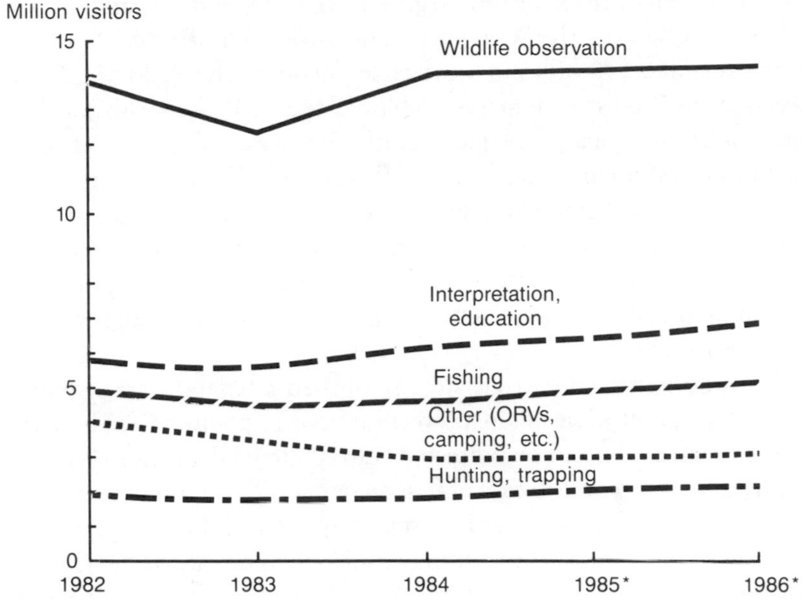

Million visitors

* Data are estimated.
Source: National Audubon Society.

wilderness. Lands designated as wilderness are managed by BLM (0.4 million acres), USFS (32.6 million acres), FWS (19.3 million acres), and the National Park Service (36.8 million acres).[67]

How to determine the suitability of lands for classification as wilderness has been a source of continuing debate. Most eastern national forest lands were originally eliminated from wilderness consideration by USFS because of extensive road building and logging during the last century.[68] Congress addressed this issue in late 1974 with enactment of the Eastern Wilderness Act which established 16 wilderness areas comprising 207,000 acres. It suggested that roadless areas that had been altered by human forces could not be disqualified from wilderness classification if they had been mostly restored to their original state by natural forces over time.[69]

Wilderness designation issues, particularly those regarding lands managed by BLM, will continue to be major sources of controversy in the coming years. Meanwhile, increased attention almost certainly will be given to questions regarding management of these areas in light of previous human disturbances and continuing intervention.

Wild and Scenic Rivers

Of the nearly 3.6 million miles of rivers and streams in the United States, 7,365 miles in 72 rivers or river segments have been designated as wild or scenic rivers under the Wild and Scenic Rivers Act of 1968.[70] In 1986, Congress added 140 miles in six river segments to the Wild and Scenic Rivers System.[71] This program was established to protect rivers with outstanding scenic, recreational, geologic, wildlife, historical, or cultural values in free-flowing condition.[72] Rivers are classified as "wild," "scenic," or "recreational," depending how close the river and its surrounding habitat are to their natural state.[73] Rivers designated for protection are managed under plans approved by the secretary of the interior or the secretary of agriculture, depending on which department administers the land through which a given river flows.[74]

The Wild and Scenic Rivers Act established a federal-state system of river conservation. The main protection tool is planning, although a designated river also can be protected through federal acquisition of surrounding land and prohibition of federal dam building. Designations are made by an act of Congress or by a state request and the approval of the secretary of the interior.[75] A river may continue to be owned by state and local governments; about 10 percent of the Wild and Scenic River System is managed by the states.[76] In some cases, rivers are managed in partnership with the federal government.[77]

National Scenic and Historic Trails

The National Trail System Act was passed by Congress in 1968 to promote the development of a national network of scenic, recreational and connecting trails.[78] In 1978, Congress authorized the addition of historic trails to this network.[79] As of 1986, eight national scenic trails (almost 14,500 miles) and six national historic trails (nearly 10,700 miles) had been designated.[80] Approximately 20 percent of these designated trail miles have been developed for public use.[81] Two—the Appalachian Trail and the Pacific Crest Trail—were designated in the act itself, which also identified 14 others for study.[82] By their very nature, designated trails are devoted primarily to hiking and primitive camping, among other things.[83]

The National Trail System Act encourages federal, state, and local agencies to work together to establish scenic trails, preserve their natural setting, and protect them from incompatible development. As with wild and scenic rivers, federal ownership is not mandated. The Appalachian Trail, for example, is protected by a combination of federal and state acquisitions, easements, and purchase by private land trusts and trail clubs.[84]

State Areas

Although they receive less attention than federally owned lands, state parks and other lands actually play a bigger role in satisfying the public's recreational demands. On less than one-seventh the acreage of national parks, state parks and related areas reported more than twice the visitation in 1985.[85]* The 1986 survey by the President's Commission on Americans Outdoors reported that 33 percent of the respondents visited state lands that year.[87]

States have set aside 61.8 million acres of forests, parks, and natural and wildlife areas that provide distinctive scenic, natural, cultural, and historic resources, as well as serve recreational needs.[88] Almost 6,000 units (about 22 percent of the total area) are designated as state parks and related areas.[89] Alaska accounted for more than one-quarter of all state park lands in 1985. Acreage per capita in 1985 varied from 7.9 acres per 1,000 persons in Mississippi to a high of 6,290 acres per 1,000 persons in Alaska, with Wyoming a distant second high at 246 acres per 1,000 persons.[90]

Since 1955, the area set aside as state parks has doubled, while visitation has more than tripled (figure 5.6).[91] In 1986, these units served over 675 million visitors.[92]† Day use has almost always accounted for 85 to 95 percent of the total, although overnight visitation has increased from 6.0 to 9.7 percent of the total since 1955.[94]

A 1985 Conservation Foundation survey revealed that state parks are facing even more stress from budgetary constraints and increased usage than federal lands. Funding is by far the most pressing concern for state park directors. Federal funds have dwindled, in part explaining a nationwide 17 percent decrease between 1980 and 1985 in spending by state parks systems. This drop is more severe than that for either local or national parks or for state activities in general during that period.[95] Many states are responding to these cuts by establishing or raising user fees or generating new sources of funding from special taxes, lotteries, and mineral extraction fees.

---

*These statistics include Alaskan state parks, which in 1985 had 3.1 million acres and reported 1.9 million visits. If Alaska is excluded from calculations of area for both national and state parks, state parks have about one-third the acreage of the national system.[86]

†This information is based on data collected by the National Association of State Park Directors. In 1955, the data included Baxter State Park in Maine and Adirondack Park and Catskill Park in New York; in 1986, these parks were excluded. Incomplete information prevents accurate adjustment of 1955 data to exclude the acreage and visitation rates of these very large state parks, which in 1985 totaled over 2.6 million acres and were administered by separate state agencies.[93]

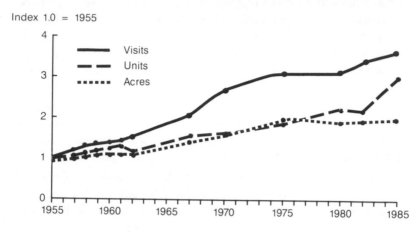

Figure 5.6
State Park Trends in the United States, 1955–1985

Index 1.0 = 1955

Source: Resources for the Future; U.S. Department of the Interior.

The contribution of user fees to state park capital development funds rose from 26.3 percent in 1977-1980 to 50.4 percent in 1981-1984 in the 10 states reporting their use.[96]

State park directors also report concern over deteriorating facilities, protecting sensitive ecological areas, promoting less popular parks, developing more visitor facilities, and serving special groups such as the handicapped and the elderly.[97] In response to these concerns, states have stepped up marketing of parks, instituted programs to improve stewardship of cultural and natural resources, and reformed park management structure to better use volunteer and nonprofit groups.[98]

Local Parks

City or community parks have the smallest acreage (5.7 million acres of county and regional land and 3 million acres of municipal recreation land), yet they also have the highest visitation of all public recreation areas.[99] Thirty-nine percent of Americans responding to the 1986 survey by the President's Commission on Americans Outdoors stated that they visited city or community parks or recreation areas often or very often.[100] More than three-fourths of American adults used a local park, pool, beach, or outdoor recreation area in their community in 1985 and nearly one-fourth of them did so at least 25 times that year.[101] Noted constraints to visiting developed recreation resources in cities were poor location and inappropriate development of existing facilities, safety concerns, interstate corridors that divide neighborhoods, and lack of regular public transportation. These factors frequently limit access to nearby facilities for many urban-surburban residents.[102]

In addition to recreation, areas set aside by localities for open space play an important role in fostering quality design and liveability. In 1986 the President's Commission on Americans Outdoors found that a total of 8.7 million acres in 87,600 units were administered by a region, county, or municipality. The amount of acreage in these areas was at least twice as high in the north-central region compared to the northeastern, southern, or western regions.[103]

There is no nationwide data available on trends for local parks, although some regions have collected information over the years. The Regional Plan Association of the tristate area of the New York City urban area (New Jersey, New York, and Connecticut) found that 40 percent of the nearly 992,000 acres of vacant land converted for use from 1964 to 1984 was preserved as open space, while the other 60 percent was developed.[104] According to this study, open space was preserved not only by localities but also by other levels of government and the private sector.

Local recreation areas, too, suffer from diminishing funds and space, increasing visitation, and growing metropolitan development of potential future sites. Aid from federal and state governments is declining, while competition for funds from other public services is growing.[105] Opportunities for creating new local recreational areas and open space have diminished as land acquisition costs have increased and fiscal budgets have become increasingly constrained. However, with some innovation, potential space for recreation is not completely limited by economics. Sparked by the rediscovery of designed urban parks and the use of incentives and other tools, urban waterfronts, abandoned industrial areas, and railroad right-of-ways are being reclaimed throughout the country and converted to provide open space and recreational opportunities on land previously dedicated to other purposes.[106]

Private Initiatives

Private lands also provide recreational opportunities. According to the President's Commission on Americans Outdoors, 56 percent of survey respondents participate in outdoor activities on privately owned land.[107]

Conservation on private lands is frequently motivated by government incentives. Programs involving easements, reduced tax assessments for dedicated farms or other open space, and cooperative agreements with landowners can often provide effective alternatives to public ownership.[108] Farmowners have allowed dispersed recreation on their lands for years; however, concerns over vandalism, liability, and changing agricultural practices may discourage future public access.[109]

Cooperative partnerships between public and private sectors can work to protect open lands. For example, through a series of transactions involving the Appalachian Trail Conference and its affiliates, a 66-acre parcel was acquired several years ago for a trail right-of-way, scenic protection, and additional public use including a hostel.[110] (The activities of private land trusts are discussed in the "Wildlife" section.) Services at local public parks and recreation facilities, which have been traditionally provided by public agencies, are being contracted to private companies or civic groups. It is estimated that most municipalities contract 10 to 20 percent of park and recreation services.[111] In the future, many parks and protected areas will depend more heavily on compatible uses of adjacent private lands and on effective support from private organizations.

WETLANDS

Wetlands—including areas such as coastal salt marshes, bottomland hardwood forests, prairie potholes, playa lakes, and the wet tundra of Alaska[112]—account for only 5 percent of the land surface in the 48 contiguous states. But they are among the earth's most productive terrestrial habitats. Nearly one-third of the nation's endangered and threatened species live in or are dependent on wetland habitats,[113] and millions of waterfowl use them for breeding and wintering grounds every year.[114] Coastal wetlands provide nursery and spawning grounds for 60 to 90 percent of U.S. commercial fisheries.[115] The National Marine Fisheries Service estimates that destruction of these wetlands between 1954 and 1978 cost the nation $208 million annually in lost fisheries income alone.[116]

Wetlands also have an important role in moderating the hydrologic cycle, controlling floods, reducing erosion, recharging groundwater, and improving water quality.[117] In assessing alternatives for flood protection along the Charles River near Boston, the U.S. Army Corps of Engineers concluded that wetlands protection was the most cost-effective approach. It estimated that destruction of the surrounding wetlands would cause flood damage averaging $17 million a year.[118] In the process of moderating surface runoff, wetlands allow more water to seep into the ground, restoring groundwater supplies and filtering nutrients and other pollutants from the water flowing through them.[119]

But farmers, foresters, developers, highway builders, and other government and private institutions also see the conversion of wetlands as providing substantial benefits. Wetland soils are often very rich and productive. They are often the only low-cost, large, undeveloped areas located near urban populations, making them economically attractive as sites for highways, shopping centers, residential developments, and commercial and industrial centers. Valuable deposits of oil, gas, and other fuels or minerals can underlie them. And, in some cases, officials see their existence as a health and aesthetic nuisance.

Historically, wetlands were often seen as useless swamps and marshes that would best be eliminated. The federal Swamp Land Acts of the middle 19th century granted individual states over 65 million acres of wetlands for conversion to agricultural land.[120] Today, a growing appreciation of the other values of wetlands has resulted in substantial efforts being made to protect, or even to create, them. Yet wetland areas continue to be lost at a rapid rate, both from direct conversion and from degradation due to accumulation of pollutants, invasion of nonnative vegetation, salt water intrusion, and diversion of their natural water sources.

Distribution and Status

Today less than half of the original 215 million wetland acres found in the contiguous United States remain.[121]* According to the most recent U.S. Fish and Wildlife Service (FWS) inventory, 99 million acres of estuarine and freshwater wetlands remained in the 48 contiguous states in the mid-1970s.[124] Perhaps 3 to 4 million more acres have disappeared since that estimate was made.[125] An additional 223 million acres of wetlands (primarily tundra) are found in Alaska.[126]

---

*There are nearly as many variations on the definition of wetlands used in legislation and inventories as there are types of wetlands, making it difficult to accurately quantify wetlands or assess the protection offered by regulations.[122] However, the definition developed by the Fish and Wildlife Service in 1979 is being used increasingly as the national standard for wetland identification. Under this definition, wetlands are described as "lands transitional between terrestrial and aquatic systems where the water table is usually at or near the surface or the land is covered by shallow water."[123] Attempting to characterize wetlands from an ecological standpoint by including consideration of vegetation, soil, and hydrology, the Fish and Wildlife Service further defines wetlands as areas that support vegetation adapted for growth in water or saturated soils, contain hydric soils, or contain sufficient water at some point during the growing season to stress plants and animals lacking adaptations for life in water-saturated soils.

The distribution of these wetlands is uneven, ranging from nearly 60 percent of Alaska's land area and over 25 percent of the land area in Florida and Louisiana to well under 5 percent of the land area in many of the western states.[127] According to the 1982 National Resources Inventory, wetlands on nonfederal land in the contiguous United States total over 76 million acres, the majority of which are concentrated in a few areas of the country such as the Southeast and the northern Midwest* (figure 5.7).

A recent inventory of coastal wetlands, undertaken by the National Atmospheric and Oceanic Administration (NOAA), concluded that the 22 states in the contiguous United States† bounded by the Atlantic and Pacific oceans and the Gulf of Mexico contain over 11.3 million acres of coastal wetlands. The methodology and definitions used for this inventory do differ from those used in other recent studies, so its results cannot be directly compared with other results. Nevertheless, the NOAA inventory does enable a relative assessment of the amounts of wetlands in various coastal states. It concluded that over half of the coastal wetland acreage is found along the Atlantic coast (37.3 percent along the southeastern coast and 15.3 percent along the northern coast), and that most of the remaining coastal wetlands are found along the Gulf of Mexico (45.9 percent). In contrast, the Pacific coast contains only 1.4 percent of the coastal wetlands found in the contiguous United States.[128]

FWS estimates that, between the 1950s and the mid-1970s, some 9 million acres of wetlands in the contiguous 48 states were converted to other uses—an annual average of 458,000 acres, of which 439,000 were freshwater wetlands and 19,000 were estuarine wetlands.[129] Although this rate has since slowed, due in part to declining rates of agricultural drainage and increasing regulation,[130] the Office of Technology Assessment estimates that 300,000 acres of freshwater and estuarine wetlands continue to be destroyed each year,[131]‡ implying that an additional 3 million acres may have been lost from the mid-1970s to the mid-1980s.

---

*To maintain continuity in data collection over recent decades, the National Resources Inventory uses a slightly different definition of wetlands than is currently used by the Fish and Wildlife Service.

†Inclusion of Alaska, Hawaii, and the Great Lakes states (Illinois, Indiana, Michigan, Minnesota, Ohio, Wisconsin) raises the number of states with coastal wetlands to 30; these states are often included as coastal states in regulatory programs.

‡The Office of Technology Assessment indicates that this estimate may be 10 to 20 percent off due to data uncertainties and variability.

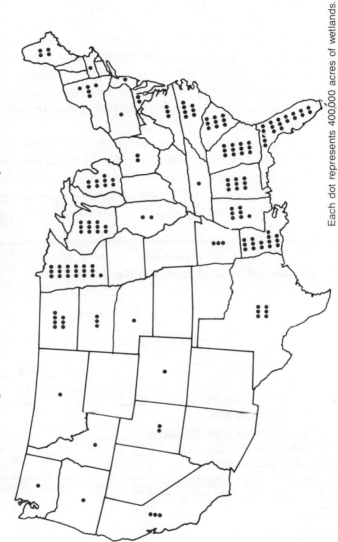

Figure 5.7

Wetland Acreage in the Coterminous United States, by State, 1982*

Each dot represents 400,000 acres of wetlands.
* Does not include wetlands on federal lands.

Source: U.S. Soil Conservation Service.

Areas such as the coastal marshes of Louisiana, the Mississippi bottomland hardwoods, the prairie potholes of the northern Midwest, and the pocosin wetlands of North Carolina have suffered particularly severe losses (figure 5.8). Additionally, natural wetlands have been almost entirely eliminated in California and Iowa, which have lost 91 and 99 percent of their original wetland acreage, respectively.[132]

A net loss of 373,000 acres of saltwater vegetated wetlands occurred between the mid-1950s and the mid-1970s, representing 7.6 percent of the total 1950s acreage.[133] The greatest losses occurred predominantly in Atlantic and Gulf coast states.[134] Most of these losses resulted from urban development, dredging of marinas and canals,[135] and other modifications of the natural hydrologic cycle.

One area that continues to experience dramatic losses is Louisiana's coastal marshes, which contain nearly 2.9 million wetland acres representing 25.4 percent of the nation's coastal wetlands.[136] More than one-third of the annual U.S. seafood harvest comes from the Gulf of Mexico,[137] and many of the gulf's fish and shellfish rely on Louisiana's extensive marshes for spawning

Figure 5.8

Examples of Wetland Losses in the United States*

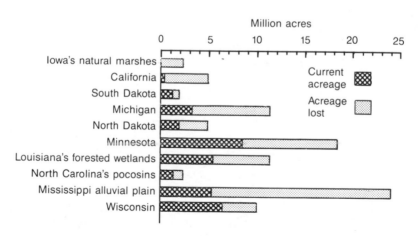

* These examples are compiled from studies conducted independently, and, therefore, survey methods and time periods may differ.

Source: U.S. Fish and Wildlife Service.

grounds and for nurseries. These marshes, along with Louisiana's barrier islands, also serve as a buffer that reduces hurricane damage to heavily populated areas.[138]

In Louisiana, one of the most serious problems is saltwater intrusion that is occurring because of rising sea levels. This rising has accelerated beyond the point where natural marsh-building processes can compensate for the loss. Channelization and canal construction have increased rates of saltwater intrusion, and subsidence of coastal land has increased as a result of extraction of groundwater, minerals, oil, and gas. Further, the construction of levees has destroyed the natural rhythm of flooding, eliminating infusions of freshwater and sediment.[139] As a result, it is estimated that these valuable marshlands are currently disappearing at a rate between 22,000 and 25,000 acres per year.[140]

Inland freshwater or palustrine wetlands sustained nearly 97 percent of the wetland losses between the mid-1950s and the mid-1970s, representing a net loss of 11 million acres (11 percent of the total) of vegetated freshwater wetlands.[141] According to FWS, 87 percent of these losses were the result of conversion to agricultural land, with most of the the remainder (8 percent) due to the conversion of wetlands to urban uses (figure 5.9).[142] Loss of freshwater wetlands to saltwater vegetated wetlands may be due to intrusion of saltwater into freshwater wetlands.

Many of the losses in palustrine wetlands have occurred in the bottomland hardwoods of the lower Mississippi River floodplain. These wetlands, located primarily in Louisiana, Arkansas, and Mississippi, play an important role in flood control, are important for fish and wildlife, and serve to filter fertilizers, pesticides, and eroding soil from the water. Over recent decades, millions of acres have been converted for agriculture, primarily for soybeans.[143] During the 20 years covered by the National Wetland Trends Study, these bottomland hardwoods were converted at a rate of 190,000 acres per year, representing an annual conversion rate of approximately 1.6 percent of the region's wetland acreage or more than three times the national conversion rate of 0.5 percent.[144] Today, only 5.2 million acres of wetlands, or a little over 20 percent of the region's original wetland acreage, remain in this area.[145]

A second area of notable palustrine wetland losses is the prairie potholes of the Midwest. These wetlands, scattered throughout the agricultural land of North and South Dakota and Minnesota, are extremely important for waterfowl production; nearly 50 percent of the ducks in North America

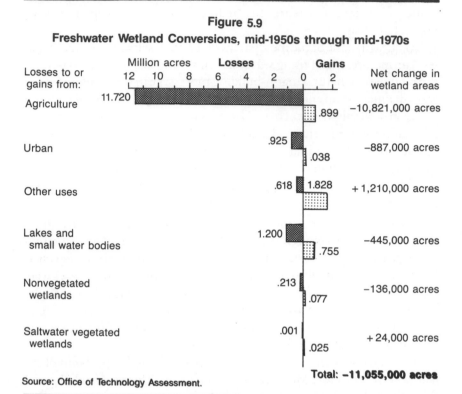

Figure 5.9
Freshwater Wetland Conversions, mid-1950s through mid-1970s

Source: Office of Technology Assessment.

Total: −11,055,000 acres

come from these small, glacially created depressions in the landscape. Over the last several decades, many of these pothole wetlands have been destroyed through conversion to agriculture. The Dakotas, for example, originally contained an estimated 7 million acres of pothole wetlands; today, less than 50 percent of that total remains. Similarly, Minnesota has lost over 9 million of its original 18 million acres of pothole wetlands.[146] Efforts have been made to safeguard these wetland areas for waterfowl, primarily through the purchase of conservation easements under the Water Bank Program and the Migratory Bird Conservation Fund, but agricultural conversion of these areas remains high.

Some 70 percent of the nation's pocosin wetlands, originally covering over 2.5 million acres, are found in North Carolina. Although these shrubby, evergreen-dominated bogs are freshwater wetlands, they are particularly important in stabilizing water quality in coastal estuaries,[147] and their disturbance may threaten North Carolina's commercial fisheries.[148] Through conversion to agriculture or pine plantations and, increasingly, peat mining, the pocosins have been reduced to an estimated 1.5 million acres, only 695,000 of which remain undisturbed.[149]

Direct conversion is not the only factor affecting the status of wetlands. Many wetlands remain but are degraded by problems such as accumulation of pollutants, diversion of wetlands' natural water and sediment sources, and invasion of nonnative vegetation. Most assessments of wetland status have not focused on these threats and only recently have attempts begun to inventory wetland quality.

A prime example of this degradation is the 5,900-acre Kesterson National Wildlife Refuge located in the San Joaquin Valley in California. In 1983, high levels of deformities and reproductive failure began to be observed in the avian populations at the refuge. The deformities have been attributed to the accumulation of high concentrations of selenium from the irrigation drainage water flowing into the refuge.[150]

Kesterson, although the most widely publicized example, may not be an isolated occurrence. In 1986, FWS completed an inventory of potential contaminant problems in the National Wildlife Refuge System, identifying 78 refuges with potential contamination problems, most of which include wetlands.[151] (See chapter 9.) Wetland areas are particularly susceptible to such contamination because of their unique ability to trap pollutants.

Degradation of wetland habitats may be physical as well as chemical. Another problem threatening wetlands is insufficient water, since water increasingly is being diverted for urban or agricultural use. The resulting lowering of the water table is degrading and perhaps destroying wetlands in some areas. For example, diversion of water to meet growing demand in Los Angeles is currently diminishing the biological integrity of Mono Lake and its surrounding wetlands.[152]

Management

Since the early 1970s, increasing efforts have been made by all levels of government and by private groups to stem these wetlands losses. The most common of these have involved regulation, economic incentives for wetlands protection, and acquisition of priority wetlands by both governmental and nongovernmental organizations.

The principal federal regulatory protection program for wetlands was established by Section 404 of the 1972 amendments to the Federal Water Pollution Control Act (now called the Clean Water Act).[153] This provision requires permits for discharging dredged or fill materials into U.S. waters and their adjacent wetlands.

By the late 1970s, the Corps of Engineers was receiving over 10,000 Section 404 permit applications annually. Over the last few years, however, this number has declined to approximately 8,000 applications per year, and the number of permits issued has dropped accordingly. In contrast, the proportion of permits denied, although still only a small percentage of the applications received, has been increasing steadily, from just over 1 percent in 1974 to nearly 4 percent in 1985 (figure 5.10). The impact of the law, however, extends well beyond the permits denied. For instance, the Office of Technology Assessment estimated that in 1981 nearly one-third of the permits were modified before being issued to reduce impacts, and an additional 14 percent were withdrawn by the applicant (figure 5.11).[154] Furthermore, 404 regulations presumably prevent some developments planned for wetland areas from getting past the design stage,

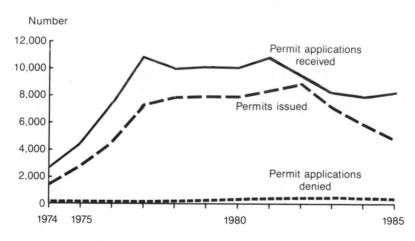

Figure 5.10
Permitting Activities Relating to the
Dredging and Filling of Wetlands, 1974–1985

Source: U.S. Army Corps of Engineers.

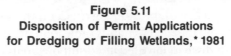

Figure 5.11
Disposition of Permit Applications
for Dredging or Filling Wetlands,* 1981

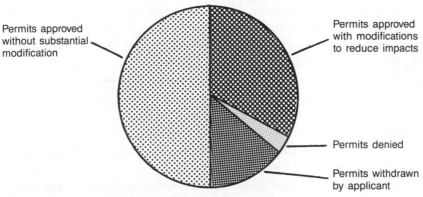

Permits approved without substantial modification

Permits approved with modifications to reduce impacts

Permits denied

Permits withdrawn by applicant

* Applications submitted under Section 404 of the Clean Water Act of 1977.

Source: Office of Technology Assessment.

although there are no reliable sources of information on this.* The 404 process, however, exempts "normal farming, silviculture and ranching practices," the major cause of freshwater wetlands loss, from the permitting process.[156]

Two recent decisions have clarified the extent of the corps's Section 404 jurisdiction and reaffirmed the U.S. Environmental Protection Agency's (EPA's) authority to veto permit decisions. In *U.S.* v. *Riverside Bayview Homes*, the U.S. Supreme Court supported a broad definition of wetlands under the corps' Section 404 jurisdiction, ruling that Section 404 permits are required for dredge or fill activities in wetlands adjacent to navigable waters, even if they are not inundated or regularly flooded by navigable waters.

A second controversial action was taken in 1986 when EPA vetoed a corps permit for construction of a shopping mall on 50 acres of red maple

---

*Some estimates have been made, however, including one put forth by the National Marine Fisheries Service that in 1981 the 404 program, in conjunction with state regulations, served to reduce coastal conversion by 70 to 85 percent.[155]

swamp in Attleboro, Massachusetts. This action reaffirmed EPA's right to veto corps permit decisions, providing a check on the corps's decisions.

Many states have also initiated wetlands protection programs. Although Michigan is the only state to have assumed responsibility for administering the Section 404 program within its boundaries,[157] as of 1983, 13 coastal states required a permit for dredge or fill activities in coastal wetlands.[158] In addition, encouraged by the Coastal Zone Management Act of 1972,* 23 coastal states have developed coastal zone management programs that are designed in part to decrease coastal wetland conversion.[160]†

Inland wetlands have not received similar attention. As of 1983, only seven states had programs explicitly regulating inland wetlands. However, some states do provide a degree of inland wetland protection as a component of broader regulatory efforts applying to areas such as floodplains, shorelines, or wild and scenic rivers.[163]

In recent years, the federal government has also enacted legislation removing some of the tax and other economic incentives that earlier programs had provided for wetlands conversion. The Coastal Barrier Resources Act of 1982,[164] covering 186 coastal barrier units along the Atlantic and Gulf of Mexico coasts,[165] removed federal insurance and subsidies for development from 700 miles of designated barrier islands and their adjacent wetlands.[166]

The "Swampbuster" provision of 1985 Food Security Act denies many subsidies to farmers producing crops on converted wetlands.[167] In addition, the Tax Reform Act of 1986 eliminated certain tax incentives for conversion of wetlands, including favorable capital gains treatment for land "improved" by drainage.[168]

Wetland acquisition represents another important means of protecting

---

*The Coastal Zone Management Act provides financial assistance to states setting up coastal management plans that include wetland protection measures.[159]

†Some estimates indicate that these regulations, along with federal regulatory programs, have dramatically reduced wetland losses. For instance, the Fish and Wildlife Service estimates that, following passage of the Wetlands Act of 1973 (and concurrent implementation of the federal Section 404 program), the destruction of coastal wetlands in Delaware dropped by more than 95 percent, from nearly 444 acres per year between 1954 and 1971 to an average of 20 acres per year between 1973 and 1979.[161] The service documented similar reductions in loss in New Jersey since passage of the Wetlands Act of 1970.[162] However, the role played by these regulatory programs cannot be isolated from other factors such as changes in the economy or decreasing available wetland, which also may play a role in this decreasing conversion rate.

wetlands. The federal government has, either by direct acquisition or through purchase of conservation easements, protected millions of wetland acres with funds from the Migratory Bird Hunting Stamp Act, passed in 1934, and the Water Bank Act, passed in 1970.[169] The Migratory Bird Hunting Stamp Act authorized the sale of "duck stamps" to hunters[170] with receipts to be used for acquisition of waterfowl habitat. Since the fund was established, over $189.5 million has been used to purchase nearly 1.9 million acres of waterfowl habitat, primary wetlands, and an additional 1.2 million acres have gained protection through the sale of conservation easements.[171]*

The Water Bank Act provides landowners with annual per-acre payments for agreeing to preserve specified wetlands over a 10 year period.[174] To date, most efforts have focused on the prairie potholes region of the Dakotas and Minnesota.[175] In 1986, 549,445 acres were under lease, 161,086 of which were wetlands.[176]

Nongovernmental efforts—for instance by the National Audubon Society, Ducks Unlimited, and the Nature Conservancy—also play an important role in wetland protection. The Nature Conservancy initiated a five-year, $55 million National Wetlands Conservation Project in January 1983 to preserve outstanding wetland habitats, to encourage cooperative efforts between public and private agencies, and to promote greater public awareness regarding wetlands and aquatic systems. By 1986, this program had acquired nearly 175,000 acres of wetlands.[177]

Another major program involves better identification and mapping of wetlands. FWS's National Wetlands Inventory, begun in 1977, had mapped wetlands in 45 percent of the contiguous United States by late 1986, covering perhaps 85 percent of coastal wetlands in those states, as well as a large proportion of freshwater wetlands.[178] The inventory had also mapped wetlands in 12 percent of Alaska.

---

*Acquisition of wetlands threatened by agricultural conversion has been accelerated over the last two decades by the Wetlands Loan Act of 1961, which provides interest-free loans and advance appropriations against future duck stamp sales.[172]

The 1986 Emergency Wetlands Resources Act provides further funding for the Migratory Bird Conservation Fund, authorizing the doubling of the cost of duck stamps over a five-year period and specifying that an amount equal to the annual import duties collected on firearms and ammunition, estimated at $10 million annually, be added to the fund for wetlands conservation. Furthermore, the act authorizes expenditures aimed specifically at wetlands acquisition from the Land and Water Conservation Fund, which draws primarily on receipts from offshore oil and gas leases.[173]

Finally, increasing attention is being given to opportunities to create or restore wetlands where they have already been lost or degraded. One of the most ambitious of such restoration projects involves the dechannelization of the Florida's Kissimmee River, transformed in the 1960s by the Corps of Engineers from a meandering 98-mile river into a 48-mile canal.[179] This channelization, in addition to negatively affecting water quality in Lake Okeechobee, resulted in the direct drainage of 40,000 acres of wetlands and facilitated drainage of an additional 100,000 acres.[180] The negative impacts of the channelization project soon became evident, and in 1976 the Florida legislature passed the Kissimmee River Restoration Act, mandating the restoration of the river. In response to this act, the South Florida Water Management District began a restoration demonstration project designed to divert water back into former oxbows and marshlands, in an effort to recreate approximately 1,300 acres of floodplain marsh over a 12-mile stretch of the river. Proposed restoration of other sections of the river would recreate another estimated 17,500 to 20,000 acres of wetlands, at a total estimated cost of $97 to $134 million.[181]

In addition to being expensive, the creation of new wetlands is an uncertain proposition. It has been attempted for only a few simple wetlands such as salt marshes,[182] and to date little evidence exists that more complex wetland ecosystems, such as forested swamps, can be created. Furthermore, it is not clear that such artificial wetlands can adequately replace natural wetlands.[183] Nonetheless, this may already be the only answer in some areas, if any of this type of habitat is to exist.

These various efforts to stem the conversion of wetlands have generated substantial controversy, as well as sometimes imposing large costs on the owners and potential developers of the lands. As the amount of wetlands continues to decline, the issue is likely to become even more contentious and the costs—of conversion, protection, or restoration—even larger. Yet many wetlands and wetland losses, at least until the Food Security Act of 1985,[184] have been largely unaffected by these efforts. Many believe that a better way to manage these unusually valuable resources must be found.

WILDLIFE

The attention paid to protecting wetlands reflects the increasing concern about the condition of wildlife both in the United States and abroad. (See chapter 9.) Wildlife provide many important benefits. They supply raw materials for food, medicine, and industrial products; genetic material for the selection and improvement of domesticated plants and animals; and recreation, aesthetic, and cultural benefits.

Wildlife conservation in the United States originally focused on reversing declines in populations of game species.[185] Research and management efforts have increasingly come to recognize the importance of nongame species—including invertebrates and plants as well as vertebrates—although game species still receive most of the research and management funds.[186]

Unfortunately, the available information on most wildlife populations and conditions is inadequate to support effective management efforts. Data for U.S. species are selective, available primarily for species of commercial or recreational importance, for particular nongame species, and for species on selected federal lands. When data are available, they are widely scattered, and little attempt has been made to synthesize these findings into a comprehensive assessment of the status of U.S. wildlife.[187] Some countries have attempted to improve this situation by initiating comprehensive surveys; however, the United States is not one of them.[188]

Game Species

Even for game species, the statistics on populations are neither adequate nor encouraging. The most comprehensive long-term data are FWS's compilation of waterfowl populations and USFS's estimates of large game and other mammal species on their lands.

Waterfowl

According to FWS, breeding populations of 10 duck species have declined or remained the same over the past 30 years (figure 5.12). In 1986, duck breeding populations totaled 30.9 million for 10 major species in North America, 14 percent below the 1955-1985 average. For individual species, the 1986 numbers ranged from 34 percent above (redhead) to 44 percent below (northern pintail) the 30-year average.[189]

Long-term trends are more telling than year-to-year averages since annual weather conditions and other factors can cause dramatic year-to-year fluctuations in populations. For example, the 1985 total population estimates were 18 percent lower than in 1984, but the 1986 estimates were 13 percent higher than in 1985. Most species show more representative population trends over a longer period. For example, both the mallard and northern pintail populations increased between 1985 and 1986. But the 1985 levels were the lowest ever estimated, and the 1986 levels were still 24 percent lower than the 30-year average for mallards and 44 percent lower than that for pintails.[190] Black duck populations, which are not included in the survey of 10 duck species, have been declining for at least 33 years. One index showed the 1982-1983 population at only 30 percent of what it was in 1949-1950.[191]

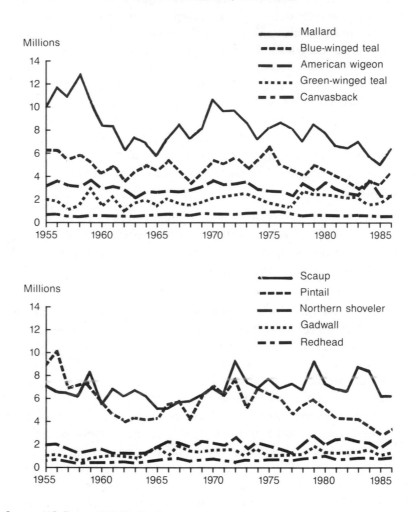

Figure 5.12
Estimated Breeding Populations of 10 Duck Species in the United States, 1955–1986

Source: U.S. Fish and Wildlife Service.

One explanation for these declines is a lack of suitable habitat. Dry conditions in the early 1980s and expanded agricultural activities have reduced the number of wetlands with suitable nesting cover.[192] To aid in the recovery of duck populations, controversial federal hunting regulations for 1985 stipulated a 25 percent reduction from the 1984 take.[193] According to one assessment, the regulations, in conjunction with rain in the drought-stricken prairies, have led to increases in 8 of the 10 species' breeding populations from the record low levels of 1985.[194] For example, the estimated population of northern pintails increased 9 percent; redheads, 36 percent; gadwall, 13 percent; and green-winged teal, 38 percent.[195]

Goose populations are surveyed at different times of the year, depending on the species, on either their breeding or wintering ground. FWS surveys estimated the 1985 and 1986 goose populations at 6 and 5.5 million, respectively, for four major species found in the United States.[196] Generally, the goose populations in three of the four management flyways are in fair condition.

Several species of Pacific Flyway geese, however, are not faring as well. Four species that nest on Alaska's Yukon-Kuskokwim delta have shown tremendous declines over the past two decades. Emperor geese, 90 percent of which nest on the delta, declined by nearly 49 percent between 1964 and 1985. The Pacific black brant population, half of which nests in the area, has declined by 22 percent since 1980. Pacific white-fronted goose populations have declined by more than 80 percent between the late 1960s and 1984. But the most dramatic declines were seen in cackling Canada geese, whose numbers dropped over 94 percent from 380,000 in 1965 to 21,000 in 1984. Recent debate has focused on whether these declines are due to spring hunting at the north end of the flyway or destruction of wetland habitat at the south end. Hunting pressure on the breeding grounds has increased due to growing Eskimo populations and the use of more effective hunting gear, while winter habitat has declined due to pollution, drainage, and reclamation.[197]

In an attempt to remedy the situation, state and federal wildlife agencies and Eskimo representatives from the delta signed, in March 1985, the Yukon-Kuskokwim Delta Goose Management Plan, designed to restore goose populations to higher levels. According to FWS, the plan is working and some species have already shown increases.[198]

Large Game

USFS estimates of certain species on its lands generally have shown stabilizing and, in a few cases, increasing trends since 1960 (figure 5.13).[199] The mule deer and the timber wolf are two notable exceptions, with both species showing significant decreases in the past quarter-century. Few data are available to make comparisons between populations on other federal and privately owned lands.

Efforts to restore overhunted game populations have been successful in numerous cases, due in part to hunting and fishing regulations and changes

Figure 5.13
Populations of Selected Large Animals on U.S. Forest Service Lands, 1960–1984

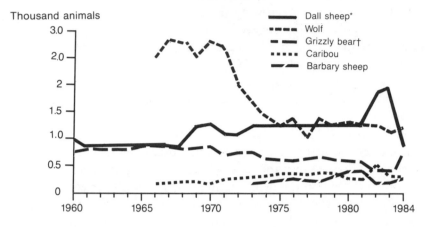

Thousand animals

Dall sheep*
Wolf
Grizzly bear†
Caribou
Barbary sheep

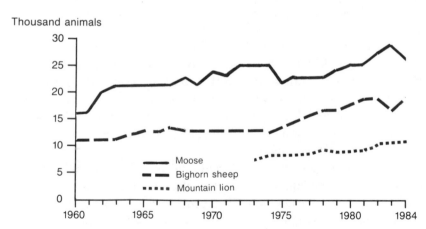

Thousand animals

Moose
Bighorn sheep
Mountain lion

Figure 5.13 (continued)
Populations of Selected Large Animals on U.S. Forest Service Lands, 1960–1984

Thousand animals

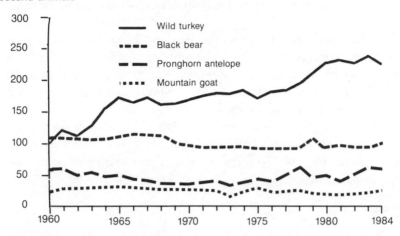

Thousand animals

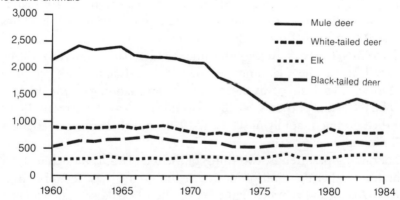

* New censusing techniques show dall sheep populations for 1984 lower than previous year's estimates.

† Alaska populations not included.

Source: U.S. Forest Service.

in management practices or land use. One of the most noted examples is the whitetail deer, which was estimated to number fewer than 500,000 around 1890 in the eastern United States, with few found in the Great Plains.[200] As a result of intensive game management strategies, nearly 3 million were harvested by hunters in 1980, about half of them in the eastern United States.[201]

The wild turkey and American bison have also shown substantial population increases over time. By 1984, the number of wild turkeys had more than doubled from the estimated 99,000 in 1960 (figure 5.13) and had reached 100 times its 1930 level of about 20,000 individuals. The increase is due, in part, to transfer of the birds from regions where survival rates had remained high to regions where populations were low or declining.[202] Overhunting decreased populations of millions of American bison to only a few hundred by 1900. Today, as a result of protection efforts, numbers range near 100,000.[203]

Fisheries

Commercial fisheries are a natural resource of major economic importance. Commercial U.S. vessels in U.S. waters landed 6.3 billion pounds, valued at $2.3 billion, in 1985 (figure 5.14), a slight decrease from the 1984 landings of 6.4 billion pounds, valued at $2.42 billion.[204] Shellfish landings increased from their 1984 levels, as did sea herring, Alaska pollack, and Pacific salmon landings. At the same time, North Atlantic trawl fish, Pacific mackerel, and anchovy landings declined.[205] Trends in finfish catch since 1973 increased overall, partly because of increased landings of menhaden, used for industrial purposes. Shellfish landings increased in the late 1970s and then declined rapidly in the early 1980s, mostly because of changes in shrimp and crab catch.

Continuing past trends, two-thirds of the total U.S. fish catch in 1985 came from either the Gulf of Mexico or the Pacific coast region (which includes Alaska and Hawaii) (figure 5.15). The 1985 Alaskan catch totaled over 1.2 billion pounds, a record.[206] The catch in other regions of the country has not changed appreciably since 1973.

Data on landings do not necessarily reflect fish stocks, however. Increased effort may temporarily result in an increased catch, even if stocks are actually decreasing. Regulatory changes may also come into play. For instance, the decline in yellowfin tuna catch in the early 1980s occurred after regulations were introduced to limit allowable incidental take of porpoises in purse seine nets used for tuna fishing.[207]

Figure 5.14
U.S. Commercial Fisheries Landings*, 1973–1985

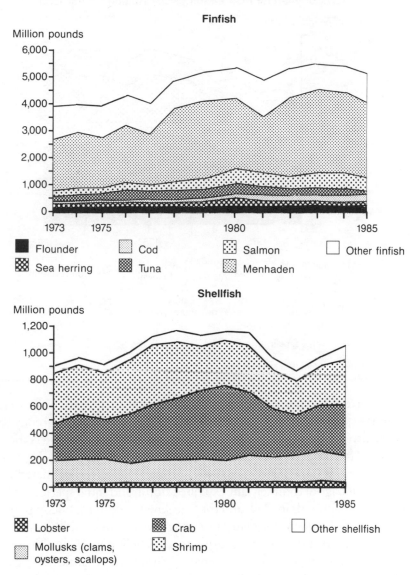

Finfish

Million pounds

Legend:
- Flounder
- Cod
- Salmon
- Other finfish
- Sea herring
- Tuna
- Menhaden

Shellfish

Million pounds

Legend:
- Lobster
- Crab
- Other shellfish
- Mollusks (clams, oysters, scallops)
- Shrimp

* Catch of U.S. flag vessels returning to ports within the 50 states.

Source: National Marine Fisheries Service.

Figure 5.15
U.S. Commercial Fish Landings, by Region,* 1973–1985

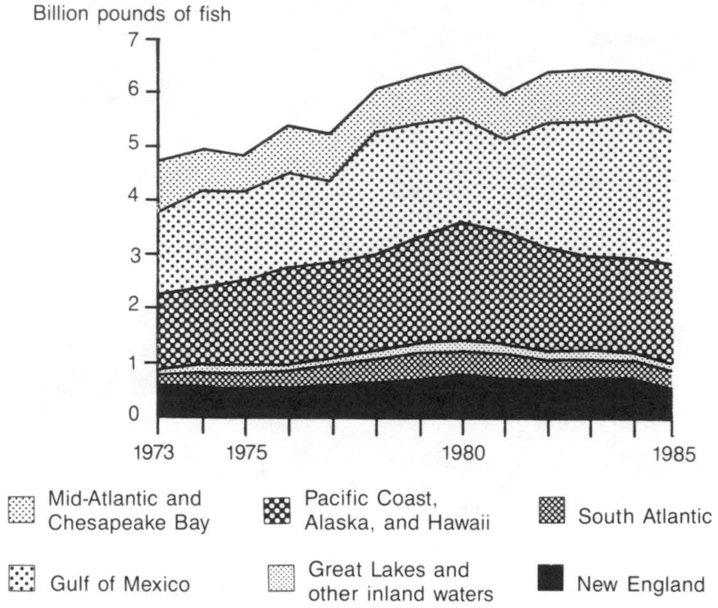

Billion pounds of fish

Mid-Atlantic and Chesapeake Bay

Pacific Coast, Alaska, and Hawaii

South Atlantic

Gulf of Mexico

Great Lakes and other inland waters

New England

* Catch of U.S. flag vessels returning to ports inside the 50 states.

Source: National Marine Fisheries Service.

A survey examining fish stocks in the Northeast suggests that overall biomass (poundage) levels have remained relatively constant in recent years. This survey, conducted by the Northeast Fisheries Center of the National Marine Fisheries Service, assesses finfish and shellfish resources off the Atlantic coast from Cape Hatteras to Nova Scotia. The survey estimated that total poundage of commercially exploited finfish and squid species reached 17.6 billion pounds in 1968 and then declined to only 4.2 billion pounds by 1975. Subsequent estimates rose to an average of 7.3 billion pounds for 1977-1978 and then rose sharply to 17.4 billion in 1979; this jump, however, was attributed to an anomalous sample for Atlantic herring and Atlantic mackerel. From 1980 to 1984, estimates have fluctuated around an average of 7.3 billion pounds.[208]

Some individual species of fish in U.S. waters have been so overfished that their populations have reached precarious levels. In these situations, a single bad season could reduce the populations to levels from which recovery might be unlikely. The Alaskan king crab is a prime example. The catch dropped from 185 million pounds in 1980 to less than half that amount a year later (figure 5.16).[209] By 1982, the catch was less than 40 million pounds, and the 1985 catch of 15.4 million pounds was the lowest since 1958.[210] The drop in numbers has been especially high in the Bering Sea and Aleutian Islands. The precise cause of the decline is unknown, but research by National Marine Fisheries Service and Alaska Fisheries Center scientists indicate that the factors involved include fishing, reproductive failure, high predator levels, and disease.[211]

Recreational fishing is of surprising importance to the condition of fisheries. In 1985, 30 percent of all marine finfish used for food was caught recreationally. Over 17 million anglers took 70.8 million fishing trips on which they caught 425 million fish weighing an estimated 717.3 million pounds.[212]

Inland fisheries are also important both recreationally and economically. In 1980, 45 percent of all identified recreational fishing expenditures were exclusively for freshwater fishing (14 percent were for saltwater fishing, and 41 percent were unspecified).[213] In fiscal year 1985, over 29 million people purchased fishing licenses to fish inland waters and paid $122 million in excise taxes on fishing equipment.[214]

Over the past several years, the inland fisheries of the United States have experienced increasing threats from small hydroelectric dams on streams

Figure 5.16
Alaskan King Crab Catch, 1978–1985

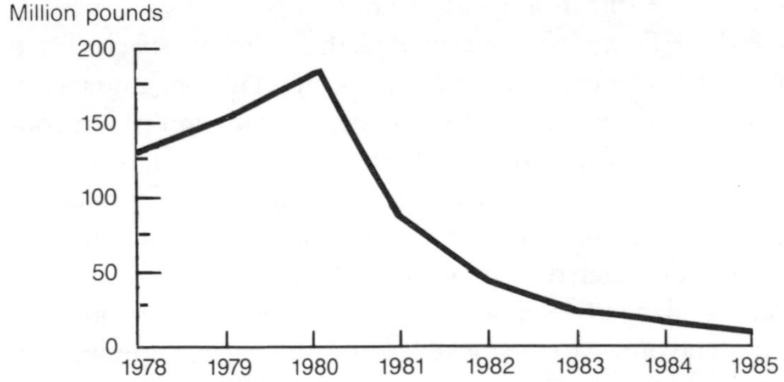

Source: National Marine Fisheries Service.

and rivers, from aquatic contamination, and from increasing acidification. Dams particularly affect anadromous fish, those that live in the open ocean as adults but migrate upstream to breed. The dams are frequently impassable, preventing the fish from reaching spawning grounds.[215]

Attempts to revive one species of anadromous fish, the Atlantic salmon, are showing success. This species has suffered severely from impassable dams, water pollution, overfishing, and stream acidification.[216] Efforts to bring back the salmon have included restricting the take from recreational fishing, restoring access to spawning and nursery habitat, and maintaining artificial propagation programs. During the past decade, roughly 6.6 million salmon smolts and 5.5 million fry and/or parr have been released. The number of adult salmon returning upstream to spawn, generally has increased since 1970.[217]

Contaminants severe enough to warrant a ban on consumption have been found in some inland and coastal species. PCBs (polychlorinated biphenyls) were found in striped bass in the Hudson Bay over a decade ago and subsequently in many locations along the East Coast, resulting in a ban on striped bass fishing. In some cases, the situation is deteriorating; the area along Long Island covered by the ban was extended oceanward in May 1986, when high levels of PCBs were found in fish caught at the eastern end of the island.[218]

Nongame Endangered and Threatened Species

Nongame species make up the huge majority of wildlife. Of the estimated 3,699 vertebrate species native to the continental United States and its coastal waters, only 17 percent are classified as game species. Vertebrates themselves account for less than 3 percent of the earth's currently described species.[219] Nongame species face threats as great, if not greater, than species being exploited directly.[220] Eighty-five percent of all the vertebrate species listed as endangered in 1976 were nongame. An additional 450 nongame species could be listed as endangered by 1990 if current population trends continue.[221] Although the importance of these species may be less obvious than that of game species, they do have economic and aesthetic value. In 1980, it was estimated that more than $1 billion was spent on nonconsumptive activities related to nongame wildlife.[222]

Passage of the Endangered Species Act in 1973[223] represent a major U.S. effort to identify and preserve endangered game and nongame species both in the United States and abroad. As of November 1986, 928 species had been listed as endangered or threatened, at least in some locations, and 425 of those were U.S. species.[224] Under this act, only 12 species have been delisted to date. Five were due to extinction, 2 to taxonomic changes, 2 to discovery of previously unknown populations, and the remaining 3 (Pacific island bird species delisted in 1985) to population recovery as a result of protection under the act.[225] Sixty new species were listed in 1985, including 8 mammals, 2 birds, 13 fish, 2 invertebrates, and 35 plants.[226] Although the 60 listings in 1985 represented a significant increase over the early 1980s (4 listings in 1981, 10 in 1982), they did little to reduce the backlog of over 3,900 species still awaiting action.[227]

A breakdown by taxonomic group illustrates a trend toward increased recognition of endangered species other than large vertebrates (figure 5.17). In the early years of the act, four-fifths of the species listed were mammals or birds. The other one-fifth were primarily reptiles, fish, and a few amphibians. By the late 1970s, however, plants, crustacea, clams, insects, and snails were appearing on the list, indicating greater breadth in the species considered.[228]*

Under the Endangered Species Act, plans identifying actions that would increase the probability of recovery must be completed for all U.S. species listed. As of August 1986, FWS had completed 197 of these plans (figure 5.18), covering 231 (or 56 percent) of the U.S. species listed.[229]† This is a dramatic increase over 1982, when only 30 percent of listed species had recovery plans.[230] Nevertheless, after several active years, recovery plan development in 1985 was less than half the 1984 rate.[231]

As of 1986, 47 states and territories had cooperative agreements with FWS covering endangered animals; 26 had agreements covering endangered plants.[232] Under these agreements, the states receive federal funding for up to 75 percent of their endangered species programs.[233]

Completion of a recovery plan does not necessarily assure a species' survival. For instance, a population of black-footed ferrets (*Mustela nigripes*), for which a recovery plan was approved in 1978, was discovered near Meeteetse, Wyoming, in 1981. Three years later, the population was estimated at 128 individuals, and attempts at captive breeding were planned with the goal of establishing additional populations. However, by August 1985, their numbers had dropped by more than half, as the surrounding colonies of prairie dogs (the ferrets' primary food source) were devastated

---

*By early 1986, plants, crustacea, clams, insects, and snails represented 20 percent of the species listed.

†Some recovery plans cover more than one species, while in other instances a single species may have more than one recovery plan.

Figure 5.17
Listed Endangered and Threatened Species, by Taxonomic Group, 1973–1985

Number of species

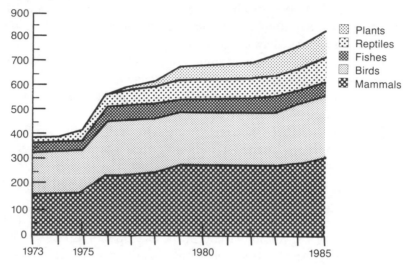

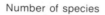

Number of species

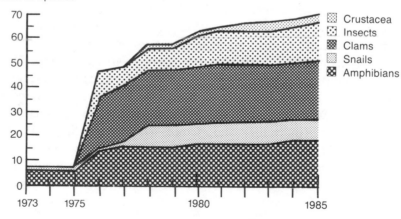

Source: U.S. Fish and Wildlife Service.

Figure 5.18
Listed U.S. Endangered and Threatened Species
With and Without Recovery Plans, 1975–1986

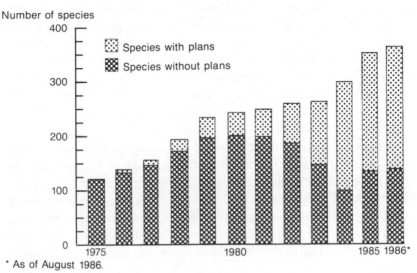

* As of August 1986.

Source: U.S. Fish and Wildlife Service.

by a plague epidemic. Further ferret deaths since then have been attributed to canine distemper, so that the number of wild ferrets is now between 3 and 10, with an additional 7 in captivity.[234]

Marine Mammals

Sixteen marine mammal species were listed as endangered and three as threatened as of January 1986.[235] Their populations have experienced declines for over a century, usually attributed to direct overexploitation by humans.

Recognition of these population declines resulted in the passage of the Marine Mammal Protection Act of 1972.[236] This act places a moratorium on taking or importing products from marine mammals except for those taken for scientific research, public display, or incidental to commercial fishing.[237]

Eight of the endangered marine mammal species are whales.[238] Commercial whaling has led to severely reduced populations over the past two centuries. Only the eastern population of the North Pacific gray whale and perhaps the western population of the North Atlantic humpback whale may have recovered from these attacks.[239] Three stocks of great whales appear to be nearing extinction—the western North Pacific gray whale, the east Greenland-Spitsbergen bowhead whale, and the North Pacific right whale.[240] Other endangered species include the blue, humpback, and right whales. Blue whale populations were reduced from 200,000 in precommercial times to 10,000 in 1966 when protection efforts were instituted. The population is now estimated at 11,000. Humpback populations are also severely depleted, numbering about 10,275 worldwide. Right whales, protected since 1938, still have severely depleted populations, numbering fewer than 4,000 worldwide.[241]

Protection of marine mammals, which live outside national boundaries, poses particular problems. Therefore, multinational agreements form an important part of the protection strategy. The International Whaling Commission (IWC), established as a multinational decision-making body, placed a five-year moratorium on commercial whaling to take effect in late 1986, following a three-year phaseout period.[242] Nevertheless, several countries have filed objections to the moratorium, and extensions and exceptions have been made.[243]

Cultural concerns enter into decisions when protecting marine mammals as well. Even though only a remnant population of the endangered bowhead whale has remained in the West Arctic for several years, the hunt for the bowhead was long permitted by the IWC because of its importance in native Eskimo culture. In 1977, however, concern over low numbers and increasing harvests by the Eskimos led to an IWC moratorium on all bowhead harvests. As a compromise, the ban was replaced the following year with strict quotas for strikes and captures by the natives. The Eskimos and IWC have had much debate on the allowed numbers. In the last few years, because of improved census techniques, IWC has increased its population estimates, and the 1985 estimate of 4,417 has provided a basis for arriving at a resolution on quotas that is acceptable to both IWC and the Eskimos.[244]

Some species of marine mammals have shown signs of recovery since protective actions, including IWC decisions and the Endangered Species and Marine Mammal Protection acts, were taken. The Guadalupe fur seal, once believed extinct, now numbers about 1,600, and its population is increasing. The gray whale, though once severely depleted by coastal whaling and still threatened in some locations, has increased overall to about 17,000 animals.[245]

Birds

Most, though not all, nongame bird populations generally seem to be holding steady, according to an annual Breeding Bird Survey (BBS) conducted by FWS and the Canadian Wildlife Service.* Of the 410 species having sample sizes large enough for analysis, 73 percent showed no statistically significant increasing or declining trends in population between 1965 and 1979. Sixteen percent showed significant increases, and 11.2 percent showed significant decreases.[247]

Although less standardized in method than the Breeding Bird Survey, the Christmas Bird Count (CBC), conducted in the winter rather than breeding season, is another source of data on bird populations.[248] The CBC indicates that raptor populations have been recovering since reaching their lowest levels prior to the DDT (dichloro-diphenyl-trichloro-ethane) ban in 1972. Seven raptor populations show predominantly increasing or, in the case of the peregrine falcon, stable trends from the early 1970s to the early 1980s. The Harris Hawk is an exception to this pattern, although data indicate that it may actually be recovering after a low point in the late 1970s.[249]

Some bird species are showing significant declines. A 1982 FWS report identified 28 nongame migratory bird species with declining or unstable populations. This analysis was based on BBS data as well as information from other surveys. The species were selected based on one or more of the following characteristics: apparent population decline, small population size, and/or restricted habitat. Of these species, 9 are marsh or wading birds, 5 are birds of prey, 3 are marine birds, 4 are shore birds, and 7 are passerines.† Coastal and wetland species account for 64 percent of those identified; habitat loss and degradation is apparently the primary factor in most of the declines.[250]

More than half of the 650 bird species in the United States migrate to Central and South America to overwinter.[251] This includes 57 percent of

---

*This survey utilizes bird counts along a series of standardized roadways to obtain information on nearly 500 bird species. It is designed to serve primarily as a population index, providing information on long-term trends rather than accurate population estimates. It provides some of the most comprehensive data on the status of bird populations in North America. However, because of the methods employed, species not found close to roadways and those that breed in northern Canada may not be adequately represented.[246]

†Passerines consist mainly of perching songbirds.

the migratory species listed by FWS as having declining or unstable populations.[252] Many biologists attribute much of the decrease in their population to destruction of their winter habitat in the neotropics. Deforestation
has been occurring rapidly in these areas over the last 20 years.[253] Other
problems may include fragmentation of desirable forests in the United States
and the contamination of air, land, and water by toxic pollutants, acid
rain, or pesticides.[254]

Programs to Protect Wildlife

The federal government has assumed primary responsibility for managing
migratory species and endangered species, as well as managing wildlife
on federally owned lands. Otherwise, states have the primary responsibility
for wildlife management.[255] Funding for state game management programs
comes primarily from state license fees and federal excise taxes.

In 1985, revenue from hunting licenses was over $300 million and that
from fishing licenses was over $282 million.[256]* Two sources—excise taxes
on hunting equipment established by the Pittman-Robertson Federal Aid
in Wildlife Restoration Act of 1937 and excise taxes on fishing equipment
begun under the Dingell-Johnson Sport Fish Restoration Act of
1951—provided nearly $243 million in fiscal year 1985.[258] Since their incep-
tion, Pittman-Robertson has generated more than $1.6 billion for state
wildlife restoration efforts while Dingell-Johnson has raised more than $622
million for state fishery restoration efforts.[259] Another source of revenue,
the sale of duck stamps, which must be purchased for waterfowl hunting,
has contributed more than $268 million to the federal government for
wetlands acquisition.[260]

The traditional emphasis on game species management has long been
reflected in funding availability. Nearly 90 percent of U.S. wildlife species
are nongame, but just 10 percent of U.S. wildlife dollars are spent to understand or benefit them.[261] In an attempt to reduce the inequitable allocation of funds to nongame programs in the states, the Fish and Wildlife
Conservation Act of 1980 authorized federal aid to states for preparation
and implementation of vertebrate nongame programs.[262] However, no
money had been appropriated to implement the act by the end of 1986.

---

*More than $4.4 billion has been paid to state wildlife agencies for hunting licenses and
more than $4 billion has been paid for fishing licenses since tabulation of hunting and fishing
license revenues began in 1923 and 1933, respectively.[257]

Several states have developed innovative approaches for funding nongame management.* About two-thirds of the states now offer tax checkoffs that allow individuals to contribute money toward wildlife programs from their income tax returns (figure 5.19). In 1984, $8.96 million was collected through this mechanism, with the bulk coming in New York ($1.7 million), Minnesota ($643,500), and California ($511,000). Other innovative approaches to funding nongame programs include small increases in state sales tax (Missouri), funds generated through purchase of personalized license plates (Washington and California), and development of endowment funds (Illinois and Indiana).[265]

Still, most state and federal nongame wildlife programs are underfunded and incomplete. The diversity of plants and animals covered under wildlife programs is increasing, but gaps in the conservation effort remain. The Fish and Wildlife Conservation Act covers only vertebrate species,[266] overlooking the more subtle importance of vegetation that filters water or insects that pollinate plants. The Endangered Species Act, while utilizing a more comprehensive definition of wildlife, addresses only species that have been labeled endangered or threatened.[267] A more adequate approach encompassing the interaction of all wild species, communities, and ecosystems would clearly be preferable, but such an approach would require substantially more money.

Government and private organizations are setting aside increasing amounts of land for wildlife protection. At the federal level, FWS administered a 90.4-million-acre network of lands and water in 1985 for wildlife and public use, most of which was part of the National Wildlife Refuge System.[268] At the end of fiscal year 1985, this system included 432 national wildlife refuges comprising 88.3 million acres (77.1 million in Alaska) or 97.6 percent of the agency's total acreage; 58 coordination areas totaling 0.4 million acres; and 150 waterfowl production areas, concentrated in the upper Midwest, comprising 1.7 million acres.[269] Five additional national wildlife refuges totaling 70,000 acres were added in fiscal year 1986, bringing the total number of refuges to 437.[270] FWS also operates 80 fish hatcheries, a number of which provide interpretive information for the public.[271]

---

*In 1986, 46 states had some form of nongame program under way.[263] In 1985, five states—California, Missouri, Florida, Colorado, and New York—spent more than $1 million each on nongame and endangered species.[264]

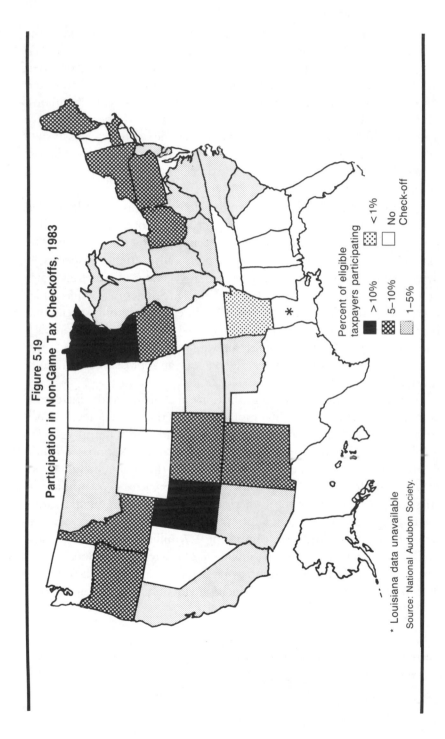

Figure 5.19
Participation in Non-Game Tax Checkoffs, 1983

Percent of eligible
taxpayers participating

> 10%
5–10%
1–5%
<1%
No
Check-off

* Louisiana data unavailable
Source: National Audubon Society.

FWS's primary mandate is to provide suitable habitat for various species of wildlife.[272] The National Wildlife Refuge System is the only extensive network of federally owned lands reserved chiefly for wildlife conservation.[273] The richness of wildlife on the refuges is remarkable, including more than 220 species of mammals, more than 600 species of birds, 250 species of reptiles and amphibians, over 200 species of fish, and uncounted numbers of plant species. Many of the listed U.S. endangered species can be found on refuge system land, and the protection of these lands is often a chief factor in the species' continued survival.[274]

Habitat management programs within the system are comprehensive and diverse. Some of the refuges are intensively managed to provide benefits to indigenous endangered species, migratory birds, or large game species. However, in the majority of refuges, intensive management is deemed unnecessary since productivity has remained high.[275] Recently, concern has emerged for the quality of the environment on these lands as more and more evidence of potentially harmful chemicals has been documented. (See chapter 9.)

The Alaskan refuges, 54 million acres of which were designated by the Alaska National Interest Lands Conservation Act in 1980, are subject to special provisions to accommodate historical and cultural traditions.[276] Subsistence taking of fish and game by residents is permitted in Alaskan refuges, whereas refuges in the lower 48 states only allow hunting and fishing for recreation (and then only if compatible with the purposes for which a refuge is established).[277] Although the Alaskan refuges account for 85 percent of the acreage of the National Wildlife Refuge System, they receive just over 10 percent of the funding. For instance, in 1986 Alaskan refuges were appropriated $11.5 million out of a total budget for refuge operation and maintenance of $105.6 million.[278] In general, in comparison with those refuges in Alaska, refuges in the contiguous United States are smaller, more intensively managed, and more heavily visited, since they are close to population centers. The relatively low funding for Alaskan refuges reflects these factors, as well as the newness and remoteness of these areas.

State fish and game agencies also manage lands and other facilities for wildlife propagation and protection. The total acreage owned by state fish and wildlife agencies is not compiled annually. However, land acquired by the states through Pittman-Robertson and Dingell-Johnson funds—totaled over four million acres from 1938 to 1984.[279]

Lands set aside for other uses can also provide important wildlife habitat. For instance, the national forests provide habitat for about 3,000 species of fish and wildlife. USFS lands contain half of the big-game and coldwater fish habitat in the nation and are vital to 185 threatened and endangered species listed under the Endangered Species Act. This particularly includes those species requiring large, undisturbed areas, such as the grizzly bear, California condor, and gray wolf, and those inhabiting old-growth stands, such as the red-cockaded woodpecker and the northern spotted owl.[280] Habitat management is the responsibility of USFS, while management of animal populations is that of the states.[281]

Similarly, the largest federal land management agency, the Bureau of Land Management, has an extensive and diverse collection of lands providing valuable fish and wildlife habitat. BLM lands support one of every five large game animals in the United States, including most of the caribou, brown bears, grizzly bears, desert bighorn sheep, moose, mule deer, and pronghorn antelope. Numerous small game and nongame wildlife also inhabit BLM lands, including over 100 federally listed endangered and threatened species of plants and animals.[282]

Most wildlife, however, must depend at least to some extent on the almost 60 percent of the nation's land that is in private ownership.[283] Private land protection programs are playing an increasingly important role in protecting valuable areas for wildlife and other purposes as pressures rise to limit public expenditures for maintenance and development of parks and protected areas.[284] Land trusts—nonprofit, tax-exempt organizations—are becoming more and more common, particularly at the local, state, and regional levels.[285] By 1985, some 535 land trusts were critical in preserving over 700,000 acres of land.[286] Through 1986, The Nature Conservancy completed over 4,000 projects protecting nearly 2.6 million acres in 50 states, Latin America, the Caribbean, and Canada, emphasizing areas of unique ecological importance.[287] The Trust for Public Land, started in 1973, assisted public agencies and, to a lesser degree, private nonprofit organizations in the acquisition of 344,110 acres of land for 366 projects in 27 states by the end of 1986.[288]* The National Audubon Society owned or leased about 80 sanctuaries in 1986, used for education as well as preservation, covering approximately 250,000 acres.[290] Other organizations have made similar contributions to preserve open space for the conservation of natural, cultural, and historic resources, including the provision of wildlife habitat.

Rural land, undeveloped by its owners or developed by using practices conducive to wildlife—for example, hedgerows or small-grain cover crops

---

*The Nature Conservancy maintains many of its own properties in preserves, but some of its acquisitions, and nearly all those of the Trust for Public Land, are turned over to government agencies for management. Therefore, it is not accurate simply to add these lands to government totals.[289]

on farms and shrubs near homes—is a significant potential source of wildlife habitat. Provisions in the Food Security Act of 1985 may help to expand conservation activities on farmland through easements.* As of October 1986, 9.1 million acres were enrolled in this program (see chapter 6).[292]

The demands on the nation's lands and waters will continue to grow. Present budget limitations are unlikely to dissipate in the near future. As a result, using private land for conservation is becoming more and more important.[293] In the East, federal tax laws have stimulated much private land conservation. It remains to be seen how changes in these laws as a result of the Tax Reform Act of 1986 will affect these incentives. (See chapter 1.)

REFERENCES

Text

1. Outdoor Recreation Policy Review Group, *Outdoor Recreation for America—1983* (Washington, D.C.: Resources for the Future, 1983), p. 1.

2. Ibid., pp. 6, 11.

3. U.S. Department of the Interior, National Park Service, *1982-1983 Nationwide Recreation Survey* (Washington, D.C.: U.S. Government Printing Office, 1986), p. 34.

4. Outdoor Recreation Policy Review Group, *Outdoor Recreation for America—1983*, p. 15.

5. Executive Order 12503, "Presidential Commission on Outdoor Recreation Resources Review," January 31, 1985, see 50 Fed. Reg. 4491 (1985); and Executive Order 12529, "President's Commission on Americans Outdoors," August 19, 1985, see 50 Fed. Reg. 33329 (1985).

6. Market Opinion Research, *Participation in Outdoor Recreation among American Adults and the Motivations which Drive Participation*, prepared for the President's Commission on Americans Outdoors (Washington, D.C.: Market Opinion Research, 1986), p. 143.

7. President's Commission on Americans Outdoors, *Americans Outdoors: The Legacy. The Challenge* (Washington, D.C.: Island Press, 1987), p. 49.

8. Ibid., p. 39.

9. Market Opinion Research, *Participation in Outdoor Recreation*, p. 34.

10. National Park Service, *1982-1983 Nationwide Recreation Survey*, pp. 30-32.

11. Ibid.

12. President's Commission on Americans Outdoors, *Americans Outdoors*, p. 56.

13. National Park Service, *1982-1983 Nationwide Recreation Survey*, p. 36.

14. U.S. Department of Commerce, Bureau of the Census, *Governmental Finances in 1983-84*, series GF84, no. 5 (Washington, D.C.: U.S. Government Printing Office, 1985), p. 19. Expenditure data relate to the fiscal year ending on June 30 of that year or at some

---

*A conservation easement is a deed that restricts certain land-use rights on a parcel of land.[291]

date within the previous 12 months. Ibid., p. v.

15. President's Commission on Americans Outdoors, *Americans Outdoors*, p. 254.

16. Ibid., pp. 142, 168, 254.

17. 16 USCA §§ 3101-3233 (Supp. 1984); Wendy S. Lee, "The National Wildlife Refuge System," in National Audubon Society, *Audubon Wildlife Report 1986* (New York: National Audubon Society, 1986), p. 450; and "Congress Clears Alaska Lands Legislation," in *Congressional Quarterly Almanac, 96th Congress, 2nd Session . . . 1980* (Washington, D.C.: Congressional Quarterly, 1981), p. 575.

18. U.S. Department of the Interior, National Park Service, "Federal Recreation Fee Report 1985: A Report to Congress," photocopy, pp. 16, 33-34.

19. Market Opinion Research, *Participation in Outdoor Recreation*, p. 86.

20. For a discussion of this issue with regard to the National Park System, see The Conservation Foundation, *National Parks for a New Generation: Visions, Realities, Prospects* (Washington, D.C.: The Conservation Foundation, 1985), pp. 72-73.

21. National Park Service, "Federal Recreation Fee Report," pp. 16, 33-34. Data for National Park Service is as of December 31, 1985, while all other data is from September 30, 1985. For Bureau of Land Management: U.S. Department of the Interior, Bureau of Land Management, *Public Land Statistics 1985* (Washington, D.C.: U.S. Government Printing Office, 1986), pp. 6-7; for Forest Service: U.S. Department of Agriculture, Forest Service, *Land Areas of the National Forest System as of September 30, 1985* (Washington, D.C.: U.S. Government Printing Office, 1986), pp. 14-32; for Fish and Wildlife Service: U.S. Department of the Interior, Fish and Wildlife Service, Division of Realty, *Annual Report of Lands under the Control of the U.S. Fish and Wildlife Service as of September 30, 1985* (Washington, D.C.: U.S. Fish and Wildlife Service, 1985), p. 3; for National Park Service: photocopy provided by U.S. Department of the Interior, National Park Service, "National Park Service, Summary of Acreages, 12/31/85"; for Corps of Engineers: personal communication with Phil Parsley, Corps of Engineers, October 1986; for Bureau of Reclamation: personal communication with Terry Cooper, Bureau of Reclamation, October 1986; for Tennessee Valley Authority: photocopy provided by Tennessee Valley Authority, Division of Land and Economic Resources, "TVA Fee Land as of September 30, 1985."

22. Ibid.

23. U.S. Department of the Interior, National Park Service, *National Park Statistical Abstract 1985* (Denver: National Park Service, 1986), p. 4.

24. National Park Service, *1982-1983 Nationwide Recreation Survey*, p. 43.

25. Carlton S. Van Doren, "The National Park System," in Carlton S. Van Doren, ed., *Statistics on Outdoor Recreation*, pt. 2, *The Record since 1956* (Washington, D.C.: Resources for the Future, 1984), p. 171; National Park Service, *National Park Statistical Abstract 1985*, p. 4; and The Conservation Foundation, *National Parks for a New Generation*, pp. 60-63.

26. National Park Service, *National Park Statistical Abstract*, pp. 4, 39.

27. Information provided by Mike Walsh, U.S. Department of the Interior, National Park Service, January 1987; and The Conservation Foundation, *National Parks for a New Generation*, p. 2.

28. Information provided by the U.S. Department of the Interior, National Park Service, "Physical and Living Resources, National Park System, 1880-1980," table A-14.

29. "Congress Clears Alaska Lands Legislation," in *Congressional Quarterly Almanac 1980*, p. 575.

30. The Conservation Foundation, *National Parks for a New Generation*, p. 64; and Van Doren, "The National Park System," p. 176.

31. The Conservation Foundation, *National Parks for a New Generation*, pp. 58-63.

32. Thomas J. Knudson, "Cool U.S. Park on Fringe of a Desert," *New York Times*, December 15, 1986.

33. National Park Service, *National Park Statistical Abstract*, p. 6.

34. Ibid., p. 4.

35. 16 USCA § 1.

36. P.L. 99-500; "NPS Shoots for February 1 to Implement New Entrance Fee," *Federal Parks and Recreation* 4, no. 21 (1986):5.

37. National Park Service, "Federal Recreation Fee Report 1985," p. 16; and U.S. Department of Agriculture, Forest Service, *Land Areas of the National Forest System as of September 30, 1985*, p. 1.

38. Katherine Barton and Whit Fosburgh, "The U.S. Forest Service," in National Audubon Society, *Audubon Wildlife Report 1986*, p. 124.

39. U.S. Department of Agriculture, Forest Service, *Report of the Forest Service, Fiscal Year 1985* (Washington, D.C.: U.S. Department of Agriculture, 1986), p. 118.

40. Ibid., pp. 22-23.

41. Ibid., p. 23.

42. Ibid., p. 22.

43. Ibid., pp. 120-21.

44. Allan S. Mills, "Recreational Use of National Forests," in Van Doren, ed., *Statistics on Outdoor Recreation: The Record since 1956*, p. 192.

45. U.S. Forest Service, *Report of the Forest Service*, p. 22.

46. Ibid., pp. 25, 120-21.

47. Barton and Fosburgh, "The U.S. Forest Service," *Audubon Wildlife Report 1986*, p. 128.

48. President's Commission on Americans Outdoors, *Americans Outdoors*, p. 60.

49. U.S. Department of Agriculture, Forest Service, *Final Environmental Impact Statement: 1985-2030, Resources Planning Act Program*, FS-403 (Washington, D.C.: U.S. Forest Service, 1986), pp. 2-30, 3-5.

50. Ibid., p. 2-42.

51. U.S. Forest Service, *Report of the Forest Service*, p. 23.

52. U.S. Bureau of Land Management, *Public Land Statistics 1985*, pp. 6, 42.

53. Katherine Barton, "Wildlife and the Bureau of Land Management," in National Audubon Society, *Audubon Wildlife Report 1986*, p. 497.

54. U.S. Bureau of Land Management, *Public Land Statistics 1985*, pp. 5-7, 122.

55. E. Glenn Carls and Brian Hay, "Bureau of Land Management," in Van Doren, ed., *Statistics on Outdoor Recreation: The Record since 1956*, p. 223.

56. U.S. Bureau of Land Management, *Public Land Statistics 1985*, p. 44.

57. Wendy S. Lee, "The National Wildlife Refuge System," in National Audubon Society, *Audubon Wildlife Report 1986*, pp. 428-29.

58. Ibid., p. 429; and Dennis Drabelle, "The National Wildlife Refuge System," in National Audubon Society, *Audubon Wildlife Report 1985* (New York: National Audubon Society, 1985), p. 164.

59. Drabelle, "The National Wildlife Refuge System," p. 164.

60. Lee, "The National Wildlife Refuge System," p. 428.

61. Ibid., p. 433.

62. Ibid., p. 429.

63. 16 USCA §§1131-36.

64. Information provided by Bob Turnage, The Wilderness Society, January 1987.

65. Information provided by Nobby Reedy, The Wilderness Society, February 1987.

66. The Wilderness Society, "Wilderness Lands in the United States" (Washington, D.C.: Wilderness Society, 1984).

67. Information provided by Bob Turnage, The Wilderness Society, January 1987; and The Conservation Foundation, *National Parks for a New Generation*, p. 65.

68. Barton and Fosburgh, "The U.S. Forest Service," p. 121.

69. William E. Shands and Robert G. Healy, *The Lands Nobody Wanted* (Washington, D.C.: The Conservation Foundation, 1977), pp. 45-46; and P.L. 93-622 (88 Stat. 2096).

70. 16 USCA §§1271-87; President's Commission on Americans Outdoors, *Americans Outdoors*, p. 149; American Rivers Conservation Council, "Congress Protects 524 River Miles on 13 Rivers," news release, October 17, 1986, p. 4; and U.S. Department of the Interior, National Park Service, "Summary: Status of the Wild and Scenic Rivers Program," photocopy, May 1985.

71. American Rivers Conservation Council, "Congress Protects 524 River Miles on 13 Rivers," p. 4.

72. 16 USCA §1271.

73. 16 USCA §1273(b).

74. The Conservation Foundation, *National Parks for a New Generation*, p. 66.

75. Barton and Fosburgh, "The U.S. Forest Service," pp. 121-22.

76. The Conservation Foundation, *National Parks for a New Generation*, p. 66; and President's Commission on Americans Outdoors, *Americans Outdoors*, p. 62.

77. The Conservation Foundation, *National Parks for a New Generation*, p. 66.

78. 16 USCA §§1241-51.

79. U.S. Department of the Interior, National Park Service, *National Trails Assessment* (Washington, D.C.: U.S. Department of the Interior, 1986), p. 6.

80. U.S. Department of the Interior, National Park Service, "Status of the National Trails System," February 27, 1986, p 2; and information provided by Bob Karotko, U.S. Department of the Interior, National Park Service, November 1986.

81. The Conservation Foundation, *National Parks for a New Generation*, p. 66; and information provided by Bob Karotko, U.S. Department of the Interior, National Park Service, November 1986.

82. U.S. Department of the Interior, "National Trails System" attachment to "Status of the National Trails System," February 27, 1986, pp. 2-3.

83. For a discussion of user perspectives, see U.S. Department of the Interior, *National Trails Assessment*, pp. 33-38.

84. The Conservation Foundation, *National Parks for a New Generation*, p. 66.

85. Phyllis Myers and Ann Christine Reid, "State Parks in a New Era: A Survey of Issues and Innovations" (Washington, D.C.: The Conservation Foundation, 1986), p. 2.

86. Ibid.

87. Market Opinion Research, *Participation in Outdoor Recreation*, p. 86.

88. President's Commission on Americans Outdoors, *Americans Outdoors*, p. 50; and Myers and Reid, "State Parks in a New Era," p. 2.

89. President's Commission on Americans Outdoors, *Americans Outdoors*, p. 50; and National Association of State Park Directors, "Annual Information Exchange 1987" (Austin, Tex.: Texas Parks and Wildlife Department, 1987), p. 4.

90. Myers and Reid, "State Parks in a New Era," pp. 2, 7.

91. Van Doren, "State Park Systems," in Van Doren, ed., *Statistics on Outdoor Recreation: The Record Since 1956*, pp. 238, 244.

92. National Association of State Park Directors, "Annual Information Exchange 1987," p. 10.

93. Myers and Reid, "State Parks in a New Era," p. 2.

94. Van Doren, "State Park Systems," p. 244; and National Association of State Park Directors, "Annual Information Exchange 1987," p. 10.

95. Myers and Reid, "State Parks in a New Era," p. ix.

96. Ibid., pp. 23-26.

97. Ibid., p. ix.

98. Ibid., p. x.

99. President's Commission on Americans Outdoors, *Americans Outdoors*, p. 67.

100. Market Opinion Research, *Participation in Outdoor Recreation*, p. 86.

101. Ibid., p. 94.

102. Barry Tindall and Michael Rogers, "Report on Outdoor Recreation Supply: An Overview," prepared for the President's Commission on Americans Outdoors, April 11, 1986, p. 5.

103. President's Commission on Americans Outdoors, "Interstate, State and Substate Recreation Resources," January 1986, tables 1 and 2; and President's Commission on Americans Outdoors, *Americans Outdoors*, p. 67.

104. Hooper Brooks, "Open Space Preservation in the New York Urban Region from 1960 to the 21st Century: A Midpoint Review," prepared for the Regional Plan Association, May 1986, p. 15.

105. Barbara Quinn, "Parks Face Squeeze Play," *American City and County* 101 (1986):35.

106. President's Commission on Americans Outdoors, *Americans Outdoors*, pp. 133-48, 150; see also Quinn, "Parks Face Squeeze Play," p. 38; and Joe Morris and Terri Stone, "Private Choices for Public Parks," *American City and County* 101 (1986):34.

107. Market Opinion Research, *Participation in Outdoor Recreation*, p. 86.

108. President's Commission on Americans Outdoors, *Americans Outdoors*, p. 203.

109. Ibid., p. 202; and Tindall and Rogers, "Report on Outdoor Recreation Supply," p. 8.

110. "ATC/TATL Acquire Bears Den," *Trail Lands*, Summer 1984, p. 1; and The Conservation Foundation, *National Parks for a New Generation*, pp. 151-52.

111. Morris and Stone, "Private Choices for Public Parks," pp. 36, 38.

112. U.S. Department of the Interior, Fish and Wildlife Service, *Wetlands of the United States: Current Status and Recent Trends* (Washington, D.C.: U.S. Government Printing Office, 1984), p. 2.

113. U.S. Environmental Protection Agency, Office of Policy, Planning and Evaluation, *Wetlands Strategic Options*, draft, February 21, 1986, p. 5.

114. U.S. Fish and Wildlife Service, *Wetlands of the United States*, p. 1.

115. U.S. Department of Commerce, National Oceanic and Atmospheric Administration, Strategic Assessment Branch, *National Estuarine Inventory: Living Marine Resources*

Components, West Coast (Rockville, Md.: National Oceanic and Atmospheric Administration, 1986), p. 1.2.

116. U.S. Fish and Wildlife Service, *Wetlands of the United States*, p. 36.

117. For more extensive discussion of wetland values see, John A. Kusler, *Our National Wetland Heritage: A Protection Guidebook* (Washington, D.C.: Environmental Law Institute, 1983), chapter 1; U.S. Fish and Wildlife Service, *Wetlands of the United States*, pp. 13-26; and U.S. Congress, Office of Technology Assessment, *Wetlands: Their Use and Regulation* (Washington, D.C.: U.S. Government Printing Office, 1984), chapter 3.

118. U.S. Fish and Wildlife Service, *Wetlands of the United States*, p. 21.

119. John A. Kusler, *Our National Wetland Heritage*, p. 7.

120. U.S. Fish and Wildlife Service, *Wetlands of the United States*, p. 33; and 43 USCA §§982 et seq. (1964).

121. U.S. Fish and Wildlife Service, *Wetlands of the United States*, p. 29.

122. For a sampling of definitions used in wetland protection ordinances, see appendix B of Kusler, *Our National Wetland Heritage*, pp. 131-38.

123. U.S. Department of the Interior, Fish and Wildlife Service, *Classification of Wetlands and Deepwater Habitats of the United States* (Washington, D.C.: U.S. Government Printing Office, 1979), p. 3.

124. W. E. Frayer et al., *Status and Trends of Wetlands and Deepwater Habitats in the Coterminous United states, 1950s to 1970s* (Fort Collins, Colo.: Colorado State University, 1983), p. 3.

125. Based on the Office of Technology Assessment's estimates of 300,000 acres of wetland per year reported in U.S. Office of Technology Assessment, *Wetlands*, p. 11.

126. U.S. Office of Technology Assessment, *Wetlands,* p. 87; and Laurie Marcus, "Alaska Wetlands: An Opportunity for Protection," *National Wetlands Newsletter* 7, no. 6 (1985):11.

127. U.S. Fish and Wildlife Service, *Wetlands of the United States*, p. 28.

128. U.S. Department of Commerce, National Oceanic and Atmospheric Administration, *An Inventory of Coastal Wetlands of the U.S.A.* (Washington, D.C.: U.S. Government Printing Office, 1986), pp. 4-6.

129. Ibid. Estimated annual *vegetated* wetland conversions during this time period were 500,000 acres. This figure is higher than the conversion rates for *all* wetlands because some wetlands were converted to nonvegetated wetlands.

130. U.S. Office of Technology Assessment, *Wetlands,* p. 87.

131. Ibid., p. 11.

132. U.S. Fish and Wildlife Service, *Wetlands of the United States*, p. 34.

133. U.S. Office of Technology Assessment, *Wetlands*, p. 93.

134. The five states in which the greatest estuarine losses occurred during this period were Florida, New Jersey, Louisiana, Texas, and California. U.S. Fish and Wildlife Service, *Wetlands of the United States*, p. 36.

135. Frayer et al., *Status and Trends of Wetlands and Deepwater Habitats in the Coterminous United States, 1950s to 1970s*, p. 24.

136. U.S. National Oceanic and Atmospheric Administration, *An Inventory of Coastal Wetlands of the USA*, p. 6.

137. U.S. Department of Commerce, National Oceanic and Atmospheric Administration, National Marine Fisheries Service, *Fisheries of the United States, 1985*, Current Fishery Statistics no. 8368 (Washington, D.C.: National Marine Fisheries Service, 1986), p. 3; and Frederick Turner, "Losing it in Louisiana," *Wilderness* 49, no. 171 (1985):43.

138. Turner, "Losing it in Louisiana," p. 43.

139. U.S. Fish and Wildlife Service, *Wetlands of the United States*, p. 38; and Sherwood M. Gagliano, "The Private Sector Role in Managing Louisiana's Coastal Wetlands," testimony before the President's Commission on American Outdoors, New Orleans, Louisiana, May 9, 1986.

140. Sherwood Gagliano, of Coastal Environments, Inc., estimates an annual loss of 22,000 acres; alternatively, the Fish and Wildlife Service gives a figure of 25,000 acres. For more details see Gagliano, "The Private Sector Role in Managing Louisiana's Coastal Wetlands"; and U.S. Fish and Wildlife Service, *Wetlands of the United States*, p. 38.

141. Palustrine losses (11 million acres) were higher than overall wetland losses (9 million acres) during this time period because a portion of these freshwater wetlands were converted to other wetland types. Frayer et al., *Status and Trends of Wetlands and Deepwater Habitats in the Coterminous United States, 1950s to 1970s*, p. 3.

142. U.S. Fish and Wildlife Service, *Wetlands of the United States*, p. 32.

143. Ibid., p. 48.

144. U.S. Office of Technology Assessment, *Wetlands*, p. 89.

145. U.S. Fish and Wildlife Service, *Wetlands of the United States*, p. 48.

146. Ibid., pp. 34, 42.

147. Ibid., p. 49.

148. Ibid.; and William C. Reffalt, "Wetlands in Extremis," *Wilderness* 49, no. 171 (1985):35.

149. U.S. Fish and Wildlife Service, *Wetlands of the United States*, pp. 32, 34.

150. U.S. Department of the Interior, Fish and Wildlife Service, Division of Refuge Management, *Preliminary Survey of Contaminant Issues of Concern on National Wildlife Refuges* (Washington, D.C.: U.S. Department of the Interior, 1986), p. A-44.

151. The contamination problems cited include DDT, PCBs, asbestos, heavy metals, selenium, and other trace elements, and excessive nutrients. Ibid., pp. 1-14.

152. T. R. Vale, "Mono Lake, California: Saving a Lake or Serving a City," *Environmental Conservation* 7, no. 3 (1980):190-92; and Gordon Young, "The Troubled Waters of Mono Lake," *National Geographic* 60 (1981):504-19.

153. 33 USCA §§1251 et seq.

154. U.S. Office of Technology Assessment, *Wetlands*, p. 12.

155. Ibid., p. 11.

156. U.S. Environmental Protection Agency, Office of Water Planning and Standards, *A Guide to the Dredge or Fill Permit Program* (Washington, D.C.: U.S. Environmental Protection Agency, 1979), p. 6.

157. "Michigan Receives Dredge and Fill Permit Authority," *National Wetlands Newsletter* 6, no. 5 (1984):10-12.

158. Kusler, *Our National Wetland Heritage*, p. 65.

159. 16 USCA §§1451 et seq. (1985).

160. National Audubon Society, *Audubon Wildlife Report 1985*, p. 214.

161. Delaware Department of Natural Resources and Environmental Control, Wetlands Section, *Wetlands of Delaware* (Dover, Del.: Department of Natural Resources and Environmental Control, 1985), p. 60.

162. U.S. Department of the Interior, Fish and Wildlife Service, National Wetlands Inventory, *Wetlands of New Jersey* (Washington, D.C.: U.S. Department of the Interior, 1985), pp. 102-5.

163. These states are Massachusetts, Connecticut, Rhode Island, Minnesota, Michigan, New Hampshire, and New York. Kusler, *Our National Wetland Heritage*, p. 65.

164. 16 USCA §§3501 et seq. (1985).

165. U.S. Department of the Interior, Coastal Barriers Study Group, *Draft Report to Congress on the Coastal Barrier Resources System* (Washington, D.C.: U.S. Department of the Interior, 1985), p. ix.

166. U.S. Fish and Wildlife Service, *Wetlands of the United States*, p. 37.

167. U.S. Department of Agriculture, Office of Information, "News Backgrounder," June 25, 1986, pp. 5, 8.

168. Ralph E. Heimlich, "Economics of Wetland Conversion: Farm Programs and Income Tax," *National Wetland Newsletter* 8, no.4 (1986):7-8; F. Kaid Benfield, Justin R. Ward, and Anne E. Kinsinger, "Assessing the Tax Reform Act: Gains, Questions, and Unfinished Business" (Washington, D.C.: Natural Resources Defense Council, 1986), p. 4; and P.L. 99-198, December 23, 1985, 99 Stat. 1354.

169. U.S. Office of Technology Assessment, *Wetlands*, pp. 72-74; 16 USCA §§1301 et seq. (1985); and 16 USCA §§718 et seq. (1985).

170. 16 USCA §§715K et seq. (1985).

171. U.S. Department of the Interior, Migratory Bird Conservation Commission, *1985 Annual Report* (Washington, D.C.: U.S. Department of the Interior, 1985), pp. 17, 20.

172. U.S. Office of Technology Assessment, *Wetlands*, p. 72; and U.S. Department of the Interior, Migratory Bird Conservation Commission, *1985 Annual Report*, p. 2.

173. U.S. House of Representatives, Committee on Merchant Marine and Fisheries, "Wetlands Bill Heads From the Hill," news release, October 15, 1986.

174. U.S. Department of Agriculture, Agricultural Stabilization and Conservation Service, "Water Bank Program Description" (Washington, D.C.: U.S. Department of Agriculture, n.d.), p. 2.

175. U.S. Office of Technology Assessment, *Wetlands*, p. 73.

176. U.S. Department of Agriculture, Agricultural Stabilization and Conservation Service, "Compilation of Status Agreements—Water Bank Program" (Washington, D.C.: U.S. Department of Agriculture, 1986), pages unnumbered.

177. The Nature Conservancy, "National Wetlands Conservation Project—Fact Sheet," Summer 1985, pp. 1, 3-6; George H. Fenwick, "The Nature Conservancy's National Wetlands Conservation Project," *National Wetlands Newsletter*, vol. 7, no. 1 (1985):12-13; and personal communication with Krishna Roy, the Nature Conservancy, Office of Communication, September 8, 1986, and David Morine, Director of Land Acquisitions, the Nature Conservancy, September 9, 1986.

178. U.S. Department of the Interior, Fish and Wildlife Service, National Wetlands Inventory, *National Wetlands Inventory Briefing Book—FY1986* (Washington, D.C.: National Wetlands Inventory, 1986), photocopy, sect. III; and Bill O. Wilen, "National Wetlands Inventory Mapping," in Alan W. Voss, ed., *Remote Sensing and Land Information Systems in the Tennessee Valley Region*, proceedings of the Forum on Remote Sensing and Land Information in the Tennessee Valley Region, Chattanooga, Tenn., October 24-25, 1984 (Falls Church, Va.: American Society for Photogrametry and Remote Sensing, 1986), p. 75.

179. Mollie Glover Palmer, "Restoration of the Kissimmee River," *National Wetlands Newsletter* 8, no. 1 (1986):8-9.

180. U.S. Fish and Wildlife Service, *Wetlands of the United States*, pp. 40-41.

181. Palmer, "Restoration of the Kissimmee River," pp. 8-10.

182. Joseph K. Shisler, "Evaluation of Artificial Salt Marshes in New Jersey," *National Wetlands Newsletter* 8, no. 3 (1986):4.

183. Francis C. Golet, "Critical Issues in Wetland Mitigation: A Scientific Perspective," *National Wetlands Newsletter* 8, no. 5 (1986):5.

184. P.L. 99-198, December 23, 1985, 99 Stat. 1354.

185. John H. Fitch, *The Need for Comprehensive Wildlife Programs in the United States: A Summary*, prepared for the Council on Environmental Quality (Washington, D.C.: U.S. Government Printing Office, 1980), pp. 2-3.

186. Ibid., pp. 4, 18.

187. Laura Tangley, "A National Biological Survey." *BioScience* 35 (1986):686.

188. Ibid., and Laura Tangley, "A New Plan to Conserve the Earth's Biota," *BioScience* 35 (1985):335-36.

189. U.S. Department of the Interior, Fish and Wildlife Service and Canadian Wildlife Service, *1986 Status of Waterfowl and Fall Flight Forecast* (Washington, D.C.: U.S. Fish and Wildlife Service, 1986), p. 22.

190. Ibid.

191. "Dark Days for Black Ducks," *Cooperative Research Newsletter*, Cornell Laboratory of Ornithology, 22, no. 36 (1986):2.

192. U.S. Fish and Wildlife Service and Canadian Wildlife Service, *1986 Status of Waterfowl and Fall Flight Forecast*, p. 14.

193. William J. Chandler, "Migratory Bird Protection and Management," in National Audubon Society, *Audubon Wildlife Report 1986*, p. 234.

194. "Ducks Respond to Reduced Harvest and Rain," *Outdoor News Bulletin*, Wildlife Management Institute, August 1, 1986, p. 4.

195. U.S. Fish and Wildlife Service and Canadian Wildlife Service, *1986 Status of Waterfowl and Fall Flight Forecast*, p. 22.

196. Ibid., p. 4.

197. George Laycock, "Doing What's Right for the Geese," *Audubon* 87, no. 11 (1985):123-25.

198. Ibid., p. 120; and Chandler, "Migratory Bird Protection and Management," pp. 241-42.

199. See, for example, U.S. Department of Agriculture, Forest Service, Wildlife and Fisheries, *Wildlife and Fish Habitat Management in the Forest Service, Fiscal Year 1984* (Washington, D.C.: U.S. Forest Service, 1985), pp. 52-53.

200. Daniel A. Poole and James B. Trefethen, "Maintenance of Wildlife Populations," in Howard B. Brokaw, ed., *Wildlife in America* (Washington, D.C.: U.S. Government Printing Office, 1978), p. 341.

201. U.S. Department of the Interior, Fish and Wildlife Service, *A Summary of Selected Fish and Wildlife Characteristics of the 50 States* (Washington, D.C.: U.S. Fish and Wildlife Service, 1984), p. 27, table C.1.

202. Ted Williams, "Resurrection of the Wild Turkey," *Audubon* 86, no. 1 (1984):71.

203. Defenders of Wildlife, *Saving Endangered Species: Amending and Implementing the Endangered Species Act* (Washington, D.C.: Defenders of Wildlife, 1986), p. 16.

204. U.S. National Oceanic and Atmospheric Administration, *Fisheries of the United States, 1985*, p. iv; and U.S. Department of Commerce, National Oceanic and Atmospheric Administration, National Marine Fisheries Service, *Fisheries of the United States, 1984*, Current Fishery Statistics 8360 (Washington, D.C.: National Oceanic and Atmospheric

Administration, 1985), p. iv.

205. National Oceanic and Atmospheric Administration, *Fisheries of the United States, 1985*, pp. vi-vii.

206. Ibid., p. 4.

207. U.S. Department of Commerce, National Oceanic and Atmospheric Administration, National Marine Fisheries Service, *Proposed Amendments to Regulations Governing the Taking of Marine Mammals Associated with Tuna Purse Seining Operations* (Washington, D.C.: National Oceanic and Atmospheric Administration, 1985), p. 1.

208. U.S. Department of Commerce, National Oceanic and Atmospheric Administration, National Marine Fisheries Center, *Status of the Fishery Resources off the Northeastern United States for 1985*, NOAA Technical Memorandum NMFS-F/NEC-42 (Springfield, Va.: National Technical Information Service, 1985), pp. 1, 2, 25.

209. U.S. Department of Commerce, National Oceanic and Atmospheric Administration, National Marine Fisheries Service, *Fisheries of the United States, 1981*, Current Fishery Statistics 8200 (Washington, D.C.: National Oceanic and Atmospheric Administration, 1982) p. 2.

210. U.S. Department of Commerce, National Oceanic and Atmospheric Administration, National Marine Fisheries Service, *Fisheries of the United States, 1982*, Current Fishery Statistics 8300 (Washington, D.C.: National Oceanic and Atmospheric Administration, 1983), p. 2; and National Marine Fisheries Service, *Fisheries of the United States, 1985*, p. ix.

211. National Oceanic and Atmospheric Administration, *Fisheries of the United States, 1984*, p. ix.

212. National Oceanic and Atmospheric Administration, *Fisheries of the United States, 1985*, supplement. Data regarding recreational fishing are from telephone and intercept surveys and thus, are somewhat subjective.

213. U.S. Department of the Interior, Fish and Wildlife Service, and U.S. Department of Commerce, Bureau of the Census, *1980 National Survey of Fishing, Hunting, and Wildlife-Associated Recreation* (Washington, D.C.: U.S. Government Printing Office, 1982), p. 10.

214. U.S. Department of the Interior, Fish and Wildlife Service, Division of Federal Aid, "Statistical Summary for Fish and Wildlife Restoration: Fiscal Year 1986" (Washington, D.C.: U.S. Fish and Wildlife Service, 1986), tables VIII and I.

215. See, for example, Lloyd A. Phinney, "Chinook Salmon of the Columbia River Basin," and Lawrence W. Stolte, "The Atlantic Salmon," both in National Audubon Society, *Audubon Wildlife Report 1986*, pp. 729-32 and 706-8, respectively.

216. Stolte, "The Atlantic Salmon," pp. 703, 706-8.

217. Ibid., pp. 704, 708.

218. Susan Pollack, "PCBs in Stripers Prompt Total Ban For N.Y. Fishery," *National Fisherman*, July 1986, p. 19.

219. Fitch, *The Need for Comprehensive Wildlife Programs in the United States*, p. 1; and Edward O. Wilson, "The Biological Diversity Crisis," *BioScience* 35, no. 11 (1985):700.

220. International Union for Conservation of Nature and Natural Resources, *World Conservation Strategy* (Gland, Switzerland: International Union for Conservation of Nature and Natural Resources, 1980), sects. 3.11-3.12. IUCN lists habitat destruction as the most serious threat to species, followed by exploitation and introduction of exotic species.

221. Fitch, *The Need for Comprehensive Wildlife Programs in the United States*, p. 4.

222. Ibid., p. 5.

223. 16 USCA §§1531-43 (1985).

224. U.S. Department of the Interior, Fish and Wildlife Service, Endangered Species Program, *Endangered Species Technical Bulletin* 11, nos. 10 and 11 (1986):12.

225. Defenders of Wildlife, *Saving Endangered Species*, p. 13.

226. U.S. Department of the Interior, Fish and Wildlife Service, Office of Endangered Species, "Number of Species Listed per Calendar Year, 3/31/86," photocopy.

227. Ibid.; and Defenders of Wildlife, *Saving Endangered Species*, p. 11.

228. U.S. Fish and Wildlife Service, "Number of Species Listed by Calendar Year, 3/31/86."

229. *Endangered Species Technical Bulletin* 11, nos. 8 and 9 (1986):16.

230. U.S. Department of the Interior, Fish and Wildlife Service, Office of Endangered Species, "Endangered Species Program: Number of Species Listed as Endangered, Reclassified, or Delisted 1963-1985 (Excluding Emergency Rules), March 31, 1986," photocopy; and U.S. Department of the Interior, Fish and Wildlife Service, Office of Endangered Species, "Status of Recovery Plans: July 1, 1986," photocopy, pp. 1-8.

231. Defenders of Wildlife, *Saving Endangered Species*, p. 16.

232. *Endangered Species Technical Bulletin* 11, nos. 10 and 11 (1986):12.

233. Dennis Drabelle, "The Endangered Species Program," in National Audubon Society, *Audubon Wildife Report 1985*, p. 78.

234. Michael J. Bean, "The Endangered Species Program," in National Audubon Society, *Audubon Wildlife Report, 1986*, p. 370; and *Endangered Species Technical Bulletin* 10, no. 11 (1985):7-8.

235. U.S. Department of Commerce, National Oceanic and Atmospheric Administration, National Marine Fisheries Service, "Marine Mammals Listed as Endangered or Threatened under U.S. Law, 1/31/86" (unpublished).

236. 16 USCA §§1361-62, 1371-84, 1401-7 (1985).

237. U.S. Department of Commerce, National Oceanic and Atmospheric Administration, National Marine Fisheries Service, *Annual Report 1984/85: Marine Mammal Protection Act of 1972* (Washington, D.C.: National Oceanic and Atmospheric Administration, 1985), p. 1.

238. National Oceanic and Atmospheric Administration, "Marine Mammals Listed as Endangered or Threatened under U.S. Law."

239. Ibid.; and Jeffrey M. Breiwick and Howard W. Braham, "The Status of Endangered Whales," *Marine Fisheries Review* 46, no. 4 (1984):4.

240. Breiwick and Braham, "The Status of Endangered Whales," p. 5.

241. Michael Weber, "Marine Mammal Protection," in National Audubon Society, *Audubon Wildlife Report 1985*, p. 206.

242. Lynton Keith Caldwell, *International Environmental Policy: Emergence and Dimensions* (Durham, N.C.: Duke University Press, 1984), p. 247.

243. National Oceanic and Atmospheric Administration, *Annual Report 1984/85*, pp. 27-28; and Thomas W. Netter, "Conservationists Fear Breakdown in Whaling Moratorium," *New York Times*, August 19, 1986.

244. Tina Berger, "Bowhead Estimates Revised Upward; Hunt Issues Ease," *Oceanus*

29, no. 1 (1986):81, 83-84.

245. Weber, "Marine Mammal Protection," pp. 203, 205.

246. Council on Environmental Quality, *Environmental Quality 1982* (Washington, D.C.: U.S. Government Printing Office, 1982), p. 266, table A-25.

247. Danny Bystrak, "The Breeding Bird Survey," *Sialia*, Spring 1979.

248. Gregory S. Butcher, "Population Trend Analysis Using the Breeding Bird Survey and the Christmas Bird Count," draft, August 1, 1986, p. 1.

249. "Raptor Rebound," *Cooperative Research Newsletter* 22, no. 36 (1986):3.

250. U.S. Department of the Interior, Fish and Wildlife Service, Office of Migratory Bird Management and Patuxent Wildlife Research Center, "Nongame Migratory Bird Species with Unstable or Decreasing Population Trends in the United States," 1982, photocopy, pp. 2-3, 6, 10.

251. John H. Rappole et al., *Nearctic Avian Migrants in the Neotropics*, prepared for U.S. Department of the Interior, Fish and Wildlife Service (Washington, D.C.: U.S. Government Printing Office, 1983), p. i.

252. U.S. Fish and Wildlife Service, "Nongame Migratory Bird Species with Unstable or Decreasing Population Trends in the United States," p. 12.

253. Peter Steinhart, "Trouble in the Tropics," *National Wildlife* 22, no. 1 (1983):16, 18.

254. Joseph Wallace, "Where Have All the Songbirds Gone?' *Sierra* 71, no. 2 (1986):45-46.

255. William J. Chandler, "State Wildlife Conservation: An Overview," in National Audubon Society, *Audubon Wildlife Report 1986*, p. 581.

256. "Fewer Hunters Pay More in '85," *Outdoor News Bulletin*, August 1, 1986, p. 1.

257. Ibid.

258. 16 USCA §§669 et seq. 777-777k (1985); and U.S. Fish and Wildlife Service, "Statistical Summary for Fish and Wildlife Restoration," table I.

259. U.S. Fish and Wildlife Service, "Statistical Summary for Fish and Wildlife Restoration," table I.

260. "Fewer Hunters Pay More in '85," p. 1.

261. Joyce M. Kelly, "Nongame Wildlife: More Than Just An Identity Crisis in Wildlife Management," speech delivered November 12, 1986.

262. 16 USCA §§2901-11 (1985).

263. Chandler, "State Wildlife Conservation," p. 580.

264. Susan Cerulean and Whit Fosburgh, "State Nongame Wildlife Programs," in National Audubon Society, *Audubon Wildlife Report 1986*, p. 639.

265. Ibid., pp. 638-41.

266. Michael J. Bean, *The Evolution of National Wildlife Law* (New York: Praeger Publishers, 1983), p. 229.

267. Ibid., p. 331.

268. U.S. Fish and Wildlife Service, *Annual Report of Lands under Control of the U.S. Fish and Wildlife Service*; and Lee, "The National Wildlife Refuge System," p. 413.

269. U.S. Fish and Wildlife Service, *Annual Report of Lands Under Control of the U.S. Fish and Wildlife Service*, pp. 2-3. Coordination of wildlife management areas are federally owned, typically part of a Bureau of Reclamation or Army Corps of Engineers water resources project, and jointly managed by the purchasing agency, Fish and Wildlife Service, and the state. Lee, "The National Wildlife Refuge System," p. 415.

270. Information provided by Bill Swanson, U.S. Fish and Wildlife Service, January 1987.

271. U.S. Fish and Wildlife Service, *Annual Report of Lands Under Control of the U.S. Fish and Wildlife Service*, p. 22.

272. J. M. Westphal, "Recreation Use of Lands Administered by the U.S. Fish and Wildlife Service," in Van Doren, *Statistics on Outdoor Recreation: The Record Since 1956*, p. 202.

273. Lee, "The National Wildlife Refuge System," p. 413.

274. Laura Riley and William Riley, *Guide to the National Wildlife Refuges* (Garden City, N.Y.: Anchor Press/Doubleday, 1979), p. 1.

275. U.S. Fish and Wildlife Service, *Preliminary Survey of Contaminant Issues of Concern on National Wildlife Refuges*, pp. iii-iv.

276. Lee, "The National Wildlife Refuge System," p. 449.

277. Ibid., p. 451.

278. Ibid., p. 453.

279. Chandler, "State Wildlife Conservation," p. 588.

280. Barton and Fosburgh, "The U.S. Forest Service," pp. 1, 102.

281. U.S. Department of Agriculture, Forest Service, *Report of the Forest Service, Fiscal Year 1985* (Washington, D.C.: U.S. Forest Service, 1986), p. 25.

282. Katherine Barton, "Wildlife and the Bureau of Land Management," in National Audubon Society, *Audubon Wildlife Report 1986*, p. 497.

283. James A. Lewis, *Landownership in the United States, 1978*, Agriculture Information Bulletin no. 435 (Washington, D.C.: U.S. Government Printing Office, 1980), p. 3.

284. Neil Sampson, "The Availability of Private Lands for Recreation," in Task Force on Recreation on Private Lands, *Recreation on Private Lands: Issues and Opportunities* (Washington, D.C.: Task Force on Recreation on Private Lands, 1986), p. 11.

285. Council on Environmental Quality, *Environmental Quality 1984: 15th Annual Report of the Council on Environmental Quality* (Washington, D.C.: U.S. Government Printing Office, 1986), p. 374.

286. President's Commission on Americans Outdoors, *Americans Outdoors*, p. 190.

287. The Nature Conservancy, "Background Information 1986," December 1986, photocopy, p. 1.

288. Information provided by Bryan Holly, Trust for Public Land, January 1987.

289. Ibid.; and the Nature Conservancy, "Background Information 1986," p. 1.

290. Information provided by Frank Dunston, National Audubon Society, January 1987.

291. James D. Riggle, "Using Private Land Trusts and Conservation Easements to Provide Recreational Opportunities on Private Lands," in Task Force on Recreation on Private Lands, *Recreation on Private Lands*, p. 55.

292. President's Commission on Americans Outdoors, *Americans Outdoors*, p. 204.

293. Task Force on Recreation on Private Lands, *Recreation on Private Lands*, p. 1.

Figures

5.1. U.S. Department of Commerce, Bureau of the Census, *Governmental Finances in 1983-84* (Washington, D.C.: U.S. Government Printing Office, 1985), p. 19, and previous annual issues. Price deflators from U.S. Department of Commerce, Bureau of the Census, *Statistical Abstract of the United States 1985* (Washington, D.C.: U.S. Government Printing Office, 1985), p. 470.

5.2. Data for National Park Service is as of December 31, 1985, while all other data is from September 30, 1985; for Bureau of Land Management: U.S. Department of the Interior,

Bureau of Land Management, *Public Land Statistics, 1985* (Washington, D.C.: U.S. Government Printing Office, 1986), pp. 6-7; for Forest Service: U.S. Department of Agriculture, Forest Service, *Land Areas of the National Forest Service as of September 30, 1985* (Washington, D.C.: U.S. Government Printing Office, 1986), pp. 14-32; for Fish and Wildlife Service: U.S. Department of the Interior, Fish and Wildlife Service, Division of Realty, *Annual Report of Lands under the Control of the U.S. Fish and Wildlife Service as of September 30, 1985* (Washington, D.C.: U.S. Fish and Wildlife Service, 1985), p. 3; for National Park Service: photocopy provided by U.S. Department of the Interior, National Park Service, "National Park Service, Summary of Acreages, 12/31/85"; for Corps of Engineers: personal communication with Phil Parsley, U.S. Army Corps of Engineers, October 1986; for Bureau of Reclamation: personal communication with Terry Cooper, Bureau of Reclamation, October 1986; for Tennessee Valley Authority: photocopy provided by Tennessee Valley Authority, Division of Land and Economic Resources, "TVA Fee Land as of September 30, 1985."

5.3. Wildlife areas include national wildlife refuges and related areas. The National Wilderness Preservation System was created in 1964. The lands are managed by four agencies. In 1985, the system included national parks (36.8 million acres), national wildlife refuges (19.3 million acres), national forests (32.1 million acres), and land managed by the Bureau of Land Management (0.37 million acres). For National Parks: U.S. Department of the Interior, National Park System, *Index of the National Park System and Affiliated Areas as of January 1, 1975* (Washington, D.C.: National Park Service, 1975); "Updated Addenda of October 22, 1976" for the *Index*, 1975; information provided by the U.S. Department of the Interior, National Park Service; analysis to account for revisions drawn from The Conservation Foundation, *National Parks for a New Generation: Visions, Realities, Prospects* (Washington, D.C.: The Conservation Foundation, 1985); photocopy provided by National Park Service, "National Park Service, Summary of Acreages, 12/31/85." For wildlife areas: U.S. Fish and Wildlife Service, *Annual Report of Lands under the Control of the U.S. Fish and Wildlife Service as of September 30, 1985*, p. 3, and previous annual issues. For wilderness areas: Council on Environmental Quality, *Environmental Statistics* (Springfield, Va.: National Technical Information Service, 1979), p. 44; U.S. Department of Agriculture, Forest Service, Recreation Management Staff, *Wilderness Fact Sheet*, February 15, 1979, December 30, 1980, and January 17, 1983; and unpublished data from Forest Service, National Park Service, Fish and Wildlife Service, Bureau of Land Management and The Wilderness Society.

5.4. The Conservation Foundation, *National Parks for a New Generation*, p. 64.

5.5. Wendy Smith Lee, "The National Wildlife Refuge System," in National Audubon Society, *Audubon Wildlife Report 1986* (New York: National Audubon Society, 1986), p. 429.

5.6. Data through 1979: Carlton S. Van Doren, "State Park Systems," in Marion Clawson, ed., *Statistics on Outdoor Recreation*, p. 1, *The Record through 1956* (Washington, D.C.: Resources for the Future, 1984), pp. 238, 244, tables 72, 77. Data after 1979: U.S. Department of the Interior, National Park Service, *Federal Recreation Fee Report*, 1979-1985 eds., report prepared for the U.S. Senate, Committee on Energy and Natural Resources, and U.S. House, Committee on Interior and Insular Affairs (Washington, D.C.: U.S. Department of the Interior, published annually).

5.7. U.S. Department of Agriculture, Office of Information, "Highly Erodible Land and Wetland Conservation Provisions of the Food Security Act of 1985," *Backgrounder*, June 25, 1986, p. 8.

5.8. U.S. Department of the Interior, Fish and Wildlife Service, *Wetlands of the United States: Current Status and Recent Trends* (Washington, D.C.: U.S. Government Printing Office, 1984), p. 34.

5.9. U.S. Congress, Office of Technology Assessment, *Wetlands: Their Use and Regulation* (Washington, D.C.: U.S. Government Printing Office, 1984), p. 92.

5.10. Ibid., p. 12.

5.11. Information provided by U.S. Army Corps of Engineers, Permitting Office, June 1986.

5.12. U.S. Department of the Interior, Fish and Wildlife Service, and Canadian Wildlife Service, *1986 Status of Waterfowl and Fall Flight Forecasts* (Washington, D.C.: U.S. Fish and Wildlife Service, 1986), p. 22, table 4.

5.13. Council on Environmental Quality, *Environmental Quality 1982*, table A-21, p. 262; U.S. Department of Agriculture, Forest Service, Wildlife and Fisheries Staff; and U.S. Department of Agriculture, Forest Service, *Wildlife and Fish Habitat Management in the Forest Service, Fiscal Year 1984* (Washington, D.C.: U.S. Forest Service, 1985), pp. 114-18, appendix G, and previous annual issues.

5.14. U.S. Department of Commerce, National Oceanic and Atmospheric Administration, National Marine Fisheries Service, *Fisheries of the United States, 1985*, Current Fisheries Statistics no. 8380 (Washington, D.C.: National Oceanic and Atmospheric Administration, 1986), pp. 1-3, and previous issues.

5.15. Ibid., p. 3, and previous issues.

5.16. Ibid., p. 2, and previous issues.

5.17. U.S. Department of the Interior, Fish and Wildlife Service, Office of Endangered Species, "Number of Species Listed per Calendear Year, 3/31/86," photocopy.

5.18. Memorandum, U.S. Department of the Interior, Fish and Wildlife Service, Office of Endangered Species, "Status of Recovery Plans: July 1, 1986," photocopy; and memorandum from acting chief, U.S. Fish and Wildlife Service, Office of Endangered Species, to associate director, Federal Assistance, p. 15.

5.19. Susan Cerulean and Whit Fosburgh, "State Nongame Wildlife Programs," in National Audubon Society, *Audubon Wildlife Report 1986*, pp. 640-41.

PART II
Issues

Chapter 6

Agriculture and the Environment in a Changing World Economy

By many measures, U.S. agriculture in the 1980s has been in the throes of its most serious economic difficulties since the Great Depression of the 1930s.[1] Faced with low prices for the crops, livestock, and milk they sell, even many efficient farmers are finding it difficult to repay their debts, let alone make a profit. Families that have farmed for generations are losing their land and livelihood. Events of the 1980s have even robbed meaning from the old saying that farmers "live poor but die rich," for the chief source of that posthumous wealth—the value of farmland—has fallen precipitously. As farmers' fortunes have plummeted, U.S. taxpayers have spent a fortune on government farm programs. Indeed, in 1986, federal government expenditures to support commodity prices and farmer income ($25.5 billion)[2] roughly equaled the value of agricultural exports ($26.5 billion).[3]

From an economic perspective, U.S. agriculture clearly has gone from boom to bust, essentially within one decade. The picture, moreover, is even bleaker from an environmental or resource conservation perspective. During the export-led agricultural boom years of the 1970s, conservationists and environmentalists decried the increases in soil erosion, groundwater depletion and contamination, and pollution of surface waters, as well as the loss of wetlands, hedgerows, and other wildlife habitat that accompanied the push to expand crop production. Nevertheless, agriculture still constitutes the largest remaining source of pollutant loadings to the United States' streams and lakes.[4] Furthermore, in the past few years, farm chemicals—

341

fertilizers and pesticides—have emerged as a significant threat to the nation's groundwater. Environmentally, it matters little if agricultural production is geared to expanding export markets, as was the case in the 1970s, or to mounting stockpiles, as has happened in the 1980s. The potential for damage to resources and the environment remains serious.

In other countries, agricultural change in recent years often has had even more serious effects on resource use and environmental quality than has been the case in the United States. Those problems are not yet well known within this country. However, conservationists and environmentalists here and elsewhere are increasingly taking a global view of the ways in which changes in agriculture or agricultural policy in one country may affect both agriculture and the environment in others.

The challenge before policy makers in the United States and other countries is to develop and implement policies that simultaneously help farmers to adjust to the volatile economic forces they face today and provide increased protection to natural resources and the environment. This study examines the resource and environmental impacts associated with contemporary agriculture. Although it primarily concentrates on production of major crops in the United States—emphasizing those impacts that could be affected by economic, technological, and policy changes under way, or foreseen, for U.S. agriculture—it also presents brief case studies from Brazil, Europe, Central America, and China to illustrate a few of the many environmental consequences of recent agricultural change around the globe.

PROFILE OF A CHANGING U.S. AGRICULTURE

Change is hardly new to U.S. agriculture. Indeed, few sectors of the U.S. economy have experienced the economic and technological upheaval agriculture has over the past 50 years. Some of the farm sector's changes—for example, fluctuations in agricultural exports—have been short-term and unpredictable. Others have been under way for decades and are somewhat easier to predict: technological change and the evolving structure of the farm sector, to name two.

Farming in the United States is not a single homogeneous enterprise, but a collection of quite diverse activities. In terms of area, the most important crops are corn, wheat, soybeans, and hay; together they occupy more than three-quarters of total U.S. cropland. Production of the first three of these commodities is heavily oriented toward exports. Cotton, tobacco, and rice are other important export crops that occupy a far smaller area but have a relatively high value of production. The most valuable single agricultural commodity, however, is not any of these crops but beef. Although there is some import of beef (mainly hamburger from Australia and New Zealand) and some export, the beef cattle industry depends mainly on domestic demand. Pork, poultry, and milk production are other major agricultural enterprises, and they too depend mostly on domestic demand.[5]

Changing Economic Circumstances

By far the most significant economic development in the U.S. farm sector since the 1970s has been the internationalization of the nation's agriculture. Rapid increase in grain and soybean exports beginning in 1973 (figure 6.1) led the United States to be firmly established as the dominant force in world agricultural trade by the end of the 1970s. Between 1976 and 1979, the United States supplied 40 percent of all wheat moving across national borders anywhere in the world, as well as 64 percent of soybeans, 60 percent of coarse grains, and 32 percent of cotton being traded. This did not mean that U.S. farmers "fed the world"; in fact, world trade comprised only about 15 percent of total world consumption of grains and oilseeds.[6] Rather, the export boom meant that the United States had become the main buffer for fluctuations in world food supply and demand. When domestic supplies in other countries grew tight or their incomes permitted it, they bought grain and soybeans from the United States. When those

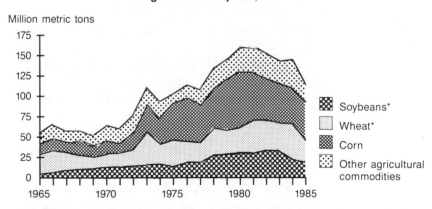

Figure 6.1
U. S. Agricultural Exports, 1965–1985

Million metric tons

Legend:
- Soybeans*
- Wheat*
- Corn
- Other agricultural commodities

* "Wheat" includes wheat flour; "soybeans" includes soybean meal.

Source: U.S. Department of Agriculture.

countries' domestic supplies were ample or their ability to purchase was constrained, the United States could be counted on to retain commodities in stock.

Several demand-related developments produced the export boom of the 1970s. Growing income enabled consumers around the world to "upgrade" their diets; wheat products were substituted for maize and rice, and meat consumption increased.[7] As meat production increased, so did the demand for U.S. corn and soybeans used for cattle, hog, and poultry feed. Some of the vast revenues received by major oil exporting countries during the 1970s returned to the United States in the form of food export demand.[8] A relatively weak U.S. dollar kept farm export prices low. The most important sources of demand were the middle-income developing countries, Eastern Europe, and Japan.[9] Another large factor was that the Soviet Union and, to a lesser extent, China sought to maintain and upgrade domestic food consumption, even in years of poor harvests, by buying U.S. grain.[10]

After peaking in 1981 at $43.8 billion, the value of U.S. farm exports fell to only $26.5 billion by 1986.[11] There were several reasons for this decline: The 1980-82 world recession reduced consumer incomes, debt repayment problems made it difficult for developing countries and Eastern Bloc nations to maintain import levels, and a steady climb in the value of the dollar relative to other world currencies began to raise the effective price of U.S. products. Most of these factors were the result of macroeconomic forces (such as the growing U.S. budget deficit and resulting high interest rates) that originated outside the farm sector.[12]

But the supply side of the world food balance changed, too, as other nations responded to the explosion in agricultural trade and prices of the 1970s. Some countries were uncomfortable with their dependence on U.S. farm products and adopted policies to encourage domestic production in the name of national self-sufficiency. Other nations saw the possibility of earning foreign exchange and entered markets in direct competition with the United States. Brazil began to grow larger amounts of soybeans and citrus, exporting them to markets traditionally supplied by U.S. farmers.[13] The European Economic Community turned from being a major importer of U.S. wheat to being a major exporter.[14] India and China modernized their agriculture, boosting yields and production.[15] Traditional food exporters, including Canada, Argentina, and Australia, stepped up production.[16]

As a result of all these developments over the last decade, U.S. agriculture became heavily dependent on earnings from a volatile, increasingly competitive international market. At the peak of the export boom in 1981,

64 percent of U.S. wheat production was destined for export markets; four years later, exports were absorbing only 38 percent of the wheat crop. Over the same interval, U.S. corn exports fell from 25 percent to 14 percent of production, and soybeans from 40 percent to 32 percent.[17] Production climbed fairly steadily over this period* while domestic demand increased only modestly, so stocks accumulated and U.S. commodity prices declined.[18] So did farm income, which in 1979 had been as high as $31.7 billion; in 1983, farm income was only $15 billion.[19]

The deep recession in the U.S. farm economy during the 1980s has had other economic consequences, as well:

• Between February 1981 and February 1986, farm real estate values dropped sharply throughout the U.S. grain belt—falling by 58 percent in Iowa, 50 percent in Nebraska, 52 percent in Minnesota, 48 percent in Illinois and Indiana, and 45 percent in Ohio. Iowa farmland that brought an average of $1,999 per acre in 1981 sold for $841 in 1986.[20]

• The sharp drop in land values reduced the collateral most commercial farmers had used to secure the large loans they needed to expand their production in the 1970s. Very high interest rates on those debts at the end of the 1970s resulted in severe debt repayment problems for a sizable proportion of farms. By 1984, U.S. Department of Agriculture (USDA) studies showed that 37,000 farms were, in effect, bankrupt; their debts exceeded the value of their assets.[21]

• As agricultural markets weakened, the total cost of government programs to support prices for crops and milk skyrocketed, from $4 billion in 1981 to an average of $14 billion per year between 1982 and 1985.[22] At that expenditure level, the Congressional Budget Office identified agriculture as the most heavily "supported" industry in the country.[23] But USDA analysts estimated that total costs would rise further, to $25.5 billion or more in 1986.[24]

The rapid decline in commodity prices and farm income, however, has not resulted in significantly scaled back production—even though U.S. farmers in the 1970s had rapidly expanded their production in response to the high prices that then existed (figure 6.2). Capital investments and land-use patterns usually make it easier for individual farmers to expand production than to contract it. Even if commodity prices drop, farmers

---

*The year 1983 was an exception to these trends because the U.S. Department of Agriculture's "payment-in-kind" program and a serious drought in the Corn Belt reduced corn production sharply.

Figure 6.2
U. S. Production of Corn, Wheat, and Soybeans, 1970–1986

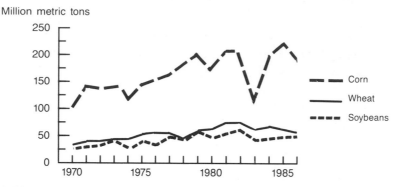

Million metric tons

* 1986 data are projected.

Source: U.S. Department of Agriculture.

may for a time continue planting the same area of land, using the same equipment and same quantities of fertilizer and other inputs (depending on their price levels) that earned reasonable profits only when crop prices were higher. Many farmers have large fixed costs (purchased land and equipment), which they must try to recoup, and they cannot readily shift to the production of other goods. Frequently, farmers cannot even shift to other agricultural commodities, because commercial farms tend to specialize in a few commodities. Government commodity programs have made production adjustments by farmers even less likely by bolstering crop prices and offering direct cash payments to farmers at artificially high levels.

Changing Structure of Agriculture

Several interrelated structural characteristics of U.S. agriculture—the number of farms, their average size, the distribution of ownership and control of basic resources (land and water) and economic clout among farms of various size, and land ownership and tenancy patterns—have undergone enormous change over the past 50 years.

The number of farms has fallen from 6.1 million in 1940 to 2.2 million today, and average size has increased from 175 acres to 441 acres per farm.[25] Four percent of the nation's farms—with annual sales totaling over $250,000—account for over half of U.S. farm production, while 72 percent of U.S. farms have farm product sales of less than $40,000 annually and collectively account for only 11 percent of total sales.[26] Typically, owners of these small farms earn nearly all of their net income from nonfarm jobs.

Even though over 90 percent of U.S. farmland is still family owned or operated,[27] the traditional image of the small-scale family farmer is becoming less and less valid. A 1986 report by Congress's Office of Technology Assessment (OTA) forecast that another 1 million U.S. farms (most of them moderate-size or small) will disappear in the United States by the year 2000. OTA projects that, by that date, 75 percent of U.S. agricultural production will come from the 50,000 largest farms.[28] Though some authorities predict a much slower rate of farm attrition, no one expects a halting, much less a reversal, of the long-term trend toward fewer, larger, more economically powerful farms. Several forces will almost certainly continue to drive this trend: technology, which over time has eliminated the need for much labor in agriculture; public policies, which favor large farms because commodity program and income tax benefits are in direct proportion to farm size; and opportunities to earn higher incomes in nonfarm jobs.

Modern farms have also become increasingly specialized,[29] deriving much more of their income from sales of a few commodities, such as cash crops (wheat, corn, or soybeans), milk, or beef than did farms at the end of World War II. Diversified crop-and-livestock farms have become fewer over time, and a large proportion of them are small.

Land ownership and tenure patterns are also changing. Although more than 67 percent of the land that comes onto the market is purchased by active or retired farmers (the rest is purchased by nonfarm investors),[30] over the past few decades an increasing amount of farmland has been operated by tenants.[31] The average farmer today owns only about 60 percent of the land that he or she farms and rents the rest.[32]

Changing Resource, Production, and Technological Inputs

Agricultural productivity is usually characterized by the amount of product output per unit of input—land, labor, applied chemicals, or technology. Increased productivity can result from changing (*a*) production's *extensiveness*, the amount of land used for agriculture or for production of specific crops, or (*b*) its *intensiveness*—for example, achieving higher crop yields per acre of land, higher milk or beef production per head of livestock, higher output of poultry per unit of feed or labor, and so forth.

The United States' endowment of natural resources, its use of chemicals

---

Figure 6.3
Resources Used in U.S. Agricultural Production, 1964–1985

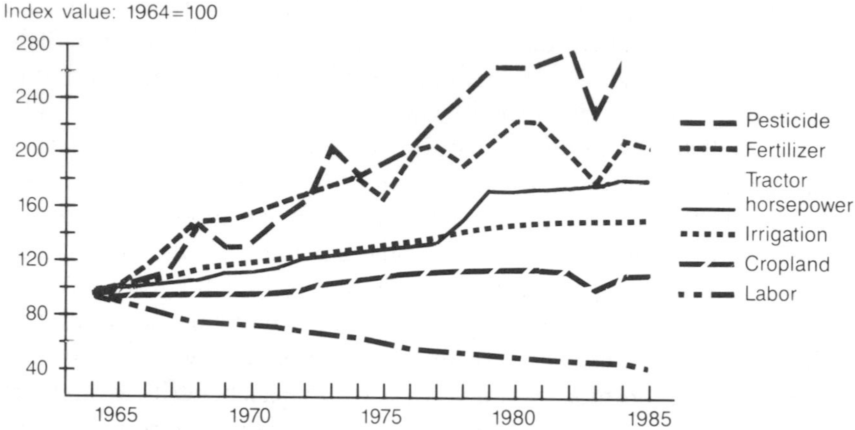

Index value: 1964=100

Sources: U.S. Department of Agriculture, U.S. Environmental Protection Agency, Irrigation Journal

---

such as fertilizers and pesticides, and its advanced technology have increasingly enabled it to produce high levels of agricultural output with little labor (figure 6.3). The type and amount of inputs used have also been changing dramatically in recent decades.

Land Use

The United States has large amounts of naturally fertile land, particularly in the Midwest, where the combination of soils, rainfall, and growing season is close to ideal for grain production. The total amount of land included in the nation's cropland base (including that cropland not currently used to grow crops) has, since around 1920, changed little from its current level of 470 million acres.[33] In response to high commodity prices in the 1970s, however, U.S. farmers brought 55 million acres of land into crop production between 1970 and 1981 and increased output by 51 percent.[34] The amount of this land actually used for crops in 1985 was estimated at 374 million acres, roughly the same as 1984 but down about 3 percent from the peak year of 1981.[35]

Most of the land that was brought into production during this period had previously been idled under government programs or was converted from pasture, forest, or wetlands.[36] Three regions accounted for 58 percent of the increase in cropland between 1972 and 1981: the Corn Belt (14.7 million acres), Lake States (8 million acres), and Southern Plains (8.2

Figure 6.4
Cropland Acreage in the United States, 1965–1986

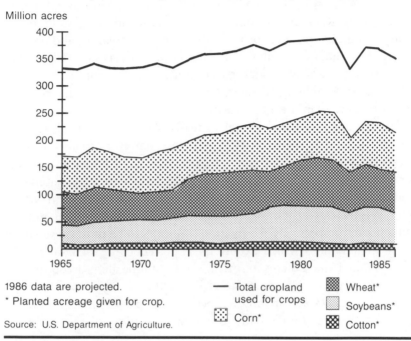

Million acres

1986 data are projected.

* Planted acreage given for crop.

Source: U.S. Department of Agriculture.

— Total cropland used for crops

▦ Wheat*

▨ Corn*

▦ Soybeans*

▨ Cotton*

million acres).[37] The principal export crops—wheat, corn, soybeans, and cotton—accounted for two-thirds of U.S. cropland used in 1981 (figure 6.4).

The regional location of crops has also changed in some cases. For example, total soybean acreage in the United States has changed little since 1981, but acreage has declined notably in the Delta (24 percent) and the Southeast (23 percent) while increasing over 6 percent in the western Corn Belt.[38] Total U.S. acreage planted to cotton has declined over the past 30 years, as intensive, high-yield production of the crop using irrigation in California and the Southwest has significantly displaced its production in the South, its native region.[39]

Economics and technical changes have also resulted in an increase in the amount of land that produces more than one crop a season. Acreage multiple-cropped in the United States nearly quadrupled between 1969 and 1982, from 3.1 million to 12.4 million acres. This expansion was driven by such factors as rising commodity prices, development of earlier maturing plant varieties, use of more supplemental irrigation, and the expansion of conservation tillage technologies.[40]

Irrigation

Because rainfall is not uniformly distributed either geographically or in the course of a growing season, U.S. farmers have become increasingly reliant on irrigation. Roughly 50 million acres of farmland are now irrigated, representing 15 percent of the nation's harvested cropland[41] and producing nearly a third of the value of all U.S. farm products sold.[42] The crops with the largest acreage under irrigation in 1982 were corn (9.5 million acres), hay (8.5 million), wheat (4.6 million), and cotton, fruit orchards, and rice (more than 3 million each).[43]

The amount of irrigated acreage increased slowly but relatively steadily until the late 1970s. Between 1978 and 1982, however, irrigated acreage declined 1.3 million acres, though this net loss was due primarily to reductions in the Southern Plains (1.5 million acres) and Mountain regions (0.7 million acres). During the same time period, the Delta States and Northern Plains increased their total irrigated acreage by 0.5 million and 0.4 million acres, respectively.[44] Irrigation continues to be most prevalent in the 17 western states, which account for 91 percent of the total water withdrawn in the United States for irrigation. California alone accounted for about 25 percent of the national total.[45] In addition, supplemental irrigation continues to expand in more temperate, humid areas such as the Southeast. Florida, for example, had 1.6 million acres in supplemental irrigation in 1982.[46]

Agricultural Chemicals

U.S. farmers have greatly increased their use of fertilizer and pesticides in recent decades. By using these chemicals, farmers are able to cultivate lands of marginal fertility and to grow a cash crop year after year without unacceptable buildup of pests or loss of soil fertility.

Fertilizer. Of the 16 chemical elements required for plant growth and development, those needed in relatively large amounts are nitrogen, phosphorus, potassium, sulfur, calcium, and magnesium.[47] In recent years, total U.S. fertilizer consumption has largely followed the amount of land planted in crops (figure 6.5). Four crops—corn, wheat, cotton, and soybeans— for an estimated 62 percent of total U.S. fertilizer use. Corn alone accounts for 44 percent, with almost all of the land in corn receiving 200 to 300 pounds of fertilizer per acre.[48]

Although these four crops are responsible for the most fertilizer consumption, the intensity of fertilizer use can be much heavier on other crops and on suburban lawns. The intensity of fertilizer use is shifting as crop-

Figure 6.5
Fertilizer Use in the United States, 1960–1985

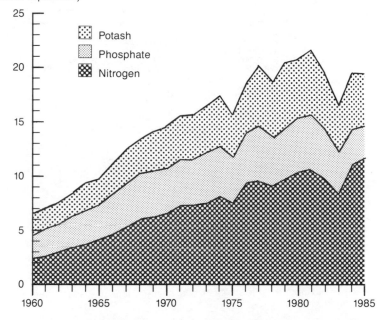

ping patterns shift. For instance, between 1984 and 1985, the Delta states showed an 8 percent decline in plant nutrient consumption while the Northern Plains showed a 10 percent increase.[49]

Pesticides. Insecticides, herbicides, fungicides, and rodenticides are widely used in the United States to protect crops from insects, weeds, fungi, and rodents. Some 1,500 different active pesticide ingredients are registered by the U.S. Environmental Protection Agency (EPA) for use in the United States.[50]*

USDA estimates that about 90 percent of the herbicides and insecticides used in 1982 on field crops were applied to only four crops: corn,

---

*No accurate, comprehensive data are kept on the quantities of pesticides used, however. USDA has conducted five surveys of pesticide use on major field crops since 1964 (as well as several smaller selected crop surveys), but these studies have not included all crops or all areas of the country. Since 1979, EPA's Office of Pesticide Programs has made annual estimates, which differ significantly from USDA figures.

Figure 6.6
Herbicide and Insecticide Use in the United States, 1971 and 1982

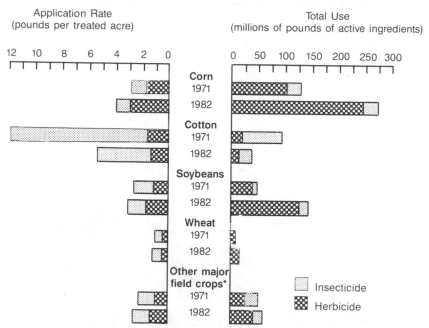

Application Rate
(pounds per treated acre)

Total Use
(millions of pounds of active ingredients)

* Other major field crops include sorghum, rice, peanuts, tobacco, rye (1971 only), barley, oats, hay, and alfalfa.

Source: U.S. Department of Agriculture.

cotton, soybeans, and wheat (figure 6.6).[51] Corn alone accounted for 54 percent of all herbicides used and 43 percent of all insecticides used on field crops.[52] Pesticides are also intensively used on certain fruit and vegetable crops. In 1980 fruits accounted for 14 percent of the total pounds of active ingredients used, while vegetables accounted for 6 percent, despite the small area devoted to these crops. Insecticides are most heavily used on citrus, while fungicides are used mainly on deciduous fruits, vegetables, and fall potatoes.[53] Pesticides are also used to fumigate stored grain.

Between 1964 and 1985, farm use of pesticides increased almost 170 percent.[54] Herbicides made up the largest part of that increase, as chemicals replaced mechanical methods of controlling weeds and monoculture systems expanded. In 1966, herbicides accounted for about 33 percent of all pesticides used for agriculture in this country.[55] Almost 88 percent of pesticides used by farmers in 1986 were estimated to be herbicides.[56]

This increased use reflects both more intensive and more widespread use of herbicides. The amount applied to corn, which accounts for the largest share of herbicide use, increased from 1.7 pounds of active ingredients per acre in 1971 to 3.1 pounds per acre in 1982. Average herbicide application rates for other major crops (excluding pasture and range) increased by 30 percent between 1971 and 1982.[57] In 1971, approximately 71 percent of all U.S. farmland acreage devoted to row crops and 38 percent of all U.S. acreage planted in small grain crops had herbicides applied. By 1982, these figures had risen to 91 and 41 percent, respectively.[58]

Important changes have also occurred in the types of pesticides produced and used. One important trend has been from DDT (dichloro-diphenyl-trichloro-ethane), toxaphene, and other persistent organochlorine compounds (63 percent of insecticide use in 1964, down to 23 percent in 1976), toward less-persistent but generally more concentrated and acutely toxic compounds such as carbamates and organophosphates.[59] (Most organochlorine compounds, including DDT, have been banned or restricted by EPA.)

In recent years, cotton has increasingly been grown using integrated pest management (IPM) technology and new synthetic pyrethroids, which are applied at about one-tenth the rate of traditional cotton insecticides.[60] This shift in the type of chemical has been a major reason for the drop in the amount of insecticides applied to major U.S. field and forage crops, a 45 percent decline between 1976 and 1982.[61]

Statistics on recent use of fertilizer and pesticides in U.S. agriculture and current projections indicate that the amount of fertilizer and pesticides used in agriculture may be stabilizing or even decreasing. A major factor in this trend may be shifts toward more efficient use of more highly concentrated compounds.[62]

Agricultural Technology

The U.S. agricultural research establishment has developed many new technologies over the years, and U.S. farmers, among the best educated and informed in the world, have eagerly adopted them. This has resulted in a substantial increase in what economists call "total factor productivity," the ratio of total output to total input. Since 1940, agricultural productivity has more than doubled. Between 1970 and 1985, total factor productivity rose an average of 2.2 percent annually.[63]

A new revolution in agricultural technology, based on biotechnology and on advanced information gathering and processing, appears to be on the horizon, and U.S. scientists are among the world leaders in its development. According to a recent study by OTA, "The effects of this new [technological] era on agricultural productivity may be more profound than those experienced from either the mechanical or chemical eras."[64]

Biotechnology promises to improve plant and animal breeds, making them more productive, more disease resistant, and better adapted to harsh environments.[65] Animal agriculture probably will be affected earlier than plant agriculture, although the impact on plants may be substantially greater in the long term.[66] The possibility of breeding animals, particularly beef and dairy cattle, that use feed more efficiently could significantly reduce the demand for U.S. feedgrains. If this happens, or if technologies are developed that greatly increase grain production per acre, the amount of land cultivated could fall; changes might also occur in the amount and distribution of fertilizer, pesticides, and energy use. New information technologies are likely to cut farmers' production costs by reducing wasted inputs—for example, by enabling more precise and timely application of animal feed, water, fertilizers, and pesticides.[67]

RESOURCE AND ENVIRONMENTAL EFFECTS OF A CHANGING AGRICULTURE

Modern U.S. agriculture has raised two broad issues for conservationists and environmentalists. First, many people are concerned about the sustainability of agricultural resource use, particularly because of the farm sector's heavy dependence on agricultural chemicals and energy, the depletion of groundwater in some areas by agricultural irrigation, and the continuing displacement of topsoil through erosion. Concerns have also been raised about the environmental side effects of agriculture: contamination of groundwater by pesticides and fertilizers, surface-water pollution with sediment and agricultural chemicals, and destruction of wildlife habitat as new lands are brought into production. Agricultural change in other countries carries with it similar environmental problems.

Agricultural Production

Three general types of change in agricultural production affect resource use and the environment: changes in the extensiveness of production, in the intensiveness of production, and in agricultural technology. Often the effects of these changes can be quite complex.

Cotton is a case in point. Soil erosion in cotton production is notoriously difficult to control under unirrigated conditions since cotton plants produce very little vegetation that can serve as protective mulch and since common production practices leave soil vulnerable to erosion, especially that caused by wind.[68] As a result, the reduction in the total area planted to cotton nationwide probably has produced net benefits for soil conservation. But the shift of cotton culture to the irrigated West has contributed to another set of concerns: about water conservation and quality, and about tapping western rivers and aquifers to increase water consumption.

At the same time, the changing use of pesticides in cotton production undoubtedly has had notable effects on the environment and on risks to human health. EPA's ban on DDT and other insecticides that once were heavily used on cotton has benefited wildlife,[69] but the organophosphates, whose usage has increased partly as a consequence, are more acutely toxic to pesticide applicators than were the banned chemicals.[70] However, IPM technology, which has also replaced the banned pesticides, represents a clear reduction in environmental dangers to human beings.[71]

The early 1980s' low commodity prices and the consequent reduced profit margins in agriculture may have led farmers to become more judicious in their expenditures on inputs than was the case in the 1970s.[72] But it is not clear that this caution has translated into tangible or even discernible benefits to resource conservation and the environment. Farmers' decisions about land and input use are strongly influenced by changes in the price of inputs or commodity prices, and those prices are subject to sudden and dramatic changes. Other things being equal, a resurgence of foreign demand and high crop prices probably would trigger increased use of inputs and possibly expansion of cropped acreage.

Finally, agricultural production-related effects can be strongly influenced by government policies. U.S. government policies and their relationship to environmental concerns are discussed later in this chapter. Other countries have also found clear relationships between their governments' agricultural policies, crop production, and the environment. This certainly was the case, for example, with the European Economic Community in the 1970s and the early 1980s (see box, ''Grain Production in the European Economic Community'').

Soil Productivity and Quality

Soil erosion can significantly reduce the productivity of agricultural lands by altering the physical characteristics of the soil, reducing its tilth and water-holding capacity. The magnitude of these changes' impacts on land productivity remains subject to debate, however. Scientists have limited

Grain Production in the European Economic Community

The nations that comprise the European Economic Community (EEC) have for centuries been both major consumers and major producers of grain. As recently as the 1960s, the EEC was a substantial net importer, because of the availability of low-cost corn and wheat from the United States, Canada, Argentina, and Australia. During the 1970s, however, an extremely generous agricultural policy administered by the EEC (the Common Agricultural Policy, or CAP) kept high tariffs on imported grain while holding prices to domestic producers at very attractive levels.[1] Europe's farmers boosted production in response. By the early 1980s, the EEC was still importing large quantities of U.S. soybeans and feed grains,[2] but it was producing more wheat and flour than it consumed —and disposing of it by subsidized sales in the world market.[3]

Sudsidized grain production in Europe has induced major changes in rural land use. Large areas of land formerly considered too steep, too infertile, or too wet for crop production have been put to the plow. In the United Kingdom, for example, the land area classified as "rough grazing," and hence unsuitable for crop use, declined by two million acres between 1961 and 1972 and by another four million acres between 1972 and 1980.[4] This land has been described as

ill-drained and so wet that cattle might only be turned out on it in high summer, pretty useless for hay, requiring tons of lime and probably only fit for a few sheep—such was a typical acre of that rough grazing. In twenty years, those seven million acres of poor land have been transformed into agriculture's tillage: wheat, barley, sugar beet and other crops that can only prosper on improved soil.[5]

In the Netherlands, the area of pasture went down by almost 250,000 acres between 1974-76 and 1983; in France, by 2.1 million.[6]

In general, land in crops remained relatively constant during the 1970s. Rather than augmenting the total stock of cropland, the pastureland newly put to the plow offset cropland that was converted to other uses, including urban or built-up uses.[7]

High grain prices (as well as high labor costs) also made mechanization attractive and encouraged expansion of the scale of production in the EEC. Traditional field configurations, some of which dated back to the Middle Ages, were enlarged and made rectangular to accommodate big, new equipment.[8] Average field sizes rose sharply, hedgerows were bulldozed, and small wetland areas drained.[9] High crop prices also encouraged heavier use of purchased inputs, such as fertilizers and pesticides.[10] For example, in West Germany, use of such inputs doubled between 1960 and 1980.[11] For the EEC as a whole, consumption of nitrogenous fertilizers rose by 55 percent between 1970 and 1983; by comparison, the rise for the United States over the same period was 37 percent.[12]

These subsidy-induced changes in European agriculture have had serious impacts on the environment. One effect has been reduction in wildlife habitat, associated with the plowing of rough areas, elimination of hedgerows and field margins, and increased crop monoculture. A study by England's Nature Conservancy Council compared unmodernized farms with hedges and seminatural grass verges with modernized farms with wire fences and sown grass. The unmodernized farms had 20 species of mammals, 37 species of birds, and 17 of butterflies; on the modernized farms, the equivalent numbers were 5, 6, and 0.[13] Related effects have been a reduction in traditional recreational access to the countryside (due to increased field size and the closing of footpaths) and a general reduction in visual variety in the rural landscape.[14] Europe's expanding agriculture also has encouraged the draining of wetlands (sometimes aided by direct subsidies from the EEC or national governments). The result has been loss of habitat for waterfowl and for anadromous fish, such as salmon.[15]

Greater use of agrichemicals has led to serious problems of water pollution. Perhaps the most serious problem is the contamination of drinking water supplies with nitrates, most of it associated with increased use of nitrogenous fertilizers.[16] High nitrate levels in water have been identified as a cause of methemoglobinemia in bottle-fed infants ("blue-baby syndrome") and have a theoretical link to human cancers.[17] The EEC has adopted a standard specifying that drinking water should not exceed a level of 11.3 milligrams per liter of nitrate as nitrogen. It has been reported that approximately 2 percent of the population of France and 8 to 9 percent of West Germans receive water exceeding the standard.[18] In the United Kingdom, a recent report by the Royal Commission on Environmental Pollution expressed concern over a continuing rise since the early 1970s in nitrate levels in some surface and groundwaters.[19]

Europe's drinking water has also been found to contain agricultural pesticides. For example, in 1985, groundwater in the province of Drenthe in the Netherlands was found to be polluted with 1,2-dichloropropane, a secondary ingredient in a pesticide used by farmers as a soil disinfectant.[20]

Pressure appears to be growing in Europe both to reduce the negative environmental impacts of agriculture and to cut the high cost of the CAP's subsidies to farmers. A promising approach to both problems would be to shift from supporting farm product prices to programs that would directly support farmers' incomes and would help marginal producers to leave agriculture. This would reduce the incentive for overproduction of subsidized products. It would probably result in reduced grain production in the EEC (creating marketing opportunities for the United States and other low-cost producers), but the removal of land from grain production might also lead to more production of dairy products and grass-fed meat, products that Europe can produce cheaply.

Another policy that is the subject of increasing interest in Europe is to give direct payments to farmers who manage their land to aid wildlife, recreation, or visual amenity. The idea, as one European expert put it, is that "if taxpayers are not interested in paying more and more for food surpluses, they may be prepared to pay to contribute to the cost of keeping the countryside attractive."[21] An EEC directive that came in force in 1985 allows member states to designate "Environmentally Sensitive Areas" within which farmers will be offered annual revenue payments in return for farming in a way that benefits landscape, wildlife, or archeology.[22] Yet other ideas are a tax on fertilizer and a restriction on application of fertilizers in areas where groundwater pollution is likely.[23]

data with which to evaluate the extent to which the yield-reducing effects of erosion and other processes may have been offset or masked by the use of fertilizers, higher yielding crop varieties, and other technologies.[73]

Productivity impacts from erosion are very site specific. Most studies show that the impacts are slight on most cropland, primarily because erosion rates are very low and soils are fairly thick. However, on certain cropland, particularly where high erosion rates correspond to relatively shallow soils, impacts can be dramatic.

Some recent analyses suggest that erosion's aggregate impact on national average crop yields likely will be less than 5 percent over 50 years, with estimates ranging from 2 percent over 30 years[74] to 10 percent over 100.[75] These estimates are conservative, however, because they assume that fertilizers, energy, irrigation, and other inputs will be economically available to farmers to offset damage that erosion may have caused to natural soil productivity.

Although some erosion of the soil by wind and water is natural, common agricultural practices accelerate soil displacement. The potential for erosion almost always increases when land is converted from less intensive uses, such as pasture or forest, to crop production; in an annual crop regime, growing vegetation no longer provides the soil with year-round protection from rain and wind. For example, according to the 1982 National Resources Inventory (NRI), sheet-and-rill erosion on cultivated cropland averages 4.8 tons per acre per year, compared to 1.4 tons per acre on pastureland and 0.7 tons per acre per year on ungrazed forestland.[76] (An erosion rate of 5 tons per acre per year represents about one one-thirtieth of an inch of soil per acre.[77])

Once land has been brought into production, the potential for erosion depends largely on the crop and the farming practices used to grow it. Among major crops (in terms of area planted), cotton has the highest average annual erosion rate, followed by soybeans, corn, wheat, and other small grains.[78] Cotton and soybeans have higher rates because fields tend to be extensively tilled and because both crops produce small amounts of vegetation to protect the soil.[79] Erosion rates for a specific crop such as corn can vary enormously on identical soils, depending on how much the soil is disturbed by the planting technique and on the amount of corn crop mulch or "residue" that remains on the soil surface after harvest. A soil may have an average annual erosion rate of 50 tons per acre per year when planted to corn three or more years in a row and thoroughly tilled. However, planting corn on identical land using no-till equipment, which leaves the soil virtually undisturbed, would reduce soil erosion to only 2 tons per acre annually.[80]

The export boom of the 1970s saw substantial increases in the United States in the acreage planted to corn, soybeans, and other row crops associated with above-average rates of soil erosion.[81] According to the 1982 NRI, sheet-and-rill erosion on land in row crops averages 6.1 tons per acre per year, 27 percent higher than the average rate for all cultivated cropland.[82]

What constitutes "excessive erosion" and "highly erodible lands" is open to debate. Most current definitions rely on erosion rates, often in relation to the "soil loss tolerance" (or "T") value. Tolerance values are considered rough indicators of the sensitivity of soils to productivity damage. Though they do not reflect off-site damage, they generally are considered to be the best currently available criteria for field applications.[83]

Figure 6.7 indicates the location of "highly erodible cropland" under one definition—land eroding in excess of three times the established T value. Under this and most definitions, the greatest concentrations of highly erodible cropland are found in the Corn Belt and Plains regions. The 69.5 million acres eroding at rates greater than "3-T" comprise about 17 percent of all cropland as defined by the Soil Conservation Service (a total of 421 million acres, including all land in grains, soybeans, specialty crops such as fruits and vegetables, and land used for hay or temporary pasture).[84]

Highly erodible land has received particular attention from policy makers in recent years because soil erosion has been found to be highly concentrated—a small proportion of the acreage in most categories of land use accounts for a large share of the total soil displacement. For example, of the 325 million acres of cropland planted to row crops and "close-grown" crops (small grains such as wheat), 7 percent accounts for 41 percent (700 million tons) of the total tonnage of soil displaced by sheet-and-rill erosion.[85] Similarly, about 5 percent of the land in row and close-grown crops accounts for 50 percent (555 million tons) of the total tonnage of wind erosion on land planted to these crops.[86]

Modern agricultural machinery also affects soil productivity and quality. Compaction of soils, caused by the impact of large tractors, pesticide-spraying trucks, crop combines, and other field equipment, can damage land productivity by creating dense layers of soil at or below the land surface, which impede root growth, water flow, and circulation of soil gases.[87] The magnitude of compaction's effects on productivity nationwide is not known, but in some areas, particularly the sandy soils of the Atlantic Coastal Plain, compaction can reduce yields sharply. Alleviating this problem often requires

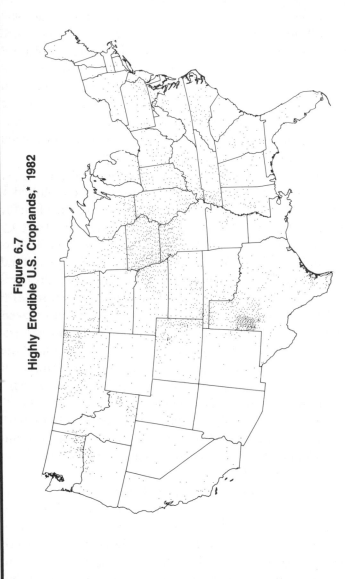

Figure 6.7
Highly Erodible U.S. Croplands,* 1982

Each dot represents 25,000 acres.

*Cropland eroding in excess of three times the established soil-loss tolerance rate ("T value").

Source: Soil Conservation Service.

costly deep plowing (''subsoiling'') to break up the compacted subsurface soil layer.[88]

Another concern is that modern cropping systems, which make heavy use of fertilizers and pesticides, may adversely affect soil biota by reducing their diversity and the size of their populations.[89] Soil microorganisms play important roles in cycling nutrients and in stabilizing soil structure in ways that foster plant growth.[90] Alteration of microbial populations from applications of farm chemicals is poorly understood but could undermine natural soil fertility and quality.

Surface-Water Pollution

As industries and municipalities succeed in cleaning up their wastewater discharges, nonpoint sources have become the major source of water pollution in many parts of the United States.[91] Reports by state water-pollution-control officials identify nonpoint sources as the primary reason that many streams still are not satisfying water-quality standards.[92]

Although the impact of soil erosion on soil productivity has been debated for years, the magnitude of its off-site effects is only beginning to be recognized. Soil particles, fertilizers, pesticides, animal wastes, and other substances washed off the land with the sediment can cause a large range of in-stream and off-stream problems after they enter waterways. Deposition of contaminants from the atmosphere can further degrade water quality. Recent, comprehensive studies by The Conservation Foundation indicate that pollution of surface water by sediments from farm fields costs society billions of dollars annually.[93]

In-stream damages are those caused by the pollutants in streams, lakes, and estuaries. They include damages to aquatic organisms, water-based recreation, water-storage facilities, and navigation. Aquatic ecosystems can be seriously affected by sediment and other attached contaminants. Sedimentation can destroy spawning areas, food sources, and habitat, while suspended sediments can directly damage fish and other aquatic wildlife. Algal growth stimulated by nutrients can block sunlight. Pesticides and other contaminants carried off agricultural lands can be directly toxic to fish.[94] A study by the U.S. Fish and Wildlife Service in association with the EPA identified agricultural sources as the primary cause of water-quality problems adversely affecting fish life in nearly 30 percent of stream miles across the United States. In about 17 percent of the stream miles, agricultural sources of pollution were considered a ''major concern.''[95] Other reports have identified agricultural runoff as a major cause of fish kills in U.S. waters.[96]

All types of water-based recreational activities are likely to be adversely affected by agricultural pollutants. The value of freshwater fishing is reduced because such pollutants can reduce fish populations and cause game fish such as trout to be replaced by low-value species.[97] Fishing is also less successful in turbid water because the fish have difficulty seeing lures.[98] Some of the same problems affect marine recreational fishing. Many marine species reproduce in estuaries or rivers, and, as the deterioration of Chesapeake Bay has demonstrated, they can be severely affected by water-quality problems in these locations.[99] In addition, boating and swimming are affected by siltation and weed growth.

Damages to water-storage facilities from sedimentation may become increasingly important because of the increasing cost and diminishing availability of new water-storage capacity in the United States. An estimated 1.4 to 1.5 million acre-feet of reservoir and lake capacity is permanently filled each year with sediment.[100] This capacity eventually will have to be replaced, and the construction costs probably will be much higher than the cost of current capacity. Currently, approximately one million acre-feet of storage capacity, costing $300 to $700 per acre-foot, is being built annually solely for the purpose of storing sediment.[101]

Other types of in-stream impacts of soil erosion include the degradation of lakes, siltation in navigation channels, impacts on commercial fisheries, and the psychological costs of dirty water. The United States spends over $500 million per year removing sediment from its harbors and waterways.[102] Much of this sediment is due to agricultural soil erosion.

Off-stream damages are those that occur before the sediment or contaminants reach a waterway, during floods, or after water is taken from a waterway to be used by industries, municipalities, or farms.[103] Sediment can cause problems in water-conveyance facilities, because some of the sediment settles out in drainage ditches before water actually reaches waterways. Each year in Illinois, for example, highway crews remove from drainage ditches sediment equal in amount to 1.4 percent of the total erosion occurring in the state.[104] The other significant cost for conveyance facilities is the annual maintenance cost of removing sediment and controlling weed growth in the 110,000 miles of irrigation canals in the United States.[105]

Sediment also contributes to flood damages in three ways. First, by causing the aggradation of streambeds, it increases the frequency and depth of flooding. Second, because suspended sediment is carried with the floodwater, the volume of the water/soil mixture is increased. And, third, many flood damages are caused by the sediment, not the water itself.[106] There are also some long-term effects to agricultural land if floods leave behind either more fertile (as in the Nile River Valley)[107] or less fertile (as in some parts of the southeastern United States)[108] silt than the original soil.

The costs of treating water for municipal and industrial uses increase because sedimentation basins must be built, chemical coagulants added, filters cleaned more frequently, and, in extreme cases, activated charcoal filters and other devices added to remove pesticides and other dissolved contaminants.[109] Treating water, however, does not eliminate all the costs to off-stream users. For instance, water-treatment facilities do not remove dissolved salts contributed by agricultural sources. These are estimated to cause $80 million in damages annually to municipal and industrial users in the lower Colorado River basin alone.[110] Nutrients and algae in the water also can cause steam-electric power plants to operate less efficiently.

Figure 6.8 summarizes The Conservation Foundation's estimates of what erosion-related pollutants are costing the United States annually. For each category, a range of costs is given, followed by a single value within that range that represents a best guess of the magnitude of the damages. The final column indicates the amount of these damages that can be attributed to cropland erosion.

Figure 6.8
Summary of Damage Costs
(in million 1980 dollars)

Type of impact	Range of estimates	Single-value estimate	Cropland's share
In-stream effects			
Biological impacts		no estimate	
Recreational	$ 950– 5,600	$2,000	$ 830
Water-storage facilities	310– 1,600	690	220
Navigation	420– 800	560	180
Other in-stream uses	460– 2,500	900	320
Subtotal—In-stream (rounded)	$2,100– 10,000	$4,200	$1,600
Off-stream effects			
Flood damages	$ 440– 1,300	$ 770	$ 250
Water-conveyance facilities	140– 300	200	100
Water-treatment facilities	50– 500	100	30
Other off-stream uses	400– 920	800	280
Subtotal—Off-stream (rounded)	$1,100– 3,100	$1,900	$ 660
Total—all effects (rounded)	**$3,200– 13,000**	**$6,100**	**$2,200**

Source: Original Conservation Foundation research.

A recent analysis by Resources for the Future (RFF) concludes that cropland erosion is responsible for over one-third of the sediment, 30 percent of the phosphorus, and 40 percent of the nitrogen entering the nation's waterways. Pastureland and rangeland combined are responsible for another 13 to 17 percent of these pollutants.[111]

At present, it is difficult to assess directly how future changes in the extensiveness and intensity of agricultural production may affect surface-water pollution. The Conservation Foundation and RFF studies document the difficulty of pinpointing the origin of nonpoint pollution from cropland. Water pollution from sediment and farm chemicals is highly site-specific; no general relationship has been established between upland erosion rates or cultivated land area and off-farm water quality impacts. However, three factors that influence sediment damage are subject to locational changes in agricultural production. The closer agricultural production is to a water body, the greater the chance it will result in increased sediment delivery. Exposure and erosion of soils composed mainly of silt and clay particles will also tend to increase the potential for sediment transport. Broad watersheds with flat floodplains usually deliver less sediment than narrow, steep watersheds.[112] Off-site damages from erosion might be mitigated by policies that encourage less intensive use of such land that is already in production, and by policies that discourage conversion of more such land to crop use in the future.

Agricultural practices can also damage water quality through atmospheric deposition of sediment and chemicals.[113] Pesticides, particularly when sprayed from airplanes, can drift off-site and contaminate water bodies. Wind-blown soil particles that carry attached chemicals may end up being deposited in lakes and other undesirable places.

Perhaps the most dramatic example of atmospheric deposition from agriculture is the case of toxaphene, previously a major cotton insecticide. Most uses of toxaphene were canceled by EPA in 1982, when it was found that large amounts of the chemical vaporized upon application and were transported in the upper atmosphere from the southern United States to the Great Lakes. The agency estimated that 3,360 to 6,720 kilograms of toxaphene were deposited into Lake Michigan in 1981, and elevated concentrations of the chemical—a suspected carcinogen—were found in fish.[114]

Groundwater Quantity and Quality

Agriculture is responsible for quantity and quality problems in the nation's groundwater. Pumping groundwater for irrigation use has resulted in significant drawdown problems in many aquifers. Such overpumping not only makes continued irrigation more expensive but may also disrupt water supplies for homes, businesses, and municipalities and decrease flows in surface streams during low rainfall periods.[115] Contaminated groundwater may require treatment before human consumption is considered safe or simply may be restricted for certain human, animal, or crop uses.

To the extent that water is recharged to aquifers in agricultural areas, it may carry with it nitrates, pesticides, salts, bacteria, and other dissolved contaminants that potentially could cause serious groundwater pollution problems.[116] Of these, nitrogen fertilizers and soluble pesticides appear to represent the greatest threats. The potential for chemical contamination of groundwater depends primarily on a chemical's properties (for example, solubility and sorption), the application rate and method, site characteristics, and climate.[117] Further, efforts to control surface runoff may exacerbate the tendency for water and its associated chemicals to percolate into groundwater aquifers.

The historical and continued use of nitrogen fertilizers in particular threatens groundwater supplies in much of the United States. Numerous studies demonstrate a relationship between nitrate concentrations in groundwater and nitrogen fertilization rates or fertilization history.[118] In the recent national nonpoint-source assessment coordinated by the Association of State and Interstate Water Pollution Control Administrators (ASIWPCA), 34 states reported known contamination of groundwater by nitrates, and 4 others reported suspected contamination.[119] The continued buildup of nitrate reservoirs in soils raises concerns about future groundwater threats.

Evidence of pesticide contamination of groundwater is mounting as well. Recent information indicates that at least 17 pesticides have been found in groundwater in 23 states as a result of agricultural practices.[120] The most noteworthy examples are Aldicarb in New York, Florida, and Wisconsin; EDB (ethylene dibromide) in Florida; and DBCP (dibromochloropropane) in California.[121] Increased monitoring efforts and capabilities continue to provide new information on the types and degree of pesticide contamination of groundwater supplies.

High salt concentrations in groundwater can result from irrigation.[122] In many arid regions, both the water and the soil have elevated salt concentrations. Irrigation can increase these levels when evapotranspiration removes pure water from the irrigation flow, leaving behind the dissolved solids (salts). This process can cause salts to build up, potentially reducing crop yields. Irrigators prevent this from occurring by applying sufficient amounts of water to flush the accumulated salts through the root zone.

Severe degradation of groundwater can result from such practices, depending on local conditions.[123] Chemigation, the application of agrichemicals directly with irrigation water, is a practice being increasingly adopted, raising more concerns about dangers to groundwater.[124] Groundwater contamination can result not only from excess irrigation water seeping into the ground but also from the chemicals being sucked down the wells when the irrigation system is turned off.[125]

Groundwater contamination and depletion problems are directly related to both the intensity of land use and the amount of land used for crop production. During the 1970s, production of cash grains and soybeans became more intensive and extensive in response to high market prices for crops, almost certainly increasing groundwater contamination and depletion. In the 1980s, despite the decline of U.S. exports, production of these crops has remained high, primarily as a result of expansion of land area, favorable weather, and incremental improvements in crop varieties. Use of pesticides, fertilizer, and irrigation water remains high, even though it has not increased sharply. A resurgence of export demand and high commodity prices probably would trigger more intensive and extensive crop production. Even while major crops are in surplus, however, groundwater resources continue to be exposed to degradation and drawdown.

Destruction of Wildlife Habitat

Often the most immediate effect of converting land to agricultural uses is the destruction of its value as wildlife habitat. Since its settlement, hundreds of millions of acres of forest, native grasslands, and wetlands have been converted to crop and livestock use in the United States. Overall, the rate of net conversion of U.S. land to cropland has slowed a great deal, though important, remaining wild areas are still threatened. However, in the developing world, especially Latin America, agricultural expansion is playing a major role in the destruction of wildlands (see boxes, " Beef Cattle Production in Central America" and "Soybean Production in Brazil").

Of particular concern in the United States is the threat agriculture poses to some of the estimated 95 million remaining acres of wetlands in the nation's coterminous 48 states.[126] Wetlands provide habitat for important commercial and recreational fish species, many species of waterfowl, fur-bearing animals, and endangered species. Inventories conducted by the U.S. Fish and Wildlife Service show that agriculture accounted for 87 percent of the 458,000 acres of wetlands lost each year between the mid-1950s and mid-1970s.[127] Much of this conversion occurred in the Mississippi Delta and Southeast regions of the country, where most of the converted wetlands

Beef Cattle Production in Central America

The raising of beef cattle on pastures created from cleared tropical forestland has been called "the single greatest cause of deforestation" in much of Central America.[1] It is also "widely considered to be the most environmentally damaging of all deforestation activities."[2] Central American cattle producers typically begin with a piece of cleared land abandoned by slash-and-burn agriculturalists after one or two seasons of cultivation. Formerly, this land would have been allowed to revert to forest, replenishing its nutrients for a subsequent cycle of clearing and cultivation. The cattle raiser, however, uses cattle to glean the remaining nutritional value available from either naturally occurring grasses or planted species (often introduced varieties from Africa). Often the grazing continues until the land is so depleted of nutrients and so badly eroded that it can no longer naturally regenerate as forest, even after its eventual abandonment. Because of this destructive quality, new forests must be cleared annually, even when cattle numbers are not expanding.

During the late 1970s, a controversy arose over what came to be called the "hamburger connection." It was charged that expansion of Central America's cattle industry—and the attendant clearing of tropical forests—was largely due to the growing demand by U.S. fast-food chains for grass-fed beef that could be made into hamburger patties and other processed convenience foods.[3] U.S.-based environmental groups were particularly concerned about the fact that Central American cattle raising had been aided by loans from the World Bank and the Interamerican Development Bank, international institutions over which the U.S. government wields considerable influence.

Prior to 1970, Central American cattle raising was concentrated in the relatively fertile Pacific coastal region. But increased cattle numbers and a rise in use of land on the Pacific side for food and cotton production have caused much of the industry's expansion to occur in the sparsely inhabited rain forests of the Caribbean slope.[4] Although data clearly support the contention that Central American cattle raising is both environmentally destructive and increasing in magnitude, the strength of the U.S. "connection" appears to be waning over time. In 1979, the United States imported some 228 million pounds of beef and veal from Central America, up more than 80 percent from 1970. But this was to represent the peak year for U.S. imports from the region; by 1984 they were only 91 million pounds, below the level of 1970.[5] Although some of the decline can be attributed to the Nicaraguan revolution, very large declines also took place in Costa Rica, Honduras, and Guatemala. The continued increase in cattle in Central America seems to be in response to growing demand from within the region, not to increased exports to the United States.

Much the same process seems to be taking place in Mexico, where growing domestic population and changing urban dietary patterns are putting strong pressures both on northern rangelands and on the tropical forests of Veracruz and Chiapas in the south.[6] Brazil has in recent years sharply increased its beef exports, some of which come from tropical forest areas, but very little of this meat is destined for the United States.[7]

Soybean Production in Brazil

At the beginning of the 1970s, Brazil annually produced 1.5 million metric tons of soybeans, or 5 percent of the amount produced in the United States.[1] By 1984, Brazil's output had multiplied tenfold, to 16.2 million tons, or 32 percent of what the United States currently produces.[2] More than two-thirds of Brazil's annual production is exported (mainly as soybean meal).[3] The United States, which once had the world soybean market virtually to itself, now faces a potent new competitor.

During the early years (1969-79) of Brazil's soybean expansion, most of the new production came from the country's southernmost states, Rio Grande do Sul, Santa Catarina, Sao Paulo, and Parana. These were traditional agricultural regions, and soybeans took over lands previously devoted to other crops. In the far South, farmers often began double-cropping soybeans with wheat, a practice that is also common in the southern reaches of the U.S. Corn Belt.

Since 1979, however, virtually all the increase in Brazilian output has come from the central and western interior of the country, principally the states of Goias, Mato Grosso, and Rondonia.[4] Much of the land going into production there is *cerrado*, a local term used for a variety of wooded grassland formations from open canopy forests to savannah-like areas with considerable amounts of low, brushy vegetation. Most had never before been plowed, having been considered too infertile for cultivation. *Cerrado* soils have limitations, but, once they have been treated with large quantities of lime and phosphorus, they have proven capable of high crop yields.[5]

Unlike Europe's wheat production, Brazil's soybean growing is not heavily subsidized. The expansion in the *cerrado* depends on the availability of large amounts of land and on energetic farmers, many of them medium-sized cultivators from the south.

The environmental effects of increased cultivation of the *cerrado* are not well documented. But some observers believe they might be substantial. "The *cerrado* is a top priority conservation area," says Russell Mittermeier of World Wildlife Fund (U.S.). "It occupies 28 percent of Brazil's land area but has not received sufficient attention in the past. Much work needs to be done to establish a representative network of protected areas while the opportunities still exist." Although soil erosion rates have not been documented for the region as a whole, the conversion of land from brushy savannah to soybeans would tend to increase the potential for erosion. Waterways in the region may already be affected by agrichemical pollution.[6]

Soybean farmers have reached the borders of Brazil's Emas National Park, created to protect important populations of endangered pampas deer, giant anteaters, armadillos, rheas, and other animals. Once buffered by vegetation identical to that within its boundaries, the park is now bordered on two sides by soybean fields and on a third by grazing land. Few of the species protected by the park are able to survive in cultivated fields; moreover, chemical and sediment runoff from the fields might pollute watercourses flowing through the park.[7]

The expansion of soybean production in southern Brazil may also have an important indirect impact on the environment outside of the *cerrado*. The conversion of cropland in Brazil's

south-central region from labor-inten-
sive crops such as coffee to mechanized soybean and wheat production is
displacing many traditional small
farmers and workers. Many of these
poor farming families migrate toward
the Amazon region in search of new
and cheaper land.[8] These new arrivals
are increasing pressure on resources
in the Amazon.

were planted to soybeans.[128] Currently, wetlands conversion is estimated
to be occuring at a pace of 300,000 to 450,000 acres per year.[129]

According to the 1982 National Resources Inventory, only 5.1 million
of the 70.7 million acres of nonfederal freshwater (''palustrine'') wetlands
were rated as having a high or medium potential for conversion to cropland.[130] However, recent analyses indicate that conversion might be economically attractive on a much larger acreage. Based on their estimated yields
and crop prices equal to season average market prices in 1985, some 13.8
million wetland acres may be profitable to drain. At higher price levels,
equal to target prices for commodity programs in 1985-86, revenue would
be sufficient to cover production and land treatment costs on an estimated
22.7 million acres of wetlands.[131]

In addition, agricultural expansion has destroyed riparian vegetation zones
in numerous locations. The removal of riparian vegetation not only directly
harms wildlife that inhabit those areas but also upsets normal patterns of
light, temperature, and dissolved oxygen in streams. Particularly in head-
waters, stream fishes like trout, which require cold water, can be replaced
by warmwater fish communities if riparian vegetation is removed.[132] Cattle
production can also cause substantial damage to these riparian areas as the
cattle concentrate in areas of the most plentiful supplies of vegetation and
water, depleting streambank vegetation and destabilizing and trampling
the streambanks themselves.[133] One observer identifies livestock grazing
as the greatest threat to the integrity of trout-stream habitat in the western
United States.[134]

Air Pollution

Agriculture's major contribution to air pollution is the dust resulting from
wind erosion. Cropland is estimated to be the major agricultural land
use contributing to wind erosion losses,[135] with air pollution from eroded
soil being related to the type of crop, cultivation practices, and the area
planted. The most severe problems probably are being experienced in
the Great Plains, particularly in Texas, Montana, and Colorado.[136] However, current estimates of wind erosion losses provided by the 1982 NRI

do not include wind erosion from the 307 million acres of federally owned rangeland in the western United States, much of which is also highly susceptible to wind erosion.[137]

Dust particles can carry fertilizers and pesticides, and some of these chemicals volatilize directly into the atmosphere. Over 50 percent of pesticides can be lost due to drift and volatilization from some pesticide application techniques.[138] In addition, air filters on various types of equipment require more frequent replacement because of wind-blown dust, and businesses that require a dust-free environment, such as those producing or assembling electronic or precision equipment, may experience increased filtration costs or increased maintenance costs.

Human Health Risks

Agricultural chemicals inevitably move through the natural environment to points that pose risks to humans from one or more exposure pathways— food consumption, drinking, inhalation, or dermal contact. The greatest health risks are apparently posed by nitrates in drinking water and pesticides in drinking water, food, and the atmosphere. The risks of pesticide poisoning via dermal contact can be very serious, mainly affecting pesticide applicators or those who enter application sites soon after the pesticides' use.

The seriousness of nitrate contamination of drinking water is unclear. One recent review of groundwater quality showed that about 20 percent of all wells in the United States showed elevated nitrate concentrations, indicating that the wells had been affected by human activities.[139] A 10 milligram per liter nitrate-nitrogen standard continues to be widely used as a benchmark for protecting human health.[140] However, the significance of nitrate levels can be addressed only in terms of *total* exposure—viewing the health risk of nitrates in groundwater to humans or animals both in the context of the amount consumed over time and in relationship to the concentrations of nitrates from other sources of exposure, such as food. One principal concern is methemoglobinemia, which can be fatal to infants;[141] more recently, nitrates in groundwater also have been identified as a potential cancer threat.[142]

Pesticides can potentially pose both acute (immediate) and chronic risks to human health. Several factors can affect pesticides' impact on human health. Technological change is especially important, because new chemicals may pose greater or less risk to human health than existing chemicals pose. Contamination of groundwater and surface water with pesticides is largely a function of persistence and solubility of the compounds, characteristics that are amenable to technological modification. Advances in application equipment and techniques can improve the efficiency of both fertilizer and pesticide use; less waste of these chemicals usually means less risk to the environment. In addition to technology, changes in the intensity of pesticide and fertilizer use, as well as in the area on which these materials are applied, affect human health by altering the quantity of the chemical introduced into the environment. Changes in quantity in turn affect the level of human exposure to potentially harmful chemicals. For example, more intensive and extensive production of corn in northern Iowa over the past decade has exposed humans who drink from certain wells to elevated levels of nitrates and pesticides.[143]

Pesticide residues can be found all over the globe, even in locations remote from the site of application. Because pesticides are developed deliberately to interfere with biological processes, the risk to humans is an obvious concern. Pesticides may pose a risk directly to human receptors or indirectly via the food chain (for example, through plant uptake or fish contamination).

Surplus Production

Historically, stockpiling has been an important means of coping with the inherent unpredictability of agricultural production. Indeed, the federal government has encouraged the accumulation of stocks as a matter of policy. However, because of high production and declining exports, the United States has accumulated excessive stocks of corn and wheat relative to total national needs (domestic and export use and emergency needs) during most of the 1980s. The government's policy reduces the economic risks to which farmers are exposed in a fickle international grain market.

Under the Food Security Act of 1985, USDA is now required to implement production controls whenever ending stocks of corn exceed 2.0 billion bushels and ending stocks of wheat exceed 1.0 billion bushels, amounts considered to be sufficient to meet domestic, export, and emergency needs from one crop season to the next.[144] For 1986, ending stocks of corn equaled 5.3 billion bushels; for wheat, the figure was 1.8 billion bushels. Conservation Foundation calculations[145] estimate residual stocks in 1986 at equivalent to 31.3 million acres of excess corn production and 22 million acres of excess wheat production.

In simplest terms, in 1986, U.S. farmers planted about 40 percent too much corn acreage and 30 percent too much wheat, even though production controls were in effect for both crops. The resulting crop surpluses cost farmers by causing depressed crop prices and reduced net farm income. The same surpluses boosted government commodity program expenditures to record levels, costing taxpayers tens of billions of dollars.[146]

But crop surpluses also represent an elevated risk of environmental impacts from the extra use of nitrogen and phosphate fertilizers and of pesticides, especially herbicides and insecticides. In 1986, U.S. corn and wheat farmers used an excess of 7.3 billion pounds of fertilizer and 110 million pounds of pesticides.

Clearly, U.S. production of corn and wheat has been poorly matched to total national needs since 1980; to varying degrees, the same can be said of rice, cotton, and other crops. It is reasonable to infer that excess production in the 1980s has also increased the risk of other types of damage to resources and the environment. National needs for corn, wheat, and other crops could have been met with less extensive use of cropland that is highly erodible, contributes to off-site sediment and runoff damages, or is subject to groundwater depletion, contamination, or salinity.

Dairy products also are produced in the U.S. in amounts far in excess of national needs, and, unlike most crops, they are not exported to a significant extent. As with crops, however, government price support programs have had a major influence on dairy production levels. Government-owned stocks of dairy products (powdered milk, butter, and cheese) have been acquired and stored at a cost of roughly $2 billion annually since the early 1980s. Stocks at the end of fiscal year 1986 reached 9.8 billion pounds of milk equivalent.[147]

The environmental effects of dairy production, like grain production, are complex. Dairy operations can be important sources of water pollution from animal wastes. But to the extent that the dairy price support program may have helped to slow the rate of decline in the number of dairy farms, it may also have reduced somewhat certain risks to resources and the environment. Dairy enterprises are located throughout the country but centered in the upper Midwest and the Northeast, many in hilly landscapes characterized by erodible, often shallow soils. Crop rotations on dairy farms commonly include soil-conserving pasture, hay, and small grains, as well as corn. Dairy production continued with the help of government programs may therefore help protect fragile land that might otherwise be planted to erosion-prone, continuous cash grains. Generally, dairy-type crop rotations are associated with lower use of fertilizers (particularly if cow manure is spread on fields) and pesticides.

COPING WITH UNCERTAINTY: ADJUSTMENT STRATEGIES FOR U.S. AGRICULTURE AND THE ENVIRONMENT

Adjustment is a term that has been in the lexicon of U.S. agricultural policy since the New Deal, when Congress passed several ''agricultural adjustment acts'' to deal with desperately low commodity prices, chronic surpluses, and dire economic hardship in farm country. Even in the 1930s, policy makers saw connections between economic adjustment in agriculture and what was then viewed as the major resource conservation problem facing the nation—soil erosion. The bold, ''emergency'' step of reducing crop surpluses by paying farmers to take land out of production was justified, in part, on grounds that soil erosion would be reduced. To some extent, that justification has been invoked ever since for various types of ''production adjustment'' programs, from the Soil Bank of the 1950s and 1960s to the payment-in-kind (PIK) program of 1983.[148]

In the late 1980s, the prevailing direction of adjustment is down. Production, it is said, must adjust to decreased demand; crop prices must adjust downward to boost exports; farmland prices and rental rates must adjust to the lower earning capacity of the land; farm lenders must adjust to losses in their loan portfolios; farmers must adjust to narrower profit margins, lower incomes and net worth, and less government support. Sometimes, adjustment spells bankruptcy and foreclosure for farmers who had been in healthy financial condition just a few years earlier.

Federal Commodity Programs

Programs to support commodity prices and transfer income to the farm sector have long been the centerpiece of U.S. farm policy. Traditionally, these programs have served to insulate farmers from the effects of a market-based economy. With the adoption of the Food Security Act of 1985,[149] however, the federal government shifted its approach somewhat, toward more market-oriented programs.

Traditional Commodity Programs

Federal commodity programs played a modest role during the United States' export boom years. Between 1975 and 1981, direct government payments to farmers averaged $1.6 billion per year, equal to about 6 percent of total net farm income. However, when exports sagged, commodity program payments mushroomed. Between 1982 and 1986, government payments averaged over $8 billion, amounting to 31 percent of net farm income. In 1983, for every dollar of net farm income, farmers received 62 cents in government payments.[150] Total goverment costs for commodity programs are much higher, however, because they include the acquisition and storage costs associated with price support loans.

Although federal commodity programs are very complex, a general familiarity with their mechanics is required to understand the important effects they have on the agricultural economy and on resource use and environmental quality.* Three principal methods employed in U.S. farm programs benefit farmers by stabilizing prices and farm incomes while providing supplies to consumers at reasonable prices. First, farmers can offer their crops as collateral for "price support loans."[151] For example, in 1986, the loan rate established by USDA and Congress for wheat was $2.40 per bushel. The highest level was $3.65 per bushel in 1983.[152] The length of the loan period is usually nine months, and farmers may place as much of their crop as they want under loan. To receive the loan, the requisite amount of crop must be placed in storage. If market prices rise above the loan rate, farmers can repay their loans, sell the crop on the market, and pocket the differences. If prices remain equal to or somewhat below the loan rate, at the end of the loan period farmers can opt to keep the money they received from the government and forfeit their commodity collateral. The government "buys" the wheat, which by law it can resell only when market prices reach specified "release" levels that are more than double loan rates. Through this mechanism, the government acquires and accumulates stocks of wheat, corn, cotton, and other crops.

A second major program benefit is the "deficiency payment," a direct cash payment made to participating farmers.[153] Congress establishes "target prices" for wheat, corn, cotton, and other major crops (but not soybeans). From 1984 through 1987, the target price for wheat was set at $4.38 per bushel, but it was scheduled to start declining in 1988.[154] If market prices fall below the target price, program participants can receive the difference between the market and target price for every bushel they produce, up to their average "program" yield. The maximum payment (and maximum government exposure) is the difference between the target price and the loan rate—in the case of wheat, $1.98 per bushel in 1986.

Production controls are a third method by which the federal government assists agriculture.[155] In return for the benefits described above, farmers usually are required to control production by idling for one year a portion of the acreage they have planted to program crops in preceding years (their program "base acreage"). From 1979 through 1986, production controls ranged from 11 million to 78 million acres, with no controls in effect for two of those years (1980 and 1981).[156] Two types of production controls are used. The first is the "acreage reduction program" (formerly called "set-asides"), which requires commodity program participants to reduce

---

*The following discussion focuses on programs for major crops: wheat, corn and other feed grains, cotton, and soybeans.

plantings by a fixed percentage. In 1986, wheat farmers had to reduce wheat plantings by 22.5 percent.[157] Usually, farmers also idle additional acreage, for which they can receive a specified amount (a "paid diversion") of cash or PIK. Paid diversions are usually voluntary but were mandatory for upland cotton and rice in 1983 and 1985, for most other commodities in 1983 and 1986, and for wheat from 1983 through 1986.[158]

Because these programs usually are voluntary, benefit levels must be sufficiently attractive for farmers to willingly reduce plantings. The record 1983 acreage retirement programs offered substantial benefits—in the form of both direct cash payments and $9.4 billion in PIK commodities[159]—and some 78 million acres were idled, about one-fifth of all cropland used for crops in 1982.[160] By the fall of 1986, corn and wheat stocks were higher than those that prompted USDA to implement the extensive land-idling programs of 1983.[161]

Price support loan levels under these programs form a "price floor" under the U.S. market. That is, participating and nonparticipating farmers receive at least the loan amount when they sell their crops, regardless of their production levels. The minimum floor price also becomes the price of U.S. grain in world markets, and other exporting nations must generally sell below that price to compete with U.S. farmers. When export demand for U.S. grain is relatively weak, as it has been since 1982, market prices hover near the loan rate but never drop very far below it. U.S. farmers are thus insulated from the market and produce crops in response to program benefit levels, often retaining resources in production beyond the point that is economically or socially efficient. Excess production merely ends up in stocks owned by the government or by farmers. Competitors can then undercut the United States in world markets by selling commodities at a price just below the U.S. floor price.

Deficiency payments, together with price support loans and diversion payments, encourage continuous production of program crops, because the payments are directly proportional to program crop production. The more farmers produce, the higher their payments. Crop rotations that incorporate hay or pasture with corn, wheat, and other crops usually reduce erosion and utilize lesser amounts of agricultural chemicals. However, farmers who follow such rotations receive less support under program rules than farmers who maximize plantings of program crops year after year.

Through these programs, the U.S. taxpayer ends up bearing much of the burden of adjustment to fluctuations in world grain supply and demand. U.S. government- and farmer-owned stocks of wheat and corn comprise a substantial proportion of total world stocks. And the United States is the only grain-exporting nation that implements production controls to boost commodity prices and farmer incomes when international market demand is weak.[162]

Despite their good intentions, conventional production controls—the acreage reduction programs and paid diversions—do not reduce production in a very cost-effective manner.[163] This is partly because farmers purposely idle below-average land, while nonparticipating farmers expand production. Moreover, because (*a*) the idling requirement extends for only one year, (*b*) farmers are not required to plant cover crops, and (*c*) environmentally sensitive lands are not targeted, these conventional production controls also have limited benefits to resource conservation and the environment.

Market-Oriented Commodity Policy

The likelihood of continued unpredictability and volatility in world agricultural markets strongly influenced the development of the Food Security Act of 1985. In principle, the 1985 farm bill committed the United States to continued reliance on international markets for a large portion of commodity sales. But the law's general intent was to reduce the government role in agriculture, with farmers to bear more of the burden of adjusting to changing market demand and prices.

One of the major changes enacted in the 1985 farm bill was a scaling down of federal price support loan levels—the guaranteed minimum price a farmer could receive from the government for wheat, corn, cotton, and other crops for participating in federal commodity programs. The act reduced government support prices for these crops to between 75 and 85 percent of the season-average market price, beginning in 1988.[164] The goal was to make the United States more competitive in world markets, make the production decisions of U.S. farmers more sensitive to market demand rather than government program benefits, and, eventually, to reduce government outlays for commodity programs. Another consequence of low U.S. subsidies and prices was likely to be to increase the cost of export subsidies that other countries must provide to undercut the U.S. price in the world market. The European Economic Community, for example, was likely to have to increase export subsidies to undersell the United States in world wheat markets.

Predicting the environmental effects of lower, "market-oriented" domestic price support levels is difficult. Lands may no longer be profitable to farm under a lower price regime if they are inherently low-yielding (perhaps due to shallow or wet soils), require large amounts of fertilizers, or are irrigated. A portion of this land may be converted to crops other than cash grains or may be devoted to pasture or trees; some land may even be abandoned. One effect of the 1985 farm bill could thus be to diminish resource and environmental impacts of commodity programs, because marginal land would be used less intensively. Just how much land would be most sensitive to a low price regime is not known, however. A considerable portion of such land may be in the Southeast, where yields of corn, soybeans, and cotton often are below the national average and pest control and fertilizer costs are relatively high. An added complication in predicting the environmental effects of the bill's move toward a free market is that production costs per unit of production often vary among fields within a given farm, because the productivity of the fields varies. A farmer may or may not eliminate use of a ''high-cost'' field solely in response to lower prices. A free-market program would eliminate incentives for a farmer to retain high-cost marginal land in production, since such land could no longer be used to satisfy government production control requirements and qualify the farmer for farm program benefits.

The pace at which such high-cost land might be forced out of production is also unclear. As discussed earlier, farmers are much more likely to increase their production in response to rising prices than they are to decrease production when prices slide. Some analyses even suggest that the immediate effect of lower prices would be a temporary increase in cultivated land in some areas, as farmers seek to maintain their total incomes by offsetting lower per-acre earnings with more extensive plantings.

It is also likely that, even on fairly productive land, lower prices will cause some farm operators to be unable to earn an adequate income, particularly if their outstanding debt obligations are high. In such cases, farms probably will change hands as the result of forced (foreclosure) or voluntary sales, often becoming parts of larger farm operations. However, there is no evidence that such changes would result in significant changes in either cropping patterns or environmental impacts.

Movement toward a more market-oriented agricultural policy also has important implications for conservation initiatives contained in the 1985 farm act (discussed next).

Resource Conservation Initiatives

Since the 1930s, several farm programs have been enacted by the federal government in the name of resource conservation. Often, the actual underlying motivation has been the provision of price supports or income maintenance. With the passage of the Food Security Act of 1985, however, the government took a major step forward in placing concerns about resources and the environment in the mainstream of U.S. agricultural policy. Title XII of the act contained five new provisions linking USDA program benefits to broad resource conservation goals. These new policies and programs could play a significant role in adjusting agricultural production to fluctuating demand levels in the future.

Policies for Highly Erodible Cropland

The 1985 farm bill included a variety of new programs designed to minimize soil erosion on cropland currently in production. Among these were the Conservation Reserve Program, conservation compliance policy, and conservation easements.

Conservation Reserve Program. One of the most important new provisions of the 1985 farm bill was the Conservation Reserve Program (CRP).[165] Under this program, the secretary of agriculture is authorized between 1986 and 1990 to enter into contracts with farmers for the purpose of converting as much as 45 million acres of highly erodible cropland currently in production into less intensive uses such as grass and trees. The goal would be to reduce erosion, improve water quality, and enhance wildlife habitat. The secretary is empowered to allow land under reserve contract to be brought temporarily into crop production in times of national emergency. Otherwise, farmers who enroll in the CRP are prohibited from haying or grazing land enrolled in the reserve, though once their contracts expire they are allowed to harvest trees that were planted on the land. If a farmer violates or breaks a contract while it is in force, USDA is to require repayment of all rental and cost-share payments, with interest.

The farm act provided USDA with the discretion to take water-quality problems into account in determining land eligibility for the CRP. As of late 1986, however, the department had not specified criteria or guidelines for identifying land that contributes to sediment or other off-site damages, but is not highly erodible under the existing definition. USDA also had not utilized discretionary authority to open the CRP to land subject to salinity or to leaching of naturally occurring toxic elements.

USDA estimated that a 40-million-acre reserve of highly erodible cropland could result in annual reductions of roughly 750 million tons of eroded soil (equal to 29 percent of estimated cropland erosion occurring on land eroding above tolerable levels), 211 million tons of sediment reaching waterways (about 23 percent of estimated sediment from cropland), and 60 million pounds of pesticides (equal to 11 percent of total 1982 pesticide use on feed grains, wheat, soybeans, cotton, tobacco, rice, and peanuts).[166] With enrollment of between 40 and 45 million acres, corn, wheat, and soybean production would be reduced by an estimated 6 to 8 percent and cotton production by as much as 20 percent.[167]

USDA also estimated that its costs of the program in the form of annual rental and cost-share payments (to defray 50 percent of the cost of establishing grass or trees), would be more than offset by reduced costs for the department's commodity programs.[168] In effect, USDA viewed the CRP as partially replacing the need for annual production control programs, which produce limited environmental benefits.

The initial farmer response to the program was disappointing. For the 1986 crop year, farmer enrollment in the CRP was about 2 million acres, well below the legislation's goal of 5 million acres.[169] This was primarily because the maximum CRP rental payment bids accepted by USDA were far less than the benefits available under annual commodity programs.[170] However, CRP enrollment reached 9 million acres in 1986; in early 1987, USDA accepted bids on another 10.6 million acres.[171]

USDA's ability to meet the enrollment goals set by Congress in the 1985 act will be determined by the economic attractiveness of the CRP vis-à-vis the annual commodity programs and market prices for corn, wheat, and other commodities. Any surge in export demand and commodity prices could discourage CRP participation, though most experts expect market prices to remain fairly low through 1990. Commodity program benefits will be the more likely source of competition. At least in the CRP's initial years, those benefits were generally more attractive to farmers than the conservation reserve. In subsequent years, the act's schedule of lower target prices and loan rates was expected to reduce the economic gap between the two programs.

However, Congress usually reexamines omnibus farm legislation during its four-to-five-year cycle, in response to economic stress in the farm sector.[172] If that tradition is followed, large income transfers to agriculture may be retained, hampering the effectiveness of the conservation reserve, though potentially increasing the potency of another new farm bill provision, "conservation compliance" (discussed below). Alternatively, Congress or the executive branch could act to increase the economic attractiveness of the CRP.

A second major CRP issue will be land eligibility. On one hand, pressure to expand eligibility for the CRP, either to favor specific geographic areas or to enhance the program's supply control potential, could result in reduced environmental benefits. On the other hand, if appropriate guidelines can be devised, it might be possible to utilize the CRP to cope with nonpoint-source water pollution or other environmental problems.

The 1985 farm bill also authorized the secretary of agriculture to implement multi-year acreage reduction programs in lieu of the current programs. Should this authority be utilized, it would bind farmers to reduce production for more than one year at a time. From the vantage point of erosion control and environmental protection, multi-year production controls can be viewed as a middle-ground position between the CRP and annual programs.

Conservation Compliance Policy. A second major, long-term provision in the Food Security Act of 1985 for dealing with highly erodible cropland was conservation compliance.[173] This policy is a noteworthy departure from past approaches in government soil conservation efforts because it utilizes disincentives rather than incentives to motivate action on the part of farmers.

The conservation compliance policy requires farmers to begin implementing by 1990 an approved, five-year soil conservation plan for any highly erodible cropland they farm. Failure to comply would render farmers ineligible for virtually all USDA programs, notably commodity programs, crop insurance, and ownership and operating loans available from USDA's Farmers Home Administration (FmHA).

Implementing regulations proposed by USDA would require the plan to stipulate conservation measures a farm operator must implement each year to remain eligible for USDA programs. By 1995, erosion on highly erodible cropland would have to be reduced to a rate between the tolerance value and twice the tolerance value.[174]

Under the proposed definition of highly erodible cropland, conservation compliance would apply to an estimated 118 million acres of cropland, about 28 percent of total cropland. According to the 1982 NRI, this cropland accounts for 1.8 billion tons of erosion per year, roughly 58 percent of total cropland erosion. If conservation compliance plans were fully implemented and erosion rates were reduced to at least twice the soil loss tolerance level, by 1995 soil erosion on U.S. cropland would be reduced by 1.2 billion tons per year, or a 40 percent reduction from the rate reported by the Soil Conservation Service (SCS) in 1982.[175]

Farmers are to be able to comply with these guidelines in a number of ways. A substantial portion of the 118 million acres is expected to qualify for the CRP, and the conservation compliance policy should provide a strong incentive for farmers to enroll in that program. Farmers also are to be able to choose to adopt a wide array of soil conservation measures, from crop rotations to conservation tillage, and to continue to crop the land, provided the measures reduce erosion to acceptable levels. Farmers could also voluntarily convert affected land to grass or trees. Finally, farmers could opt to continue to farm highly erodible cropland with no conservation measures if they were willing to forgo eligibility for USDA program benefits.

USDA estimated that erosion control measures and, in some cases, conversion of land to grass and trees, would cost farmers an average of $40 to $60 per acre to reduce erosion to the tolerance level and $25 to $45 per acre to reduce it to twice the tolerance level. Aggregate costs to farmers were estimated to range from $700 million to $1.3 billion if erosion is reduced to twice the soil-loss tolerance level, or from $1.9 billion to $2.9 billion if erosion were reduced to the T values.[176] For some farmers, these costs would be spread over as many as five years.

Apart from anticipated increases in administrative costs, it is not yet clear what the impacts of conservation compliance on government program costs will be. Farmers who remove land from production to comply will reduce crop production and government outlays. Farmers who choose to abandon the commodity programs rather than comply are not subject to production controls. If a large amount of crop production is excluded from production controls in this manner, market prices could weaken further and the government could be exposed to high program costs associated with farms that remain in the program.

The potential potency of the conservation compliance policy depends to a large degree on the value of the USDA program benefits that farmers stand to lose if they fail to comply. The value of those benefits and the degree of farmer participation in the future are difficult to predict. USDA has estimated that 80 percent of all farmers participate in at least one of the USDA programs to which the policy applies.[177] For instance, about 100,000 farm loans are made through the FmHA each year;[178] all of these loans are subject to conservation compliance, though the number of FmHA borrowers who may crop highly erodible land is not clear. Commodity program participation rates, usually stated in terms of the percent of base acres enrolled in the program, vary considerably from year to year, depending on market conditions and program provisions. When market prices are low, participation usually is fairly high for most crops. For example, the 1986 programs attracted 85 percent of the corn acreage, 84 percent of the wheat acreage, and 91 percent of the upland cotton acreage.[179]

If, as the 1985 farm bill specified, direct commodity program payments to farmers decline after 1987, farmers will have less incentive to abide by the conservation compliance policy. However, as noted in the earlier discussion of the Conservation Reserve Program, economic stress in the farm economy may lead Congress to extend sizable direct income transfers to the sector beyond 1990, providing leverage to conservation compliance. Commodity programs need not be in effect every year to provide such leverage, because farmers must be in compliance in each year they apply for commodity programs after 1990. Alternatively, Congress may act to postpone the 1990 starting date for the policy or otherwise modify it to moderate its impact on financially strapped farmers.

Although the farm bill does not authorize it, the conservation compliance concept conceivably could be applied to other resource and environmental quality problems related to cropland. Such policies might require farmers to phase-in best management practices for mitigating pollution or depletion of groundwater—a "wellbuster" policy—or for preventing off-site sediment and runoff problems. Applying conservation compliance to such problems would require development of fair, practical, and scientifically credible field procedures for identifying affected lands and for evaluating compliance.

Conservation Easements. A third provision of the 1985 farm bill affected farmers who have highly erodible land or wetlands on their farms and are unable to repay debts owed the FmHA.[180] In essence, the secretary of agriculture is authorized to forgive all or a portion of an FmHA debt if, in return, an indebted farmer places highly erodible land or wetlands in a 50-year "conservation easement." The easement, a binding rider to the land deed, would require conservation of erodible land (through conversion to grass or trees) or retention of wetlands for the duration of the easement. The amount of FmHA debt that could be forgiven is to be based on an appraisal of the economic value of the land a farmer proposes for an easement.

Proposed regulations for implementing the conservation easement provision were scheduled for publication in the fall of 1986.[181] Like other farm bill conservation provisions, conservation easements could potentially be adapted to address other resource conservation and environmental protection problems.

Policies For Potential Cropland and Wetlands

The 1985 farm bill contained two policies designed to discourage cropping on certain fragile or environmentally important lands that were not yet in production by denying USDA program benefits to farmers who cultivate such lands.

Sodbuster Policy. One policy of the act was designed to deny farmers eligibility for most USDA programs if, after the date of enactment of the law (December 23, 1985), they brought into crop production land highly susceptible to soil erosion.[182]* Farmers were to be exempted from the sod-buster policy if they follow a conservation plan approved by the SCS or their local soil and water conservation district.

Under USDA's proposed criteria, the sodbuster policy would apply to some 227 million acres of land not currently being cropped but that has potential for conversion to cropland. Approximately 99 million of these acres are in range, 74 million are in forest, 47 million are in pasture, and 7 million are in other uses.[183] One study indicates that about 668,000 acres of highly erodible land were brought into crop production annually in the early 1980s.[184]

As with conservation compliance, the potential influence of the sod-buster policy will be greatest when USDA program benefits are large.

Swampbuster Policy. Another policy specified in the 1985 farm bill was to apply the same penalties contained in the sodbuster and conservation compliance policies to farmers who, after December 1985, commence drain-ing or otherwise modifying natural wetlands to produce agricultural commodities.[185]

The swampbuster policy theoretically is to apply to any wetlands cleared for agriculture. However, USDA has estimated that about 5.1 million[186] of the 99 million acres of wetlands existing in the coterminous 48 states in the mid-1970s have significant potential for drainage and crop production; most of the readily convertible wetlands have already been altered. Among the key issues to emerge in the wake of implementing regulations proposed by USDA is the question of whether the swampbuster policy applies to farmers whose lands are drained, perhaps inadvertently, by a "third party"—for example, by an irrigation or drainage district.

Tax Policies for Potential Cropland and Wetlands

The federal income tax code traditionally has provided important economic incentives both to cultivate highly erodible land and to drain wetlands. Farmers have long been able to deduct expenses for such activities and have enjoyed favorable capital gains treatment (a lower tax rate) upon resale of highly erodible land or wetlands "improved" by cultivation or drainage.

---

*A "grandfather clause" exempted producers if their land was used to produce an agricultural commodity at least one year between 1981 and 1985. However, under the conservation compliance policy discussed previously, these grandfather exemptions were scheduled to end on January 1, 1990, after which all highly erodible cropland, regardless of its cropping history, must be farmed according to an approved conservation plan.

More recently, investment tax credits have been available for such activities.

The future use of tax policies as a tool for promoting agricultural goals is unclear, however. The Tax Reform Act of 1986 eliminated these incentives for sodbusting and wetlands conversion.[187]

International Initiatives

Recent changes in domestic farm policies may significantly reduce some of the impacts that agriculture has on the environment in the United States. But what can the United States do about such problems abroad?

Both the U.S. government and foreign governments have an important stake in making world agriculture productive, sustainable, and environmentally sound. Foreign nations, including the developing world, are increasingly important as trading partners for a wide range of U.S. products; the health of their agriculture is an important component of their general prosperity. In the long run, even U.S. farmers have an interest in seeing a healthy agricultural sector in other nations because agricultural prosperity helps create the general prosperity that leads to dietary improvements and increased imports of U.S. grain. China's increased food grain production, for example, is likely to increase rural incomes, and lead to more meat consumption—and an increased market for U.S. feedstuffs (see box, "Grain and Cotton Production in China").

However, there is little that the United States can do directly to influence policies and agricultural practices in other countries to ameliorate adverse effects on the environment or natural resources. Direct intervention is obviously impossible, and most of the more aggressive alternatives are impracticable and, diplomatically at least, undesirable. The United States could, for instance, limit imports of foodstuffs whose production has involved resource abuse. An example might be refusing to import beef grown on land that required clearing tropical rain forests. Such a policy would be virtually impossible to implement. For example, how would one distinguish imported beef raised on a planted pasture from beef raised by grazing clearings in a tropical forest? Moreover, basing import policy on the conditions under which the product is produced would invite retaliation. European countries or Japan could easily claim that corn or soybean production involves an unreasonable amount of soil erosion.

The United States can, however, take a much stronger role in demonstrating the benefits of environmentally sound agricultural policies and in providing technical assistance to other countries on how to avoid environmental degradation. Like the United States, European countries are tiring of paying their farmers high subsidies to produce more food than is needed. If the United States is successful in implementing the initiatives set forth in the Food Security Act of 1985 that jointly address environmental concerns and excess production problems, European and other countries may take an interest in adopting similar programs to discourage the use of environmentally sensitive land for intensive agricultural production. If so, the environment would benefit, and some of the burden of responding to excess production would be removed from the United States, particularly if those policies raised commodity prices in international markets.

The United States can encourage these policies by providing information on agricultural and environmental problems and technical assistance on how to deal with these problems to receptive countries. The private and nonprofit sectors may be able to help the government significantly in carrying out such activities. For example, U.S. pesticide exporters and various U.S. health and environmental groups have reached an agreement on measures that pesticide exporters should adopt to provide better information on pesticide use to farmers in Third World countries.[188] Congress and various private groups are also putting increasing pressure on international lending organizations such as the World Bank and the Interamerican Development Bank to be more environmentally sensitive in their development projects, many of which involve agriculture.[189] Similar pressures have been placed on the Agency for International Development (the principal U.S. development assistance agency), and the agency seems to have responded positively.[190]

The United States also has a role as a world technological leader. Many agricultural technologies used abroad have been first developed in the United States; many foreign-developed technologies have been inspired in part by U.S. practices. Practices such as monoculture, large-scale operations, mechanization of all phases of production, and heavy use of fertilizers, herbicides, and insecticides have been promoted in the United States by the high labor costs that have long characterized U.S. agriculture. However, in countries that have low labor costs and serious land and capital constraints, those approaches do not make nearly as much sense; yet they have been seen by researchers and policy makers as the unavoidable path to "modernizing" traditional agriculture.

The wholesale adoption of U.S. approaches abroad also may not make sense ecologically. But there is often too little research conducted to determine what makes sense and what does not. The United States could support such research efforts to help developing countries ensure that the agricultural developments they undertake are compatible with both the economic and environmental conditions that exist.

Grain and Cotton Production in China

It should come as no surprise that China, with the world's largest population, is also the world's largest grain producer (first in rice, first in wheat, second in corn). China is also the world's largest cotton grower.[1] What is remarkable is not the amount of food and fiber annually produced, but the rapidity with which production has been increasing in the last several years—a 49 percent increase between 1978 and 1984[2]—and the impacts that change has had on China's position on world agricultural markets.

China, says the U.S. Department of Agriculture, has made the transition from "customer to competitor" in key commodity markets.[3] Most experts attribute the change largely to China's shift away from communal farming toward a more market-oriented system.

Evidence has accumulated that the development of China's agriculture between the 1949 Revolution and the 1979 agricultural reforms exacted a severe price from the country's environment and land resources.[4] Much of China's land area is too steep or arid for cultivation; nearly all the good land was long ago pressed into production to feed its huge rural population. To feed a constantly growing number of people, and to offset large land losses for urban, industrial, and other built-up uses, post-Revolutionary China aggressively pushed agriculture onto marginal lands. Deserts were irrigated, lakes drained, and erodible slopes cultivated. Particular emphasis was put on greater grain production, even where the land was unsuitable to producing it.[5] Often the results were disappointing in terms of food output and devastating in terms of soil loss, water table drawdown, and habitat alteration.

China's post-1979 approach to agriculture has put much greater emphasis on giving individual peasant family units a financial incentive to raise productivity per acre and less emphasis on large-scale programs of land development or reclamation. Less emphasis is reportedly put on local self-sufficiency, more on specialization and adapting cropping to local conditions.[6] Total cultivated area actually dropped between 1978 and 1984, despite a 46 percent increase in crop output. The new market-oriented policy seems to have led to more sustainable land-use patterns, though nitrogen fertilizer use has nearly doubled.[7] Greater fertilizer use will likely increase the risk of nitrate pollution of water supplies, particularly in densely populated and heavily agricultural south China.[8]

If China continues to move toward greater agricultural diversification, both the environment and U.S. trade could benefit. Large areas of land that are too steep, arid, or otherwise unsuitable to crop production could be returned to pasture or even forest, while better land and water management could increase food crop yields on the more suitable lands. Because of poor internal transport, it might make sense for parts of China to import grain from abroad, even while other parts of the country export the same products. The United States might supply much of that grain, provided China could earn sufficient foreign exchange by exporting other agricultural or nonagricultural products.

Ultimately, however, China will have to find ways for its arable land base of only 0.1 hectare per capita (by comparison, densely populated India has 0.27 hectares per capita)[9] to provide all but a tiny fraction of its total food needs. Supplying a year 2000 national population of 1.2 billion (a total below trend growth) with an "adequate" annual grain ration of 400 kilograms per capita would require an almost 50 percent increase in grain output, and rice yields would have to be above the highest now achieved in more advanced countries.[10] Regardless of the agricultural path chosen, feeding China's huge population offers a tough challenge not only to its agriculture but to its environment as well.

Although such activities appear much less direct than those that the United States can adopt to deal with its own agriculturally related environmental problems, they could be quite effective. Other countries are increasingly indicating a growing concern for both environmental problems and large agricultural subsidies.[191] By adopting a coherent set of research, demonstration, and technical assistance activities, the United States could help foreign countries better address their own problems and help protect fragile and valuable environments abroad.

LOOKING AHEAD

Agricultural activities clearly can have a substantial impact on environmental quality. On one hand, in the United States, agriculture is the major source of some water pollutants, the major cause of wetland loss, a source of groundwater contamination in some areas, and in many other ways an adverse influence on the nation's environment. On the other hand, agricultural lands can contribute to improved environmental quality. For instance, farmland is a major source of wildlife habitat, often an important component of treasured landscape, and a site for beneficially disposing of sewage sludges. The links between agricultural activities and environmental quality are even more multitudinous and extensive in that agricultural productivity can be adversely affected by air pollution and other forms of environmental degradation.

Congress incorporated several significant provisions in the Food Security Act of 1985 that recognize these interconnections. Provisions such as the conservation reserve and "swampbuster" policy not only serve to reduce some of the more serious conflicts between agriculture and the environment but also are an important step forward in fashioning agricultural policies so that they simultaneously promote the goals of protecting farm income and enhancing environmental quality.

Other legislation and administrative initiatives at the federal, state, and local levels are supplementing the farm act's provisions. At the federal level, both Congress and EPA are developing nonpoint-source pollution control programs under the Clean Water Act,[192] procedures under the Federal Insecticide, Fungicide, and Rodenticide Act for protecting groundwater from pesticide contamination,[193] and comprehensive groundwater protection initiatives that would affect agricultural sources of pollution.[194] The U.S. Department of Agriculture is also focusing more on reducing environmental problems in its research, technical assistance, and financial assistance programs.[195] A growing number of states and localities are also undertaking initiatives dealing with some of these conflicts, and in some cases farmers face regulatory action if they fail to deal with certain environmental problems.

Support for these initiatives is becoming increasingly widespread, even within the agricultural community. As farmers understand more fully the ways in which their activities can cause environmental degradation, they increasingly support and adapt activities to reduce environmental problems as long as these activities do not affect the farmers' incomes significantly. Like other people, most farmers have no desire to drink contaminated water, destroy lakes, or poison wildlife. As evidenced by the contents of agricultural magazines, stories in rural newspapers, and the agenda of agricultural conferences, farmers are demonstrating the pride they take in being stewards of the land.

Despite the significant steps now being taken to reduce conflicts between agriculture and the environment, substantial challenges remain. The first is to implement existing agricultural and environmental programs in a manner that provides effective environmental protection without imposing excessive costs on either farmers or the implementing agencies. One reason for the delayed application of environmental protection programs to the agricultural sector has been the immense difficulty of dealing with millions of separate facilities, each with a unique combination of conditions, problems, and resources.

The second challenge is to implement these programs in such a way that they have the flexibility to respond to the possibly significant technical, economic, institutional, and social changes that may take place in the agricultural community in the coming years. Implementing the programs under static conditions would be difficult enough. Implementing them so they can adjust rapidly to these changing conditions is much more difficult— particularly since it is impossible to predict all the changes that might occur.

And a third challenge is to implement these and other agricultural programs in such a way that they also serve to protect environmental quality and improve the quality of life in other countries, particularly those that are already facing serious stresses in their efforts to develop economically. The United States may be able to do little to address these problems directly. But it would be myopic, and ultimately very costly to the United States itself, to ignore these issues altogether.

FURTHER READING

Agricultural policy is a broad and complex subject; a good introduction to it is found in William A. Galston's *A Tough Row to Hoe: The 1985 Farm Bill and Beyond* (Washington, D.C.: Roosevelt Center for American Policy Studies, 1985). Present and future effects of agricultural policy and technology on the number and size of farms, agricultural productivity, and the environment are examined in *Technology, Public Policy and the Changing Structure of American Agriculture* (Washington, D.C.: U.S. Congress, Office of Technology Assessment, 1986). *Choices*, published by the American Agricultural Economics Association, is written for a popular audience and devoted to all aspects of agricultural policy, from research to commodity programs. The U.S. Department of Agriculture's Economic Research Service, in Washington, D.C., publishes a variety of technical and nontechnical reports on agricultural policy and the farm economy, some of which bear on conservation and environmental issues. For an up-to-date and fairly comprehensive review of economic and policy developments in U.S. agriculture, consult USDA's annual *Outlook Conference Proceedings* (Washington, D.C.: U.S. Department of Agriculture).

There are several indispensable sources of agricultural statistics. The first is entitled, appropriately enough, *Agricultural Statistics*. It is compiled annually by USDA (and published by the U.S. Government Printing Office) and usually contains over 700 statistical tables on virtually every aspect of agriculture, including international trade. The *Census of Agriculture*, conducted periodically since 1850 and most recently in 1982, provides voluminous information on farm and ranch operations in the United States. (The next *Census* will cover 1987.) A separate *Census* volume treats each state and the counties therein, though for most purposes *The United States Summary and State Data* is the most useful volume to consult.

Although somewhat dated, the standard reference on trends and future prospects in world agriculture is *Agriculture: Toward 2000* (Rome: United Nations Food and Agriculture Organisation, 1981). U.S. agricultural trade performance is the subject of *A Review of U.S. Competitiveness in Agricultural Trade* (Washington, D.C.: U.S. Congress, Office of Technology Assessment, 1986). The World Bank's *World Development Report 1986* provides a useful review of agricultural trade and policy problems in both industrial and developing countries.

No good comprehensive studies are available on the implications of global agricultural trends on resource use and the environment. The annual *World Resources Report* (Washington, D.C.: World Resources Institute) devotes a chapter to developments in agriculture with emphasis on resource use and the environment. Many publications of the Worldwatch Institute (located in Washington, D.C.) examine agricultural and environmental problems from a global perspective, including the annual *State of the World* report.

For the United States, R. Neil Sampson's *Farmland or Wasteland: A Time To Choose* (Emmaus, Pa: Rodale Press, 1981) provides a general and sometimes impassioned overview of resource and environmental problems in agriculture. For another perspective, see *Resource and Environmental Effects of U.S. Agriculture* by Pierre R. Crosson and Sterling Brubaker. USDA's Soil Conservation Service analyzes the status of soil and water conservation, nonpoint pollution, and related topics in the periodic *Appraisals* it conducts by mandate of the Resource Conservation Act (the next appraisal will be available in 1987). A two-volume study by the National Research Council, *Soil Conservation: Assessing the 1982 National Resources Inventory* (Washington, D.C.: National Academy Press, 1986), analyzes the methodology and findings of the National Resources Inventory conducted by SCS in 1982. The issue of off-site pollution damages caused by agriculture is the subject of two Conservation Foundation books: *Eroding Soils: The Off-Farm Impacts* by Edwin H. Clark II, Jennifer A. Haverkamp, and William Chapman (1985); and *The Off-Site Costs of Soil Erosion*, the proceedings of a symposium held in Washington in May 1985, edited by Thomas E. Waddell (1986).

Pesticide contamination of groundwater is an important emerging issue; for a recent review, see *Pesticides in Ground Water: Background Document* (Washington, D.C.: U.S. Environmental Protection Agency, 1986). The Council for Agricultural Science and Technology (CAST), based in Ames, Iowa, frequently publishes reports dealing with a broad range of conservation and environmental issues. An example is *Agriculture and Groundwater Quality* (1985). The bimonthly *Journal of Soil and Water Conservation*, published by the Soil Conservation Society of America (in Ankeny, Iowa), covers a broad range of issues relating to agriculture's impacts on resource conservation and environmental quality. Each issue includes feature articles and commentaries accessible to nonexperts, as well as more technical research reports on scientific or policy topics.

REFERENCES

Text

1. By far the most significant development in the early 1980s was the sharp decline in asset and equity values, mainly associated with declining land prices. Real net farm income (income after adjustment for inflation) also declined from the late 1970s through the mid-1980s. Wide variations in economic conditions exist among farms. As of January 1, 1985, about 213,000 farm operators—some 13 percent of the total—were characterized as in financial stress: they had negative cash flows (cash expenses exceeded cash receipts) and debts equal to 40 percent or more the value of their assets. Collectively, this vulnerable group of farmers held 45 percent of total farm operator debt. Most of the farms experiencing these problems were cash grain and livestock farms in the Corn Belt, Lake States, and Northern Plains. However, many farms did not experience severe financial problems in the 1980s, especially those that did not incur heavy debts and high interest payments during the 1970s. See U.S. Department of Agriculture, Economic Research Service, Farm Sector Financial Problems: Another Perspective, Agriculture Information Bulletin No. 499 (Washington, D.C.: U.S. Department of Agriculture, May 1986), pp. 1, 4, 12-14.

2. Information provided by the U.S. Department of Agriculture, Agricultural Stabilization and Conservation Service, Budget Division, August 29, 1986.

3. Information provided by the U.S. Department of Agriculture, Economic Research Service, International Economic Indicators Branch, September 1986.

4. Henry M. Peskin, "Cropland Sources of Water Pollution," Environment, May 1986, p. 32.

5. U.S. Department of Agriculture, Agricultural Statistics 1985 (Washington, D.C.: U.S. Government Printing Office, 1985), pp. 301, 388-89, 392.

6. Calculated from U.S. Department of Agriculture, Foreign Agricultural Service, PSD data base figures for grains (wheat, corn, sorghum, barley, oats, rice) and oilseeds (primarily soybeans).

7. U.S. Department of Agriculture, Economic Research Service, World Agriculture: Outlook and Situation Report, WAS-43 (Washington, D.C.: U.S. Department of Agriculture, March 1986), pp. 9-12, 14-16; "Wheat Consumption: Where Will Growth Occur?", Agricultural Outlook (Washington, D.C.: U.S. Department of Agriculture, Economic Research Service, August 1986), pp. 24-27.

8. The massive increase in oil prices in the 1970s raised the demand for U.S. food from such nations as Nigeria, Mexico, and many middle eastern states. When OPEC states "recycled" their petrodollars through U.S. banks, they enabled such countries as Poland, Mexico, and the Philippines to borrow large quantities of dollars. Some of this money returned to the United States in the form of food export demand.

9. See Alan J. Webb et al., "World Agricultural Markets and U.S. Farm Policy," in U.S. Department of Agriculture, Economic Research Service, *Agricultural-Food Policy Review: Commodity Program Perspectives* (Washington, D.C.: U.S. Department of Agriculture, 1985), p. 79; and U.S. Department of Agriculture, *Agricultural Statistics 1985*, p. 518; *Agricultural Statistics 1982*, p. 535; *Agricultural Statistics 1979*, p. 571; *Agricultural Statistics 1977*, p.582; *Agricultural Statistics 1975*, p. 588; *Agricultural Statistics 1973*, p. 584.

10. See Webb et al., "World Agricultural Markets," p.86; and "China's Agricultural Revolution: From Customer to Competitor," *Agricultural Outlook* (U.S. Department of Agriculture, Economic Research Service), March 1985, p. 26.

11. Information provided by the U.S. Department of Agriculture, Economic Research Service, International Economic Indicators Branch, September 1986.

12. See Charles E. Hanrahan, "Why U.S. Agriculture Exports Have Declined in the 1980s," Congressional Research Service, Library of Congress, October 1984; and for general discussion of macroeconomic influence on agriculture, see Paul T. Prentice and David A. Torgerson, "U.S. Agriculture and the Macroeconomy," in U.S. Department of Agriculture, *Agricultural-Food Policy Review* (Washington, D.C.: U.S. Department of Agriculture, 1985), pp. 9-24.

13. U.S. Department of Agriculture, Economic Research Service, *World Indices of Agricultural and Food Production, 1975-1884*, Statistical Bulletin No. 730 (Washington, D.C.: U.S. Department of Agriculture, 1985), table 15, p.33; and for change in the U.S. share of the world market, see *Agricultural Outlook*, November 1985, p.16.

14. U.S. Department of Agriculture, Foreign Agricultural Service, *Foreign Agriculture Circular: Grains*, FG-13-85 (Washington, D.C.: U.S. Department of Agriculture, October 1985), pp. 1, 9-13.

15. "China's Agricultural Revolution: From Customer to Competitor," March 1985, pp. 23-26; and U.S. Department of Agriculture, *World Agriculture*, p. 11.

16. U.S. Department of Agriculture, *World Indices*, pp. 30, 34, 115.

17. Calculated from the U.S. Department of Agriculture, Foreign Agricultural Service PSD data base, July 1986.

18. Ibid.; The drop in corn production due to the 1983 payment-in-kind program and drought, cut deeply into stocks and temporarily boosted prices. The trends of production surpluses and low prices resumed the following year.

19. U.S. Department of Agriculture, Economic Research Service, *Economic Indicators of the Farm Sector: State Financial Summary, 1984*, ECIFS 4-5 (Washington, D.C.: U.S. Department of Agriculture, March 1986), p. 37.

20. Calculated from the U.S. Department of Agriculture, Economic Research Service, *Agricultural Resources: Agricultural Land Values and Markets, Situation and Outlook Report* (Washington, D.C.: U.S. Department of Agriculture, June 1986), table 2, p. 16.

21. U.S. Department of Agriculture, *Farm Financial Problems*, table 4, p. 14.

22. Information provided by the U.S. Department of Agriculture, Agricultural Stabilization and Conservation Service, Budget Division, September 1986.

23. U.S. Congress, Congressional Budget Office, *Federal Support of U.S. Business* (Washington, D.C.: U.S. Government Printing Office, January 1984), p. 39.

24. Information provided by the U.S. Department of Agriculture, Agricultural Stabilization and Conservation Service, Budget Division, August 1986.

25. Calculated from the U.S. Department of Agriculture, *Agricultural Statistics 1985*, tables 535 and 536, p. 372.

26. Donn A. Reimund, Nora L. Brooks, and Paul D. Velde, *The U.S. Farm Sector in the Mid-1980's*, Economic Research Service, Agricultural Economic Report No. 548 (Washington, D.C.: U.S. Department of Agriculture, May 1986), pp. 2, 4, 26.

27. Ibid., p. 11.

28. U.S. Congress, Office of Technology Assessment, *Technology, Public Policy, and the Changing Structure of American Agriculture*, OTA-F-285 (Washington, D.C.: U.S. Government Printing Office, March 1986), pp. 96-97.

29. Agapi Somwaru, *Disaggregated Farm Income By Type of Farm, 1959-82*, U.S. Department of Agriculture, Economic Research Service, Agricultural Economic Report No. 558 (Washington, D.C.: U.S. Department of Agriculture, 1986), p. 12.

30. U.S. Department of Agriculture, *Agricultural Resources: Land*, p. 23.

31. U.S. Department of Agriculture, *Agricultural Statistics 1985*, table 536, p. 372.

32. U.S. Department of Agriculture, *1986 Fact Book of U.S. Agriculture*, Miscellaneous Publication No. 1063 (Washington, D.C.: U.S. Department of Agriculture, November 1985), p. 30.

33. Total cropland is the sum of cropland used for crops, idle cropland, and cropland pasture. U.S. Department of Agriculture, *Agricultural Statistics 1985*, table 357, p. 372, and *Agricultural Statistics 1980* (Washington, D.C.: U.S. Government Printing Office, 1980), table 602, p. 419.

34. Calculated from the U.S. Department of Agriculture, Economic Research Service, *Economic Indicators of the Farm Sector: Production and Efficiency Statistics, 1984*, ECIFS 4-4 (Washington, D.C.: U.S. Department of Agriculture, February 1986), table 1, p. 5, and table 13, p. 17.

35. U.S. Department of Agriculture, Economic Research Service, *Cropland Use and Supply: Outlook and Situation Report*, CUS-2 (Washington, D.C.: U.S. Department of Agriculture, 1985), pp. 5, 7.

36. Ibid., p. 8-9, 16.

37. Ibid., table 3, p. 7.

38. Calculated from the U.S. Department of Agriculture, Economic Research Service, *Oil Crops: Outlook and Situation Report*, OCS-10 (Washington, D.C.: U.S. Department of Agriculture, March 1986), table 9, p. 22.

39. U.S. Department of Agriculture, Economic Research Service, *Cropland Use and Supply: Outlook and Situation Report*, p.9-10.

40. U.S. Department of Agriculture, *Cropland Use*, pp. 24-25.

41. Calculated from U.S. Department of Agriculture, *Agricultural Statistics 1985*, table 539, p. 374; and U.S. Department of Agriculture, *Cropland Use*, table 1, p. 5.

42. Calculated from the U.S. Department of Commerce, Bureau of Census, *1982 Census of Agriculture*, Vol. 1, part 51 (Washington, D.C.: U.S. Department of Commerce, 1986), table 3, p. 2.

43. Ibid., table 41, pp. 20-23.

44. U.S. Department of Agriculture, *Agricultural Statistics 1985*, calculated from table 539, p. 374.

45. U.S. Department of the Interior, Geological Survey, *Estimated Use of Water in the United States in 1980*, USGS Circular 1001 (Reston, Va.: U.S. Geological Survey,

1983), p. 18.

46. Rajinder Singh Bajwa, *Analysis of Irrigation Potential in the Southeast: Florida. A Special Report*, U.S. Department of Agriculture, Economic Research Service (Washington, D.C.: U.S. Department of Agriculture, November 1985), p. 4.

47. M. A. Tabatabai, "Atmospheric Deposition of Nutrients and Pesticides", in Frank W. Schaller and George W. Bailey, eds., *Agricultural Management and Water Quality* (Ames, Iowa: Iowa State University, 1983), p. 93.

48. Calculated from the U.S. Department of Agriculture, Economic Research Service, *Agricultural Resources: Inputs Outlook and Situation Report*, AR-1 (Washington, D.C.: U.S. Department of Agriculture, February 1986), table 8, p. 10 and table 10, p. 11.

49. Ibid., table 7, p. 9.

50. Information provided by U.S. Environmental Protection Agency, Office of Pesticide Programs, September 1986.

51. Calculated from the U.S. Department of Agriculture, Economic Research Service, *Inputs Outlook and Situation*, IOS-2 (Washington, D.C.: U.S. Department of Agriculture, October 1983), table 2, p. 4 and table 4, p. 5.

52. Ibid.

53. Walter Ferguson, *Pesticide Use on Selected Crops: Aggregated Data. 1977-80)*, Economic Research Service, Agriculture Information Bulletin No. 494 (Washington, D.C.: U.S. Department of Agriculture, 1985), pp. 2, 7, 8.

54. U.S. Environmental Protection Agency, Office of Pesticide Programs, "Pesticide Industry Sales and Usage: 1985 Market Estimates," September 1986, table 8.

55. U.S. Department of Agriculture, Economic Research Service, *Quantities of Pesticides Used by Farmers in 1966*, Agricultural Economic Report No. 179 (Washington, D.C.: U.S. Department of Agriculture, April 1970), p. 6.

56. Information provided by U.S. Department of Agriculture, Economic Research Service, September 1986.

57. Calculated from U.S. Department of Agriculture. *Inputs Outlook*, table 2, p. 4; and U.S. Department of Agriculture, *Agricultural Statistics 1985*, pp. 1, 15, 19, 30, 38, 43, 50, 61, 93, 117, 124.

58. U.S. Department of Agriculture, Economic Research Service. *Inputs Outlook*, p.4.

59. Calculated from U.S. Department of Agriculture, Economic Research Service. *Quantities of Pesticides Used by Farmers in 1964*, Agricultural Economic Report No. 131, January 1968, p. 22; and Theodore R. Eichers, Paul A. Andrilenas, and Thelma W. Anderson, *Farmers' Use of Pesticides in 1976*, Economics, Statistics, and Cooperatives Service, Agricultural Economic Report No. 418 (Washington, D.C.: U.S. Department of Agriculture, December 1978), p. 16.

60. U.S. Department of Agriculture, *Inputs Outlook*, p. 8.

61. Ibid., calculated from p. 5.

62. Information provided by U.S. Environmental Protection Agency, Office of Pesticide Programs, September 1986.

63. Calculated from U.S. Department of Agriculture, *Economic Indicators: Production and Efficiency*, table 69, p. 68.

64. Office of Technology Assessment, *Technology. Public Policy and Changing Structure*, p. 4.

65. Ibid., pp. 31-32.

66. Ibid., p. 32.

67. Ibid., p. 6-8.

68. Information provided from the U.S. Department of Agriculture, Soil Conservation Service, September 1986; and Katherine H. Reichelderfer, *Do USDA Farm Program Participants Contribute to Soil Erosion*, Agricultural Economic Report No. 532 (Washington, D.C.: U.S. Department of Agriculture, Economic Research Service, April 1985), pp. 27-30.

69. The dramatic decline in population of such species as peregrine falcons and ospreys has been tied to the effects of organochlorine pesticides such as DDT on their reproductive success. Evidence of its effect on wildlife was an important influence on EPA's decision to ban DDT in 1972. In recent years, these species have gradually increased in number. See The National Audubon Society, *Audubon Wildlife Report 1986* (New York: National Audubon Society, 1986), pp. 811, 813, 819-20, 897-98.

70. George W. Ware, *Fundamentals of Pesticides*, (Fresno, Calif.: Thompson Publications, 1982), pp. 216, 219-21.

71. Integrated pest management (IPM) is an approach to pest control that minimizes use of pesticides by maximizing naturally occuring controls such as predators and parasites, utilizing nonchemical methods such as habitat modification, and timing control actions to the biological cycles of the pest. IPM may be able to reduce the use of pesticides by as much as half. Office of Technology Assessment, *Technology. Public Policy and Changing Structure*, p.210.

72. Indicated by leveling off or decline of most farm inputs. See U.S. Department of Agriculture, *Economic Indicators: Production and Efficiency*, table 57, p. 56.

73. U.S. Congress, Office of Technology Assessment, *Impacts of Technology on U.S. Cropland and Rangeland Productivity* (Washington, D.C.: U.S. Government Printing Office, August 1982), pp. 34-35.

74. Pierre Crosson and Anthony Stout, *Productivity Effects of Cropland Erosion in the United States* (Washington, D.C.: Resources for the Future, 1983), p. 3.

75. W. E. Larson, F. J. Pierce, and R. H. Dowdy, "The Threat of Soil Erosion to Long-term Crop Production," *Science*, 219 (1983):219-465.

76. National Research Council, Board on Agriculture, *Soil Conservation: Assessing the National Resources Inventory*, vol. 1 (Washington, D.C.: National Academy Press, 1986), table 1-4, p. 8.

77. Ibid., p. 8.

78. Information provided by U.S. Department of Agriculture, Soil Conservation Service, September 1986.

79. Ibid.

80. National Research Council, *Soil Conservation*, p. 45.

81. For planted acreage, see U.S. Department of Agriculture, *Agricultural Statistics 1985*, pp. 61, 129. For relative erosion rates, see Paul E. Rosenberry and Burton C. English, "Erosion Control Practices: The Impact of Actual Versus Most Effective Use," in National Research Council, *Soil Conservation : Assessing the National Resources Inventory*, vol. 2, table 4, p. 211.

82. National Research Council, *Soil Conservation*, vol. 1, table 3-1, p. 39.

83. "The T value is defined as the maximum rate of annual soil loss (in tons/acre/year) that will permit crop productivity to be sustained economically and indefinitely. For cropland soils, T values have been estimated to range from 1 to 5 tons/acre/year; 71.4

percent of these soils have been assigned the maximum value of 5 tons/acre/year, and another 11.5 percent have a T value of 4 tons/acre/year. For the generally shallower rangeland soils, T values ranged from 1 to 3 tons/acre/year." National Research Council, *Soil Conservation*, vol. 1, p. 9.

84. Information provided by U.S. Department of Agriculture. Soil Conservation Service, October 1986.

85. National Research Council, *Soil Conservation*, vol. 1, table 3-1, p. 13.

86. Ibid., pp. 13-16.

87. Office of Technology Assessment, *Impacts of Technology on Productivity*, pp. 42-43.

88. Ibid., p.43-44.

89. David Pimentel and Clive A. Edwards, "Pesticides and Ecosystems", *BioScience* 32 (1982):595-600; and Office of Technology Assessment, *Impacts of Technology*, pp. 230-232.

90. Office of Technology Assessment, *Impacts of Technology*, p. 226-228.

91. Association of State and Interstate Water Pollution Control Administrators, *America's Clean Water: The States' Nonpoint Source Assessment 1985* (Washington, D.C.: Association of State and Interstate Water Pollution Control Administrators, 1985), p. 3.

92. U.S. Environmental Protection Agency, Office of Water Regulations and Standards, *National Water Quality Inventory: 1984 Report to Congress*, EPA 440/4-85-029 (Washington, D.C.: U.S. Environmental Protection Agency, August 1985), p. 3.

93. Edwin H. Clark II, Jennifer A Haverkamp, and William Chapman, *Eroding Soils: The Off-Farm Impacts* (Washington, D.C.: The Conservation Foundation, 1985), p. 175.

94. Ibid., p. xv.

95. Robert D. Judy et al., *1982 National Fisheries Survey. vol. 1. Technical Report: Initial Findings*, prepared for U.S. Department of the Interior, Fish and Wildlife Service and U.S. Environmental Protection Agency, Office of Water, FWS/OBS-84/06 (Washington, D.C.: U.S. Department of the Interior, 1984), p. 28.

96. U.S. Environmental Protection Agency, *Fish Kills Caused by Pollution. Fifteen-Year Summary 1961-1975*, EPA-440/4-78-011 (Washington, D.C.: U.S. Government Printing Office, 1979), table 3, p.8; and U.S. Environmental Protection Agency, *Fish Kills Caused by Pollution in 1976*, EPA-440/4-79-024 (Washington, D.C.: U.S. Government Printing Office, 1979), table 2, p. 5; and U.S. Environmental Protection Agency, "Fish Kills by Source of Pollution, 1977-1980" (unpublished).

97. Ohio Environmental Protection Agency, Ohio Water Quality Management Plan, Office of the Planning Coordinator, "Scioto River Basin Agriculture Report," May 1981, revised January 1983, p. 79.

98. G.W. Bennett, D.H. Thompson, and S.A. Parr, "A Second Year of Fisheries Investigations at Fort Lake, 1939," Illinois Natural History Survey, Urbana, Ill., Biological notes no. 14, 1940 cited in R.E. Sparks, *Effects of Sediment on Aquatic Life* (Havana, Ill.: Illinois Natural History Survey, 1977), p. 6.

99. J.C. Ritchie, "Sediment, Fish, and Fish Habitat," *Journal of Soil and Water Conservation*, 27 (1972):125.

100. F.E. Dendy, "Sedimentation in the Nation's Reservoirs," *Journal of Soil and Water Conservation* 23, no.4 (1968):135-7.

101. Clark, Haverkamp, and Chapman, *Eroding Soils*, p. 148.

102. Ibid., pp. xiv, xvi, 76.

103. Ibid., p. xvii.

104. A.G. Taylor et al., "Costs of Sediment in Illinois Roadside Ditches and Rights-of-Way," Collection of Reports on Effects and Costs of Erosion in Illinois (Illinois Environmental Protection Agency, October 1978), p. 1.

105. U.S. Department of Commerce, Bureau of the Census, 1978 Census of Agriculture, vol. 4, "Irrigation" (Washington, D.C.: U.S. Government Printing Office, 1982), p. 266.

106. Clark, Haverkamp, and Chapman, Eroding Soils, p. xvii.

107. Fairfield Osborn, Our Plundered Planet (Boston: Little, Brown and Co., 1948), pp. 109-10.

108. Stanley W. Trimble, Man-Induced Soil Erosion on the Southern Piedmont, 1700-1970 (Soil Conservation Society of America, 1974); J.H. Stallings, Soil Conservation (Englewood Cliffs, N.J.: Prentice-Hall, 1957); and Hugh Hammond Bennett, Soil Conservation (New York: McGraw-Hill Book Co., 1939).

109. Clark, Haverkamp, and Chapman, Eroding Soils, p. xviii.

110. Estimated from U.S. Department of the Interior, Bureau of Reclamation, Colorado River Water Quality, Colorado River Water Quality Improvement Program, Status Report (Washington, D.C.: U.S. Government Printing Office, 1983), pp. 5, 21. Total damages are $113 million, and municipal and industrial damages account for 70 percent of these.

111. L.P. Gianessi, H.M. Peskin, P. Crosson, and C. Puffer, "Nonpoint Source Pollution: Are Cropland Controls the Answer?" report prepared for the U.S. Environmental Protection Agency by Resources for the Future, February 14, 1986 (unpublished).

112. Vladimir Novotny and Gordon Chesters, Handbook of Nonpoint Pollution: Sources and Management (New York: Van Nostrand Reinhold Co., 1981), p. 188; Leonard P. Gianessi and Henry Peskin, "Analysis of National Water Pollution Control Policies: 2. Agricultural Sediment Control," Water Resources Research 17, no. 4 (1981):805; and Oswald Rendon-Herrero, "Estimation of Washload Produced on Certain Small Watersheds," Journal of the Hydraulics Division, American Society of Civil Engineers 100 (1974):843.

113. Council on Environmental Quality, Environmental Trends (Washington, D.C.: U.S. Governmental Printing Office, 1981) p. 92.

114. C.P. Rice, P.J. Samson, and G. Noguchi, Project Summary: Atmospheric Transport of Toxaphene to Lake Michigan, prepared for U.S. Environmental Protection Agency, Environmental Research Laboratory, Research and Development, EPA-600/S3-84-101 (Washington, D.C.: U.S. Government Printing Office, 1984), p. 2; and Council on Environmental Quality, Environmental Quality: 1982 (Washington, D.C.: U.S. Government Printing Office, 1983), pp. 51-52.

115. U.S. Department of the Interior, Geological Survey, National Water Summary 1983, Water Supply Paper 2250 (Washington, D.C.: U.S. Government Printing Office, 1984), p. 40; and U.S. Geological Survey, "Basic Ground-Water Hydrology," Water-Supply Paper 2220 (Washington, D.C.: U.S. Government Printing Office, 1984), pp. 76-77.

116. Vladimir Novotny and Gordon Chesters, Handbook of Nonpoint Pollution (New York: Van Nostrand Reinhold Company, 1981), pp. 257, 287-89.

117. Ibid., pp. 231-32.

118. George R. Hallberg, "Agricultural Chemicals and Groundwater Quality in Iowa:

Status Report 1985'' (Ames, Iowa: Iowa State University Cooperative Extension Service, December 1985), p. 1; and U.S. Geological Survey, *National Water Summary 1984: Hydrologic Events, Selected Water-Quality Trends, and Ground-Water Resources* (Washington, D.C.: U.S. Government Printing Office, 1985), pp. 98-99.

119. Association of State and Interstate Water Pollution Control Administrators, *America's Clean Water: The States' Nonpoint Source Assessment 1985* (Washington, D.C.: Association of State and Interstate Water Pollution Control Administrators, 1985), p. 17.

120. Cohen, Eiden, and Lorber, "Monitoring Ground Water for Pesticides," *Evaluation of Pesticides in Ground Water*, American Chemical Society Symposium series no. 315 (Washington, D.C.: American Chemical Society, 1986), pp. 170-196.

121. Patrick W. Holden, *Pesticides and Groundwater Quality: Issues and Problems in Four States*, prepared for the National Research Council, Board on Agriculture (Washington, D.C.: National Academy Press, 1986), p. 3.

122. Council for Agricultural Science and Technology, "Agriculture and Groundwater Quality," report no. 103 (Ames, Iowa: Council for Agricultural Science and Technology, 1985), p. 17.

123. Ibid.

124. The Conservation Foundation, "A Guide to Groundwater Pollution Problems, Causes, and Government Responses," in *Groundwater Protection* (Washington, D.C.: The Conservation Foundation, 1987).

125. Colorado Department of Health, *Public Comments on Groundwater Quality Protection Issues and Alternatives*, August 1983.

126. According to the most recent national wetlands inventory conducted by the U.S. Fish and Wildlife Survey, W.E. Frayer, T.J. Monahan, D.C. Bowden and F.A. Graybill, *Status and Trends of Wetlands and Deepwater Habitats in the Conterminous United States, 1950s to 1970s* (Ft. Collins, Colo.: Colorado State University, 1983), 99 million acres of wetlands remained in the lower 48 states in the mid-1970s and these were being converted at a rate of 458,000 acres per year. More recently, in U.S. Congress, Office of Technology Assessment, *Wetlands: Their Use and Regulation*, OTA-0-206 (Washington, D.C.: Office of Technology Assessment, March 1984), the OTA estimates that 300,000 acres of wetland are being converted annually. Based on these figures, the remaining wetland area is approximately 95 million acres.

127. Ralph W. Tiner, *Wetlands of the United States: Current Status and Recent Trends*, for U.S. Department of the Interior, Fish and Wildlife Service (Washington, D.C.: U.S. Government Printing Office, March 1984), p. 31.

128. Ibid., p. 34.

129. U.S. Department of Agriculture, "Environmental Assessment for the Wetland conservation Provisions of the Food Security Act 1985," June 1986, p. 1.

130. Ralph E. Heimlich and Linda L. Langer, "Swampbusting in Perspective," *Journal of Soil and Water Conservation* 41 (1986):220.

131. Ibid.

132. For a good assessment of this problem, see Bruce W. Menzel, "Agricultural Management Practices and the Integrity of Instream Biological Habitat," in Frank W. Schaller and George W. Bailey, eds., *Agricultural Management and Water Quality* (Ames, Iowa: Iowa State University Press, 1983), pp. 305-29.

133. William S. Platt, "Livestock Grazing and Riparian Stream/Ecosystems—An Overview," in Oliver B. Cope, ed., *Proceedings of the Forum-Grazing and Riparian Stream/*

Ecosystems, Denver, Colorado, November 3-4, 1978 (Trout Unlimited, March 1979), pp. 42-43.

134. Behnke and Zarn, *Biology and Management of Threatened and Endangered Western Trouts*, U.S. Forest Service General Technical Report RM-28 (Fort Collins, Colo.: Rocky Mountain Forest and Range Experiment Station, 1976); cited in Platt, "Livestock Grazing and Riparian/Stream Ecosystems," in Cope, *Proceedings*, p. 43.

135. National Research Council, *Soil Conservation*, vol. 1, table 1-4, p. 8.

136. Unpublished data from 1982 National Resources Inventory, tables 16a and 17a.

137. Information provided by U.S. Department of the Interior, Bureau of Land Management, Division of Rangeland Resources, September 1986.

138. For a review of experimental findings, see Douglas A. Haith and Raymond C. Loehr, eds., *Effectiveness of Soil and Water Conservation Practices for Pollution Control*, EPA-600/3-79-106 (Athens, Ga.: U.S. Environmental Protection Agency, October 1979), pp. 218-22 and table 9-8, pp. 240-43. For an overview of pesticide application and movement through the environment, see David Pimentel and Lois Levitan, "Pesticides: Amounts Applied and Amounts Reaching Pests," *BioScience* 36 (1986):86-91.

139. U.S. Geological Survey, *National Water Summary 1984: Hydrologic Events, Selected Water-Quality Trends, and Ground-Water Resources* (Washington, D.C.: U.S. Government Printing Office, 1985), pp. 95-96.

140. Ibid., p. 95.

141. Council for Agricultural Science and Technology, "Agricultural and Groundwater Quality," report no. 103 (Ames, Iowa: Council for Agricultural Science and Technology, 1985), p. 29.

142. Ibid., p. 29.

143. George R. Hallberg, "Agricultural Chemicals and Groundwater Quality in Iowa: Status Report 1985," pp. 1-6.

144. Lewrene K. Glaser, *Provisions of the Food Security Act of 1985*, Economic Research Service, Agriculture Information Bulletin No. 498 (Washington, D.C.: U.S. Department of Agriculture, April 1986), p. 12.

145. Excess stocks for wheat and corn are based on August 1986 estimates of ending stocks less the respective levels that trigger acreage reduction programs under the 1985 Food Security Act. For wheat, excess stocks are: 1.8 bil. bu. ending stocks – 1 bil. bu. trigger stock = 0.8 bil. bu. excess stocks. For corn: 5.3 bil. bu. ending stocks – 2 bil. bu. trigger stock = 3.3 bil. bu. excess stocks. Excess stocks were converted to acreage estimates using average yields for 1980 through 1986 (estimated): wheat 36.3 bu./acre, corn 105.5 bu./acre. (Information on stocks and yields provided by U.S. Department of Agriculture, Agricultural Stabilization and Conservation Service, September 1986.) The resulting acreage estimates were 31.3 million acres excess corn production and 22.0 million acres excess wheat production relative to ending stocks in 1986. This overcapacity in 1986 is partly the result of large ending stocks accumulated in previous years.

Nitrogen and phosphorus fertilizer use (nutrient equivalent) associated with this overcapacity was estimated using the following assumptions: for corn, 97 percent of acreage treated with 140 lbs./acre of nitrogen and 86 percent treated with 60 lbs./acre of phosphate; for wheat, 77 percent of acreage treated with 60 lbs./acre of nitrogen and 48 percent treated with 35 lbs./acre of phosphate; these assumptions reflect average 1985 application rates obtained from U.S. Department of Agriculture, *Agricultural Resources: Inputs*, AR-1, table 10, p. 11. Total fertilizer use associated with excess production in 1986 equalled

5.9 billion pounds for corn and 1.4 billion pounds for wheat.

Herbicide and insecticide use (active ingredients) associated with this overcapacity were estimated using the following assumptions: for corn, 95 percent of acres treated with 3.1 lbs./acre herbicide and 37 percent treated with 1 lb./acre insecticide; for wheat, 42 percent of acres treated with 0.5 lbs./acre herbicide and 3 percent treated with 0.9 lbs. per acre insecticide (these assumptions reflect average 1982 application rates obtained from U.S. Department of Agriculture, *Inputs: Outlook*, IOS-2, tables 1 and 2, p. 4 and table 4, p. 5). Total pesticide use associated with excess production in 1986 equaled 104.5 million pounds for corn and 5.2 million pounds for wheat.

146. Information provided by U.S. Department of Agriculture, Agricultural Stabilization and Conservation Service, Budget Division, September 1986.

147. Information provided by U.S. Department of Agriculture, Agricultural Stabilization and Conservation Service, Commodity Analysis Division, September 1986.

148. For a good review of U.S. agricultural policy, see Wayne D. Rasmussen, "Historical Overview of U.S. Agricultural Policies and Programs," in U.S. Department of Agriculture, Economic Research Service, *Agricultural-Food Policy Review: Commodity Program Perspectives*, Agricultural Economic Report no. 530 (Washington, D.C.: U.S. Department of Agriculture, July 1985).

149. The Food Security Act of 1985 (P.L. 99-198), commonly referred to as the "1985 Farm Bill," was signed into law December 23, 1985. It provides a five-year framework for the U.S. secretary of agriculture to administer various agriculture and food programs.

150. Calculated from U.S. Department of Agriculture, Economic Research Service, *Economic Indicators of the Farm Sector: State Financial Summary, 1984* (Washington, D.C.: U.S. Department of Agriculture, 1986), p. 37.

151. For a general description of "price-support loans" see Penelope C. Cate and Geoffrey S. Becker, "Federal Farm Programs: A Primer," 84-232 ENR (Washington, D.C.: Library of Congress, Congressional Research Service, December 1984), pp. 20-21.

152. Glaser, *Provisions*, p. 85.

153. For a general description of deficiency payments, see Cate and Becker, "A Primer," pp. 25-29.

154. Glaser, *Provisions*, pp. 25-29.

155. For a general description of production controls, see Cate and Becker, "A Primer," pp. 32-37.

156. Information provided by the U.S. Department of Agriculture, Agricultural Stabilization and Conservation Service, September 1986.

157. Glaser, *Provisions*, p. 85.

158. Ibid., pp. 85-86.

159. Information provided by the U.S. Department of Agriculture, Stabilization and Conservation Service, Budget Division, September 1986.

160. Information provided by the U.S. Department of Agriculture, Stabilization and Conservation Service, Budget Division, September 1986. Calculated using "cropland used for crops" in 1982 from U.S. Department of Agriculture, Economic Research Service, *Cropland Use*, p. 5.

161. Information provided by the U.S. Department of Agriculture, Agricultural Stabilization and Conservation Service, September 1986. See footnote 145.

162. Information provided by the U.S. Department of Agriculture,, Foreign Agricultural Service, September 1986.

163. For a discussion of this, see Milton H. Ericksen and Keith Collins, "Effectiveness of Acreage Reduction Programs," in U.S. Department of Agriculture, Economic Research Service, *Agricultural-Food Policy Review* (Washington, D.C.: U.S. Department of Agriculture, 1985), pp. 166-184.

164. Glaser, *Provisions*, p. 7.

165. For a brief discussion, see Glaser, *Provisions*, pp. 47-49; and U.S. Department of Agriculture, Office of Information, *Backgrounder-Conservation Reserve Program* (Washington, D.C.: U.S. Department of Agriculture, January 13, 1986).

166. Estimated impacts of the Conservation Reserve Program were based on a 40-million-acre reserve comprised of land eroding in excess of two times the T value or land in capability classes VI through VIII; U.S. Department of Agriculture, *Environmental Assessment for Conservation Reserve Program Authorized Under the 1985 Farm Bill*, January 1986, Table 11, p. 30. However, the criterion was subsequently altered to land eroding in excess of 3-T or land in capability classes VI through VIII. The impacts for this definition of highly erodible cropland were not estimated by USDA but should be similar to the original estimates. Further changes in CRP criteria were anticipated as this report was being prepared.

167. U.S. Department of Agriculture, *Environmental Assessment for CRP*, figure 10, p. 39.

168. Ibid., table E.3, p. vi.

169. Information provided by the U.S. Department of Agriculture, Agricultural Stabilization and Conservation Service, October 1986.

170. In 1986, the substantial benefits made available to farmers under USDA's commodity price and income support programs, coupled with sharply lower market prices resulting from lowered commodity loan rates, resulted in a high level of program participation. Many farmers found it to their economic advantage to use highly erodible cropland to satisfy the acreage reduction requirements of the commodity programs instead of enrolling the land in the CRP. Numerous economic factors entered into farmers' decisions about enrolling in the CRP including crop yields on highly erodible land, the proportion of base acres to total cropland on the farm, the farm operator's financial situation, assumptions about future commodity program benefits, and whether operators owned or operated eligible land. Information obtained from the Soil Conservation Service, and Agricultural Stabilization and Conservation Service, U.S. Department of Agriculture, October 1986.

171. Information provided by U.S. Department of Agriculture, Soil Conservation Service, March, 1987.

172. Between the 1981 and 1985 acts, Congress enacted five laws that altered various aspects of commodity programs for dairy, cotton, tobacco, feed grains, rice, and wheat. For a listing of major agricultural legislation, see Glaser, *Provisions*, appendix 2, pp. 87-90.

173. For a brief description see Glaser, *Provisions*, pp. 45-47.

174. 51 Fed. Reg. 23504 (1986).

175. U.S. Department of Agriculture, *Environmental Assessment* for the "Highly Erodible Land Conservation Provisions of the Food Security Act of 1985," June 1986, p. 30. Percent reduction calculated from table 13, p. 29 for alternative 2, erosion potential 8.

176. Ibid., pp. 35-36.

177. U.S. Department of Agriculture, Office of Information, "Highly Erodible Land and Wetland Conservation Provisions of the Food Security Act of 1985," *Backgrounder*, June 25, 1986, p. 19.

178. Information provided by the U.S. Department of Agriculture, Farmers Home

Administration, October 1986.

179. Information provided by the U.S. Department of Agriculture, Agricultural Stabilization and Conservation Service, September 1986.

180. For a brief description see Glaser, *Provisions*, pp. 55-56.

181. Information provided by the U.S. Department of Agriculture, Farmers Home Administration, October 1986.

182. For a brief description, see Glaser, *Provisions*, pp. 46-47.

183. U.S. Department of Agriculture, "Environmental Assessment for Highly Erodible Land," table 10, p. 24.

184. Calculated from Clayton W. Ogg, "New Cropland in th 1982 NRI: Implications for Resource Policy," in National Research Council, *Soil Conservation*, vol. 2, table 2, p. 258 and table 3, p. 260.

185. For a brief description, see Glaser, *Provisions*, p. 47. For an analysis of "swampbuster" and agricultural conversion of wetlands see Ralph E. Heimlich and Linda L. Langner, "Swampbusting in Perspective," *Journal of Soil and Water Conservation* 41 (1986):219-224.

186. U.S. Department of Agriculture, "Environmental Assessment for the Wetland Conservation Provisions of the Food Security Act 1985" (Washington, D.C.: U.S. Department of Agriculture, June 1986), p. 11.

187. Anne E. Kinsinger, "A Preliminary Review of the Conference Committee's Tax Reform Package" (Washington, D.C.: Natural Resources Defense Council, August 1986), p. 36; see also William D. Anderson and Nelson L. Bills, "Soil Conservation and Tax Policy," *Journal of Soil and Water Conservation* 41 (1986):225-28.

188. "A Meeting of Minds on Pesticides Ads Overseas," *Chemical Week*, November 9, 1983, pp. 29-30.

189. See "Critics Fault World Bank for Ecological Neglect," *Conservation Foundation Letter*, November-December 1984, pp. 1-7; Bruce M. Rich, "The Multilateral Development Banks, Environmental Policy, and the United States," *Ecology Law Quarterly* 12 (1985):681-745; and "Environmental Reform of World Bank Lending Mandated by Recently Passed U.S. Law," *World Environment Report*, January 8, 1986, pp.3-4.

190. H. Jeffrey Leonard, "Political and Economic Causes of Third World Environmental Degradation," in H. Jeffrey Leonard, ed., *Divesting Nature's Capital: The Political Economy of Environmental Abuse in the Third World* (New York: Holmes and Meier, 1985), p. 98.

191. European Economic Community Commission, Agricultural Information Service, *Perspectives for the Common Agricultural Policy: The Green Paper of the Commission* (Brussels: European Economic Community Commission, 1985).

192. Clean Water bills that addressed nonpoint-source problems passed the House of Representatives (H.R. 8, H.Rpt. 99-189) and Senate (S. 1128, S.Rpt. 99-50) in 1985; U.S. Environmental Protection Agency, *Final Report on the Federal/State/Local Nonpoint Source Task Force and Recommended National Nonpoint Source Policy* (Washington, D.C.: U.S. Environmental Protection Agency, January 1985).

193. Amendments to the Federal Insecticide, Fungicide, and Rodenticide Act passed the House (H.R. 2482) and the Senate (S. 2792) in 1986; and U.S. Environmental Protection Agency, Office of Ground-Water Protection, *Pesticides in Ground Water: Background Document* (Washington, D.C.: U.S. Environmental Protection Agency, May 1986).

194. A proposal for comprehensive national action to protect groundwater was introduced to the Senate (S. 1836) in November 1986 to focus congressional attention on this issue; and U.S. Environmental Protection Agency, Office of Ground-Water Protection, *Ground-Water Protection Strategy* (Washington, D.C.: U.S. Environmental Protection Agency, August 1984).

195. Peter C. Myers, "Offsite Effects of Soil Erosion: What We Can Co," in Thomas E. Waddell, ed., *The Off-Site Costs of Soil Erosion*, Proceedings of a Symposium held in May 1985 (Washington, D.C.: The Conservation Foundation, 1986), pp. 103-10.

Boxes

Grain Production in the European Economic Community

1. The EEC countries, as defined here, are Belgium, Denmark, France, West Germany, Greece, Ireland, Italy, Luxembourg, Netherlands, and the United Kingdom. Spain and Portugal joined in 1986 and are not included in the data presented. For an overview of EEC agriculture and of current agricultural policy issues, see European Economic Community Commission, Agricultural Information Service, *Perspectives for the Common Agricultural Policy: The Green Paper of the Commission* (Brussels: European Economic Community Commission, 1985). For the role of the EC in world grain trade see U.S. Department of Agriculture, Foreign Agricultural Service, *Foreign Agriculture Circular: Grains* (Washington, D.C. U.S. Department of Agriculture, October 1985).

2. Donna U. Vogt and Jasper Womach, *The Common Agricultural Policy of the European Community and Implications for U.S. Agricultural Trade* (Washington, D.C.: Congressional Research Service, 1984), p. 3.

3. Ibid., p. 8.

4. Richard Body, *Agriculture: The Triumph and the Shame* (London: Temple Smith, 1983), p. 40.

5. Ibid., p. 40.

6. Food and Agriculture Organization of the United Nations, *FAO Production Yearbook* (Rome: FAO, 1985), p. 55.

7. Ibid., p. 55.

8. Richard Westmacott, "Reminders of the Rural Landscape," *Landscape Design* 2 (1985):12-17.

9. Ibid.

10. Ibid.

11. Hartwig de Haen, "Interdependence of Prices, Production Intensity and Environmental Damage from Agricultural Production," *Zeitschrift fur Umweltpolitik* 8 (1985):199-219.

12. Organisation for Economic Cooperation and Development, *OECD Environmental Data, Compendium 1985* (Paris: Organisation for Economic Cooperation and Development, 1985), p. 205.

13. Westmacott, "Reminders of the Rural Landscape."

14. For an up-to-date review of environmental impacts, see European Parliament, Committee on the Environment, Public Health and Consumer Protection, *Report on Agriculture and the Environment*, Document A 2-207/85 (February 1986). An appended report by the Parliament's Committee on Agriculture, Fisheries and Food notes (p. 58) that there has been "considerable talk of 'agriculture damaging the environment'", but again it

is difficult to say to what extent this is happening. Even the Agriculture Committee, however, admits (p. 62) that "To summarise, under the CAP regime, with its emphasis on high production and intensive farming, there has been a whole range of deleterious environmental effects, although, as stated before, it would appear that the precise scale of these problems has not been quantified."

15. Edward Maltby, *Waterlogged Wealth* (London: International Institute for Environment and Development, 1986), p. 151.

16. Annette Kovar, "Nitrate Pollution: The European Experience," A Report to the German Marshall Fund of the United States, September 1985, p. 1.

17. Ibid., pp. 4-5.

18. Ibid., p. 14.

19. "Nitrate Pollution, Farm Waste," *International Environment Reporter*, February 8, 1984, p. 44.

20. "Pesticide Byproduct Found As Pollutant in Drinking Water in Province of Drenthe," *International Environment Reporter*, July 10, 1985, pp. 229-230.

21. Graham Avery, "Prosperity With Responsibility" (Address given at the 40th Oxford Farming Conference, January 1986).

22. Committee on the Environment, Public Health and Consumer Protection, European Parliament, *Report on Agriculture and the Environment*, February 3, 1986.

23. "Nitrate Pollution from Agriculture Cited; Government Rejects Regulation of Farmers," *International Environment Reporter*, January 8, 1986, pp. 7-8.

Beef Cattle Production in Central America

1. George Ledec, "The Political Economy of Tropical Deforestation," in H. Jeffrey Leonard, ed., *Divesting Nature's Capital: The Political Economy of Environmental Abuse in the Third World* (New York: Holmes and Meier, 1985), p. 204.

2. Douglas R. Shane, "Hoofprints on the Forest: An Inquiry into the Beef Cattle Industry in the Tropical Forest Areas of Latin America," report prepared for Office of Environmental Affairs, U.S. Department of State, March 1980, p. 8.

3. See Norman Myers, "The Hamburger Connection: How Central America's Forests Became North America's Hamburgers," *Ambio*, vol. 10 (1981):3-8.

4. James Nations and H. Jeffrey Leonard, "Grounds of Conflict in Central America," in Andrew Maguire and Janet Walsh Brown, eds., *Bordering on Trouble*, (Washington, D.C.: World Resources Institute, 1986), p.72.

5. Calculated from U.S. Department of Agriculture, *Agricultural Statistics 1985* (Washington, D.C.: U.S. Government Printing Office, 1985), table 447, p. 301.

6. See Victor Manuel Toledo, "La Guerra de las Reses," in E. Leff, ed., *Medio Ambiente y Desarrollo en Mexico* (in press, 1986). Mexican beef exports to the United States, which mainly come from nontropical northern Mexico, have oscillated greatly from year to year and have been negligible since 1979; and U.S. Department of Agriculture, *Agricultural Statistics 1985*, table 447, p. 30.

7. Exports of fresh and frozen beef from South America to the United States are largely restricted by federal regulations aimed at preventing the spread of hoof-and-mouth disease. Brazil does export canned and cooked meat to the United States, but this accounts for less than 10 percent of total Brazilian meat exports. For observations on Brazilian beef production, see Edward C. Wolf, "Managing Rangelands," in Lester R. Brown, ed., *State of the World, 1986* (New York: W.W. Norton, 1986), pp. 71-72.

Soybean Production in Brazil

1. Calculated from the U.S. Department of Agriculture, *Agricultural Statistics 1973* (Washington, D.C.: U.S. Government Printing Office, 1973), table 189, p. 132.

2. Calculated from the U.S. Department of Agriculture, *Agricultural Statistics 1985* (Washington, D.C.: U.S. Government Printing Office, 1985), table 174, p. 128.

3. Information provided by Ed Allen, U.S. Department of Agriculture, Foreign Agricultural Service, September 1986.

4. Ibid.

5. Ibid.

6. Stephen Graham, "Down But Not Out in Brazil," *Sierra* 71 (1986):33-37.

7. Kent H. Redford, "Emas National Park and the Plight of the Brazilian Cerrados," *Oryx* 19 (1985):210-214; and personal communication from Kent H. Redford, August 1986.

8. Philip Fearnside, "Spatial Concentration of Deforestation in the Brazilian Amazon," *Ambio* 15 (1986):74-81.

Grain and Cotton Production in China

1. Information provided by International Economic Division, Economic Research Service, U.S. Department of Agriculture,, August 1986.

2. "China's Agricultural Revolution: From Customer to Competitor," *Agricultural Outlook* (U.S. Department of Agriculture, Economic Research Service), March 1985, pp. 23-26.

3. Ibid., p. 23.

4. See E.B. Vermeer, "Agriculture in China—A Deteriorating Situation," *The Ecologist*, vol. 14, no. 1 (1984); Vaclav Smil, *The Bad Earth: Environmental Degradation in China* (Armonk, N.Y.: M.E. Sharpe, 1984); Harold L. Barrows et al., "Report on China: An American View of How That Nation Manages its Soil Resources," *Journal of Soil and Water Conservation*, November-December 1983, pp. 315-18; Wang Huijiong, Li Jinchang, and Li Poxi, "Natural Resources and Environmental Protection of China's Agriculture" (Beijing: Technical-Economic Research Center, State Council of China, 1984).

5. Smil calls this China's "grain-first" policy and attributes it to the Maoist concern for "taking grain as the key link." See Smil, *The Bad Earth*, pp. 16, 62-68, 183.

6. *Agricultural Outlook* (March 1985), pp. 19-20.

7. Ibid., p. 24.

8. Smil, *The Bad Earth*, p.143.

9. Huijiong, Jinchang, and Poxi, "Natural Resources and Environmental Protection of China's Agriculture," p. 4.

10. Smil, *The Bad Earth*, p. 192. /ftx/

Figures

6.1. For wheat and wheat flour, corn, 1965-84: Information provided by U.S. Department of Agriculture, Economic Research Service, August 1986; for soybeans and soybean cake, 1965-85: ibid.; for total export quantities, 1965-85: U.S. Department of Agriculture, Economic Research Service, *Foreign Agricultural Trade of the United States: Calendar Year Supplement*, (Washington, D.C.: U.S. Department of Agriculture, 1986), table

2, p. 2; for corn, wheat, and wheat flour, 1985: ibid., table 4, p. 5-6.

6.2. For wheat, 1970-83: U.S. Department of Agriculture, *Agricultural Statistics 1985* (Washington, D.C.: U.S. Government Printing Office, 1985), p. 1; for corn, 1970-83: ibid., p. 30; for soybeans, 1970-83: ibid., p. 125; using conversion factors pp. v-vii; for wheat, soybeans, corn, 1984-85: *Agricultural Outlook* (U.S. Department of Agriculture, Economic Research Service) August 1986, p. 49.

6.3. For pesticides, 1964-84: U.S. Environmental Protection Agency, Office of Pesticide Programs, "Pesticide Industry Sales and Usage: 1984 Market Estimates," September 1985, table 8; for fertilizer 1964-83: U.S. Department of Agriculture, Economic Research Service, *Economic Indicators of the Farm Sector: Production and Efficiency Statistics, 1984*, ECIFS 4-4 (Washington, D.C.: U.S. Department of Agriculture, 1986), p. 26; for tractor horsepower, 1964-83: ibid., p. 30; for labor, 1964-78: ibid., p. 31; for cropland, 1965-83: ibid., p. 17; for fertilizer 1984-85: U.S. Department of Agriculture, Economic Research Service, *Agricultural Resources: Inputs Outlook and Situation Report*, AR-1 (Washington, D.C.: U.S. Department of Agriculture, February 1986), p. 10; for tractor horsepower, 1984-85, labor, 1979-85, and cropland, 1984-86: information provided by U.S. Department of Agriculture, Economic Research Service, August 1986.

6.4. For corn, 1965-69: U.S. Department of Agriculture, *Agricultural Statistics 1980* (Washington, D.C.: U.S. Government Printing Office, 1980), p. 30; for wheat, 1965-69: ibid., p. 1; for soybeans, 1965-69: ibid., p.129; for cotton, 1965-69: ibid., p. 61; for corn, 1970-83: U.S. Department of Agriculture, *Agricultural Statistics 1985*, p. 30; for wheat, 1970-83: ibid., p. 1; for soybeans, 1970-83: ibid., p. 124; for cotton, 1970-83: ibid., p. 61; for corn, wheat, soybeans and cotton, 1984-86: information provided by U.S. Department of Agriculture, National Agricultural Statistics Service, August 1986; for cropland, 1965-83: U.S. Department of Agriculture, *Economic Indicators: Production and Efficiency*, p. 17; for cropland 1984-86: information provided by the U.S. Department of Agriculture, Economic Research Service, August 1986.

6.5. For 1960-83: U.S. Department of Agriculture, *Economic Indicators: Production and Efficiency*, pp.27-29; for 1984-85: U.S. Department of Agriculture, *Agricultural Resources: Inputs Outlook*, p. 10. Data converted to metric tons.

6.6. For herbicide use: U.S. Department of Agriculture, Economic Research Service, *Inputs: Outlook and Situation*, IOS-2 (Washington, D.C.: U.S. Department of Agriculture, 1983), p. 4; for insecticide use: ibid., p. 5; planted acreage, 1971 and 1982 for corn: U.S. Department of Agriculture, *Agricultural Statistics 1985*, p. 30; for cotton: ibid., p. 61; for soybeans: ibid., p. 124; for wheat: ibid., 1; for acreage of other major field crops: ibid., pp. 15, 19, 38, 43, 50, 93, 117, 267 and U.S. Department of Agriculture, *Agricultural Statistics 1973* (Washington, D.C.: U.S. Government Printing Office, 1973), pp. 242, 243.

6.7. Map provided by U.S. Department of Agriculture, Soil Conservation Service, National Mapping Division, Ft. Worth, Texas, 1986. Data are from the 1982 National Resources Inventory. Each dot represents 25,000 acres.

6.8. Edwin H. Clark II, Jennifer A. Haverkamp, and William Chapman, *Eroding Soils: The Off-Farm Impacts* (Washington, D.C.: The Conservation Foundation, 1985). figure ES1, xiv.

Chapter 7

America's Waste:
Managing for Risk Reduction

Modern societies generate large amounts of waste of many types. In the United States, about 50,000 pounds of waste is produced for each of our 240 million residents every year. Figure 7.1 shows the approximate number of pounds of different types of waste produced per person in 1984. Figure 7.2 shows the proportions that are released to the air and dumped into the water or onto the land each year. If all of it could be neatly deposited in the backyard, the average sized family each year would create a pile approximately 10 feet on a side and 28 feet high.* Each household would spend approximately one and one-half hours a day carrying its wastes to this pile, assuming an average of 20 pounds and five minutes a trip.

These rough numbers substantially underestimate the amount of waste actually produced, for they are based predominantly on dry weight measurements; they assume that all the water has been removed from wastes that are normally produced in liquid form. The estimates also ignore all of the wastes produced abroad in manufacturing goods imported by the United States (although they do include the wastes associated with producing U.S. exports).

Most Americans do not imagine that they generate so much waste, for they do so only indirectly. The amount of waste produced directly by all households is about 3 percent of the total waste load. Per household per

---

*This assumes a waste density of 40-60 pounds per cubic foot and an average household of 2.7 persons.

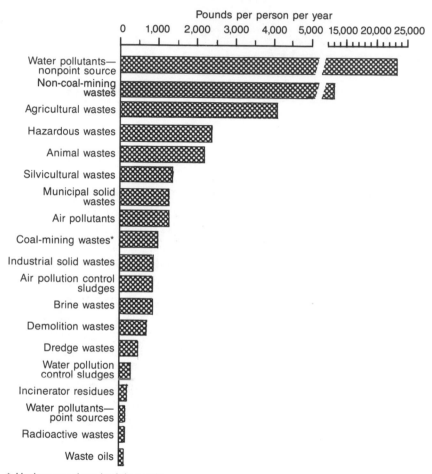

Figure 7.1
Estimated Annual Waste Production
in the United States

* Underground coal mining only.
All values are estimated dry weights except for "Hazardous wastes." Some wastes may
be double-counted.

Source: The Conservation Foundation.

Figure 7.2
Relative Amounts of Waste Originally Released to Air, Water, and Land

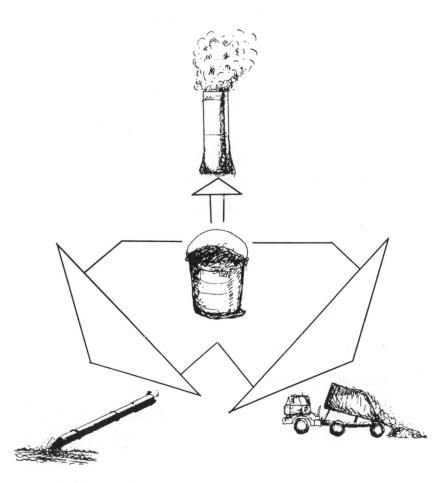

Source: The Conservation Foundation.

year, this waste consists of about 3,600 pounds of garbage, 120,000 gallons of wastewater that ends up as about 180 pounds of wastewater sludge, 64 pounds of pollutants emitted to the air by wood stoves, and 210 pounds from family automobiles.[1] The rest of society's total is generated by industry in the manufacture and distribution of goods for human use— goods ranging from tubes of toothpaste to nuclear missiles.

But the distinction between what is produced directly and what is produced indirectly is not important here. Nor is the total amount of waste produced. Many wastes create relatively few problems. Some provide benefits, and perhaps should not be considered wastes at all.* The most important question is how much damage wastes can do to our health and environment—both immediately and in the future. To answer this question, the risks posed by both the wastes themselves and society's techniques for managing them must be assessed. Such an assessment requires sophisticated understanding of the different parts of the waste management system, including generation, transportation, storage, treatment, and disposal.

Is about 50,000 pounds of waste per person per year unreasonably high? That depends on how effectively our waste management system protects the public. Many programs to control wastes have not been as effective as they might have been in reducing risk. They often have done little more than shift the wastes from one medium—water, land, or air—to another, without regard to whether risks are being reduced in the process. By contrast, the most effective, as well as most economical, way to reduce the risks associated with wastes in many cases is to reduce the amount that is generated and released to the environment.

TYPES AND AMOUNTS OF WASTE

Although it is obvious that modern societies produce large amounts of waste, what constitutes waste is not always clear. In the first place, one person's waste may be another's raw material. The problem of defining and measuring waste becomes particularly tricky when one attempts to distinguish among the different types of waste. In some cases, wastes are categorized simply by the medium to which they are released. In others, they may be identified by their origins, for example, construction debris, mine tailings, or municipal wastes. Sometimes wastes are defined according to their

---

*Economists define waste as a nonproduct stream of material or energy, the value of which is less than the costs of collection, transport, and use.[2]

physical characteristics—whether they are gaseous, liquid, or solid. Other times they are classified according to the type of risk or problem they create—for example, solid wastes, hazardous wastes, and radioactive wastes.

These different ways of classifying wastes are reflected in the fragmented legal system used to control them. Some laws focus on where the wastes are discharged (for example, to the air or water), some on the source of the wastes (for example, coal mining), some on how they are disposed of (for example, in underground injection wells), and some on the characteristics of the waste (for example, toxic or radioactive). Because a single waste stream may be managed under different programs, the wastes may be tallied more than once. For instance, liquid wastes released by a copper mine may be simultaneously reckoned by one government office or another as water pollutants, mining wastes, hazardous wastes, and wastes released to land. On the other hand, if a waste such as animal manure is not managed by any of these offices, it may not be counted at all.

Classification and measurement are further complicated because many waste management systems transform waste or transfer it to a point where it may be counted again. Thus, contaminants can be removed from a wastewater stream and either dumped on the ground—creating solid wastes—or incinerated—creating both air wastes and, with the remaining ash, solid wastes. Similarly, air pollution control devices can create solid wastes or water wastes. In some cases, waste may be chemically or physically converted to a form no longer counted as waste, even though it may still cause problems. For example, both air and water pollution control devices frequently convert organic (that is, carbon-containing) wastes to carbon dioxide (CO_2) and water, which they release to the atmosphere. In most cases, this CO_2 disappears from the accounting system. Yet it is still a waste product, for it contributes to the atmospheric CO_2 overload.

Another problem is how to measure a given amount of waste. If waste is diluted with clean water, does this increase the amount of waste generated? It does under some measurement systems. For example, a ton of soluble solid waste diluted to a 1 percent mixture (that is, 99 percent water and 1 percent "waste") will produce twice the waste by volume that it would produce if diluted to a 2 percent mixture, and 100 times the amount of waste that existed originally. On the other hand, the amount of air used to dilute a gaseous air stream is not usually counted, only the weight of the waste materials themselves.

The measurement problem is compounded by the fact that the amount of waste generated often depends on how it is processed before discharging it to the environment. For instance, assume someone has 75 pounds of pure carbon black to get rid of. If it were pure enough, it should not enter the waste stream at all, for it would be worth about $450.00 at 1986 retail prices.[3] If it were dumped into the garbage, it would be counted as 75 pounds of solid waste. If it were incinerated, however, it would be counted as 175 pounds of gaseous waste if burned inefficiently (producing carbon monoxide among other things) or as 275 pounds if burned efficiently (producing carbon dioxide).* If it were pulverized and dumped in a stream, it would be counted twice—once as 75 pounds of suspended solids and a second time as 200 pounds of biochemical oxygen demand (BOD) or chemical oxygen demand (COD).

Why even try to measure waste production? In the past, waste was largely ignored until it began to pose a public health problem or destroy a natural resource such as groundwater. Then a regulatory program was developed. Today, for the most part, only regulated wastes are tracked and measured; information on unregulated wastes is difficult or impossible to come by. It is useful, however, to step back occasionally and make sure that some serious problems are not eluding the regulatory net and that existing programs are in fact providing solutions to the problems that stimulated their adoption, instead of just shifting the problems elsewhere.

Considering the many difficulties involved in defining wastes, and considering the fact that many estimates are based on large extrapolations from small surveys or on theoretical analyses, any waste estimates are highly uncertain. With full recognition of these limitations, some estimates are presented below. The wastes are defined chiefly by the medium to which they are released because this distinction comports best with current regulatory programs and, therefore, with current estimates.

Air

The U.S. Environmental Protection Agency (EPA) estimates that a total of 153 million tons of waste was released to the air in 1984.[4] Forty-eight percent of the total was contributed by transportation, 16 percent by electric utilities, and 14 percent by industries. The EPA estimates do not cover all sources of wastes, but only major point sources and types of pollutants regulated under the Clean Air Act. The estimates do not, for instance, include the volatile chemicals and other gases released by wastewater treatment facilities; nonpoint sources such as wind-blown dust or pesticides attached to this dust; or the volatilized portion of animal manure, agriculture,

---

*Because carbon dioxide is usually not considered a waste, the efficient burning of the carbon black would usually result in it disappearing from the accounts entirely.

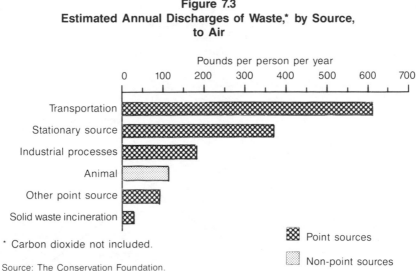

Figure 7.3
Estimated Annual Discharges of Waste,* by Source,
to Air

Pounds per person per year

* Carbon dioxide not included.

Source: The Conservation Foundation.

or silvicultural waste. Figure 7.3 shows the numbers of pounds of waste per person per year emitted to the air. It includes more wastes than the EPA estimate, but does not include the huge amounts of carbon dioxide. Researchers analyzing the problem of increasing atmospheric carbon dioxide have estimated that, globally, human sources—such as power plants, automobiles, industrial plants, and home and business space heating— release about five billion metric tons of carbon to the atmosphere annually.[5]* EPA's current programs, however, do not consider carbon dioxide to be a waste.

Most air pollutants—such as sulfur dioxide, nitrogen oxides, and carbon monoxide—are released in gaseous form. But "particulates," small solid particles released to the air, might be classified as solid wastes under some schemes. Some of the gaseous pollutants may adsorb onto these small particles (either before or after release to the air) and thus become part of the solid wastes.

As indicated in figure 7.4, however, many of the wastes initially headed for release to the air are instead collected in an air pollution control device and then transferred either to the land (in most cases) or water (less commonly). In the collection process, the amount of waste may be increased

---

*Large amounts are also released as a result of deforestation activities.

Figure 7.4
Final Destination of Wastes
Originally Released to
Air

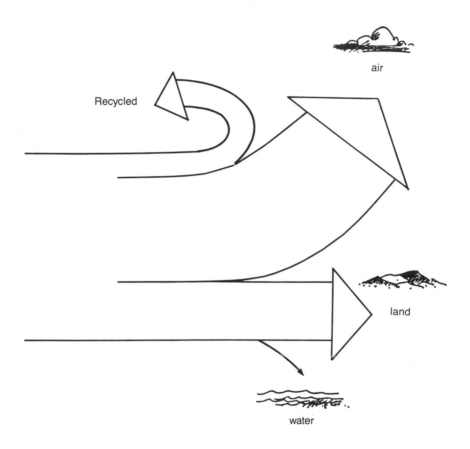

Source: The Conservation Foundation.

dramatically. For instance, one type of wet scrubber uses a great deal of water and a little more than one pound of powdered lime to capture one pound of sulfur dioxide. This process converts the original one pound of air pollution to two to four pounds[6] of very wet solid waste, which typically is partially dried and disposed of on the land.

Water

No government agency makes any official estimates of the amount of wastes released to the nation's waterways. However, Resources for the Future (RFF) has developed a large information base that provides such estimates for both point sources regulated under the Clean Water Act (such as industrial and municipal sewage plants) and nonpoint sources (such as runoff from farms and city streets) that are not regulated.[7]

The RFF estimates indicate that a substantial majority of the conventional pollutants—averaging* nearly three billion tons of suspended solids, seven million tons of nitrogen, and two million tons of phosphorus per year—come from unregulated nonpoint sources of pollution.

Municipal sewage treatment plants can also release large amounts of both conventional and nonconventional pollutants, particularly if industries that discharge wastewater to them do not pretreat their wastes. The United States has invested some $56 billion since 1972 ($37.2 billion from the federal government) attempting to control this source, but EPA's most recent survey indicates that another $44.4 billion of new construction is required to provide adequate wastewater treatment facilities for all municipal systems for the current population.[8] Even after the treatment facilities are constructed, they might not be operated properly. Industrial point sources, having largely adopted pollution controls under the requirements of the Clean Water Act, are now responsible for smaller amounts of most conventional pollutants than either nonpoint sources or municipal treatment plants.

Other water pollutants are sludges, industrial wastes, dredge spoils, and other "solid" wastes that are carried offshore in barges and dumped in designated ocean dumping sites, as well as some industrial and municipal sewage effluent that is delivered to the ocean via pipelines. The amounts of some of these wastes have decreased since revisions to the ocean dumping regulations were made in 1977. Dumping of sewage sludge has, however, increased; in 1983 it was 60 percent greater than in 1977.[9]

Figure 7.5 shows that nonpoint sources and dredge material contribute most of the water pollutants. Where the wastes enter the water affects the amount of damage. Pipelines continuously releasing wastes to estuaries are likely to do more damage than barges dumping wastes into the open ocean, for example. However, many of the pollutants from wastewater treatment plants that would otherwise go to the water now go to either the

---

*Nonpoint source figures are long-term averages. The amounts can differ greatly from year to year.

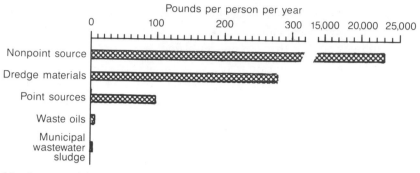

**Figure 7.5
Estimated Annual Discharges of Waste, by Source,
to Water**

All values are estimated dry weights.

Source: The Conservation Foundation.

land or the air (figure 7.6). Air emissions result from the incineration of wastewater sludges, the bacterial degradation of organic wastes, and the intentional "air stripping" of volatile pollutants. Much larger amounts of water-borne wastes are converted to sludge and disposed of on land.

Land

Because it is not as homogeneous as water or air, land traditionally has not been defined as a medium accepting waste. There is no Clean Land Act, and no "Office of Land" exists at EPA. Instead the focus has been on the various sources that discharge wastes to land and the methods by which these wastes are managed.*

The largest amount of waste, aside from nonpoint releases to water, is currently discharged to land (figure 7.7). Some of it, such as air pollution control and wastewater sludge (approximately 800 pounds per person), is waste that otherwise would have been discharged to the air or the water in the absence of pollution control requirements. About 5 percent of the wastes that normally would be disposed of on the land are recycled and diverted from the waste stream.[10]

---

*The term *managed* is used in this analysis to incorporate the whole process of waste transport, storage, treatment, and disposal.

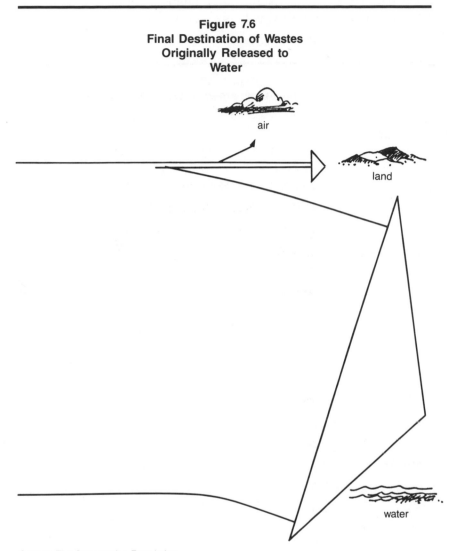

Figure 7.6
Final Destination of Wastes
Originally Released to
Water

air

land

water

Source: The Conservation Foundation.

As noted, many of these estimates are very uncertain. The estimates for industrial solid wastes, for instance, may vary from 50 to 350 million tons per year.[11] Most of these wastes are disposed of on company property, and, except for the hazardous wastes defined under the Resource Conservation and Recovery Act (RCRA), companies are not required to report the amounts generated. The volumes of agricultural, animal, and mining wastes are also very uncertain, but they probably account for the largest amount of wastes discharged to land.

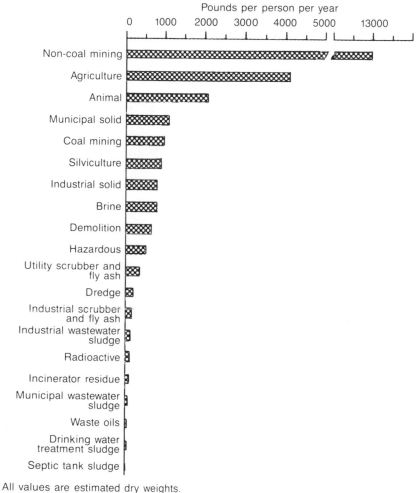

Figure 7.7
Estimated Annual Discharges of Waste, by Source, to Land

All values are estimated dry weights.

Source: The Conservation Foundation.

Much close attention is paid to some dangerous waste streams, such as radioactive wastes and wastes defined as hazardous under EPA's implementation of RCRA. Infectious wastes, such as those generated by hospitals, are also of concern. On the basis of the available information, the United States appears to generate about 2,400 pounds of hazardous wastes (wet weight), 120 pounds of radioactive wastes, and 60 pounds of infectious wastes per person per year.[12] Although the total is small in comparison to the amounts of less hazardous waste disposed of on land (perhaps 24,000 pounds per person per year), wastes in those three categories probably create the greatest risks.

Information about the composition of these wastes is even more uncertain than information about their quantities. Even for hazardous wastes, little is known about the relative importance of their components. Clearly these wastes include substantial amounts of water, but no one knows how much—it could well be over 75 percent.[13]*

Much work has been done to determine the composition of municipal solid waste. According to one of the more recent investigations, the largest component (37 percent) is paper, with yard wastes at 18 percent. Metals account for 10 percent and plastics for 7 percent (figure 7.8).

Few of the wastes disposed of on land end up elsewhere (figure 7.9). The major exceptions are those that are recycled, thereby leaving the waste stream entirely, and those that are incinerated, thereby being converted to gases and released to the air. (Incineration is used on approximately 6 percent of municipal solid waste, 5 percent of hazardous waste,† and 25 percent of municipal sewage sludge.) Relatively small amounts of wastes are now diverted to the water (except for those carried off the land during storms or leached through the soil), but discharging wastes through waste-water treatment plants may become more common as stricter controls are placed on land disposal and underground injection.

RISKS AND DAMAGES

The best way to make sense out of the complex components and paths of waste streams is to examine the different kinds and degrees of risk and damage they create. Different waste streams create different risks or damages

---

*Because of this uncertainty, the hazardous waste estimates are the only ones not presented on a dry weight basis.

†About four-fifths of this was burned in boilers or kilns rather than EPA-approved incinerators.[14]

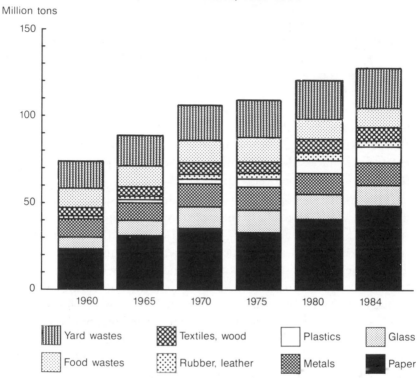

Figure 7.8
**Major Components of the Municipal Solid Waste Stream
in the United States, 1960–1984**

Million tons

Yard wastes	Textiles, wood	Plastics	Glass
Food wastes	Rubber, leather	Metals	Paper

* Wastes discarded after material recovery, but before energy recovery.
Source: U.S. Environmental Protection Agency.

to humans or ecosystems that are exposed to them. Some of these risks and damages are created directly. If pesticide residues are dumped into sewers and not removed by a wastewater treatment plant, they may kill the fish in a stream; air pollution can cause respiratory diseases.

Some of the risks and damages also can be created indirectly. If pesticide residues are removed by a wastewater treatment plant, they can accumulate in sludge that then may be put in a landfill. From there, they can leach into water or volatilize into the air. Air pollutants can fall to earth and contaminate lakes and streams or soil. Trichloroethylene (TCE) placed in a landfill can evaporate, creating a potential air pollution risk to people downwind,[15] or it can leach to groundwater, making it unfit to drink.

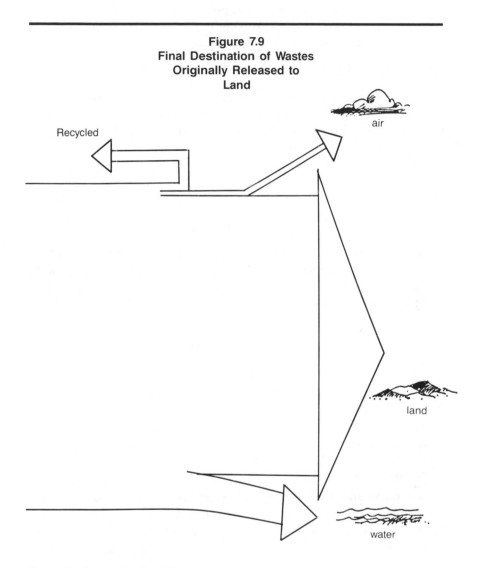

**Figure 7.9
Final Destination of Wastes
Originally Released to
Land**

Recycled

air

land

water

Source: The Conservation Foundation.

Assessing the risks associated with a waste stream requires evaluation of two factors. The first is the hazard associated with the waste—that is, the inherent potential of the waste to cause harm. The second is the likelihood that populations or ecosystems—especially those of greatest vulnerability or sensitivity—will be exposed to that hazard. If there is no potential harm, there is no risk or potential damage. Likewise, if there is no exposure, no damage will occur.

Assessment of Hazards

Some wastes create serious health hazards. In extreme cases, brief exposure can cause instant death or permanent physical damage. In other cases, human health risks only manifest themselves many years later or are only likely to result from continued exposure over a long period of time. Often, the wastes create very little, if any, risk to human health, but cause various other types of damage—discoloring the paint on cars, causing the stone in buildings to deteriorate, making beaches unfit for swimming and lakes too polluted for fish, or just creating an aesthetic nuisance, as with litter. In other cases, the risks remain unknown.

The duration of a hazard also differs from one waste stream to another. Some radioactive wastes pose risks for a few days and others for thousands of years. Metals do not degrade, but they may change into more or less hazardous forms. Some wastes degrade very rapidly, but the resulting substances may be either more or less hazardous than the original. TCE, one of the most common groundwater contaminants, may be transformed into vinyl chloride or 1,2-dichloroethylene, substances that are 2.5 and 5 times more potent than the initial solvent.[16]

A single source of waste can create several different types of damage. An abandoned waste dump may threaten both the health of humans living nearby and the survival of wildlife in an adjacent stream. It may create an aesthetic nuisance as well. Clearly, these various hazards are difficult to compare.

The degree of the hazard depends on the characteristics of both the waste and the environment into which it is released. Acid drainage, for instance, is much less likely to be a hazard in western than in eastern coal mines because the western coal has a lower sulfur content and because the drier environment is likely to result in the sulfur being converted to sulfuric acid at a much slower rate.[17]

Assessment of Exposure

The second step in assessing risk is to determine the extent to which people and the environment are, or will be, exposed to the hazards. Wastes dangerous to human health obviously would affect more people if they were released in heavily populated areas. Sediment from eroding land probably would cause more damage if it entered sensitive environments such as the upper reaches of salmon spawning streams, where it could severely inhibit the hatching of salmon eggs, than it would if it entered the main stem of the Missouri River, where the fish are less likely to be harmed by silt.

The extent of exposure is affected by the tendency of the waste to migrate after it is released. Wastes released to the air usually move easily and therefore can rapidly result in widespread exposure. Wastes released to the ground are less likely to disperse widely and therefore may result in less exposure.

However, it is not just the number of people or the extent of the environment exposed that is of concern, but the intensity of the exposure as well. Releases to the air typically disperse widely and are likely to be very diluted; the extent of the exposure thus may be at least partially offset by its reduced intensity. (Temperature and wind affect the rate of dispersion.) Hazardous wastes released to groundwater from land may cause higher levels of exposure, but for fewer people.

It can be very difficult to estimate the size of a population subject to exposure. Analyzing the potential risk from exposure to groundwater when a hazardous-waste landfill leaks is a case in point. The amount of leakage from the landfill is contingent more on what cannot be predicted—imperfections in the liner materials, cracks developing as the wastes settle, accidental ruptures or spills—than on what can be predicted. Depending on the type of soil and the type of material that is leaking, some wastes may not migrate far from the site but rather become bound to soil particles.

The degree of exposure to those wastes that migrate to groundwater depends on a number of factors: the type and concentration of the waste; the rate at which it degrades and its degradation products; the pattern of groundwater movement in the aquifer; the extent to which people use the aquifer as a source of water for drinking and other purposes; and whether the groundwater is sufficiently well monitored to detect the contamination and thereby allow measures to be taken to prevent exposure. Furthermore, to predict total exposure from a landfill, it is necessary to consider exposure through air, surface water, and soil.

It can be equally difficult to estimate the sensitivity of people or an environment subject to exposure, although studying such targets of exposure is a rapidly developing field. Certainly the effects of exposure can be magnified when sensitivity is greater. A person with asthma is likely to be more vulnerable to air pollutants from a waste facility than other people. A child may inhale more of a pollutant than an adult because of a higher metabolic rate and greater physical activity, or ingest more because children eat soil. That is true for lead, for example. [18] If a person is already exposed to a chemical from some source, added exposure from another source may trigger or exacerbate an effect. Thus, many different factors—including a person's health, age, and other exposure to chemicals—affect his or her sensitivity.

Any evaluation of the relative seriousness of different types of risks also should take into account public perception. As figure 7.10 shows, 4 types of accidents involving hazardous materials (which usually result in wastes to be cleaned up) are among the top 10 hazards perceived as major concerns by local emergency organizations.[19] The general public also ranks exposure to hazardous substances through accidents or waste management failures as very high among its concerns. In addition, factors other than anxieties about health or environmental damage can influence attitudes about the location of waste facilities. Two such factors are increased traffic and concern that the image of the neighborhood might be damaged. Thus,

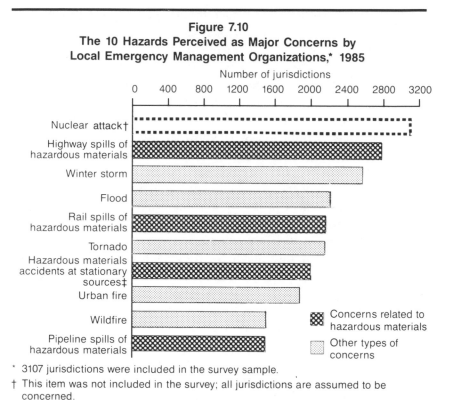

Figure 7.10
The 10 Hazards Perceived as Major Concerns by Local Emergency Management Organizations,* 1985

* 3107 jurisdictions were included in the survey sample.

† This item was not included in the survey; all jurisdictions are assumed to be concerned.

‡ Includes plants using hazardous materials and hazardous waste management facilites.

Source: Federal Emergency Management Agency.

siting a municipal waste facility may be no less a contentious issue than siting a hazardous waste facility.

Limitations of Risk Assessment

The science of risk assessment is relatively undeveloped. The National Research Council concluded in a 1984 report that fewer than 2 percent of the chemicals currently used for commercial purposes have been tested sufficiently for a complete health hazard assessment to be made.[20] Adequate information to support even a partial hazard assessment is available for only 14 percent of the chemicals; for 70 percent, no information is available. Moreover, these percentages refer only to human health hazards. In general, environmental hazards are even less well understood, and as indicated above, exposure assessments also are apt to be uncertain.

Thus, the apparently rational approach of ranking wastes according to their risks or potential damages may be somewhat less straightforward in actual application. This is not to suggest that the concept should be abandoned and all wastes treated as if they present the same type and degree of risk. That would result in expenditure of resources to deal with wastes that cause relatively little damage at the cost of ignoring more toxic wastes.

The challenge is to improve risk assessment and use a better understanding of risks to tailor the existing schemes for regulation and management of wastes.

HOW WASTES ARE REGULATED

At least 11 federal laws and many more state laws govern different aspects of waste management (see figure 7.11). Both the uncertainty of much of our knowledge about risk and the fragmented nature of the laws limit their effectiveness at reducing risk from waste. These laws (a) protect a particular part of the environment from being used for unlimited waste disposal, (b) relate to a specific type or source of waste, (c) specify procedures for management, and (d) provide for cleanup.

The Clean Air Act's major purpose is "to protect and enhance the quality of the nation's air resources so as to promote the public health and welfare and the productive capacity of its population."[21] Of the many laws that protect water resources, three constitute the primary regulatory framework. The Clean Water Act aims to "restore and maintain the chemical, physical, and biological integrity of the nation's waters."[22] The Marine Protection, Research, and Sanctuaries Act regulates "the dumping of all types of materials into ocean waters."[23] The Safe Drinking Water Act protects public water systems and underground sources of drinking water.

Figure 7.11
Major Federal Laws Regarding Waste

Statute	Waste management objective	Pollutants/wastes covered*	Regulatory approach	Basis for controls	Primary transfers to another medium
Clean Water Act; 33 USC §1251 et seq.	Protect and improve surface water quality	All discharges to surface waters, including 126 priority toxic pollutants	Effluent limitations; water quality standards	Technology and cost	Sludge to land; air emissions from treatment plant and sludge incineration
Marine Protection, Research and Sanctuaries Act; 16 USC §1401 et seq.	Limit dumping into ocean	All wastes except oil and sewage in the ocean	All dumping prohibited unless permitted	Potential damages of dumping; cost; availability	
Safe Drinking Water Act; 40 USC §300f-300j-10 (Supp. 1977); P.L. 99-339	Protect public drinking water supply	Contaminants found in drinking water and wastes injected into deep wells	Drinking water quality standards; proper construction and operation of injection wells	Health risks; cost of treatment technology	
Clean Air Act; 42 USC §7401 et seq.	Protect and improve air quality	All emissions to air	Air quality standards and emissions limitations	Health risks and environmental damages	Sludge and incinerator residues to land
Resource Conservation and Recovery Act; 42 USC §6901 et seq.	Control hazardous and solid wastes; encourage waste reduction and recycling	Hazardous and solid wastes	Waste tracking system and management standards for treatment, storage and disposal facilities	Risk and cost	Air through incineration; water through sewage treatment plants

Statute	Waste management objective	Pollutants/wastes covered*	Regulatory approach	Basis for controls	Primary transfers to another medium
Comprehensive Environmental Response, Compensation, and Liability Act; 42 USC §9601 et seq.; P.L. 99-499	Clean-up of abandoned hazardous waste sites; emergency response	All hazardous wastes found at sites	Site clean up	Risk and cost	Air through volatilization, incineration and dust
Surface Mining Control and Reclamation Act; 30 USC §1201 et seq.	Control pollution from surface coal mines	Surface coal mining wastes	Management practices	Potential damages and cost	Releases to water
Nuclear Waste Policy Act; 42 USC §10101 et seq.	Control disposal of high-level radioactive wastes	Commercial high-level radioactive waste	Prohibits disposal except in geological repositories	Performance and design standards	
Low Level Radioactive Waste Policy Act; 42 USC §2021b et seq.	Control disposal of low-level radioactive waste	Commercial low-level radioactive waste	Performance standards for waste disposal facilities through interstate compacts	Performance and design standards	
Uranium Mill Tailings Radiation Control Act; 42 USC §7901 et seq.	Manage uranium mill tailings	Uranium mill tailings	Standards for remedial action	Health and environmental impact; technology	Air from dust
Toxic Substances Control Act; 15 USC §2601 et seq.	Prevent unreasonable risk from chemical substances	Wastes from the production or use of industrial chemical substances	Limitations on manufacture, use & disposal of industrial chemical substances	Risk and cost	

* Includes all substances that could be controlled under the acts.

The Resource Conservation and Recovery Act has multiple goals. It protects one part of the environment and also sets up a management system for specified hazardous wastes. It can be viewed as a land protection statute. The act states that "although land is too valuable a national resource to be needlessly polluted by discarded materials, most solid waste is disposed of on land in open dumps and sanitary landfills."[24] The Superfund law (officially the Comprehensive Environmental Response, Compensation and Liability Act, or CERCLA) regulates one aspect of waste management—the identification and cleanup of spills and abandoned waste management sites.

Other laws provide for management of specific sources or types of wastes. The purpose of the Surface Mining Control and Reclamation Act is to protect society and the environment from adverse effects of surface mining. Two laws provide for the development of management facilities for radioactive wastes—one law for high-level wastes (the Nuclear Waste Policy Act) and the other for low-level wastes (the Low-Level Waste Policy Act). The Uranium Mill Tailings Radiation Control Act is similar to the Superfund law in that it provides for cleaning up inactive tailings piles, but it also strengthens the Nuclear Regulatory Commission's authority at active milling facilities.[25]

Laws aimed at controlling products also can affect what wastes are released to the environment. The Toxic Substances Control Act provides authority to regulate industrial chemicals presenting an unreasonable risk. Other laws cover consumer products, pesticides, foods, drugs, and cosmetics.[26]

The extent to which implementation of these laws reduces risk and damage depends on whether the wastes selected for regulation are those most likely to cause risk or damage, whether the control is equal to the degree of risk, and whether transfers of the risk to other places or generations are avoided.

Choosing the Wastes

Each new environmental law or modification of existing laws in the past several decades reflects increased knowledge about the risks from waste. Actions under the air and water pollution control laws started out by regulating a few large-volume pollutants that were known to cause damage to health and the environment. Implementation of the Clean Water Act focused primarily on reducing discharges of "conventional" pollutants such as organic matter, sediment, nutrients, salts, and bacteria from "point sources"—industries and municipal waste water treatment plants that discharge their wastes through sewer pipes. National ambient air quality standards were initially established under the Clean Air Act for sulfur dioxide, carbon monoxide, nitrogen dioxide, particulates, hydrocarbons, and photochemical oxidants.[27] Some of these pollutants, such as lead, were found to cause more serious and widespread problems than initially realized. Accordingly, for example, lead in gasoline has been increasingly tightly regulated under the Clean Air Act.[28]

Concern has grown over the large number of toxic pollutants present in the environment at low concentrations. As a result, the Clean Water and Clean Air acts have both undergone revision. The 1977 amendments to the Clean Water Act added a list of 126 "priority pollutants" based on criteria of persistence, toxicity, and potential for exposure to organisms. A decade later, the evidence indicates that additional substances should be controlled. One study found that of the 50 most frequently occurring organic compounds in industrial wastewater, only 14 are priority pollutants. Thus, by one exposure criterion, water pollutants regulated under the Clean Water Act may not include those most likely to present a risk.[29] Another study has shown that pollutants listed as hazardous under RCRA are more prevalent in the wastewater of some manufacturers, such as that from major organics industries, going to sewage treatment plants than are priority pollutants regulated under the Clean Water Act. (RCRA pollutants that are discharged to sewage treatment plants are exempt from RCRA controls, but they are not regulated under the Clean Water Act unless they are also priority pollutants.)[30]

EPA has set standards for only seven hazardous air pollutants in addition to the list of conventional pollutants regulated under the Clean Air Act. Hazardous air pollutants are selected because they "may reasonably be anticipated to result in an increase in mortality or an increase in serious irreversible, or incapacitating reversible illness."[31] Many more unregulated substances are emitted into the air, but so far only a few areas have done systematic monitoring to determine their presence.

RCRA covers a larger number of specific substances—about 450—than the Clean Air and Clean Water acts. However, the adequacy of its complex definition of hazardous waste, which also relies on four characteristics, has been a subject of much debate.[32] Amendments to RCRA in 1984 added more wastes to those covered earlier, including wastes burned in boilers and kilns and those produced in small quantities.[33] EPA has not yet decided how to handle some large-volume wastes such as muds from oil drilling.

EPA has designated a larger number of specific chemicals under the Superfund law. As of early 1987, there were 717 substances for which releases had to be reported to the federal government so that remedial action could be considered. Reporting on about 400 chemicals is required for emergency planning.[34]

Existing laws attempt to identify the wastes likely to cause the most risk or damage. This task can be quite difficult, however, because of both the sheer number of potential waste sources and the difficulties that exist in demonstrating damage. About 70,000 industrial chemicals, as well as mixtures of chemicals, can end up as waste.[35] Acute health effects and some chronic health effects are known through workplace studies or animal testing; the environmental behavior and effects and extent of exposure are likely to be unknown. Moreover, mixtures of wastes may have different effects from individual components and may behave differently in the environment. They may degrade more or less rapidly, for example. Thus, the extent of risks and potential for damage from many wastes have not been identified.

One available tool for gathering necessary information is the Toxic Substances Control Act, which gives EPA the authority to require that industrial chemicals be tested for adverse effects and to collect existing data.[36] Recently EPA has proposed using this authority to obtain information on environmental transport and toxicity of 73 substances found in wastes.[37]

Numerous factors determine which wastes actually get regulated. Information about adverse effects and exposures does not automatically lead to regulation of those wastes with the greatest potential for damage. Visibility in the news media and litigation by union, community, or public interest groups also are likely to play an important role.

Choosing the Controls

The stringency of regulations is not necessarily commensurate with a waste's potential for harm if it is released to the environment. Other factors besides reducing the risk influence the regulations. These factors include the availability of pollution control technology, the source of pollution that is being controlled, the knowledge about different types of hazards, and the financial resources available for controlling a particular type of waste.

Regulations often require a specific form of technology be used to control releases to the environment. Thus, under RCRA, landfills used for hazardous wastes must have liners.[38] These regulations are based on the assumption that releases should be controlled to the extent possible within certain (usually unspecified) economic limits. Another argument for requiring a particular form of technology rather than a level of risk reduction is that not enough is known about potential adverse effects of toxic pollutants to set such a level. In addition, the technology may simultaneously prevent release of numerous pollutants.

The stringency of the regulation may depend on the cost and difficulty of regulating a source of waste. Under the Clean Water Act, more attention has been paid to reducing releases from industrial facilities than to those from public facilities or nonpoint sources.[39] The normally lower cost and ease of implementing controls for new products or plants has sometimes led to stricter controls for them, even though the risk may not be as great as that from existing sources. New industrial chemicals usually are easier for EPA to regulate than existing ones under the Toxic Substances Control Act and therefore may be regulated even though they pose less risk than chemicals already on the market.

If large financial resources are available and a hazard is well understood, much more money may be spent to manage it. Thus, the funds are available to place high-level waste generated by nuclear power plants in geologic depositories. It is estimated that disposing of that waste will cost between $150,000 and $240,000 per ton placed in the planned depositories,[40] but $14.2 million worth of electricity will be generated for each of those tons.[41] In contrast, only $30 to $250 a ton is spent on landfilling hazardous wastes.[42]

A regulation also may focus on just one hazard of a waste. Hospital wastes, for example, may be infectious, toxic, and radioactive. Procedures for handling them have not always taken into account all the hazards. For example, although low-level radioactive wastes that also are solvents are now frequently incinerated, they once were usually put in landfills because only the radioactivity, not the potential to leach through soil, was considered.

Governmental agencies increasingly take the degree to which a regulation reduces the hazard of a waste and exposure to it into account in preparing regulations. The appropriateness of the factors considered and the adequacy of the models used to estimate the risk are almost always disputed, however, given the state of existing knowledge of adverse effects and the development of assessment methodologies. Other factors such as the availability of technology and resources will always be significant considerations in deciding how to control wastes.

Transfers in Time and Place

Passage of the various federal environmental laws has sometimes been described as a shell game that moves wastes from one part of the environment to another. RCRA recognizes this by stating:

> As a result of the Clean Air Act, the Water Pollution Control Act, and other Federal and State laws respecting public health and the environment, greater amounts of solid waste (in the form of sludge and other pollution treatment residues) have been

created. Similarly, inadequate and environmentally unsound practices for the disposal or use of solid waste have created greater amounts of air and water pollution and other problems for the environment and health.[43]

In some ways, in addition to its role in protecting land, RCRA is becoming a water and air protection statute. Groundwater monitoring is required for land disposal facilities. The 1984 amendments to RCRA also provide authority to control air releases from hazardous waste facilities. In addition, they require that corrective measures be taken to rectify release of hazardous waste to any medium from any solid waste management unit at any facility seeking a RCRA hazardous waste management permit.[44]

A common measure of success for the Clean Air and Clean Water acts, however, remains the percentage of pollutants removed from air and water. Less attention has been paid to transfers of pollutants to other media, despite some provisions that require consideration of that issue. An exception is the transfer of contamination by sludge. Since 1977, the Clean Water Act has required EPA to issue regulations for the disposal or utilization of sludge. As of early 1987, however, these regulations still had not been issued. (Some states and local communities do regulate disposal of sludge.)[45]

Although a principal intent of the 1984 RCRA amendments was to encourage the use of waste management methods that reduce risk, they may also encourage the transfer of some wastes back to air and water through incineration or sewage treatment.

Cross-media transfers have been dealt with largely by depending on the EPA regulatory programs responsible for keeping the separate waste-receiving media clean. That is partly because these programs have the requisite expertise. The air program is considering the need to regulate emissions from incinerators that burn land and water treatment wastes.[46] It is also studying air releases from landfills, surface impoundments, and land treatment facilities.[47] Presumably, smaller amounts of waste will remain to be emitted in these second-time releases. But controls may also take longer and cost more when they are imposed sequentially by different media programs rather than designed for all media together, with a selection of controls that most reduce the total risk.

Transfers occur not only across media but from one community to another. Superfund wastes have frequently been moved from one landfill to another. Methods chosen for cleanup have usually been the least expensive, technologically feasible alternatives. Often, long-term costs have not been adequately considered. A recent study of EPA cleanup actions and future plans shows that 25 percent or fewer of all such activities involve using treatment methods to reduce waste's toxicity, rather than merely containing or moving the waste to another site.[48] The 1986 amendments to Superfund require that, in selecting cleanup methods, their permanence be given greater weight.

In sum, the current regulatory structure contains significant weaknesses. Some large-volume wastes likely to cause damage, such as the conventional air and water pollutants, are regulated. Some wastes known to be persistent and toxic or to have other harmful effects when released in smaller amounts are also regulated. Other known sources of waste with potential to cause damage, such as nonpoint sources, have not been controlled because it is difficult to do so. And most of the approximately 70,000 industrial chemicals in commercial use, many of which are likely to be released to some extent as waste, have yet to be assessed for risk. Thus, laws and regulations, in effect, are usually only roughly related to the potential for damage. They are only beginning to take into account the long-term risks related to waste management methods. The methods currently used and those available for use are discussed next.

HOW WASTES ARE MANAGED

Waste management techniques are divisible into four general categories. The first is reduction in the amount of waste generated by changing products or processes or in the amount of waste that is released into the environment by recycling. The second is waste treatment, which includes a host of techniques for physically, biologically, or chemically treating waste streams to reduce the amount or hazard of the wastes ultimately released to the environment. The third is waste containment—storing or disposing of the wastes to reduce the extent of exposure. The fourth—and traditionally most common—technique is waste dispersal; that is, diluting wastes or moving them to a different site.

Three recent studies indicate the extent these four methods are now used to manage hazardous waste. In a 1985 report, the Congressional Budget Office (CBO) analyzed how wastes generated by 70 industries in 1983 were managed.[49] The study included wastes then regulated as hazardous under RCRA, as well as waste oils, PCBs (polychlorinated biphenyls), scrubber sludges, air pollution control dusts, and some liquid hazardous waste streams. The study found that almost 30 percent of the wastes were treated (primarily in sewage treatment plants), and two-thirds were managed by containment (primarily in deep wells, impoundments, and landfills). This study did not estimate direct releases to the air or water (figure 7.12).

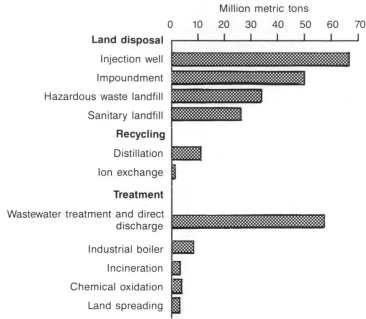

Figure 7.12
Selected Management Practices Used by Major Industries
for Potentially Hazardous Wastes,* 1983

Million metric tons

Land disposal
Injection well
Impoundment
Hazardous waste landfill
Sanitary landfill
Recycling
Distillation
Ion exchange
Treatment
Wastewater treatment and direct discharge
Industrial boiler
Incineration
Chemical oxidation
Land spreading

* Includes hazardous wastes defined under Resource Conservation and Recovery Act of 1984 Amendments plus waste oils, PCBs, industrial scrubber sludges, air pollution control dusts, and certain liquid waste streams.

Source: Congressional Budget Office

Two other reports offer additional clues to how chemical companies manage their wastes. One, conducted by the Chemical Manufacturers Association, examines the practices used by about 700 of its members (figure 7.13). Most of these companies' hazardous waste is handled under the Clean Water Act. Of the less than 1 percent of hazardous waste in solid form, about three-fifths is handled by attempted containment in surface impoundments or landfills. A study by INFORM analyzed the releases of eight chemicals from 29 organic chemical plants.[50] It found that 23 percent were released to the air, 42 percent were released as wastewater, and 35 percent were contained as solid wastes. (Both these studies classified deep-well injection under wastewater. EPA, however, considers it to be containment.)

These studies show that containment is the most common method of management for solid hazardous wastes. They also indicate the importance

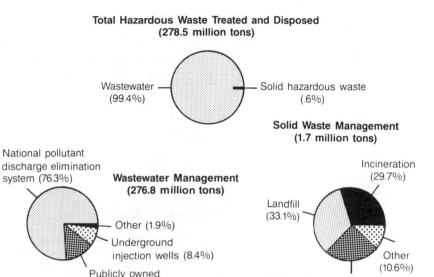

Figure 7.13
**Management of Hazardous Wastes by 725 Companies
in the United States, 1984**

Total Hazardous Waste Treated and Disposed
(278.5 million tons)

Wastewater
(99.4%)

Solid hazardous waste
(.6%)

Solid Waste Management
(1.7 million tons)

National pollutant
discharge elimination
system (76.3%)

**Wastewater Management
(276.8 million tons)**

Incineration
(29.7%)

Landfill
(33.1%)

Other (1.9%)

Underground
injection wells (8.4%)

Other
(10.6%)

Publicly owned
treatment works (13.2%)

Surface impoundment
(26.3%)

Source: Chemical Manufacturers Association.

of wastewater treatment and the apparently relatively small role played by waste reduction.

However, these studies examine only a small number of either the 70,000 chemicals that may be released into the environment or the thousands of companies that generate wastes. Thus, there is only fragmented information about how wastes are being managed.

Reduction and Recycling

While society's interest in reducing the amount and toxicity of waste has intensified in recent years, there still is no agreement on the appropriate terminology to use, as figure 7.14 illustrates. Some definitions of reduction include recycling; others are limited to source reduction through product or process changes, including good housekeeping practices, that take place within an industrial facility. Some definitions focus only on reducing the amount of waste, while others stress reducing toxicity. Definitions often do not include diluting or concentrating wastes as a type of reduction, al-

---

Figure 7.14
Examples of Waste Reduction Definitions
from Recent Reports

Group	Definitions
INFORM Cutting Chemical Wastes, 1985	*Waste reduction at source:* Source of waste altered to reduce or eliminate waste before generation (does not include recycling or treatment). Explicitly includes CWA and CAA as well as RCRA toxic wastes regardless of medium to which released.
Environmental Defense Fund Approaches to Source Reduction, 1986	*Source reduction:* Any technique that reduces amount of hazardous substance that society's waste management system must handle (includes recycling but not incineration or dewatering). Pertains mainly to RCRA wastes.
U.S. Office of Technology Assessment Serious Reduction of Hazardous Waste, 1986	*Waste reduction:* In-plant practices that reduce, avoid, or eliminate generation of hazardous waste so as to reduce risk to health and environment (does not include recycling). Pertains to all nonproduct hazardous outputs from an industrial operation into all environmental media even within permitted limits. Includes corrosive, flammable, explosive, and infectious, as well as toxic, wastes.
Office of Solid Waste, U.S. Environmental Protection Agency Minimization of Hazardous Waste, 1986	*Waste minimization:* Activity that reduces (1) total volume or quantity, (2) toxicity, or (3) both. Includes recycling but not dilution or concentration. Pertains to RCRA wastes. *Source reduction:* Reduction or elimination of waste generation at the source, usually within a process. (May include treatment and recycling within a process.) Pertains to RCRA wastes.
E.I. du Pont de Nemours and Co.	*Waste reduction:* Reduction in quantity or volume, or both, of wastes (called "tabulated wastes") that either require treatment or disposal, or are RCRA wastes burned for fuel. "Tabulated wastes" include all RCRA wastes except that which is recycled or used as a commercial product; and all other discarded materials except those treated by industrial wastewater treatment or publicly owned wastewater treatment works, burned for fuel, reclaimed or recycled. (Air emissions, garbage, and ash from coal combustion not included).

---

though EPA does recognize them as a step in treatment of waste.[51] In this report, waste reduction refers to the use of a raw material, product, or process change inside the plant that prevents the generation of waste. Recycling refers to actions that occur after the waste has been generated and has left the plant at which it originated. Recycling usually involves making a new product from waste. Here, the definition includes reuse (reusing a product or material in the same form for the same purpose). Recovery (converting the waste to energy) is discussed under incineration.

Waste reduction and recycling can each eliminate the need for long-term containment and monitoring of wastes to prevent later health or environmental damage. However, from a risk reduction perspective, it is preferable never to produce the waste, because less hazard is created. Recycling can cause added risk through releases of waste during treatment and transportation. Residues remain even though there is no longer a need for long-term control of whatever waste is recycled.

Reduction

The amounts and types of waste produced by a plant result from many choices. What fuels and raw materials are used? What products with what characteristics are made? What manufacturing processes are selected? What maintenance practices are followed?

Waste reduction can result from modification of any of these factors. One product can be substituted for another. For instance, replacing insulation made from urea-formaldehyde with mineral wool means no formaldehyde will be released to the environment.[52] Similarly, one process can replace another. Changing from a solvent- to a water-based process to coat medicine tablets eliminated 24 tons of air pollution per year at a 3M pharmaceutical plant.[53] Using sodium hydrosulfite instead of zinc hydrosulfite to bleach pulp helped some manufacturers meet effluent standards for zinc.[54]

Wastes can also be segregated to reduce contamination. This may involve good housekeeping processes such as preventing nonradioactive material from entering low-level radioactive waste bins or preventing leaks of volatile substances to the air. Changes that involve recirculating air or water back into the production process may reduce the amount of waste.

Various studies have long emphasized the potential for waste reduction. In the early 1970s, Resources for the Future's residuals management program stressed the role of product and process changes in much of its research.[55] The Electric Power Research Institute is in the 10th year of its Integrated Environmental Control research program for coal-fired plants. It has found that environmental control systems costs can be reduced up to 50 percent by integrating different types of pollution controls and reusing wastes within a plant.[56]

North Carolina has taken the lead among about 10 states in encouraging plants to develop waste reduction programs.[57] Its Pollution Prevention Pays Program serves as an information clearinghouse and provides training and technical assistance to the state's industries. The program works with small businesses and communities as well as larger ones. It provides a single source of assistance on waste reduction regardless of whether the reduction affects air, water, or land pollution.[58]

Industries that generate large amounts of hazardous waste, such as those in the chemical and metals processing sectors, have reported more and more examples of waste reduction.[59] These reports indicate that creative efforts to reduce waste have been taking place and that the opportunities can be significant, depending on the industry. One report estimates that as much as 80 percent of some waste solvents can be recovered by distillation and that wastewater from cyanide and metal liquids can be reduced by up to half, with 50 percent of the metals recovered.[60] According to a study by the federal Office of Technology Assessment (OTA), recycling materials within an industrial process and changes in plant operation are the most frequently used methods of reduction. Two other approaches that are sometimes used are changing technology and changing products. These approaches, however, may affect product quality and customer acceptance and commonly require skills other than those of environmental engineers.[61]

INFORM's previously cited detailed study of 29 organic chemical plants found that waste reduction is neither widespread nor well documented. The study identified 44 waste reduction practices at 12 companies. (See box.) One company responded but presumably had no examples of waste reduction, while 16 plants were unwilling to provide information. The report found that data usually are not available to measure the success of the measures taken; that is, the percentage of total waste reduced. This is due partly to concern about confidentiality, but it is also a result of the government's collecting information on general categories of wastes in a fragmented and incomplete manner.[62]

Waste reduction efforts often offer the best opportunities for completely eliminating the potential risk or damage from particular wastes. Nevertheless, the replacement products or processes need to be carefully analyzed to see if they have hazards of their own. For instance, substituting polyvinyl chloride pipe for asbestos cement pipe will reduce asbestos wastes, but it will also increase the generation of vinyl chloride gas, a carcinogen that must be carefully controlled to avoid exposure to workers.[63]

The role of waste reduction in the future depends on the incentives involved and on how the generators of the waste react to them. CBO estimates that waste reduction measures taken in response to incentives in the 1984

Examples of Waste Reduction Practices

Companies can reduce the wastes they generate through a wide variety of practices. In its study, INFORM divided the hazardous waste reduction practices used by 29 organic chemical plants into five categories: process change, product reformulation, chemical substitution, equipment change, and operational change.

Process changes can range from altering process conditions (for example, temperature) to implementing new chemical or technological methods. Ciba-Geigy completely eliminated the use of mercury at its Toms River, New Jersey, plant through a process change it initiated in 1983. Prior to the change, the plant was using 2,280 pounds of mercury annually in the manufacture of anthraquinone dyes, which are widely used for dyeing cotton. Most of that mercury was ending up as air, water, or solid wastes. Concerned about the environmental and health effects of mercury, Ciba-Geigy's corporate research group developed a new dye-manufacturing process that eliminated the mercury-requiring sulfonation step.[1]

Sometimes, hazardous waste production can be reduced or eliminated by *reformulating a product* without changing the basic manufacturing process. Monsanto, for example, altered the formula for an industrial adhesive it produced in its Port Plastics Plant in Addyston, Ohio, to eliminate the need for filtering the product. As a result, the company no longer had any hazardous filtrate or filters that required disposal.[2]

By *substituting a nonhazardous chemical* for a hazardous one in any production process, quantities of hazardous waste can be significantly reduced. In 1971, a Union Oil plant in La Mirada, California, completely eliminated the use of mercury as a biocide in the latex it was selling to paint manufacturers, replacing it with another, less hazardous chemical.[3]

A relatively simple *equipment change* in any stage of a manufacturing process may promote waste reduction. In 1983, when an employee discovered cumene escaping from a pressure control vent, a USS Chemicals plant in Ironton, Ohio, was able to reduce the amount of this material emitted into the air by adding a condenser to existing equipment. The condensed gas was then returned directly to the phenol process unit. USS Chemicals was thereby able to recover 400,000 pounds of cumene, one of the plant's major raw materials, in the first year, saving the plant $100,000. The cost of installation of the condenser was $5,000.[4]

Operational (or housekeeping) changes include alterations in the way hazardous wastes are handled in a plant, such as spill minimization and more conservative use of chemicals. In 1982, at its plant in Fremont, California, Borden was able to reduce phenol wastes discharged from its plant by making a simple change in operational practices. Borden uses water to rinse the filters that remove large particles of phenol-containing resinous material from products as they are loaded into tank cars. Previously, this rinsewater was sent to floor drains where it contaminated all wastewater that was discharged to a municipal sewage treatment plant. With the change, the rinsewater is now collected in a 250-gallon recovery tank and reused as rinsewater when a new batch of phenolic resin is produced.[5]

RCRA amendments could lower the total amount of hazardous waste generated by 14 percent in 1990. Furthermore, it says that if industry does not alter its practices in response to increasing costs of land disposal, waste generation might grow 6 percent.[64] As figure 7.15 shows, reduction of waste generation would limit the increase in funds needed to manage hazardous wastes by 1990. OTA concludes that not enough is known to make estimates about waste reduction's potential as a management technique. However, the study found that "there are substantial opportunities for waste reduction, even though it is not possible to give numbers for specific wastes and industries."[65]

Recycling

Recycling can reduce significantly the amount of wastes released to the environment and therefore the risks associated with their disposal. However, it can also create risks of its own.

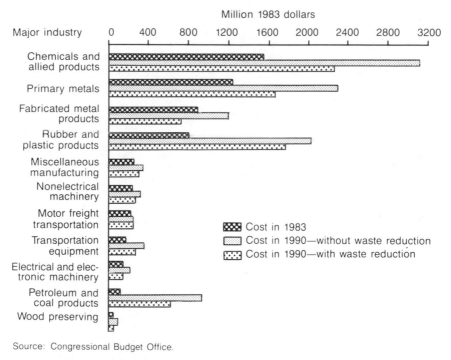

Figure 7.15
Estimated Expenditures for Hazardous Waste Management,
1983 and 1990

Source: Congressional Budget Office.

Recycling has always played a part in waste management. In agriculture, about 50 percent of the manure produced is economically recoverable.[66] Nearly half of copper and lead scrap metals are currently recycled; other metals are recycled at lower rates.[67] Community recycling of solid wastes, which early in the century was a part of municipal waste programs in large cities, emerged again in the 1970s, based this time on a concern about energy and environmental conservation.[68] In the 1980s, the need for alternatives to landfills (because of both space and leaching problems) has resulted in additional attention being given to recycling.

Increasingly, cities have been building collection and processing systems to serve residential and commercial institutions and to link their waste systems with the existing flow of materials in the recycling industry. Some 400 to 500 U.S. cities have curbside separation programs, but recycling still plays a relatively small part in management of solid waste.[69] Only a few communities such as Groton, Connecticut; Austin, Texas; San Francisco; and Davis, California, recycle more than 20 percent of their wastes.[70]

Recycling of hazardous wastes is apparently increasing, although confusion over how to define recycling and reduction makes it difficult to know how much. Solvent recovery may account for most of the hazardous wastes now recycled. About 4 percent of hazardous wastes are distilled to recover solvents.[71] One indication of interest in this form of recycling is a service offered by Safety-Kleen, which picks up used solvents from dry cleaners and replaces them with clean solvents.[72] Such services may grow now that small waste generators are covered by the RCRA hazardous waste management requirements.

Burning of waste is a form of recycling usually known as resource recovery. The Economic Development Council of Northeastern Pennsylvania has proposed a power plant that would burn culm, a low-sulfur waste from anthracite mining.[73] Burning waste for fuel is a common form of on-site recovery for chemical plants. One plant saved as much as $175,000 a month on fuel costs by burning the one million pounds of phenol tarry wastes it generated each month.[74] But the risks of air pollution are such that these practices will be regulated much more closely under amendments to RCRA.

Recycling has not occurred as expected in the nuclear power sector. Initially, fuel for nuclear power plants was to be reprocessed for reuse. Economic factors have made that unprofitable, and environmental problems have added other drawbacks.[75] One reprocessing plant never operated because of design problems; the other closed because of groundwater contamination.[76] Reprocessing also could result in additional worker exposure and increase the availability of weapons materials to terrorists.

Recycling is a particularly complicated part of the waste management system. It is most easily performed close to the initial production process—for example, in reusing wastewater or applying animal wastes to land. Otherwise, managers must cope with collection problems and with uncertain sources and waste composition at one end and uncertain markets (often the major obstacle) at the other.

Recycling may involve increased handling of the materials, with greater risk to workers involved in separating, transporting, and processing the waste streams. Also, due to transportation costs, recycling facilities need to be near both the supply of waste materials and the market for the recycled materials. Thus, they often are located in or near urban areas, creating a potentially high level of human exposure in case of accidental release.

As noted, recycling can create risks. If it involves processing a waste stream to remove contaminants, pollution can be generated. Thus, metal recyclers may burn the plastic coating off electrical wire to reclaim the copper. Disposing of the wire as waste in a sanitary landfill would probably create little risk, whereas the air pollution from the burning may be resulting in substantially more.

In other cases, a recycling process may not directly release contaminants to the environment, but rather allow them to accumulate on site and increase the risk of accidental release. Indeed, about 10 percent of the sites currently on the Superfund list for priority cleanup are former recycling facilities.[77]

Recycling reduces the amount of waste released to the environment and so reduces risk over the longer term. However, it must be done carefully. Since recycling uses many of the treatment techniques described in the next section, it poses the same risks and has the same advantages as those techniques.

Treatment

Treatment uses physical, chemical, and biological processes to reduce the amount of a waste or transform it into substances that will cause less harm or no harm. Treatment usually is employed in conjunction with other management approaches such as recycling, containment, and dispersal.

The traditional waste treatment devices for air and water pollution control typically have depended on simple physical separation to remove pollutants, which often has had substantial drawbacks. For example, "primary" wastewater treatment allows heavier suspended materials to settle out of the waste stream before its release to the environment. While such a system can remove about two-thirds of the suspended solids, it will control only about one-third of the biochemical oxygen demand and less than one-fourth of the nutrients, two other indicators of pollution.[78]

Similarly, baghouses and electrostatic precipitators are physical means of capturing particles that otherwise would be emitted to the air. Such devices can reduce emissions of total suspended particulates very efficiently, but are relatively ineffectual in removing gaseous pollutants such as sulfur dioxide.

Recent laws seek to substantially increase the use of treatment to remove pollutants from waste streams.[79] The need is to adopt more modern, sophisticated techniques.

Wastewater Treatment

Sewage treatment plants are the best known and probably the most frequently used treatment facilities. More than 15,000 such plants were operating in the United States in 1984.[80] They had a total flow capacity of 36 billion gallons per day. Although initially intended to treat domestic wastes that are for the most part biodegradable, many of these plants now handle large quantities of metal and persistent organic wastes. Nearly one-fourth of the industrial hazardous wastes included in the CBO study were sent to sewage treatment plants. Of 29 organic chemical plants studied by INFORM, 17 released some wastes to such facilities.[81]

Although a variety of sewage treatment systems have been used, most, as noted, have depended on simple physical separation of suspended solids and on the biological conversion of organic compounds into carbon dioxide. These systems may also degrade other types of pollutants and kill pathogens.

The extent to which sewage treatment plants emit wastes to the environment is beginning to be analyzed more completely. A New Jersey study recently showed that such plants can release higher levels of metals and other compounds than industrial facilities.[82] The transfer of metals and persistent organic substances to sludge has long been a concern. The same study showed that 48 of 49 sludges tested at 16 plants were considered unsuitable for application on land.

Wastes also are transferred to air. A Philadelphia sewage treatment plant is the largest stationary source discharging some volatile organic substances in the city—even surpassing refineries. A treatment plant in California's Santa Clara Valley was similarly found to be an important source of air emissions.[83]

An EPA report to Congress on the discharge of hazardous wastes to publicly owned treatment plants estimates the extent to which compo-

Figure 7.16
Percentage of Pollutants Released by Different Routes
from a Typical Wastewater Treatment Plant

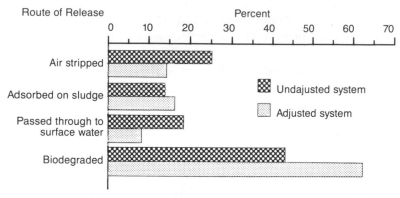

Source: U.S. Environmental Protection Agency.

nent pollutants are degraded or merely transferred to other parts of the environment once they enter sewer lines.[84] The report concludes that, if a sewage treatment plant is not properly adjusted to cope with the types of pollutants it receives, more than half of those pollutants may be released directly to the air, passed through to surface water, or adsorbed on sludge (figure 7.16). (In addition to other volatilized pollutants released to the air, the biodegradation process releases carbon dioxide.) Even if a plant is properly tuned to the incoming waste load, major transfers still can occur; for example, more than one-third of the waste typically is not biodegraded.

Little is known about the extent of releases to groundwater. The magnitude of leaks to groundwater from the system of sewers and collection pipes is unknown.[85]

Releases can differ greatly from facility to facility, depending on factors such as the properties of the compounds, the type of waste stream, the operation of the treatment plant, and the design of the collection system.[86] Certainly, wastewater treatment plants are a far-from-foolproof way to reduce risks. They must be designed, operated, and maintained properly to avoid just collecting hazardous constituents from a wide area and releasing them at one location. The net effect can otherwise be detrimental to both human health and environmental quality.

Incineration

Although a relatively small percentage of wastes are now burned, incineration is probably the most rapidly growing treatment technique for both domestic and industrial solid wastes. As of 1985, approximately 55 incinerators were burning municipal garbage, about 40 were incinerating municipal sewage sludge, and, by September 1986, about 330 incinerators were burning RCRA hazardous wastes.[87] The chemical industry is increasing its use of incineration; between 1982 and 1984, the percentage of *solid* hazardous wastes so treated rose from nearly 16 percent to almost 28 percent, according to surveys by the Chemical Manufacturers Association.

Many different facilities can be used to burn waste. The CBO survey indicates that most burning takes place in industrial boilers, not in facilities designed primarily for hazardous waste incineration.[88] Cement kilns are also used, particularly for acidic wastes, because the cement kiln can neutralize the acid. More unusual is the rotary kiln operated by the Cincinnati Metropolitan Sewer District; it burns wastes from several stages of treatment at sewage facilities, as well as some industrial wastes.[89]

Other thermal technologies besides incineration are also being developed. For instance, wet-air oxidation, in which oxygen is bubbled through aqueous waste under high pressures and temperatures, can be used for wastes that are not concentrated enough to burn economically but are too toxic to be biodegraded in sewage treatment plants.[90]

Like sewage treatment facilities, incinerators operate largely by converting organic compounds into carbon dioxide and other constituents. They are disposed of in the air or on the land; from 20 to 50 percent of incinerated solid wastes by weight may end up as ash or scrubber sludge for land disposal, with the rest entering the air.[91]

The greatest concern about risk from incineration now centers on possible releases of dangerous metals and chemical compounds. Incineration can volatilize metals such as cadmium and mercury and release them as air pollutants.[92] Metals in particulate form may be captured by scrubbers and transferred to landfills in sludge. The incineration process may modify the chemical form of the metal cadmium so that it is more soluble and therefore more likely to leach from ash disposed of in a landfill. However, burning may decrease the solubility of chromium and lead. Such chemical changes also can increase or decrease the likelihood that metals will be taken up by living organisms.

If the incineration process is incomplete, new compounds not part of the original waste can be formed. Dioxins and related compounds are particularly worrisome. Some of the compounds undergo further chemical changes after they are released. Current research on the transformation of organic emissions from combustion indicates that these emissions may react with other pollutants already in the atmosphere to become more mutagenic.[93]

The problems associated with incineration relate both to resource recovery facilities built by communities to handle garbage and to RCRA hazardous waste facilities. Even when release levels are very low, they may still present a risk. Over long periods of time, both metals and persistent organic wastes will accumulate in the environment. One report concludes that garbage incinerators may become the largest stationary source of heavy metals in the state of New York.[94]

The extent of the risks from incineration is determined by the composition of the materials being burned, the temperature of incineration, how well releases to air and land are controlled, and the care taken in operating and maintaining the facility. The location of the facility is also important, a fact that has led to substantial interest in the possibility of incinerating hazardous wastes offshore on seagoing vessels.

CBO estimates that the amount of hazardous waste incinerated may triple or quadruple by 1990, depending on the extent of recycling and reduction.[95] It suggests that incineration will be used for organic liquid, sludge, and solid waste. An OTA report summarizes studies of the market for incineration and concludes that there exists a significant and growing shortfall in incineration capacity. An estimated 20 percent of hazardous wastes (as defined by RCRA) are appropriate for incineration, it concludes. About one-third of the wastes that can be incinerated are solvents that could be recycled instead.[96]

Land Treatment

Land treatment is a technique that involves the controlled application of waste to soil through spraying, spreading, or injecting a short distance beneath the surface.[97]* Nationwide, approximately 25 percent of municipal wastewater treatment sludge is land-spread at more than 2,600 sites.[99] Land treatment also is commonly used for petroleum wastes. However, only 3 percent of the total industrial wastewaters and sludges are thought to be suitable for this approach.[100]

---

*Under RCRA, however, land treatment is considered to be a disposal technique.[98]

In land treatment, the organic constituents of the waste are degraded by naturally occurring organisms in the soil, much as they are in other biological treatments. Nondegradable compounds may bind onto soil particles and be immobilized.

If not carefully controlled, land-spreading can result in harmful wastes washing off into lakes or streams, leaching into groundwater, and volatilizing into the air. Wastes may also contaminate crops grown on the land. (Half of the land used for treating municipal sewage sludge is also used for pastureland or cropland.[101]) Heavy metals in the sludge may be picked up by the crops, making them unsuitable for food.

The state of New Jersey, for instance, found that almost none of the sludges it tested met guidelines for land-spreading because the level of contamination was too high.[102] Nevertheless, under the right conditions and with suitable wastes, land treatment is appealing because of its relatively low costs and because it improves the condition of the soil and recycles the nutrients.

Other Means of Physical and Chemical Treatment

A variety of other physical, chemical, and biological treatment systems are available or are being developed to deal with specific types of wastes. Scrubbers help control air pollution by removing particles from the gas flow. The ways in which this is done vary depending on the scrubber design. One of the simplest designs sprays water down a tower onto the rising dirty gases. Often the water contains reagents such as lime, which reacts chemically with flue gas to remove sulfur dioxide from a gaseous waste stream.[103]

Automobile emission controls rely predominantly on catalytic converters, which oxidize carbon monoxide and unburned hydrocarbons into carbon dioxide and water vapor, and on the reduction of nitrogen oxides into pure nitrogen and oxygen.

Probably the most common forms of chemical wastewater treatment are flocculation, neutralization, and chlorination. Flocculation involves mixing a compound such as alum into the wastewater to induce suspended solids to settle out. In neutralization, acids are added to alkaline wastes or alkalies to acidic wastes. Chlorination involves adding chlorine to wastewaters to kill bacteria.

Increasing attention is also being paid to biological waste treatment. Experiments are being conducted to isolate bacteria capable of degrading hazardous substances. Some of these experiments involve injecting such bacteria into the ground to degrade pollutants that already contaminate groundwater.

Finally, if the wastes cannot be degraded, they may require stabilization. This is a combination of physical and chemical treatment that converts hazardous waste into a form that impedes leaching into the environment after disposal. In 1984, eight commercial hazardous waste firms reported that approximately 7 percent of all wastes in landfills were stabilized before disposal.[104]

Substances such as asphalt, polyester resins, cement, and fly ash are used as solidification agents.[105] The agents react with the wastes, solidifying through a cementation process with or without a chemical reaction or through an encapsulation process that immobilizes the waste by coating it with an impenetrable material. These processes are likely to be more successful with inorganic wastes than with organic wastes.

All treatment methods, including stabilization, involve some risks. Any method may require transportation of the wastes to a central treatment facility, which increases the risk of spills and accidents. Some physical treatments may not reduce the hazard of the waste, but only increase its concentration. All systems create some residues, which may be very hazardous and difficult to contain. Furthermore, any methods must be monitored carefully to ensure that they operate as intended.

Attempted Containment

As the control of waste dispersal has increased, the most popular category of waste management has become containment.[106] Wastes are injected into deep geological formations, buried in landfills, or stored in surface impoundments. The theory is that if wastes are adequately contained, the risks they create will be very low even if the wastes are extremely hazardous, for there will be no exposure.

Landfills are the most common form of municipal waste disposal and are used for a substantial proportion of industrial wastes as well. The evolution from open dumps—which are little more than a form of waste dispersal—to properly located and operated sanitary landfills has occurred over the past 10 to 20 years. EPA contractors estimate that there were approximately 16,000 such landfills in operation in 1984.[107] The total number has probably dropped substantially over the past decade because municipalities often find it increasingly expensive and politically difficult to open new landfills as the old ones become filled.

Hazardous wastes also are disposed of in landfills. In its analysis of hazardous waste management practices used in the United States in 1983, CBO estimated that about 23 percent of the wastes it studied were disposed of in some sort of landfill.[108] A little over half of those wastes were placed in sites constructed with special liners to prevent leakage, and the rest were placed in unlined facilities. Earlier EPA-sponsored studies, using a more restricted definition of hazardous wastes, had concluded that the proportion of total hazardous wastes disposed of in landfills was much less.[109]

Most recent studies agree that deep-well injection has become the most popular method for disposing of hazardous wastes, at least in terms of waste volume. CBO's survey indicated that 25 percent of the wastes it studied were disposed of in this manner.[110] However, these wastes are likely to contain much larger amounts of water than those disposed of in landfills, so the actual amount of undiluted wastes injected into deep wells may be much less than 25 percent. EPA figures indicate that 46 Class I hazardous waste injection wells are in operation in the United States.[111]

Another widely used containment technique is surface waste impoundment. According to the CBO report, 19 percent of the wastes it includes are managed in this way.[112] An EPA survey estimates that over 180,000 such impoundments exist in the United States, ranging in size from a few hundred square yards to hundreds of acres.[113] These sites are used for agricultural, industrial, and mining wastes, municipal sewage sludges, and brines from oil and gas extraction. Many of the impoundments actually are used not for disposal but rather for temporary storage or treatment.

A wide variety of other containment facilities also are used for waste storage or disposal. Hazardous wastes are stored in everything from small drums to large storage tanks. High-level radioactive wastes are stored in stainless steel tanks until permanent repositories can be found for them deep underground. Low-level wastes generated from defense and federal research facilities are disposed of at federal sites. Commercially generated low-level radioactive wastes currently are buried in three landfills, located in Nevada, South Carolina, and Washington. Each state, however, is responsible for providing facilities for this type of waste by 1993. They may form compacts with other states to build a facility and exclude low-level wastes from states outside the compact to which they belong.[114]

The term *attempted containment* is used advisedly for all the facilities in this category because their effectiveness typically is uncertain. Although much greater efforts are now being made to prevent waste leakage, no type of containment is guaranteed to be leakproof. Unlined landfills and impoundments are a significant source of groundwater contamination.[115] According to an impoundment survey by EPA, 70 percent of industrial impoundments are unlined and 30 percent are located in permeable soils overlying usable aquifers.[116] Wastes injected through wells also can migrate up into aquifers through unknown fissures and abandoned oil and gas wells, or along the casing of the injection well itself.

Landfills and impoundments can release significant amounts of waste into the air as well. Volatile chemicals evaporate from both. Anaerobic degradation of organic wastes in landfills generates methane gas, which can escape and carry off other substances as well. It also can explode.

Assumptions about what constitutes adequate containment of wastes on land have changed dramatically in the past decade. In the early 1970s, landfills began to be designed to handle more dangerous wastes. Today, more attention is paid to liners, systems for collecting leachate (initially developed in the 1950s) or runoff, top cover, and ways of monitoring groundwater quality.[117] Some attention is given to limiting air emissions. Environmental protection measures such as groundwater monitoring and liners are now required for landfills and impoundments that handle hazardous waste. Protective requirements for deep wells and solid waste facilities are being developed. And it is now assumed that some wastes eventually will escape from containment facilities regardless of the measures adopted. Therefore, long-term monitoring is necessary, as are limitations on what wastes are ever placed in containment facilities.

As containment practices change and new facilities become more expensive and difficult to locate, the number of land disposal facilities is likely to drop. Already 1,000 such facilities for hazardous wastes have closed because they were unable to meet the requirements, such as groundwater monitoring, of the 1984 RCRA amendments.[118] (See box.) Partly because of these facilities' limited ability to degrade or contain wastes, the 1984 provisions banned some wastes from being managed by land disposal.[119] In the United States, landfills are likely to be used increasingly for residues from treatment processes. There are some indications that treatment in tanks is replacing treatment in surface impoundments.[120] An example of waste reduction as incentives change is provided by a California chemical company that reduced one type of waste it generated from 350 cubic yards to 25 cubic yards a year when the cost of landfilling tripled.[121]

Dispersal

Dispersal operates on the principle that, if the concentration of pollution can be sufficiently dissipated, little hazard will result. Dispersal assumes that by reducing the concentration of a pollutant, the risks it poses will be low, even if exposure to it is widespread. However, if the wrong types of wastes are released in too large amounts in the wrong locations (for example, near population concentrations), this rationale is violated. Even with dispersal in low concentrations over a wide area, various physical and biological processes such as sedimentation or bioaccumulation can reconcentrate pollutants to harmful levels in localized critical areas such as wetlands. Some pollutants can also be transformed into more hazardous substances. In the early 1970s, these processes threatened biological activity in parts of the Great Lakes.[122]

Although the pollution control programs enacted since the late 1960s have substantially reduced the use of dispersal as an intentional or unintentional waste management technique,* it continues to be prevalent. Furthermore, many wastes continue to be dispersed into the environment with little or no control, although the extent to which this is the case is not reliably known.

Many wastes also are released to the environment by unintentional dispersal; that is, accident and spillage. Each time a substance is transferred from one place to another, spillage is likely to occur. For instance, EPA estimates that on average one 55-gallon drum of hazardous waste is spilled or otherwise "lost" for every five trucks shipping hazardous materials.[124] Accidental discharges also are a major problem at manufacturing and commercial facilities. The release of methyl isocyanate from the Union Carbide Corporation's chemical plant in India and the releases of such substances in West Virginia's Kanawha Valley are particularly dramatic examples.[125]

Quite aside from accidents, even the best pollution abatement devices usually provide less than 100 percent control and therefore disperse wastes to some extent. An efficiently run municipal wastewater treatment plant is designed to remove only 80 to 90 percent of the biochemical oxygen demand and suspended solids and less than half of the nutrients in the sewage.[126] And many treatment plants operate far more inefficiently than that. Permits, particularly for older facilities, can be quite generous in allowing regular releases. For instance, the permit for a steel plant in Baltimore allows it to release up to 38 million tons of cyanide a year into the Chesapeake Bay.[127]

Dispersal will never be completely eliminated. It may be the preferred method of disposal when a waste degrades before it damages health or

---

*For example, Exxon has saved more than five million pounds of volatile chemicals since 1975, primarily by installing floating roofs on storage tanks to reduce evaporation losses at its Bayway plant.[123]

Wastes on the Niagara Frontier

In adopting the Resource Conservation and Recovery Act (RCRA) Amendments of 1984 and the Superfund Amendments of 1986, Congress attempted to answer many difficult questions about managing wastes. For example, To what extent should society use alternatives to trying to contain wastes in their present leaky sites? Should wastes be incinerated, sent to wastewater treatment plants, or handled by newer treatment techniques? What risks do newer technologies present? How much should be spent to clean up waste sites in comparison to other ways of reducing risk from exposure to waste?

The importance of these questions is illustrated by the experience of New York's Niagara Frontier in generating and disposing of waste. This area, long known as the scenic site of a world-class waterfall, has gained a second reputation. It is now a symbol of waste management methods that did not work. As a region where innovative remedial and treatment approaches are being tried, it may also eventually become known for use of newer clean-up technologies that work better.

The spectacular falls that drew tourists to the 37-mile Niagara River flowing from Lake Erie to Lake Ontario have also attracted steel, petrochemical, and chemical industries looking for cheap power. Together with municipal and federal governments, these industries have used 215 sites for land disposal in Erie and Niagara counties in the United States. Sixty-one of these sites (and five more on the Canadian side) have been identified as having significant potential to contaminate the Niagara River.[1] In addition, at least nine major industrial plants and six wastewater treatment plants on the U.S. side

discharge into the environment.

The seepage of wastes into basements from the nearby Love Canal waste site in the 1970s was one indication that the land disposal sites were not containing the wastes as planned. Monitoring of groundwater and the river water now indicates that wastes are moving from other land disposal sites as well as entering the river directly from industrial and wastewater treatment plants. Hyde Park landfill, for example, is located about 2,000 feet from Niagara Gorge. Between 1953 and 1974, more than 80,000 tons of chemicals, many of them known to be very toxic (for example, trichlorophenol, chlorobenzenes, and Lindane), were placed in this site. They are now leaching or draining to the gorge face and into the river.[2] Other waste sites and storm sewers also contribute toxics to the river. A task force has identified 261 chemicals present in the river water, sediment, and biota.[3] In February 1987, Canada and the United States set a target of reducing the level of persistent toxic chemicals going into the Niagara River from point and nonpoint sources by 50 percent by 1996.

A Niagara River Action Plan prepared by the U.S. Environmental Protection Agency's (EPA's) Region 2 summarizes the actions being taken under the U.S. Clean Water Act, RCRA, and the Comprehensive Environmental Response, Compensation, and Liability Act by municipal, state, and federal governments to clean up wastes in the region.[4] The Niagara Falls Wastewater Treatment Plant, which was the most significant contributor of organic priority pollutants and phenols to the river, has been repaired. Its activated carbon treatment system had been out of operation almost since it was first installed in 1978. Permits for major point sources are being reviewed and limitations on toxic releases increased. The wastewater treatment plants are working on industrial pretreatment programs.

Controlling the nonpoint sources remains much more difficult. Twenty hazardous waste management facilities in the Niagara Frontier are either being granted permits or closed under RCRA. Remedial work is under way at four sites, including Hyde Park and Love Canal. The New York State Department of Environmental Conservation is testing plasma arc technology to deter-

mine if it should be used to treat organic hazardous wastes leaching from Love Canal. Millions of dollars are being spent by private companies and governments on efforts to clean up containment that did not contain and treatment that did not treat.[5]

The experience of the Niagara Frontier holds an important lesson that waste managers across the country are beginning to heed. It is largely because of problems such as Niagara's that the focus of waste management is shifting from land disposal to treatment and that emphasis on reducing the volume and toxicity of wastes is increasing.

the environment. The best method depends, as noted, on what type of waste is released, how much is released, when and where it is released, and what happens to it afterward.

CHOOSING A WASTE MANAGEMENT SYSTEM

Private firms, government agencies, legislatures, and citizen groups are often caught up in the process of trying to select the "best" management method for a waste. The perfect method would be one that eliminated all risk at a reasonable cost. But, as the overview presented above demonstrates, perfect answers to the management problem do not exist. Every technique has its advantages and disadvantages. In almost no case can a technique guarantee the elimination of risk. And, in many cases, the question of reasonable cost is certainly open to discussion. The risk caused by managing a waste in a particular way is likely to differ from one waste stream to another and sometimes from one location to another.

Unfortunately, too little usually is known about the advantages and disadvantages of alternative management techniques to allow a fully informed choice. As a result, managers often lurch from one solution to another without careful analysis, only to discover that the favored new solution also causes problems. For instance, incineration was widely touted as a solution, much superior to landfills, for the municipal garbage problem before the extent of air releases and their effects were studied and the need for regulations addressed. This solution is now encountering opposition because of concern about hazardous air emissions from incinerators.[128]

All too often, managers fixate on a single part of the waste management system. They fail to analyze the entire problem by looking at how wastes change form and move among several media. Managers need to look at wastes from "cradle to grave," for there can be several "graves," and they can be hard to locate.

The Information Gap

Clearly, managers need better information. They could make better risk assessments and management decisions if they knew the answers to such fundamental questions as what wastes are released into the environment, what potential risks these wastes create, and how alternative waste management techniques change these risks.

The first priority is to get more information about what wastes are entering the environment, how they are entering, and in what quantities. Because current pollution control programs independently address separate parts of the problem, rarely is an effort made to get a comprehensive picture of release to the environment. The adoption of a "mass-balance" approach can help provide such a picture both for an individual plant and for regulatory agencies.

In a mass balance, analysts attempt to identify what happens to the entire amount of a specific chemical substance that either enters or is produced by a plant. This can be done as part of performing an audit of company products, processes, and operations to identify opportunities for reducing the amount and toxicity of waste generated.[129]* To be useful in devising ways of reducing waste, the audit needs to include information about plant processes and operations.

Besides its value in devising ways to reduce waste, the information on amounts released into different media directly or through treatment processes is useful to state and local governments in planning for emergencies, in setting priorities for regulatory action, and in ensuring that proposed regulations avoid the tendency simply to move wastes from one medium to another without reducing risk. The reports on releases need to be updated regularly and supported by monitoring of releases. Present information systems provide fragmentary data that usually relate only to emissions that are allowed by existing permits rather than those actually occurring.

---

*This kind of audit differs from an environmental audit in that the latter is performed to review problems in complying with environmental laws rather than to trace where a substance goes and how releases can be reduced.

Cities such as Philadelphia and states such as New Jersey and Maryland have established at least partial emission inventories. New Jersey selected a list of about 150 large-volume chemicals with known effects and asked companies to submit information about the amounts of the chemicals entering a plant, used in a product, and emitted directly to the environment or sent to sewage treatment plants or other treatment or disposal facilities.[130] The collected data were used to locate waste facilities requiring cleanup. Also, areas of the state with potentially high levels of exposure to specific chemicals from one or many sources were identified. Further monitoring of these areas is being undertaken. The 1986 amendments to the Superfund law provide for a federal emissions inventory similar to that used in New Jersey.[131]

Developing accurate emissions inventories can be difficult. Important process information often is confidential within companies. Mass balances can be hard to calculate, especially when by-products are formed by a process. And inventories, such as the one established under Superfund, may rely only on estimates of amounts of wastes entering each medium, rather than require new monitoring.[132]

Mass balances can provide better information about exposure. But they need to be combined with improved understanding of the hazards associated with the chemicals to support a truly risk-based system of waste management. The distressing lack of information about the hazards of commonly used chemicals is emphasized by the National Research Council's study mentioned earlier under "Limitations of Risk Assessment."[133] Correcting this ignorance should be a primary goal. Otherwise, the very expensive mistakes will continue—from the perspectives of both economics and environmental health—and excessive attention will be paid to substances that pose relatively little risk while too little will be done about the more dangerous ones.

Better risk assessments can be achieved by developing better methodologies for testing the wide range of potential effects that wastes may have. Much attention has been focused on cancer, and the ability to assess the risk from carcinogens has increased considerably in the past 10 years. Comparable progress needs to be made in improving methods to assess other types of health and environmental effects. After all, exposure to some chemicals can affect people's reproductive, immune, and nervous systems and can cause other problems as well.[134]

Also needed is improvement of the current simplistic and crude understanding of what happens to substances once they are released in the environment. How are they transported and transformed? Do these processes result in unexpected, indirect exposures—particularly in association with other substances—that may be more serious than the direct exposures?

Exposure is typically assumed to take place primarily through one medium, and each pathway through the environment is usually assessed independently. For instance, the test for transport under RCRA considers only leaching to groundwater, not how much of a substance may be emitted to air; yet for a volatile organic compound, that emission may be significant. More research is needed on how chemicals move between the soil and air and the soil and water and on biochemical transformations that may contaminate food and water.[135] Models and monitoring play complementary roles in this process.

The Elements of Choice

Even with substantially more information, choosing the best waste management method under any set of conditions will not be easy. All of the management techniques are bound by the fundamental laws of chemistry, physics, and thermodynamics. These dictate that waste, once created, cannot disappear. It can only be changed physically or transformed to other substances in hopes of making it less hazardous or moved from one place to another in hopes of reducing exposure. The basic choice in managing a waste is deciding whether it makes more sense to reduce the intrinsic hazard or to change the exposure—or a combination of the two.

Considerations of Risk

The state of California has done some analyses to allow a better comparison of the relative risks of different management techniques. One study analyzes the differences in emissions to air from three ways of handling volatile organic wastes—incineration, landfilling, and recycling. The report estimates that burning 50 tons of such waste in a rotary kiln results in only 9 percent of the volatile organic air emissions that land disposal of the same waste causes. However, incineration also releases particulates, acid gases, and sulfur and nitrous oxides not released by the landfill. Use of wet-air oxidation for volatile organic wastes produces very few air emissions, although some hydrocarbons may need to be controlled with scrubbing towers followed by adsorption with activated carbon. If the organic wastes are recycled to recover solvents, emissions can occur during distillation, filtration, and land disposal of residues, but they can be reduced with controls.[136]

Such comparisons provide companies making waste management choices with some basis for selection, but a broader approach is needed if overall risk reduction is to be considered. What happens to the volatile organic compounds released? How rapidly do they degrade? Depending on the location of the facility, some may degrade to a nonharmful level before sensitive people or environments are exposed. Other substances may accumulate in the atmosphere or other parts of the environment or degrade into more harmful substances.

Location can also substantially affect risk. There is little question that past practices in siting both production and waste management facilities sometimes increased rather than reduced exposure to wastes that could cause damage. Waste sites now operating and/or being cleaned up are frequently located in urban, industrialized areas. Superfund sites are most often storage or disposal facilities with contaminated groundwater in highly populated urban states.[137] Some former waste dumps containing hazardous waste were converted for use as parks and building sites. Wetlands were sometimes filled with contaminated dredge materials.

If one looks beyond RCRA and Superfund wastes to the emission of air pollutants, release patterns are similar. Three percent of the U.S. land area, occupied by 36 percent of the nation's population, receives 39 percent of the hydrocarbon air emissions. The same area is responsible for 34 percent of chemical production and hosts 38 percent of all hazardous waste facilities.[138] Mining and dredging sites are likely to be more isolated, but they may endanger sensitive environments in some circumstances.

Physical location standards for waste producing and management facilities, such as those being developed in many states, can help reduce exposure in the future. The location of aquifers, floodplains, and fault zones are a few of the criteria to be considered. But attention also needs to be paid to risks caused by the entire waste management system, including storage and transport.

Most wastes are managed at the point of generation. Even industrial hazardous wastes are primarily managed and disposed of on site.[139] A major advantage of on-site management is that no transportation is needed. Transportation and waste handling are major potential causes of waste spills and other environmental releases.

Another advantage of on-site management is that large numbers of people, or extremely valuable or sensitive environmental areas, are not usually located immediately adjacent to industrial facilities. Thus, the exposure potential may be reduced. However, on-site management can increase the potential exposure of the plant's employees and, particularly if there are releases to the air and the plant is in an urban area, of a large number of other workers and residents.

Trade-offs among types of risk are often involved in deciding how to deal with waste. The decision whether to incinerate on land or on an ocean vessel is an example. Ocean incineration raises the risk of accidents, since wastes may need to be transported for long distances. Barges, which would be used at some stages, have a relatively high spill rate.[140] The risk to the marine environment from ocean incineration is largely unknown. Yet the alternative of land incineration raises uncertainty about effects on human health from air releases. As this example indicates, choices of *where* to manage waste can make a difference in the degree and types of risk, as well as in what communities will be exposed. Unfortunately, the present fragmented management programs are not usually organized in a way that allows the trade-offs to be evaluated.

Considerations of Cost and Incentives

Waste management, as indicated in figure 7.17, can run over $1,000 per ton for certain types of hazardous wastes. On the other hand, when materials can be recycled or energy recovered, management can generate a net income.

The net costs of the alternative management options clearly provide strong financial incentives favoring some treatment techniques over others. And, as would be expected, the least-cost systems are not necessarily those promising the greatest reductions in risk. A fundamental question for policy makers is how the incentives can be adjusted to stimulate waste generators to adopt those techniques that do offer the most risk reduction for their waste stream.

Regulations, of course, can provide the strongest incentives, depending on the severity of the noncompliance penalties, the efforts devoted to inspecting and enforcing compliance, and how clearly and carefully the conditions of noncompliance are specified. A regulatory program, however, is likely to be more successful if other incentives reinforce its goals.

As a result of court decisions and statutory changes, liability has become an increasingly important incentive affecting the actions of everyone involved in the waste management system.[141] Firms producing wastes can be held liable for the damages the wastes may cause many years after they are produced, regardless of who was actually responsible for their disposal. These changes provide very strong incentives for firms to reduce the amount of dangerous wastes they generate or to ensure that these wastes are managed to eliminate their risk as much as possible.

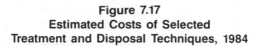

Figure 7.17
Estimated Costs of Selected
Treatment and Disposal Techniques, 1984

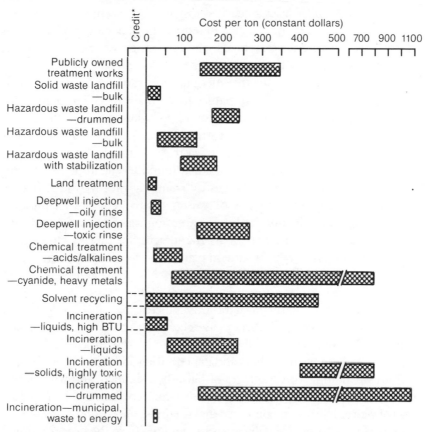

* The range of values for wastes being sold is unknown.

Source: Office of Technology Assessment; State of California, Air Resources Board; Connecticut Hazardous Waste Management Service; Environmental Defense Fund; National Solid Wastes Management Association; Environmental Protection Agency; Council on Environmental Quality.

California and New York are among about 20 states attempting to reinforce these incentives by taxing waste generation roughly according to the risks that the wastes may present.[142] Funds raised by these taxes can be used to help support the costs of cleanup or recycling programs as well as waste treatment facilities. Such a tax can improve incentives in two ways: the tax itself provides an incentive to reduce the generation of hazardous wastes, and the revenues can be used to lower the cost of more desirable waste management systems.

Fees charged by wastewater treatment facilities can, if properly designed, provide similar incentives. Such charges are normally based on volume plus charges for specific materials or indicators of pollution such as oil and grease. A study of 101 plants in nine industries showed that even a low level of most charges was enough to result in waste discharges being reduced, often by more than 10 percent.[143] The study found several instances of companies responding to sewer charges by changing processes so that they reduced the amounts or types of wastes discharged. For example, a corrugated-box production facility began using water contaminated with heavy metals in another part of its manufacturing process rather than discharging it to the sewage treatment plant. However, a more recent survey by INFORM did not find any clear indications of sewer charges stimulating waste reduction efforts at organic chemical plants.[144]

Both regulatory and financial incentives increasingly favor reduction of waste. In a recent report, EPA states its belief that the higher cost of managing waste and financial liability will combine with the difficulties in siting new waste management facilities and in permitting and cleaning up facilities already operating, with shortages of liability insurance, and with public concern about toxic chemicals to provide strong incentives for the reduction of waste. The report points out that there also are economic, technical, and regulatory barriers to reducing waste ranging from the need for capital and concerns about technical quality to the effect on existing environmental permits. However, the agency recommends to Congress that consideration of regulatory approaches to reducing waste be delayed until the effect of existing incentives is seen.[145]

The information obtained from mass-balance analyses described above not only can help companies determine the need for waste reduction but also can assist in measuring the extent to which risk is being reduced as practices change.

Efforts to establish effective risk-based incentive schemes will inevitably encounter a number of difficulties. A perfect scheme, in which a waste generator would be charged for the precise amount of risk that its wastes create, is no doubt impossible. But the question of incentives cannot be ignored. They already exist, and waste generators are responding to them. The challenge is to develop incentive schemes that can be implemented and that further rather than counteract the goal of minimizing the risk associated with society's waste management system.

CONCLUSIONS

Waste management decisions will never be easy. They will always involve extremely complicated trade-offs among different types of risks and damages. They will always, at least implicitly, involve placing some economic value on the different types of risks and on the probability of their occurring. They will always involve substantial elements of politics and public perception. The decision-making process can never be perfect.

But that process can be improved. As argued above, it would benefit substantially from more and better information. It would also benefit from removal of many current institutional blinders. The study of the risk implications of alternative management methods that was performed by the California Air Resources Board illustrates the limitations that can weaken analysis and action. Because its mandate does not extend to wastewater and waste reduction, the board's report did not include an assessment of how risk would be reduced if the waste stream were released to wastewater or if efforts were made to reduce releases through process or product changes in the plant.

No longer can the waste problem be addressed in such a piecemeal manner. Removing wastes from air and water and placing them on land may only delay and change the location of damage. So may diluting waste in air and water. There is no easy answer. A choice that reduces risk from waste will always require considering the waste's potential to cause damage and the degree to which different management methods can reduce exposure to the waste. Managing wastes requires the same careful attention as manufacturing a product. Risk is likely to be reduced in direct relation to the extent that waste management becomes a part of the production process rather than afterthought.

FURTHER READING

Morton Lippmann and Richard B. Schlesinger provide an unusually broad view of the nature, sources, effects, and environmental behavior of wastes in *Chemical Contamination in the Human Environment* (New York: Oxford University Press, 1979). Written as an introduction for environmental health scientists, the book also describes legal and technical controls, though those descriptions are now somewhat dated. Allen V. Kneese and Blair T. Bower stress the economic, technological, and institutional aspects of waste management in *Environmental Quality and Residuals Management* (Baltimore: Johns Hopkins University Press, 1979). The U.S. Environmental Protection Agency's *Environmental Outlook 1980* (Washington, D.C.: U.S. Government Printing Office, 1980) provides the most complete summary of the amounts of wastes generated and released to all parts of the environment. *Environmental Quality* (Washington, D.C.: U.S. Government Printing Office), produced annually since 1970 by the Council on Environmental Quality, documents the changing focus of research and action on waste.

"Risk Assessment and Risk Control," a chapter in *State of the Environment: An Assessment at Mid-Decade* (Washington, D.C.: The Conservation Foundation, 1984) and also published separately, provides a broad view of assessing risk and includes suggestions for further reading in this field.

Much of the writing on waste in the past decade has analyzed the implementation of waste laws. Most of the emphasis has been on hazardous waste. The Office of Technology Assessment has issued a series of reports that outline policy options and summarize the legal, scientific, and technical issues involved in managing waste. They include *Hazardous Waste Management* (1983), *High-Level Radioactive Wastes* (1983), *Superfund Strategy* (1985), *Serious Reduction of Hazardous Waste* (1986), and *Marine Waste Management* (in press). The reports are available from the U.S. Government Printing Office. Richard C. Fortuna and David J. Lennett describe the legal requirements governing wastes covered by RCRA in *Hazardous Waste Regulation: The New Era* (New York: McGraw-Hill, 1986). The *Environmental Law Reporter* has prepared a *Superfund Deskbook* (Washington, D.C.: Environmental Law Institute, 1986).

The literature on waste reduction has expanded rapidly in the past two years. In addition to the Office of Technology Assessment's report mentioned above, new publications in this area include D. Sarokin, W. Muir,

C. G. Miller, and S. R. Sperber, *Cutting Chemical Wastes* (New York: INFORM, 1985); Environmental Defense Fund, *Approaches to Source Reduction: Practical Guidance from Existing Policies and Programs* (New York: Environmental Defense Fund, 1986); and U.S. Environmental Protection Agency, Office of Solid Wastes, *Report to Congress: Minimization of Hazardous Wastes*, Executive Summary (Washington, D.C.: U.S. Environmental Protection Agency, 1986). INFORM's report documents waste reduction practices of organic chemical companies in three states. The Environmental Defense Fund and a report in preparation by the Natural Resources Defense Council address state options. The EPA report to Congress describes current incentives for waste reduction. It also analyzes the extent of waste reduction in 22 industrial processes.

Environmental Science and Technology is particularly valuable because it takes a comprehensive view of pollution control rather than focusing on one type of pollutant or environmental medium. Its articles cover both the effectiveness of treatment technologies and the behavior of wastes in the environment. *JAPCA* now describes itself as "the international journal of air pollution control and hazardous waste management." This reflects the decision of the Air Pollution Control Association to broaden its focus to cover hazardous waste as of January 1987. The *Water Pollution Control Journal* covers wastes released to water. The Solid Waste Management Association publishes *Waste Age*, a monthly aimed mainly at operators of waste facilities. These monthly periodicals are complemented by *Hazardous Waste & Hazardous Materials*, a quarterly edited at the Tufts University Center for Environmental Management that brings together articles from engineers, policy analysts, and health and environmental scientists.

REFERENCES

Text

1. U.S. Department of Commerce, Bureau of the Census, *Statistical Abstract of the United States 1986*, 106th ed. (Washington, D.C.: U.S. Government Printing Office, 1984), pp. 6, 39, 204, 205, tables 3, 54, 353, 355; U.S. Environmental Protection Agency, Office of Municipal Pollution Control, *1984 Needs Survey Report to Congress: Assessment of Needed Publicly Owned Wastewater Treatment Facilities in the United States*, EPA 430/9-84-011 (Washington, D.C.: U.S. Environmental Protection Agency, February 1985), p. C-15, table C-5; JRB Associates, "Inventory of Air Pollution Control, Industrial Wastewater Treatment and Water Treatment Sludges," report for the U.S. Environmental Protection Agency,

December 1983, table 5.1, p. 5-2; personal communication with Jeff Tealander, U.S. Environmental Protection Agency, Research Triangle Park; and "EPA to Regulate Emissions from Wood Burning Stoves," *The New York Times*, October 5, 1986.

2. Blair T. Bower, ed., *Regional Residuals Environmental Quality Management Modeling*, research paper R-7 (Washington, D.C.: Resources for the Future, 1977), p. 2.

3. Personal communication with Tricon Colors, Elmwood Park, N.J., January 20, 1987.

4. U.S. Environmental Protection Agency, Office of Air Quality, Planning and Standards, "National Air Pollutant Emissions Estimates, 1940-1984," EPA-450/4-85-014 (Washington, D.C.: U.S. Environmental Protection Agency, January 1986), pp. 11-16.

5. G.M. Woodwell, *The Role of Terrestrial Vegetation in the Global Carbon Cycle: Measurement by Remote Sensing*, SCOPE 23 (New York: John Wiley and Sons, 1984), p. 4; and World Resource Institute, Institute for Environment and Development, *World Resource 1986: An Assessment of the Resource Base that Supports the Global Economy* (New York: Basic Books, 1986), p. 174.

6. Richard W. Goodwin, "Air Pollution Clean Wastes: Dry Versus Wet," *Journal of Energy Engineering* 109, no. 3 (1983):131.

7. Leonard Gianessi and Henry Peskin, *The RFF Environmental Data Inventory* (Washington, D.C.: Resources for the Future, April 1986), p. 13, table 4.

8. U.S. Environmental Protection Agency, *1984 Needs Survey Report to Congress*, pp. 26-27.

9. Personal communication with K. Wagner, Office of Technology Assessment; and U.S. Environmental Protection Agency, Office of Water, Regulations and Standards, *Report to Congress January 1981-December 1983: On Administration of the Marine Protection, Research, and Sanctuaries Act of 1972, as Amended (P.L. 92-532) and Implementing the International London Dumping Convention* (Washington, D.C.: U.S. Government Printing Office, January 1981-December 1983), p. 9, table III, and p. 10, Figure II.

10. William Rutala and Felix Sarubbi, "Management of Infectious Waste from Hospitals," *Infection Control* 4, no. 4 (1983):198.

11. National Solid Wastes Management Association, "Basic Data: Solid Waste Amounts, Composition and Management Systems," *NewsFacts*, Technical Bulletin 85-6, 1984.

12. U.S. Congress, Congressional Budget Office, *Hazardous Waste Management: Recent Changes and Policy Alternatives* (Washington, D.C.: U.S. Government Printing Office, May 1985), p. 24; and U.S. Department of Energy, *Spent Fuel and Radioactive Waste Inventories, Projections and Characteristics* (DOE/RW-0006, Rev. 1), December 1985.

13. Calculations are by The Conservation Foundation, 1986, drawing from the Congressional Budget Office, *Hazardous Waste Management* report, p. 24.

14. Congressional Budget Office, *Hazardous Waste Management*, p. 24.

15. California Air Resources Board, *An Assessment of the Volatile and Toxic Organic Emissions from Hazardous Waste Disposal in California* (Sacramento: California Air Resources Board, February 1982), pp. 31-32.

16. R. D. Kleopfer et al., "Field Investigation of Uncontrolled Hazardous Waste Sites, 1983," technical report submitted to U.S. Environmental Protection Agency, contract

68-01-6056, cited in State of California, Commission for Economic Development, *Poisoning Prosperity: The Impact of Toxics on California's Economy* (Sacramento: California Commission for Economic Development, June 1985), p. 109; and R.D. Kloepfer et al.,"Anaerobic Degradation of Trichloroethylene in Soil," *Environmental Science and Technology* 19 (1985):277-79.

17. National Research Council, Committee on Ground-Water Resources in Relation to Coal Mining, *Coal Mining and Ground-Water Resources in the United States* (Washington, D.C.: National Academy Press, 1981), pp. 82-88.

18. Ada and Frank Graham, "Lead Poisoning and the Suburban Child," *Today's Health*, March 1974, cited in Louis Freedberg, *America's Poisoned Playgrounds: Children and Toxic Chemicals* (Oakland: Youth News, 1983), pp. 32, 36.

19. "Jurisdiction Responses to Federal Emergency Management Agency, Hazardous Incident Capability Assessment Multi-Year Development Plan," 1985, cited in U.S. Office of Technology Assessment, *Transportation of Hazardous Materials*, OTA-SET-304 (Washington, D.C.: U.S. Government Printing Office, July 1986), p. 218, Table 5-7.

20. National Research Council, Commission on Life Science, Board on Toxicology and Environmental Health Hazards, *Toxicity Testing: Strategies to Determine Needs and Priorities* (Washington, D.C.: National Academy Press, 1984), p. 33.

21. 42 USC §7401(b)(1).

22. 33 USC §1251(a)

23. 33 USC §1401(b)

24. 42 USC §6901(b)(1)

25. League of Women Voters Education Fund, *The Nuclear Waste Primer: A Handbook for Citizens* (New York: Nick Lyons Books, 1985), pp. 31-34, 38.

26. Consumer products are regulated by the Consumer Product Safety Act (15 USC §2051 et seq.). The Federal Insecticide, Fungicide, and Rodenticide Act (7 USC §135 et seq.) regulates pesiticides. The Federal Food, Drug, and Cosmetic Act (21 USC §301 et seq.) regulates food, drugs, and cosmetics.

27. Since national air quality standards were set, a standard has also been established for lead, the standard for photochemical oxidants has been revised and changed to one for ozone—the principal component of smog—and the hydrocarbon standard has been withdrawn as superfluous.

28. U.S. Comptroller General, *Air Pollution: EPA's Efforts to Reduce and End the Use of Lead in Gasoline* (Washington, D.C.: U.S. General Accounting Office, 1986), p. 3.

29. Walter M. Shackelford and David M. Cline, "Organic Compounds in Water," *Environmental Science and Technology* 20 (1986):652.

30. U.S. Environmental Protection Agency, Office of Water Regulations and Standards, *Report to Congress on the Discharge of Hazardous Wastes to Publicly Owned Treatment Works* (Washington, D.C.: U.S. Government Printing Office, 1986). The differences between RCRA and Clean Water Act controls are discussed on pages 1-1 through 1-2 and 1-7 through 1-10. Wastewater from organics industries are discussed on page E-4.

31. Clean Air Act, §112.

32. Under RCRA (42 USC §6903(5)), hazardous waste is defined as "a solid waste, or combination of solid wastes, which because of its quantity, concentration, or physical, chemical, or infectious characteristics may—(A) cause, or significantly contribute to an increase in mortality or an increase in serious irreversible, or incapacitating reversible, illness; or (B) pose a substantial present or potential hazard to human health or the environment when improperly treated, stored, transported, or disposed of, or otherwise managed."

33. Under RCRA (42 USC §6924(q)), EPA must set standards for facilities that burn fuel that contains hazardous substances. Cement kilns are specifically prohibited from burning such fuels in cities until EPA promulgates regulations defining de minimus quantities of hazardous substances in such fuels below which such resource recovery facilities are exempt. Under section 42 USC §6921(d), EPA must promulgate standards for generators of between 100 and 1,000 kilograms of hazardous waste per month.

34. "EPA Proposes New Reportable Quantities for 340 Superfund Toxics," *Inside EPA*, January 16, 1987, p. 3.

35. The Conservation Foundation, *State of the Environment: An Assessment at Mid-Decade* (Washington, D.C.: The Conservation Foundation, 1984), p. 63.

36. 15 USC §2601(b).

37. "Studies To Be Proposed Under TSCA Section 4 for 73 Chemicals Named By Solid Waste Office," *Chemical Regulation Reporter*, Jan. 16, 1987, p. 1323. Under § 8(d) of TSCA, EPA has already promulgated a rule (51 *Fed. Reg.* 2890) requiring that health and safety data be collected on 33 chemicals found in waste. Some of the chemicals listed are found in water as well. EPA has also proposed the collection of such data on an additional list of 107 chemicals nominated by the agency's offices of solid waste, water, and others inside out outside of EPA (51 *Fed. Reg.* 27562).

38. EPA promulgated regulations on landfills in 40 CFR §264.301 (1985) and on suface impoundments in 40 CFR §264.220 (1985).

39. Council on Environmental Quality, *Environmental Quality 1984* (Washington, D.C.: U.S. Government Printing Office, 1986), pp. 81-2.

40. 1985 Dollars. Calculations made from DOE docments give a range of values because the cost of the disposal facility will depend on the site characteristics as well as the period of time over which it is used. Since no permanent nuclear waste diposal has ever been attempted in the United States, the actual cost may vary considerably. See U.S. Department of Energy, Office of Civilian Radioactive Waste Management, *Nuclear Waste Fund Fee Adequacy: An Assessment* (Washington, D.C.: U.S. Government Printing Office, 1986).

41. U.S. Department of Energy, Energy Information Adminstration, *World Nuclear Fuel Cycle Requirements 1986,* (Washington, D.C.: U.S. Government Printing Office, 1986), pp. 57, 60; and U.S. Department of Engery, Energy Information Adminstration, *Monthly Review,"* July 1986, p. 100.

42. Office of Technology Assessment, *Technologies and Management Strategies for Hazardous Waste Control,* OTA-M-196 (Washington, D.C.: U.S. Government Printing Office, March 1983), p. 197.

43. 42 USC §6901(b)(3).

44. Air releases from hazardous waste facilities are regulated under 42 USC §6924(n). Corrective measures for facilities seeking permits are required under 42 USC §6924 (u).

45. 16 ELR 20693, 8-86, *Natural Resources Defense Council, Inc.* v. *U.S. Environmental Protection Agency.*

46. U.S. Environmental Protection Agency, *A Strategy to Reduce Risks to Public Health From Air Toxics* (Washington, D.C.: U.S. Environmental Protection Agency, 1985), p. 13.

47. 51 Fed. Reg. 38957.

48. Henry S. Cole, Ken Silver, and Terry Lave, *Out-of-Sight, Out-of-Mind: EPA Superfund Clean-ups Continue to Leave Large Volumes of Hazardous Wastes in the Ground*, January 1986, p. ES3.

49. Congressional Budget Office, *Hazardous Waste Management*, pp. 9, 11, 17.

50. David Sarokin et al., *Cutting Chemical Wastes: What 29 Organic Chemical Plants Are Doing to Reduce Hazardous Wastes* (New York: INFORM, 1985), pp. 55, 67.

51. U.S. Environmental Protection Agency, *Report to Congress: Minimization of Hazardous Waste: Executive Summary and Fact Sheet* (Washington, D.C.: U.S. Environmental Protection Agency, October 1986), p. v.

52. Office of Technology Assessment, *Technologies and Management Strategies for Hazardous Waste Control, Volume II—Working Papers: Part D. Alternatives for Reducing Hazardous Waste Generation Using End-Product Substitution* (Washington, D.C.: National Technical Information Service, April 1983), p. 1-6.

53. 3M, Environmental Engineering and Pollution Control Department, "Riker Innovation Meets Air Regulation," *Ideas: A Compendium of 3P Success Stories* (St. Paul, Minn.: 3M, n.d.).

54. U.S. Environmental Protection Agency, Effluent Guidelines Division, *Guidance Manual for Pulp, Paper, and Paperboard and Builders' Paper and Board Mills Pretreatment Standards*, July 1984, pp. 3-1 and 3-2.

55. Allen V. Kneese and Blair T. Bower, *Environmental Quality and Residuals Management* (Baltimore: Johns Hopkins University Press, 1979).

56. Robert Carr, "Integrated Environmental Control in the Electric Utility Industry," *Integrated Environmental Controls for Fossil-Fuel Power Plants: Challenges-Techologies Strategies*, Proceedings of the 3rd Symposium (Pittsburgh: Air Pollution Control Association, February 1986), p. 29.

57. Office of Technology Assessment, *Serious Reduction of Hazardous Waste: For Pollution Prevention and Industrial Efficiency*, OTA-ITE-317 (Washington, D.C.: U.S. Government Printing Office, September 1986), pp. 51-52.

58. Ibid., pp. 216-20.

59. League of Women Voters of Massachusetts, Environmental Management Center of Tufts University, and U.S. Environmental Protection Agency, *Waste Reduction: The Untold Story* (National Academy of Sciences Conference Center, June 19-21, 1985, Woods Hole, Massachusetts) (Boston: League of Women Voters of Massachusetts, 1985).

60. Congressional Budget Office, *Hazardous Waste Management*, p. 45.

61. Office of Technology Assessment, *Serious Reduction of Hazardous Waste*, pp. 83-84.

62. Sarokin et al., *Cutting Chemical Wastes*, p. 35.

63. Office of Technology Assessment, *Technologies and Management Strategies for Hazardous Waste Control, Volume II-Working Papers: Part D*, p. 3-36.

64. Congressional Budget Office, *Hazardous Waste Management*, p. xiv.

65. Office of Technology Assessment, *Serious Reduction of Hazardous Waste*, p. 26.

66. Donald L. Van Dyne and Conrad B. Gilbertson, *Estimating U.S. Livestock and Poultry Manure and Nutrient Production*, prepared for U.S. Department of Agriculture, Economics, Statistics, and Cooperatives Service, ESCS-12 (Washington, D.C.: National Technical Information Service, March 1978), p. 5.

67. National Association of Recycling Industries, "Domestic Consumption and Exports—1980-1985," *Annual Review of Scrap Metal for 1984* (New York: National Association of Recycling Industries, March 1986).

68. Richard Hertzberg, "New Directions in Solid Waste and Recycling," *BioCycle*, January 1986, p. 22.

69. Ibid.

70. Environmental Defense Fund, *To Burn or Not To Burn: The Economic Advantages of Recycling over Garbage Incineration for New York City* (New York: Environmental Defense Fund, August 1985), p. C-1.

71. Congressional Budget Office, *Hazardous Waste Management*, p. 24.

72. U.S. Environmental Protection Agency, Office of Policy Analysis, *Survey of Selected Firms in the Commercial Hazardous Waste Management Industry: 1984 Update* (Final Report prepared by ICF) (Washington, D.C.: U.S. Environmental Protection Agency, September 30, 1985), p. 4-2.

73. "Technology," *Environmental Science and Technology* 20 (1986):310.

74. Sarokin et al., *Cutting Chemical Wastes*, p. 122.

75. Office of Technology Assessment, *Managing the Nation's Commercial High-Level Radioactive Waste* (Washington, D.C.: U.S. Government Printing Office, March 1985), pp. 67-68, 84.

76. League of Women Voters Education Fund, *The Nuclear Waste Primer*, p. 28.

77. U.S. Environmental Protection Agency, Office of Emergency and Remedial Response, *National Priorities List Fact Book, June 1986* (Washington, D.C.: U.S. Government Printing Office, 1986), p. 23.

78. Council on Environmental Quality and U.S. Environmental Protection Agency, *Municipal Sewage Treatment: A Comparison of Alternatives* (Washington, D.C.: U.S. Government Printing Office, February 1974), pp. 73, 41, A-2.

79. 42 USCA. §§6901 et seq. (1986); and Superfund Amendments and Reauthorization Act of 1986 (PL99-499, October 17, 1986), as published in *Environment Reporter—Current Developments*, October 24, 1986, pp. 995-1005.

80. U.S. Environmental Protection Agency, *1984 Needs Survey Report to Congress*, p. C-13.

81. Sarokin et al., *Cutting Chemical Wastes*, p. 65, Table 5-5.

82. Robert T. Mueller, Tessie W. Fields, and Leslie McGeorge, *The Occurrence and Fate of Toxic Substances in New Jersey Sewage Treatment Facilities*, CN-409 (Trenton, N.J.: New Jersey Department of Environmental Protection, Office of Science and Research, September 1986), p. 54.

83. U.S. Environmental Protection Agency, Office of Policy Analysis/Office of Policy, Planning and Evaluation, *Santa Clara Valley Integrated Environmental Management Project: Revised Stage One Report* (Washington, D.C.: U.S. Environmental Protection Agency, May 1986), p. 3-51.

84. U.S. Environmental Protection Agency, Office of Water Regulations and Standards, *Report to Congress on the Discharge of Hazardous Wastes to Publicly Owned Treatment*

Works, EP/530-SW-86-004 (Washington, D.C.: U.S. Government Printing Office, February 1986), pp. 4-1, 5-7.

85. Ibid., p. 4-9.

86. Ibid., p. 4-1.

87. Robert Gould, ed., *1986-87 Resource Recovery Yearbook* (New York: Governmental Advisory Associates, 1986), p. 34; information provided by U.S. Environmental Protection Agency, Office of Water, March 1987; U.S. Environmental Protection Agency, Information Management Staff, Office of Solid Waste, *Summary Report on RCRA Permit Activities for September 1986* (Washington, D.C.: U.S. Environmental Protection Agency, October 15, 1986), Figure 2; and Environmental Planning Lobby, *The Financial and Environmental Impact of Garbage Incineration* (Albany, NY: Environmental Planning Lobby, July 11, 1985), p. 2.

88. Congressional Budget Office, *Hazardous Waste Management*, p. 24.

89. California Air Resources Board, *Technologies for the Treatment and Destruction of Organic Wastes as Alternatives to Land Disposal* (Sacramento, Calif.: California Air Resources Board, August 1982), p. 13.

90. Benjamin L. Blaney, "Treatment Technologies for Hazardous Wastes: Part II. Alternative Techniques for Managing Solvent Wastes," *Journal of the Air Pollution Control Association* 36 (1986):282.

91. K. Carlson, "Dry Absorption System at Refuse Incineration Plant Malmoe—Experiences from Six Months Operations" (Berlin, West Germany: E. Freitag-Verlag, Recycling International, 1982), pp. 668-73, cited in State of California, Air Resources Board, Stationary Source Division, *Air Pollution Control at Resource Recovery Facilities: Final* (Sacramento: California Air Resources Board, May 1984), pp. 129, R-10; and Environmental Defense Fund, *To Burn or Not to Burn*, p. A-1.

92. Office of Technology Assessment, *Ocean Incineration: Its Role in Managing Hazardous Waste*, OTA-0-313 (Washington, D.C.: U.S. Government Printing Office, August 1986), pp. 120-21.

93. Matt Jantunen et al., "Rapid Changes in Peat Fly Ash Mutagenicity after Release into the Atmosphere: A Controlled Dilution Bag Study," *Environmental Science and Technology* 20 (1986):684.

94. Environmental Defense Fund, *To Burn or Not To Burn*, p. 2.

95. Congressional Budget Office, *Hazardous Waste Management*, p. 49.

96. Office of Technology Assessment, *Ocean Incineration*, pp. 9, 75-76.

97. R.C. Loehr, "Multi-Media Aspects of Waste Management" (draft), 1986, pp. 16-17.

98. Ibid.

99. U.S. Environmental Protection Agency, *1984 Needs Survey Report to Congress*, p. C-27.

100. U.S. Environmental Protection Agency, Office of Toxic Substances, *Methods for Assessing Exposure to Chemical Substances, Volume 3: Methods for Assessing Exposure from Disposal of Chemical Substances* (Washington, D.C.: U.S. Government Printing Office, September 1983), p. 95.

101. Ibid., p. 94.

102. Mueller et al., *The Occurrence and Fate of Toxic Substances in New Jersey Treatment Facilities*, p. 56.

103. Gilbert Masters, *Introduction to Environmental Science and Technology* (New York: John Wiley and Sons, 1974), p. 243; and California Air Resources Board, *Air Pollution Control at Resource Recovery Facilities*, p. 129. 104. U.S. Environmental Protection Agency,

Survey of Selected Firms in the Commercial Hazardous Waste Management Industry: 1984 Update, p. 3-5.

105. New Jersey Department of Environmental Protection, Division of Waste Management, *Proposed New Jersey Solid Waste Management Plan Update: 1985-2000* (Trenton, N.J.: New Jersey Department of Environmental Protection, July 15, 1985), p. 64.

106. Congressional Budget Office, *Hazardous Waste Management*, p. 24.

107. Gary Brown, Scotty Fallah, and Cassie Thompson, *Census of State and Territorial Subtitle D Non-Hazardous Waste Programs*, prepared for U.S. Environmental Protection Agency, Office of Solid Waste (Rockville, Md.: Westat, Inc., September 1986), p. 49.

108. Congressional Budget Office, *Hazardous Waste Management*, p. 24.

109. Westat, Inc., *Final Report: National Survey of Hazardous Waste Generators and Treatment, Storage and Disposal Facilities Regulated under RCRA in 1981*, prepared for U.S. Environmental Protection Agency, Office of Solid Waste (Rockville, Md.: Westat, Inc., April 1984), p. 205.

110. Congressional Budget Office, *Hazardous Waste Management*, p. 24.

111. Information Management Staff, *Summary Report on RCRA Permit Activities for September 1986*, October 15, 1986.

112. Congressional Budget Office, *Hazardous Waste Management*, p. 24.

113. U.S. Environmental Protection Agency, Office of Drinking Water, *Surface Impoundment Assessment: National Report* (Washington, D.C.: U.S. Environmental Protection Agency, December 1983), pp. 5, 72, 74.

114. League of Women Voters, *The Nuclear Waste Primer: A Handbook for Citizens*, pp. 28-29, 34, 57-60.

115. Office of Technology Assessment, *Protecting the Nation's Groundwater from Contamination, Vol. II* (Washington, D.C.: U.S. Government Printing Office, 1984), pp. 269, 272, 274.

116. U.S. Environmental Protection Agency, *Surface Impoundment Assessment: National Report*, pp. 8-9.

117. Office of Technology Assessment, *Technologies and Management Strategies for Hazardous Waste Control* (Washington, D.C.: U.S. Government Printing Office, 1983), pp. 174-176.

118. Laurie Rich and Donald R. Canon, "Hazardous Waste Management: New Rules Are Changing the Game," *Chemical Week* 139, no. 8 (1986):39.

119. 42 U.S.C.A. §6924 (1986).

120. *1985 Survey of Selected Firms in the Commercial Hazardous Waste Management Industry*, U.S. Environmental Protection Agency, November 1986, p. 2-13.

121. Sarokin et al., *Cutting Chemical Wastes*, p. 32.

122. U.S. Environmental Protection Agency, Office of Planning and Management, Program Evaluation Division, *National Accomplishments in Pollution Control: 1970-1980: Some Case Histories* (Washington, D.C.: U.S. Environmental Protection Agency, 1980), pp. 29-33.

123. Sarokin et al., *Cutting Chemical Wastes*, pp. 312-13.

124. "EPA Draft Study Shows 38 Gallons Per 200 Drum Shipment Lost in Transport," *Inside EPA Weekly Report*, October 28, 1983, p. 11; and Mark Abkowitz et al., "Assessing the Risks and Costs Associated with Truck Transport of Hazardous Wastes," draft final

report prepared for U.S. Environmental Protection Agency, Office of Solid Waste (Washington, D.C.: U.S. Environmental Protection Agency, n.d.). 125. Wil Lepkowski, "Bhopal: Indian City Begins to Heal but Conflicts Remain," *Chemical and Engineering News*, December 2, 1985, p. 18; and Word Worthy, "U.S. Chemical Undustry Moving to Assume No More Bhopals," *Chemical and Engineering News*, January 6, 1986, p. 9.

126. Council on Environmental Quality and U.S. Environmental Protection Agency, *Municipal Sewage Treatment: A Comparison of Alternatives*, pp. 41, 91.

127. "Federal Facilities That Flout the Law," *The Washington Post*, June 1, 1986.

128. Bureau of National Affairs, "State Solid Waste Management Programs Vary Widely But Face Similar Problems, Such as Capacity, Siting Limits," *Environmental Reporter— Current Developments*, October 3, 1986, pp. 844, 845.

129. Office of Technology Assessment, *Serious Reduction of Hazardous Waste*, pp. 92-93.

130. New Jersey Department of Environmental Protection, Office of Science and Research, *New Jersey Industrial Survey: Final Report* (Trenton, N.J.: New Jersey Department of Environmental Protection, 1986), Executive Summary and pp. 3, 32.

131. U.S. Congress, *Congressional Record*, 99th Cong., 2d sess., 1986, p. H9071.

132. Ibid., p. H9072.

133. National Research Council, *Toxicity Testing*.

134. See, for example, Child Trends, *Improving Assessment of the Effects of Environmental Contamination on Human Reproduction*, September 1986.

135. Council on Environmental Quality, Office of Environmental Quality, *Report on Long-Term Environmental Research and Development* (Washington, D.C.: Council on Environmental Quality, March 1985), p. 2-3.

136. California Air Resources Board, *Technologies for the Treatment and Destruction of Organic Wastes as Alternatives to Land Disposal*, pp. 91-99.

137. Michael R. Greenberg, *Hazardous Waste Sites: The Credibility Gap* (New Brunswick, N.J.: Center for Urban Policy Research, 1984), p. 128.

138. Currie, *The Geographic Approach to Integrated Environmental Management: Rationale, Objectives, and Methods* (Washington, D.C.: U.S. Environmental Protection Agency, January 1983), p. 2.

139. Westat, Inc., *Final Report: National Survey of Hazardous Waste Generators and Treatment, Storage and Disposal Facilities under RCRA in 1982*, pp. 127-29.

140. Testimony of Dr. Richard A. Denison, Office of Technology Assessment, to House Committee on Merchant Marine and Fisheries, Subcommittee on Oceanography, "The Role of Ocean Incineration in the Management of Hazardous Wastes," December 3, 1985, pp. 5, 6, 17, 18.

141. Rich and Canon, "Hazardous Waste Management," p. 30.

142. Office of Technology Assessment, *Superfund Strategy* (Washington, D.C.: U.S. Government Printing Office, April 1985), pp. 45-48.

143. Urban Systems Research and Engineering, Inc., and Resource Analysis, CDM, *Responses to Local Sewer Charges and Surcharges: Final Report, Volume I*, prepared for Council on Environmental Quality, October 1979, pp. 61, 73.

144. Sarokin et al., *Cutting Chemical Wastes*, pp. 129, 131. 145. U.S. Environmental Protection Agency, *Report to Congress: Minimization of Hazardous Waste*, pp. vi, vii, x, xv, xxvi.

Boxes

Examples of Waste Reduction Practices

1. David J. Sarokin et al., *Cutting Chemical Wastes: What 29 Organic Chemical Plants Are Doing to Reduce Hazardous Wastes* (New York: INFORM, Inc., 1985), pp. 83, 87.
2. Ibid., pp. 91, 399.
3. Ibid., pp. 91, 475.
4. Ibid., pp. 93, 485.
5. Ibid., pp. 97, 183.

Wastes on the Niagara Frontier

1. Niagara River Toxics Committee, "Report of the Niagara River Toxics Committee: Summary and Recommendations," October 1984, p. 7.
2. Toby Vigod, "The Hyde Park Landfill Case: Canadian Citizen Action in the U.S. Courts," a report to Environment Canada, March 1982, pp. 3-5.
3. Niagara River Toxics Committee, Report of the NRTC," p. 14.
4. U.S. Environmental Protection Agency, Region 2, "Niagara River Action Plan," May 1986, pp. 1-2.
5. Ibid., p. 2.

Figures

7.1. For nonpoint-source water pollutants: Leonard P. Gianessi et al., "Nonpoint Source Pollution: Are Cropland Controls the Answer?" (Washington, D.C.: Resources for the Future, 1986), table 1. For point-source water pollutants: Ibid.. For noncoal mining wastes: U.S. Environmental Protection Agency, *Report to Congress: Wastes from the Extraction and Beneficiation of Metallic Ores, Phosphate Rock, Asbestos, Overburden from Uranium Mining, and Oil Shale* (Washington, D.C.: U.S. Government Printing Office, 1985), p. ES-9. For agricultural wastes: U.S. Environmental Protection Agency, *Environmental Outlook, 1980* (Washington, D.C.: U.S. Government Printing Office, 1980), p. 585; and U.S. Department of Agriculture, *Agricultural Statistics, 1985* (Washington, D.C.: U.S. Government Printing Office, 1985), pp. 392 and 470. For hazardous wastes: Congressional Budget Office, *Hazardous Waste Management: Recent Changes and Policy Alternatives* (Washington, D.C.: U.S. Government Printing Office, 1985), p. 24. For animal wastes: Information provided by U.S. Department of Agriculture, Soil Conservation Service, September 1986. For silvicultural wastes: U.S. Environmental Protection Agency, *Environmental Outlook, 1980*, p. 583. For municipal solid wastes: Franklin Associates, Ltd., *Characterization of Municipal Solid Waste in the United States, 1960 to 2000*, prepared for U.S. Environmental Protection Agency, Office of Solid Waste (Prairie Village, Kans.: Franklin Associates, 1986), pp. 1-12, 3-17. For air pollutants: U.S. Environmental Protection Agency, Office of Air and Radiation, *National Air Pollutant Emission Estimates, 1940-1984* (Research Triangle Park, N.C.: U.S. Environmental Protection Agency, 1986), pp. 11-16. For coal mining wastes: U.S. Department of Energy, Energy Information Administration, *1985, Annual Energy Review* (Washington, D.C.: U.S. Government Printing Office, 1986), p. 165; and William S. Doyle, *Deep Coal Mining Waste Disposal Technology* (Noyes Data, 1976), p. 312. For industrial solid wastes: Franklin Associates, *Characterization of Municipal Solid Waste in the United States, 1960 to 2000*, p. 2-4. For air pollution control sludge: JRB

Associates, Inc., "Inventory of Air Pollution Control, Industrial Wastewater Treatment and Water Treatment Sludges," prepared for U.S. Environmental Protection Agency (McLean: JRB Associates, 1983), pp. 3-3 to 3-5 and Edison Electric Institute, *Report and Technical Studies on the Disposal and Utilization of Fossil-Fuel Combustion By-Products*, vol. 1 (Washington, D.C: Edison Electric Institute, 1982), pp. 18, 21. For brine wastes: Donald Feliciano, "Underground Injection of Wastes" (Washington, D.C.: Congressional Research Service, 1983), p. CRS-13; and U.S. Office of Technology Assessment, *Protecting the Nation's Groundwater from Contamination*, vols. 1 and 2, OTA-0-276 (Washington, D.C.: U.S. Government Printing Office, 1984), p. 269. For demolition wastes: U.S. Environmental Protection Agency, *Environmental Outlook, 1980*, pp. 585-86. For dredge wastes: Information provided by U.S. Office of Technology Assessment, December 1986. For water pollution control sludge: JRB Associates, "Inventory of Air Pollution Control, Industrial Wastewater Treatment and Water Treatment Sludges," pp. 3-15, 3-43; Robert K. Bastian, "EPA Comprehensive Review of Municipal Sludge Management Alternatives," mimeo (Washington, D.C.: U.S. Environmental Protection Agency, Office of Water, n.d.), p. 6; and information provided by U.S. Environmental Protection Agency, Office of Water, August 1986. For incinerator residue: National Ash Association, "Ash at Work," vol. 16, no.3 (Washington, D.C.: National Ash Association, 1984), p. 4. For radioactive wastes: Information provided by U.S. Environmental Protection Agency, Office of Solid Waste and Emergency Response, December 1986. For waste oils: Vaughn S. Kimball, *Waste Oil Recovery and Disposal* (Noyes Data Corporation, 1985), pp. 2-3.

7.2. For sources to air: U.S. Environmental Protection Agency, *National Air Pollutant Emission Estimates, 1940-1984*, pp. 11-16; JRB Associates, "Inventory of Air Pollution Control, Industrial Wastewater Treatment and Water Treatment Sludges," p. 3-5; and National Ash Association, "Ash at Work," p. 4. For sources to water: JRB Associates, "Inventory of Air Pollution Control, Industrial Wastewater Treatment and Water Treatment Sludges," pp. 3-15, 5-8, 5-9, 3-23, 4-25; information provided by U.S. Environmental Protection Agency, Office of Water, August 1986; U.S Environmental Protection Agency, Center for Environmental Research Information, *Use and Disposal of Municipal Wastewater Sludge*, EPA 625/10-84-003 (Cincinnati, Ohio: U.S. Environmental Protection Agency, 1984), pp. 10, 27, 37, 46, 56; National Research Council, *Disposal of Industrial and Domestic Wastes: Land and Sea Alternatives* (Washington, D.C.: National Academy Press, 1984), p. 163; Bastian, "EPA Comprehensive Review of Municipal Sludge Management Alternatives," p. 4; Congressional Budget Office, *Hazardous Waste Mangement*, p. 24; Kimball, *Waste Oil Recovery and Disposal*, pp. 2-3; information provided by U.S. Office of Technology Assessment, December 1986; and Gianessi et al., "Nonpoint Source Pollution," table 1. For sources to land: U.S. Environmental Protection Agency, *Report to Congress: Wastes from the Extraction and Beneficiation of Metallic Ores, Phosphate Rock, Asbestos, Overburden from Uranium Mining, and Oil Shale*, p. ES-8 to ES-10; U.S. Environmental Protection Agency, *Environmental Outlook, 1980*, pp. 583, 585-86; U.S. Department of Agriculture, *Agricultural Statistics, 1985*, pp. 392, 470; Congressional Budget Office, *Hazardous Waste Management*, p. 24 (hazardous waste converted to dry weight using the following assumptions—wastes to injection wells, 5 percent solids; to surface impoundments, 10 percent solids; to landfills, 20 percent solids; to land treatment, 15 percent solids); information provided by U.S. Department of Agriculture, Soil Conservation Service, September 1986; Franklin Associates, *Characterization of Municipal Solid Waste in the United States, 1960 to 2000*, pp. 1-12, 3-17; U.S. Department of Energy, Energy Information Administration, *1985, Annual Energy Review*, p. 165; Doyle, *Deep Coal Mining Waste Disposal Technology*, p. 312; JRB Associates, "Inventory of Air Pollution Control, Industrial Wastewater Treatment and Water Treatment Sludges," pp. 3-3 to 3-5, 3-15, 3-43; Edison Electric Institute, *Report and Technical Studies on the Disposal and Utilization of Fossil-Fuel Combustion By-Products*, pp. 18, 21; Donald Feliciano, "Underground Injection of Wastes," p. CRS-13; U.S. Office of Technology Assessment, *Protecting the Nation's Groundwater from Contamination*, p. 269; information provided by U.S. Office of Technology Assessment, December 1986; Bastian, "EPA Comprehensive Review of Municipal Sludge Management Alternatives," p. 6; information provided by U.S. Environmental Protection Agency, Office of Water, August 1986; National Ash Association, "Ash at Work," p. 4; information provided by U.S. Environmental Protection Agency, Office of Solid Waste and Emergency Response, December 1986; Kimball, *Waste Oil Recovery and Disposal*, pp. 2-3 (recycled portion of wastes to land equals approximately 10 percent).

7.3. Donald L. Van Dyne and Conrad B. Gilbertson, "Estimating U.S. Livestock and Poultry Manure and Nutrient Production" (Washington, D.C.: U.S. Department of Agriculture, Economics, Statistics, and Cooperatives Service, 1978), pp. 2-4; Information provided by U.S. Department of Agriculture, Soil Conservation Service, September 1986; and U.S. Environmental Protection Agency, *National Air Pollutant Emission Estimates, 1940-1984*, pp. 11-16.

7.4. U.S. Environmental Protection Agency, *National Air Pollutant Emission Estimates, 1940-1984*, pp. 11-16; JRB Associates, "Inventory of Air Pollution Control, Industrial Wastewater Treatment and Water Treatment Sludges," p. 3-5; and National Ash Association, "Ash at Work," p. 4.

7.5. Gianessi et al., "Nonpoint Source Pollution," table 1; information provided by U.S. Office of Technology Assessment, December 1986; Kimball, *Waste Oil Recovery and Disposal*, pp. 2-3; and U.S. Environmental Protection Agency, *Use and Disposal of Municipal Wastewater Sludge*, p. 56.

7.6. JRB Associates, "Inventory of Air Pollution Control, Industrial Wastewater Treatment and Water Treatment Sludges", pp. 3-15, 5-8, 5-9, 3-23, 4-25; information provided by U.S. Environmental Protection Agency, Office of Water, August 1986; U.S. Environmental Protection Agency, *Use and Disposal of Municipal Wastewater Sludge*, pp. 10, 27, 37, 46, 56; National Research Council, *Disposal of Industrial and Domestic Wastes*, p. 163; U.S. Environmental Protection Agency, *Report to Congress on the Discharge of Hazardous Wastes to Publicly Owned Treatment Works* (Washington, D.C.: U.S. Environmental Protection Agency, 1986), pp. 1-10 to 1-12; Bastian, "EPA Comprehensive Review of Municipal Sludge Management Alternatives," p. 6; Congressional Budget Office, *Hazardous Waste Mangement*, p. 24; Kimball, *Waste Oil Recovery and Disposal*, pp. 2-3; information provided by U.S. Office of Technology Assessment, December 1986; and Gianessi et al., "Nonpoint Source Pollution," table 1.

7.7. For noncoal mining wastes: U.S. Environmental Protection Agency, *Report to Congress: Wastes from the Extraction and Beneficiation of Metallic Ores, Phosphate Rock, Asbestos, Overburden from Uranium Mining, and Oil Shale*, p. ES-8 to ES-10. For agricultural wastes: U.S. Environmental Protection Agency, *Environmental Outlook, 1980*, p. 585; and U.S. Department of Agriculture, *Agricultural Statistics, 1985*, pp. 392, 470. For hazardous wastes: Congressional Budget Office, *Hazardous Waste Management*, p. 24 (hazardous waste converted to dry weight using the following assumptions: wastes to injection wells, 5 percent solids; to surface impoundments, 10 percent solids; to landfills, 20 percent solids; to land treatment, 15 percent solids). For animal wastes: Information provided by U.S. Department of Agriculture, Soil Conservation Service, September 1986. For silvicultural wastes: U.S. Environmental Protection Agency, *Environmental Outlook, 1980*, p. 583. For municipal solid wastes: Franklin Associates, *Characterization of Municipal Solid Waste in the United States, 1960 to 2000*, pp. 1-12, 3-17. For coal mining wastes: U.S. Department of Energy, Energy Information Administration, *1985, Annual Energy Review* p. 165; and Doyle, *Deep Coal Mining Waste Disposal Technology*, p. 312. For industrial solid wastes: Franklin Associates, *Characterization of Municipal Solid Waste in the United States, 1960 to 2000*, p. 2-4. For air pollution control sludge: JRB Associates, "Inventory of Air Pollution Control, Industrial Wastewater Treatment and Water Treatment Sludges," pp. 3-3 to 3-5; and Edison Electric Institute, *Report and Technical Studies on the Disposal and Utilization of Fossil-Fuel Combustion By-Products*, pp. 18, 21. For brine wastes: Feliciano, "Underground Injection of Wastes," p. CRS-13; and U.S. Office of Technology Assessment, *Protecting the Nation's Groundwater from Contamination*, p. 269. For demolition wastes: U.S. Environmental Protection Agency, *Environmental Outlook, 1980*, pp. 585-86. For dredge wastes: Information provided by U.S. Office of Technology Assessment, December 1986. For water pollution control sludge: JRB Associates, "Inventory of Air Pollution Control, Industrial Wastewater Treatment and Water Treatment Sludges," pp. 3-15, 3-43; Bastian, "EPA Comprehensive Review of Municipal Sludge Management Alternatives," p. 6; and information provided by U.S. Environmental Protection Agency, Office of Water, August 1986. For incinerator residue: National Ash Association, "Ash at Work," p. 4. For radioactive wastes: Information provided by U.S. Environmental Protection Agency, Office of Solid Waste and Emergency Response, December 1986. For waste oils: Kimball, *Waste Oil Recovery and Disposal*, pp. 2-3.

7.8. Franklin Associates, *Characterization of Municipal Solid Waste in the United States, 1960-2000*, p. 1-6.

7.9. For noncoal mining wastes: U.S. Environmental Protection Agency, *Report to Congress: Wastes from the Extraction and Beneficiation of Metallic Ores, Phosphate Rock, Asbestos, Overburden from Uranium Mining, and Oil Shale*, pp. ES-8 to ES-10. For agricultural wastes: U.S. Environmental Protection Agency, *Environmental Outlook, 1980*, p. 585; and U.S. Department of Agriculture, *Agricultural Statistics, 1985*, pp. 392, 470. For hazardous wastes: Congressional Budget Office, *Hazardous Waste Management*, p. 24 (hazardous waste converted to dry weight using the following assumptions: wastes to injection wells, 5 percent solids; to surface impoundments, 10 percent solids; to landfills, 20 percent solids; to land treatment, 15 percent solids). For animal wastes: Information provided by U.S. Department of Agriculture, Soil Conservation Service, September 1986. For silvicultural wastes: U.S. Environmental Protection Agency, *Environmental Outlook, 1980*, p. 583. For municipal solid wastes: Franklin Associates, *Characterization of Municipal Solid Waste in the United States, 1960 to 2000*, pp. 1-12, 3-17. For coal mining wastes: U.S. Department of Energy, Energy Information Administration, *1985, Annual Energy Review*, p. 165; and Doyle, *Deep Coal Mining Waste Disposal Technology*, p. 312. For industrial solid wastes: Franklin Associates, *Characterization of Municipal Solid Waste in the United States, 1960 to 2000*, p. 2-4. For air pollution control sludge: JRB Associates, "Inventory of Air Pollution Control, Industrial Wastewater Treatment and Water Treatment Sludges," pp. 3-3 to 3-5; and Edison Electric Institute, *Report and Technical Studies on the Disposal and Utilization of Fossil-Fuel Combustion By-Products*, pp. 18, 21. For brine wastes: Feliciano, "Underground Injection of Wastes," p. CRS-13; and U.S. Office of Technology Assessment, *Protecting the Nation's Groundwater from Contamination*, p. 269. For demolition wastes: U.S. Environmental Protection Agency, *Environmental Outlook, 1980*, pp. 585-86. For dredge wastes: Information provided by U.S. Office of Technology Assessment, December 1986. For water pollution control sludge: JRB Associates, "Inventory of Air Pollution Control, Industrial Wastewater Treatment and Water Treatment Sludges," pp. 3-15, 3-43; Bastian, "EPA Comprehensive Review of Municipal Sludge Management Alternatives," p. 6; and information provided by U.S. Environmental Protection Agency, Office of Water, August 1986. For incinerator residue: National Ash Association, "Ash at Work," p. 4. For radioactive wastes: Information provided by U.S. Environmental Protection Agency, Office of Solid Waste and Emergency Response, December 1986. For waste oils: Kimball, *Waste Oil Recovery and Disposal*, pp. 2-3 (recycled portion of wastes to land equals approximately 10 percent).

7.10. Federal Emergency Management Agency, *Hazard Identification, Capability Assessment, and Multi-Year Development Plan (HICA/MYDP)* (Washington, D.C.: Federal Emergency Management Agency, 1985).

7.11. Clean Water Act, 33 U.S.C. §§ 1251 et seq. Marine Protection, Research and Sanctuaries Act, 16 U.S.C. §§ 1401 et seq. Safe Drinking Water Act, 40 U.S.C. §§ 300f—300j-10 (Supp. 1977). P.L. 99-339. Clean Air Act, 42 U.S.C. §§ 7401 et seq.; Resource Conservation and Recovery Act, 42 U.S.C. §§ 6901 et seq.; Comprehensive Environmental Response, Compensation, and Liability Act, 42 U.S.C. §§ 9601 et seq, P.L. 99-499. Surface Mining Control and Reclamation Act, 30 U.S.C. §§ 1201 et seq. Nuclear Waste Policy Act, 42 U.S.C. §§ 10101 et seq.; Low-Level Radioactive Waste Policy Act, 42 U.S.C. §§ 2021b et seq.; Uranium Mill Tailings Radiation Control Act, 42 U.S.C. §§ 7901 et seq.; Toxic Substances Control Act, 15 U.S.C. §§ 2601 et seq.

7.12. Congressional Budget Office, *Hazardous Waste Management*, p.24.

7.13. Chemical Manufacturers Association and Engineering-Science, Inc., *Results of the 1984 CMA Hazardous Waste Survey* (Washington, D.C.: Chemical Manufacturers Association, 1986), pp. 21, 25, 33.

7.14. David J. Sarokin et al., *Cutting Chemical Wastes: What 29 Organic Chemical Plants Are Doing to Reduce Hazardous Wastes*, (New York: INFORM, Inc., 1985), pp. 8-9; Environmental Defense Fund, *Approaches to Source Reduction* (Berkeley, Calif.: Environmental Defense Fund, 1986), p. 8; U.S. Office of Technology Assessment, *Serious Reduction of Hazardous Waste: For Pollution Prevention and Industrial Efficiency*, OTA-ITE-317 (Washington, D.C.: U.S. Government Printing Office, 1986), p. 3; U.S. Environmental Protection Agency, *Report to Congress: Minimization of Hazardous Waste*, Executive Summary and Fact Sheet, October 1986, p.ii; and information provided by E. I. du Pont de Nemours and Co., November 1986.

7.15. Congressional Budget Office, *Hazardous Waste Management*, p. 51.

7.16. U.S. Environmental Protection Agency, *Report to Congress on the Discharge of Hazardous Waste to Publicly Owned Treatment Works*, pp. 5-7.

7.17. For all costs, except treatment at publicly owned treatment works: U.S. Office of Technology Assessment, *Technologies and Management Strategies for Hazardous Waste Control* (Washington, D.C.: U.S. Government Printing Office, 1983), p. 197; Donald Ames et al., *Technologies for the Treatment and Destruction of Organic Wastes as Alternatives to Land Disposal* (Sacramento, Calif.: Air Resources Board, 1982), p. 102; Connecticut Hazardous Waste Mangement Service, *Connecticut Hazardous Waste Management Plan: 1985-2005 (Hartford, Conn.: Connecticut Hazardous Waste Mangement Service*, 1986), table 9; Environmental Defense Fund, *To Burn or Not to Burn: The Economic Advantages of Recycling Over Garbage Incineration for New York City* (New York: Environmental Defense Fund, 1985), p.17; National Solid Wastes Management Association, "Tipping Fee Survey," Technical Bulletin 86-2 (Washington, D.C.: National Solid Wastes Management Association, 1986), pp.2-3. For publicly owned treatment works: U.S. Council on Environmental Quality and U.S. Environmental Protection Agency, Office of Planning and Evaluation, *Municipal Sewage Treatment: A Comparison of Alternatives* (Washington, D.C.: U.S. Government Printing Office, 1974), pp. 88-91 (one gallon of sewage weighs 8.34 pounds and is .08 percent solids).

Chapter 8

Toxics in the Air: Reassessing the Regulatory Framework

One day seven years ago, James L. Repace, a physicist at the U.S. Environmental Protection Agency (EPA), strapped on a small air pollution monitor and wore it for 24 hours while he went through all his daily activities. The monitoring results showed higher exposures to particulate pollution indoors than outdoors. They suggested that the quality of indoor air deserves much greater attention in the United States.[1]

Beyond that conclusion, however, Repace's exposure to particulates for that day raises intriguing questions that underscore the difficulty of assessing risks from air pollutants (figure 8.1). Did the single "peak" exposure in the kitchen by itself cause harm? Would repeated peak exposures in the kitchen each night for several years cause harm? Would the chronic exposures to lower concentrations of particulates cause harm over many years? Do these lower concentrations of particulates interact with other pollutants in low or high concentrations to produce harm? Are any of the particulates, such as those from the diesel truck or from tobacco, especially carcinogenic and therefore more worrisome than other particulates? Alternatively, are the health effects from these exposures insignificant?

In an ideal world, policy makers would have answers to these questions, both for particulates and for a multitude of other pollutants, and might be able to respond with a carefully crafted strategy designed to reduce risks effectively and efficiently. Unfortunately, the lack of such definitive answers complicates policy making for many toxic air pollutants.

It is no exaggeration to characterize current understanding of the risks

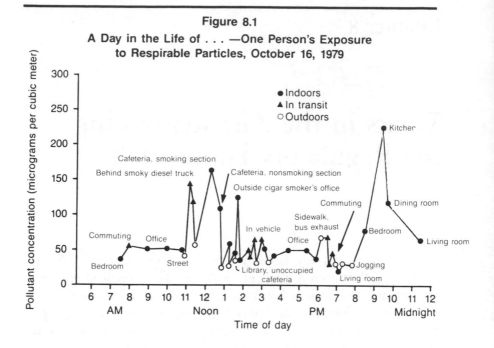

Figure 8.1

A Day in the Life of . . . —One Person's Exposure to Respirable Particles, October 16, 1979

Source: U.S. Environmental Protection Agency.

posed by airborne contaminants as primitive. Much still needs to be learned about where exposures occur and what health effects and environmental damages result. Estimates of exposures indoors must be added to those for outdoor exposures to assess the total exposure, and total risk, for human populations. The contributions of airborne pollutants to contamination of land and water must also be weighed.

The political and institutional environment in which these risk issues are grappled with is much different now than it was at the beginning of the environmental decade of the 1970s. First, at a time when the nation's environmental risk problems seem more complex than ever, the federal government is facing a burdensome national debt and is under enormous pressure to reduce spending.[2] Second, even though state regulatory programs suffer from many of the weaknesses that have surfaced in federal regulatory programs, many state agencies are stronger than they were in the early 1970s, and several have crafted innovative responses to newly emerging air pollution problems.[3] Third, while the industrial community still contains far too many "bad actors," a significant reservoir of environmental expertise has developed in the private sector.[4]

In contemplating risk management policies—how decisions should be made and by whom, and the prospects for success of alternative incentives, requirements, penalties, and exhortations—this new institutional environment must be recognized. The following considers how well existing institutions have responded to the threats posed by various air pollutants, what new approaches might be taken, and what some of the problems are in developing a risk-based approach to managing airborne toxic substances.

RISKS FROM AIRBORNE TOXIC SUBSTANCES

The risk that a chemical will harm humans is a function of (a) the chemical's toxicity and (b) the extent of human exposure to the chemical. But risk frequently is difficult to assess. Much scientific research and public attention has focused on cancer. Inferences about the risks of cancer for humans, however, often must be drawn from experiments on animals; the deductive leaps involved are quite large and are characterized by considerable scientific uncertainty. The risks of other health effects—damage to various organ systems, reduced resistance to disease, genetic damage, and birth defects—are not always understood. Some effects may occur immediately or may not surface for many years. Some exposures may lead to instant death and others to serious irreversible illness; while still other exposures may produce less serious, seemingly reversible health effects.*

Uncertainties about when and where exposures to contaminants occur further confound judgments about health risks. Exposures can occur outdoors, in homes, offices, and factories, and in cars, buses, airplanes, and other vehicles. Furthermore, humans may receive doses of some of the same chemicals in multiple ways—from the air, from food, and from water.

---

*Scientists have come to distinguish "exposure" from "dose," noting that exposure to a chemical can occur without a dose of it being received by one of the body's sytems. This chapter ignores this distinction. Risk managers also must take into account impacts on the environment. These impacts can take many forms, including reductions in population of animal species and damage to forests and crops.[5]

While it is difficult to assess the risks from routine emissions of and exposures to airborne contaminants, it seems even harder to judge potential risks from accidents. Sophisticated techniques have been developed for judging the likelihood of accidents, often drawing on historical data, but these techniques are only as good as the numerous assumptions underlying them and the adequacy of the historical data.[6]

Perhaps more important, numerical judgments assessing the likelihood of an accident and the associated deaths or injuries may have only limited relevance in framing public policy for reducing risks. Public decisions to limit risks are shaped heavily by public perceptions. The prospects of a low-probability accident that may have grave consequences in the future (like a meltdown of a nuclear power plant) may cause more alarm than higher-probability risks that are more likely to occur but that may be less dramatic (like the health and environmental impacts of mining and burning coal to produce electric power).[7]

Indoor Air Pollution

Hundreds of toxic chemicals pervade the indoor environments of homes, offices, public buildings, and vehicles. The risks to human health from some of these pollutants indoors might be greater than risks from those pollutants outdoors, even though national efforts to control pollution have primarily focused on pollutants outdoors.[8] Some pollutants that are regulated outdoors—for example, carbon monoxide and nitrogen dioxide—have been found by some researchers in indoor concentrations exceeding the ambient standards established for acceptable concentrations in the atmosphere.[9]* The risks indoors might be greater than the risks outdoors also because most people spend most of their time indoors. Moreover, the very young, the elderly, and those who are ill—three groups that might spend an especially large amount of time indoors—can be particularly sensitive to elevated concentrations of pollutants.[10]

Some of the most dramatic findings regarding indoor exposures have emerged from EPA's Total Exposure Assessment Methodology (TEAM) project. The TEAM researchers attempted to examine total human exposure to selected pollutants by measuring levels of pollutants indoors and outdoors and in drinking water, and then relating these levels to levels in the breath of study participants.[11] Perhaps the most striking findings are those

---

*An ambient standard describes a permissible concentration of pollution in the atmosphere. Concentrations exceeding the standard generally are regarded as constituting a threat to human health. Ambient standards are distinguishable from emission standards, which refer to the permissible amounts of pollution a source may emit to the atmosphere.

shown in figure 8.2. The upper graph in the figure shows measured concentrations of selected organic compounds in indoor and outdoor air in heavily industrialized Bayonne and Elizabeth, New Jersey. For all the substances measured, indoor concentrations were substantially higher than outdoor concentrations.[12] It is conceivable that, in this highly industrialized community, pollutants generated outdoors simply build up indoors, but the lower graph suggests this is not necessarily so. It shows that, in rural, nonindustrial Devils Lake, North Dakota, indoor concentrations of the organic compounds also far exceeded the outdoor levels.[13]

The TEAM researchers concluded that personal exposures to almost every chemical measured were greater than levels measured in outdoor air.* A variety of indoor sources were implicated, including consumer products and building materials. (Visiting two types of sites outside the home—dry cleaners and automobile service stations—also exposed those monitored to elevated levels of certain pollutants.) The researchers found that, in most cases, the impact of indoor sources on exposures far outweighed the impact of such traditionally regulated major industrial sources as chemical plants, petroleum refineries, and petrochemical plants.[14]

The TEAM project has made it clear that indoor exposures to chemicals are significant. But the limits of the research must also be acknowledged. Because of monitoring and related measurement problems, the researchers looked only at one group of chemicals, the so-called volatile organic compounds. Their exposure studies did not examine pesticides and metals.[15] Accordingly, the TEAM studies should not be viewed as a comprehensive analysis of indoor and outdoor exposures to airborne pollutants.

Pollutants in the Home

Some of the pollutants found indoors are particularly pernicious. The effects of smoking tobacco on smokers are well known, but the presence of smokers in a household may increase health risks to others as well. Tobacco smoke contains over 3,800 chemical compounds, including benzene and other carcinogens.[16] In 1986, a National Research Council review of studies of passive smoking estimated that nonsmoking spouses of smokers face a 30 percent increase in their chance of incurring lung cancer, as compared to nonsmoking spouses of nonsmokers.[17]† The reviewers also concluded

---

*Personal exposures were measured by monitors worn by those participating in the study.

†One researcher has estimated that exposure to tobacco smoke caused between 25 percent and 46 percent of the roughly 7,000 lung cancer deaths in 1985 of women who had never smoked, and between 14 percent and 37 percent of roughly 5,200 such deaths in men.[18]

Figure 8.2
Indoor and Outdoor Concentrations of Selected Toxic Organics

Bayonne and Elizabeth, New Jersey, Fall 1981

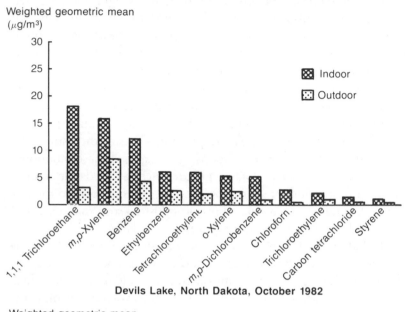

Devils Lake, North Dakota, October 1982

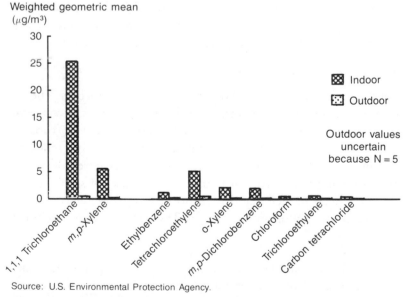

Source: U.S. Environmental Protection Agency.

that, for smokers' children, the risk of suffering respiratory problems increases between 20 and 80 percent as compared to nonsmokers' children, depending on the symptom examined and the number of smokers in the house. Harm to children is sufficiently evident that the committee recommended eliminating children's exposure to tobacco smoke.[19]

Radon is another especially dangerous home pollutant. In contrast to many of the other contaminants of concern, radon is produced by nature, not by humans. It is a decay product of uranium, and the radon itself decays into "radon daughters." Radon and its daughters can penetrate into homes through openings in foundations and through water supplies. The radon daughters attach themselves to particulate matter in indoor air, are inhaled, and can cause lung cancer.[20]

Radon appears to be a very serious public health problem, the magnitude of which has only begun to become apparent during the past several years. Perhaps the most extreme case found to date is that of Stanley Watras, an engineer at the Limerick nuclear power plant in Pennsylvania. According to warning devices designed to detect excess radiation from workers leaving the plant, he registered very high levels of radiation when he entered the plant. It turned out that radon levels in his home were creating a cancer risk equivalent to having 455,000 annual chest x-rays.[21] Less extreme situations also give cause for concern, however. In the Reading Prong area of Pennsylvania, where the ground contains large amounts of uranium, researchers found that 20 of 2,690 homes surveyed contained 1.0 working level (WL) of radon.[22]* At this level, individuals have a 44 to 77 percent chance of contracting lung cancer in their lifetime.[23] Forty-four percent of the homes were above .02 WL, a level at which there is a 1 to 5 percent lifetime risk of getting cancer.[24] Scientists estimate that, of the approximately 100,000 deaths of Americans from lung cancer each year, radon causes perhaps 5,000 to 20,000.[25]†

Those figures are based on calculations that assume that individuals are exposed to a certain level of radon for their entire lives—assumed to be 70 years. Risks drop if a shorter period of exposure is assumed. For example, if individuals are exposed to 1.0 working level of radon for only 10

---

*Working level is a commonly used unit of measurement for radon.

†The basis for estimating risks from radon is somewhat stronger than that for estimating risks from other carcinogens, because data on the incidence of cancer are available from studies of uranium miners exposed to radon. However, even these data provide uncertain guidance, because the uranium miners were exclusively male and may have been heavier-than-average smokers.[26]

years rather than for 70, cancer risks drop from 44 to 77 percent to 14 to 42 percent.[27]*

The risks from other indoor contaminants are even less well understood than those from radon, but the measured presence of these contaminants indoors certainly gives pause. Indoor combustion sources, such as wood-burning stoves, can produce large amounts of particulates. EPA has estimated that, by the end of 1983, over 10 million wood-burning stoves were in use, emitting an estimated 2.7 million tons of particulates.[29] Of these tons, 20,000 were estimated to be polycyclic organic matter (POM).[30] Several POM compounds are among the most potent animal carcinogens known to exist, although the magnitude of their carcinogenic risk to humans is uncertain.[31] Wood stoves can raise indoor pollutant levels, particularly when the devices leak and have poorly fitting gaskets, when their doors are opened, and when emissions from short chimneys are drawn indoors by household ventilation systems.[32]†

Consumer products used within the home are yet another major source of pollutants. Some products—such as paint thinners and wood conditioners—already bear labels suggesting their use only in well-ventilated areas.[35] New furniture, wood paneling, and other new home furnishings can emit formaldehyde. Formaldehyde concentrations can be a problem in newly constructed mobile homes, which not only rely heavily on materials containing this solvent but also typically are more tightly sealed than conventional homes and therefore are less well ventilated.[36]

---

*The risks from radon seem quite high when viewed in isolation, and they certainly are high when compared to many of the risks that EPA tries to protect against in its traditional air pollution control programs. For example, in issuing rules requiring controls on radionuclide emissions from underground mines, EPA took action because the emissions were estimated to increase the lifetime risk of fatal lung cancer for people near mines by between 1 in 1,000 (0.1 percent) and 1 in 100 (1 percent). The "potential risk" to a person living near multiple mine vents was characterized by EPA as being 1 in 10. During the peak uranium production period of 1978 to 1982, exposures to radon-222, the principal radionuclide emitted from mines, were estimated to have caused one to four fatal cases of cancer per year.[28]

†Wood-burning stoves also have contributed to violations outdoors of national standards for concentrations of particulates and for carbon monoxide.[33] This has been the case not only in bucolic resort communities that have no industry, but also in areas where controls on traditional industrial sources of pollution otherwise would have reduced ambient concentrations of particulates to acceptable levels.[34]

Consumer efforts to reduce energy costs also can contribute to indoor air quality problems. Filling spaces around windows and doors and other insulation measures can impede both the entry of relatively clean outdoor air and the exit of relatively dirty indoor air, causing indoor levels of pollutants to rise. However, research shows that the pollution levels in a home typically are influenced more by the sources of pollutants than by the amount of air flowing in and out.[37]

Tobacco smoke, radon, particulates, and organic chemicals are only a few of the many pollutants found indoors. In many cases the risks to human health from pollutants in the home are difficult to assess. More research on indoor risks is needed—both on exposures to pollutants indoors and on the toxicity of those pollutants.

Pollutants in the Office

The cleaning products, tobacco smoke, and furnishings that cause air quality problems in homes also contribute to air quality problems in office buildings. In addition, buildups of allergens and bacteria in building ventilation systems can pose special risks to office workers. These are but a few of a long list of office building contaminants.

"Sick building syndrome" or "tight building syndrome" is the label that has been attached to health problems caused by poor indoor air quality in office buildings. The problems, often found in new or recently renovated office buildings, can include eye, nose, and throat irritation, headaches, high rates of respiratory infections, nausea, and dizziness, among others. Serious contamination of new and renovated buildings has sometimes required extended evacuation of the premises.[38] As is the case with pollution in homes, the magnitude of airborne risks in offices is difficult to assess.

Air Quality in Vehicles

Vehicles are yet another indoor environment in which exposure to pollutants occurs. For years, drivers have been cautioned against the hazards of carbon monoxide leakage into automobiles from faulty exhaust systems. But carbon monoxide may not be the only pollutant of concern within automobiles. Preliminary results from a California study taken during peak rush hours show in-vehicle levels of six other pollutants to be three to five times measured background levels.[39]

Airplane cabins also can expose individuals to elevated levels of pollutants, especially tobacco smoke. The 70,000 flight attendants working aboard aircraft may suffer the most exposure, but millions of others are exposed, as well. In 1986, a committee of the National Research Council recommended that smoking be banned on all domestic commercial flights. Other pollutants of concern within aircraft include infectious microorganisms and fungal spores.[40]

Indoor Air Risks in Industry

Government traditionally has treated occupational health risks separately from other health risks.[41] But a comprehensive assessment of exposure to chemicals should include all sources. Hence, it is appropriate to treat workplace risks from airborne pollutants in conjunction with risks from other indoor and outdoor sources.

For some pollutants, like the asbestos that harms shipyard workers, the scientific evidence demonstrates clear risks to human health.[42] But for many other substances, the evidence is less definitive. Data developed by the National Institute of Occupational Safety and Health (NIOSH) and other organizations during the 1970s, for just 30 hazardous substances, suggest that millions of American workers are exposed to airborne contaminants in their workplaces.[43] But the data often are not very precise; "exposure" may refer to regular or frequent exposures to a substance or simply to working with a substance regardless of whether exposure actually occurred.[44]

Judging health risks in workplaces is complicated further by the difficulty of linking information about exposures to information about resulting diseases. Many occupational diseases are indistinguishable from nonoccupational ones and often are not recognized as having specific or exclusively occupational causes. In addition, such diseases typically become manifest only after long latent periods, so their relationship to much earlier exposures may be obscured.

Published estimates of annual deaths due to occupational illness range widely from 10,000 to 210,000.[45] A Bureau of Labor Statistics survey cites 106,000 illnesses in 1983, but the Office of Technology Assessment states that, because of underreporting, this is "almost certainly an underestimate."[46] When relatively good information on particular occupational diseases is available, it indicates the existence of major threats to human health. For example, in 1979, an estimated 84,000 active workers suffered from acute byssinosis (a disease related to cotton dust). In 1978, an estimated 59,000 workers were believed to suffer from silicosis, a disease caused by the silica dust used as an abrasive in sand blasting and polishing.[47]

Cancer is a major occupational illness. Figure 8.3, based on NIOSH data,

Figure 8.3
The 10 Leading Work-Related Diseases and Injuries
in the United States, 1982

Type of disorder/injury	Examples
1. Lung diseases	asbestosis, byssinosis, silicosis, coal workers' pneumoconiosis, lung cancer, occupational asthma
2. Musculoskeletal injuries	disorders of the back, trunk, upper extremity, neck, lower extremity; traumatically induced Raynaud's phenomenon
3. Cancers (other than lung)	leukemia, mesothelioma; cancers of the bladder, nose, and liver
4. Amputations, fractures, eye loss, lacerations, and traumatic deaths	——
5. Cardiovascular diseases	hypertension, coronary artery disease, acute myocardial infarction
6. Disorders of reproduction	infertility, spontaneous abortion, teratogenesis
7. Neurotoxic disorders	peripheral neuropathy, toxic encephalitis, psychoses, extreme personality changes (exposure-related)
8. Noise-induced loss of hearing	——
9. Dermatologic conditions	dermatosis, burns (scaldings), chemical burns, contusions (abrasions)
10. Psychologic disorders	neuroses, personality disorders, alcoholism, drug dependency

Source: Office of Technology Assessment.

displays the 10 leading work-related diseases and injuries in the United States in 1982. Occupational lung diseases (including cancer) ranked first, and occupational cancers (other than lung cancer) ranked third.[48]

Reproductive disorders are an increasingly great concern. Figure 8.3 shows reproductive disorders as ranking sixth among work-related diseases and injuries. Despite this high ranking, the exact risk to reproductive health from airborne and other pollutants in the workplace environment is unclear. The Office of Technology Assessment has noted that no reliable estimates are available of the numbers of workers exposed to hazards, the levels of exposure, and the toxicity of the agents to which workers are exposed.[49]

Tobacco smoking contributes to occupational health disorders, just as it contributes to elevated levels of contamination in nonmanufacturing indoor environments. Figure 8.4 shows the enormous impact smoking can

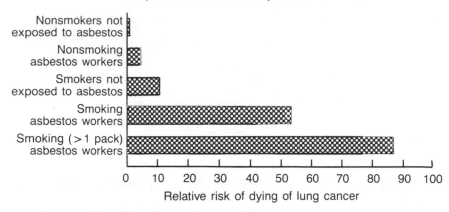

Figure 8.4

Relative Risk of Dying of Lung Cancer due to Smoking and Occupational Asbestos Exposure*

Relative risk of dying of lung cancer

* Includes asbestos workers, but not other workers exposed to asbestos.

Source: Surgeon General of the United States.

have on the incidence of lung cancer among workers exposed to asbestos; heavy-smoking asbestos workers are 17 times more likely than nonsmoking asbestos workers to die of lung cancer.[50] Evidence also indicates that cotton textile workers who smoke experience a greater incidence of byssinosis and more severe byssinosis than do nonsmoking workers.[51] In general, smoking can both add to and multiply the health risks from exposures to toxic materials in the workplace, although its effects vary from substance to substance.

Routine Outdoor Emissions

The most recent extensive analysis of risks from routine releases of air pollutants outdoors suggests that between 1,300 and 1,700 cancer cases each year may be attributable to the toxic pollutants analyzed.[52]* The study, published by EPA in mid-1985, focuses not on the more common pollutants like sulfur dioxide and nitrogen dioxide, for which national outdoor ambient standards and regulatory programs have been established, but on some of the less-common and less-regulated but more hazardous pollutants.

---

*For perspective, it should be noted that there were 850,000 cancer cases and 440,000 cancer deaths in the United States in 1983.[53]

The figures indicate that the risk of cancer from routine emissions of certain toxic substances outdoors may be relatively small compared to the possible risk from some other toxic substances indoors. However, the EPA study may have underestimated the number of outdoor threats to human health. Indeed, the authors clearly stressed the limits and uncertainties of their work.[54] The study covered only 15 to 45 toxic substances, a fraction of the total number present in outdoor air. The study considered only inhalation, not the ingestion of air pollutants via food and water. It did not cover all sources or accidental releases. It did not examine risks due to compounds formed in the atmosphere. While it addressed the additive effects of pollutants, it did not address their multiplicative effects.* Finally, it considered only cancer risks, not risks of genetic effects, birth defects, or other health risks. These caveats underscore the tentative, skeletal character of knowledge about risks to human health from airborne toxic substances.

On the other hand, the EPA study may have made some assumptions that overestimated the risk of cancer from toxic pollutants in outdoor air. For example, the guidelines EPA uses to assess carcinogenicity may overstate the risk of cancer to humans because they are based on many conservative assumptions. Moreover, the EPA assessments of carcinogenicity assume that individuals are exposed to toxic substances outdoors for their entire lives, when in fact much of people's lives is spent indoors.[56]

The EPA analysis estimated that area sources (that is, widespread but individually small sources) account for over 75 percent of the cancer attributable to the pollutants studied. These area sources include motor vehicles, home heating, use of solvents, and gasoline marketing. The remaining 25 percent is accounted for by large point sources, such as chemical production plants, steel mills, and petroleum refineries. The analysts noted, however, that these large point sources also frequently seem to create pockets of high individual risk of getting cancer.[57] The analysts also noted that "nontraditional" sources of airborne toxic substances, such as publicly owned sewage treatment plants and hazardous waste treatment, storage, and disposal facilities, may pose important risks in some locations.[58]

Of the pollutants studied, metals (for example, chromium, cadmium, and arsenic) contributed about 30 percent of the estimated cancer threat to public health. Products of incomplete combustion (for example, organic particulates like benzo[a]pyrene) contributed 40 percent and organic vapors

---

*Even additive effects might be substantial. One of the assessments conducted for the study suggested that simultaneous exposure to 10 to 15 pollutants in some areas might make the chances of getting cancer between 1 in 1,000 and 1 in 10,000.[55]

(for example, benzene, chloroform, carbon tetrachloride, and other solvents) contributed about 30 percent.[59]

Critics of the EPA study, including environmentalists and members of Congress dissatisfied with EPA's past efforts to control toxic air pollutants, have stressed the limited nature of the EPA analysis and have publicized data underscoring the large quantities of toxic pollutants, including both suspected and proven human carcinogens, which are released routinely by American industry. For example, drawing on 80 chemical companies' responses to questions posed by his subcommittee, the House Subcommittee on Health and the Environment, U. S. Representative Henry Waxman (D-Calif.) noted that more than an estimated 60 million pounds of toxic chemicals are discharged into the air annually from the plants of those responding.[60] But the committee survey, like so many studies of airborne toxic substances, is incomplete. It focused primarily on larger companies, and these companies used varied data bases for their submissions.[61]

Besides data on emissions or exposures, another way to estimate risks from airborne and other pollutants is to assess the prevalence of health problems in industrialized areas. A Tulane University study reported that residents living within a mile of major chemical production facilities have an incidence of cancer more than four times the national average.[62] Elevated cancer rates also have been reported in neighborhoods near chemical plants in Charleston, West Virginia.[63] However, these and similar studies, while suggestive of problems, must be interpreted with great caution. In assessing associations suggested by such studies, attention must be paid to long-term trends and to the influence of such factors as diet and smoking.[64]

Even if breathing ambient levels of toxic pollutants does not unambiguously threaten humans, emissions to the atmosphere may still create risks. Research has shown that transfers of pollutants from air to water and soil contribute to raised levels of PCBs in the Great Lakes and of cadmium in local food supplies.[65]*

The sad state of data on outdoor emissions, exposures, and effects inevitably leads to a familiar refrain—more research is needed. Choices among policies for controlling pollution will continue to be made under conditions of pervasive uncertainty.

---

*Transfers in the opposite direction must also be acknowledged—efforts to control water pollution and dispose of hazardous waste on land can create air pollution problems.[66]

Accidental Releases

In December 1984, release of methyl isocyanate at Union Carbide's Bhopal, India, plant killed at least 1,700 people and injured at least 14,000 others.[67] The accident startled the world. In this country, it substantially increased the attention paid to preventing and minimizing damage from catastrophic accidents, spurred by public worry that something similar could occur in the United States. Agencies at all levels of government increased data gathering and accident prevention and response activities. Many companies and trade associations enhanced existing programs and launched new ones, all intended to reduce risks from accidents.[68]

The public perceptions that influence public policy in the United States are shaped heavily by the few accidents that cause catastrophic loss of lives and property. Bhopal has entered the language of public and political discourse as a synonym for a community chemical disaster. For those who wondered whether a "Bhopal" could happen in the United States, it did not help that nine months later the Union Carbide facility in Institute, West Virginia, suffered an accident in which release of toxic fumes produced breathing problems, burning eyes, nausea, and dizziness in about 135 local residents. This happened after assurances were given by Union Carbide and regulatory officials alike that operations in Institute were being conducted safely.[69]

Other accidents in the mid-1980s also have contributed to public concerns. In November 1984, an explosion in a liquified petroleum gas facility in a Mexico City suburb killed 503 persons and injured more than 4,000.[70] In January 1986, a tank at a Diamond Shamrock paint pigment plant in Ashtabula, Ohio, exploded, killing 2 persons and injuring at least 18; all deaths and injuries were limited to the plant.[71] In January 1986, 1 worker died and 40 persons were injured when a cylinder of uranium hexafluoride ruptured at a Kerr-McGee uranium processing facility in Gore, Oklahoma.[72]

EPA and other agencies have attempted to go beyond reports of individual accidents, reviewing records of incidents for the patterns of error and impact they might disclose. For example, a study of chemical accidents produced for EPA in late 1985 reported over 6,900 accidents for the period from 1980 to mid-1985.[73]* The report focused on states with a heavy con-

---

*Since the EPA study was not intended to be comprehensive, it understates the total number of industrial accidents involving chemicals.

centration of chemical plants, including Texas, Ohio, New Jersey, and California. The 138 recorded fatalities and 4,717 recorded injuries stemmed from only about 7 percent of the accidents. Four common chemicals—chlorine, ammonia, hydrochloric acid, and sulfuric acid—were released in over one-fourth of the cases where there were deaths or injuries.[74]

In that study, transportation mishaps accounted for 25 percent of all accidents and 33 percent of those causing death or injury. Among the in-plant accidents causing death or injury, equipment failures were the cause of over 27 percent, and operator error was implicated in 13 percent. The causes of 40 percent of the plant accidents producing casualties were unknown.[75]

This EPA report is a reminder of how frequently accidents occur and of how little is known about their causes and impacts. Information about actual human exposures to the toxic substances released in accidents is especially poor.

Rethinking Airborne Risks

Americans live in a chemical soup. Human exposures to this soup transcend the artificial institutional boundaries between indoor air and outdoor air, between occupational and nonoccupational environments, and between routine emissions and accidental releases. Risks to human health are present in both indoor and outdoor air, but limited knowledge about exposures and toxicity makes it difficult to determine which human environments are the most threatening. Notwithstanding this uncertainty, the information that has emerged in recent years makes it clear that:

- contamination of indoor environments must be moved much higher on public and private research agendas than it has been in the past;
- much more attention must be paid to assessing hot spots of routine toxic emissions; and
- greater emphasis must be placed on understanding the causes of, and means of preventing, industrial accidents.

FEDERAL STRATEGIES FOR MANAGING AIRBORNE TOXIC SUBSTANCES

At present, federal authority to deal with toxic air pollutants is widely dispersed throughout the government. Much responsibility lies with EPA, but additional duties are vested in the Occupational Safety and Health Administration (OSHA) and the Consumer Product Safety Commission

(CPSC). A number of other agencies also share responsibility for dealing with accidents that pollute air, land, and water.

The Clean Air Act

The Clean Air Act, administered by EPA, is the nation's principle vehicle for combating air pollution. Two of the act's major components, enacted in 1970, require EPA (*a*) to establish national *ambient* air quality standards for the most common pollutants and (*b*) to establish *emission* standards for less common but particularly hazardous pollutants.[76]

The program to achieve ambient standards has emphasized the reduction of routine emissions outdoors of the most widely occurring pollutants. These include sulfur dioxide, particulates, carbon monoxide, nitrogen dioxide, and the chemicals that contribute to formation of ozone.* With federal guidance and financial assistance, state and local pollution control agencies were required to develop and implement regulatory programs designed to meet the standards by December 31, 1982, or, in some cases, by December 31, 1987. Significant progress has been made, but much more remains to be achieved.

Section 112 of the Clean Air Act mandated that "hazardous" pollutants be subject to a different, more stringent regulatory strategy, intended to encourage quick regulation of substances capable of causing serious harm at relatively low concentrations. EPA was also given authority to regulate "hazardous" fuels and fuel additives.[78] Hazardous substances were defined as those contributing to increases in mortality, serious irreversible illness, or incapacitating but reversible illness. Once EPA designated a substance as hazardous, it was supposed to quickly propose controls on sources of the contaminant, and sources were supposed to comply quickly.

The law did not give EPA any deadline for listing substances as hazardous. Congress evidently did not expect the provision to apply to very many chemicals. The Senate report on the legislation stated that "it is clear that (the definition of a hazardous air pollutant) will encompass a limited number of pollutants."[79] The report mentioned only four substances: asbestos, cadmium, mercury, and beryllium.

By 1980, EPA had listed seven pollutants as hazardous and had regulated only four.[80] While this restraint might seem consistent with Congress's view

---

*These are sometimes referred to as "criteria pollutants" because the standards are based on compilations of information labeled "criteria."[77] See the "Status and Trends" chapters of this book for a discussion of the progress made in meeting national ambient air quality standards.

in 1970 that few substances would need to be addressed, it now seems grossly inconsistent with the growing awareness of the plethora of potentially hazardous airborne pollutants. Moreover, as early as 1977, it was evident that Congress was dissatisfied with EPA's inaction. That year, Congress added a new section to the Clean Air Act, naming several substances for which a listing determination had to be made within one or two years.[81] EPA was unable to meet the deadlines.

During the past several years, under considerable pressure from Congress and from environmentalist lawsuits, EPA has devoted more resources to implementing Section 112. By mid-1986, however, only eight pollutants had been listed, and final regulations had been published for only seven of them.[82]*

Ironically, EPA's program to control the common pollutants for which national ambient standards have been set (the criteria pollutants) may have done more to reduce risks from hazardous air pollutants than has been done by the agency's regulatory programs specifically targeted to the latter. This has occurred because the controls designed to capture the criteria pollutants also have reduced emissions of hazardous pollutants.† Using both emission estimates and monitored levels of concentrations, EPA has estimated that, as a result of efforts to control criteria pollutants, the cancer incidence for 16 "toxic" pollutants was reduced by more than 50 percent (from 17.5 cases to 6.8 cases per million) between 1970 and 1980.[84]‡

EPA's continuing efforts to reduce levels of pollutants for which national ambient air quality standards have been set may further reduce exposures to hazardous pollutants. For example, if EPA imposes further controls on emissions from automobiles or from service stations to promote

---

*"Notices of intent to list"—EPA's preliminary determinations that substances are potentially toxic—were published for 9 other substances, and decisions not to list were published for another 11 substances. Decisions on 2 additional substances were also published. One was referred to state and local governments for action, while the other EPA intended to regulate under several different statutes.[83]

†One explanation for this is that, while an administrative distinction is made between criteria pollutants and hazardous pollutants, one pollutant often will fall in both categories. For example, a metal may be regulated as a hazardous pollutant. But, if it is emitted as a particulate, it may be controlled by devices designed to help a company meet an emission standard for particulates.

‡EPA's estimates of the impact of controls for criteria pollutants were developed as part of its previously discussed study of outdoor airborne toxic substances.[85] EPA attached many caveats to these data.

attainment of the ambient standard for ozone, these strategies will have the collateral effect of reducing emissions of benzene.[86] Benzene, a proven carcinogen,[87] is one of the few substances EPA has listed under Section 112. Furthermore, as EPA refines its strategies for regulating particulates, it is reasonable to presume that reductions in toxic substances within the particulate category will continue.

EPA's Air Toxics Strategy

Responding to the changing scope of air pollution problems, EPA announced in 1985 a "comprehensive action agenda" intended to strengthen existing programs and launch new ones directed at airborne risks.[88] Building on the results of its previously discussed study of risks from airborne toxic substances and stressing that it must concentrate on those substances presenting the greatest health risks, EPA announced plans to expand its program for emergency preparedness and response; expand its multimedia studies of local toxic-pollutant problems; help states build strong regulatory programs of their own and, when appropriate, refer localized air pollution problems to states for evaluation and action; and regulate area (that is, small, but numerous and broadly distributed) sources of complex toxic emissions that appear to account for a significant portion of controllable health risks.[89]

EPA's program for managing industrial accidents includes publication of a list of approximately 400 chemicals that could produce acute adverse health effects if released into the air accidentally.[90] The list is supplemented by chemical profiles describing the properties and characteristics of each chemical. EPA is developing guidelines on use of the list to help state and local officials and organizations in contingency planning, and it intends to provide suitable training in emergency planning and response.[91]

EPA also intends to reduce emissions to the air caused by pollution control efforts in other media. For example, under provisions of the Resource Conservation and Recovery Act, the agency is planning to limit emissions to the air from hazardous waste dumps, and under the Clean Water Act the agency is attempting to limit emissions to the air from municipal sewage treatment plants.[92] The agency also intends to explore the use of its other statutory authorities (for example, the Toxic Substances Control Act) to reduce airborne risks.[93]

Many environmentalists have criticized the EPA strategy. They suggest that the accident program stresses response rather than prevention; that the program of referral to states represents yet another form of federal abdication of responsibility for controlling airborne toxic substances; and that

EPA's actions under Section 112 continue to be too slow and too feeble.[94] Many state officials, while recognizing that some toxic-pollutant problems are primarily local in nature, disagree with the specific elements of EPA's referral program. Not surprisingly, these officials decry the lack of sufficient federal funding assistance for state airborne toxic substance programs.[95]

EPA's strategy attempts to interweave many disparate actions into a coherent approach to airbone toxic substances. However, state officials and environmentalists are concerned that EPA is unwilling to take sufficiently tough action against identified risks.

The Occupational Safety and Health Act

The Occupational Safety and Health Act assigns to OSHA principal responsibility within the federal government for protecting health and safety in industrial environments.[96] After initially emphasizing the "safety" side of its mission in the early to middle 1970s, OSHA turned increasing attention to the "health" side. This included setting standards and establishing reporting and monitoring requirements for toxic pollutants.[97] However, the OSHA program for protecting workers from these health hazards has moved at a very slow pace.

From 1971 to 1984, OSHA developed 18 separate health standards, or about three rules every two years. Most govern airborne toxic substances, including some substances regulated or considered for regulation by EPA outdoors. The standards establish exposure limits for some substances but, for others, simply create new requirements governing work practices and medical surveillance.[98]*

Standard-setting activity in the private sector contrasts sharply with the snail's pace of OSHA's action. Standards developed by two voluntary standard-setting organizations, the American Conference of Governmental Industrial Hygienists (ACGIH) and the American National Standards Institute, establish "Threshold Limit Values" (TLVs) for workday exposure.[100]† These private organizations evidently are able to revise their standards quite readily; ACGIH updates its limits each year. Shortly after it was created, OSHA adopted as its own approximately 400 standards developed by the

---

*As of April 1985, some of these standards were being reconsidered by OSHA, and some were under judicial review.[99]

†The TLVs usually are eight-hour time-weighted average values. The standards often also contain a short-term limit. However, they do not include elements one might find in government-developed regulations—for example, exposure monitoring, medical surveillance, record keeping, or other informational provisions.[101]

private organizations.[102] Unfortunately, OSHA's limits are not readily updated, and remain "virtually frozen" at the levels set by ACGIH in the late 1960s.[103]

The Consumer Product Safety Act

The Consumer Product Safety Act assigns responsibility for protecting consumers from hazardous products to CPSC. This commission has jurisdiction over products produced for consumer home or recreational use, but pesticides, drugs, and other items regulated by other agencies are excluded.[104]*

Concern with pollutants inside the home was not a major motivation behind establishment of CPSC, but the commission has taken a number of actions to reduce risks from indoor pollutants. It banned the sale of urea formaldehyde foam for insulation of schools and houses. (The ban subsequently was overturned in court, but public concern and attendant publicity essentially ended use of the insulation.) CPSC also banned artificial fireplace logs and patching compounds containing asbestos, negotiated with manufacturers to end the use of asbestos in household hair dryers, and required that unvented gas space heaters bear precautionary labels and automatically shut off when oxygen levels drop.[107]

In view of the emerging evidence of high levels of pollutants in some homes from consumer products, CPSC may continue to play an important role in reducing airborne risks. However, the commission's average yearly budget since 1981 has been substantially lower than its budget during the late 1970s, so its ability to take aggressive regulatory action remains uncertain.

Federal Authorities and Accident Response

The discussion above emphasizes the fragmentation and limited scope of programs that focus mainly on routine emissions of airborne toxics. The same problems are associated with the management of accidental releases of toxic substances into the air. The Department of Transportation, which regulates rail and highway shipments of hazardous substances, and the Federal Emergency Management Agency, which responds to a wide variety of disaster situations, play major roles in accident prevention and re-

---

*CPSC also administers the Federal Hazardous Substances Act, which provides it with additional authority to act against toxic air pollutants.[105] For example, it is considering action to reduce consumer exposure to methylene chloride.[106]

sponse. EPA and OSHA also have responsibility for accidents. Figure 8.5, which shows federal, state, and local responsibilities for hazardous materials in the state of Washington, lists these and other federal agencies that may be responsible for preventing or responding to accidental releases.

OVERCOMING FRAGMENTATION AND SPEEDING CONTROL AT THE FEDERAL LEVEL

Federal action against toxic airborne pollutants has been fragmented and slow. How might programs be better organized and action speeded? Integration of programs might allow systematic action to be taken against pollutants that present both indoor and outdoor exposure problems. Integrated strategies, in theory, would take into account the incidence of exposure in various locations and the authorities available to government agencies to reduce that exposure. They then would use those various agencies to develop the most effective, efficient reduction of risk. This section looks at devices for improving integration of federal government activities and speeding regulatory activity.

Improved Coordination of Existing Activities

Various coordinating devices such as interagency committees and memoranda of understanding are sometimes quite effective. In the absence of strong and clear statutory authorization for comprehensive management of air pollution problems, such coordinating mechanisms could do much to improve the overall federal response.

Greater attention must be paid to the systematic collection of information on exposures to, and health effects of, airborne toxic substances. A coordinated research program involving the many federal agencies concerned with public health, pollution control, and consumer and occupational safety could maximize use of scarce federal research resources and might help ensure that the potentially greatest risks are well characterized. For example, the 15 agencies concerned with indoor air participate in an interagency Council on Indoor Air Quality (CIAQ), which is supposed to develop a coordinated program of research. The council is cochaired by 4 federal agencies. It has been entangled in interagency disagreements, and members of Congress concerned about indoor air quality have been quite dissatisfied with its work.[108] Nevertheless, the committee's existence reflects the fact that researching the many elements of indoor air risks requires crossing numerous jurisdictional boundaries.

Coordination across jurisdictional lines does not require a broad "umbrella" like a CIAQ but can be done on an ad hoc basis. For example, CPSC recently requested EPA's Clean Air Science Advisory Committee

Figure 8.5
Federal, State, and Local Agencies Having Hazardous Materials Responsibilities in the Puget Sound, Washington, Area as of April 1981

	Premarket testing	Manufacture	Handling	Storage	Use	Labeling	Package/container design	Packaging/placarding	Shipping papers	Transportation equipment	Inspections—process/storage	Inspections—transportation	Notification	Response/containment	Cleanup, mitigation, disposal	Accident reporting equipment
Federal:																
Federal Highway Administration (U.S. Department of Transportation)						●	●	●	●	●			○	○		●
Federal Railroad Administration (U.S. Department of Transportation)			●			●	●	●	●	●			●	○	○	●
U.S. Coast Guard			●			●	●	●	●	●	●	●	●	●	●	●
Federal Aviation Administration (U.S. Department of Transportation)			●			●	●	●	●	●		●	●	○	○	●
Office of Pipeline Safety (U.S. Department of Transportation)			●					●				●	●	○	○	●
National Transportation Safety Board (U.S. Department of Transportation)													●			●
Environmental Protection Agency	●	●		●	●	●	◐	●				●	●	●	●	●
Federal Emergency Management Agency													●	○		●
Department of Health and Human Services		●	●	●									●			
Nuclear Regulatory Commission		●	●	●	●								◐	◐	◐	◐
Bureau of Alcohol, Tobacco and Firearms (U.S. Treasury)				●	●								●			
Department of Defense, Explosives Safety Board		●	●	●	●								◐	◐	◐	
Department of the Army														◐		
State:																
Department of Emergency Services													●	◐	○	
Labor and Industry		○	○	○	○							○		◐	○	
Department of Social and Health Services		○	○	○	○						○	○	◐	◐	○	●
Department of Agriculture			◐	◐	◐							◐	◐			
Department of Ecology	●													○	○	●
Washington Utilities and Transportation Commission							●	●	●	●						●
Washington State Patrol							●	●	●				●	●	○	●
Local:																
City fire	○	●	●	●		○							●	●	○	
City building department		●	●	●												
City police								●								
County fire				○	○							○	●	●	○	
County police								●								
City/county Department of Emergency Services													○	○		
City/county health department														●		

○ — Limited regulatory authority
◐ — Scope of authority depends on type of substance, location of spill or identity of carrier or discharger
● — Major regulatory authority

Source: Office of Technology Assessment.

to review for the commission the potential health hazards associated with exposure to nitrogen dioxide emitted from household consumer products. This is the first review conducted by the advisory committee for an agency other than EPA, and it is being paid for with CPSC funds provided under an interagency agreement.[109]

Within the federal government one potentially important vehicle for integrating control of airborne and other toxic compounds is the Toxic Substances Control Act (TSCA). TSCA gives EPA broad authority to gather information on chemicals and to impose regulatory controls if it can reasonably conclude that the commercial use or disposal of a chemical presents an unreasonable risk of injury to human health or the environment. TSCA is a broad statute, which, says EPA, "allows regulation of a chemical substance based on all its risks and thereby allows the government to remedy the deficiencies in other statutes that can deal only with parts of the risk."[110]

Section 4(f) of TSCA requires the EPA administrator to undertake a priority review of risks from a toxic substance when the administrator is informed that the chemical may present a serious risk to human health. The administrator then has 180 days to take appropriate regulatory action pursuant to other provisions of TSCA or to announce that the risk from the substance is not unreasonable.[111]

In mid-1985, EPA launched a priority review of the chemical methylene chloride after being notified that the substance caused cancer in tests on mice.[112] Because exposures to methylene chloride occur in many human environments (the workplace, homes, and elsewhere) and from different media (for example, air and water), EPA is exploring regulatory alternatives under TSCA; the Clean Air Act; the Safe Drinking Water Act; the Federal Insecticide, Fungicide, and Rodenticide Act; and other applicable statutes.[113] EPA also is considering, in cooperation with other agencies, the use of statutes administered by those agencies.

EPA has not invoked Section 4(f) very often,[114] and it has not yet published the results of the investigation of methylene chloride. As a result, it is not easy to predict how well Section 4(f) will function in the future as a vehicle for integrated risk assessment.

Section 9 of TSCA requires the EPA administrator to report to other federal agencies if the administrator determines (*a*) that a substance poses an unreasonable risk and (*b*) that the unreasonable risk could be prevented or reduced to a sufficient extent by another federal agency. These other agencies, in turn, reply to EPA by taking any of several steps ranging from launching a regulatory action to doing nothing. In the latter case, EPA remains free to act against the substance.[115]

When it enacted Section 9, Congress intended to make sure that EPA employed its own regulatory remedies only after thoroughly considering the potential of adequate regulatory action by other agencies.[116] Only on a few recent occasions has the agency used Section 9 either to make referrals to other agencies or to take action itself. EPA's first referral was of 4,4'-methylenedianiline (4,4'-MDA), exposure to which occurs almost exclusively in workplaces. OSHA responded by establishing a "mediated rule-making" advisory committee to assist in developing a workplace standard.[117]

EPA's second referral was of 1,3-butadiene, to which humans are exposed in both workplaces and outdoors. OSHA intends to revise its existing occupational standard to reduce risks identified by EPA.[118] In addition, EPA intends to consider listing 1,3-butadiene as a hazardous substance under Section 112 of the Clean Air Act.[119]

The EPA administrator may also conclude that no referral to another agency is in order because no other agency can reduce the risk to a sufficient extent. For example, EPA declined to refer asbestos to other agencies for action, preferring instead to phase out its use.[120] In this instance, EPA determined that OSHA would not be able to reduce risks to workers sufficiently and that referral to OSHA and other agencies would result in a fragmented assessment of risks, potentially duplicative regulatory efforts, and inefficient control.[121]*

New Laws Redefining Agency Authority

Legislation amending and reauthorizing Superfund in October 1986, gives EPA the lead authority within the federal government to assess risks from indoor air pollutants and to report the results to Congress by October 1988.[123] Congress requires EPA to gather information on sources and levels of indoor air pollution. The agency is mandated to conduct research on devices for measuring indoor air quality and on techniques for reducing indoor pollution. Finally, EPA must assess appropriate federal actions to reduce environmental and health risks associated with indoor air pollutants.

---

*EPA's decision to retain jurisdiction was quite controversial. The president's Office of Management and Budget (OMB) had tried to force a referral from EPA to OSHA. However, following a congressional investigation and a scathing congressional report condemning OMB, EPA proceeded to take its own action against asbestos.[122]

The same legislation also expands EPA's authority concerning industrial accidents and routine emissions of toxic pollutants. Title III, the Emergency Planning and Community Right-To-Know Act of 1986, establishes an ambitious national program that requires industries to estimate and report emissions of large numbers of pollutants and requires state and local governments to plan responses to chemical emergencies (see box). The complex requirements apply to a host of chemicals, with the applicability of a particular requirement depending on whether a chemical is labeled as "hazardous," "extremely hazardous," or "toxic."[124] These provisions provide a firm statutory basis for EPA's fledgling accident response work, encourage development of the information base needed to identify high-risk situations, and serve as a prod to state action.

Superfund Reauthorization Includes Major New Accident Response and Toxic Emission Reporting Requirements[1]

When it amended and reauthorized the federal Superfund in October 1986, Congress enacted the "Emergency Planning and Community Right-To-Know Act of 1986." The law contains major new authority relating to (1) emergency planning, (2) emergency notification, (3) "community-right-to-know" reporting on chemicals, and (4) emissions inventories.

Emergency Planning

The law requires states to establish state emergency planning commissions, emergency planning districts, and local emergency planning committees. These are to develop and implement emergency response plans, with the participation of facilities that produce, use, or store "extremely hazardous" substances. The extremely hazardous substances covered by this provision are those previously listed as part of the emergency preparedness component of EPA's air toxics strategy.

Emergency Notification

The law requires owners and operators of facilities to notify the state commission and local committees of releases of both extremely hazardous substances and those chemicals reportable under the provisions of Superfund. Only releases above certain levels must be reported.

Community Right-to-Know Reporting

This requires owners or operators of facilities to provide information on the manufacture, use, and storage of chemicals present at their facilities. The information must be provided to the state commission, local committees, and local fire department and must be made available to the general public.

Emissions Inventory

Owners or operators of certain facilities must submit toxic chemical release forms annually to EPA if they manufacture, process, or use specific toxic chemicals in excess of certain thresholds. EPA is required to compile this information and make it available to the public through such means as computerized data bases.

This new legislation should enhance understanding of the magnitude of airborne risks and hasten their regulation. It should raise airborne toxic substances even higher on the federal agenda, provide for more assertive action and policy leadership by federal agencies, and support agency efforts to obtain OMB approval of budget requests for programs aimed at toxic air pollutants.

STATE AND LOCAL PROGRAMS FOR MANAGING AIRBORNE RISKS

With its emphasis on reducing emissions of criteria air pollutants, the federal government has largely dictated the air pollution control agenda in the United States for more than a decade. However, the slow pace of federal efforts to address risks from less-common airborne toxic substances has prompted some state and local governments to move ahead of the federal government in developing innovative policies. These initiatives are a reminder of the vitality and responsiveness of these governments. The state and local innovations also provide important tests for new approaches that ultimately might be applicable nationwide.

State and local efforts indicate that fragmentation per se is not necessarily bad. Fragmented authority can encourage a constructive interagency and intergovernmental competition to protect public health, promote testing of a wide range of innovative approaches, and provide enhanced protection against risk—in contrast to those situations where responsibility is centralized in a single agency or level of government that lacks the ability or will to move off dead center.

The relative difficulty or cost of addressing a problem often determines the most effective level of management.[125] For example, funding or conducting basic research on health effects of pollutants most appropriately rests at the federal level, since the research results produce national benefits and state and local governments usually lack the capability to conduct or fund such work. The federal government also can play a major role in testing technologies and setting standards, although this need not preclude state and local governments from research and testing. Similarly, through CPSC and other entities, the federal government can set standards for or ban products that have a national market.

But state and local governments historically have played some important regulatory roles that could effectively enable them to reduce airborne risks. For example, state and local building codes are the principal rules governing construction and operation of buildings. Perhaps the most effective way to promote new construction that minimizes risks from indoor air pollutants is for state and local governments to make appropriate changes in those codes.

The point was made earlier that fragmentation of responsibility can be advantageous, at least compared to having one agency that has principal responsibility but that is reluctant to act. This is well illustrated, in the intergovernmental context, by experience with a "hazard communication standard" issued by OSHA that required the labeling of toxic and hazardous substances in the workplace.[126] Such a standard was proposed during the closing days of the Carter administration. It was sought by labor and opposed by industry. When the proposal was withdrawn by the Reagan administration, organized labor and other groups persuaded 17 states and dozens of localities to adopt their own disclosure requirements. Figure 8.6 lists the many states that, by 1985, had enacted laws requiring disclosure of the presence of hazardous materials to either workers or local officials. Industry groups became concerned about the diverse regulatory requirements resulting from state and local regulation. Threatened by such regulatory fragmentation, they encouraged the Reagan administration to issue a federal regulation. The new federal regulation, however, is weaker than many of the state and local requirements it preempts.[127]

State and local government regulations regarding routine emissions of toxic air pollutants vary widely in scope. A number of state programs derive ambient standards or guidelines from the occupational limits developed by OSHA and other organizations. State and local governments setting these standards often require industries to submit information on their emissions. If it is demonstrated that the ambient standards or guidelines are being exceeded by an existing source or would be exceeded by a newly constructed source, the industries are required to reduce their emissions. For example, Philadelphia has been developing guidelines for 99 contaminants. On the basis of both emissions data and modeling, the city will require reductions in pollution from those sources whose emissions are deemed a threat to human health.[128]

The state and local programs' use of guidelines based on occupational limits, as a shortcut to implementation of controls, may be a somewhat speedier approach to decision making than the risk assessment process used by EPA under Section 112 of the Clean Air Act.* In part, the state and local governments' approaches reflect their very limited resources to conduct scientific analysis, but the approaches also reflect the urgency some governments feel to act, even in the face of considerable scientific uncertainty. Because of the scientific uncertainties involved, however, the amount

---

*EPA has opted to regulate only "significant" risks and to consider economic costs and technological feasibility in deciding whether to regulate. This approach has been quite controversial, and is discussed later.

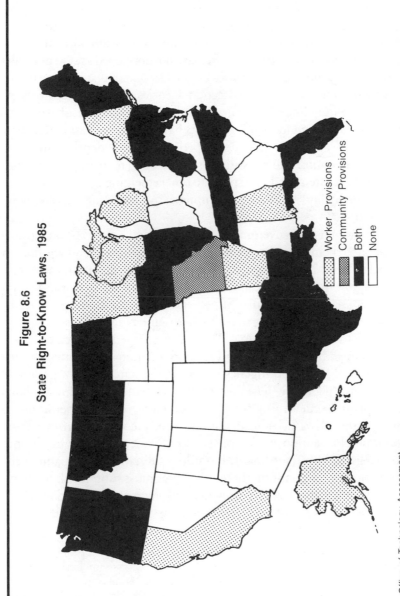

Figure 8.6

State Right-to-Know Laws, 1985

Worker Provisions

Community Provisions

Both

None

Source: Office of Technology Assessment.

of risk reduction likely to result from the state and local programs cannot be judged with much precision.* It is also important to note that many of these programs were launched only recently, so their impact on emission levels is not yet very pronounced.

State and local governments also have moved forward with programs to address indoor air quality, but these have not developed as systematically as programs for routine outdoor emissions of toxic air pollutants. State health departments, environmental protection agencies, and other bureaus often are on the front line of the war against formaldehyde and asbestos contamination. State and local governments have passed increasing numbers of laws to restrict smoking, have developed programs to identify dangerous radon contamination and to assist those affected in reducing radon exposures, and have attempted to respond to other emerging problems relating to indoor air quality.[130] Coherent, comprehensive state programs are, however, a rarity.[131]

Many state and local governments have developed hazard response teams to respond to chemical emergencies, and they often are closely coordinated with federal teams. But in terms of comprehensive legislation, most state and local governments have not moved much farther than the federal government had before the new Superfund reauthorization. In 1985, Illinois became one of the first states to enact an emergency response law, the Illinois Chemical Safety Act. The act covers chemical releases to soil and water in addition to releases to air, and it requires companies to submit "chemical safety contingency plans" to the state by July 1, 1986.[132]

In January 1986, New Jersey adopted a law requiring chemical plants to have plans for preventing the accidental release of toxic chemicals. In contrast to those laws focusing on response to accidents, New Jersey's Toxic Catastrophe Prevention Act emphasizes prevention. The act establishes an initial list of 11 extraordinarily hazardous substances. Companies generating, storing, or handling these substances must submit risk management programs to the state Department of Environmental Protection. Companies are required to provide considerable information to the state,

---

*The workplace exposure limits were not intended for use in nonoccupational environments. In adapting them for nonoccupational environments, state and local officials use some fraction of the workplace exposure limits, because workers in occupational environments are presumed to be healthy, while persons to be protected in nonoccupational environments may be less healthy, especially sensitive individuals in the general population. The stringency of a guideline for a particular substance can vary tremendously among jurisdictions, because regulators may use different fractions (1/100 versus 1/420, for example) of the workplace exposure limits.[129]

including descriptions of equipment, maintenance programs, and training procedures. If a company fails to act, the state can step in to prepare a plan. The department can conduct routine inspections to make sure plans are being carried out. And it can expand the list of substances for which plans must be developed.[133]

The activism of state and local governments, as compared to the posture of federal government, can cause significant problems. First, having various state and local entities go through their own scientific reviews and standard-setting processes can be redundant. However, such inefficiency can be reduced through information sharing. As part of its air toxics strategy, EPA has established an airborne toxic substance clearinghouse, readily accessible by computer, which details various state activities. Through the clearinghouse, states can find out what ambient standards and guidelines other states have established and what emission limits other states have imposed.[134]

Second, while state and local actions should produce health and environmental benefits in some areas, they can be used as an argument against significant federal regulatory steps. Delays in federal intervention may leave at some risk the citizens of those states and localities where political, economic, or other factors discourage the establishment of effective programs for regulating airborne toxic substances.

Third, in state and local battles over establishing programs, states may be played off against one another; multistate industries may argue that stringent regulation of toxic substances will prompt them to shift production (and jobs) to those states where regulations do not drive up the marginal costs of production.

Fourth, the diversity of state and local programs may leave industries subject to a confusing array of different requirements, thereby spurring industry to seek preemptive, and possibly weaker, federal regulation.

Yet, as demonstrated above, state and local activism has positive aspects as well. First, in those areas where state and local programs have been adopted, citizens may gain protection not available from the federal government. Second, states can develop control priorities based on their particular problems, rather than respond to priorities established on a nationwide basis by federal regulators; thus, the greatest risks may be addressed first. Third, because of their diversity, states may develop some noteworthy innovative approaches that merit emulation by other state and local governments and, perhaps, by the federal government. State and local governments can benefit from each others' experiences, copying the most successful risk assessment and management strategies and, hopefully, avoiding those that have worked less well.

THE ROLE OF THE PRIVATE SECTOR IN REDUCING RISKS

A significant reservoir of environmental expertise has developed in the private sector. Designers of new government programs should take into account past efforts of the private sector to address airborne risks; they should also consider the incentives that exist for private organizations to continue and expand their activities. Private programs take many forms, including, for example, voluntary standard setting by private organizations whose main purpose is the development of standards; accident prevention and response networks developed by trade associations and individual companies; individual companies' environmental auditing procedures designed to reduce environmental liabilities; and the entrepreneurial efforts of the pollution control industry.

While government obviously should play a major part in undertaking research on the risks from airborne toxic substances and on setting compliance standards, an important research role can be, and is being, played by the private sector. This is particularly evident with indoor air pollution. The American Society for Testing and Materials (ASTM), a voluntary private organization that formulates standards on a consensus basis, is developing standards for measuring indoor air quality.[135]* The American Society of Heating, Refrigerating, and Air Conditioning Engineers (ASHRAE) is revising its standards for indoor air quality.[137] As noted previously, the American Conference of Governmental Industrial Hygienists sets consensus standards for workplace exposures to toxic risks. ACGIH covers approximately 200 more substances than OSHA, and its standards are more current than OSHA's, but its recommendations do not have the force of law that OSHA's do.[138] While voluntary standards set by ASTM, ASHRAE, and other such organizations are not legally binding, they often are incorporated into building codes and thus become binding.

The private sector also has an important role to play in developing new monitoring technologies for data gathering. If regulators want to assess quickly the scope of certain indoor air problems, their task would be made that much easier by the availability of inexpensive monitors. Such monitors would also be important to home buyers and other individuals concerned about radon, formaldehyde, and other dangerous substances. The private sector is sure to respond to this growing demand.

---

*ASTM produces many different standards, based on different consensus efforts. It may produce a company standard, an industry standard, or a professional standard. It also develops what it calls "Full Consensus Standards," based on work by "all the several elements of the community that have an interest in . . . the standards."[136]

Private activity also is important in the realm of industrial accidents. One of the most well known private-sector accident response activities is the Chemical Transportation Emergency Center (CHEMTREC), operated by the Chemical Manufacturers Association (CMA) since 1971. CHEMTREC maintains files on more than 90,000 chemicals and products and provides information on immediate steps to be taken in response to emergency discharges. More than 2,000 companies or groups depend on CHEMTREC as the communication center for their emergency response systems.[139]

Since the Bhopal accident, CHEMTREC has been incorporated into a larger National Chemical Response and Information Center. The center includes CHEMNET, a mutual-aid network that speeds experts to the scene of accidents, a chemical referral system for the public to obtain information about chemicals and chemical products, and additional information services.[140]

A major CMA effort, the Community Awareness and Emergency Response Program (CAER), is designed to work with both companies and communities in developing emergency response plans.[141] Since CAER's inception, the chemical industry has developed and distributed thousands of emergency planning and communication manuals, conducted nationwide seminars for thousands of industry managers, and started CAER-related activities at approximately 1,400 locations.[142]

The American Institute of Chemical Engineers is another private organization that has stepped up its accident prevention activity. Its recently organized Center for Chemical Process Safety has produced *Guidelines for Hazard Evaluation Procedures*, a compendium of approaches for assessing hazards from industrial processes.[143] The manual provides a guide for plant managers attempting to develop risk management priorities. The center also has initiated several projects to reduce the likelihood and severity of chemical plant accidents.

Individual companies wary of liability associated with accidents and waste disposal have some economic incentive to reduce risks from hazardous substances. Some of the largest companies are reducing their storage of hazardous materials, attempting to reduce reliance on toxic materials in products, and developing internal audit systems to police compliance with regulatory requirements and to reduce risks.[144] Nevertheless, new legislation has been needed because the private marketplace still provides an insufficient incentive for many other companies to reduce risks.

Individual companies' environmental auditing programs can be useful devices for gathering information on routine emissions, accidental discharges, and risk reduction opportunities, and can be an important element of corporate risk management.[145] However, the extent to which corporations are obligated to share with regulators the results of their audits has been controversial.[146] So while environmental auditing may usefully reduce risks at various corporate locations, it may not necessarily help regulators to make risk management decisions.

These are but a few of the many private-sector activities that help reduce risks to human health and the environment from airborne toxic substances. The challenge facing those who design government programs is deciding how to take maximum advantage of the skills, knowledge, and successful risk management programs of the private sector, while also designing programs that reduce airborne risks caused by those in the private sector who lack the funding, knowledge, or desire to take appropriate action.

TARGETING RISKS FOR CONTROL: ANALYTICAL APPROACHES AND CHALLENGES

A wide range of tools is available for reducing risk to human health and the environment from airborne toxic substances. A long, but not exhaustive, list includes:

- government bans on products;
- required or voluntary standards limiting emissions; specifying strength, durability, and other characteristics of storage vessels, pipes, and other materials; and defining safe work practices;
- voluntary industry changes in products to reduce emissions from product manufacture and use;
- information strategies to promote private behavior that reduces emissions, reduces demand for polluting products, or reduces risks to human populations and the environment from accidental releases of toxic substances;
- government financial subsidies to promote emission reductions or assist in reducing the impacts of emissions;
- administrative and judicial sanctions and financial penalties to compensate for past damages from emissions and to discourage future emissions; and
- use of economic incentives (for example, raised insurance premiums or nonavailability of insurance) within the private sector to discourage routine emissions and reduce industrial accidents.

These strategies can be used singly or in combination both to reduce existing risks and to prevent future ones. Some of these strategies involve choices made by the private sector, while others involve requirements dictated by the public sector.

It seems entirely appropriate to establish as management principles the ideas that (*a*) big risks should be managed before small ones, (*b*) dollars should be spent where they will buy the biggest reductions in risk, and (*c*) the likely speed and effectiveness of risk reduction activities should be weighed when designing risk management programs. These principles suggest an orderly approach to cleaning up the air. They recognize the impossibility of achieving zero risk from air pollution or of acting against all significant risks simultaneously and quickly.

Yet while these principles may be appealing, their practical application creates some thorny problems. Information and analytical methods available may be inadequate. The needed institutions may not be in place. Political support may be lacking. A given approach may be regarded as unfair by those who believe government should protect them from all risks that they incur involuntarily. Decision makers also may have difficulty reconciling the desirability of targeting the biggest, most controllable risks with the delays that inevitably accompany the analysis needed to choose such targets in the first place.

Moreover, setting priorities and choosing among alternative options is never as rational as the management principles suggest. New scientific discoveries, catastrophes, and other factors will skew government agendas for action.

Improved Risk Assessment

A better assessment of the total risk to human health and the environment from all airborne toxic substances is needed. This requires improved knowledge of health effects and better information on human exposures, including a greater understanding of how airborne toxic substances move into and from land and water.[147] The federal government must continue funding and conducting such research and encouraging or requiring the private sector to do the same. Since much of the recent debate over controlling toxic air pollutants has emphasized cancer, it is especially important to pay greater attention to noncancer health risks.

Risk assessment is permeated with nonscientific value judgments.[148] The seeming precision of quantitative estimates can mask enormous uncertainties and controversial assumptions. Moreover, excessive emphasis on risk assessment—particularly on a chemical-by-chemical basis—can lead to paralysis by analysis.

Nevertheless, risk assessment can help distinguish large risks from small ones and thereby direct resources where they are most needed. For example, a risk assessment might show that a routinely released airborne chemical is not likely to produce more than one cancer case in 100 years in the general population, and also is unlikely to increase significantly the risk to those living immediately around major emission sources. It therefore may make sense to ignore that chemical and to focus instead on controlling one believed to produce hundreds of cancer cases.

Amid much controversy, EPA has attempted to make greater use of risk assessment in its regulation of hazardous air pollutants under Section 112 of the Clean Air Act. EPA's new approach is illustrated by its withdrawal, in 1984, of emission standards it had proposed for several industries that routinely emit benzene to the atmosphere.[149] EPA contended that the withdrawn standards would have eliminated only one case of cancer every 30 years.[150] At the same time, EPA proposed to retain standards for other sources of benzene.[151] For example, the agency proposed controls on benzene emissions from coke by-product plants, whose emissions are estimated to cause about two cases of leukemia per year.[152] The proposed controls would reduce cancer cases to less than one each year.

EPA sometimes decides to take regulatory action even when the total number of annual cancer cases is low, but when risks to the most exposed individuals are fairly high. For instance, in announcing its intention to list cadmium as a hazardous airborne substance, EPA estimated that cadmium emissions cause only 3 to 7 cases of cancer per year; however, the most exposed population stands a 3-in-1,000 lifetime chance of getting cancer from cadmium emissions.[153] In a similar notice for chloroform, EPA estimated only 13 annual cases for cancer but indicated that the lifetime risk to those exposed from emissions from pulp and paper mills is a relatively high 1 in 100.[154]

EPA has used the same risk assessment techniques to rule out listing of pollutants as hazardous under Section 112. For example, EPA declined to list the chemical hexachlorobenzene, estimating that cancer cases would total between 1 every 700 years and 1 every 4,500 years and that the maximum risk to any individual would be from 1 in 10,000 to 2 in 1,000,000.[155]

In court actions contesting many of EPA's recent decisions under Section 112, environmentalists (and some states) have challenged EPA's use of such risk assessments.[156] The suits indicate a strong wariness of risk assessment methodology. They view it as "too incomplete, too primitive, and too uncertain" and as not including all important health effects.[157] Critics worry that the government may not act to protect those who live in sparsely populated areas, because few lives are at stake. And they sense that EPA's emphasis on risk assessment is a smoke screen for a general reluctance to regulate, a reluctance that is unfair to those citizens involuntarily exposed to risks from air pollution.

Policy makers using information on risks face many difficult decisions. For example, how might a wide range in credible estimates of risks be taken into account in deciding whether to manage a risk and what management option to select? What if alternative scientific models indicate that the risk of an exposed individual getting cancer from a toxic chemical might be either 1 in 10,000 or 1 in 1,000,000 during his lifetime? How should non-cancer health risks, which may be even less well quantified, be taken into account? To what level should estimated risk be reduced—1 in 10,000 or 1 in 1,000,000? These are but a few of many hard issues.

Consideration of Costs

Some of the most readily implemented or inexpensive measures to reduce airborne risks may already have been employed in addressing the most common air pollutants outdoors. How should the government consider costs when deciding to manage additional airborne risks?

The Occupational Safety and Health Act, the Consumer Product Safety Act, and many provisions of the Clean Air Act provide that costs be taken into account when regulatory decisions are made. For some decisions, the standards set must be economically "feasible"[158] and for others a "reasonable" relationship must exist between the costs and benefits of a regulatory standard.[159]

A major exception to the explicit incorporation of cost considerations into decision making is the Clean Air Act's provision for setting national ambient air quality standards for common pollutants.[160] Section 112 of the Clean Air Act also does not explicitly mention cost as a factor to be taken into account in setting emission standards.[161] EPA, however, attempts to take the feasibility and cost of controls into account when considering regulations on sources' emissions. In doing so, EPA has argued that Section 112 does not prohibit it from considering the costs of controls.[162]

Environmentalists maintain that EPA is on shaky legal ground with that position.[163]* The environmentalists' legal argument is premised on a far more fundamental concern about the unfairness of requiring health to be

---

*Environmentalists have filed a host of lawsuits challenging EPA's position on costs. In the first of these to be decided, a three-judge panel of the D.C. Circuit Court of Appeals held (by a 2-1 vote) that EPA could take the feasibility and cost of controls into account.[164]

traded-off against economic well-being, particularly when individuals are involuntarily exposed to pollution and when trade-offs may not be necessary. The "unfairness" argument has been cogently advanced by Natural Resources Defense Council Attorney David Doniger:

> When the [EPA] Administrator urges the American people to accept a philosophy of deliberately trading off lives and health against the economic costs of pollution controls ("risk management"), he is . . . swimming against the strong tide of public opinion. Section 112 of the Clean Air Act embodies the public's adherence to a fundamental goal that no one should be required to sacrifice his or her life or health on account of air pollution. . . ."[165]

The premium that Americans place on protecting human life, especially from involuntarily incurred risks, is reflected well in Doniger's argument. However, as environmental law scholar Phillip Reed has noted, the position taken by environmentalists in their challenge to EPA's decision making under Section 112 "seems to push the agency to the extreme of shutting down industries to save at most a handful of lives over a period of decades." Reed goes on to add that the environmentalists are not really arguing for zero-emission standards that would shut down industry but simply are pressing EPA to push industry harder than the agency is inclined; unfortunately, the environmentalists do not offer concise legal grounds for saying where the line should be drawn.[166]

Environmentalists are as wary of cost calculations as they are of risk assessments, and understandably so. Cost estimates may not take into account technological innovations that can reduce the costs of compliance with a standard. When OSHA promulgated a standard for controlling cotton dust in 1978, it estimated compliance costs to be $1 billion. But a post-standard analysis in 1982 pegged the costs at $245 million. The availability of newer production equipment, which increased productivity and reduced cotton dust exposures, was responsible for this enormous difference between projected and actual costs.[167]

Difficult questions face the policy maker attempting to take costs into account. Should a formal ceiling be placed on how much money will be spent to prevent a case of cancer? If so, what should that amount be? If calculations suggest that 90 percent of a population highly at risk can be protected for what is considered a reasonable amount of money, but costs rise dramatically to protect the remaining 10 percent, should government protect them all? These can be troublesome issues.

In sum, cost-effectiveness analysis and risk assessment can have valuable applications, yet care must be exercised in their use. They help to order information, identify uncertainties, and clarify the bases for decisions. But tyranny of numbers must be avoided. An appropriately cautious view of risk and cost estimates has been expressed by EPA Administrator Lee Thomas. He told his staff that they should not eliminate "otherwise feasible and sensible options . . . on the basis of any specific 'rules of thumb' that, in turn, are based on estimated risk ranges, population incidence, or cost-per-incidence avoided." [168]

Controllability of Risk

The perceived controllability of risk should be a third major factor influencing the selection of risks to manage and the approaches to use. Government may not always be able to reduce risks, even when it is evident that risks are significant and are not being controlled sufficiently by the private sector. The controllability of a risk may depend on a host of considerations, such as the availability of technology, the ability of government officials to administer risk reduction programs, and public support for government efforts. Errors in judging the controllability of risks can create a gulf between the expectations for and the realities of risk reductions from government programs.

Technology

Government decisions to require or encourage reductions in risks are made easier when technological fixes can be employed. In deciding which risks to control and which control options to select, government decision makers often must ask the following questions:

- Do monitoring technologies exist that permit measurement of risks and assessment of compliance with regulatory requirements?
- Do technologies exist that allow emissions of pollutants to be readily controlled? If they are not presently available, does development of such technologies appear imminent? Can it be speeded by government intervention? What form of government intervention might be most effective?
- Are substitute technologies or products available, or likely to be developed, for use in place of products or technologies that presently produce significant airborne risks? What are the risks from these substitutes compared to those from existing sources?

Government regulatory programs often are biased toward technological fixes, because it is relatively easy to write regulations requiring use of particular technologies, because officials believe they have a good sense of how effective such technologies will be, and because it often is easy for enforcement personnel to determine whether required technological fixes have been made. Even when the technology is available, however, technological fixes may not always be successful in reducing risk. They may not work as well as expected. There may be unanticipated side effects (like the transferring of risks by pollution control devices from air to water and soil), or the human component of technological fixes (for example, operation and maintenance activities that assure that equipment works correctly) may be flawed.

Amenability to Administration

Government perception of a risk's controllability also is influenced heavily by how easily management strategies can be implemented and how successful these strategies are likely to be. Decision makers often must ask questions like the following:

- Is new legislative authority needed, or could existing authority be used?
- Using existing authority, how easy would it be to piggyback new requirements onto existing programs? To what extent would new risk control initiatives undercut existing ones, and would this undercutting either hamper existing control efforts or foster bureaucratic resistance to new ones?
- What administrative resources would be required to develop a given program and monitor compliance? Would there be only a short-term demand for these resources, or would the risk reduction program require continued administration for many years?
- Is the program readily enforceable? Could a high level of voluntary compliance be expected?
- Through what channels would requirements be communicated and reinforced? How great are the chances of program failure because of poor communication, and what actions would be required to minimize these? To what extent can public participation and oversight be built into the program?
- If government does not act, what incentives exist for risk reduction within the private sector? Might private action prove more timely and more effective than government action?

These and similar hard questions constitute, in effect, an "implementation assessment." They must be posed at the time program options are first being explored. The answers can help assess the validity (or falseness) of important assumptions about how effective particular programs are expected to be and what demands they will make on both the public and private sectors.

Public Support

A third important element of controllability of risks is public support. Just as strong public demand can push government to action, strong public resistance to government risk reduction programs may also exist. Tobacco provides a clear example. The adverse health impacts of tobacco are enormous, yet a ban on cigarettes probably would be no more successful than the ban on liquor was 60 years ago. While some restrictions on smoking in public places have been adopted, federal policy has called simply for warning smokers of tobacco's hazards. Individual smokers are free to ignore the warnings, pay higher insurance premiums, and take the chance of dying younger.[169]

Cultural norms such as those precluding a tobacco ban are a substantial barrier to government action. However, proliferating state and local restrictions on smoking in public places[170] and the increasing visibility of corporate efforts to restrict smoking and to encourage abstinence[171] all suggest that the cultural acceptability of smoking is slipping. More far-reaching government action against smoking may become easier if this slippage continues.

Tobacco is such a special case that it would be easy to draw too many generalizations from it. But the reliance on labeling for tobacco reflects to some degree the view that the government should not be the nation's nanny and should not protect citizens from risks they appear to incur voluntarily. Examples of the strength of this belief include successful efforts to repeal state laws requiring motorcyclists to wear helmets[172] and congressional action repealing federal regulations requiring seatbelts to be connected before cars can be driven.[173]

These and other instances of public resentment of government efforts to reduce risk are a reminder that risk assessment, cost-effectiveness, and other analytical approaches that stress logical, well-ordered decision making may not count for much in the political arena. Even if a compelling case initially can be made for the effectiveness and reasonable cost of a program, public resistance may prevent effective implementation or lead to a program's demise.

For tobacco and for many indoor threats (for example, pesticides and other household chemicals), it often is argued that risks are incurred voluntarily. However, research shows that many risks are not incurred as voluntarily as it appears. Individuals may not be aware of some risks; they may tend to discount whatever information they might have about the magnitude of risks; or they may not have the freedom or money to reduce the risks to which they are exposed.[174] Furthermore, although the costs of incurring a risk might at first seem restricted to one voluntary individual, thereby eliminating the rationale for government action to prevent harm to others, tobacco smoking and other voluntary activities can put other people at risk.[175]

In manufacturing environments, the voluntarism argument has an economic dimension—the notion that wages in some industries are higher to compensate workers for the higher risks they incur.[176] But in industry, too, worker awareness and assessment of risk, and real freedom to walk away from a job, may be quite limited.[177]

These caveats about voluntarism and the questionable efficacy of labeling notwithstanding, labeling and other strategies of information disclosure can be expected to play a major role in efforts to reduce risks from airborne toxic substances. They will be employed when the benefits of a substance, or the lack of less toxic substitutes, preclude banning its use; when political pressures preclude more stringent regulatory action; or when a more demanding regulatory requirement would be very difficult to implement.

Conflicts Inherent in Risk-Based Management Strategies

Several tensions are inherent to the process of developing risk-based management strategies. As policy makers and others work to devise new strategies, they should keep these various conflicts in mind.

One conflict is between action and analysis. How much must be known about a risk before action is taken? The Clean Air Act emphasizes expedited, precautionary decision making. The public's fear of accidents and cancer, as well as the dynamics of congressional decision making, predisposes legislators to push for rapid administrative decision making within tight deadlines. Yet much of this chapter implies a need for more detailed study as a prerequisite to effective action. Establishing the proper balance between action and analysis will continue to be a major challenge.

A second conflict is between chemical-by-chemical and category-by-category approaches to pollution control. The latter can be expected to reduce risks from many toxic substances simultaneously. For example, controls on particulate and organic chemical emissions from municipal incinerators will capture a large number of toxic substances included in those two categories.[178] Similarly, broad programs to reduce emissions of volatile organic compounds from auto exhaust and from refueling autos, designed to help communities meet the ambient air quality standard for ozone, will reduce emissions of benzene and ethylene dibromide.[179] Regulatory action against major sources of multiple toxic pollutants may be a far speedier risk reduction strategy than targeting risks on a pollutant-by-pollutant basis. However, some individual chemicals inevitably will not be contained by broad strategies, and programs targeted at individual chemicals will continue to be necessary.

A third conflict is between programs to regulate pollution outdoors and proposals to increase regulation of pollution indoors. Some proponents of the existing strategy for outdoor pollutants fear that the awakened concern for indoor exposures may lead to a weakening of controls outdoors. But there are many reasons for maintaining outdoor pollution regulations—such as continuing nonattainment of outdoor standards that should be met, the need to lower outdoor contributions to pollution in other media, and the desirability of protecting visibility. Moreover, broad control programs for the outdoors can help reduce exposure to some airborne toxic substances that also are a part of the indoor problem.

These tensions are exacerbated by the fact that the federal government currently devotes very limited resources to environmental problems. More funding is needed, but even if it is provided, efforts must be made to use it most effectively; trade-offs must be made among competing risk reduction programs.

THE NEED FOR INTEGRATED APPROACHES

Airborne toxic substances pose such challenges that ample opportunity exists for governments, private-sector organizations, and individuals to aid in the task of risk reduction. This is illustrated by the many opportunities available to reduce risks indoors and to lessen the chance of industrial accidents.

Some risks are incurred in exclusively private environments (for example, owner-occupied private homes) where individuals have considerable control over many of the risks to which they are subject and of which they are aware. In other private environments, individuals may be subject to risks of which they are unaware (for example, purchasers of homes with high levels of radon). Still other risks are incurred in more public spaces, such as office buildings and commercial establishments. Here, individuals may have little or no control over the risks. Clearly, the reduction and avoidance of risks needs to be addressed by individuals, companies, building and plant managers, and different levels of government.

They have available a cornucopia of techniques to reduce risks from airborne toxic substances indoors, including the following:

- Public and private programs to develop or certify inexpensive monitors for measuring indoor air pollution (to inform homeowners of existing problems meriting attention and to reduce consumer fraud).

- State and local government programs to reduce pollution in indoor public spaces (through restrictions on smoking and revisions in building codes).
- State and local programs to ensure fuller disclosure of indoor air problems in real estate transactions (for example, requiring radon tests or disclosure of urea formaldehyde foam insulation), and use of financial incentives and sanctions to encourage disclosure of indoor pollution (for example, public and private dealers in the secondary mortgage market might insist on disclosure of radon, formaldehyde, and other problems before purchasing loans).
- Efforts by utilities to assist the public in reducing risks associated with energy conservation measures (these programs could be piggybacked onto existing energy conservation and equipment installation programs).
- Voluntary technological changes by individual companies and adoption by trade associations of voluntary standards to reduce emissions of pollutants from products used indoors (for example, development of low emission burners by manufacturers of gas stoves).
- Continuing efforts by the building design and operation community (architects, managers, and others) to encourage new approaches to building design and operation that reduce risks posed by indoor pollutants.
- Continuing federal efforts to restrict hazardous products or require prominent disclosure of the indoor air pollution risks they pose.[180]*

Responding to potential risks of accidents in an integrated fashion may require a mix of public- and private-sector initiatives similar to those appropriate for attaining indoor air quality. Emphasis should be on prevention of accidents. Systematic gathering of information on causes of accidents, with the goal of remedying obvious defects in design and procedures, is

---

*Although national ambient air quality standards were adopted for use in combating outdoor air pollution, a system of such standards (including related emission standards, and enforcement by federal, state, and local environmental officials) is not likely for indoor environments. However, federal ambient air quality guidelines that can be the basis either for suggested remedial measures by homeowners or for decisions by realtors, lending agencies, and other parties are a plausible approach. For example, EPA has recently published guidelines for homeowner response to elevated levels of radon in homes, and these guidelines are likely to have implications for other parties concerned about real estate.[181]

crucial. Government and voluntary standards, education and training, substitution of less-toxic materials in manufacturing processes, and sufficient government regulation to protect citizens from industries that lack the will or capability to reduce risks—all have a role to play.

When the environmental decade of the 1970s began, the United States launched itself in a headlong rush to clean up the nation's air and water. It is now evident that airborne toxic substances present a complex problem that requires a more systematic analysis of threats to human health and the environment. In managing these risks, much greater attention will have to be paid to distinguishing significant from insignificant threats. Finally, if the new generation of risks from airborne toxic substances is to be adequately addressed, new forms of creative partnerships will be needed among agencies, among different levels of government, and between the public and private sectors.

FURTHER READING

The most comprehensive assessment of the magnitude of risks from air toxics is "The Air Toxics Problem in the United States: An Analysis of Cancer Risks for Selected Pollutants," prepared by the U.S. Environmental Protection Agency (EPA). This study, informally referred to as "the six-month study," is reproduced in U.S. Congress, House of Representatives, Committee on Energy and Commerce, Subcommittee on Health and the Environment, *Toxic Release Control Act of 1986*, 99th Cong., 1st. sess. (1985).

The *Journal of the Air Pollution Control Association* and papers delivered at the association's annual meetings are a rich source of recent research findings on and analyses of risks from toxic air pollutants. Copies of the papers can obtained for a fee from the association (P.O. Box 2861, Pittsburgh, PA 15230). Good overviews of the major issues can be found in two journal articles—Joseph Cannon, "The Regulation of Toxic Air Pollutants: A Critical Review" (May 1986); and "The Regulation of Toxic Air Pollutants: Critical Review Discussion Papers" (September 1986).

Environmental Science and Technology also publishes numerous related articles. For example, D. Kent Berry summarizes EPA's recent efforts to upgrade its air toxics program in "Air Toxics" (July 1986).

Phillip D. Reed, "The Trial of Hazardous Air Pollution Regulation," *Environmental Law Reporter* (March 1986), offers an excellent summary of the major points of dispute between environmentalists and EPA in the implementation of Section 112 of the Clean Air Act.

On indoor air pollution, Isaac Turiel, *Indoor Air Quality and Human Health* (Stanford, Calif.: Stanford University Press, 1985), provides a good overview for the interested lay reader. A more technical treatment is provided by R.C. Diamond and D.T. Grimsrud, *Manual on Indoor Air Quality* (Palo Alto, Calif.: Electric Power Research Institute, 1984). Two other overview articles are Ken Sexton, "Indoor Air Quality: An Overview of Policy and Regulatory Issues," *Science, Technology, and Human Values* (Winter 1986); and Robert Repetto, "Indoor Air Pollution and Public Policy," *Environment International* (vol. 8, no. 1, 1982). The American Lung Association (1740 Broadway, New York, NY 10019) publishes brief brochures on the topic, and EPA has similar materials such as "A Citizen's Guide to Radon." The Consumer Federation of America publishes a newsletter, *Indoor Air News*, which provides brief summaries of upcoming conferences and recent developments (1424 16th Street NW, Washington, DC 20336), and Action on Smoking and Health serves as a clearinghouse for information on efforts to reduce smoking (2013 H Street NW, Washington, DC 20006).

The Chemical Manufacturers Association (2501 M Street NW, Washington, DC 20037) is perhaps the best source of information on industrial relases. It can provide detailed information on its Community Awareness and Emergency Response program and National Chemical Response and information Center.

The Conservation Foundation has published an overview of the issues involved in risk management in its chapter "Risk Assessment and Risk Control," in *State of the Environment: An Assessment at Mid-Decade* (1984). This report also is available as a separate publication.

REFERENCES

Text

1. Stephen Budiansky, "Indoor Air Pollution," *Environmental Science and Technology* 14 (1980):1,023.

2. Jonathan Rauch, "Politics of Budget Reduction Remains Deadlocked Despite Balanced Budget Act," *National Journal*, January 4, 1986, pp. 15-21; and Jonathan Rauch, "Pete Domenici Stands at Center of Storm as Budget Deficit Crisis Comes to Head," *National Journal*, February 1, 1986, pp. 263-266.

3. The Conservation Foundation, *State of the Environment: An Assessment at Mid-Decade* (Washington, D.C.: The Conservation Foundation, 1984), p. 446.

4. On corporate environmental management, see Frank B. Friedman, "Managing and Resolving Corporate Environmental Issues," *The Environmental Forum* 3, no. 10 (1985):28-32.

5. For further discussion, see Wayne R. Ott, "Total Human Exposure: An Emerging Science Focuses on Humans as Receptors of Environmental Pollution," *Environmental Science and Technology* 19 (1985):880-86.

6. U.S. General Accounting Office, *Probabilistic Risk Assessment: An Emerging Aid to Nuclear Power Plant Safety Regulation*, Report to the Chairman, U.S. Congress, House Committee on Energy and Commerce, Subcommittee on Energy Conservation and Power (Gaithersburg, Md.: U.S. General Accounting Office, June 1985).

7. The Conservation Foundation, *State of the Environment: An Assessment at Mid-Decade*, p. 274. Risk assessment and management issues are explored more fully in this edition.

8. Neil Orloff, "Climbing the Pollution Learning Curve," *Wall Street Journal*, November 5, 1985.

9. John D. Spengler and Ken Sexton, "Indoor Air Pollution: A Public Health Perspective," *Science*, July 1, 1983, p. 9.

10. Ken Sexton, "Indoor Air Quality: An Overview of Policy and Regulatory Issues", *Science, Technology, and Human Values* 11, no. 1 (1986):53-67.

11. U.S. Environmental Protection Agency, "Briefing on TEAM Study for the Assistant Administrator for Air and Radiation, October 11, 1984"; and Lance A. Wallace, "Personal Exposures, Indoor and Outdoor Air Concentrations, and Exhaled Breath Concentrations of Selected Volatile Organic Compounds Measured for 600 Residents of New Jersey, North Dakota, North Carolina and California," *Toxicological and Environmental Chemistry* (forthcoming).

12. Lance A. Wallace, E.D. Pellizzari, and S.M. Gordon, "Organic Chemicals in Indoor Air: A Review of Human Exposure Studies and Indoor Air Quality Studies," in R.B. Gammage, *Indoor Air and Human Health*, Proceedings of the Seventh Life Sciences Symposium, Knoxville, Tennessee, October 29-31, 1984 (Chelsea, Mich.: Lewis Publ., 1985), p. 364.

13. U.S. Environmental Protection Agency, *Briefing on TEAM Study*; Wallace, "Personal Exposures, Indoor and Outdoor Air Concentrations, and Exhaled Breath Concentrations"; and Wallace, Pellizzari, and Gordon, "Organic Chemicals in Indoor Air," p. 364.

14. Lance A. Wallace, "Estimating Risk from Measured Exposures to Six Suspected Carcinogens in Personal Air and Drinking Water in 600 U.S. Residents" (Paper delivered at the 79th Annual Meeting of the Air Pollution Control Association, Minneapolis, Minnesota, June 22-27, 1986), pp. 2, 4, 20; and Wallace, "Personal Exposures, Indoor and Outdoor Air Concentrations, and Exhaled Breath Concentrations", p. 21.

15. Lance A. Wallace et al., "The Total Exposure Assessment Methodology (TEAM) Study: Direct Measurement of Personal Exposures through Air and Water for 600 Residents of Several U.S. Cities," in Yoram Cohen, ed., *Pollutants in a Multimedia Environment* (New York: Plenum Press, 1986), pp. 289-316; and Lance A. Wallace, "Cancer Risks from Organic Chemicals in the Home," APCA Specialty Conference in Risk Management, Air Pollution Control Association, April 8-10, 1986, p. 2.

16. U.S. Environmental Protection Agency, Office of Air and Radiation, Office of Policy, Planning and Evaluation, "The Air Toxics Problem in the United States: An Analysis of Cancer Risks for Selected Pollutants," in U.S. Congress, House Committee on Energy and Commerce, *Toxic Release Control Act of 1985: Hearings on H.R. 2576*, 99th Congress, 1st sess., June 11 and 19, 1985, p. 428; National Research Council, Board on Environmental Studies and Toxicology, Committee on Passive Smoking, *Environmental Tobacco Smoke*

(Washington, D.C.: National Academy Press, 1986), pp. 2, 37; "Cracking Down on Wood-Stove Pollution," *Consumer Reports*, October 1985, p. 595; and Isaac Turiel, *Indoor Air Quality and Human Health* (Stanford, Calif.: Stanford University Press, 1985), p. 71.

17. National Research Council, *Environmental Tobacco Smoke*, p. 11.

18. Ibid., Appendix D, p. 296.

19. Ibid., p. 9.

20. Turiel, *Indoor Air Quality and Human Health*, pp. 34, 37.

21. "Radioactive Gas in Soil Raises Concern in Three State Area," *New York Times*, May 19, 1985; and U.S. Congress, House Committee on Science and Technology, Subcommittee on Natural Resources, Agricultural Research and Development, *Hearing on Radon and Air Pollution*, 99th Cong., 2d sess., 1986, p. 87.

22. U.S. Comptroller General, *Air Pollution Hazard of Indoor Radon Could Pose a National Health Problem*, Report to the Pennsylvania Congressional Delegation, U.S. House of Representatives (Washington, D.C.: U.S. General Accounting Office, June 1986), p. 24.

23. U.S. Environmental Protection Agency, Office of Air and Radiation, and U.S. Department of Health and Human Services, Center for Disease Control, *A Citizen's Guide to Radon: What Is It and What to Do about It* (Washington, D.C.: U.S. Environmental Protection Agency, August 1986), p. 9.

24. Ibid.; and U.S. Comptroller General, *Air Pollution Hazard of Indoor Radon*, p. 24.

25. Turiel, *Indoor Air Quality and Human Health*, p. 78; and "Concern over Radon in Homes Triggers Plan for National Survey," *Chemical and Engineering News*, April 28, 1986, pp. 19-20.

26. "Concern over Radon in Homes Triggers Plan for National Survey," pp. 19-20.

27. U.S. Environmental Protection Agency and U.S. Department of Health and Human Services, *A Citizen's Guide to Radon*, p. 9.

28. 50 Fed. Reg. 15387 (1985). The "potential risk" to a person living near multiple mine vents was characterized by EPA as being 1 in 10 (10 percent).

29. 51 Fed. Reg. 4801 (1986); "Cracking Down on Wood-Stove Pollution," *Consumer Reports*, October 1985, p. 595; and J. A. Cannon, "Air Quality Effects of Residential Wood Combustion," *Journal of the Air Pollution Control Association* 34 (1984):896.

30. 51 Fed. Reg. 4801 (1986).

31. Ibid.; and 49 Fed. Reg. 31680 (1984).

32. "Cracking Down on Wood-Stove Pollution," p. 595.

33. Ibid.; and Cannon, "Air Quality Effects of Residential Wood Combustion," p. 896.

34. "Cracking Down on Wood-Stove Pollution," p. 595; and Cannon, "Air Quality Effects of Residential Wood Combustion," p.896.

35. Wallace, "Estimating Risk from Measured Exposures to Six Suspected Carcinogens," pp. 2, 4, 20; Wallace, "Cancer Risks from Organic Chemicals in the Home," p. 2; Turiel, *Indoor Air Quality and Human Health* pp. 16, 19, 21, 71; and Robert K. McLellan, "The Health Hazards of Office Work," *Toxic Substances Journal* 5 (1983-84):168, 170.

36. McLellan, "The Health Hazards of Office Work," pp. 168, 170; and Turiel, *Indoor Air Quality and Human Health*, p. 21.

37. Sandia National Laboratories, "Indoor Air Quality Handbook for Designers, Builders, and Users of Energy Efficient Residences," in Kelly Collins, ed., *Air Pollution: The Architects' Response*, a symposium, San Francisco, November 9-10, 1984 (Sacramento, Calif.: California Council, The American Institute of Architects, 1985), pp. 5-1 to 5-25.

38. George Rand, "Caution: The Office Environment May Be Hazardous to Your Health—The Need for an Ecological Approach to its Design," *American Institute of Architects Journal*, October 1979, p. 38; McLellan, "The Health Hazards of Office Work," p. 71; and Jan A. J. Stolwijk, "The Tight Building Syndrome," *Toxic Substances Journal* 5 (1983-84):155.

39. "Vehicle Riders Exposed to More Toxic Air, Indoor Models Need Work, Research Finds," *Air/Water Pollution Report*, September 15, 1986, p. 356.

40. National Research Council, Commission on Life Sciences and Commission on Physical Sciences, Mathematics, and Resources, Committee on Airliner Cabin Air Quality, *The Airliner Cabin Environment: Air Quality and Safety* (Washington, D.C: National Academy Press, 1986), as summarized in Pepper Leeper, "Cleaning up the Air in Commercial Airliners," *National Research Council News Report* 36, no. 8 (1986):4-10.

41. The most obvious distinction is the separation of responsibilities between OSHA and other agencies.

42. Laura Punnett, "Airborne Contaminants in the Workplace," in Mary Gibson, ed., *To Breathe Freely: Risk, Consent, and Air* (Totowa, N.J.: Rowman and Allanheld, 1985), pp. 39-41.

43. Ibid., pp. 40-41.

44. Ibid., p. 39.

45. U.S. Office of Technology Assessment, *Preventing Illness and Injury in the Workplace* (Washington, D.C.: U.S. Government Printing Office, 1985), p. 37.

46. Ibid.

47. Ibid., p. 43.

48. For a lengthy list of occupational cancer hazards, see Ibid., p. 43.

49. Ibid., p. 48; and U.S. Office of Technology Assessment, *Reproductive Health Hazards in the Workplace* (Washington, D.C.: U.S. Government Printing Office, 1985), p. 3.

50. U.S. Department of Health and Human Services, Public Health Service, *The Health Consequences of Smoking, Cancer and Chronic Lung Disease in the Workplace: A Report of the Surgeon General* (Rockville, Md.: U.S. Department of Human Services, 1985), pp. 216-17.

51. Ibid., p. 16.

52. U.S. Environmental Protection Agency, "The Air Toxics Problem in the United States," p. 404.

53. Ibid.

54. Ibid.

55. Ibid.

56. Ibid., pp. 407, 422, 428; and "Cracking Down on Wood-Stove Pollution," p. 595.

57. U.S. Environmental Protection Agency, "The Air Toxics Problem in the United States," pp. 490-491.

58. Ibid., pp. 404-405.

59. Ibid., p. 428; and U.S. Environmental Protection Agency, "Air Toxics Facts," circa May 1985, p. 2.

60. Henry A. Waxman, "Toxic Chemicals in Our Air Supply: The Need for Action to Protect the Public Health," *Journal of the Air Pollution Control Association* 35 (1985):1,021.

61. Ibid; and Stuart Diamond, "Problems of Toxic Emissions: Officials Find Lack of Data a Hindrance," *New York Times*, May 20, 1985.

62. Waxman, "Toxic Chemicals in our Air Supply," p. 1,022.

63. Ibid.

64. Michael Greenberg, "Cancer Atlases: Uses and Limitations," *The Environmentalist* 35 (1985):189-90; and Michael Greenberg, "Does New Jersey Cause Cancer: It's How You Live, Not Where, That Counts," *The Sciences* 26, no. 1 (1986):43.

65. The Conservation Foundation, *State of the Environment 1982* (Washington, D.C.: The Conservation Foundation, 1982), p. 64; and The Conservation Foundation, *State of the Environment: An Assessment at Mid-Decade*, p. 340.

66. Previous *State of the Environment* reports have described such transfers.

67. Wil Lepkowski, "Bhopal," *Chemical and Engineering News*, December 2, 1985, p. 18; and B. Bowonder, Jeanne X. Kasperson, and Roger E. Kasperson, "Avoiding Future Bhopals," *Environment* 27, (1985):10.

68. Waxman, "Toxic Chemicals in our Air Supply," p. 1021; and Ward Worthy, "U.S. Chemical Industry Moving to Assure No More Bhopals," *Chemical and Engineering News*, January 6, 1985, pp. 9-16.

69. The August 1985 accident at Institute occurred in a part of the plant not examined by OSHA in its post-Bhopal inspection of the facility. U.S. Congress, House Committee on Education and Labor, Subcommittee on Health and Safety, *OSHA Oversight: Workers Health and Safety at Union Carbide, Institute, WV, Facility*, 99th Cong., 1st sess., 1986, p. 33; and Worthy, "U.S. Chemical Industry Moving to Assure No More Bhopals," p. 9.

70. "Mexico's Previous Disaster," *Newsweek*, November 11, 1985, p. 14.

71. "Two Killed in Ohio in Chemical Blast," *New York Times*, January 18, 1986.

72. "Toxic Chemical Spill at Oklahoma Plant Kills One, Injures 40 Others, NRC Says," *Environmental Reporter—Current Developments*, January 10, 1986, p. 1,711.

73. Industrial Economics, Inc., Management Technology and Data Systems, Inc., and P.E.I. Associates, Inc., "Acute Hazardous Events Data Base," executive summary, prepared for U.S. Environmental Protection Agency, Office of Toxic Substances, Economics and Technology Division (Springfield, Va.: National Technical Information Service, December 1985), p. 2.

74. Ibid.; and "Statistics on Toxic Chemical Accidents Compiled," *Chemical and Engineering News*, October 14, 1985, p. 7.

75. Industrial Economics, Inc., et al., "Acute Hazardous Events Data Base," exhibit N.

76. 40 C.F.R. 50 (1984)

77. 42 U.S.C.A. §7408 (1983)

78. Phillip D. Reed, "The Trial of Hazardous Air Pollution Regulation," *Environmental Law Reporter* 16 (1986):10,067; and 42 U.S.C.A. §7542 (1983)

79. Gregory Westone, ed., *Air and Water Pollution Control Law: 1980* (Washington, D.C.: Environmental Law Institute, 1980), p. 171.

80. Reed, "The Trial of Hazardous Air Pollution Regulation," p. 10068.

81. "The Regulation of Toxic Air Pollutants: Critical Review Discussion Papers," *Journal of the Air Pollution Control Association* 36 (1986):990; and 42 U.S.C.A. §7422 (1983).

82. "The Regulation of Toxic Air Pollutants," p. 990.

83. Ibid.

84. U.S. Environmental Protection Agency, "The Air Toxics Problem in the United States," p. 405.

85. U.S. Environmental Protection Agency, *A Strategy to Reduce Risks to Public Health From Air Toxics* (Washington, D.C.: U.S. Environmental Protection Agency, June 1985), p. 7.

86. U.S. Environmental Protection Agency, Office of Air and Radiation, Office of Air Quality Planning and Standards and Office of Mobile Sources, *Evaluation of Air Pollution Regulatory Strategies for Gasoline Marketing Industry*, executive summary (Washington, D.C.: U.S. Environmental Protection Agency, July 1984), pp. 1-18.

87. 42 Fed. Reg. 29332 (1977).

88. U.S. Environmental Protection Agency, *A Strategy to Reduce Risks to Public Health from Air Toxics*, p. 1.

89. Ibid., pp. 1-2.

90. *Environment Reporter—Current Developments*, December 20, 1985, pp. 1,638-47.

91. U.S. Environmental Protection Agency, *A Strategy to Reduce Risks to Public Health from Air Toxics*, pp. 30-35.

92. Ibid., pp. 8-9.

93. U.S. Comptroller General, *EPA's Efforts to Identify and Control Harmful Chemicals in Use* (Washington, D.C.: U.S. General Accounting Office, June 1984); and D. Ken Berry, "Air Toxics: What Is the Problem and How Do We Deal with It?", *Environmental Science and Technology* 20 (1986):649.

94. U.S. Congress, *Toxic Release Control Act of 1985*, pp. 302-303.

95. "EPA Revised Air Toxics Policy Results in Increased Activity bbt Problems Remain with Funding, States, Environmentalist Challenges," *Environmental Reporter—Current Developments*, October 11, 1985, p. 1,037.

96. U.S. Office of Technology Assessment, *Preventing Illness and Injury in the Workplace*, pp. 219, 223, 226.

97. Ibid., p. 228.

98. Ibid.

99. Ibid

100. Ibid., pp. 206-207, 227.

101. Ibid., pp. 206, 259.

102. Ibid., p. 227.

103. Ibid., p. 260.

104. Laurence S. Kirsch, "Behind Closed Doors: Indoor Air Pollution and Government Policy," *The Harvard Environmental Law Review* 6 (1982):374-82.

105. 15 U.S.C.A. §§1261-1276 (1982).

106. 51 Fed. Reg. 29778 (1986).

107. Kirsch, "Behind Closed Doors," pp. 380-82, 140; and Turiel, *Indoor Air Quality and Human Health*, p. 24.

108. See, for example, "Field Study Battle Delays CIAQ Reply to Boland on Indoor Air Research," *Inside EPA Weekly Report*, June 13, 1986; "EPA to Revamp Indoor Air Multi-pollutant Field Study Following CIAQ Protest," *Inside EPA Weekly Report*, December 6, 1985, p. 6; "CIAQ, Sour on National Indoor Air Survey, Searches for New Priorities," *Inside EPA Weekly Report*, January 3, 1986, p. 5; Edward P. Boland, chairman, U.S. Congress, House Subcommittee on HUD-Independent Agencies, letter to Lee M. Thomas, administrator, U.S. Environmental Protection Agency, January 16, 1986; and "House Panel

Demands Interagency Group Submit Indoor Air Plan within 60 Days," *Inside EPA Weekly Report*, February 7, 1986, p. 3.

109. U.S. Environmental Protection Agency, Science Advisory Board, Office of the Administrator, *Report of the Scientific Advisory Committee: Review of U.S. Consumer Product Safety Commission's Health Effects and Exposure Assessment Documents on Nitrogen Dioxide* (Washington, D.C.: U.S. Environmental Protection Agency, May 1986).

110. 51 Fed. Reg. 3753 (1986).

111. 15 U.S.C.A. §2603(f) (1982).

112. 50 Fed. Reg. 42037 (1985); reprinted in *Environment Reporter—Current Developments*, October 25, 1985, p. 1,109-19.

113. Ibid., pp. 1,109, 1,114-15.

114. U.S. Comptroller General, *EPA's Efforts to Identify and Control Harmful Chemicals in Use*, pp. 15-16; and 50 Fed. Reg. 42037 (1985).

115. 50 Fed. Reg. 27676 (1985).

116. U.S. Congress, House Committee on Interstate and Foreign Commerce, *Legislative History of the Toxic Substances Control Act*, committee reprint prepared by the Library of Congress, 95th Congress, 1st sess., 1976, p. 84.

117. 50 Fed. Reg. 27674 (1985); and 51 Fed. Reg. 24452 (1986).

118. 50 Fed. Reg. 41393 (1985); and 51 Fed. Reg. 35003 (1986).

119. 50 Fed. Reg. 41466 (1985).

120. 51 Fed. Reg. 3738 (1986).

121. U.S. Congress, House Committee on Energy and Commerce, Subcommittee on Oversight and Investigations, *EPA Asbestos Regulations: Report on a Case Study on OMB Interference in Agency Rulemaking*, 99th Congress, 1st sess., pp. 4, 44-46; and 51 Fed. Reg. 3753 (1986).

122. 51 Fed. Reg. 3738 (1986).

123. Title IV of the Superfund Amendments and Reauthorization Act of 1986, *Congressional Record*, October 3, 1986, p. 9,076.

124. *Environmental Reporter—Current Developments*, October 24, 1986, pp. 1,001-2.

125. The Conservation Foundation, *State of the Environment: An Assessment at Mid-Decade*, p. 421.

126. The Conservation Foundation, *State of the Environment: An Assessment at Mid-Decade*, p. 448; and "Right to Know: A Regulatory Update on Providing Chemical Hazard Information" (Washington, D.C.: Bureau of National Affairs, 1985), pp. 1-3.

127. The Conservation Foundation, *State of the Environment: An Assessment at Mid-Decade*, p. 448.

128. State and Territorial Air Pollution Program Administrators and the Association of Local Air Pollution Control Officials (STAPPA/ALAPCO), *Toxic Air Pollutants: State and Local Regulatory Strategies*, a survey (Washington, D.C: STAPPA/ALAPCO, January 1984), p. 117.

129. J. Held and R. Harkop, "Present Applications of the TLV Approach to Setting State Guidelines and Standards: Consistencies and Problems" (Paper delivered at the 79th Annual Meeting of the Air Pollution Control Association, Minneapolis, Minnesota, June 22-27, 1986), p. 3; Steve P. Hui, John B. Batchelder, Jr., and Stanley V. Dawson, "The Merits of Quantitative Risk Assessment vs. TLV Approaches to Non-Criteria Pollutant Standards" (Paper delivered at the 79th Annual Meeting of the Air Pollution Control Association, Minneapolis, Minnesota, June 22-27, 1986); Radian Corporation, *National Air Toxics*

Information Clearinghouse: NATICH Data Base Report on State and Local Agency Air Toxic Activities, final report, vol. 1, prepared for U.S. Environmental Protection Agency, Office of Air Quality Planning and Standards, Strategies and Air Standard Division (Research Triangle Park, N.C.: U.S. Environmental Protection Agency, 1986), pp. 29-166, 173-84; and State and Territorial Air Pollution Program Administrators and the Association of Local Air Pollution Control Officials, *Toxic Air Pollutants*, p. 25.

130. For a sampling of past state activities, see Robert S. Bernstein et al., ''State Monitoring of Non-Occupational Exposure to Indoor Air Pollution,'' Proceedings of the 3rd International Conference on Indoor Air Quality and Climate (Stockholm: Swedish Council for Building Research, 1984), p. 239.

131. Ken Sexton and Jerome J. Wesolowski, ''Safeguarding Indoor Air Quality: California Lawmakers and Health Experts Have a Program to Address the Problem,'' *Envionmental Science and Technology* 19 (1985):305.

132. U.S. Office of Technology Assessment, *Transportation of Hazardous Materials* (Washington, D.C.: U.S. Government Printing Office, July 1986), pp. 220-21, 230-32; and *Illinois Legislative Service*, 1985 1st special sess., Act 84-852 (St. Paul, Minn.: West), p. 359.

133. Joseph F. Sullivan, ''Jersey Acts to Curb Toxic Accidents,'' *New York Times*, January 1, 1986; copies of the law are available from New Jersey's Department of Environment Protection.

134. Radian Corporation, *National Air Toxics Information Clearinghouse*, vol. 1.

135. American Society for Testing and Materials, Committee D-22 on Sampling and Analysis of Atmospheres, ''Minutes of the Organizational Meeting on Indoor Air, March 12-13, 1985, Philadelphia, Pa.'' (Philadelphia: American Society for Testing and Materials, n.d.), pp. 1, 2, 44; and American Society for Testing and Materials, ''Workshop of Interpretation and Use of Result from Indoor Air Monitoring Surveys'' (Philadelphia: American Society for Testing and Materials, n.d.).

136. American Society for Testing and Materials, ''Questions Most Frequently Asked About ASTM'', a brochure (Philadelphia, Pa.: American Society for Testing and Materials, undated).

137. American Society of Heating, Refrigerating and Air-Conditioning Engineers, ''Institutional Notes,'' *Journal of the Air Pollution Control Association* 35 (1985):274.

138. U.S. Office of Technology Assessment, *Preventing Illness and Injury in the Workplace*, pp. 260-61.

139. Worthy, ''U.S. Chemical Industry Moving to Assure No More Bhopals,'' p. 12.

140. Chemical Manufacturers Association, ''Air Toxics Control Policy of Chemical Manufacturers Association (CMA),'' a CMA Board of Director's Report (Washington, D.C.: Chemical Manufacturers Association, January 28, 1986), pp. 2-3.

141. Ibid., p. 2; and Worthy, ''U.S. Chemical Industry Moving to Assure No More Bhopals,'' p. 11.

142. Chemical Manufacturers Association, ''Air Toxics Control Policy,'' p. 2.

143. Worthy, ''U.S. Chemical Industry Moving to Assure No More Bhopals,'' pp. 14-15.

144. Monsanto Company, ''One Year Later: Report of the Monsanto Product and Plant Safety Task Force'' (St. Louis, Mo.: Monsanto Company, December 1985), pp. 2, 3, 7.

145. John Palmisano, ''The Evolution of Environmental Auditing: Implications for Firms and for Regulators'' (Paper delivered at the 76th Annual Meeting of the Air Pollution Control Association, Atlanta, Georgia, June 1983); Richard A. Penna et al., ''Environmental

Auditing. The Policy and the Prospects," *The Environmental Forum* 2, no. 1 (1983):16-20; William Hall, "Environmental Audits—A Corporate Response to Bhopal," *The Environmental Forum* 4, no. 4 (1985):36-41; Mark B. Friedman, "Managing and Resolving Corporate Environmental Issues," *The Environmental Forum* 3, no. 1 (1985):28-32; and Arthur D. Little, Inc., "Annotated Bibliography on Environmental Management," prepared for U.S. Environmental Protection Agency, Office of Policy, Planning and Evaluation, Office of Standards and Regulations, Regulatory Reform Staff (Washington, D.C.: U.S. Environmental Protetion Agency, November 1985).

146. Ibid.

147. The Conservation Foundation, *State of the Environment: An Assessment at Mid-Decade* (Washington, D.C.: The Conservation Foundation, 1984), pp. 332-39; National Research Council, *Epidemiology and Air Pollution* (Washington, D.C.: National Academy Press, 1985), p. 22; and U.S. Environmental Protection Agency, Office of Management Systems and Evaluation, *Environmental Progress and Challenges: An EPA Perspective* (Washington, D.C.: U.S. Environmental Protection Agency, June 1984), p. 12.

148. The Conservation Foundation, *State of the Environment: An Assessment at Mid-Decade*, pp. 265-66.

149. 49 Fed. Reg. 23558 (1984).

150. "EPA Background Paper Outlining Risk Assessment Rationale, Regulatory Plan for Controlling Benzene under Clean Air Act," *Environment Reporter—Current Developments*, December 23, 1983, pp. 1,484-87.

151. 49 Fed. Reg. 23528 (1984).

152. 49 Fed. Reg. 23522-25 (1984).

153. 50 Fed. Reg. 42002 (1985).

154. 50 Fed. Reg. 39627 (1985).

155. 50 Fed. Reg. 32632 (1985).

156. See, for example, *Environmental Defense Fund* v. *Thomas* (D.C. Circuit, No. 84-1524 et al.); *Natural Resources Defense Council, Inc.* v. *Thomas* (D.C. Circuit, No. 84-1387 et al.

157. Rochelle L. Stanfield, "Air Toxics Debate Clouded by Mistrust, Philosophical Dispute over Remedies," *National Journal*, June 29, 1985, p. 1,518.

158. 29 U.S.C.A. 655(b)(5) (1985).

159. 15 U.S.C.A. 2058(f)(3)(E) (1982); and 42 U.S.C. §7411 (1983)

160. 42 U.S.C. §7409. (1983)

161. 42 U.S.C. §7412. (1983)

162. National Commission on Air Quality, *To Breathe Clean Air* (Washington, D.C.: U.S. Government Printing Office, March 1981), pp. 76-77; and Reed, "The Trial of Hazardous Air Pollution Regulation," p. 10,068. For EPA's description of how it takes risks and costs into account, see the benzene proposed rule-making notice, 49 Fed. Reg. 23522 (1984). See also 51 Fed. Reg. 27598, 27966-27968 (1986).

163. Reed, "The Trial of Hazardous Air Pollution Regulation," p. 10068.

164. *Natural Resources Defense Council, Inc.* v. *U.S. Environmental Protection Agency*, 25 ERC 1105-1129 (CA DC Circ., 11-4-86).

165. "The Gospel of Risk Management: Should We Be Converted?' *Environmental Law Reporter* 14 (1984):10,222.

166. Reed, "The Trial of Hazardous Air Pollution Regulation," p. 10,072.

167. U.S. Office of Technology Assessment, *Preventing Illness and Injury in the Workplace*, p. 89.

168. "Thomas: High Cost-Per-Life-Saved Can't Be Sole Basis for Shunning Rule Option," *Inside EPA Weekly Report*, October 11, 1985, pp. 1, 9.

169. John Urquhart and Klaus Heilman, *Risk Watch: The Odds of Life* (New York: Facts on File Publications, 1984), pp. 85-90.

170. "Rhode Island's New No-Smoking Law Requires Employers to Set Policy," *Air/Water Pollution Report*, November 3, 1986, p. 426.

171. "Businesses Increasingly Adopt Limits on Smoking: Companies Set Up Separate Work Areas Despite Organized Opposition," *Washington Post*, June 18, 1986.

172. John D. Graham, "Automobile Crash Protection: Institutional Responses to Self-Hazardous Behavior," in Susan G. Hadden, ed., *Risk Analysis, Institutions and Public Policy* (Port Washington, N.Y.: Associated Faculty Press, 1983), p. 50.

173. John D. Graham and Patricia Gorham, "NHTSA and Passive Restraints: A Case of Arbitrary and Capricious Deregulation," *Administrative Law Review*, 35 (1983):193-252.

174. Susan G. Hadden, *Read the Label Reducing Risk by Providing Information* (Boulder, Colo.: Westview Press, 1986), pp. 218-19, 226.

175. U.S. General Accounting Office, *Probabilistic Risk Assessment*.

176. W. Kip Viscusi, "Market Incentives for Safety. Federal Regulation Should Complement, not Contradict, the Market Forces Working to Promote Safety," *Harvard Business Review* 63, no. 4 (1985):133-38.

177. Patrick Derr et al., "The Double Standard," *Environment* 23, no. 7 (1981):6-32; "Chemical Hazards at Work: Whose Business?' *The Harvard Environmental Law Review* 9 (1985):351; and Dorothy Nelkin, "Workers at Risk," *Science*, October 14, 1983, p. 125.

178. Natural Resources Defense Council, *Petition to the United States Environmental Protection Agency for the Regulation of Emissions from Municipal Solid Waste Incinration* (New York: Natural Resources Defense Council, August 5, 1986).

179. U.S. Environmental Protection Agency, Office of Air and Radiation, Office of Air Quality Planning and Standards and Office of Mobile Sources, *Evaluation of Air Pollution Regulatory Strategies for Gasoline Marketing Industry*, executive summary (Washington,D.C.: U.S. Environmental Protection Agency, July 1984).

180. Some of these measures are listed in Spengler and Sexton, "Indoor Air Pollution," pp. 9-17. See also Sexton, "Indoor Air Quality," pp. 53-67; U.S. Department of Energy, Bonneville Power Administration, *Environment and Power: Home Weatherization and Indoor Air Pollutants* (Portland, Oreg.: Bonneville Power Administration, November 1984); U.S. Department of Energy, Bonneville Power Administration, *Issue Background: Energy Efficient New Homes and Indoor Pollutants* (Portland, Oreg.: Bonneville Power Administration, July 1985); Janet Raloff, "Cleaner Cooking with Gas: Environmentalists May Have Prompted a Renaissance in Kitchen-Range Designs," *Science*, January 14, 1984, pp. 28-31; and American Institute of Architects and American Institute of Architects, California Council, *Indoor Pollution: The Architects' Response*, a symposium, San Francisco, November 9-10, 1984 (Sacramento, Calif.: American Institute of Architects, California Council, 1985).

181. U.S. Environmental Protection Agency, Office of Public Affairs, *Radon Reduction Methods: A Homeowner's Guide* (Washington, D.C.: U.S. Environmental Protection Agency, August 1986); American Society for Testing and Materials, "Minutes of the Organizational meeting on Indoor Air," pp.1, 2, 44; and American Society for Testing and Materials, "Workshop of Interpretation and Use of Results from Indoor Air Monitoring Surveys."

Box

1. This box is based on EPA's summary of the new legislation, reprinted in *Environmental Reporter—Current Developments*, October 24, 1986, pp. 1001-2.

Figures

8.1. Stephen Budiansky, "Indoor Air Pollution," *Environmental Science and Technology* 14 (1980):1,024.

8.2. E. D. Pellizzari et al., *The Total Exposure Assessment Methodology (TEAM) Study: Bayonne and Elyzabeth, New Jersey, Devils Lake, North Dakota, and Greenberg, North Carolina*, final report (Washington, D.C.: U.S. Environmental Protection Agency, 1987), vol. 2.

8.3. U.S. Office of Technology Assessment, *Reproductive Health Hazards in the Workplace* (Washington, D.C.: U.S. Government Printing Office, 1985), p. 43.

8.4. U.S. Department of Health and Human Services, Public Health Service, *The Health Consequences of Smoking, Cancer and Chronic Lung Disease in the Workplace: A Report of the Surgeon General* (Rockville, Md.: U.S. Department of Human Services, 1985), p. 217.

8.5. U.S. Office of Technology Assessment, *Transportation of Hazardous Materials: State and Local Activities* (Washington, D.C.: U.S. Government Printing Office, 1986), p. 42.

8.6. Ibid., p. 60.

Chapter 9

Protection of Biological Diversity: The Challenges of a Broadening Perspective

The long battle to save the California condor exemplifies some of the frustrations and policy dilemmas that society faces in attempting to protect the earth's biological resources. By September 1985, as far as anyone knew, only 6 California condors remained in the wild. Another 21 were in captivity. During the previous winter, 6 wild birds had disappeared, reducing the world's total population by 18 percent.[1] In the view of some scientists, this population was already below the minimum size needed for long-term survival; even if the current population were to grow, the descendants might well be afflicted with genetic problems.

Many causes have contributed to the California condor's plight. Humans have killed the birds for sport or as nuisances that were thought to attack farm animals. (This killing of condors had persisted after the hunting of nongame birds was banned in California in 1905 and even after the condor was given special protection in a 1953 law.) Human population growth and agricultural and other economic development in south-central California have reduced the condor's habitat. Finally, and perhaps most important in recent years, the condor has ingested deadly chemicals—including lead shot, predator-control poisons, and insecticides.[2]

What could government do to help save the California condor? A number of options were considered in the early 1980s, but each posed problems—and none guaranteed success. Some of these options focused on the bird's habitat. Lands could be purchased to set aside remaining portions of the natural habitat. Controls could be placed on unreserved lands to prevent threatening development. Efforts could be made to protect condors from chemical contamination by restricting the use of pesticides and lead shot in the area where they lived.

Beyond habitat protection, the remaining population could be more actively managed. Food could be provided that was free from contamination. The birds could be closely monitored. Most aggressively and controversially, the remaining birds could be captured and held—at least until their numbers increased and their habitat could be secured—to ensure protection from the many threats that already had depleted their ranks.

None of these proposals would be sufficient in and of itself. It was too late to preserve all the habitat the condor naturally depended on because much of it already had been developed for other purposes. The cost of acquiring such land and returning it to its natural state would have been prohibitive. Protecting habitat that could not be acquired would have been slow and uncertain. Providing uncontaminated carrion would have been easy but would have solved only a small part of the problem. Capturing the birds might well have offered the best protection to those still alive, but there would have been no guarantee that they would breed in captivity. In addition to problems of efficiency and cost, proposals to hold the remaining birds in captivity might have raised ethical questions. In spite of these problems, the U.S. Fish and Wildlife Service, in conjunction with the California Department of Fish and Game and the National Audubon Society, initiated a condor protection program incorporating all of the elements mentioned above.[3]

In January 1987, several thousand acres of condor habitat were purchased by the federal government to comprise a major portion of the Bitter Creek National Wildlife Refuge. By then, however, the condor had suffered continuing setbacks. In 1986, one of the birds apparently had died from lead poisoning caused by its eating carrion containing lead shot, and one of the two eggs laid that year had not hatched. By the summer of 1986, only three birds—and more important, no breeding pairs—were known to be left in the wild. In April 1987, the last remaining wild condor was captured and transported to the San Diego Zoo for the captive breeding program, bringing the total number of birds in captivity to 27.[4]

Well-known species such as the California condor are only the most publicized victims of forces that are reducing the earth's biological diversity. Numerous species of animals, birds, plants, and insects are rapidly disappearing. Many disappear without ever being identified and named.

Biologists are rapidly learning more about the dimensions of the earth's biological domain, the threats that it faces, and what can be done to protect it. Recent explorations, mainly in tropical rain forests, have revealed that the earth's biota is much more diverse than previously thought. In the last few years, biologists have dramatically increased their estimate of the number of species that exist.[5]

Popular opinion and public policy in the United States are gradually embracing the goal of protecting biological diversity. The Endangered Species Act, passed in 1973, requires measures to protect even those plant and animal species that lack immediate and obvious human utility.[6] Since enactment, the threatened and endangered species list maintained under the act has become taxonomically diverse. In 1973, nearly 82 percent of the listed species were mammals or birds. By 1985, these two groups constituted only 59 percent of the total, due to an addition of large numbers of insects, clams, crustacea, and plants.[7] (See chapter 5.)

More recently, legislative and policy initiatives have focused on requiring foreign aid programs and multilateral lending institutions to take greater account of the effects of their actions on biological resources and to take steps to promote conservation strategies. For example, congressional action in 1985 led the U.S. Agency for International Development (AID) to develop a U.S. strategy for conserving biological diversity in the developing world.[8]

This chapter explores the current state of efforts to protect biological diversity in the United States, the threats that imperil these resources, and some of the difficult challenges ahead to counteract those threats. However, the need for conservation is worldwide. Indeed, some of the most critical needs and greatest opportunities lie outside the United States—in Brazil, for example, and Indonesia and Madagascar, and numerous other countries where resources are particularly diverse. Each country must tailor its choice of conservation methods not only to varying biological systems but also to its own economic and political conditions and opportunities.

WHAT IS BIOLOGICAL DIVERSITY?

Biological diversity, in the words of scientist Paul R. Ehrlich, "is the tens of millions of distinct species—and the billions of distinct populations—of plants, animals, and microorganisms that share Earth with us."[9] Simply put, it is the variety of species in ecosystems as well as the genetic variability within each species. Maintaining biological diversity involves conserving a wide array of life forms, from obscure plants and insects to well-known species such as polar bears and whales. Efforts to conserve biological diversity (or biodiversity) embrace three types of conservation:

- the protection of individual species;
- the protection of communities of species and the ecosystems of which they are a part, such as tropical forests, wetlands, virgin prairies, and coastal mangroves; and
- the preservation of diverse gene pools within species, or genetic diversity.[10]

In the United States, game species, such as pheasant, trout, and deer, have received the most attention from policy makers. Now, nongame species, such as the California condor, are brought to the public's attention almost daily by television, magazines, newspapers, and mail solicitations. Some—such as the panda, grizzly bear, and various types of whales—generate substantial publicity and aggressive preservation efforts. Other endangered species have garnered little attention. For example, few people have heard of the Tecopa pupfish, Sampson's pearly mussel, or long-jaw cisco, all of which have been declared extinct in the last five years.[11]

The survival of a species in the wild depends on a well-functioning ecosystem. By conserving such ecosystems, it is possible not only to protect one particular species, but many other species as well. The members of an ecosystem live together in complex, interlocking ways, such that the fate of one species is closely tied to that of others.[12] Because of this interdependence, ecosystems have a certain amount of resilience. Yet they also react to perturbation with long-term changes, often in complex and unpredictable ways. For example, a human-caused decrease in the population of one species is likely to trigger an increase in another species that uses the same resources, just as the near extirpation of the wolf in the United States may have promoted the ascendancy of the coyote.[13]

The third type of diversity is genetic. Genetic diversity is the variation among the members of a population, all of which are genetically unique. It determines that some roses have red blooms and others yellow, that some types of wheat will be resistant to drought and others not, that some chickens will be best for producing meat and others eggs.

WHY PROTECT THE DIVERSITY OF BIOLOGICAL RESOURCES?

For many conservationists, protecting the biological resources of the earth is a moral imperative requiring no economic or practical justification; the diversity of biological resources represents a natural endowment that human stewards must not squander.[14]

Aldo Leopold, who wrote eloquently about the need for a land ethic that appropriately recognizes the value of all life, saw the issue also in a more pragmatic way:

> If the biota, in the course of aeons, has built something we like but do not understand, then who but a fool would discard seemingly useless parts? To keep every cog and wheel is the first precaution of intelligent tinkering.[15]

For many policy makers, moral and aesthetic arguments require some bolstering. And there are, to be sure, economic and other pragmatic arguments for protecting species, ecosystems, and genetic diversity.

Agriculture

Biological diversity holds out two important opportunities for agriculture: (*a*) a source of genetic materials for improving strains of crop plants that are under cultivation and (*b*) a source for development of "new" crop species.[16]

Agricultural productivity in the United States and abroad has been influenced substantially by the use of "germ plasm" (genetic materials) from wild species. The U.S. Department of Agriculture credits $1 billion annually of increased crop productivity to the introduction of genetic characteristics from wild species into major U.S. crop plants. Much of the increase since 1930 in the yields of a few well-known crops—corn up 333 percent, potatoes up 297 percent, cotton up 157 percent, tomatoes up 230 percent—has been attributed to the use of germ plasm.[17]

Selective breeding, the key feature of crop development, is designed to diminish the genetic variability of crop species and narrow the range of genetic characteristics in each cultivar. While these techniques are beneficial in the short term, the long-term implications can be negative. For example, domestic species often end up being less resistant to disease than are their wild relatives. *Zea diploperennis*, a species of wild corn discovered in 1977 in Mexico, is resistant or immune to several major diseases that plague domestic corn.[18]

Disease resistance is just one example of the potential contribution of wild species to domestic needs. The wide range of genetic characteristics found in wild species may potentially contribute to increased crop yield, pest resistance, and greater tolerance for environmental variablities such as heat and drought.

The potential contribution of wild species to the development of "new" crops may in the long term be even more important than the contributions of specific genetic characteristics. Given the fact that only a small percentage of the total estimated plant species have been evaluated in any detail, the future of crop development seems bright. The Jojoba plant is a well-known example of a wild species brought into domestic production in recent years. The seeds of this desert shrub are rich in liquid wax, especially valuable as an industrial lubricant and therefore as an alternative to sperm whale oil.[19]

Health and Medicine

The diversity of wild plant and animal species also provides enormous potential for both the development and testing of new drugs. By one estimate, some 25 percent of the prescription medicines currently sold in the United States are based on chemicals derived originally from wild plants.[20] Wild species are estimated to be even more important in Europe and especially in developing countries, where many people depend directly on the curative powers of the plants themselves rather than on derived drugs.[21]

The range of naturally active ingredients found in wild species is so great that chemical derivatives are used as local anesthetics and muscle relaxants in surgery; as the source of active ingredients in the contraceptive pill; for treatment of high blood pressure, leukemia, and many other diseases.[22] The sap of certain trees in the Amazon has been found to be very effective against fungal skin infections.[23] Economically, a single drug, cascara sagrada (from the tree *Rhamnus purshiana*), used to treat constipation, accounts for 20 percent of a U.S. laxative market that totaled $350 to $400 million in 1975, according to one estimate.[24]

Because the pharmacological properties of only a few species have ever been tested, wild species continue to hold substantial promise for the development of new drugs. Moreover, as one medical researcher has noted, "without naturally occurring active principles, it seems probable that neither the principle nor the activity would otherwise have been discovered. Put yourself in the place of a chemist who would like to develop a remedy for cardiac insufficiency; methods currently available would not lead him to synthesize a digitoxin-like molecule without knowledge of the natural prototype."[25]

Tourism and Recreation

Places such as parks, reserves, and wildlife refuges, where people go to see wild species and other natural features, contribute enormously to the economy. Recent studies have found that Americans alone spend some $30 billion a year "on wildlife-associated recreation: $16.25 billion fishing; $7.15 billion hunting; and $6.6 billion in nonconsumptive (or nonharvesting) ways such as whale watching, feeding wild birds, and photographing wildflowers.''[26] These figures most likely do not reflect the additional millions of dollars spent each year by visitors to national and state parks. An estimated 83.2 million Americans in 1980 enjoyed observing, studying, or photographing wildlife in its natural habitat, while more than the 42 million Americans fished for recreation and 17.4 million hunted.[27] Large numbers of people sign up for boat trips to look at whales; over 25 million Americans maintain bird feeders at home;[28] and an increasing number of photographic safaris travel through Africa and Central America.

"Ecosystem Services"

In addition to acting as a haven for all the individual species within it, an ecosystem often provides other benefits that humans take for granted: the biologically mediated recycling of nutrients, purifying of water, flood control, breakdown of pollutants, protection of soil, fixation of solar energy, and other so-called ecosystem services that sustain life.[29] The U.S. Army Corps of Engineers estimates that a 40 percent reduction in wetland area along the Charles River in Massachusetts would result in a two- to four-foot increase in flood peaks and thus cause an additional $3 million in flood damages annually.[30] Certain wetland plants are so efficient at removing wastes that artificial waste-treatment systems are using them.[31]

The costs of protecting ecosystems, and the services they provide, though sometimes significant, are generally not nearly as great as the costs of returning degraded ecosystems to a functional level. Although development pressures continue, the state of Florida is spending millions to acquire land, alter levees and canals, and reflood drained marshes in hopes of restoring natural waterflow patterns to the Everglades. Additionally, more than $7 billion is to be spent over the next 40 years to buy surrounding land critical to the restoration effort.[32] Even with such large expenditures, it is uncertain whether the water-flow patterns and wildlife populations will ever return to their original state. (See box, "Restoring the Everglades Ecosystem.")

Lack of Information

One of the most compelling arguments for protecting diversity is that so little is known about what exists and what is being lost. There is no consensus on how many species exist in the world, the potential usefulness of most of them, or the rate at which they are disappearing.

The severe limit of existing knowledge is apparent when considering the issue of the number of species that inhabit the planet. In total, about 1.7 million species have been formally named under the system Linnaeus established in 1753. Some 751,000 are insects; about 440,000, plants,

Restoring the Everglades Ecosystem

Early in this century, Florida Governor Napolean Bonaparte Broward began zealously to drain the Everglades.[1] At that time, the grassy marshland—actually, a slow-moving sheet of water—covered most of the Florida peninsula south of Lake Okeechobee.[2] A total of 9,000 square miles was included in the Kissimmee River-Lake Okeechobee-Everglades ecosystem.[3]

As Broward and his successors worked to reclaim the land for agriculture, towns, and industry, they significantly altered this natural sheet flow, which was a key element for continued survival of the Everglades ecosystem.

A long-time visitor to the Everglades recalls when "you could hear the panther scream at night. In the morning, the birds were so thick you would have to shoo them away."[4] The panther then was plentiful throughout the Southeast, but urbanization has reduced its numbers to an estimated 30 in the entire Everglades region.[5] Over a dozen other Everglades animals are listed under the Endangered Species Act.[6] For some, like the West Indian manatee, decline is associated with stress from recreational boating activities along the coast. For others, such as the snail kite, decline is linked directly to the loss of suitable habitat from the alteration of the Everglades ecosystem. During the last 40 years, the population of freshwater wading birds in Everglades National Park at the southern tip of the Everglades ecosystem, has declined by 90 percent.[7]

Valuable ecosystem services have been altered as well. Water flowing through the Everglades southward to the coast used to recharge the Biscayne aquifer, the only supply of fresh water for southeast Florida.[8] However, water tables have dropped, and in 1980-1981, after a year-long drought, an underground wedge of saltwater

moved inland, tainting the water supply.[9] Fresh water flowing into the estuaries of the Everglades once created one of the most productive fisheries in the world, where 90 percent of the commercially valuable fish from the Florida Bay spent a portion of their life cycle.[10] By December 31, 1985, fish and shellfish populations in the bay had declined to the point where the National Park Service banned commercial fishing. The slow movement of water also served to nourish the soil and enable filtering of high levels of nutrients and vectors of disease by marsh vegetation. Prior to drainage, the water moved an average of a foot a day through the Everglades, thus controlling both flooding in the rainy season and fires in the dry season.[11] With the advent of channelization, wildfires increased nearly eightfold in one affected county.[12]

To be sure, even after a century of draining, the Everglades still present a striking and varied system of marshes, sloughs, prairies, pinelands, hardwood hammocks, and mangrove islands. Some of the inhabitants, particularly birds, now seem to be recovering, thanks both to the cooperative efforts of federal, state, local, and private organizations and to other influences, such as the ban on DDT in the early 1970s. But beneath the surface is an ecological time bomb.

Over the years, Lake Okeechobee was diked, and a series of levees and canals channeled the flow. In the late 1940s, the U.S. Army Corps of Engineers initiated a flood control project that entailed construction and improvement of 1,400 miles of canals and levees and the installation of tide gates, floodgates, and huge pumps to drain potential farmland.[13] Highways built through the Everglades further blocked the southward flow of water. Most devastating to the Everglades ecosystem was the channelization of the Kissimmee River in the 1950s and 1960s, which led to an 80 percent loss of its marshlands.[14]

The hard-fought effort to create Everglades National Park was intended to protect a portion of this unique, pristine wilderness. However, the boundaries, which include nearly 1.4 million acres, were drawn by politics, not ecology, and water flow to the park could not be isolated from the manipulated ecosystem around it. The park lies virtually at the mouth of a water supply restricted by the complex maze of levees and dikes.

A scientific study team working inside the park since 1976 has gathered extensive data on the extent and effects of the radically changed environment in the Everglades region and the implications for resource management problems in the park. The disrupted terrain has affected the health of indigenous species and made them less able to withstand the rapid invasion of exotic plants and animals.[15] Prolonged reductions in water flow to the park have converted some wetlands into upland ecosystems. At the other extreme, sudden large discharges destroy the nests of wading birds and alligators.

New programs are taking a revolutionary approach. The whole Everglades drainage basin is being regarded as an integrated system rather than as an assortment of separate streams, marshes, and lakes. To undo the damage, water flows are being managed so that they simulate natural conditions more closely. In 1983, the South Florida Water Management District agreed to a National Park Service plan for releasing water into the park to simulate seasonal flows.[16] In November of that year, Congress enacted legislation requiring an experimental two-year water delivery program for the Everglades to be monitored by the Corps of Engineers.[17] The corps has modified levees and canals to reduce the large and sudden volumes of discharge in certain park locations.

Former U.S. Fish and Wildlife Service biologist and Everglades expert Arthur R. Marshall developed an ambitious plan for repair of the entire ecosystem. His repair plan called for dechannelizing the Kissimmee, removing spillways and levees that were blocking water flow south of Lake Okeechobee, installing culverts under the roadways, and generally providing for a relatively natural flow from Lake Okeechobee to and through the national park and preserve.[18] In response, Governor Bob Graham initiated a seven-point "Save Our Everglades" emergency program in 1983, which included a demonstration restoration of a portion of the Kissimmee River and state acquisition and reflooding of a 95-square-mile area between Lake Okeechobee and Big Cypress National Preserve.

Progress has been made on these plans. Structures on the Kissimmee canal and alteration of water levels have caused substantial flow through the old river oxbows and reflooding of the historic river floodplain along a 12-mile stretch of the river for the first time since channelization. Highway construction has begun, including several design features to improve the natural overland sheet flow of water and underpasses and fencing to allow animals to pass safely from one side to the other. Experimental water delivery systems continue, and land acquisition efforts are under way.[19]

The hopes are that, as a result, in the year 2000 the Everglades "will look and function more as it did in 1900 than it does today."[20]

including algae and fungi; 47,000, vertebrates; and the rest, invertebrates and microorganisms. Yet millions of species have yet to be identified. As one expert observed: "How many species of organisms are there on Earth? We don't know, not even to the nearest order of magnitude."[33]

Until the early 1980s, estimates of the number of species typically ranged between 3 and 10 million, most of which were believed to be insects. However, recent studies in tropical rain forests have shown that those regions probably harbor many more species than biologists thought. One estimate suggests that the earth may contain as many as 30 million species of insects alone, the majority of them in rain forests.[34] More thorough examination of biologically rich but sparsely surveyed coral reefs may further boost estimates of the earth's species.

The number of extinctions is even less clear.[35] The discovery that species are far more numerous than previously thought suggests that extinctions, too, are far more frequent than estimated earlier. The extinction rate is a matter of some controversy. According to one authority, 15 to 20 percent of the species that inhabited the earth in 1980 are likely to have been lost by the turn of the century.[36] If there are 30 million species, this rate would mean losses of 4.5 to 6 million species. This estimate is vigorously disputed by some,[37] although the fact that great losses will be suffered as tropical forests are cleared seems indisputable. Further, as a recent report by the Office of Technology Assessment concluded,

> global and national data and projections may mask the localized nature of resource degradation, diversity loss, and the consequences of both. Large inaccessible areas of forest, for example, may make the global deforestation rate seem moderate, but destruction of especially diverse forests in local areas . . . proceeds at catastrophic rates.[38]

THREATS

Biological resources today are under tremendous stress. Hunting and harvesting are often assumed to be the main culprits. [39] Ultimately, however, they are probably less important than some other threats—notably, loss of suitable habitat and chemical poisoning of that habitat.[40]

Many organisms are exposed to a variety of human-caused threats. A single species may be hunted for food and clothing, have its habitat reduced by development, and be controlled as a nuisance.[41] Chemical pollution can be another threat in degrading habitat and destroying specific plants and animals.

As a population is decreased in size and fragmented by these processes, there is a greater probability that it will become extinct due to genetic and demographic effects or because of random ecological disasters such as fires and floods. Even an apparently widespread species with many separate, small subpopulations may ultimately become extinct if each subpopulation itself has a high probability of vanishing.[42]

In some instances, one form of human activity may increase risks from another. New development such as houses and roads may not only lead to a species' decline because of habitat loss but also leave the remaining population more vulnerable to hunters. For instance, the woodland caribou, a U.S. endangered species found only in northeastern Washington and northern Idaho, is threatened by illegal hunting facilitated by new roads built by the U.S. Forest Service.[43]

Harvesting and Killing

Excessive commercial harvesting has caused the virtual elimination of several species of rhinoceroses, seals, and wild cats.[44] And hunting for sport, unless carefully regulated as it usually is in the United States, has been and may continue to be a particular threat to certain larger animals. Even in the United States, however, some wild species' populations have plummeted in part due to overharvesting, including several species of Pacific Flyway geese and, some scientists say, the Alaska king crab.[45]

In many other countries, harvesting is a far more serious problem.[46] There is enormous global trade in smuggled wildlife and wildlife products—from butterflies and parrots to lizard skins and elephant tusks. The annual U.S. share of international trade in live animals, ivory, and skins is valued at a minimum of $4 billion, according to one estimate. Up to one-third of this trade is illegal.[47]

Species may be threatened by nuisance controls, which can be particularly damaging when broad-gauge poisons are used. Heavy pesticide spraying, for instance, can directly or indirectly eliminate a wide range of species, both beneficial and bothersome.*

Habitat Destruction

The problems of habitat destruction, fragmentation, and degradation threaten more resources and may be more difficult to solve than those caused by direct killing and harvesting. Valuable habitats are being destroyed at unprecedented rates around the world.[49]

---

*A recent report showed that the U.S. Environmental Protection Agency consistently violated the Endangered Species Act by failing to take required action to protect endangered species from pesticides despite danger alerts from the U.S. Fish and Wildlife Service.[48]

Deforestation is perhaps the single greatest cause of decline in global biological diversity. Loss of diversity is greatest in the tropical forests because the rate of deforestation there is rapid and the communities being destroyed contain many species. An estimated 29,000 to 36,000 square miles are being cleared each year to provide fuel wood, timber for export, and new land for raising crops and livestock.[50]

Some types of nonforest terrestrial habitats have all but disappeared in many parts of the world. Prior to the 1850s, tallgrass prairies occupied a quarter of a billion acres in central North America; today, less than 1 percent of this prairie remains.[51] In the United States, grassland remnants have been identified, but a proposed tall-grass prairie national park and preserve still has not been established.[52] Overgrazing in the arid regions of the world is one primary reason why as many as 23,000 square miles of land are being destroyed or seriously degraded by desertification each year.[53]

Wetlands and marshes, too, are being extensively destroyed for farmland and urban development. Some 80 percent of the 300,000 to 500,000 acres of wetlands cleared in the United States each year are converted to agricultural uses.[54] Large wetland areas along the Mississippi River in Louisiana are being lost in part because flood-control projects have eliminated the annual replenishment of silt that these areas depend on and because channels cut for boats have allowed saltwater to intrude upon freshwater systems.[55] (See chapter 5.)

Perhaps the most biologically diverse saltwater communities under severe assault are coral reefs—among the more fragile, complex, species-rich ecosystems on the planet. Reefs are imperiled by fishing with dynamite, commercial collection of corals, and extensive mining for concrete production. Furthermore, relatively small amounts of silt deposited on a coral reef, from a dredging operation or from deforestation and erosion on land, can interfere with the feeding of the coral polyps that build the reef.[56]

The problem of very long-term, if not irreversible, damage affects many natural communities. In forests where large areas have been cleared, natural regeneration may not occur because seed sources may not be available, symbionts (such as nitrogen-fixing bacteria) may have been removed, and soils may have been degraded. This is particularly true in tropical forests, where climax species have large and poorly dispersed seeds, where close interdependence with microorganisms is probably common, and where nutrients are rapidly leached from exposed soils. Reforestation by planting can provide wood and watershed protection, but it will rarely replace the natural forest. Plantations are often of a single species and generally lack most of the forest's original plant and animal inhabitants.

True reestablishment of a community may eventually occur if sources of seeds or colonizing animals are available, but the more severe the degradation, the longer the community may take to repair itself. As described later, in the section on habitat restoration, people may speed up the regeneration process, but complete restoration or natural regeneration may be impossible in some cases.

Habitat Degradation

Biological diversity is threatened not only by outright physical destruction of habitat. Many habitats have been seriously polluted and degraded through chemical contamination and the invasion of exotic species.

Chemical Contamination

The widely publicized experience at California's Kesterson National Wildlife Refuge illustrates the seriousness of chemical contamination problems. In 1983, alarming numbers of waterfowl with severe birth defects appeared there; many eggs never hatched. The cause was high levels of selenate (a form of the element selenium) dissolved in irrigation runoff that subsequently entered the refuge (see chapter 5). Research is under way to better understand what happened at Kesterson and what might be done about it; remedial steps are beginning to be taken.[57]

Concerned about the extent of contamination problems in the National Wildlife Refuge System, the U.S. Fish and Wildlife Service (FWS) undertook a preliminary survey of its refuges. This survey, the results of which are summarized in figure 9.1, found that evidence of chemical contamination in the 430 refuges was sufficiently strong to call for corrective action in 9 cases. For another 26 cases, enough information existed to justify indepth monitoring and analysis of possible problems. For an additional 43 cases, direct evidence of contamination was insufficient to justify action, but circumstantial evidence suggested a possible problem. The sources of contamination included toxic waste dumps, industrial and municipal wastewater discharges, and irrigation return flows.[58]

These recent revelations about contamination are particularly disturbing, for refuges are places specifically established to protect wild species. The threats to wild plants and animals resulting from chemical contamination have been recognized for decades, however. The pesticide DDT

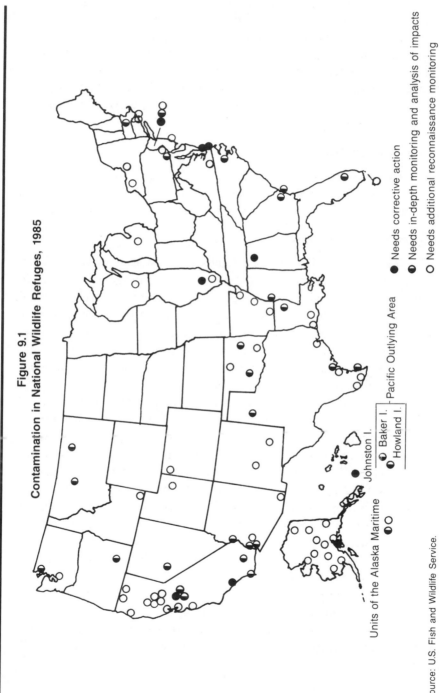

Figure 9.1
Contamination in National Wildlife Refuges, 1985

● Needs corrective action
◑ Needs in-depth monitoring and analysis of impacts
○ Needs additional reconnaissance monitoring

Units of the Alaska Maritime

Johnston I.

● Baker I. ─ Pacific Outlying Area
○ Howland I.

Source: U.S. Fish and Wildlife Service.

(dichloro-diphenyl-trichloro-ethane) was implicated in the rapid population declines of eagles, falcons, and other raptors.[59] Oil spills may be accompanied by the death of large numbers of seabirds and other aquatic wild species. Contamination with polychlorinated biphenyls (PCBs) is strongly implicated in the decline of Baltic seals, including the grey seal, whose numbers dropped from 20,000 in the 1940s to a few thousand individuals in the early 1980s.[60]

Concern has been growing, sharply and internationally, over acid precipitation and its degradation of habitat. The effects on aquatic life have been particularly damaging. Lakes and streams with increased acidity frequently suffer decreased fish populations. Young fish may be more susceptible to the negative effects of high acidity (including death) and its capacity to mobilize heavy metals. Acid precipitation, along with overharvesting, has been named as one of the causes of the recent, rapid decline of striped bass populations. The annual commercial catch of striped bass decreased 90 percent from 1973 to 1983 (recreational declines were comparable). During this 10-year period, the catch from the Chesapeake Bay plummeted from 14.7 to 1.7 million pounds, and the North Carolina catch dropped from 1.7 million to 360,000 pounds.[61]

Problems Related to Exotic Species

The introduction of exotic species into habitats, through planned release or escape, may also endanger native species—by spreading disease, inflicting environmental damage, adversely affecting commercial and recreational use of fish and wildlife, and causing other resource management problems.[62]

A 1980 National Park Service survey of 326 park system units in the United States revealed a total of 210 problems related to exotic species.[63] For example, the exotic tamarisk, or salt cedar, has become a problem in parks of the arid Southwest, where the tamarisk's high water consumption is decreasing water availability for indigenous resources.[64] In Florida, a species of Australian eucalyptus (*Melaleuca quinquefolia*) has spread rapidly over the last several decades. Like the tamarisk, *Melaleuca* demands plenty of water and is drying up areas of the Everglades at the expense of indigenous plant and animal life.[65] The full effects of the encroachment of most exotic species are generally complex and difficult to predict, but may be far-reaching.

THE CHALLENGES AHEAD: PRESERVING BIOLOGICAL DIVERSITY

To counteract the many threats to biological diversity, decision makers face difficult choices. With limited funds and staff, one could, for example, be forced to choose between committing another million dollars to protect a single hard-pressed species and purchasing a tract of virgin forest threatened with logging to protect several less-publicized species and perhaps others not yet identified.

In all probability, many species, ecosystems, and gene pools will continue to be lost, while others will be saved. The core issues are: What should energies be focused on trying to save? How should those energies be allocated among various strategies, such as setting up reserves, restoring damaged habitat, regulating illegal trade, and so forth, to maximize protection efforts for biological resources? And how should broader constituencies be built for conservation?

These are not easy questions to answer. Consider the battle to save the California condor. Should so many resources be allocated to that one species? Could they be better used on other species, or in setting up and managing reserves? Which ones? Would the money even be available for reserves or other species if it were not going to the condor? If the resources are to be allocated to the condor, how should they be apportioned among various strategies—for example, regulating against lead shot, setting up a reserve, or providing space and care in a zoo?

Unfortunately, such choices usually must be made despite substantial uncertainty and ignorance. For example, although most warm-blooded vertebrates (birds and mammals) are believed to have been discovered, named, and described, scientists frequently lack the information needed to determine the survival status of these species or to protect them adequately if they are found to be in jeopardy. Information about the values and needs of ecosystems—and threats to them—is often lacking.

Even for such celebrated and threatened wild species as the grizzly bears of Yellowstone National Park, the most elementary data—the size of the park's grizzly population, for instance—are often in dispute.[66] In the case of many tropical birds, scientists may be able to do no more than establish that a species has disappeared from a particular locale, with little or nothing known about the existence, location, or size of other wild populations of the species.[67]

Although research is needed to reduce this ignorance, decisions and actions cannot be put off, since to do so might cause the needless loss of biological resources that later could be found to have had substantial value. The need is to act as wisely as possible in the face of uncertainty.

Just as efforts to protect biological resources and counteract the threats they are under have stepped up in recent years, so has understanding of the efficacy of those efforts. New capability to address the problems facing biological resources has come as a result of advances in the field of conservation biology and experience and insights gained in other fields of wildlife management and habitat protection.

For instance, over the past 12 years, the Nature Conservancy has developed and continually refined procedures for identifying and ranking natural areas.[68] As a result, it can better focus its acquisition and management activities on properties that contain rare or threatened species or ecosystems. World Wildlife Fund* has conducted an evaluation of the tropical Andes to identify existing protected areas and potential new areas with the objective of developing a system of protected areas that will conserve the vast biological diversity of the region.[69] Over the same period, an increasing number of developing countries have begun to measure the richness of their biological resources as a criterion for the establishment of reserves. Through biogeographical censuses, scientists are trying to identify areas that harbor endangered species or that are important centers of endemism (areas containing many species not found elsewhere).

Nevertheless, efforts to protect biological diversity are not growing as fast as the threats. The goal of conservation means that protection efforts must be focused on ecosystems and genetic diversity as well as species. It is not enough to answer the traditional question, How many wild species and which species can or should be saved? Other questions also must be addressed: How many ecosystems of what size should be conserved? How many members of an individual species must be protected for species survival? In using and analyzing conservation strategies, it is important to understand how they apply—to species, ecosystems, and gene pools—what their strengths and limitations are, and how they will need to be advanced and refined in the coming years to adapt to rapidly changing conditions and scientific understanding.

Species Management

Individual species and categories of species have traditionally attracted the most public interest and support among wildlife-related efforts. Management tools have followed from this, having long been directed at animals that the public is most concerned about.

Game species have traditionally received the most attention (see chapter 5). Predator control, supplemental feeding, and domestic propagation, in addition to hunting regulations, are techniques that have been used to protect these species. Humans have hunted wolves for centuries, one

*World Wildlife Fund is affiliated with The Conservation Foundation.

of the justifications being to eliminate an undesirable predator. Hatcheries and stocking of inland waters have been used to enhance fish populations.

In recent years, attention to species-level efforts, reflecting public interest, has broadened to include endangered and nongame species. In its endangered species recovery programs, FWS has adopted such aggressive management techniques as attaching radio transmitters to the few remaining California condors and monitoring their movements to better understand survival requirements.[70] The endangered Florida panther has received similar attention.[71] Transportation of eggs or young individuals is often used to relocate a species to a protected area or to establish a new population. Eggs from peregrine falcons living in captivity (and thus free from pesticide contamination) have been placed into the nests of wild peregrines or related species, thereby increasing the number of successfully hatched young. Each year since 1977, between 1,000 and 3,000 Kemp's ridley sea turtles' eggs have been removed from nests in Mexico and hatched in a laboratory. Upon hatching, some young have been returned to Mexico, while the remainder have been reared where they were hatched and then released into protected national park waters in the Gulf of Mexico.[72]

International efforts to protect species have also increased. The Convention on International Trade in Endangered Species and Wild Fauna and Flora (commonly known as CITES), signed by 21 countries in 1973, is a global mechanism to control trade in all rare and threatened species.[73] Since 1975, when the treaty came into force, 95 countries have become parties to CITES, making it the most widely supported of any conservation convention in the world. (Over half of these parties are developing countries, where wild species are sometimes crucial for local industries, food, and tourism.[74]) As a result, trade in wild species has a functioning international regulatory framework and a secretariat to oversee implementation.[75]

Clearly, some species attract more interest than others. The amount of resources devoted to, say, grizzly bears and condors is staggering compared to what is allocated to species of beetles, frogs, and cacti. For example, projected expenditures by FWS alone for California condor and whooping crane recovery efforts in 1985 were $833,000 and $5,706,100, respectively—whereas projected expenditures by the same agency in 1985 for many endangered plants were negligible.[76]

Focusing protection strategies on individual species quickly runs into problems. One is that popular attention, and through it political support, can focus only on a limited number of species at one time. These fortunate few tend to be what one observer has called "the charismatic megafauna—big, fierce, or attractive animals."[77] Other species with less charismatic attributes have a more difficult time competing for attention, though they may be just as important.

The focus on a few select, popular species does, however, have an important role to play in galvanizing public interest and support. Condors, grizzly bears, and panthers, important in and of themselves, serve a broader purpose as well: they act as so-called flagship species for attracting attention and resources to protection efforts that might not otherwise be available.

Moreover, measures used for flagship species often provide increased protection for other endangered species and other members of native ecosystems. The key is to ensure that these species are protected while using the support for them to enhance the biological resources they are dependent on and the broader efforts devoted to biological diversity in general.

Multiple Techniques

Management of the endangered whooping crane is an example of how multiple techniques can be used to increase a species' chances of survival. In an attempt to establish a second population, eggs are being transferred from both the wild flock nesting at Wood Buffalo National Park in Canada and a captive flock in Maryland to sandhill crane nests in Grays Lake National Wildlife Refuge in Idaho. The cranes are also protected during migration by a monitoring network and kept away from areas that may be hazardous due to disease, chemicals, or danger of accidental shooting. Since a major cause of death in migrating whooping cranes is collision with power lines, utility companies have been asked to make the lines visible with bright aircraft marker balls. Whooping crane habitat management includes burning, cutting, or grazing to control vegetation height and increase insect availability. Crops, including corn and chufa, are planted at many refuges, and fresh water is pumped in to decrease the probability of diseases such as botulism and avian cholera.[78]

The success of these management techniques is reflected in population increases. In 1985, the world population of whooping cranes in the wild was about 170, more than 11 times the 1941 population of 15. The rate of increase of the world population was initially slow but has risen dramatically since 1967, when the transfer of eggs to build a captive population at Pautuxent, Maryland, began.[79]

In some instances, if threats in the wild can be sufficiently reduced, species management techniques may need to be adopted only until a viable population reestablishes itself. But, in other cases, particularly if aggressive management is used as a substitute for habitat acquisition and protection, such management may become a permanent necessity if the species is to survive.

Ex Situ Conservation

When efforts to protect a species from the many threats it faces in the wild are not sufficient by themselves, ex situ (that is, off-site) conservation may be considered. The case of the peregrine falcon provides an example. In the early 1970s, peregrine falcons in the United States were headed for extinction. The eastern population had already vanished; the western population was following hard after. The culprit was DDT, a persistent pesticide that accumulated in the food chain of falcons and other birds. The accumulated high levels of DDT caused the shells of the birds' eggs to become much thinner, and they often broke before hatching. Although DDT was banned in 1972, it persisted in the environment. The peregrine falcon's reproductive rate continued to plummet, endangering the species' survival.[80]

A captive breeding program was undertaken at Cornell University in 1970, and methods for breeding and raising peregrines in captivity were developed. In 1973 the first 20 peregrine young were produced, and since 1976 over 50 young have been raised each year. Reintroduction of the captive-bred birds has been highly successful.[81]

Types of Ex Situ Conservation. Ex situ conservation methods may be separated into two categories. The first group of methods, used to save the peregrine falcon, involves creating situations in which captive populations continue to reproduce normally, even though matings may be controlled. Examples are populations kept in zoos, botanical gardens, game parks, agricultural stations, fish hatcheries, and facilities specially dedicated to raising rare species.

The second ex situ conservation category includes facilities like seed and germ plasm banks, where the goal is to store genetic information in the form of seeds and frozen embryos. In the future, storage of a variety of pure, isolated, or synthesized genetic materials (DNA sequences) could be possible. Collectively, these facilities have been likened to genetic libraries for space-efficient storage of genetic variability.[82]

Zoos, botanical gardens, and other breeding facilities are the traditional ways of conserving organisms out of their environment. Successful captive propagation depends on careful research and the creation of environmental conditions appropriate to the species. With good facilities, planning, knowledge, and luck, mortality may be significantly reduced from what it would be in the wild. Populations of rare plants or animals can be raised and released into suitable habitat. Some of the more successful captive breeding programs have involved golden lion tamarins, Arabian oryxes, peregrine falcons, Przewalski's horse, and European bison.[83]

Even in the recent past, many of the institutions specializing in exhibition paid little attention to the needs of rare species, which often could be replaced from the wild more cheaply and easily than they could be bred. When the animals were bred, genetic records were rarely used, because inbreeding and other genetic problems were not well understood.[84]

This situation is changing. Many institutions have evolved a more sophisticated conservation ethic, necessitated in part by tighter restrictions on trade in rare species. The $35,000 cost of a female bongo antelope[85] is an excellent incentive for developing the facilities needed for producing baby bongos.

Management methods today have become more sophisticated. For years, efforts to maintain viable populations of endangered golden lion tamarins in captivity were unsuccessful; second-generation individuals were unable to raise their offspring.[86] In time, breeders discovered that the problem lay in the common practice of removing juveniles from the family group when their younger siblings were born, under the supposition that their presence might harm the newborns. This isolation prevented the juveniles from learning how to care for their own offspring. For this species, as for some others, intensive research has paid off. However, adequate research tends to be the exception rather than the rule.

An increasing number of zoos and botanical gardens have made ex situ conservation of rare species a major goal and have even begun to coordinate management of their collections. The recently formed Center for Plant Conservation in Massachusetts, for example, was organized by over a dozen leading botanical gardens and arboretums to create a natural collection of endangered wild plants.[87] Species Survival Plans for zoo animals, administered by the American Association of Zoological Parks and Aquariums, attempt to manage all captive specimens of a rare species coherently and with concern for genetic requirements. The plans are designed to ensure that frequent interchanges of individuals among zoos, determined by analysis of genetic records, will decrease the probability of inbreeding problems, while maintaining enough separation of populations to avoid catastrophic losses due to disease.[88] In some cases, analyses of captive populations have indicated a need to capture fresh wild stock so that genetic diversity can be added to the captive population. In principle, captive populations could provide the same service to wild populations.

Drawbacks of Ex Situ Conservation. Although ex situ techniques will likely play an increasing role in species conservation, particularly with emergency measures, a number of drawbacks exist. One of the weaknesses inherent in any method of ex situ conservation is that even sizable collections represent only a sampling of individuals and may not include all the important genetic traits. A founding population may not include enough genetic variability for long-term survival. Successive generations may experience genetic deterioration.

For long-term survival, ex situ populations require careful, sustained management based on good research. Continuity of care over the years is vital. A fire, a cut in government funding, a power loss, a poor administrator—any of these could cause the loss of irreplaceable specimens. For example, a lack of continuity in management has resulted in the loss of extensive numbers of plant genotypes, including over two-thirds of a collection of 4,000 samples of soybean seed from Asia and the near-total loss of several grape species collections.[89]

No matter what measures are taken, it may be difficult or impossible to breed some species in captivity. Moreover, another major issue, raised in the controversy over how to save the California condor, is whether captive populations can be successfully reintroduced into the wild. They may fail to learn the behavior necessary for survival and reproduction in another habitat. It is the long-term selection of genes for survival in captivity and the loss of genes useful for survival in the wild that results in domesticated animals and plants. Also, the natural habitat of some species may change during the time they are being captive-bred; when released, they might be unable to cope with the new environment.

A final limitation on the contributions of ex situ measures is that they can only deal with a limited number of species. There is only so much "captive habitat." In 1980, according to a report compiled for the American Association of Zoological Parks and Aquariums, North American zoos maintained self-sustaining populations of only 96 species.[90] Populations of other species in zoos were too small to survive in the long term without the addition of new breeding stock. For example, there is at present captive habitat for approximately 300 rhinos.[91] Even if all these facilities were devoted to just one of the five recognized species of rhino, that would be barely enough for the animal's long-term survival, given what is known about the minimum population sizes needed to sustain large mammals.

The number of species that can be maintained in zoos, moreover, is always a function of money. The yearly maintenance costs for a family of gorillas, for instance, easily exceed $50,000.[92] Because of limited resources, institutions and, by extension, society face tough decisions about which species and strains to concentrate on.

Habitat Management

Paying attention simply to individual species—whether in the wild or ex situ—will not by itself sustain and conserve biological diversity. The most cost-efficient, and sometimes only, means of protecting large numbers of species and associated ecological processes is through the conservation of habitat: by establishing reserves that encompass ecosytems and natural communities and by fashioning strategies to protect and restore nonreserve habitat.

The Role of Ecosystem Reserves

National parks, nature reserves, and other protected areas are the cornerstones of most national strategies to preserve wild plants, animals, and ecological communities. According to a 1985 survey by the International Union for Conservation of Nature and Natural Resources (IUCN), almost 1.7 million square miles, or 3.2 percent of the world's land, has some sort of protected status (figure 9.2). In the United States, about 7.2 percent of the land was protected in some way (see chapter 5).[93]

If suitable habitat is available, reserves can confer important benefits: (a) they may provide protection for an entire ecosystem, not just for species of particular interest; (b) they are likely to provide recreational, aesthetic, natural resource conservation, and other environmental benefits to the surrounding area; and (c) they are likely to be inexpensive to maintain compared to the amount of diversity they protect and, if acquired before other uses contend for the land, relatively inexpensive to create.

In most areas of the world, there are not enough properly located reserves of sufficient size to adequately protect biological diversity. Moreover, the ones already established provide less security to biological resources than most people think, sometimes because of inadequate internal management and often because of encroaching activities on lands outside their boundaries. Recent studies have shown this to be painfully true in the United States, despite the existence of strong managing institutions like the National Park Service and the Fish and Wildlife Service and strong public support for these areas.

The national parks in the western United States are among the areas that have been held longest as public reserves. It is now being discovered that they may not provide all the protection expected of them. To most

Figure 9.2
Protected Natural Areas as a Percentage of Total Area,
by Country, 1985

1 Less than 1%

2 1- 5%

3 5-10%

4 More than 10%

Alaska, Hawaii, and Puerto Rico treated separately from contiguous United States; Greenland treated
separately from Denmark; Spitsbergen treated separately from Norway.
Source: International Union for Conservation of Nature and Natural Resources.

Americans, these parks represent the essence of wild, primitive America: spectacular scenery, vast tracts of pristine forests, and, in particular, abundant wildlife. They contain a great diversity of plants and animals. For most park visitors, however, the wild species of greatest interest are the native mammals, especially large ones such as bear and elk.

Recent advances in biological understanding have made it clear that such isolated populations of plants and animals, surrounded by spreading human development, are prone to extinction and that large mammals and rare species are at greatest risk.[94] The effect is correlated with area size: the smaller the area to which a group of species is newly restricted, the greater the number of extinctions likely to occur.

America's national parks are no exception to this chilling rule. A recent study indicates that, if current trends continue, future generations of visitors to Yosemite, Zion, Mt. Rainier, and other famous parks may be left with a tamer and more sterile scene, from which many species of wild mammals will have disappeared.

Based on a review of park sighting records and scientific literature, a researcher has found that many species of mammals had disappeared from park areas even before the parks were created and that the loss of mammalian populations has continued since then. In 12 of the 14 parks with complete records on numbers of mammalian species dating from their establishment, a total of 44 mammalian populations have disappeared, usually because habitat within the parks was inadequate to sustain viable populations over time due to isolation and habitat loss outside the park.[95]

In practice, species protection is, at best, only one of the factors determining the size, location, and management of reserves. Commonly, historical accidents and financial opportunity have also been important factors, especially in determining reserve size and location. Instead of a single large reserve that might best meet ecological requirements, a government might create two smaller reserves to please two constituencies. Instead of a reserve in a biologically rich but distant area, officials may choose one close to a national capital for its recreational benefits and political impact. These factors help build important constituencies and are unlikely to disappear in the future.

Designing Reserves. Reserve creation is critical for protecting biological resources, and reserve expansion may be necessary to secure areas already set aside. As more has been learned about how populations respond when they are isolated in reserves, it has become increasingly clear that careful design is crucial for long-term survival of the species reserves are created to protect.[96] Unfortunately, few existing reserves encompass entire ecosystems or include sufficient habitat for all the wild species that originally used the area.*

Research is under way to determine how rapidly species are lost from reserves of particular sizes. How much more rapidly will species be lost from small reserves than from larger ones? Will more total species be saved in one large reserve than in two smaller ones having the same total area? What kinds of species will be lost most rapidly? Current research is directed toward determining the minimum viable population necessary for long-term survival of selected species and to estimating how large reserves must be to accommodate the plant and animal species indigenous to them. The Minimum Critical Size of Ecosystems Project being sponsored by World Wildlife Fund and Brazil's National Institute for Amazon Research (INPA) is a 20-year project that will provide data on which to base design and management criteria for national parks and reserves, particularly in the Amazon forest.[98] (See box, "Determining the Minimum Critical Size of Reserves.")

Setting up reserves is more complicated than just opting for the largest areas possible. Because of environmental catastrophes, such as forest fires and epidemics, several small reserves could offer more safety than a single large one. Thus, if one population of a species were lost, a second might still be safe. To mitigate risk, FWS proposes to ensure California sea otters against a massive oil spill or similar catastrophe by establishing a new colony around the outermost of the Channel Islands to complement the present colony surviving off the Big Sur area of central California.[99]

Location also is an important factor in reserve design. It is obviously best to locate reserves where they can protect as many unique or imperiled species as possible. In Brazil, for example, there is an attempt to create reserves in areas in which an especially high degree of speciation appears to have occurred and which continue to be centers of diversity.[100] As noted earlier, the Nature Conservancy has selected areas throughout the United States

---

*One way of mitigating the genetic and demographic problems caused by reserves that are too small is to connect the reserves to each other with protected corridors of suitable habitat. These corridors can allow the interchange of genes between what would otherwise be isolated populations. The effectiveness of reserve corridors depends on their biological composition, width, length, and number and on the mobility of the species in question. A drawback of corridors is that they may offer an opportunity for disease or exotic invaders to spread more rapidly among the connected populations. In terms of their design and management, corridors may resemble extensions of reserves, or they may be more like buffer zones in which certain human activities are limited but not prohibited.[97]

Determining the Minimum Critical Size of Reserves

As the demand for each acre of habitable or arable land increases, much of the world's wildlife habitat is being destroyed, so that, by the end of the 20th century, it may be restricted to specially established parks and reserves. As surrounding land is converted to other uses, undisturbed natural areas will become islands in an altered landscape. Will such reserves be able to support the species they were designed to protect? How large an area will be required to maintain the natural array of species? How will neighboring land-use practices affect the reserves? How will the isolation of wild populations affect species diversity over the long term? Current knowledge of the conditions necessary to sustain viable populations is limited, but research is under way in hopes of answering these questions.

In 1979, World Wildlife Fund and Brazil's National Institute for Amazon Research (INPA) joined in a 20-year effort "to identify the minimum area of rain forest that will support natural communities with their characteristic variety of plant and animal life."[1] This Minimum Critical Size of Ecosystems Project (MCS) is examining the changes in natural communities that occur when once-continous tracts of Brazil's Amazon forest are fragmented into isolated reserves. According to the theory of island biogeography, the number of species that can inhabit an island—be it land in the ocean or a patch of jungle amid pasture—depends on the size of the island and its proximity to a species pool.[2] When an ecosystem is reduced to small isolated areas, species are lost in each area until a new equilibrium is reached. Equations have been derived to determine

the rate of species loss, but as ecologist John Terbourgh admits, scientists do not know very much about why species go extinct on isolated islands or in forest remnants. All the mathematics does is describe the rate at which they go extinct."[3]

The MCS project is designed to study not only the rate but also the mechanisms and patterns of species loss. Reserves of 1, 10, 100, and 1,000 hectares (2.5, 25, 250, and 2,500 acres, respectively) are demarcated, studied for baseline information, and isolated when surrounding areas are cleared for pasture. Long-term investigations of how the animal and plant populations respond to isolation are then carried out in each reserve. Twenty-two such reserves are in active study, and, of these, 10 have been isolated. One 10,000-hectare tract will be left intact to represent the original forest. It is hoped that study of these isolated forest fragments will help in the design of reserves that best preserve the biological diversity of the Amazon Basin. The MCS project should also contribute to a general understanding of ecological processes. There will, however, be limitations in extrapolating results to other regions. Ecosystems vary greatly and must be studied individually, if not as intensely as in this project, to evaluate conservation options.

Early results already show that the decreased area is insufficient to meet the specialized requirements of some species. Fruit-eating monkeys disappeared from one 10 hectare reserve because they could not find a continuous food supply, but less-specialized leaf-eating monkeys have survived.[4] After an initial influx of birds due to the destruction of surrounding habitat, the activity and almost certainly the number of understory bird species (those that live below the forest canopy) has dropped below preisolation levels. Part of the decline in bird species is due to the disappearance of birds that feed on the insects flushed by swarming army ants; an army ant colony requires about 30 hectares of habitat, and birds that follow these ants need several times that area to find enough colonies that are swarming on any given day. Ant-following birds disappeared from the 10-hectare reserve before the ants did. Evidence suggests that corridors connecting fragments to continuous forest may enable small areas to support these birds.[6] More subtle species interactions that do not depend on food supply also have proved to be important. For example, three frog species that breed in the standing water of peccary wallows disappeared after peccaries abandoned a small reserve.[7]

Such area effects were the original focus of the project, but "edge effects," changes resulting from the sharp edge created between primary forest and open pasture, have also been found to have great impact on reserves. The increased penetration of light and hot, dry winds coming from the surrounding clearing have altered the microclimate well into the reserve interior. Within the outer 100 meters of a 100-hectare reserve, air temperature has been found to differ by as much as 4.5°C (8°F) and relative humidity by as much as 20 percent. For 1 and 10 hectare reserves, whole areas have been affected.[8]

Changes in the physical environment have precipitated biological changes. Light-loving butterflies have penetrated 200 to 300 meters into the reserves, where they may now compete with butterflies of the forest interior.[9] Bird populations have diminished at reserve margins. Forest understory birds appear to avoid the sharp edges of the reserves, and few birds typically found at forest margins have invaded.[10] Tree mortality within small reserves has increased, as well as tree falls along windward margins. Researchers estimate that, within a decade, the 1- and 10-hectare reserves will consist entirely of secondary woody vegetation.[11]

These edge-related changes indicate that biological reserves must include buffer zones hundreds of meters wide to maintain a relatively stable core area.[12] Fortunately, about three years after isolation, the growth of vines and weedy trees along the forest margins is expected to block light and wind, thereby helping to restore the original conditions of temperature and humidity to the forest interior.[13] However, these small reserves will still protect far fewer rain forest species than would be protected on the same amount of land within a larger, virgin rain forest environment.

Studies such as this one, which take an ecological perspective, are the most likely to provide information valuable in land-use planning and creation of reserves. As the project's coprincipal investigator Thomas E. Lovejoy states, "The goals of conservation aren't simply to protect the full array of plant and animal species on the planet, but rather also to protect them in their natural associations so that the relationships between species are preserved and the evolutionary and ecological processes are protected."[14]

for acquisition and protection based on a scientific assessment of their potential contribution to the preservation of individual species or communities.

Another criterion for choosing reserve sites is habitat heterogeneity. A population's chances of survival may be increased by having variable habitat within its range. The Bay checkerspot butterfly, for instance, hatches more young on south-facing slopes in wet years and north-facing slopes in dry years. Some populations on slopes facing only one direction have become extinct, while small populations on slopes with differing orientations persist.[101]

Managing Reserves. The 1980 *State of the Parks* survey undertaken by the National Park Service uncovered diverse pressures on park resources in the United States. The problems reported in the survey varied in scale and magnitude from park to park. Aesthetic degradation was the most frequently reported threat, followed by air pollution, logging and mining, the encroachment of exotic plants and animals, visitor impacts and pollution, and water quantity or quality problems. The source of more than half of the reported pressures was outside park boundaries. No major park was free from outside pressures on its resources.[102] As discussed earlier, there is also severe habitat degradation in U.S. wildlife refuges.

In general, there can be an inverse relationship between size and the amount of management necessary in a reserve—the larger the reserve, the less management required. But maintaining and restoring natural processes even in large reserves, particularly those accommodating people—as visitors or inhabitants—can be difficult. In many instances, there is disagreement about why a particular resource is under stress or what should be done about it. On one hand, there is a tendency toward natural-process management, where nature is left to manage more of itself. On the other hand, because most areas are no longer pristine, some active management is needed to maintain or restore naturalness.[103]

What, for example, is to be done about exotic species? Efforts are being made to remove black rats from California's Channel Islands so the native deer mouse can safely return. Attempts are also under way to eliminate the wild boar from Great Smoky Mountains National Park to allow the native vegetation to reestablish itself and to reduce the boar's competition with indigenous black bears. Mountain goat removal is being proposed at Olympic National Park, where this exotic species is destabilizing plant populations, endangering several species of wildflowers, and causing soil erosion.

But the control of exotic species raises some difficult management issues for agencies concerned with natural area protection. In the Everglades, for example, attempts are made to remove exotic species such as Brazilian holly by bulldozing, burning, and mowing, as well as through treatment with herbicides.[104] The costs of removal are often high, however, and some herbicides kill nontarget species.

What happens when natural-process management threatens the very survival of popular species—such as the grizzly bear—in a particular reserve? Should special attention and human intervention be devoted to that species, at the risk of interfering with natural processes and diverting funds and staff from other biological resources? Might efforts to protect one species have unacceptable ecological consequences for others? Are there species that will not be able to exist in natural reserves because their management is not feasible or is simply too costly?

One of the most controversial current issues in grizzly bear management in Yellowstone National Park is supplemental feedings. Advocates of these feedings say that, given the decline of the bear population, the park service should enhance survival by providing food, primarily by dumping animal carcasses in the forests far away from people. This would not only relieve the problems caused by bears begging and stealing from people and foraging through garbage dumps. It is claimed that it would also help keep the bears within park boundaries, protected from poachers and other outside influences. These advocates believe that keeping the bear in Yellowstone is important; if this takes supplemental feedings, and a turn away from natural-process management, they maintain, so be it.[105] Supplemental feedings have not been adopted,[106] and the grizzly bear in Yellowstone has not yet arrived at the point of no return. But the debate about what to do about the grizzly continues.

Because of the effects of internal use, adjacent land uses, boundary designations, and past practices, new and existing reserves may require more active management in the future. The degree to which active management intervention in reserves is necessary is a matter of philosophic orientation as well as scientific judgment. Since few reserves, including the 2.2-million-acre Yellowstone National Park, encompass entire ecosystems, are functioning as complete natural systems, and are free from the effects of human activities inside and outside their boundaries, simple laissez-faire management will not be sufficient in many cases. Answers to questions concerning how much and what types of intervention will be needed to maintain "naturalness" must be developed and refined as more experience is accumulated.

Problems of reserve design and management are of international concern. Kenton R. Miller, director general of IUCN, has observed that many of the world's current reserves provide inadequate protection:

> Existing reserves have been selected according to a number of criteria, including the desire to protect nature, scenery, and watersheds, and to promote cultural values and recreational opportunities. The actual requirements of individual species, populations and communities have seldom been known, nor has the available information always been employed in site selection and planning for nature reserves. The use of lands surrounding nature reserves has typically been inimical to conservation, since it has usually involved heavy use of pesticides, industrial development, and the presence of human settlements in which fire, hunting, and firewood gathering feature as elements of the local economy. Recent studies demonstrate that most existing protected areas are small, have odd shapes, and are at considerable distances from one another. Few have species lists. Most have no research program. Research on the effective boundary for conservation purposes versus actual legal boundaries has only recently been initiated. The fact is that most national parks and nature reserves will rapidly become green islands surrounded by agriculture, logging operations, urbanizations, and encroaching desert.[107]

New Kinds of Reserves. Conflicts in reserve creation and management values are likely to broaden as more reserves begin to incorporate areas where human settlement is part of the landscape to be nurtured. Even if people are not living within a reserved area, future population growth and efforts at economic development may bring human land use literally "up to the fence." The mere act of establishing a reserve may attract people to the area, and their presence and activities can limit the protection the reserve provides. In the United States, for instance, development along the boundaries of national parks and wildlife refuges has become one of the major threats to the integrity of these areas.[108]

As populations increase, wild lands decrease. When people live on and use valuable lands, attempts to establish traditional reserves can have serious economic, social, and political drawbacks. Economic needs or development pressures in many desirable reserve areas may be strong. Worldwide, this is leading to more ambitious and complex responses, namely, the creation of fewer traditional parks and more reserves that permit multiple uses.

In the United States, the Pinelands National Reserve in New Jersey was designed to allow traditional uses of the area to continue while development is controlled to protect critical natural and cultural resources. A state-created commission oversees management of the area, which contains no federally owned land.[109] Cape Cod National Seashore in Massachusetts was one of the first areas to combine a mixture of public and private land and various uses into a reserve.[110] Proposals for similar "greenline parks" in various places in the United States incorporate a variety of landowners, human settlements, and economic uses along with resource protection.[111]

In countries such as Nepal, Panama, and Peru, reserves are similarly being established that include villages within or along their borders. Planning and operating these reserves involve finding economic opportunities for the affected human population that are compatible with the reserve's purposes.[112]

These are dramatic departures from the usual common perception of a national park or refuge. They require an array of management tools, especially where private land is involved. (See box, "Reserves and Supplementary Measures to Protect Privately Owned Land.") These new types of reserves are not without problems, for the natural resources, including wild species, sometimes suffer in competition with human needs and desires. Yet coordinated land-use arrangements are preferable to the alternative of no protection and the simple loss of more species.

The Importance of Nonreserve Habitat

Techniques, policies, and funds for creating and maintaining reserves, while vital and necessary, fall far short of being adequate measures for preserving biological diversity. More attention must be directed at the larger landscape. There will never be enough room on reserves to support all of the earth's important biological resources. Moreover, some species, such as migratory birds, cannot be easily managed solely through a system of reserves. And the impacts from activities on lands outside reserve boundaries will require increasing attention to the economic forces and institutional processes that foster that development.

Even with active and effective reserve and species management, the habitats used by many species and populations will remain largely outside reserves. If the fate of these species were dependent solely on the establishment of reserves, most would soon be added to lists of the endangered or extinct. Therefore, an important question is: How can nonreserved lands be managed to help protect the biological resources that depend on them? This applies not just to lands adjacent to existing reserves but to the broader landscape as well.

Frequently this will involve management plans that integrate economic and conservation goals. In Peru, for example, the National Agrarian University (Universidad Nacional Agraria-La Molina), supported by World Wildlife

Reserves and Supplementary Measures to Protect Privately Owned Land[1]

In the United States, a growing number of areas rely on supplementary protection measures for privately owned land. They vary in permanence, public costs and landowner compensation, degree of resource protection, and provision of public access. Some of the most important measures are:

• *Partial ownership.* Instead of acquiring all ownership rights in parkland ("fee-simple" ownership), a managing agency may acquire partial ("less-than-fee") ownership. Partial ownership often takes the form of an easement, although there are variants such as acquisition of development rights. Partial ownership is sometimes used in combination with other techniques; for example, land may be acquired and resold subject to deed restrictions that limit future development or use.

Whatever its form, partial ownership typically restricts the use of property for the purpose of achieving scenic, or conservation, objectives or providing limited public access. For example, an easement may prevent a landowner from cutting trees or modifying structures without approval by the managing agency. Easements can also require an owner to take certain action, such as providing safe trails for public use or maintaining wildlife habitat.

Easements are used extensively in some units of the National Park System, including the Blue Ridge Parkway and Sawtooth National Recreation Area (managed by the U.S. Forest Service) and with less frequency in a number of others.

Easements may be purchased by the managing agency or donated by a landowner, who may then take advantage of income tax deductions.

• *Acquisition and lease.* Acquisition and lease can be considered a variant of conventional acquisition since the government agency becomes and remains the owner of the land. Instead of managing the land, however, the agency leases it to an individual or corporation, sometimes to the former owner in which case it is called acquisition and leaseback. For example, a rancher in a greenline park might sell his ranch to the managing agency and lease it back for continued ranching; the terms of the lease would determine how the land could be used.

• *Land exchange.* Land exchanges, too, usually involve ownership in fee by the government agency. What is distinctive about land exchanges is that the private owner receives another piece of property instead of cash. Federal laws contain detailed procedures and requirements that must be satisfied before an exchange can be accomplished. For this reason, and because the federal government does not have a good inventory of potential trading stock, exchanges are not widely used, although there has been a movement to make them easier to employ.

• *Land-use regulations.* Regulations such as zoning can affect not only the use of private land within reserves but also that land's value and thus the price that the government must pay to acquire it. Since the agency itself may have no general authority to regulate the use of private land, any land-use regulations governing private land in reserves may need to be adopted by state or local governments.

In several park system units created since 1960, including Cape Cod and Fire Island national seashores, local zoning regulations play a key role in park protection. In these units, the National Park Service cannot condemn specified lands within park boundaries so long as owners use them in accordance with local regulations that the

U.S. Department of the Interior has found compatible with park policy.

• *Developer contributions.* Under state or local laws, developers must sometimes make contributions to resource conservation. For example, the California Coastal Commission requires a developer to earmark four acres for preservation or public use for each acre of wetland developed. Such contributions can sometimes be used to extend protection of parklands, although the approach raises several legal and administrative issues.

• *Private stewardship.* In a variety of ways short of binding legal agreements, and often as a result of informal consultation with reserve officials, landowners within reserves have long modified the ways they manage their property in deference to the needs of the area. Some places—for example, Santa Monica Mountains National Recreation Area—are taking vigorous initiatives to develop cooperative park service/landowner programs with respect to such activities as planting native species and encouraging compatible residential design and good land planning.

• *Incentives and assistance for landowners.* Incentives and assistance for landowners can be used alone or in combination with measures such as easements, zoning, or reliance on private stewardship. In either case, such "sweeteners" supplement the regulatory process. They can also be useful to secure positive action by a property owner—for example, the provision of access across private property to a river or the maintenance of a trail.

Until 1986, federal tax incentives played an important role in fostering the donation or bargain sale of important natural areas to private land trusts such as the Nature Conservancy and in promoting preservation and rehabilitation of historic buildings. The donor of land or of a restrictive easement could take a charitable tax deduction. In the case of historic buildings, the federal tax code allowed developers a 25 percent credit for approved preservation expenditures. Tax and financial incentives also could be an important adjunct to other protection techniques. In mid-1987, however, it remained unclear what effect recent changes specified in the Tax Reform Act of 1986 will have on these incentives. In addition, continuing federal budget deficits make the likelihood of any new incentives uncertain.

• *Technical assistance and grants-in-aid to governments.* Many local governments, particularly in semideveloped rural areas, do not have the financial resources or expertise to deal with complex land-use planning issues. Yet the success of a greenline effort—that is, one involving a mix of landowners and land uses—usually depends on a cooperative and knowledgeable local partner.

In a few instances, notably at Pictured Rocks and Sleeping Bear Dunes national lakeshores, Congress has authorized federal land managing agencies to provide grants to local regulatory and planning agencies. At Sleeping Bear Dunes, the park service helped fund economic impact studies for two counties soon after the park was established a decage ago. Other economic impact studies have been performed at Cape Cod and Redwood National Park.

Perhaps the most ambitious use of incentives to stimulate local planning occurs in New York State's Adirondack park, where the Adirondack Park Agency pays up to 87 percent of a local government's cost of preparing local land-use plans. The agency also develops model ordinances and helps train local zoning officers. Between 1973 and 1982, the agency provided assistance to 84 communities in the park at a cost of more than $1.4 million.

Fund, has devised a strategy for sustained-use management of the mangrove ecosystem in that country, where marine resources have been exploited through harvesting and habitat alteration to maximize yields. The strategy is to coordinate the activities of different local agencies and manage the resources so as to perpetuate those biological processes in the estuaries and mangroves that sustain both the ecosystem and the area's economic base.[113]

In the United States, all levels of government have established programs to encourage conservation on nonreserved lands. Some programs operate indirectly. For example, the National Environmental Policy Act of 1969 and the Fish and Wildlife Coordination Act, as amended in 1965, require consideration of the adverse impacts on environmental and wild-species resources caused by federally funded or permitted projects.[114] They also require examination of alternatives to minimize those impacts.

State programs provide technical advice and materials to landowners for habitat improvement projects on farms and ranches. Some also offer tax credits for conservation easements or contracts for maintenance of compatible land uses. The 1986 Reinvest in Minnesota Resources Act pays farmers to take their most erodible and marginal lands out of production and convert them into wildlife habitat.[115] The cost of Nebraska's Private Lands Habitat Program is shared by the state through stamp sales to hunters (75 percent) and by local districts through taxation (25 percent). As of 1981, 35,000 acres had been enrolled in the program.[116]

Habitat degradation on agricultural lands is a major problem because so many acres are involved and because the conversion of land to agricultural use typically renders the area largely inhospitable to wildlife. For example, World Wildlife Fund is supporting a study of the effects of traditional and alternative agricultural practices on migratory birds in Mexico's Yucatan Peninsula. Mayan farmers are being encouraged to use small-scale, intensive farming techniques aimed at increasing their net income *and* reducing forest habitat destruction. If this alternative to extensive slash-and-burn agriculture becomes widely accepted, it could help to slow the decline of the migratory birds dependent on these tropical forest lands.[117]

The U.S. Department of Agriculture has made some attempt to promote farmland management techniques that provide food and protection for wild species and reduce threats to them. One goal of the Conservation Reserve Program established by the 1985 Food Security Act is to increase wildlife habitat. Farmers who enroll highly erodible land in the program will establish a vegetative core of grass or trees that, in principle, should provide food and shelter for wild animals, particularly game birds.[118] However, it is not yet clear whether land in the conservation reserve program will in fact be managed by farmers in ways that are beneficial to wild species. (See chapter 6.)

Of course, farmers can take actions on their own to improve habitat or minimize damage to wild species. Various tactics—such as delaying plowing until spring so that waste grain and other food is available to wild animals during the winter months, retaining wild hedgerows, controlling overgrazing, and keeping livestock out of certain areas during nesting seasons— are available to improve the ability of farmland to sustain wild species.[119] In many cases, these techniques have the added advantages of reducing soil erosion and improving productivity.

Some large industrial landowners have voluntarily undertaken wildlife enhancement efforts. Tenneco Oil, for example, has undertaken a project to maintain a 5,000-acre marsh it owns in Louisiana. The installation and operation of water control structures prevents saltwater intrusion from destroying the marsh, protecting the company's rights to oil and gas resources and preserving valuable wildlife habitat.[120]

Most "nonreserved" federal lands—that is, lands that are not primarily used for maintenance of wild species—are forest and range areas owned by the Forest Service and the Bureau of Land Management (BLM). These lands are managed under multipurpose or "multiple use" mandates. Wildlife and watershed protection needs are considered along with human needs for timber, beef, minerals, and recreation.

Over the last decade, BLM and the Forest Service sometimes have increased their consideration of wild species' needs. In 1985, for example, BLM used nearly $600,000 in appropriations and contributions to undertake recovery efforts for the desert bighorn sheep, some 80 percent of which are found on federal lands. With these funds, BLM reintroduced the species into four new areas in Arizona, built 14 water facilities, and conducted two habitat- and population-monitoring projects and one lamb-mortality study. Additional funds were appropriated for fiscal year 1986 with the expectation that private contributions would again match the appropriation.[121]

The fact that many populations of wild species may overlap several different governmental jurisdictions and private properties poses unique problems. Thus, achievement of habitat preservation goals requires substantial cooperation among various land managers and owners.

Private lands and federally owned forests and rangeland set aside for multiple-use management will become increasingly important for sustaining wild species in the United States. Fortunately, many types of land use are compatible with wildlife needs. For example, careful selective harvesting of trees can provide a sustained economic return, yet leave adequate stocks for reseeding and for animal needs. Owners of a private 5,000-acre tract of oak and pine forest in southern New Jersey harvest approximately 1,000 cords of wood per year, yet are also paid $550 per year by each person hunting on their land.[122] In Louisiana, hunting rights may yield as much as $10 per acre per year, and rates are rising.[123]

Habitat Restoration. Sometimes a natural community may be so damaged by pollution, deforestation, or other factors that it cannot be revived with simple protection or modest management efforts alone. In such cases, intensive efforts may be made to recreate the original community by essentially "replanting it" or by changing environmental conditions so that it can replant itself. In the United States, replacement of several types of saltwater and freshwater marshes destroyed by development and dredging has been mandated by environmental laws.[124] With respect to plant species, at least, the restored communities often can be returned to conditions very similar to the original.[125] However, attention is rarely given to restoring small animals, such as insects and mollusks, to these communities.

Restoration efforts range from simple preparation of a site for natural colonization by a native species to a complex effort to plant many species in ways that mimic natural succession. In recent years, exotic grasses in the California habitat of the endangered Lange's metalmark butterfly have been hand-cleared to reduce competition with auriculate buckwheat, the native species on which the butterflies lay their eggs.[126] With freshwater wetlands, recolonization of marsh plants can sometimes be facilitated by grading the disturbed area to reconstruct the hydrologic conditions under which the plants thrive. However, natural colonization alone will not always suffice, as when a forest has been so extensively cleared that no seed sources remain. In such cases, soil preparation, planting, and weeding may all be necessary.

One ambitious restoration project now under way is the attempt to transform degraded lands surrounding a Costa Rican dry tropical forest reserve into additional forest. The new forest will form a corridor between the present dry forest and nearby moist forest, so that migratory animals, particularly moths and other insects, dependent on both types of forest can journey back and forth.[127] In some areas, tropical forest lands cleared for agriculture have been abandoned as soil quality has deteriorated. These lands have little value today, but reserves might be established on them and recovery efforts undertaken.[128] (See box, "Restoring the Everglades Ecosystem.")

Clearly there are many opportunities to restore damaged lands for wild species. Restored areas might help conserve rare species by functioning as corridors or buffer zones adjacent to reserves. Such areas can provide habitat for remnant populations threatened by development or introduced from captive breeding facilities.

Better management of nonreserved lands in general could substantially benefit many types of biological resources; in a conflict with more profitable uses of the land, however, wild species are likely to lose out. In the future, governments will have to become even more creative in encouraging compatible land use through regulations and incentives so that wildlife habitat protection is more beneficial to the landowner. Conservationists, for their part, must work toward channeling economic development into areas that will not disrupt valuable habitat, and seeing that sound environmental planning is undertaken when development does occur.

CONCLUDING THOUGHTS

In this "age of extinction," as Dr. Thomas E. Lovejoy has called it, powerful forces are diminishing the vast biological richness of the earth.[129] Countervailing protective forces, although stronger than a generation ago, are only beginning to come to grips with the problem.

Information—about what species exist, where they are concentrated, how and where they are most threatened, how to design and manage reserves—will permit more efficient allocation of the limited resources available for protection. It remains crucial that scientific knowledge continue to be sought and technical solutions continue to be developed.

At present, however, the constituency for protecting biological diversity as such remains thin. Many people who would be sympathetic with the aim are unfamiliar with the term or, if they have run across it, find it unmoving. For a variety of economic, political, and social reasons, the practical opportunities to preserve biological diversity often do not take advantage of the optimum technical solutions. A strategy is needed to bridge science and policy. To fashion that strategy, conservationists must search for allies and must establish priorities among protection approaches.

One element of a strategy to conserve biodiversity is a vision of the richness of life on earth and the moral and ethical arguments associated with this vision. As a declaration at a major interfaith conference on environmental conservation in 1986 stated: "We have a responsibility to life, to defend it everywhere, not only against our own sins, but also against those of others. We are all passengers, together, in the same fragile and glorious world."[130] These arguments can have an increasing impact—much as the wilderness vision has strengthened wildlands protection measures in the United States during the past generation.

Another strategic element should be to increase awareness of the economic benefits of diverse species, ecosystems, and gene pools to agriculture, medicine, and other quantifiable sectors. Until recently, conservationists did not focus much on the broader issues involving integrating conservation and economic goals more effectively to protect wild species. This has begun to change, especially as reserves have faced mounting pressures from the civilizations that surround them, as environmental concerns have become more institutionalized in government programs, and as conservationists have recognized the indisputable links between an area's needs for economic growth and its environmental goals. Much more work, however, needs to be done.

In fashioning their strategies, those committed to preserving biodiversity need to make choices. Effective support for protection will require a broad coalition of people—of politicians, hunters, pharmaceutical firms, development economists, for example—with diverse interests and methods to forestall destruction. Only by establishing priorities can such a coalition hope to ensure that limited resources are employed effectively. Focusing funds in one reserve or one country may mean important needs are not addressed elsewhere; an all-out effort to protect one species may be bought with the extinction of others. This is not welcome news. By exerting leadership and helping to determine the choices, however, one avoids having them imposed by others.

As time goes on and changes occur in human sensitivities, the values that are perceived in biological diversity may also evolve. In describing a place he visited in South America, Edward O. Wilson wrote:

> To the south stretches Surinam eternal, Surinam serene, a living treasure awaiting assay. I hope that it will be kept intact, that at least enough of its million-year history will be saved for the reading. By today's ethic its value may seem limited, well beneath the pressing concerns of daily life. But I suggest that as biological knowledge grows the ethic will shift fundamentally so that everywhere, for reasons that have to do with the very fiber of the brain, the fauna and flora of a country will be thought part of the national heritage as important as its art, its language, and that astonishing blend of achievement and farce that has always defined our species.[131]

FURTHER READING

The chapter on "Ecology and Natural Resources—Biological Diversity" in *Environmental Quality 1980: 11th Annual Report of the President's Council on Environmental Quality* (Washington, D.C.: U.S. Government Printing Office, 1980) provides a useful overview of the concept of and issues involved in biological diversity—the benefits of diversity, the causes of its reduction, and some strategies and policies for its conservation. Two other overviews published at about the same time are *The Global 2000 Report to the President: Entering the Twenty-first Century* (Washington, D.C.: U.S. Government Printing Office, 1980), which called attention to loss of species between now and the year 2000, and a chapter in Julian Simon and Herman Kahn, *The Resourceful Earth: A Response to Global 2000* (New York: Basil Blackwell, 1980), which cautions that the problem of such loss needs deeper thought and more wide-ranging analysis.

Several conferences in the early 1980s, notably the U.S. Conference on Biological Diversity, November 16-18, 1981—cosponsored by the U.S. Agency for International Development, the U.S. Departments of State, Agriculture, the Interior, and Commerce, the Smithsonian Institution, and the National Science Foundation—was convened to stimulate such analysis. Norman Myers's *A Wealth of Wild Species* (Boulder, Colo: Westview Press, 1983) further popularized the value of species preservation. Several recent studies are providing the underpinnings for increased attention to biological diversity issues. The U.S. Office of Technology Assessment issued several backround papers and then a comprehensive study in the spring of 1987, *Technologies to Maintain Biological Diversity* (Washington, D.C.: U.S. Government Printing Office). *World Resources 1986* and *World Resources 1987* by the World Resources Institute and the International Institute for Environment and Development contain chapters on wildlife and threatened species issues. And *Environmental Quality 1984: 15th Annual Report on the Council on Environmental Quality* (Washington, D.C.: U.S. Government Printing Office, 1986) chronicles the rise of biological diversity as an environmental concern, as well as potential responses.

The emerging field of conservation biology is the subject of a book edited by Michael Soule, *Conservation Biology: The Science of Scarcity and Diversity* (Sunderland, Mass.: Sinauer Associates, 1986). A new journal, entitled *Conservation Biology*, is being published by Blackwell Scientific Publishers. Current issues in biodiversity are frequently the subject of articles in *BioScience*, a monthly journal.

New evidence of the economic values of wildlife resources in the United States is the subject of Christine Prescott-Allen and Robert Prescott-Allen, *The First Resource* (New Haven, Conn.: Yale University Press, 1986). In terms of wildlife resources in the United States, the National Audubon Society has published two annual reports that examine the current status in wildlife and describe recent events and trends in their management by public and private agencies. Legal issues regarding wildlife and biological diversity are thoroughly covered and presented for the expert and lay person alike in a revised and expanded edition by Michael Bean, *The Evolution of National Wildlife Law* (New York: Praeger Publishers, 1983). Finally, *International Wildlife Law, An Analysis of Treaties Concerned with the Conservation of Wildlife* by Simon Lyster (Cambridge, England: Grotius, 1985) merits notice as a unique reference.

REFERENCES

Text

1. Mark J. Palmer, "Too Late for the Condor?" *Sierra* 71, no. 1 (1986):33.

2. John Ogden, "The California Condor," in National Audubon Society, *Audubon Wildlife Report 1985* (New York: National Audubon Society, 1985), p. 392-93.

3. Ibid., p. 393-97.

4. Jay Mathews, "Last Wild Condor of Species Netted," *Washington Post*, April 20, 1987.

5. Richard Conniff, "Inventorying Life in a 'Biotic Frontier' Before It Disappears," *Smithsonian* 17, no. 6 (1986):80-81.

6. 16 USCA §§1531-43 (1985); see also Michael J. Bean, *The Evolution of National Wildlife Law* (New York: Praeger Publishers, 1983), pp. 330-31.

7. U.S. Department of the Interior, Fish and Wildlife Service, Office of Endangered Species, "Number of Species Listed by Calendar Year, 3/31/86", 1986 (photocopy). However, despite these gains, listing of insects, clams, crustacea, and plants still lag far behind their actual populations among the world's biota.

8. Laura Tangley, "A New Plan to Conserve the Earth's Biota," *Bioscience* 35 (1985):334-35. The "U.S. Strategy on the Conservation of Biological Diversity: An Interagency Task Force report to Congress" was delivered to Congress in 1985. In 1986, AID completed a follow-up document entitled "Action Plan on Conserving Biological Diversity in Developing Countries I."

9. Paul R. Ehrlich, "Habitats in Crisis," *Wilderness* 50, no. 176 (1987):12.

10. For further discussion, see U.S. Congress, Office of Technology Assessment, *Technologies to Maintain Biological Diversity*, OTA-F-330 (Washington, D.C.: U.S. Government Printing Office, 1987), pp. 37-43; Robert E. Jenkins, "The Preservation of Natural Diversity"; in The Nature Conservancy, *The Preservation of Natural Diversity* (Washington, D.C.: The Nature Conservancy, 1975); and The Ecological Society of America, *Conserving*

Biological Diversity in Our National Forests, prepared for The Wilderness Society (Washington, D.C.: The Wilderness Society, 1986).

11. U.S. Department of the Interior, Fish and Wildlife Service, *Endangered and Threatened Wildlife and Plants* (Washington, D.C.: U.S. Government Printing Office, 1986), p. 30.

12. Paul R. Ehrlich and Harold A. Mooney, "Extinction, Substitution, and Ecosystem Services," *BioScience* 33, no. 4 (1983):249, 254.

13. John Yurus, "Song Dog in the Suburbs," *Animal Kingdom* 89, no. 3 (1986):36.

14. Ehrlich, "Habitats in Crisis", p. 14.

15. Aldo Leopold, *A Sand County Almanac* (New York: Sierra Club/Ballantine Books, 1966), p. 190.

16. Norman Myers, *A Wealth of Wild Species* (Boulder, Colo.: Westview Press, 1983), pp. 27-42, 63-75.

17. Steven C. Witt, *Biotechnology and Genetic Diversity* (San Francisco: California Agricultural Lands Project, 1985), p. 13-14. According to Witt, over half of the increased yields in these species can be attributed to genetic improvements, with the remaining increases due to "inputs" such as irrigation, fertilizer, pesticides, herbicides and farm machinery.

18. Ibid., pp. 14, 16; and Christine Prescott-Allen and Robert Prescott-Allen , *The First Resource* (New Haven, Conn.: Yale University Press, 1986), pp. 329-30.

19. Myers, *A Wealth of Wild Species*, pp. 152-55.

20. Norman R. Farnsworth and Ralph W. Morris, "Higher Plants—The Sleeping Giant of Drug Development," *American Journal of Pharmacy* 148 (1976):46-47.

21. Myers, *A Wealth of Wild Species*, pp. 92-94.

22. "Searching for Cures in the Rainforest," *World Wildlife Fund News*, September-October 1986, p. 3.

23. Personal communication with Mark Plotkin, World Wildlife Fund, October 28, 1986.

24. Prescott-Allen and Prescott-Allen, *The First Resource*, p. 104.

25. International Union for Conservation of Nature and Natural Resources, *World Conservation Strategy* (Gland, Switzerland: International Union for Conservation of Nature and Natural Resources, 1980), sect. 3.7.

26. Prescott-Allen and Prescott-Allen, *The First Resource*, p. 363.

27. U.S. Department of the Interior, Fish and Wildlife Service, and U.S. Department of Commerce, Bureau of the Census, *1980 National Survey of Fishing, Hunting, and Wildlife-Associated Recreation* (Washington, D.C.: U.S. Government Printing Office, 1982), pp. 4-5.

28. William W. Shaw and William R. Mangun, *Nonconsumptive Use of Wildlife in the United States*, Fish and Wildlife Service Resource Publication 154 (Washington, D.C.: U.S. Department of the Interior, 1984), p. 10.

29. Walter E. Westman, "How Much Are Nature's Services Worth?" *Science* 197 (1977):961; and Ehrlich, "Habitats in Crisis," pp. 14-15.

30. U.S. Congress, Office of Technology Assessment, *Wetlands: Their Use and Regulation* (Washington, D.C.: U.S. Office of Technology Assessment, 1984), p. 45.

31. Ralph W. Tiner, Jr., *Wetlands of the United States: Current Status and Recent Trends* (Washington, D.C.: U.S. Government Printing Office, 1984), p. 18.

32. Jeffery Kahn, "Restoring the Everglades," *Sierra* 71, no. 5 (1986):41.

33. Edward O. Wilson, "The Biological Diversity Crisis," *BioScience* 35 (1985):700.

34. Ibid.; Coniff, "Inventorying life in a 'Biotic Frontier' Before It Disappears," p. 81.

35. U.S. Office of Technology Assessment, *Technologies to Maintain Biological Diversity*, pp. 4, 74.

36. Council on Environmental Quality and U.S. Deparment of State, *The Global 2000 Report to the President: Entering the Twenty-first Century*, vol. 2 (Washington, D.C.: U.S. Government Printing Office, 1980), pp. 328-31.

37. Julian L. Simon and Aaron Wildavsky, "On Species Loss, the Absence of Data, and Risks to Humanity," in Julian L. Simon and Herman Kahn, ed., *The Resourceful Earth* (New York: Basil Blackwell, 1984), pp. 171-83.

38. U.S. Office of Technology Assessment, *Technologies to Maintain Biological Diversity*, p. 74.

39. International Union for Conservation of Nature and Natural Resources, *World Conservation Strategy*, sects. 4.1-9.

40. Ibid., sects. 3.11-12.

41. See National Audubon Society, *Audubon Wildlife Report, 1985* and *Audubon Wildlife Report, 1986*, for case studies discussing the varied threats to United States species.

42. For further discussion of the threats facing small populations, see Mark L. Shaffer, "Minimum Population Sizes for Species Conservation," *BioScience* 31 (1981):131-34; and Peter F. Brussard, "Minimum Viable Populations: How Many are Too Few?' *Restoration & Management Notes*, Summer 1985, pp. 21-25.

43. U.S. Department of the Interior, Fish and Wildlife Service, Endangered Species Program, "Woodland Caribou Listed as Endangered in Emergency Rule," *Endangered Species Technical Bulletin* 8, no. 1 (1983).

44. World Resources Institute and International Institute for Environment and Development, *World Resources 1986* (Washington, D.C.: World Resources Institute and International Institute for Environment and Development, 1986), p. 90.

45. National Audubon Society, *Audubon Wildlife Report 1985*, pp. 426-57.

46. Gary E. Machlis and David L. Tichnell, *State of the World's Parks* (Boulder, Colo.: Westview Press, 1985), p. 50. In a survey of national parks worldwide, the authors found that in 74 of the 98 parks surveyed, illegal removal of animal life was perceived as a threat.

47. "Traffic Stems Illegal Trade," *WWF News*, July-August 1986, pp. 1-2.

48. James Serfis, Richard Tinney, and Roger E. McManus, "The Environmental Protection Agency's Implementation of the Endangered Species Act with Respect to Pesticide Registration," report prepared by the Center for Environmental Education for the President's Council on Environmental Quality and the U.S. Environmental Protection Agency, July 1986.

49. International Union for Conservation of Nature and Natural Resources, *World Conservation Strategy*, sect. 3.11.

50. Norman Myers, "Tropical Deforestation and a Mega-Extinction Spasm"; in Michael E. Soule, ed., *Conservation Biology: The Science of Scarcity and Diversity* (Sunderland, Mass.: Sinauer Associates, 1986), pp. 399-400.

51. Steven Jay Parcells, "How Long the Tallgrass . . . ?" *National Parks and Conservation Magazine* 52, no. 4 (1980)4.

52. Michael D. Lemonick, "A Preserve of Splendid Grass," *Time*, July 14, 1986, p. 42; and Philip Shabecoff, "National Park Takes Root in Oklahoma," *New York Times*, July 23, 1985.

53. "A Decade of Debate: The Biosphere," *Ambio* 11, no. 4 (1982):220-22.

54. U.S. Office of Technology Assessment, *Wetlands: Their Use and Regulation*, pp. 6, 11, 91.

55. Ralph W. Tiner, Jr., *Wetlands of the United States*, p. 38.

56. Rodney V. Salm, "Coral Reefs of the Western Indian Ocean: A Threatened Heritage," *Ambio* 12, no. 6 (1983):349-53.

57. U.S. Department of the Interior, Fish and Wildlife Service, Division of Refuge Management, "Preliminary Survey of Contaminant Issues of Concern on National Wildlife Refuges," 1986, p. A-44; and "Tragedy at Kesterson Reservoir: Death of a Wildlife Refuge Illustrates Failings of Water Law," *Environmental Law Reporter* 15 (1985):10,387.

58. U.S. Fish and Wildlife Service, "Preliminary Survey of Contaminant Issues of Concern on National Wildlife Refuges," pp. 6-7.

59. "Monitoring Bird Populations," *Cooperative Research Newsletter*, Summer 1986, p. 1.

60. "The Case of Baltic Seals," *Ambio* 9, nos. 3-4 (1980):182.

61. Whit Fosburgh, "The Striped Bass", in National Audubon Society, *Audubon Wildlife Report 1985*, p. 421.

62. National Wildlife Federation, Resolution No. 15, 48th meeting of the National Wildlife Federation, Atlanta, Georgia, March 15 - 18, 1984.

63. U.S. Department of the Interior, National Park Service, Office of Science and Technology, *State of the Parks 1980. A Report to the Congress* (Washington, D.C.: National Park Service, 1980), pp. 2, 15.

64. The Conservation Foundation, *National Parks for a New Generation: Visions, Realities, Prospects* (Washington, D.C.: The Conservation Foundation, 1985), p. 128.

65. Walter R. Courtenay, Jr., "The Introduction of Exotic Organisms" in Howard P. Brokaw, ed., *Wildife and America: Contributions to an Understanding of American Wildlife and Its Conservation* (Washington, D.C.: Council on Environmental Quality, 1978), p. 238.

66. Alston Chase, "The Last Bears of Yellowstone," *The Atlantic Monthly*, February 1983, p. 67.

67. Personal communication with Pieter Oyens and Martha Hays-Cooper, World Wildlife Fund, October 31, 1986.

68. Anne M. Byers, "The Nature Conservancy and Species Diversity," *Nature Conservancy News* 32, no. 1 (1982):22; and The Nature Conservancy, "Fact Sheet: Natural Heritage Programs, 1986."

69. Personal communication with Curtis Freese, World Wildlife Fund, October 31, 1986.

70. John Ogden, "The California Condor"; in The National Audubon Society, *Audubon Wildlife Report 1985*, p. 395.

71. Juanita Greene, "Panthers at the Vanishing Point," *National Parks* 59, nos. 7-8 (1985):18-20.

72. A.R. Weisbrod, "On the Biology and Management of Species Threatened with Extinction," *Trends in Natural Resources* 19, no. 1 (1982):17-19.

73. 27 U.S.T. 1087; T.I.A.S. No. 8249. For more information regarding CITES and earlier international wildlife trade regulations, see Tim Inskipp and Sue Wells, *International Trade in Wildlife* (London: International Institute for Environment and Development, 1979), pp. 4-27.

74. Information provided by TRAFFIC(USA), May 1987; and Inskipp and Wells, *International Trade in Wildlife*, pp. 5, 7-9.

75. For more detailed information on CITES and its regulatory framework, see Simon Lyster, *International Wildlife Law: An Analysis of International Treaties Concerned with the Conservation of Wildlife* (Cambridge: Grotius Publications, 1985), pp. 239-77.

76. U.S. Department of the Interior, Fish and Wildlife Service, Office of Endangered

Species, Recovery Plan Cost Programs.

77. Hal Salwasser, "Managing Ecosystems for Viable Populations of Large Vertebrates," draft report presented at the Scientific Conference of the Greater Yellowstone Coalition, Yellowstone National Park, May 30, 1986.

78. James C. Lewis, "The Whooping Crane"; in National Audubon Society, *Audubon Wildlife Report 1986*, pp. 671-72.

79. Ibid., p. 670.

80. "Monitoring Bird Populations," p. 1.

81. John H. Barclay and Tom J. Cade, "Restoration of the Peregrine Falcon in the Eastern United States," *Bird Conservation* 1 (1986):1.

82. Witt, *Biotechnology and Genetic Diversity*, p. 64.

83. Frankel and Soule, *Conservation and Evolution*, pp. 138-39; and Barclay and Cade, "Restoration of the Peregrine Falcon in the Eastern United States," pp. 3-39.

84. Ralls and Ballou, "Extinction: Lessons from Zoos"; in Christine M. Schonewald-Cox et al., eds., *Genetics and Conservation* (Menlo Park, Calif: Benjamin Cummings, 1983), pp. 164-65.

85. Personal communication with Betsy Dresser, Cincinnati Zoo, February 6, 1986.

86. Adelmar F. Coimbra-Filho and Russell A. Mittermeier, "Hybridization in the Genus *Leontopithecus*, *L.r. rosalia* (Linnaeus, 1766), x *L.r. chrysomelas* (Kuhl, 1820) (Callitrichidae, Primates)," *Revista Brasileira de Biologia* 36, no. 1 (1976):129-37.

87. Frank Thibodeau, "Saving the Pieces—A New Center for Plant Conservation," *Restoration and Management Notes*, Winter 1984, pp. 71-72.

88. American Association of Zoological Parks and Aquariums, *Species Survival Plans* (Wheeling, W.Va.: American Association of Zoological Parks and Aquariums, n.d.).

89. Prescott-Allen, *Genes from the Wild* (London: International Union for Conservation of Nature and Natural Resources, 1983), pp. 92-93.

90. Ralls and Ballou, "Extinction: Lessons from Zoos"; in Schonewald-Cox et al., eds., *Genetics and Conservation*, pp. 164-65.

91. Thomas J. Foose, "The Relevance of Captive Populations to the Conservation of Biotic Diversity"; in Schonewald-Cox et al., eds., *Genetics and Conservation*, pp. 376-79.

92. William Conway, "The Practical Difficulties and Financial Implications of Endangered Species Breeding Programs," *International Zoo Yearbook 24/25* (London: Zoological Society of London, 1986), pp. 210-19.

93. World Resources Institute and International Institute for Environment and Development, *World Resources 1986*, table 7.1, pp. 282-83.

94. Bruce A. Wilcox, "Insular Ecology and Conservation"; in Michael E. Soule and Bruce A. Wilcox, eds., *Conservation Biology: An Evolutionary-Ecological Perspective* (Sunderland, Mass.: Sinauer Associates, 1980), pp. 114-16.

95. William Dubois Newmark, "Mammalian Richness, Colonization, and Extinction in Western North American National Parks," Ph.D. dissertation, University of Michigan, 1986, abstract and p. 28.

96. For a further discussion of nature reserve design and the consequences of insularization, see Frankel and Soule, *Conservation and Evolution*, pp. 101-22; Bruce A. Wilcox, "Insular Ecology and Conservation"; in Soule and Wilcox, eds., *Conservation Biology*, pp. 95-227; and John Terborgh and Blair Winter, "Some Causes of Extinction"; in Soule and Wilcox, eds., *Conservation Biology*, pp. 119-33.

97. Larry D. Harris, *The Fragmented Forest* (Chicago: University of Chicago Press, 1984), pp. 84-87.

98. Personal communication with Pieter Oyens and Martha Hays-Cooper, World Wildlife Fund, October 31, 1986.

99. Rachel T. Saunders, "A Safe Harbor for the Sea Otter," *Sierra* 71, no. 5 (1986):26, 28.

100. Personal communication with Curtis Freese, World Wildlife Fund, October 31, 1986.

101. Bruce A. Wilcox and Dennis D. Murphy, "Conservation Strategy: The Effects of Fragmentation on Extinction," *American Naturalist* 125 (1985):881-83.

102. National Park Service, *State of the Parks 1980*, pp. 3-6.

103. Robert Michael Pyle, "Management of Nature Reserves"; in Soule and Wilcox, eds., *Conservation Biology*, pp. 320-321.

104. Noel Vietmeyer, "Casuarinea: Weed or Windfall", *American Forests* 92, no. 2 (1986):26; and The Conservation Foundation, *National Parks for a New Generation*, p. 128.

105. Alston Chase, "The Last Bears of Yellowstone", *The Atlantic Monthly* 251, no. 2 (1983):63-73.

106. Alston Chase, *Playing God in Yellowstone* (Boston: Atlantic Monthly Press, 1986), p. 182-83.

107. Kenton R. Miller, "Foreword"; in Larry D. Harris, *The Fragmented Forest*, pp. xii-xiii.

108. The Conservation Foundation, *National Parks for a New Generation*, p. 126; and Chase, "The Last Bears of Yellowstone," p. 72.

109. The Conservation Foundation, *National Parks for a New Generation*, p. 63.

110. Ibid., pp. 157-69.

111. Ibid., pp. 225, 258.

112. Personal communication with Michael Wright, World Wildlife Fund, October 31, 1986.

113. Personal communication with Curtis Freese, World Wildlife Fund, October 31, 1986.

114. 42 USCA §§4321 et seq. (1983); 16 USCA §§661-67e (1983) (amended in 1958); see also Bean, *The Evolution of National Wildlife Law*, pp. 181-201.

115. July 28, 1986, news release from Rep. John Rose, District 63A, Minnesota, "Minnesota Conservation Bill Selected as National Model."

116. Carl R. Madsen, "Wildlife Habitat Development and Restoration Programs"; in Robert T. Dumke, George V. Burger, and James R. March, eds., *Wildlife Management on Private Lands*, proceedings of Symposium: Wildlife Management on Private Lands, May 3-6, 1981, Milwaukee, Wisconsin (Madison, Wisc.: The Wildlife Society, 1981), pp. 210-11.

117. "Can a New Agriculture Save Migratory Birds?" *Focus*, newletter of World Wildlife Fund, September/October 1986, pp. 1, 3.

118. Lewrene K. Glaser, *Provisions of the Food Security Act of 1985*, Agriculture Information Bulletin No 498 (Washington, D.C.: U.S. Government Printing Office, 1986), pp. 46-47.

119. U.S. Congress, Office of Technology Assessment, *Technologies to Benefit Agriculture and Wildlife, Workshop Proceedings* (Washington, D.C.: U.S. Government Printing Office, 1985), pp. 13-18.

120. *Outdoor News Bulletin*, September 21, 1984, p. 5.

121. Katherine Barton, "Wildlife and the Bureau of Land Management;" in National Audubon Society, *Audubon Wildlife Report 1986*, p. 508.

122. Deborah A. Boerner, "Firewood, Game, Tax Dollars, and Land Stewardship,"

American Forests 91, no. 9 (1985):47-49.

123. Jim Conrad, "Hunting for Forest Income, *American Forests* 91, no. 9 (1985):45-46.

124. Millicent L. Quammen, "Measuring the Success of Wetlands Mitigation," *National Wetlands Newsletter*, September-October 1986.

125. William R. Jordan III, "Hint of Green—Making Marshes along the Atlantic Coast," *Restoration and Management Notes*, Summer 1983, pp. 4-10.

126. Paul A. Opler and Lee Robinson, "Lange's Metalmark Butterfly"; in National Audubon Society, *Audubon Wildlife Report 1986*, p. 914. Further attempts are being made to increase the amount of available habitat within Antioch Dunes National Wildlife Refuge by transforming part of an abandoned vineyard into dunes and planting nursery raised buckwheat.

127. Daniel H. Janzen, "How to Grow a Tropical National Park," paper presented at a symposium, "Tropical Forest Conservation: What can be done? What can we do?' December 4-6, 1985, National Zoological Park, Washington, D.C.; Jamie Murphy, "Growing a Forest from Scratch", *Time*, December 29, 1986, p. 65.

128. Thomas E. Lovejoy, "Rehabilitation of Degraded Tropical Forest Lands," reprinted from *The Environmentalist* 5 (1985); International Union for Conservation of Nature and Natural Resources, *Rehabilitation of Degraded Tropical Rainforest Lands* (Gland, Switzerland: International Union for Conservation of Nature and Natural Resources, 1977).

129. Thomas Lovejoy, "Education, Zoos, and the 'Age of Extinction," keynote address at the American Association of Zoological Parks, Northeast Regional Conference, Burnet Park Zoo, Syracuse, New York, March 16, 1987.

130. "The Assisi Declarations," *WWF News*, November-December 1986, p.3.

131. Laura Tangley, "Biological Diversity Goes Public," *BioScience* 36, no. 11 (1986): 710.

Boxes

Restoring the Everglades Ecosystem

1. Nelson M. Blake, *Land into Water—Water into Land: A History of Water Management in Florida* (Tallahassee, Fla.: University Presses of Florida, 1980), pp. 95-100.

2. Jeffery Kahn, "Restoring the Everglades," *Sierra* 71, no. 5 (1986):41.

3. Kerry Gruson, "Flooding Pores Threat to Everglades Ecology," *New York Times*, July 25, 1983, p. A10; Steven Yates, "Florida's Broken Rain Machine," *The Amicus Journal* 4, no. 2 (1982):48.

4. Bill Belleville, "The Everglades: Headed for Death Before It Is Ever Understood," *ENFO*, August 1983, p. 1.

5. "Save Our Everglades, Report Card No. 6," May 9, 1986; William R. Mangun, "Wetlands and Wildlife Resource Issues," *National Wetlands Newsletter*, November-December 1983, p. 8

6. Keith Hansen, "A Trickle of Hope for the Everglades," *Environment* 28, no. 5 (1986):16; Belleville, "The Everglades," p. 4.

7. Belleville, "The Everglades," p. 2; Hansen, "A Trickle of Hope for the Everglades," p. 20.

8. Bob Graham, "Erasing Man's Mark in the Everglades," *National Parks* 59, nos. 7-8 (1985):14.

9. Kahn, "Restoring the Everglades," p. 41.

10. Graham, "Erasing Man's Mark in the Everglades," p. 14.

11. Ibid.

12. Kahn, "Restoring the Everglades," p. 42.

13. Hansen, "A Trickle of Hope for the Everglades," p. 17; P. C. Rosendahl and P. W. Rose, "Freshwater Flow Rates and Distribution within the Everglades Marsh," in *Proceedings of the National Symposium on Freshwater Inflow to Estuaries*, San Antonio, Texas, September 9-11, 1980. Because of the much publicized water quantity problems of the 1960s, Congress subsequently guaranteed to the park a minimum annual delivery of 315,000 acre-feet per year.

14. Hansen, "A Trickle of Hope for the Everglads," pp. 17-18.

15. Ibid., pp. 19, 41.

16. Belleville, "The Everglades," p. 6; Hansen, "A Trickle of Hope for the Everglades," p. 41.

17. Ibid.

18. Rose Mary Mechem, "In Florida, The Grass Is No Longer Greener," *National Wildlife* 20, no. 6 (1982):55; Yates, "Florida's Broken Rain Machine," p. 53.

19. "Save Our Everglades, Third Anniversary Report Card," August 22, 1986.

20. "Save Our Everglades, Report Card No. 2," March 30, 1983.

Determining the Minimum Critical Size of Reserves

1. Thomas E. Lovejoy, "Minimum Critical Size of Ecosystem Project," World Wildlife Fund project description, 1985, p. 1.

2. See R. H. MacArthur and E. O. Wilson, *The Theory of Island Biogeography* (Princeton, N.J.: Princeton University Press, 1967); for a discussion of how the theory applies to the Minimum Critical Size project, see Sam Iker, "Islands of Life in a Forest Sea," *Mosaic*, September-October 1982, pp. 25-30.

3. Iker "Islands of Life in a Forest Sea," p. 29.

4. Roger Lewin, "Parks: How Big Is Big Enough?" *Science* 225 (1984):612.

5. Thomas E. Lovejoy et al., "Ecological Dynamics of Forest Fragments"; in T. C. Whitmore and A. C. Chaddwick, eds., *Tropical Rainforest: Ecology and Management* (Oxford, England: Blackwell Scientific Publications, 1983), pp. 377-84.

6. Thomas E. Lovejoy et al., "Edge and Other Effects of Isolation on Amazon Forest Fragments"; in Michael E. Soule, ed., *Conservation Biology: The Science of Scarcity and Diversity* (Sunderland, Mass.: Sinauer Associates, 1986), pp. 277-80.

7. Lewin, "Parks," p. 612.

8. Lovejoy et al., "Edge and Other Effects of Isolation on Amazon Forest Fragments," pp. 258-62.

9. Ibid., p. 270.

10. Ibid. pp. 265-70.

11. Thomas E. Lovejoy et al., "Ecosystem Decay of Amazon Forest Remnants"; in Matthew H. Nitecki, ed., *Extinctions* (Chicago: University of Chicago Press, 1984), pp. 316-21.

12. Lovejoy et al., "Edge and Other Effects of Isolation on Forest Remnants," p. 284.

13. Per Ola and Emily d'Aulaire, "Lessons from a Ravaged Jungle," *International Wildlife* 16, no. 5 (1986):40; Lovejoy et al., "Ecosystem Decay of Amazon Forest Remnants," p. 321.

14. Iker, "Islands of Life in a Forest Sea," p. 29.

Reserves and Supplementary Measures to Protect Privately Owned Land

1. Adapted from The Conservation Foundation, *National Parks for a New Generation:*

Visions, Realities, Prospects (Washington, D.C.: The Conservation Foundation, 1985), pp. 260-62.

Figures

9.1. Information provided by U.S. Department of the Interior, Fish and Wildlife Service, Division of Realty,, September 30, 1985.

9.2. International Union for Conservation of Nature and Natural Resources, "1985 United Nations List of National Parks and Protected Areas" (Gland, Switzerland: International Union for Conservation of Nature and Natural Resources, 1985), in World Resources Institute and International Institute for Environment and Development, *World Resources 1986* (Washington, D.C.: World Resources Institute and International Institute for Environment and Development, 1986), p. 283; unpublished data provided by International Union for Conservation of Nature and Natural Resources, Conservation Monitoring Centre, Cambridge, England, August 1986.

Index

Regular numerals indicate materials in text; italicized numerals indicate figures.